S0-CJN-316

Understanding
Human Development
Dialogues with Lifespan Psychology

Understanding
Human Development
Dialogues with Lifespan Psychology

Edited by

Ursula M. Staudinger
Dresden University
Germany

Ulman Lindenberger
Saarland University
Germany

Kluwer Academic Publishers
Boston/Dordrecht/New York/London

Distributors for North, Central and South America:
Kluwer Academic Publishers
101 Philip Drive
Assinippi Park
Norwell, Massachusetts 02061 USA
Telephone (781) 871-6600
Fax (781) 681-9045
E-Mail: kluwer@wkap.com

Distributors for all other countries:
Kluwer Academic Publishers Group
Post Office Box 322
3300 AH Dordrecht, THE NETHERLANDS
Telephone 31 786 576 000
Fax 31 786 576 254
E-Mail: services@wkap.nl

Electronic Services <http://www.wkap.nl>

Library of Congress Cataloging-in-Publication Data

Understanding human development: dialogues with lifespan psychology / edited by
Ursula M. Staudinger, Ulman Lindenberger.
    p.cm.
    Includes bibliographical references and indexes.
    ISBN 1-40207-198-1
    1. Developmental psychology.   I. Staudinger, Ursula M., II. Lindenberger, Ulman

  BF713.5 .U53   2003
  155—dc21

                      2002073182

Copyright © 2003 by Kluwer Academic Publishers

All rights reserved. No part of this work may be reproduced, stored in a retrieval system, or transmitted in any form or by any means, electronic, mechanical, photo-copying, microfilming, recording, or otherwise, without the written permission from the Publisher, with the exception of any material supplied specifically for the purpose of being entered and executed on a computer system, for exclusive use by the purchaser of the work.

Permission for books published in Europe: permissions@wkap.nl
Permission for books published in the United States of America: permissions@wkap.com

Printed on acid-free paper.   Printed in the United States of America.

Cover design by Ulrich Knappek

To Paul B. Baltes
UMS and UL

CONTENTS

FOREWORD

K. Warner Schaie

I am pleased to write a foreword for this interesting volume, particularly as over many years, I have had the privilege of interacting with the editors and a majority of the contributors in various professional roles as a colleague, mentor, or research collaborator. The editors begin their introduction by asking why one would want to read yet another book on human development. They immediately answer their question by pointing out that many developmentally oriented texts and other treatises neglect the theoretical foundations of human development and fail to embed psychological constructs within the multidisciplinary context so essential to understanding development.

This volume provides a positive remedy to past deficiencies in volumes on human development with a well-organized structure that leads the reader from a general introduction through the basic processes to methodological issues and the relation of developmental constructs to social context and biological infrastructure. This approach does not surprise. After all, the editors and most of the contributors at one time or another had a connection to the Max Planck Institute of Human Development in Berlin, whether as students, junior scientists, or senior visitors. That institute, under the leadership of Paul Baltes, has been instrumental in pursuing a systematic lifespan approach to the study of cognition and personality. Over the past two decades, it has influenced the careers of a generation of scientists who have advocated long-term studies of human development in an interdisciplinary context.

The volume begins with a section on the architecture of lifespan development. This section reprints Baltes's seminal 1997 article on the incomplete architecture of humans to lay the foundation for discussions of life-stage differences in evolutionary selection benefits as well as the secular changes in cultural efficiency. This is followed by applications of the selective optimization with compensation (SOC) theory to basic developmental processes, including a novel economic perspective. SOC theory plays a prominent role in the next section, which details a lifespan view on self and personality. Here concepts of gains and losses and efforts to reconcile the conflicting themes of continuity and change in adults provide prominent themes. The section on lifespan views of intelligence and cognition traces new directions that have not been broadly covered previously. This material is followed by several important contributions on new methodological approaches for the study of change, including issues in molecular and quantitative genetics.

What is perhaps most interesting and useful in this volume is the final section, which includes comments from related fields and disciplines. Although many developmental psychologists have begun to pay attention to other disciplines, we have heard relatively little from our colleagues that specifically addresses developmental issues. The final eight contributions span the fields of education, anthropology, sociology, sociobiology, social psychology, and experimental psychology. All these contributions contain important efforts to view human development as a core process that deserves to be incorporated into the theoretical structure of many disciplines.

The contributors to this volume represent a thoughtful selection of some of the most productive and creative thinkers on human development in the United States and Western Europe. I was greatly stimulated by reading this wealth of new thoughts on human development, and I know that no reader will put down this book without having been influenced and steered into new directions.

ACKNOWLEDGMENTS

In a metaphorical sense, this book is the long-term result of our meeting at the Max Planck Institute of Human Development in Berlin in August 1985. At that time, we both became doctoral fellows at the Institute and started to work with Paul B. Baltes. Over the years, we were more and more excited by lifespan psychology in our respective fields of study—the mechanics and the pragmatics of the mind. We were about to leave the Institute to take on our first professorships at different universities when the idea for this book was born. It was our intention to bring together and start a dialogue among scholars from different disciplines engaged in the investigation of human development. To our contributing authors—without whose willingness to contribute to such an interdisciplinary experiment located between fields, our project would have been doomed to end before it began—we offer a warm thank you. We would like to express our heartfelt gratitude to Paul B. Baltes for his outstanding mentorship and intellectual encouragement over the years and to the Max Planck Society for providing such an exquisite working environment.

We wish to express our gratitude to Ulrich Knappek for his continued assistance in the preparation of this volume. Christian Seeringer and Yvonne Brehmer very carefully prepared the Indices. Last, but not least, we would like to thank Kluwer Academic Publishers, and particularly Christiane Roll and Marianna Pascale, for their support in the whole process. The production process was supported by the diligent work of Mary Panarelli, Tracey O'Connell and Susan Detwiler. Our expressions of gratitude to colleagues and staff, however, are not meant to detract from our responsibility as editors. This concerns particularly the selection of topics and authors. Considering the complexity of its theme, it is perhaps not surprising that this book cannot offer definite or comprehensive coverage. Other researchers and lines of scholarship could have been involved. Despite these limitations, we are hopeful that the book with its unique discursive format provides new perspectives.

LIST OF CONTRIBUTORS

Margret M. Baltes (deceased Jan., 1999)
Free University
Berlin, Germany

Paul B. Baltes
Max Planck Institute for Human
Development
Lentzeallee 94
14195 Berlin, Germany

Jürgen Baumert
Max Planck Institute for Human
Development
Lentzeallee 94
14195 Berlin, Germany

Jere Behrman
William R. Kenan Professor
of Economics
Department of Economics
University of Pennsylvania
542 McNeil Building
3718 Locust Walk
Philadelphia, PA 19104-6297, U.S.A.

Jochen Brandtstädter
Fachbereich I—Psychologie
Universität Trier
Tarforst, Gebäude D
54286 Trier, Germany

Laura L. Carstensen
Department of Psychology
Stanford University
Jordan Hall, Building 420
Stanford, CA 94305-2130, U.S.A.

Avshalom Caspi
Social, Genetic, and Developmental
Psychiatry Research Centre
Institute of Psychiatry
III Denmark Hill
De Crespigny Park
London SE5 8AF, U.K.

C. Robert Cloninger
Wallace Renard Professor of Psychiatry
Department of Psychiatry
School of Medicine
Washington University in St. Louis
Campus Box 8134
St. Louis, MO 63130, U.S.A.

Elizabeth Dowling
Tufts University
Medford, MA 02115, U.S.A.

Paolo Ghisletta
Center for Interdisciplinary
Gerontology
University of Geneva
Route de Mon Idee 59
1226 Thonex, Geneve, Switzerland

Gerd Gigerenzer
Max Planck Institute for Human
Development
Lentzeallee 94
14195 Berlin, Germany

Jutta Heckhausen
Department of Psychology
and Human Behavior
School of Social Ecology
3340 Social Ecology II
University of California, Irvine
Irvine, CA 92697-7085, U.S.A.

Hilde M. Huizenga
Faculty of Psychology
University of Amsterdam
Roeterstraat 15
NL-1018 Amsterdam, the Netherlands

Thomas B. L. Kirkwood
University of Newcastle
Institute for Ageing and Health
Newcastle General Hospital
Westgate Road
Newcastle upon Tyne NE4 6BE, U.K.

Reinhold Kliegl
Department of Psychology
University of Potsdam
P.O.Box 601553
14415 Potsdam, Germany

Olaf Köller
Friedrich-Alexander-Universität
Erlangen Nürnberg
Department of Psychology
Regensburger Str. 160
90478 Nürnberg, Germany

Gisela Labouvie-Vief
Department of Psychology
Wayne State University
71 West Warren
Detroit, MI 48202, U.S.A.

Richard M. Lerner
Eliot-Pearson Department of Childhood
Development
Tufts University
105 College Ave
Medford, MA 02115, U.S.A.

Ulman Lindenberger
Psychology Department
Building 1
Saarland University
Im Stadtwald
66123 Saarbrücken, Germany

Heiner Maier
Max Planck Institute for Demographic
Research
Doberaner Str. 114
18057 Rostock, Germany

Karl Ulrich Mayer
Max Planck Institute for Human
Development
Lentzeallee 94
14195 Berlin, Germany

Ulrich Mayr
Department of Psychology
University of Oregon
Eugene, OR 97403-1227, U.S.A.

Gerald E. McClearn
Biobehavioral Health Department
The Pennsylvania State University
0101 Gardner House
University Park, PA 16802, U.S.A.

Jürgen Mittelstrass
School of Philosophy
Constance University
P.O.Box 5560
78434 Constance, Germany

Peter Molenaar
Faculty of Psychology
University of Amsterdam
Roeterstraat 15
NL-1018 Amsterdam, the Netherlands

John R. Nesselroade
Department of Psychology
Gilmer Hall
University of Virginia
Charlottesville, VA 22903, U.S.A.

Brent W. Roberts
Department of Psychology
University of Illinois
603 East Daniel Street
Champaign, IL 61820, U.S.A.

Susanna Lara Roth
Tufts University
Medford, MA 02115, U.S.A.

Klaus Rothermund
Fachbereich I—Psychologie
Universität Trier
Tarforst, Gebäude D
54286 Trier, Germany

Timothy A. Salthouse
Department of Psychology
Gilmer Hall
University of Virginia
Charlottesville, VA 22904-4400, U.S.A.

K. Warner Schaie
College of Human Development
The Pennsylvania State University
S-110 Henderson Drive
University Park, PA 16802, U.S.A.

Kai U. Schnabel
Department of Psychology
University of Michigan
1012 East Hall, 525
East University
Ann Arbor, MI 48109-1109, U.S.A.

Wolf Singer
Max Planck Institute for Brain Research
Deutschordenstrasse 46
60528 Frankfurt am Main, Germany

Jacqui Smith
Max Planck Institute for Human
Development
Lentzeallee 94
14195 Berlin, Germany

Ursula M. Staudinger
Department of Psychology
Dresden University
01062 Dresden, Germany

James W. Vaupel
Max Planck Institute for
Demographic Research
Doberaner Str. 114
18057 Rostock, Germany

Henry M. Wellman
Center for Human Growth and
Development
University of Michigan
300 North Ingalls Building
Ann Arbor, MI 48109, U.S.A.

1 Why Read Another Book on Human Development? Understanding Human Development Takes a Metatheory and Multiple Disciplines

Ursula M. Staudinger

Dresden University, Dresden, Germany

Ulman Lindenberger

Saarland University, Saarbrücken, Germany

The Idea

The description, explanation, and enhancement of development in individuals and groups of individuals are seen as important goals of scientific inquiry in most of the social, behavioral, and life sciences. At the same time, scholars working in these three research traditions increasingly agree that cultural and biological processes interact in the co-construction of human ontogeny. This broad and growing consensus provides a fertile common ground for scientific exchange. In the process, communication across research traditions and disciplines, while acknowledging necessary differences in terminology and methodology, needs to establish a common conceptual framework. Psychology, with its links to sociology, cultural anthropology, and history, on the one hand, and to cognitive neuroscience, evolutionary biology, and developmental biology, on the other, appears to be in a good position to mediate such a framework. The general goal of the present volume is to explore the tenability of this assertion.

Specifically, the book features lifespan psychology, a metatheoretical framework that was first proposed by Paul B. Baltes (1987, 1997; see also Baltes, Lindenberger, & Staudinger, 1998; Baltes, Staudinger, & Lindenberger, 1999). Lifespan psychology articulates the two major sources of human development, biology and culture, and posits three central developmental mechanisms—selection, optimization, and compensation (Baltes, 1997). Development, in the lifespan sense, is not reduced to growth but encompasses growth, stability, and decline fromconception to the end of life.

Embedded within the more general goal of promoting interdisciplinary discourse about human ontogeny and transdisciplinary theorizing, the specific goal of this volume is to invite scholars from neighboring fields to interrogate the central tenets of lifespan psychology.

To serve these goals, the present volume follows a novel format. It is organized around a target article by Baltes (1997) that features the overall lifespan framework for understanding human development. The following chapters provide discussion of the lifespan framework from other disciplines and from other perspectives within psychology. We hope that this particular format will bring to life the book's subtitle— "Dialogues with Lifespan Psychology." Clearly, lifespan psychology alone cannot explicate the architecture of human development. Biology, demography, neuroscience as well as economics, educational science, and philosophy are also needed—just to mention a few. The interdisciplinary focus of the book reflects our view that understanding human development necessitates a systemic approach (see also Lerner, Dowling, & Roth, this volume; Molenaar, Huizenga, & Nesselroade, this volume).

Historical Background

To begin, it may be useful to consider some of the historical background of the lifespan approach to human development. Already in 1777 Johann Nicolaus Tetens, who is considered the founder of the field of developmental psychology in Germany, published his major work in which he described human development as a lifelong phenomenon (cf. Lindenberger & Baltes, 1999). In other European countries, such as England, and in the United States, developmental psychology emerged around the turn of the century with a strong emphasis on child development. In recent decades, however, a lifespan approach has become more prominent in North America, as well, for several reasons. Interdisciplinary synergism has been one of them. Especially in sociology, related to scholars such as Bernice Neugarten or Glen Elder, lifecourse sociology took hold as a powerful intellectual force.

The first West Virginia Conference on lifespan development (Goulet & Baltes, 1970; see also Thomae, 1959)—which turned into a series of conferences as well as a book series titled *Life-span Development and Behavior* (first editors P. B. Baltes and O. G. Brim)—probably marks the emergence of lifespan psychology as a modern metatheoretical framework and a psychological field of study. An article in the *Annual Review of Psychology* documents the establishment of lifespan psychology during the early 1980s (Baltes, Reese, & Lipsitt, 1980). In the late 1990s, the continued importance of lifespan psychology is demonstrated by contributions to the latest edition of the *Handbook of Child Development* (Baltes, Lindenberger, & Staudinger, 1998) and a second *Annual Review of Psychology* article (Baltes, Staudinger, & Lindenberger, 1999). Over the years, lifespan theorizing strengthened its interdisciplinary basis. This is perhaps seen most clearly in an article published by Baltes (1997) in the *American*

Psychologist. Therefore, the present volume features this article as a target for exchange across disciplines.

What Is the Metatheory All About? Major Tenets of Lifespan Psychology

Defining Development

In lifespan psychology, development is not defined in juxtaposition to aging, as is usually the case in models of development exclusively informed by biology. Rather, *development* and *aging* are used synonymously and are defined as selective age-related change in adaptive capacity. Adaptive capacity encompasses psychological functions (such as self-regulation and working memory) as well as structures (such as personality traits and knowledge systems). Age-related changes in adaptive capacity involve increases, as much as maintenance, transformation, and decreases.

Central to this definition of development and aging is the proposition that gains and losses coexist in human development from conception to death; the traditional equations—"child development = gain" and "aging = loss"—are called into question and ultimately dissolved. Instead, lifespan psychology investigates the etiology and modifiability of age-related changes in the *ratio* of gains and losses. The basic assumption is that with increasing age, losses are on an increasing trajectory and gains are on a decreasing trajectory. Two further assumptions are central. First, classifications of gains and losses are context-specific; their recognition requires knowledge of, and theories about, age-associated changes, societal rules, historical periods, and individual differences. Second, and more radically, lifespan psychology posits the dialectics of gains and losses (Riegel, 1976)—that is, any gain, at any age, entails a loss, and vice versa (e.g., Baltes, 1987).

In general agreement with depicting development as a gain-loss dynamic, Wellman (this volume) suggests that developing a culture for old age should not be limited to compensating losses or supporting the maintenance of levels of functioning but should also comprise the cultivation of the gain aspects of losses. In old and very old age, indeed, a lot of evidence documents the "loss-triggers-gain" association but at the same time illustrates the existential limits of that association (Smith, this volume). Exploring in depth the different meanings of gains and losses in old and very old age contributes to weakening the effect of the negative age stereotype that discounts the possibility of maintenance and growth in old age.

Sources of Development

Human development at any given time in life comprises gains and losses and is the result of interacting forces. It cannot be reduced to either biology or culture (for a review of interactionism in developmental science, see, e.g., Lerner, 1984). The human genome cannot unfold without a given context, and this context influences the way it unfolds (see Kirkwood, this volume; Singer, this volume). And certainly, culture needs an organism on which to unfold its influences (see Köller, Baumert, & Schnabel, this volume; Mayer, this volume).

The nature-nurture debate has a long history that has been stimulated by recent developments in quantitative genetics (McClearn, this volume). The complexities of gene-gene and gene-environment developmental interactions are progressively uncovered. In basic agreement with Molenaar, Huizenga, and Nesselroade (this volume), McClearn concludes that a comprehensive view of human ontogeny needs to embrace the language, concepts, and methods of developmental systems theory, such as network causality, hierarchical organization, catastrophes, bifurcations in chaotic systems, and feedback loops. In this context, the actions and intentions of the developing individual constitute—besides biology and culture—a third, emergent source of influence on development (e.g., Brandtstädter & Rothermund, this volume). Intentional human behavior (such as actions) and its corollaries (such as choice, self, life goals, and so on) are closely linked to the openness of human ontogeny.

The dynamics between biology and culture described by Baltes (1997) provide the basic script for lifespan changes in many functional domains. For example, in the domain of cognitive performance, measures assessing individual differences in processing efficiency (such as measures more closely related to biology) are generally negatively related to age during adulthood and old age. In contrast, measures assessing individual differences in the cumulative products of past processing (such as measures more closely related to culture) tend to show little or no decrements during adulthood. This developmental dissociation between "process" and "product" measures (Hebb, 1949) is at the heart of several two-component theories of cognition, such as the theory of fluid and crystallized intelligence by Cattell (1971) and Horn (1989) or the theory of the mechanics and pragmatics of cognition by Baltes (1987, this volume; for a comparison, see Lindenberger, 2001).

At a more specific level of analysis, Salthouse (this volume) discusses and empirically examines various explanations for the widespread absence of negative age-cognition relations in the pragmatics of cognition. The data presented in his chapter are well explained by the migration hypothesis, a term proposed by Salthouse (this volume), according to which individuals tend to "migrate" from lower to higher levels of knowledge with advancing age. From the other end of the lifespan, however, Wellman (this volume) questions the expertise analog (such as proceeding through the accumulation of the specific to the general) as a description of cognitive development during early childhood. He provides convincing evidence that early development, at least in certain cases, proceeds from the general and abstract to the specific and concrete, and not the other way around, as the transition from novices to experts generally would suggest.

Through the innovative use of existing methodological tools (such as experimental age simulations) and the development of new ones (such as time-accuracy functions),

Kliegl, Krampe, and Mayr (this volume) further differentiate the distinction between "process" and "product" mentioned above. They suggest that processing serving the production of novel ideas is more negatively affected by advancing age than processing that dwells on the retrieval of existing knowledge (see also Sternberg, 1985).

Another example for the interaction between biology, culture, and person is the self and personality domain. Again, we find a biological basis, the mechanics of life, that is reflected in basic emotional (positive, negative) and motivational (approach, avoidance) tendencies, as well as basic activity patterns (Staudinger & Pasupathi, 2000). In countless interactions with cultural contexts, these basic biological components of self and personality become regulated, differentiated, and enriched (Cloninger, this volume). As a result individuals develop their pragmatics of life. They possess highly complex emotional patterns ranging from guilt to pride, goal systems encompassing, for instance, the pursuit of a professional career and the construction of meaning in life, as well as multifaceted personality characteristics and self definitions (Staudinger & Pasupathi, 2000). This developmental course, however, should not be mistaken as a devaluation of biological forces. The synergistic operation of biology and culture is maintained throughout life, notwithstanding the fact that in very old age biological powers decrease. Decreases in biological functioning may lead to reduced vitality and psychological energy and influence goal pursuit, the emotional budget and the personality structure accordingly (see also Roberts & Caspi, this volume; Smith, this volume). At the same time, the resources propelling self-regulatory processes are reduced, and, thus, in very old age the biological basis of self and personality shines through more strongly than during adulthood (Staudinger & Pasupathi, 2000).

Processes of Development

The developmental sources of biology, culture, and person are linked to different developmental processes. In biology, the developing organism is described at first as *maturing* and later as *senescing* (see Kirkwood, this volume; Singer, this volume). From a cultural point of view, development is *learning* (see Köller, Baumert, & Schnabet, this volume; Mayer, this volume). And finally, *actions* taken by the developing human being contribute to development. The dynamic relations between intentionality and ontogenetic time are considered both as a resource for action and a source of meaning (see Brandstädter & Rothermund, this volume). It is by means of these three processes that biology, culture, and person interact and produce development and aging (see Li, in press, for an attempt to specify those interactions).

The development of the human brain and of human cognition may serve as illustration for the interaction among these three processes. During pregnancy, infancy, and childhood, brain structures mature. These processes, however, are *not* following a fixed biological maturation program but rather interact with and depend on contextual characteristics such as plasma composition or nutrition (see Kirkwood, this volume; Singer, this volume). Further, there is intrinsic chance of genome expression that adds to the variability of maturational processes. Turning to work on cultural learning, we realize how closely human cognition and intelligence are intertwined with the social and material context in which we develop (e.g., Tomasello, 1999). With the emergence of the ability to select, the developing individual further complicates or better enriches the etiology of brain and cognitive development. Which are the learning contexts the individual selects, and which contexts are avoided? What is the individual's motivational structure? To demonstrate how deeply such personal choices interact with biological processes, consider evidence from research on brain plasticity. Research on brain plasticity suggests, for instance, that a person who opted for and over years pursued a career as a professional string player at the same time affects the structural and functional aspects of her cortical organization. As a result of years of practicing to play a string instrument, the cortical representations of fingers of the left hand were found to be increased (e.g., Elbert, Pantev, Wienbruch, Rockstroh, & Taub, 1995).

The pervasiveness of epigenetic (e.g., person-specific) processes in human ontogeny has important consequences for developmental methodology. As argued by Molenaar, Huizinga, and Nesselroade (this volume), the conceptually privileged unit of analysis in human ontogeny is the developing individual. However, most of developmental psychology routinely utilizes statistical methods that focus on differences among individuals such as standard longitudinal or cross-sectional factor analysis. Methods with an explicit focus on intraindividual change, such as time-series analysis or dynamic factor analysis, are notoriously underused in psychology. (Note that the situation is somewhat different in lifecourse sociology; cf. Blossfeld, Hamerle, & Mayer, 1991). Specifically, when lifespan researchers use interindividual-difference methods to study within-person change, they tacitly assume that individuals are homogeneous with respect to the number, structure, and relative importance of developmental causes. Available empirical evidence (such as the molecular genetics of epigenesis; cf. McClearn, this volume) and theoretical considerations (such as developmental systems theory; Lerner, Dowling, & Roth, this volume) strongly suggest that the homogeneity assumption is generally incorrect. Under conditions of heterogeneity, however, the structure of interindividual variation as revealed by standard interindividual-difference methods does not yield an approximation of within-person changes. This mismatch between theoretical intentions and research design is likely to go unnoticed in standard applications of interindividual difference methods because they will tend to work properly in a technical sense. Put simply, the best way to find out about the degree of heterogeneity among different developmental systems (that is, different developing individuals) is to study it. As John Nesselroade and others have argued for quite some time (Baltes, Reese, & Nesselroade, 1977; Nesselroade & Bartsch, 1977), formal comparisons of multivariate individual developmental trajectories (cf. Molenaar & Nesselroade, 1998) are ideally suited for this purpose. Molenaar, Huizenga, and Nesselroade (this volume) strengthen this argument through formal simulations, and we hope that their line of reasoning will entice researchers in developmental psychology and in other developmental disciplines to make increased use of research designs that focus on the observation of change processes within individuals.

Plasticity of Development

Human development is the result of variable and interacting systems of influence and any observable developmental trajectory is but one possible manifestation of a large but not infinite range of alternative trajectories (cf. Tetens, 1777; for a recent review of plasticity, see Li, in press). Thus, for any given individual, at any given age, and for any given psychological dimension, alterations in developmental context carry the potential to funnel developmental trajectories in more or less desired directions. In this context, the notions of plasticity, reserve capacity, and latent potential are used in lifespan psychology to denote the difference between realized and maximum potential. In principle, however, the notion of plasticity also includes deviations in the negative direction. These phenomena and processes related to the maintenance or regaining of levels of functioning under conditions of stress are subsumed under the concept of resilience (e.g., Staudinger, Marsiske & Baltes, 1995).

In this vein, Lerner, Dowling, and Roth (this volume) argue that human development is best understood as a system comprising the person within context. This system consists of subsystems (such as biological organism, cognition, personality, motor performance, family, neighborhood, and nation) that show intra- and intersystemic co-actions. Given this systemic nature, human development demonstrates great plasticity. The plasticity of human development is also pivotal for philosophical anthropology. It is captured there by the notion of world-openness (see Mittelstrass, this volume). But beyond its malleability and variability, philosophical anthropology is also interested in the constants of human development.

A central goal of lifespan psychology is to chart the magnitude of plasticity and the extent to which it covaries with age. Probably the most direct strategy to examine age changes in the range and limits of plasticity is through active experimental intervention (Baltes & Kliegl, 1992). Another strategy is to explore the range and malleability of developmental pathways is the study of "turning points" in naturalistic settings (Caspi, 1998; Magnusson & Stattin, 1998; Rutter, 1996; Staudinger et al., 1995). Finally, a third strategy is to document differences in behavior across cultures or historical time (Flynn, 1987). Despite large differences in method, the common theme of these research strategies is to better understand the nature of human plasticity.

The conceptual emphasis on age changes in plasticity needs to be accompanied by the search for methods that allow for valid and reliable assessment of intraindividual change. Nesselroade and Ghisletta (this volume) present a historical and systematic summary of the measurement and structural representation of change. In line with Molenaar, Huizenga, and Nesselroade (this volume), they invite developmental researchers to move toward more dynamical models for representing developmental change. One of the models they propose in this context, dampenend linear oscillators (e.g., Boker & Nesselroade, 2001), has its origins in the natural sciences (e.g., physics). The general lesson to be learned is that lifespan psychology may profit from methodological exchange with fields remote in substance but equipped with a rich set of methodological tools for representing change.

The Role of Constraints (Enabling, Disabling) and Opportunity Structures in Lifespan Development

The plasticity of human development is regulated by the properties and interactions of its constituent resources: biology (maturation), culture (learning), and person (action). A first set of constraints, both enabling and disabling, refers to the biological script that governs the life course. During infancy and early childhood, maturation and learning produce a system of enabling constraints that facilitate the acquisition of complex performances. Language development may serve as an example. It has been suggested, on the basis of formal simulations, that young children's short working-memory span may facilitate the acquisition of grammar because it facilitates an initial focus on simple sentences (Elman, 1993). Such a constraint may be called enabling because it fosters ontogenetic development (see also Wellman, this volume).

Enabling constraints are especially prominent early in life but continue to exist throughout the entire life span. With increasing adult age, however, and especially after the end of the reproductive phase, disabling constraints due to senescence become more prominent. As Baltes (1997) poignantly argued, biological sources of development deplete with increasing age. Evolution did not yet have enough time or means to optimize later phases of the lifespan. Consequently, cultural sources have to compensate for this depletion. In this sense, cultural sources of development gain special importance in old age. Plasticity in old age, however, is diminished due to the depletion of resources (not only the biological ones), and consequently the efficiency of cultural compensation is reduced (Baltes, 1997). Age-graded decrements in evolutionary selection benefits in humans and other mammalian species are predicted by disposable soma theory (Kirkwood, 1977, 1997) and antagonistic pleiotropy theory (Williams, 1957). Kirkwood (this volume) summarizes both theories and convincingly argues that they provide a more compelling account of human senescence than rival explanations such as the notion of a programmed death.

Maier and Vaupel (this volume) critically investigate the last tenet of the lifespan architecture—that the efficiency of cultural compensation is reduced—by using the sample case of the extension of longevity and show that during the last 30 to 40 years mortality reductions have been highest at highest ages (that is, 90 or 100 years). Very much in line with lifespan theory, they use the case of gender-specific change in mortality rates to argue for the interaction between biological, evolutionary, and historical forces in supporting survival. Finally, the authors raise the stimulating question of whether the age-related efficiency of culture may vary depending on cultural-historical context rather than show general age-related decline.

Certainly, the biological script is complemented by a sociocultural script. Social opportunity structures and cultural tasks such as the school setting, professional settings, or retirement constrain and enable the range of possible experiences and actions and thus contribute to developmental outcomes. In this sense, the scientific agendas of lifespan psychology and lifecourse sociology are intertwined. Mayer (this volume) suggests that the two research traditions could remedy some of their weaknesses by more exchange. Using the conceptual tools of lifecourse sociology, lifespan psychology could profit from considering the effects of institutional and other forms of socioeconomic regulation on the development, stability, and change of normative orientations at the psychological level of analysis. Conversely, lifespan psychology could help lifecourse sociology in filling "the black box of the actor" by providing concepts that focus on interindividual differences in processes such as control and goal striving, control beliefs, and selective optimization with compensation.

From the perspective of the educational sciences, Köller, Baumert, and Schnabel (this volume) argue that schools represent powerful contexts for cognitive development. Schools are highlighted as environments that place a considerable number of constraints on students' actions. To enhance educational outcomes, the patterns of constraints provided by school contexts should be synchronized with age-graded changes in the students' capabilities and needs.

A third set of constraints on the plasticity of development is "orthogonal" to the biological and cultural constraints and describes three logics according to which biology and culture unfold their enabling and disabling constraints. The first logic is age. Depending on an individual's age, biology and culture have different developmental effects. The second logic is history. And this refers to the fact that depending on historical time, biological and cultural constraints differ. And finally the third logic is person-specific and acknowledges the fact that biological and cultural constraints unfold their interactions in a highly idiosyncratic manner.

For instance, personality traits increase in consistency *with age* and are mostly consistent across adulthood, and yet they retain the capacity for change throughout the adult life course (see Roberts & Caspi, this volume). This proposition is in line with lifespan theory that argues for the dialectic between continuity and change. Evidence is provided for why personality is consistent as well as for why it changes. Identity structure—that is, the *person-specific* logic—is offered as an important link to understand age-related increases in consistency. Considering the historical logic, it has been demonstrated that given certain *historical contexts*, such as the student and peace movement of the 1960s and 1970s, personality development during these times showed changed trajectories (for instance, that autonomy showed earlier peaks; Baltes, Reese, & Nesselroade, 1977).

In her commentary, Labouvie-Vief (this volume) offers still another logic, and that is the logic of gender and how it contrains and enables development. She argues that leaving out gender from a theory of development is usually symptomatic for a number of other deletions. This omission may lead to hosting many dualities of development, such as gains and losses or cognition and emotion or symbolism and logic, without offering mechanisms of integration.

Regulatory Processes in Human Development: Selection, Optimization, and Compensation (SOC)

Due to the plasticity of human development, models of developmental regulation are of utmost importance to developmental science. Among existing regulatory models, the model of selection, optimization, and compensation (SOC) (Baltes & Baltes, 1990) has been introduced and is described in a number of chapters of this volume as a potent means to describe, explain, and predict developmental regulation in various developmental subsystems ranging from the biological through the psychological to the societal levels of development. Selection is an inextricable part of development. Each developmental step implies that other steps are not taken and thus that selection has taken place. Selection by itself, however, is not enough. After selection, optimization has to take place, and sometimes optimization is possible only through compensation for lost means. In some of the chapters, the interplay between intentional and subintentional processes in developmental regulation is introduced as a fascinating research topic (Cloninger, this volume; Heckhausen, this volume).

Baltes and Baltes (1990) have argued that the three processes of selection, optimization, and compensation are universal almost in the sense of anthropological constants (see Mittelstrass, this volume) but that the combination and content are highly idiosyncratic. M. Baltes and Carstensen (this volume) specify in great detail the three central mechanisms of developmental regulation and their interaction as well as empirical evidence for their contribution to successful aging. Among others, selection, compensation, and optimization are, for instance, discussed as mechanisms promoting continuity as well as change in personality structure across the life span (see Robert & Caspi, this volume). Or aging individuals may be able to protect cognitive performance levels in a given domain of life (such as their professional life) against decreases in innovative solutions by allotting more time to this domain (optimization), at the cost of reducing or eliminating the time allocated to other domains (selection). For instance, Kliegl, Krampe, and Mayr (this volume) discuss possible consequences of differential rates of slowing for various types of cognitive operations from a selection, optimization, and compensation perspective (see also M. Baltes & Carstensen, this volume; Freund, Li, & Baltes, 1999). Specifically, they suggest that aging individuals may be able to protect a given domain of life (such as their professional life) against the decreasing likelihood of coming up with novel solutions by allotting more time to this domain, at the cost of reducing or eliminating the time allocated to other domains.

Gigerenzer (this volume) compares the concept of the adaptive toolbox (Gigerenzer, Todd, & ABC Group, 1999) with the SOC metatheory. Conceived within the general framework of evolutionary psychology, the adaptive toolbox contains a collection of domain-specific heuristics that can function quickly and effectively for solving specific problems when used in the proper environment. SOC metatheory may help to shed light on the regulation and coordination of this behavioral repertoire.

Alternative models of developmental regulation argue that selection, compensation, and optimization can be subsumed under primary and secondary control (Heckhausen, this volume) or embedded in a model of self-regulation that contrasts two basic processes—goal pursuit and goal adjustment (see Brandtstädter & Rothermund, this volume). From an economist's perspective, Behrman (this volume) argues that the lifespan architecture postulated by P. Baltes (1997) does not distinguish between total and marginal costs and benefits and does not provide a formal algorithm for optimization. In this context, both Behrman (this volume) and Mittelstrass (this volume) insist that selection, compensation, and optimization are interdependent.

Looking Back and Looking Ahead

The search for common conceptual ground in the study of human ontogeny was a main motive for editing this volume. By initiating conceptual exchange between lifespan psychology and other disciplines in the social, behavioral, and life sciences, we hope to enrich lifespan psychology through exchange with other disciplines and to establish a common, transdisciplinary framework for articulating the dynamics between culture and biology in human ontogeny.

In retrospect, it seems to us that the first goal was more realistic than the second. We feel that lifespan psychology has profited considerably from the multifaceted and diverse interrogations by scholars working in the related fields documented in this volume. As for the establishment of a common conceptual framework that transcends disciplinary boundaries, we feel reminded of what Piaget (and others before him) once called "le recul de l'objet": the goal seems to recede as one approaches it. For good reasons, the quest for a transdisciplinary framework about human ontogeny will never come to an end. Rather, discipline-specific innovation and transdisciplinary coordination are equally important, and what matters is to have an open eye for both.

References

Baltes, P. B. (1987). Developmental psychology. In G. L. Maddox (Ed.), *The encyclopedia of aging* (pp. 170–175). New York: Springer.

Baltes, P. B. (1997). On the incomplete architecture of human ontogeny: Selection, optimization, and compensation as foundation of developmental theory. *American Psychologist, 52*, 366–380.

Baltes, P. B., & Baltes, M. M. (1990). Psychological perspectives on successful aging: The models of selective optimization with compensation. In P. B. Baltes & M. M. Baltes (Eds.), *Successful aging: Perspectives from the behavioral sciences* (pp. 1–34). New York: Cambridge University Press.

Baltes, P. B., & Kliegl, R. (1992). Further testing of limits of cognitive plasticity: Negative age differences in a mnemonic skill are robust. *Developmental Psychology, 28*, 121–125.

Baltes, P. B., & Brim, O. G. J. (1978). *Life-span development and behavior.* (Vol. 2). New York: Academic Press.

Baltes, P. B., Lindenberger, U., & Staudinger, U. M. (1998). Life-span theory in developmental psychology. In R. M. Lerner (Ed.), *Handbook of child psychology* (5th ed.), Vol. 1, *Theoretical models of human development* (pp. 1029–1143). New York: Wiley.

Baltes, P. B., Reese, H. W., & Nesselroade, J. R. (Eds.). (1977). *Lifespan developmental psychology: An introduction to research methods.* Montery, CA: Brooks Cole (reprinted Hillsdale, NJ: Erlbaum, 1988).

Baltes, P. B., Reese, H. W., & Lipsitt, L. P. (1980). Life-span developmental psychology. *Annual Review of Psychology, 31*, 65–110.

Baltes, P. B., Staudinger, U. M., & Lindenberger, U. (1999). Lifespan psychology: Theory and application to intellectual functioning. *Annual Review of Psychology, 50*, 471–507.

Blossfeld, H.-P., Hamerle, A., & Mayer, K. U. (1991). Event-history models in social mobility research. In D. Magnusson, L. R. Berman, G. Rudinger, & B. Törrestad (Eds.), *Problems and methods in longitudinal research* (pp. 212–235). Cambridge, MA: Cambridge University Press.

Boker, S. M., & Nesselroade, J. R. (2002). A method for modeling the intrinsic dynamics of intraindividual variability: Recovering the parameters of simulated oscillators in multi-wave data. *Multivariate Behavioral Research, 37*, 127–160.

Caspi, A. (1998). Personality development across the life course. In N. Eisenberg (Ed.), *Handbook of child psychology (5th ed.), Vol. 3, Social emotional, and personality development* (pp. 311–387). New York: Wiley.

Cattell, R. B. (1971). *Abilities: Their structure, growth, and action.* Boston: Houghton Mifflin.

Elbert, T., Pantev, C., Wienbruch, C., Rockstroh, B., & Taub, E. (1995). Increased cortical representation of the fingers of the left hand in string players. *Science, 270*, 305–307.

Elman, J. L. (1993). Learning and development in neural networks: The importance of starting small. *Cognition, 48*, 71–99.

Flynn, J. R. (1987). Massive IQ gains in 14 nations: What IQ tests really measure. *Psychological Bulletin, 101*, 171–191.

Freund, A., Li, K. Z. H., & Baltes, P. B. (1999). The role of selection, optimization, and compensation in successful aging. In J. Brandtstädter & R. M. Lerner (Eds.), *Action and self-development: Theory and research through the lifespan* (pp. 401–434). Thousand Oaks, CA: Sage.

Gigerenzer, G., Todd, P. M., & The ABC Group. (1999). *Simple heuristics that make us smart.* New York: Oxford University Press.

Goulet, L. R., & Baltes, P. B. (Eds.). (1970). *Life-span developmental psychology: Research and theory.* New York: Academic Press.

Hebb, D. O. (1949). *The organization of behavior.* New York: Wiley.

Horn, J. L. (1989). Models of intelligence. In R. L. Linn (Ed.), *Intelligence: Measurement, theory, and public policy* (pp. 29–73). Urbana: University of Illinois Press.

Kirkwood, T. B. L. (1977). Evolution of aging. *Nature, 270*, 301–304.

Kirkwood, T. B. L. (1997). The origins of human aging. *Philosophical Transactions of the Royal Society, London, B, 352*, 1765–1772.

Lerner, R. M. (1984). *On the nature of human plasticity.* New York: Cambridge University Press.

Li, S.-C. (in press). Biocultural orchestration of cognition: Concerted biological and cultural influences in turning the mind's epigenesis across life span. Psychological Bulletin.

Lindenberger, U. (2001). Lifespan theories of cognitive development. In N. J. Smelser & P. B. Baltes (Eds.), *International Encyclopedia of the Social and Behavioral Sciences* (pp. 8848–8854). Oxford, England: Elsevier.

Lindenberger, U. (2000). Intellectual Development across the Life Span: Overview and Selected Empirical Evidence. *Psychologische Rundschau, 51*, 135–145.

Lindenberger, U., & Baltes, P. B. (1999). Lifespan Developmental Psychology (Lifespan Psychology): Honoring Johann Nicolaus Tetens (1736–1807) *Zeitschrift für Psychologie, 207*, 299–323.

Magnusson, D., & Stattin, H. (1998). Person-context interaction theories. In R. M. Lerner (Ed.), *Theoretical models of human development*, Vol. 1, *Handbook of child psychology* (pp. 685–759). New York: Wiley.

Molenaar, P. C. M., & Nesselroade, J. R. (1998). A comparison of pseudo-maximum likelihood and asymptotically distribution-free dynamic factor analysis parameter estimation in fitting covariance-structure models to block-Toeplitz matrices representing single-subject multivariate time series. *Multivariate Behavioral Research, 33*, 313–342.

Nesselroade, J. R., & Bartsch, T. W. (1977). Multivariate experimental perspectives on the construct validity of the trait-state distinction. In R. B. Cattell & R. M. Dreger (Eds.), *Handbook of modern personality theory*. New York: Hemisphere.

Riegel, K. F. (1976). The dialectics of human development. *American Psychologist, 31*, 689–700.

Rutter, M. (1996). Transitions and turning points in developmental psychopathology: As applied to the age span between childhood and mid-adulthood. *International Journal of Behavioral Development, 19*, 603–626.

Staudinger, U. M., Marsiske, M., & Baltes, P. B. (1995). Resilience and reserve capacity in later adulthood: Potentials and limits of development across the life span. In D. Cicchetti & D. Cohen (Eds.), *Developmental psychopathology*, Vol. 2, *Risk, disorder, and adaptation* (pp. 801–847). New York: Wiley

Staudinger, U. M., & Pasupathi, M. (2000). Life-span perspectives on self, personality and social cognition. In T. Salthouse & F. Craik (Eds.), *Handbook of cognition and aging* (pp. 633–688). Hillsdale, NJ: Erlbaum.

Sternberg, R. J. (1985). *Beyond IQ. A triarchic theory of human intelligence.* New York: Cambridge University Press.

Tetens, J. N. (1777). *Philosophical Trials on Human Nature and Its Development.* Leipzig: Weidmanns Erben & Reich.

Thomae, H. (1959). *Developmental Psychology.* Göttingen: Hogrefe.

Tomasello, M. (1999). *The cultural origins of human cognition.* Cambridge, MA: Harvard University Press.

Williams, G. C. (1957). Pleiotropy, natural selection and the evolution of senescence. *Evolution, 11*, 398–411.

I
The Overall Architecture of
Lifespan Development

2 On the Incomplete Architecture of Human Ontogeny: Selection, Optimization, and Compensation as Foundation of Developmental Theory

Paul B. Baltes

Max Planck Institute for Human Development, Berlin, Germany

Abstract

Drawing on both evolutionary and ontogenetic perspectives, the basic biological-genetic and social-cultural architecture of human development is outlined. Three principles are involved. First, evolutionary selection pressure predicts a negative age correlation, and, therefore, genome-based plasticity and biological potential decrease with age. Second, for growth aspects of human development to extend further into the life span, culture-based resources are required at ever-increasing levels. Third, because of age-related losses in biological plasticity, the efficiency of culture is reduced as life span development unfolds. Joint application of these principles suggests that the lifespan architecture becomes more and more incomplete with age. *Degree of completeness* can be defined as the ratio between gains and losses in functioning. Two examples illustrate the implications of the lifespan architecture proposed. The first is a general theory of development involving the orchestration of three component processes: selection, optimization, and compensation. The second considers the task of completing the life course in the sense of achieving a positive balance between gains and losses for all age levels. This goal is increasingly more difficult to attain as human development is extended into advanced old age.

During the last decade, we have witnessed a vigorous effort to strengthen the link between evolutionary and ontogenetic perspectives in the study of human behavior.

Originally published in *American Psychologist, 52* (1997), 366–380. Reprinted with permission.

In this spirit, the purpose of this article is to offer a general framework of the biological and cultural architecture of human development across the life span. With this approach, which considers both evolutionary and ontogenetic arguments, I hope to identify the foundational structure that any general theory of human development must have.

Many of the arguments presented owe their line of reasoning to theoretical propositions associated with lifespan developmental psychology (P. B. Baltes, 1979, 1987; P. B. Baltes, Lindenberger, & Staudinger, in press; Elder, in press; Featherman, 1983; Labouvie-Vief, 1982). The arguments are also consistent with more recent theoretical efforts claiming that ontogenesis is inherently a system of adaptive change involving as foundational elements the orchestration of three subprocesses: selection, optimization, and compensation (M. M. Baltes & Carstensen, 1996; P. B. Baltes & Baltes, 1980, 1990; Heckhausen & Schulz, 1995; Marsiske, Lang, Baltes, & Baltes, 1995; Nesselroade & Jones, 1991).

Especially relevant for the present article is the notion that since the classical work of Tetens (1777), life span scholars proceeded in their theoretical efforts from the basic assumption that human development essentially is incomplete. In this article, I contend that this incompleteness of what I call the biological and cultural architecture of lifespan development is less promising than an unfinished Schubert symphony. The situation is more like an ill-designed building in which inherent vulnerabilities, as old age is reached, become more and more manifest.

The incompleteness of lifespan human development results primarily from two conditions. Incompleteness results first from the fact that biological and cultural co-evolution (Durham, 1991) has not come to a standstill but is an ongoing process. Second, and most important, incompleteness results from the fact that the biological and cultural architecture of human ontogeny is relatively undeveloped for the second part of the lifespan (P. B. Baltes, 1991; P. B. Baltes & Graf, 1996). Neither biological nor cultural evolution has had sufficient opportunity to evolve a full and optimizing scaffolding (architecture) for the later phases of life. A seeming paradox exists: Historically speaking, old age is young.

To explore this incompleteness argument and its implications for the future potentials of human development, lifespan researchers have focused their work on searching for methods to study age-related changes in plasticity (potential) and for conceptualizations that permit the definition of successful or effective human development. One general approach to this topic has been to define *successful development* as the relative maximization of gains and the minimization of losses (M. M. Baltes & Carstensen, 1996; P. B. Baltes, 1987; P. B. Baltes & Baltes, 1990; Brandtstädter & Wentura, 1995; Marsiske et al., 1995).

Such a gain-loss approach also permits the definition of degrees or completeness or incompleteness of the life span. Using the ratio between achieved gains and losses as a criterion for evaluation, the lifespan architecture would be the more complete, the more, in all age periods of the life course, individuals were to show relatively more gains than losses in functioning. Instead of gains and losses, it would be possible also to use desirable and undesirable states as criteria. Currently, as described below in more detail, this pattern of relative completeness does not exist for all phases of life. Beginning in late adulthood and certainly in old age, losses outnumber gains, and with age the balance becomes less positive (P. B. Baltes, 1987).

The determination of what is a gain or a loss in ontogenetic change is a topic of theoretical as well as empirical inquiry (see also M. M. Baltes & Carstensen, 1996; Brandtstädter, 1984; Hobfoll, 1989; Kahneman & Tversky, 1984; Labouvie-Vief, 1982; Schulz & Heck-hausen, 1996). Suffice it here to mention that the nature of what is considered a gain or a loss can change with age; involves objective in addition to subjective criteria; and is conditioned by theoretical predilection, standards of comparison, cultural and historical context, as well as by criteria of functional fitness or adaptivity.

Architecture of Lifespan Development: The Frame Resulting from Biological and Cultural Coevolution

What is the role of cultural and biological factors in ontogenesis across the life span—how do they interact and condition each other, for instance, in the sense of biocultural coevolution (Durham, 1991)? What is the zone of development, the norm of reaction, and the modifiability or plasticity (P. B. Baltes, 1987; P. B. Baltes & Schaie, 1976; Lerner, 1984, 1986; Magnusson, 1996) that one can expect to operate during ontogenesis? On the basis of genetic- and evolution-based factors and availability of cultural structures, only certain pathways can be implemented during ontogenesis, and some of these are more likely to be realized than others. Despite the sizable plasticity of *Homo sapiens* and the dynamic quality of such conceptions as norms of reaction, zone of development, or plasticity, not everything is possible in ontogenetic development. Although open, development inherently is also limited.

Figure 2.1 illustrates the main lines of argument that I submit as being the three foundational (constraining) principles of the lifespan architecture of human ontogeny (P. B. Baltes, 1994; P. B. Baltes et al., in press). Note first that the specific form (level

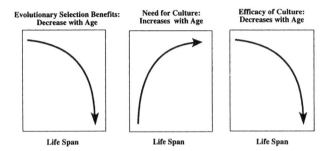

| **Figure 2.1** | Schematic Representation of Three Principles Governing the Dynamics Between Biology and Culture Across the Life Span |

shape) of the three lifespan functions depicted in Figure 2.1 is not critical. What is critical are the overall direction and reciprocal interactions between the functions displayed.

Evolutionary Selection Benefits Decrease with Age

The first foundational principle of my view of the lifespan architecture states that the benefits resulting from evolutionary selection evince a negative age correlation (Finch, 1990, 1996; Finch & Rose, 1995; Martin, Austad, & Johnson, 1996; Osiewacz, 1995; Rose, 1991; Yates & Benton, 1995). As a consequence, the human genome in older ages is predicted to contain an increasingly larger number of deleterious genes and dysfunctional gene expressions than in younger ages.

Why did whatever happened later in the life span benefit less from the optimizing power of evolutionary selection pressure? The primary reason is that reproductive fitness, the essential component of natural selection, involved the transmission of genes in the context of fertility and parenting behavior, events and processes that typically extend from conception to earlier adulthood. As a consequence, over evolutionary history, selection operated more strongly on the first half of life. Moreover, given the much shorter life span in early human evolution, selection pressure could not operate as frequently to begin with when it came to the second half of life. Most individuals died before possible negative genetic attributes were activated or their possible negative consequences could become manifest.

One concrete illustration of this aging-based weakening of evolutionary selection benefits is the existence of late-life illnesses such as Alzheimer's dementia (for other examples, see Martin et al., 1996). This disease typically does not become manifest until age 70. After age 70, however, dementia of the Alzheimer's type increases markedly in prevalence (for specific data, see below). Alzheimer's dementia is at least in part a late-life disease because reproductive fitness-based evolutionary pressure was unable to select against it. Geneticists (e.g., Martin et al., 1996) call such a situation *selection neutrality.*

There are other aspects of a biology of aging that, together and separately, imply an age-associated loss in biological potential, and whose operation amplifies the evolutionary neglect of old age (e.g., Finch, 1996; Martin et al., 1996). Many of these age-related biological losses are associated with the mechanisms of ontogenesis itself. Among the prevalent explanations for biological aging losses are wear-and-tear theories, entropy-based conceptions, as well as interpretations related to the sources of age-accumulated increases in mutations.

These various considerations about the role of genetic and biological factors converge into an unequivocal conclusion regarding the dynamics of biological factors in lifespan development. Where evolutionary selection and the ontogenetic biology of aging are concerned, the life span of humans displays an unfinished architecture, and in this instance, and certainly after physical maturity, the consequences of this incompleteness are essentially negative or dysfunctional. With age, the genetic material, associated genetic mechanisms, and genetic expressions become less effective and less able to generate or maintain high levels of functioning. Evolution and biology are not good friends of old age.

Age-Related Increase in Need (Demand) for Culture

The second cornerstone of a lifespan architecture of human ontogenesis states that there is an age-related increase in the need or demand for culture (middle part of Figure 2.1). *Culture* in this context refers to the entirety of psychological, social, material, and symbolic (knowledge-based) resources that humans have generated over the millenia, and which as they are transmitted across generations, make human development possible as we know it today (Boesch, 1991; Cole, 1996; D'Andrade, 1995; Durham, 1991; Shweder, 1991). For human ontogenesis to achieve increasingly higher levels of functioning, for instance, to live longer or to be able to read and write, there had to be a conjoint evolutionary increase in the content and dissemination of culture. And the further we expect human ontogenesis to extend itself into adult life and old age, the more it will be necessary for particular cultural factors and resources to emerge and operate to make this possible.

To appreciate the power of the evolution of such culture-based resources, consider what happened to average life expectancy in industrialized countries during the twentieth century. It was not the genetic make-up of the population that evinced marked changes during this time. On the contrary, it was economic and technological innovations that produced significant additions to average life expectancy, from an average of about 45 years in 1900 to about 75 years in 1995. Similarly, the dramatic increase in literacy rates over the last centuries in industrialized nations was not the result of a change in the genome (that requisite evolution took place at a much earlier time many millenia ago; e.g., Klix, 1993) but, above all, a change in environmental contexts, cultural resources, and strategies of education.

There is a second argument for the proposition that, with age, the need for the supportive and enriching role of culture increases. The demand for culture also increases because, as individuals reach old age, their biological potentials decline (left part of Figure 2.1). The older in age individuals are, the more they are in need of culture-based compensations (e.g., material, technical, social, economic, psychological) to generate and maintain high levels of functioning. This view of "culture as compensation" is a major tenet of many evolutionary theories in cultural anthropology (P. B. Baltes, 1991; Brandtstädter, in press; Dixon & Bäckman, 1995; Durham, 1991; Marsiske et al., 1995). Consider the evolution of clothing in its many variations as an example. At the evolutionary base is a biological lack. Humans wear cloth in part because of a thermoregulation deficit.

Age-Related Decrease in Efficiency of Culture

The right panel of Figure 2.1 illustrates the third cornerstone of the overall architecture of the life course. This foundational principle states that there is an age-related loss in the effectiveness or efficiency of cultural factors and resources. With age, and conditioned primarily by the negative biological trajectory of the life course, the relative power (effectiveness) of psychological, social, material, and cultural interventions wanes. In summary, although there continues to be plasticity in the second half of life—and its extent may even be larger than typically believed (M. M. Baltes & Carstensen, 1996; P. B. Baltes, 1987; Lerner, 1984; Willis, 1990)—the scope of plasticity of the human organism declines with age.

Take cognitive learning in old age as an example (P. B. Baltes, 1993; Birren & Schaie, 1996; Craik & Salthouse, 1992; Lindenberger & Baltes, 1995; Salthouse, 1991). The older the adult is, the more time, practice, and cognitive support it takes to attain the same learning gains. Moreover, when it comes to high levels of performance, older adults may never be able to reach the same levels of functioning as younger adults even after extensive training (P. B. Baltes & Kliegl, 1992; Ericsson & Smith, 1991; Kliegl, Mayr, & Krampe, 1994; Kliegl, Smith, & Baltes, 1989). Similar conclusions apply to lifespan changes in neuronal plasticity (Magnusson, 1996). Neuronal plasticity continues to exist across the life span, but with age it is reduced in scope and efficiency.

This third principle of an age-related reduction in cultural efficiency is likely to raise objections in social science circles. Two reasons are central. A first objection is the notion that the specifics of cultural systems, namely their symbolic form, may follow different mechanisms of efficiency. For instance, the lifespan developmental entropy costs of symbolic systems may be more favorable than those observed for basic biological processes (P. B. Baltes & Graf, 1996). Second, some social scientists argue that the concept of efficiency contains assumptions about human functioning that are inherently opposed to phenomena such as meaning of life, a sense of religion, or an understanding of one's finitude (P. B. Baltes et al., in press; Dittmann-Kohli, 1995; Rosenmayr, 1990). These are serious lines of argument. However, I submit that such perspectives, important and critical as they are for an understanding of human development, do not alter the general direction of the lifespan function outlined. In other words, the primary impact of symbolic systems and related meaning systems is on level, rate, and the lifespan extension of cultural efficiency, not on its ontogenetic directional course.

I submit that the three propositions and trajectories outlined in Figure 2.1 form a robust architecture of the lifespan dynamics between biology and culture. This architecture, including its growing incompleteness as the life course unfolds, represents the most general frame within which developmental theory is embedded. Whatever the specific content and form of a given psychological theory of human ontogeny, they need to be consistent with this architectural frame. For instance, any theory of lifespan development that were to posit "general" positive advances across broad domains of functioning in later adulthood can be judged to be false. Similarly false would be the view that development at any age could consist of pure gain. In the past, as argued for instance by Hetherington and Baltes (1988) and Labouvie-Vief (1982), such a pure-gain view of development was often held by cognitive child developmentalists.

Why is a pure-gain view of ontogenesis false? As is true for evolution, ontogenetic adaptivity and ontogenetic attainments are always local, that is, context, space and time (age) bound. In addition, development always involves selection and, therefore, a trade-off between alternative pathways and success-failure constellations. This recognition has led lifespan theorists such as Jochen Brandtstädter, Gisela Labouvie-Vief, and myself to reject any conception of development that is unilinear and based solely on the notion of growth as a unidimensional advance in quantity and quality of functioning. On the contrary, multicausality, multidimensionality, multidirectionality, and multifunctionality reign supreme in ontogenesis at all stages of the life course (M. M. Baltes, 1996; P. B. Baltes, 1987; P. B. Baltes et al., in press; Brandtstädter, in press; Labouvie-Vief, 1982; Marsiske et al., 1995; Schulz & Heckhausen, 1996; Uttal & Perlmutter, 1989).

The changing lifespan dynamics in the ratio of gains and losses are also evident at the level of subjective beliefs about the overall developmental trajectory of gains and losses across the life span (Heckhausen, Dixon, & Baltes, 1989). For instance, when asked about the typical adult developmental trajectory of a large number of attributes (such as intelligent, strong, anxious, sick, etc.), persons report a script that involves a changing ratio of gains and losses toward an increasingly less desirable balance (see left part of Figure 2.2). With increasing age, more and more of the expected changes involve losses rather than gains, although there continue to be some expectations of gains in old age, such as an increase in dignity and wisdom. And with this changing ratio between gains and losses, there is a corollary change in the expected proportion of success and failure experiences (Schulz & Heckhausen, 1996).

This lifespan script about gains and losses has consequences for the subjective experience of lifespan development. Thus, when persons of different ages are asked about what age they would like to be, they report an increasing negative discrepancy between their actual age and their desired age (Smith & Baltes, 1996). Seventy-year-olds, for instance, would like to be on average about 10 years younger. For 90-year-olds, the discrepancy is increased to about 25 years. These findings of an age-related increase in the discrepancy between actual age and desired age lend support to the reality of a growing disjuncture between body and mind—between what is desirable and what is possible. These findings also illustrate that the beliefs that individuals hold about the life course reflect the biological and cultural incompleteness of the life span and the resulting age-related increase in less desirable outcomes.

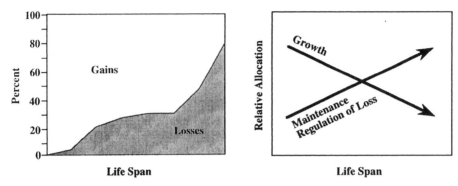

Figure 2.2   Lifespan Script of Allocation of Resources to Functions of Development

> *Note:* The left part shows subjective expectations about desirable (gains) and undesirable (losses) changes across adulthood on the basis of Heckhausen, Dixon, and Baltes (1989). The right side illustrates lifespan changes in the allocation of resources into three functions of development: growth, maintenance (resilience), and regulation of loss (Staudinger, Marsiske, & Baltes, 1995).

Lifespan Changes in the Allocation of Resources to Functions of Development

In the following section, I pursue a strategy where the implications of this overall architectural landscape of human development are examined at levels of analysis that step-by-step approximate the kind of questions that developmental psychologists study. A first step in this direction, and as illustrated in the right part of Figure 2.2, involves consideration of three general functions or outcomes of development: (a) the function of growth; (b) the function of maintenance, including recovery (resilience); and (c) the function of regulation of loss. These three functions and their associated outcomes represent the systemic whole of individual development (see also Staudinger, Marsiske, & Baltes, 1995).

With the adaptive function of growth, I refer to behaviors involved in reaching higher levels of functioning or adaptive capacity. Under the heading of maintenance and recovery (resilience), I classify behaviors involved in maintaining levels of functioning in the face of a new contextual challenge or a loss in potential. Finally, regarding regulation of loss or management, I mean behaviors that organize functioning at lower levels when maintenance or recovery (resilience) is no longer possible.

Because of the architecture outlined above, my colleagues and I argue that there is a systematic lifespan shift in the relative allocation of resources to these three functions (P. B. Baltes, 1994; P. B. Baltes et al., in press; Marsiske et al., 1995; Staudinger et al., 1995). In childhood, the primary allocation is directed toward growth; during adulthood, the predominant allocation is toward maintenance and recovery (resilience). In old age, more and more resources are directed toward regulation or management of loss. Such a characterization of the life span, of course, is an oversimplification, as individual, functional (domain), contextual, and historical differences need to be taken into account. The lifespan script is about relative probability and prevalence. Note in this context that the reallocation of resources toward maintenance of functioning and regulation of loss is facilitated by the tendency of individuals to prefer avoidance of loss over enhancement of gains (Hobfoll, 1989; Kahneman & Tversky, 1984).

The lifespan trajectories regarding investment of resources into growth, resilience, and regulation of loss also have implications for the dynamics involved in the systemic and integrative coordination of these three functions. A first telling research example is the strong interest of adult development researchers in topics such as selection of goals (Cantor & Fleeson, 1994) but especially compensation (Bäckman & Dixon, 1992; P. B. Baltes & Baltes, 1990; Dixon & Bäckman, 1995). And when considering compensation, theoretical considerations include the seemingly counterintuitive view that deficits can breed advances through innovative efforts (P. B. Baltes, 1987, 1991; Burghardt, 1984; Uttal & Perlmutter, 1989). Such a view, incidentally, is consistent with evolutionary theory, where it is widely held that during evolution, increases in adaptive capacity were enhanced by conditions of stress and challenge (anagenesis).

Another telling example of the dynamics among the functions of growth, resilience, and regulation of loss is the lifespan study of the interplay between autonomy and dependency in children and older adults (M. M. Baltes, 1996). Whereas the primary focus of the first half of life is the maximization of autonomy, in old age, the productive and creative use of dependent behavior becomes critical. According to Margret Baltes, for older adults to maintain autonomy in select domains of functioning, the effective exercise and use of dependent behavior is a compensatory must. By invoking dependency and support, resources are freed up for use in other domains "selected" for personal efficacy and growth. Similar perspectives, of course, can be applied to functioning in childhood, such as the nature of child care or motor development (Hetherington & Baltes, 1988; Labouvie-Vief, 1982; Thelen & Smith, 1994).

Selective Optimization with Compensation: An Example of a General (Systemic) Theory of Lifespan Development

In this section, I add another level of analysis and apply the basic lifespan architectural frame to the formulation of a general model of development. For this purpose, I characterize a *metatheory of development*, selective optimization with compensation (SOC), which, together with several colleagues, Margret Baltes and I have developed over the last decade (M. M. Baltes & Carstensen, 1996; P. B. Baltes, 1987; P. B. Baltes & Baltes, 1980, 1990; P. B. Baltes, Dittmann-Kohli, & Dixon, 1984; Carstensen, Hanson, & Freund, 1995; Marsiske et al., 1995).

In our work on SOC, the original intellectual motivation was the search for a general process of systemic functioning that would serve as an effective strategy for dealing with the lifespan architecture described above. We began by using the field of aging as a testing ground (P. B. Baltes & Baltes, 1990). The following everyday example was one of our early illustrations of SOC. When the concert pianist Arthur Rubinstein, as an 80-year-old, was asked in a television interview how he managed to maintain such a high level of expert piano playing, he hinted at the coordination of three strategies. First, Rubinstein said that he played fewer pieces (selection); second, he indicated that he now practiced these pieces more often (optimization); and third, he suggested that to counteract his loss in mechanical speed, he now used a kind of impression management, such as introducing slower play before fast segments, so to make the latter appear faster (compensation). Using such a SOC-related strategy and paraphrasing a quotation from Hesiod, "Half can be more than the whole."

Meanwhile, my colleagues and I have enlarged this view and emphasize that the orchestration of selection, optimization, and compensation is not unique to human aging but inherent in any developmental process (P. B. Baltes & Graf, 1996; P. B. Baltes et al., in press; Marsiske et al., 1995; see also chapter by Edelman & Tononi, 1996). Beginning with birth, if not at conception, humans select, optimize, and compensate. In this sense, we view SOC as a general frame for developmental theory. We further argue that this general theoretical approach is consistent with the lifespan architecture outlined above.

The essential nature of *selection* in ontogenesis follows from several arguments. One is that development always has a specific set of targets (goals) of functioning. Second, development always proceeds within the condition of a limited capacity, including constraints in time and resources. Moreover, selection is conditioned by the very fact that organisms possess behavioral dispositions (e.g., sensory modalities, motor repertoires, cognitive mechanics) that during evolution were selected from a pool of potentialities. Furthermore, in reflection of the left part of Figure 2.1, selection is conditioned by age-related changes in plasticity and associated losses in potential. Age-associated losses in biological potential or plasticity increase the pressure for selection.

Because most examples in this article have their origin in the field of adult development and aging, the following illustrations are taken from the field of infant and child development. The biologist Waddington (1975; see also Edelman, 1987) was perhaps the first powerful spokesperson for the notion of development as selective "canalization." A specific example of selection in early life is the acquisition of language (Levelt, 1989). Although infants around the world seem to possess the same basic dispositons for the recognition and production of language, their ontogenetic development is shaped in specific (selected) directions of sound recognition and sound production by the realization (acquisition) of a particular language. Thus, the acquisition of language involves from the ontogenetic beginning selection phenomena, with associated gains and losses in performance potential. Another concrete illustration of selection is the acquisition of cognitive stages in child development. Take Piagetian theory as an example. It has become increasingly recognized that the ontogenetic movement toward a "final" stage of formal logical reasoning is the effect of a culture-based selection process. Another approach closely related to the notion of development as selection is the work of Siegler

(1994) who treated the ontogeny of cognitive skills and strategies in children as the outcome of variability-based selection from a larger pool of potentialities.

Optimization is the hallmark of any traditional conception of development. Development is widely considered as a movement toward increased efficacy and higher levels of functioning. My colleagues and I argue that human development, as an optimizing positive change in adaptive capacity toward a set of desirable outcomes (goals), requires in concert the application of a set of behavior-enhancing factors such as cultural knowledge, physical status, goal commitment, practice, and effort. The component elements that are relevant for the task of optimization vary by domain and developmental status. And from an ontogenetic point of view, of course, the concept of optimization undergoes developmental changes in the components and mechanisms involved as well. Research on the development of expertise in children and adults is a good example (Ericsson & Smith, 1991).

Compensation, finally, is operative whenever a given set of means is no longer available, either because of direct losses of these means (e.g., hearing loss), because of negative transfer (e.g., incompatibility between goals), or because of new limiting constraints in time and energy (e.g., the exclusive consumptive focus on the tasks of resilience and regulation of loss). Compensation, then, has multiple origins and comes in varied forms.

Researchers in the field of aging have little trouble evoking examples of compensation (M. M. Baltes & Carstensen, 1996; P. B. Baltes et al., 1984; Dixon & Bäckman, 1995; Schulz & Heckhausen, 1996). This is different for researchers in the field of child development in which the prevalent view is on gain and advances in functioning. Because of our predominant concern with development as growth in childhood and with the exception of compensatory responses to pathological conditions such as deafness or blindness, we know relatively little about the functional role that compensation plays in normal child and adolescent development. A first line of thinking involves losses in means (resources), which result in the sense of "negative transfer" from advances in those means that are directly targeted for developmental enhancement. As children move toward decontextualized thinking in the formal-logical sense, for instance, their ability for play, imagery, as well as divergent modes of thinking may decline. Similarly, as adolescents opt for particular pathways of athletic development, their skills in other kinds of sports are reduced. In this instance both negative transfer and a reduced amount of practice are involved. Or consider interpersonal issues such as those associated with the emergence of autonomy during adolescence (M. M. Baltes & Silverberg, 1994). As adolescents sharpen their means of autonomy, their means of relating to their parents lose in efficacy. Consideration of the sequelae of this parent-adolescent dynamic also illustrates how losses in means can represent temporary conditions for subsequent advances, such as when adolescents and their parents at later points reach a new and possibly more advanced (egalitarian) form of communication and relatedness.

These examples already illustrate that how selection, optimization, and compensation are defined differs by theoretical framework and domains of functioning. Within

Table 2.1

Selection, Optimization, and Compensation Embedded in an Action-Theoretical
Framework (After P. B. Baltes, Baltes, Freund, & Lang, 1995; Freund & Baltes, 1996)

Selection (goals/preferences)	Optimization (goal-relevant means)	Compensation (means/resources for counteracting loss/decline in goal-relevant means)
Elective selection:	Attentional focus	Increased attentional focus
Specification of goals	Effort/energy	Increased effort/energy
Goal system (hierarchy)	Time allocation	Increased time allocation
Contextualization of goals	Practice of skills	Activation of unused
Goal commitment	Acquiring new	skills/resources
Loss-based selection:	skills/resources	Acquiring new skills/resources
Focusing on most	Modeling successful	Modeling successful others
important goal(s)	others	who compensate
Search for new goals	Motivation for	Use of external aids/help of others
Reconstruction of goal	self-development	Therapeutic intervention
hierarchy		
Adaptation of standards		

an action-theoretical framework (Boesch, 1991; Brandtstädter, in press), for instance, the following characterizations of the three components hold: Selection involves directionality, goals, or outcomes; optimization involves means to achieve success (desired outcomes); and compensation denotes a response to loss in means (resources) used to maintain success or desired levels of functioning (outcomes).

Table 2.1 illustrates the kind of category of behaviors and items my colleagues and I apply when measuring behaviors of selection, optimization, and compensation—in this case, by means of a questionnaire (P. B. Baltes, Baltes, Freund, & Lang, 1995; Freund & Baltes, 1996). The use of action-theoretical perspectives might suggest to some readers the conclusion that SOC is intended always to be a process with intention and rationality, but this is not so. Rather, each of these elements or components can be active or passive, internal or external, or conscious or unconscious. Moreover, during ontogenesis, the status of these components can change, for instance, from compensation to optimization (Marsiske et al., 1995).

The SOC theory is inherently a systemic and functionalist one. Its focus is on the whole and the coordination of its parts in terms of three functions (selection, optimization, and compensation). The theory is also highly general. Therefore, we label it a *metatheory*. Because SOC does not designate the specific content and mechanisms of developmental processes and outcomes, it is applicable to a large range of variations in goals and means. One recent example is the application of SOC to the topic of control, which results in a lifespan theory of successful aging by means of an adaptive combination of primary and secondary control (Heckhausen & Schulz, 1995; Schulz & Heckhausen, 1996).

One may wonder whether the SOC theory carries a cultural bias. Is its conceptualization specific to industrialized Westernized societies? The use of the terms *selection*,

optimization, and *compensation*, by themselves and because of their frequent association with economic criteria of productivity, may suggest such a possibility. Aside from
the context of these terms, however, I argue that this is not the case. As a metatheory,
that is, a developmental theory about developmental theories, SOC is open in regard to
its phenotypic realization. In fact, I consider it the special strength of this theory, that
it is at the same time relativistic and universalistic.

The relativity of SOC lies in the variations of physical, motivational, social, and
intellectual resources, as well as in the criteria used to define successful development
(P. B. Baltes & Baltes, 1990). SOC is definitely context- and person-conditioned. Thus,
SOC, depending on sociocultural context, individual resources, and personal preferences, can be implemented in very different ways and by different means. Take the
context of Japan as an example. If in Japan, for instance, and in comparison with Western cultures, the primary focus of social development is more on family-boundedness
and on social interdependence and less on individuality and individual competitive-
ness, as Takahashi (1990) reported, such a cultural difference can be illuminated by
representing these differences in terms of the nature of selection, optimization, and
compensation.

The universalism (generality) of SOC rests in the argument that any process of
development is expected to involve some orchestration of selection, optimization, and
compensation and that with age, because of the basic architecture of the life course,
selection and compensation become increasingly important to maintain adequate levels
of functioning and permit advances in select domains of functioning (M. M. Baltes &
Carstensen, 1996; P. B. Baltes & Baltes, 1990; Dixon & Bäckman, 1995; Marsiske et al.,
1995). One interesting and as yet uncharted challenge is to link SOC to other theories
of development (Lerner, 1986). How would one reconstruct, for instance, Piagetian or
Eriksonian theory in terms of selection, optimization, and compensation? In my view,
such an effort would be a concrete test of the generality or metatheoretical usefulness
of the SOC approach.

The Sample Case of Lifespan Intellectual Development

In the opening sections, I argued that the lifespan architecture and SOC provide a
general frame for the study and organization of any developmental phenomenon. In
this section, I have chosen the example of lifespan intellectual development to examine
the degree to which these general frameworks on development are consistent with
extant psychological research on human ontogeny (P. B. Baltes, 1993; P. B. Baltes
et al., 1984; P. B. Baltes et al., in press).

The lifespan architectural frame outlined in Figure 2.1 suggests different trajectories for biological and cultural processes. In line with this frame, it has become theoretically useful to distinguish between two main categories of intellectual functioning: the
fluid mechanics and the crystallized pragmatics. Although the fluid-crystallized distinction dates back to the early work of Hebb (1949), Cattell (1971), and Horn (1970),

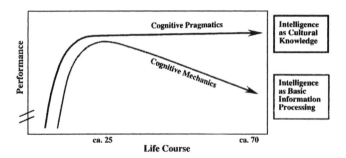

Figure 2.3   The Dual-Process Model of Lifespan Intellectual Development
Note: Modified after P. B. Baltes (1993) and Horn (1970).

embedding this distinction into the present line of theoretical argument makes these theories appear in a new and enriched framework, as Figure 2.3 illustrates.

Using a computer metaphor, one can conceptualize the fluid cognitive mechanics as reflecting the neurophysiological "hardware" (Barkow, Cosmides, & Tooby, 1992) or cognitive primitives (Salthouse, 1991) of the human brain as it was shaped by biocultural coevolution. At the operational level, we assume that the cognitive mechanics are indexed by the speed and accuracy of elementary processes of information processing: information input; visual and motor memory; and basic perceptual-cognitive processes such as discrimination, comparison, categorization, as well as their application in working memory. Because of the close connection of the fluid mechanics to the neurobiology of development, lifespan theory predicts some form of an inverted U-shape function across the life span, with decline beginning in young adulthood, if not earlier (P. B. Baltes & Lindenberger, 1997; Horn & Hofer, 1992).

The crystallized cognitive pragmatics can be understood as the culture-based "software" of the mind. They reflect the bodies of knowledge and information that cultures provide in the form of factual and procedural knowledge about the world, human affairs, socialization, and human agency (Cole, 1996; Klix, 1993). Examples of cognitive pragmatics are reading and writing skills; language; educational qualifications and professional skills; as well as knowledge about the self and about life skills that are relevant to the planning, conduct, and interpretation of life (P. B. Baltes, 1991; Brim, 1992; Smith, 1996; Staudinger, & Baltes, 1996b). The positive lifespan trajectory of the cognitive pragmatics, being primarily determined by cultural forces, can extend further into the life course than the mechanics. How far the trajectory extends is a function of two conditions. The first is the availability of cultural opportunities and their translation into programs of cognitive enhancement (P. B. Baltes, Lindenberger, & Staudinger, 1995; Willis, 1990). The second is the limitation posed by the cognitive mechanics and their lifespan trajectory.

In general, the body of lifespan work on intellectual functioning is consistent with this dual-process model of intelligence. Thus, there are distinct differences in lifespan trajectories among cognitive tasks when tasks are grouped into more biology- or culture-based ones. Beginning in adulthood, for the cognitive mechanics, negative age gradients are obtained consistently for such component processes as working memory, speed of information processing, and inhibitory efficacy (Lindenberger & Baltes, 1994; Salthouse, 1991). Age gradients for pragmatic tasks, on the other hand, such as for verbal performance tasks or for tasks of professional expertise, often evince maintenance into later phases of adulthood, and their trajectory is very dependent on life course experiential factors (P. B. Baltes, 1993; Blanchard-Fields & Hess, 1995; Ericsson & Smith, 1991; Salthouse, 1991). In addition, there is ample evidence about how the mechanics and pragmatics interact, for instance, how the cognitive pragmatics can be used to offset losses in the mechanics. Older adults, for example, who continue to be excellent typists, do so by reading further along in the text when typing to compensate for losses in reaction time (Salthouse, 1991).

In our own work over the past decades, my colleagues and I have attempted to study the development of the two basic categories of the mind with a primary focus on their maximal expression. For this purpose, we selected tasks that represented prototypes of the cognitive mechanics and pragmatics: working memory for the fluid mechanics and wisdom for the crystallized pragmatics (P. B. Baltes, 1993; P. B. Baltes, Lindenberger, & Staudinger, 1995; Kliegl et al., 1989). For each of these prototypical tasks, we studied people of different ages under optimizing conditions to understand maximum performance potential and its age-associated changes. In addition, we demonstrated that a key component of the cognitive pragmatics is its social and collaborative nature such as expressed in the facilitative effect of interactive minds (Cole, 1996; Staudinger & Baltes, 1996a). Figure 2.4 summarizes the main outcomes of our research on the dual-process model of lifespan intelligence.

In the left part of Figure 2.4, data on psychometric intelligence tests are graphed, which reflect primarily the cognitive mechanics. These findings exhibit the typical age-loss trend beginning in early adult life (P. B. Baltes & Lindenberger, 1997). Age losses, incidentally, become even more pronounced if, similar to stress tests in medicine, the focus is on maximum performance as studied by means of testing-the-limits methodology

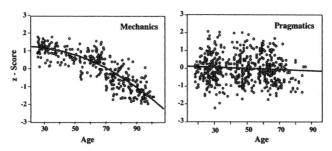

Figure 2.4   Adult Developmental Age Gradients for Measures of the Cognitive Mechanics (Lindenberger & Baltes, 1995) and the Cognitive Pragmatics (Staudinger & Baltes, 1996b)

(P. B. Baltes & Kliegl, 1992; Kliegl, Smith, & Baltes, 1990). The right side of Figure 2.4 summarizes our evidence on age correlations that involve a prototype of the cognitive pragmatics, that is, wisdom, and the results, are very different (P. B. Baltes & Smith, 1990; P. B. Baltes & Staudinger, 1993; Staudinger & Baltes, 1996b). As predicted by the lifespan architecture outlined, the lifespan trajectory of wisdom-related performance extends further into the life span. In our data on wisdom, for instance, older adults performed as well as younger adults at least up to age 70. After that age, however, performance levels seemed to decline in wisdom tasks as well. In advanced old age, the lifespan biological architecture constrains more and more what culture and individuals can accomplish.

More recently, our work has been extended to include the study of predictive correlates of old-age intelligence to test another facet of the dual-process model of intellectual development, that is, the differential mechanisms and causal factors assumed to regulate lifespan development. One example is work on intelligence in the Berlin Aging Study (Mayer & Baltes, 1996) in which 516 persons 70 to 103 years of age have been studied with an extensive battery of cognitive measures and a large set of culture- and biology-related indicators. From this evidence, I highlight four findings that demonstrate, as predicted by the lifespan architecture outlined, the powerful role of biological constraints in old age and the parallel decrease in efficacy of cultural factors (P. B. Baltes & Lindenberger, 1997; Lindenberger & Baltes, 1995, in press; Smith & Baltes, 1996).

The first finding involves the increasing cascade-like effect of the generality of cognitive aging. As shown also in the longitudinal analyses of Schaie (1988, 1994, 1996), with age, more and more of the cognitive abilities are involved in the loss pattern. Thus, when the age range of 70 to 100 years is reached, all cognitive dimensions exhibit losses (P. B. Baltes & Lindenberger, 1997). There are large individual differences in initial level and onset of the aging losses, but the pattern seems universal. The second example concerns the age-associated increase in pathological aging. In particular, people at risk for Alzheimer's disease or categorized as demented demonstrate major losses (see also M. M. Baltes, Kühl, & Sowarka, 1992).

The third exemplary finding concerns the role of culture-based life history in the regulation of cognitive aging. For instance, is old age kinder to the culturally advantaged? The basic biological architecture of the life span (see Figure 2.1) would suggest that the effect of cultural advantage may become progressively smaller as the individual ages, that is, the more the biological lifespan architecture is tested at its limits. In the Berlin Aging Study (Mayer & Baltes, 1996), the outcome supports this prediction. As shown in Figure 2.5, the negative age gradient found for the aging of a general measure of intellectual performance applied to subgroups irrespective of their social and educational life histories and current life contexts. Whereas people from culturally and socially advantaged life histories entered old age at a higher average level of functioning, their subsequent negative age patterns were identical with those

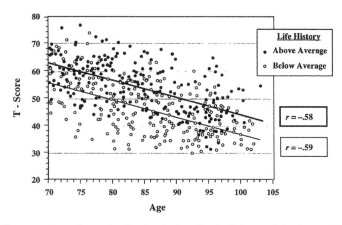

Figure 2.5   Data from the Berlin Aging Study (Mayer & Baltes, 1996)

Note: Age gradients in intellectual functioning (based on 14 tests) are identical for subgroups reflecting above-average and below-average life circumstances involving education, income, occupational status, and social prestige (Lindenberger & Baltes, 1995).

having experienced or experiencing less favorable life conditions. In other words, earlier advantages do not guard against decline.

The fourth exemplary finding is the powerful connection between physical functions and cognitive functioning that emerges in old age. In the Berlin Aging Study (Mayer & Baltes, 1996), for instance, the telling result is the extremely strong association that my colleagues and I observed between basic sensorimotor functions (such as hearing, vision, and motor balance) and intellectual functioning. In old age, individual differences in these basic sensory and sensorimotor functions were found to correlate almost perfectly with age differences in the 14 tests of cognitive functioning studied (P. B. Baltes & Lindenberger, 1997; Lindenberger & Baltes, 1994).

Figure 2.6 illustrates the powerful association of sensory with intellectual functioning in old age by comparing the raw age gradient in an overall measure of general intelligence with the age gradient obtained after statistically controlling for sensory functioning. When simple measures of hearing, vision, and motor balance are used as covariates, the entire pattern of negative age differences in general intelligence disappears. Our preferred explanatory option is to invoke a common cause (third-variable hypothesis) for this powerful association between sensorimotor and cognitive functioning that emerges in old age. We suggest that age-related changes in neurophysiological brain functioning are assumed to affect at the same time sensory, sensorimotor, and cognitive functioning. This interpretation is also supported by evidence on brain atrophy (Lindenberger & Baltes, 1996).

The pattern of these findings is fully consistent with the life span architecture outlined in Figure 2.1 and the dual-process model of intelligence. When it comes to the "hardware-like" cognitive mechanics and the speedy and accurate functioning of basic

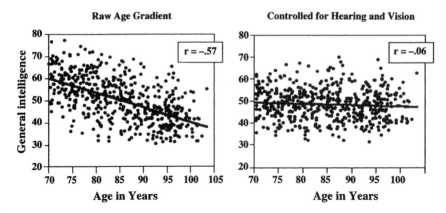

Figure 2.6   Data from the Berlin Aging Study (Mayer & Baltes, 1996)

Note: Measures of visual acuity and auditory threshold sensitivity in advanced old age predict the whole of age differences (from 70 to 100) in intellectual functioning (modified after P. B. Baltes & Lindenberger, 1997; Lindenberger & Baltes, 1994). The same pattern applies to a measure of sensorimotor balance.

mechanisms of information processing, old age takes its toll, very much consistent with what is found in biological and physical indicators of functioning. Conversely, the lifespan trajectories for cognitive pragmatics, reflecting the enhancing contribution of cultural factors and the interactive mind's conditions of life (P. B. Baltes & Staudinger, 1996), increase for a longer span of life. However, as old age is reached, the compensatory role of culture and culture-based behaviors and resources becomes less efficient. As a consequence, in advanced old age, the cognitive pragmatics such as wisdom decline as well.

The Fourth Age: The Most Radical Form of Incompleteness

In conclusion, I concentrate on advanced old age that, following the tradition described in Laslett (1991), I propose to call the *fourth age*. The nature of the fourth age (from about 80 years onward) is, in my opinion, the major new frontier for future research and theory in lifespan development as well as for efforts in human development policy. Two arguments lay the foundation for the following observations: (a) the fundamental incompleteness of the biological and cultural architecture of the life span as outlined above and (b) recent findings on advanced old age as obtained, for instance, by the Berlin Aging Study (P. B. Baltes, Mayer, Helmchen, & Steinhagen-Thiessen, 1996; Mayer & Baltes, 1996; Smith & Baltes, 1996). These findings differ in some dramatic ways from research on young-old age.

During the last decades, we have witnessed a growing success story regarding young-old age (Birren & Schaie, 1996). Because of medical, technical, social, economic and educational advances, the overall gestalt of life for 60- and 70-year-olds has made major strides in indicators of health and psychological functioning. For this period of the third age, cultural and social forces in industrialized countries have been able to offset, for the most part and for more and more individuals, the weaknesses inherent in the biological lifespan architecture.

What about advanced old age, however? What is the evidence that the same trend will continue as people increase the number of remaining years in old age as well? Thus far, the increase in life expectancy was primarily based on the reduction of mortality in younger ages. Recent demographic research by Manton, Vaupel, and others (Manton & Vaupel, 1995; Vaupel & Jeune, 1995), however, has shown that during the last decades of this century, the increase in average life expectancy was not only due to the fact that more persons reached higher ages but also to the fact that older persons live longer. Eighty-year-olds, for instance, over the last three decades in northern Europe have increased their remaining lifetime from about four years to seven years.

The basic architecture of the life span displayed in Figure 2.1 suggests that these added years will not harbor the same potential as earlier gains in life expectancy. Not surprisingly, therefore, we are witnessing a new line of inquiry in aging research. More and more of the current gerontological work concentrates on such questions as the plasticity and quality of life in old age, how to define it, and how to measure it and to assess the degree to which it shows historical cohort- and age-related changes.

A key question in this research is whether potential and quality of life are different in advanced old age than in young-old age. A recent analysis of Americans, for instance, by Crimmins, Hayward, and Saito (1996) suggested that the percentage of dysfunctional-inactive years of the remaining lifetime is 20% for 70-year-old women, whereas for 90-year-olds, close to 60% of the remaining years represent dysfunctional-inactive time (see Table 2.2). In this instance, dysfunctionality or inactivity was measured by indicators of everyday competence and independent living. These are dramatic age-related losses in functional status as people move from the third to the fourth age. The oldest old are not simply individuals who continue to stay alive because their functional status remains at the same level as that of the younger old.

Table 2.2

Quality of Life in Old Age: Dysfunctional-Inactive Proportions of Remaining Years

Age	Dysfunctional-Inactive Percentage	
	Women	Men
70	20% of 14 years	14% of 10 years
80	35% of 8 years	27% of 6 years
90	60% of 5 years	55% of 3 years

Note: Data are for U.S. residents. Aggregated from information contained in Crimmins et al. (1996). Dysfunctional-inactive life = independent living not possible (basic everyday skills).

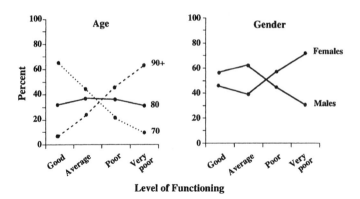

Figure 2.7   Data from the Berlin Aging Study (Mayer & Baltes, 1996)

Note: Research participants were distributed (by age and gender) into four groups differing in functional status. Groups were formed by considering a total of 23 physical, mental, and social indicators (Mayer & Baltes, 1996; Smith & Baltes, 1996).

The Berlin Aging Study (Mayer & Baltes, 1996), because of its wide age range and broad interdisciplinary assessment, offers a new window on this question of potential and quality of life in advanced old age. As shown in Figure 2.7, in one analysis (Mayer & Baltes, 1996; Smith & Baltes, in press) we used a total of 23 indicators of physical, psychiatric, psychological, social, and economic functioning. Using cluster analysis, we then explored age differences from 70 to 100 years. Note here that, because of the stratified sample used in the Berlin Aging Study, these comparisons involved equal numbers of persons in each age and gender group.

In Figure 2.7, the participants in the Berlin Aging Study ($N = 516$) were subdivided into four subgroups that descended in the quality of functional status and subjective well-being from good to average to poor and very poor. The outcome is clear. As shown in the left part of the figure, the oldest old appear much more frequently in undesirable clusters than the younger old. In the functionally best group (good), for instance, we found about 10 times more 70-year-olds than 90-year-olds. The reverse was true for the very poor group. In this extreme group of dysfunctionality, 90-year-olds were much more frequent than 70-year-olds. These are dramatic age differences in risk ratios. Although further analyses, including longitudinal, cohort-sequential, and interventive ones, need to be conducted to substantiate this pattern of results, the central outcome is unlikely to change. The oldest old are at a much higher risk for dysfunctionality than the young-old.

The right part of Figure 2.7 shows that there are also major gender differences in risks for old-age dysfunctionality (Smith & Baltes, 1996). The relative risk is significantly greater for women than men, and it becomes larger the higher the age. The female gender risk factor in the most dysfunctional group is about two. Thus, although women live longer than men, their functional status is less desirable, and this disadvantage increases with age. Although this is speculative, this gender difference may have a strong evolutionary basis. For men, because of their longer fertility and the role of dominance in reproductive fitness, selection may have favored vital biological functioning. For women and their role in nurturance, selection may have favored length of life over physical strength-related vitality of life.

This pattern of a major increase in risk for the fourth age is not only noticeable when physical variables are considered but also when the sole focus is on psychological measures such as intelligence, the self, personality, and social behavior (Smith & Baltes, 1996). On the level of individual psychological variables, and with the exception of intelligence, the negative age effects were relatively small. However, all significant age-difference effects were in the same direction, that is, toward more dysfunctionality in advanced old age. Thus, when the effects were aggregated into multivariate profiles, the negativity of the psychological aging patterns became more and more dramatic. Psychologically speaking, advanced old age presented itself more and more like a situation with high demand and stress characteristics. Advanced old age, the fourth age, is a kind of testing-the-limits situation for psychological resilience.

The relatively pessimistic picture for advanced old age is perhaps most conspicuous when the most prevalent old-age mental illness is considered, senile dementia of the Alzheimer's type. In the Berlin Aging Study (Helmchen et al., 1996; Mayer & Baltes, 1996)—and these findings are consistent with research by others—the prevalence of all diagnoses (mild, moderate, severe) of Alzheimer's dementia increased from about 2–3% in 70-year-olds, 10–15% in 80- to 90-year-olds, to about 50% in 90-year-olds. Alzheimer's disease is the condition that older persons fear most. Its manifestation is often outside the dignity that humans aspire for themselves. Currently, there is no effective therapy available. Thus, if, as demographic analyses suggest (Manton & Vaupel, 1995; Vaupel & Jeune, 1995), the recent trend of an increase in remaining lifetime for the oldest old of the population continues, it is likely that the incidences of Alzheimer's dementia will increase as well. The major exception to this prediction would be as yet uncharted medical advances in the preventive and remedial treatment of this disease.

Summary and Outlook

This article deals with the search for the most general frame of human development across the life span. The purpose is twofold: first, to stimulate developmentalists to embrace in their work the consideration of what I call the incomplete and changing architecture of the lifespan and second, to alert psychologists to the special forces and challenges of a fourth age.

Proceeding across several levels of analyses, I opened with general evolutionary considerations on the basic architecture of the life course. The proposed frame of constraints, which I judge to be fairly robust and therefore deserving of being called an architecture, contains three elements: First, evolution neglected old age, and, therefore, biological potential wanes with age. Second, for development to extend into progressively later portions of the life span, more and more culture is required. Third, because of the age-linked weakening of biological potential, the efficiency of culture decreases with age.

Informed by this biological and social architectural frame, I proceeded to identify a lifespan script in the relative allocation of resources into the three major functions of ontogenetic development: growth, maintenance (resilience), and the regulation or management of loss. Subsequently, I described a general metatheory of adaptive (successful) human development, SOC, which I concluded to be consistent with the lifespan architecture outlined and to represent a general model of effective adaptation or mastery. In a final step, I applied these general considerations to specific instantiations of developmental research and theory: the lifespan developmental study of intelligence and the nature of advanced old age.

In my view, the most pressing challenge for human developmentalists of the next century is to search for the conditions required to complete the biological and cultural architecture of the life span so that the optimization of development (in the sense of achieving a positive balance between gains and losses; P. B. Baltes, 1987) extends further and further into the later periods of the life span. Because of the robustness of the incomplete architecture of the life course, however, it is likely that extending positive human development into progressively higher ages will be increasingly more difficult. To this end, psychologists' collaboration with other disciplines engaged in remedying the incomplete architecture of the life span, such as biology, medicine, the social sciences, as well as practical anthropology, seems paramount.

A concluding observation is as follows: Although I do suggest that the optimization of human development is increasingly difficult as it is extended into advanced old age, I do not want to leave the impression that completion, in the sense of achieving a positive balance of gains and losses for all ages of life, is not possible in principle. Neither the biological matrix nor the current state of the cultural world ought to be viewed as a fixed representation of "the" nature of human aging. States of deficit and limitations, such as the fourth age, are powerful catalysts for scientific and cultural innovation. Furthermore, despite age losses in plasticity, there is latent potential for enhancement of functioning in old age as well (M. M. Baltes & Carstensen, 1996; P. B. Baltes, 1991, 1993).

In this spirit, we need to keep in mind that the future is not something we simply enter; the future is also something we help create. Of particular importance is the question of whether humankind will opt for remedying the basic incompleteness of the biological lifespan architecture through various techniques of genetic interventions aimed at the optimization of individual functioning. Despite the serious ethical issues, dilemmas, and possible misuses involved, my judgment is that it will be difficult to resist this genetic-intervention option. Why? The degree of biological incompleteness in advanced old age is a radical one. Thus, cultural and psychological factors alone would seem to be insufficient to generate for most individuals the kind of functional status in advanced old age in which gains outnumber losses and where human dignity prevails.

Notes

[*American Psychologist's*] *Editor's note.* Cheryl B. Travis served as action editor for this article. Articles based on APA award addresses are given special consideration in the *American Psychologist's* editorial selection process. A version of this article was originally presented as part of an Award for Distinguished Contributions to the International Advancement of Psychology address at the 104th Annual Convention of the American Psychological Association, Toronto, Ontario, Canada, August 1996.

Author's note. I gratefully acknowledge the many valuable discussions with and contributions by Margret Baltes, Laura Carstensen, Caleb Finch, Alexandra Freund, Ulman Lindenberger, Michael Marsiske, John Nesselroade, Jacqui Smith, and Ursula Staudinger. In addition, I thank the MacArthur Research Network on Successful Midlife Development (O. G. Brim, director) for their generous intellectual and financial support. Correspondence concerning this article should be addressed to Paul B. Baltes, Lentzeallee 94, Max Planck Institute for Human Development and Education, 14195 Berlin, Germany. Electronic mail may be sent via Internet to sekbaltes@mpib-berlin.mpg.de.

References

Bäckman, L., & Dixon, R. A. (1992). Psychological compensation: A theoretical framework. *Psychological Bulletin, 112*, 1–25.

Baltes, M. M. (1996). *The many faces of dependency in old age.* New York: Cambridge University Press.

Baltes, M. M., & Carstensen, L. L. (1996). The process of successful ageing. *Ageing and Society, 16*, 397–422.

Baltes, M. M., Kühl, K.-P., & Sowarka, D. (1992). Testing for limits of cognitive reserve capacity: A promising strategy for early diagnosis of dementia? *Journal of Gerontology: Psychological Sciences, 47*, P165–P167.

Baltes, M. M., & Silverberg, S. B. (1994). The dynamics between dependency and autonomy: Illustrations across the life span. In D. L. Featherman, R. M. Lerner, & M. Perlmutter (Eds.), *Life-span development and behavior* (Vol. 12, pp. 41–90). Hillsdale, NJ: Erlbaum.

Baltes, P. B. (1979). Life-span developmental psychology: Some converging observations on history and theory. In P. B. Baltes & O. G. Brim, Jr. (Eds.), *Life-span development and behavior* (Vol. 2, pp. 255–279). New York: Academic Press.

Baltes, P. B. (1987). Theoretical propositions of life-span developmental psychology: On the dynamics between growth and decline. *Developmental Psychology, 23*, 611–696.

Baltes, P. B. (1991). The many faces of human aging: Toward a psychological culture of old age. *Psychological Medicine, 21*, 837–854.

Baltes, P. B. (1993). The aging mind: Potential and limits. *Gerontologist, 33*, 580–594.

Baltes, P. B. (1994, August). *On the overall landscape of human development.* Invited address at the 102nd Annual Convention of the American Psychological Association, Los Angeles.

Baltes, P. B., & Baltes, M. M. (1980). Plasticity and variability in psychological aging: Methodological and theoretical issues. In G. E. Gurski (Ed.), *Determining the effects of aging on the central nervous system* (pp. 41–66). Berlin, Germany: Schering.

Baltes, P. B., & Baltes, M. M. (1990). Psychological perspectives on successful aging: The model of selective optimization with compensation. In P. B. Baltes & M. M. Baltes (Eds.), *Successful aging: Perspectives from the behavioral sciences* (pp. 1–34). New York: Cambridge University Press.

Baltes, P. B., Baltes, M. M., Freund, A. M., & Lang, F. R. (1995). *Measurement of selective optimization with compensation by questionnaire.* Berlin, Germany: Max Planck Institute for Human Development and Education.

Baltes, P. B., Dittmann-Kohli, F., & Dixon, R. A. (1984). New perspectives on the development of intelligence in adulthood: Toward a dual-process conception and a model of selective optimization with compensation. In P. B. Baltes & O. G. Brim, Jr. (Eds.), *Life-span development and behavior* (Vol. 6, pp. 33–76). New York: Academic Press.

Baltes, P. B., & Graf, P. (1996). Psychological aspects of aging: Facts and Frontiers. In D. Magnusson (Ed.), *The lifespan development of individuals: Behavioural, neurobiological and psychosocial perspectives* (pp. 427–460). Cambridge, England: Cambridge University Press.

Baltes, P. B., & Kliegl, R. (1992). Further testing of limits of cognitive plasticity: Negative age differences in a mnemonic skill are robust. *Developmental Psychology, 28,* 121–125.

Baltes, P. B., & Lindenberger, U. (1997). Emergence of a powerful connection between sensory and cognitive functions across the adult life span: A new window at the study of cognitive aging? *Psychology and Aging, 12,* 12–21.

Baltes, P. B., Lindenberger, U., & Staudinger, U. M. (1995). Die zwei Gesichter der Intelligenz im Alter [The two faces of intelligence in old age]. *Spektrum der Wissenschaft, 10,* 52–61.

Baltes, P. B., Lindenberger, U., & Staudinger, U. M. (in press). Lifespan theory in developmental psychology. In R. M. Lerner (Ed.), *Handbook of child psychology: Vol. 1. Theoretical models of human development* (5th ed.). New York: Wiley.

Baltes, P. B., Mayer, K. U., Helmchen, H., & Steinhagen-Thiessen, E. (1996). Die Berliner Altersstudie (BASE): Überblick und Einführung [The Berlin Aging Study: Overview and introduction]. In K. U. Mayer & P. B. Baltes (Eds.), *Die Berliner Alterstudie* (pp. 21–54). Berlin, Germany: Akademie Verlag.

Baltes, P. B., & Schaie, K. W. (1976). On the plasticity of intelligence in adulthood and old age: Where Horn and Donaldson fail. *American Psychologist, 31,* 720–725.

Baltes, P. B., & Smith, J. (1990). The psychology of wisdom and its ontogenesis. In R. J. Sternberg (Ed.), *Wisdom: Its nature, origins, and development* (pp. 87–120). New York: Cambridge University Press.

Baltes, P. B., & Staudinger, U. M. (1993). The search for a psychology of wisdom. *Current Directions in Psychological Science, 2,* 75–80.

Baltes, P. B., & Staudinger, U. M. (Eds.). (1996). *Interactive minds: Life-span perspectives on the social foundation of cognition.* New York: Combridge University Press.

Barkow, J. H., Cosmides, L., & Tooby, J. (Eds.). (1992). *The adapted mind: Evolutionary psychology and the generation of culture.* New York: Oxford University Press.

Birren, J. E., & Schaie, K. W. (1996). *Handbook of the psychology of aging* (3rd ed.). San Diego, CA: Academic Press.

Blanchard-Fields, F., & Hess, T. (Eds.). (1995). *Perspectives on cognitive change in adulthood.* New York: McGraw-Hill.

Boesch, E. E. (1991). *Symbolic action theory and cultural psychology.* Heidelberg, Germany: Springer.

Brandtstädter, J. (1984). Personal and social control over development: Some implications of an action perspective in life-span developmental psychology. In P. B. Baltes & O. G. Brim. Jr. (Eds.), *Life-span development and behavior* (Vol. 6, pp. 1–32). New York: Academic Press.

Bradtstädter, J. (in press). Action theory in developmental psychology. In R. M. Lerner (Ed.), *Handbook of child psychology: Vol. 1. Theoretical models of human development* (5th ed.). New York: Wiley.

Brandtstädter, J., & Wentura, D. (1995). Adjustment to shifting possibility frontiers in later life: Complementary adaptive modes. In R. A. Dixon & L. Bäckman (Eds.), *Psychological compensation: Managing losses and promoting gains* (pp. 83–106). Hillsdale, NJ: Erlbaum.

Brim, O. G., Jr. (1992). *Ambition: How we manage success and failure throughout our lives.* New York: Basic Books.

Burghardt, G. M. (1984). On the origins of play. In P. K. Smith (Ed.), *Play in animals and humans* (pp. 1–45). London: Basil Blackwell.

Cantor, N., & Fleeson, W. (1994). Social intelligence and intelligent goal pursuit: A cognitive slice of motivation. In W. D. Spaulding (Ed.), *Nebraska Symposium on Motivation: Vol. 41. Integrative views of motivation, cognition, and emotion* (pp. 125–179). Lincoln: University of Nebraska Press.

Carstensen, L. L., Hanson, K. A., & Freund, A. (1995). Selection and compensation in adulthood. In R. Dixon & L. Bäckman (Eds.), *Compensating for psychological deficits and declines: Managing losses and promoting gains* (pp. 107–126). Hillsdale, NJ: Erlbaum.

Cattell, K. B. (1971). *Abilities: Their structure, growth, and action.* Boston: Houghton Mifflin.

Cole, M. (1996). Interacting minds in a life-span perspective: A cultural/historical approach to culture and cognitive development. In P. B. Baltes & U. M. Staudinger (Eds.), *Interactive minds: Life-span perspectives on the social foundation of cognition* (pp. 59–87). New York: Cambridge University Press.

Craik, F. I. M., & Salthouse, T. A. (Eds.), (1992). *The handbook of aging and cognition.* Hillsdale, NJ: Erlbaum.

Crimmins, E. M., Hayward, M. D., & Saito, Y. (1996). Differentials in active life expectancy in the older population of the United States. *Journal of Gerontology: Social Sciences, 51B,* S111–S120.

D'Andrade, R. (1995). *The development of cognitive anthropology.* Cambridge, England: Cambridge University Press.

Dittmann-Kohli, F. (1995). *Das persönliche Sinnsystem: Ein Vergleich zwischen frühem und spätem Erwachsenenalter* [Personal meaning systems: Age differences in adult development and aging]. Göttingen, Germany: Hogrefe.

Dixon, R. A., & Bäckman, L. (Eds.). (1995). *Compensating for psychological deficits and declines: Managing losses and promoting gains.* Hillsdale, NJ: Erlbaum.

Durham, W. H. (1991). *Coevolution: Genes, culture and human diversity.* Stanford, CA: Stanford University Press.

Edelman, G. M. (1987). *Neural Darwinism: The theory of neuronal group selection.* New York: Basic Books.

Edelman, G. M., & Tononi, G. (1996). Selection and development: The brain as a complex system. In D. Magnusson (Ed.), *The life-span development of individuals: Behavioral, neurobiological and psychosocial perspectives* (pp. 179–204). Cambridge, England: Cambridge University Press.

Elder, G. H. (in press). Life-course theory. In R. M. Lerner (Ed.), *Handbook of child psychology: Vol. 1. Theoretical models of human development* (5th ed.). New York: Wiley.

Ericsson, K. A., & Smith, J. (Eds.). (1991). *Towards a general theory of expertise: Prospects and limits.* New York: Cambridge University Press.

Featherman, D. L. (1983). The life-span perspective in social science research. In P. B. Baltes & O. G. Brim, Jr. (Eds.), *Life-span development and behavior* (Vol. 5, pp. 1–59). New York: Academic Press.

Finch, C. E. (1990). *Longevity, senescence, and the genome.* Chicago: University of Chicago Press.

Finch, C. E. (1996). Biological bases for plasticity during aging of individual life histories. In D. Magnusson (Ed.), *The life-span development of individuals: Behavioral, neurobiological and psychosocial perspective* (pp. 488–511). Cambridge, England: Cambridge University Press.

Finch, C. E., & Rose, M. R. (1995). Hormones and the physiological architecture of life history evolution. *The Quarterly Review of Biology, 70,* 1–52.

Freund, A. M., & Baltes, P. B. (1996). *Selective optimization with compensation as a strategy of life-management: Prediction of subjective indicators of successful aging.* Unpublished manuscript, Max Planck Institute for Human Development and Education, Berlin.

Hebb, D. O. (1949). *The organization of behavior.* New York: Wiley.

Heckhausen, J., Dixon, R. A., & Baltes, P. B. (1989). Gains and losses in development throughout adulthood as perceived by different adult age groups. *Developmental Psychology, 25,* 109–121.

Heckhausen, J., & Schulz, R. (1995). A life-span theory of control. *Psychological Review, 102,* 284–304.

Helmchen, H., Baltes, M. M., Geiselmann, B., Kanowski, S., Linden, M., Reischies, F. M., Wagner, M., & Wilms, H.-U. (1996). Psychische Erkrankungen im Alter [Psychiatric illnesses in old age]. In K. U. Mayer & P. B. Baltes (Eds.), *Die Berliner Altersstudie* (pp. 185–220). Berlin, Germany: Akademie Verlag.

Hetherington, E. M., & Baltes, P. B. (1988). Child psychology and life-span development. In E. M. Hetherington, R. M. Lerner, & M. Perlmutter (Eds.), *Child development in life-span perspective* (pp. 1–19). Hillsdale, NJ: Erlbaum.

Hobfoll, S. E. (1989). Conservation of resources: A new attempt at conceptualizing stress. *American Psychologist, 44*, 513–524.

Horn, J. L. (1970). Organization of data on life-span development of human abilities. In L. R. Goulet & P. B. Baltes (Eds.), *Life-span developmental psychology: Research and theory* (pp. 423–466). New York: Academic Press.

Horn, J. L., & Hofer, S. M. (1992). Major abilities and development in the adult period. In R. J. Sternberg & C. A. Berg (Eds.), *Intellectual development* (pp. 44–99). New York: Cambridge University Press.

Kahneman, D., & Tversky, A. (1984). Choices, values, and frames. *American Psychologist, 39*, 341–350.

Kliegl, R., Mayr, U., & Krampe, R. T. (1994). Time–accuracy functions for determining process and person differences: An application to cognitive aging. *Cognitive Psychology, 26*, 134–164.

Kliegl, R., Smith, J., & Baltes, P. B. (1989). Testing-the-limits and the study of age differences in cognitive plasticity of a mnemonic skill. *Developmental Psychology, 26*, 894–904.

Kliegl, R., Smith, J., & Baltes, P. B. (1990). On the locus and process of magnification of age differences during mnemonic training. *Developmental Psychology, 26*, 894–904.

Klix, F. (1993). *Erwachendes Denken: Geistige Leistungen aus evolutionspsychologischer Sicht* [The evolution of thinking: The mind from an evolutionary–psychological perspective]. Heidelberg, Germany: Spektrum Akademischer Verlag.

Labouvie-Vief, G. (1982). Dynamic development and mature autonomy: A theoretical prologue. *Human Development, 25*, 161–191.

Laslett, P. (1991). *A fresh map of life: The emergence of the Third Age.* Cambridge, MA: Harvard University Press.

Lerner, R. M. (1984). *On the nature of human plasticity.* New York: Cambridge University Press.

Lerner, R. M. (1986). *Concepts and theories of human development* (2nd ed.). New York: Random House.

Levelt, W. J. M. (1989). *Speaking: From intention to articulation.* Cambridge, MA: MIT Press.

Lindenberger, U., & Baltes, P. B. (1994). Sensory functioning and intelligence in old age: A strong connection. *Psychology and Aging, 9*, 339–355.

Lindenberger, U., & Baltes, P. B. (1995). Kognitive Leistungsfähigkeit im hohen Alter: Erste Ergebnisse aus der Berliner Altersstudie [Cognitive capacity in old age: First results from the Berlin Aging Study]. *Zeitschrift für Psychologie, 203*, 283–317.

Lindenberger, U., & Baltes, P. B. (in press). Intellectual functioning in old and very old age: First results from the Berlin Aging Study. *Psychology and Aging.*

Magnusson, D. (Ed.). (1996). *The life-span development of indviduals: Behavioural, neurobiological, and psychosocial perspectives.* Cambridge, England: Cambridge University Press.

Manton, K. G., & Vaupel, J. W. (1995). Survival after the age of 80 in the United States, Sweden, France, England and Japan. *New England Journal of Medicine, 333*, 1232–1235.

Marsiske, M., Lang, F. R., Baltes, M. M., & Baltes, P. B. (1995). Selective optimization with compensation: Life-span perspectives on successful human development. In R. A. Dixon & L. Bäckman (Eds.), *Compensation for psychological defects and declines: Managing losses and promoting gains* (pp. 35–79). Hillsdale, NJ: Erlbaum.

Martin, G. M., Austad, S. N., & Johnson, T. E. (1996). Genetic analysis of ageing: Role of oxidative damage and environmental stresses. *Nature Genetics, 13*, 25–34.

Mayer, K. U., & Baltes, P. B. (Eds.). (1996). *Die Berliner Altersstudie* [The Berlin Aging Study]. Berlin, Germany: Akademie Verlag.

Nesselroade, J. R., & Jones, C. J. (1991). Multi-model selection effects in the study of adult development: A perspective on multivariate, replicated, single-subject, repeated measures designs. *Experimental Aging Research, 17*, 21–27.

Osiewacz, H. D. (1995). Molekulare Mechanismen biologischen Alterns [Molecular mechanisms of biological aging]. *Biologie in unserer Zeit, 25,* 336–344.

Rose, M. R. (1991). *The evolutionary biology of aging.* Oxford, England: Oxford University Press.

Rosenmayr, L. (1990). *Die Kräfte des Alters* [The powers of old age]. Wien, Germany: Edition Atelier.

Salthouse, T. A. (1991). *Theoretical perspectives on cognitive aging.* Hillsdale, NJ: Erlbaum.

Schaie, K. W. (1988). The hazards of cognitive aging. *Gerontologist, 29,* 484–493.

Schaie, K. W. (1994). The course of adult intellectual development. *American Psychologist, 49,* 304–313.

Schaie, K. W. (1996). *Adult intellectual development: The Seattle Longitudinal Study.* New York: Cambridge University Press.

Schulz, R., & Heckhausen, J. (1996). A life-span model of successful aging. *American Psychologist, 51,* 702–714.

Shweder, R. A. (1991). *Thinking through cultures.* Cambridge, MA: Harvard University Press.

Siegler, R. S. (1994). Cognitive variability: A key to understanding cognitive development. *Current Directions in Psychological Science, 3,* 1–5.

Smith, J. (1996). Planning about life: Toward a social-interactive perspective. In P. B. Baltes & U. M. Staudinger (Eds.), *Interactive minds: Life-span perspectives on the social foundation of congnition* (pp. 242–275). Cambridge, England: Cambridge University Press.

Smith, J., & Baltes, P. B. (1996). Altern aus psychologischer Perspektive: Trends und Profile im hohen Alter [Psychological aging: Trends and profiles in very old age]. In K. U. Mayer & P. B. Bales (Eds.), *Die Berliner Altersstudie* (pp. 221-250). Berlin, Germany: Akademie Verlag.

Smith, J., & Baltes, P. B. (in press). Profiles of psychological functioning in the old and oldest-old. *Psychology and Aging.*

Staudinger, U. M., & Baltes, P. B. (1996a). Interactive minds: A facilitative setting for wisdom-related performance? *Journal of Personality and Social Psychology, 71,* 746–762.

Staudinger, U. M., & Baltes, P. B. (1996b). Weisheit als Gegenstand psychologischer Forshung [Wisdom as a topic of psychological research]. *Psychologische Rundschau, 47,* 57–77.

Staudinger, U. M., Marsiske, M., & Baltes, P. B. (1995). Resilience and reserve capacity in later adulthood: Potentials and limits of development across the life span. In D. Cicchetti & D. Cohen (Eds.), *Developmental psychopathology: Vol. 2. Risk, disorder, and adaptation* (pp. 801–847). New York: Wiley.

Takahashi, K. (1990). Affective relationships and their lifelong development. In P. B. Baltes, D. L. Featherman, & R. M. Lerner (Eds.), *Life-span development and behavior* (Vol. 10, pp. 1–27). Hillsdale, NJ: Erlbaum.

Tetens, J. N. (1777). *Philosophische Versuche über die menschliche Natur und ihre Entwicklung* [Philosophical essays on human nature and its development]. Leipzig, Germany: Weidmanns Erben und Reich.

Thelen, E., & Smith, L. B. (1994). *A dynamic systems approach to the development of cognition and action.* Cambridge, MA: MIT Press.

Uttal, D. H., & Perlmutter, M. (1989). Toward a broader conceptualization of development: The role of gains and losses across the life span. *Developmental Review, 9,* 101–132.

Vaupel, J. W., & Jeune, B. (1995). *Exceptional longevity: From prehistory to the present.* Odense, Denmark: Odense University Press.

Waddington, C. H. (1975). *The evolution of an evolutionist.* Edinburgh, Scotland: Edinburgh University Press.

Willis, S. L. (1990). Contributions of cognitive training research to understanding late-life potential. In M. Perlmutter (Ed.), *Late-life potential* (pp. 25–42). Washington, DC: The Gerontological Society of America.

Yates, E., & Benton, L. A. (1995). Biological senescence: Loss of integration and resilience. *Canadian Journal on Aging, 14,* 106–120.

3 Age Differences in Evolutionary Selection Benefits

Thomas B. L. Kirkwood

University of Newcastle, Institute for Aging and Health, Newcastle General Hospital, Newcastle upon Tyne, U.K.

Abstract

From a biological perspective, the key to understanding the evolution of the human life history is the recognition that natural selection acts with different force on different ages. Natural selection acts through the differential survival and reproduction of genotypes. Genetic factors that exert their effects early in life have the potential to affect the whole of the organism's reproduction. Conversely, genes that exert their effects late in life have much reduced impact. This is because in the wild environment most individual organisms die young, due to extrinsic sources of mortality such as predation and starvation. For this reason, most reproduction in wild populations is due to young individuals. Although humans now live much more protected lives, the conditions under which the genetic determinants of our aging processes evolved were not very different from those that exist today for other species. The reduction in the force of natural selection with advancing age tells us that the senescent phase of the life history cannot be under direct genetic control. In other words, aging itself is not programmed. Instead, the evolutionary theories of aging suggest that senescence takes place because (1) natural selection is powerless to prevent the accumulation within the genome of genes having late deleterious effects and because (2) long-term survival requires major ongoing investment in mechanisms of cellular maintenance and repair. The second point is the basis of the disposable soma theory of aging, which attributes senescence to a gradual accumulation of damage and faults in the cells and tissues of the organism. In the context of understanding human development, the evolutionary theories of aging reinforce the recognition of older people as individuals. Biologically, each individual is likely have a different set of late-acting deleterious genes and will accumulate a unique history of somatic damage at the cellular and molecular levels.

Introduction

From a biological perspective, the key to understanding the evolution of the human life history is the recognition that natural selection acts with different force on different ages (Kirkwood, 1997). Natural selection acts through the differential survival and reproduction of genotypes. Genetic factors that exert their effect early in life have the potential to affect the whole of the organism's reproduction. Conversely, genes that exert their effects late in life have reduced impact, partly because some individuals die before they reach the age at which the gene action is experienced and partly because a fraction of reproduction occurs before the gene action is felt and is therefore unaffected (Charlesworth, 1994). We may note that this principle is true even if the life history is free from senescence and if reproduction does not decline with age. This is important because it permits the principle of a declining force of natural selection to explain the *origin* of the aging process, which would not be possible without logical circularity if aging was a necessary assumption for the principle to hold true. Indeed, one of the major aims in this chapter is to examine how age differences in evolutionary selection benefits account for the evolution of human aging and other aspects of the human life history, such as the menopause.

The aging process may be generally characterized as an increase with age in frailty and loss of adaptive response to stress, causing increased incidence and prevalence of age-related disabilities and diseases and eventually an increased risk of death. This is a trait we share with the vast majority of animal and plant species, although it may be noted that exceptions do exist (see, for example, Martinez, 1997). These exceptions are important because they are counterexamples to the common belief that the aging process is a biological inevitability, and they sharpen the challenge of trying to answer the evolutionary (why?) question of aging. Although there are important respects in which the aging process in humans differs from aging in other species, it is likely that human aging shares a common evolutionary basis with general senescence and has been subject to comparatively recent modification. Thus, in examining the impact of age differences in evolutionary selection benefits on the human aging process, it makes sense to consider the general evolutionary theory of aging first. Although it applies to all specialty areas with an interest in human ontogenesis, the logic of this argument is rarely recognized outside the field of evolutionary biology itself. A notable exception is the theoretical framework of lifespan psychology advanced by Baltes (1997, this volume), in which age differences in evolutionary selection benefits serve as a distal explanation (fundamental constraint) of age differences in behavioral plasticity.

The need for an evolutionary understanding of aging is reinforced by the emerging studies on the human genome, which promise to reveal unprecedented volumes of data on genetic factors affecting human development and aging but which also need a conceptual framework within which these data can be organized and understood. It is clear from several lines of evidence that aging and longevity are governed by genetic factors (Finch & Tanzi, 1997). First, lifespans of human monozygotic twin pairs are statistically more similar to each other than lifespans of dizygotic twins, the magnitude of this difference indicating that around a quarter to one-third of what determines lifespan is genetic. Second, there are clear lifespan differences between different inbred strains of laboratory animals. The strains experience identical environments but differ in their genomes. Third, studies of simple organisms like fruit flies, nematode worms, and yeast have identified gene mutations that affect duration of life. Evolution theory addresses the nature of these genetic factors.

Evolution of Aging and Longevity

The enigma of explaining the evolution of aging is clearly seen if we consider the natural life history of the mouse. Out of a population of newborn wild mice, 90% will be dead before age 10 months, even though 50% of the same animals reared in captivity would still be alive at age 24 months (Austad, 1997). Animals survive much longer when protected from natural hazards like predators, starvation, and cold. However, even if we keep them in an ideal environment, all the mice will die within a few years, having spent their last months in a state of visible senescence. Thus, aging is in one sense an artifact of the protected environment, since it is a state not normally seen in nature, but it is also an intrinsic biological process. The situation seen in wild mice is not, in fact, so very different from what existed in ancestral human populations. Although the early records are sparse, it appears that human life expectancy was static for many thousands of years until increases began to occur around the mid-nineteenth century among what are today's developed countries (see also Maier & Vaupel, this volume). In late nineteenth century England and Wales, for example, only 50% of the population could expect to survive past age 45, with 70% dead by age 65, whereas in the present day the figures are 96% surviving past age 45, and only 17% dead by age 65 (see Kirkwood, 1999).

The fact that aging is rarely seen in natural animal populations is an important counterargument to the first (and still popular) evolutionary explanation of aging—namely, that aging is a genetically programmed means to limit population size and avoid overcrowding. This theory is commonly attributed to Weismann (1891), who first seriously addressed the evolutionary basis of aging, but it has independently reemerged in various forms since then. A variant of the argument proposes that aging is a beneficial process to facilitate the turnover of generations and thereby aid the adaptation of organisms to changing environments. In particular, the idea of programmed aging appears attractive to many because it suggests that a so-called aging gene might exist. The flaws in these arguments have been comprehensively reviewed (e.g., see Kirkwood & Cremer, 1982), but the concept exerts such perennial attraction that they will be summarized again here. First, because aging has negligible impact on organisms in their natural environment, we can infer immediately that it does not serve to control population size (Medawar, 1952). Animals die young, as previously remarked. They do not, for the most part, live long enough for aging to exert any effect on their survival. Therefore, a basic premise of the aging-gene hypothesis can be discounted. Second, because animals die young, natural selection cannot exert a *direct* influence over the process of senescence. It is thus hard to see how an aging gene might have evolved. Indeed, the failure of natural selection to tightly control the late stages of the life history is at the heart of the modern evolutionary theory of aging, as discussed below. Third, even if neither of the above objections applied, the aging-gene concept has a major logical fault. Since aging is clearly deleterious to the individual organism, any individual in whom the hypothetical aging gene was inactivated by mutation would enjoy an advantage within the population, so freedom from aging should spread. The only way this could be prevented is by an advantage to the species or group that outweighs the disadvantage for the individual. Such arguments are very hard to construct, and no one has yet been able to suggest a plausible basis for this concept.

Once it is accepted that the aging-gene hypothesis is flawed, it becomes easier to see that the successful evolutionary explanation for aging lies in two fundamental observations: (1) natural selection is powerless to prevent the accumulation within the genome of genes having late deleterious effects, and (2) long-term survival requires major ongoing investment in mechanisms of cellular maintenance and repair. Instead of being programmed to die, as the aging-gene concept suggests, organisms are programmed to survive. However, in spite of a formidable array of survival mechanisms, most species appear not to be programmed well enough to last indefinitely. The key to understanding why this should be so and what governs how long a survival period should be provided comes from understanding how the survival patterns in wild populations affect the age differences in evolutionary selection benefits. If 90% of wild mice are dead by the age of 10 months, any investment in programming survival much beyond this point can benefit at most 10% of the population. This immediately suggests that there will be little evolutionary advantage in programming long-term survival capacity into a mouse. The argument is further strengthened when we observe that nearly all of the survival mechanisms required by the mouse to combat intrinsic deterioration (such as DNA damage, protein oxidation, and so on) require metabolic resources. Metabolic resources are scarce, as is evidenced by the fact that the major cause of mortality for wild mice is cold, due to failure to maintain adequate body temperature. From a genetic point of view, the mouse will benefit by investing any spare resource into thermogenesis or reproduction rather than into better DNA repair capacity than it requires.

This concept, with its explicit focus on evolution of optimal levels of cell maintenance, is termed the *disposable soma theory* (Kirkwood, 1977, 1997). In essence, the investments in durability and maintenance of somatic (nonreproductive) tissues are predicted to be sufficient to keep the body in good repair through the normal expectation of life in the wild environment, with some measure of reserve capacity. Thus, it makes sense that mice (with 90% mortality by 10 months) have intrinsic lifespans of two to three years, while humans (who might have experienced 90% mortality by age

50 in our ancestral environment) have intrinsic lifespans limited to about 100 years. The distinction between somatic and reproductive tissues is important because the reproductive cell lineage, or germ line, must be maintained at a level that preserves viability across the generations, whereas the soma needs to serve only a single generation. As far as is known, all species that have a clear distinction between soma and germ line undergo somatic senescence, while those animals that do not show senescence have germ cells distributed throughout their structure (Bell, 1984; Martinez, 1997).

To this analysis, we can add two important earlier perspectives drawn from evolution theory that also take account of age differences in evolutionary selection benefits. Medawar (1952) suggested that because organisms die young, there is little force of selection to oppose the accumulation within the genome of mutations with late-acting deleterious effects. This predicts that, in principle, a very large number of such genes might be distributed through the genome, possibly with a high degree of heterogeneity between one individual and another. Attempts to identify a contribution to aging from such mutations have had mixed success, but it would be surprising if they were entirely absent. Williams (1957) suggested, using an argument somewhat similar to Medawar's, that genes with beneficial effects would be favored by selection even if these genes had adverse effects at later ages. Again, the plausibility of this hypothesis rests on the fact that there is negligible survival to older ages in the wild. Williams's concept, known as the *antagonistic pleiotropy theory,* is a particularly attractive general framework to consider gene actions in aging. Some commentators have borrowed the focus on somatic maintenance from the disposable soma theory (developed independently at a later date) and applied it to the pleiotropy theory. However, the pleiotropy concept is more general in nature, and there may be pleiotropic gene actions that are unconnected with durability and maintenance of the soma (Kirkwood & Rose, 1991).

The evolutionary theories of aging thus make the following predictions, based on recognition of the importance of age differences in evolutionary selection benefits. First, there are unlikely to exist specific genes for aging. Second, genes of particular importance for aging and longevity are likely to be those governing durability and maintenance of the soma. Third, there may exist other genetically determined tradeoffs between benefits to young organisms and their viability at older ages. Fourth, there may exist a variety of gene mutations with late deleterious effects that contribute to the senescent phenotype. Fifth, it is clear that multiple genes probably contribute to the aging phenotype, and a major challenge will be to identify how many of each category exist and which are the most important.

Tradeoffs in the Human Life History

As we have shown above, a central concept in the evolutionary theory of senescence is the idea of tradeoffs between investments in somatic maintenance and in reproduction. This is a prediction that applies both on a comparative basis, when different species are compared (see Kirkwood & Rose, 1991; Kirkwood, 1992), and also when considering genetic variance between individuals within a single species. The existence of intraspecific heterogeneity with respect to genetic determinants of longevity is supported by data from human populations indicating significant heritability of lifespan (Vaupel et al., 1998). In the fruit fly *Drosophila melanogaster*, selection on late egg-laying capacity in females resulted in populations with extended lifespans but decreased early fecundity (for reviews, see Rose, 1991; Partridge & Barton, 1993), providing direct support for the concept of tradeoffs. Furthermore, an experiment selecting directly for increased lifespan revealed a similar result: the long-lived populations resulting from selection for increased lifespan showed reduced early fecundity (Zwaan, Bijlsma, & Hoekstra, 1995).

The concept of a tradeoff between resources invested in fertility and longevity is important in understanding how age differences in evolutionary selection benefits might have played a part in generating population heterogeneity with respect to genomic determinants of the human life history. In a static environment, there should be a unique optimal compromise between investments in somatic maintenance and in reproduction. However, the nature of the optimizing process is such that, within the vicinity of the optimum, the fitness peak is quite flat, and it is therefore possible to deviate from the optimum without incurring a major loss in fitness (Kirkwood & Holliday, 1986; Kirkwood & Rose, 1991). Thus, a combination of weak selection around the optimum and genetic drift might be expected to produce significant polymorphism. This tendency will have been reinforced by the fact that the real evolutionary environment is seldom static and may include unpredictable variations, which may mean that across time the optimum tradeoff varies to some degree.

To test for the presence of tradeoffs between fertility and longevity that might conform with the predictions of the disposable soma theory, Westendorp and Kirkwood (1998) analyzed an extensive data set containing life history records for British aristocrats. In making such a study, it is important to recognize that there are many ways in which nongenetic heterogeneity within populations might generate positive associations between longevity and fertility. The most obvious is through variance in socioeconomic factors, particularly wealth. Poverty typically confers increased risk of malnutrition and general ill health, resulting in reduced life expectancy and a possibly greater risk of infertility. The advantages of the data for the British aristocracy are the unusually privileged socioeconomic status of the individuals, even in times when living conditions were generally much harsher than today, and the availability of records extending over a long period of history. A disadvantage of the data is the relatively low overall fertility for the British aristocrats, a feature also commented on by earlier authors (see Cummins, 1999). However, since the purpose of the study was to compare fertility of long- and short-lived individuals within the same population, low average fecundity should not bias this comparison.

The relationships between female longevity (expressed as age at death in 10-year groups), proportion childless, age at first childbirth, and number of progeny

Table 3.1

Female Reproduction and Age at Death among British Aristocrats Adjusted for Trends over Calendar Time (abbreviated from Westendorp & Kirkwood, 1998)

Age at Death	Number	Percent Childless	Mean Age at First Childbirth	Mean Number of Children
<20	42	66%	19.1	0.45
21–30	176	39%	20.5	1.35
31–40	218	26%	23.2	2.05
41–50	210	31%	23.9	2.01
51–60	299	28%	24.6	2.40
61–70	337	33%	23.8	2.36
71–80	322	31%	24.6	2.64
81–90	247	45%	25.1	2.08
>90	57	49%	27.0	1.80

are summarized in Table 3.1 (abbreviated from Westendorp & Kirkwood, 1998), where the data were adjusted for trends over calendar time. Women who died at younger ages (before 30 years) had little opportunity to reproduce, and therefore it was not surprising that these women showed a higher proportion who died childless, a lower average age at first childbirth, and a low number of progeny. For women who died between age 31 and 60, there was an approximately constant proportion who remained childless and an approximately constant age at first childbirth. The number of progeny showed an increase with age at death, consistent with the fact that the longer a woman lived, the greater opportunity she would have had to have children. Opportunity for having further children would have ceased with menopause. Therefore, in the absence of any tradeoff between longevity and fertility it would be predicted that number of progeny should reach a plateau. However, the women who died at the oldest ages showed significantly reduced numbers of children, compared with those who died at earlier ages. Also, those women who died at the oldest ages had their first children at significantly later ages, consistent with the idea that they may have had impaired fertility.

While the causal basis of the tradeoff could not be determined from this study, the results were compatible with the prediction that individuals with increased predisposition to longevity have decreased predisposition to fertility, and vice versa. An alternative interpretation of this finding could be that biological wear and tear associated with reproduction might be the cause. Since reproductive wear and tear would be expected to affect males less than females, the data for men were also examined and found to be similar. The similarity of the tradeoffs for males and females suggested that reproductive wear and tear was not the explanation. Other environmental factors could be important—for example, if a large family increased stress and mortality risk for both parents. This was tested by entering spouse's age at death as an explanatory variable that might capture any effect of environment. It was found that although the correlation between spouses was statistically significant, it explained only 2% of the variance in age at death (Westendorp & Kirkwood, 1999), and the tradeoff was unaffected. Thus, the most likely explanation was that the data exposed an intrinsic tradeoff between genetic factors promoting fertility and longevity. This conclusion has been strengthened by later analysis of a different historical population by Lycett, Dunbar, & Voland, (2000), in which the importance of socioeconomic factors was also confirmed.

Evolution of Menopause

Menopause—the universal cessation of human female fertility at around age 50—presents an intriguing evolutionary puzzle (Williams, 1999). Why should a woman cease reproducing at a much earlier age relative to her biological lifespan potential than occurs in other mammals (Pavelka & Fedigan, 1991)? Although life expectancy in earlier times was much shorter than it is today, the evidence suggests that a fraction of the women who escaped the hazards of juvenile mortality might survive to age 50 and above (Hill & Hurtado, 1996). For these women, even if their numbers were small, ceasing reproduction early would, if other things were equal, have an adverse effect on evolutionary fitness. So why not retain fertility for longer? In physiological terms, the cause of reproductive senescence in mammalian females is the exhaustion of ovarian oocytes, accompanied by degenerative changes in the associated components of the neuroendocrine system (Gosden, 1985). However, while oocyte depletion is the trigger for menopause, there is no clear reason why the size of the initial oocyte stock should not have increased in line with human longevity. Equally, although the increase in chromosome abnormalities with maternal age points to an age-related decline in oocyte quality, which might itself offer a reason to cease reproduction, there is no compelling reason why a longer shelf life could not have evolved through better cellular repair (such as probably explains the extended functional longevity of human neurons). It is thus appropriate to ask if the ultimate reason for the existence of menopause lies in the evolutionary biology of the human life history. In particular, we consider the interplay of the age differences in evolutionary selection benefits with the special factors that characterize human evolution, such as large brain size, social structure, and extended longevity. The two major evolutionary hypotheses to explain menopause are founded on the extreme altriciality (such as immaturity and dependence) of human infants and the extensive opportunities for intergenerational cooperation within kin groups.

The altriciality of human offspring appears to be the result of a compromise driven by the evolution of an increasingly large brain in the hominid ancestral lineage and the pelvic constraint on the birth canal. The pressure to evolve increased lifespans is likely to have been driven primarily by the increase in human brain size, leading to advanced intelligence, use of language and tools, and social living, all of which will have reduced the level of extrinsic mortality and favored increased investments in somatic maintenance. Increased brain size, however, makes giving birth riskier, since the neonatal brain must pass through the birth canal, whose size is constrained by the pelvis, which in turn is restricted by mechanical constraints (Abitbol, Chervenah, & Ledger, 1996). The result appears to have been a compromise whereby, in comparison with other mammals, the human infant is born unusually altricial, with brain growth still far from complete, requiring extended postnatal development before gaining independence from the mother. A second possible explanation for the altriciality of human offspring is that adequate development of the human nervous system requires that interaction of the system with the social and physical extrauterine environment starts at a comparatively immature state. According to this line of reasoning, which has been emphasized by developmental psychologists, immaturity and plasticity may enable infants and children to acquire complex social and cognitive skills such as language (Elman et al., 1996; for related views see Gigerenzer, this volume; Singer, this volume; Wellman, this volume).

In either case, given that maternal mortality increases with age (Grimes, 1994) and that maternal death will seriously compromise the survival of any existing dependent offspring, it appears to make sense to cease having more children when the risks outweigh the benefits. Thus, one explanation of menopause proposes that a woman should cease reproducing at an age when the risk to her survival (and that of her later children) exceeds the gain from continuing to be fertile (Peccei, 1995).

Nevertheless, human infants regularly do survive the death of their mothers due to the role of kin in caring for and provisioning the very young. The second hypothesis to explain menopause is that by ceasing reproduction early; an older woman can assist her adult daughters by sharing in the burden of provisioning and protecting their grandchildren (Hill & Hurtado, 1991; Hawkes et al., 1997, 1998; O'Connell et al., 1999). Thus, although her own reproductive opportunities are curtailed, she can maximize her fitness by promoting the propagation of her genes through her daughter's children.

To examine the plausibility of these ideas, we need to consider very carefully the magnitudes of the costs and benefits of menopause in relation to the evolutionary selection forces that act at different ages. Although each hypothesis appears, in principle, plausible, evolutionary tests of these ideas have so far suggested that neither hypothesis is, on its own, sufficient to explain menopause (Rogers, 1993; Peccei, 1995; Hill & Hurtado, 1996; Shanley & Kirkwood, 2000). However, recent work by Shanley and Kirkwood (2000) indicates that a *combined* model, which takes both ideas into account, can successfully explain why menopause occurs. Thus, the evolution of menopause appears to have its roots in complex features of the human life history, including the unusual importance of kin interactions.

Intrinsic Developmental Variations Allowed by Age Differences in Selection

An aspect of the evolutionary genetics of aging that has not yet received the attention it merits is the prediction that intrinsic chance plays an important part (Finch &

Kirkwood, 2000). A major characteristic of aging is the low predictability of individual phenotypes. This is strikingly illustrated by the lifespan variations seen in isogenic populations of laboratory animals, such as mice, fruitflies, and nematode worms. The variability of the aging phenotype can be interpreted as a direct consequence of age differences in evolutionary selection benefits, in particular the declining force of natural selection with advancing age. Not only does this declining force of selection allow for the easy accumulation within populations of genetic differences affecting the later stages of life, but it also can explain the development of individual differences even when the genotype is the same. The disposable soma theory predicts that aging is caused primarily by the intrinsic accumulation of small, stochastic faults in the development and maintenance of somatic cells, tissues, and organs. These variations may have little impact on the organism at an early age, when functional reserves are high. However, they can produce marked individual differences at older ages, when functional reserves have been eroded.

A good example of how developmental variations can lead to later differences in aging is the variation in neuron numbers. In inbred laboratory rodents, neuron numbers vary 10% to 40% in young individuals, depending on the brain region (West, Slimianka, & Gundersen, 1991; Finch & Kirkwood, 2000). In humans, the range of individual values is up to 50% of the mean at all adult ages (West, 1993; Simic, Kostovic, Winblad, & Bogdanovic, 1997), and brain imaging data are consistent with these ranges in neuron numbers (Plassman et al., 1997). Intrinsic variation in the neuron numbers formed during development is a likely explanation for certain differences in cognitive aging of human twins. For example, the age of onset of Alzheimer's disease in a study of MZ cotwins (Gatz et al., 1997) differed by an average of 9.5 years (range of 4 to 16 years). The classical model would attribute this variation to environmental differences, but intrinsic differences in hippocampal size could provide one co-twin with a greater functional reserve, enabling normal cognition to persist at later ages.

At the cellular level, there is much evidence for the role of intrinsic chance variations in the general determination of cell fate and in the kinetics of cell proliferation (Potten, 1998; Abkowitz, Catlin, & Guttorp, 1996; Smith & Whitney, 1980). Multiple processes generate these intrinsic variations, some of which are particularly important during development, whereas others act during adulthood. At the molecular level, subcellular processes are subject to random diffusion, which generates extensive variations due to actions of chance (McAdams & Arkin, 1999). During the extensive proliferation of cells in developing embryos, the number and type of individual cells formed, and their distributions in developing anatomical structures, may be influenced by chance (e.g., Walsh & Cepko, 1992; Grove, Kirkwood, & Price, 1992). Somatic genome instability, resulting in somatic mutations and chromosomal abnormalities, is another important source of intrinsic variation (Vijg, 1990; King et al., 1994).

Recognizing the variability of the aging process, which derives to a large extent from age differences in evolutionary selection benefits, cautions against overenthusiastic expectations for future modification of the aging process based on human genome research. Not only does lifespan show limited heritability (about 30%) in humans and other species (Finch & Tanzi, 1997), but so do many diseases with onset in middle age or later. Genetic risk factors are being identified, such as the apolipoprotien E4 allele, the most common known risk factor for cardiovascular disease and Alzheimer disease (Meyer et al., 1998). However, carriers of this allele still show great variability in the age at which they develop the disease (Finch & Kirkwood, 2000), and some carriers remain free from disease even at very advanced ages (Corder et al., 1996). This variable "penetrance" of the risk allele is usually explained in terms of unknown interactions with other genes or environmental factors. However, it may equally be due to chance developmental variations in brain that influence the threshold for development of disease.

References

Abitbol, M. M., Chervenah, F. A., & Ledger, W. J. (1996). *Birth and human evolution: Anatomical and obstetrical mechanics in primates*. Westport: Bergin & Garvey.

Abkowitz, J. L., Catlin, S. N., & Guttorp, P. (1996). Evidence that hematopoiesis may be a stochastic process in vivo. *Nature Medicine, 2*, 190–197.

Austad, S. N. (1997). Comparative aging and life histories in mammals. *Experimental Gerontology, 32*, 23–38.

Baltes, P. B. (1997). On the incomplete architecture of human ontogeny: Selection, optimization, and compensation as foundation of developmental theory. *American Psychologist, 52*, 366–380.

Bell, G. (1984). Evolutionary and nonevolutionary theories of senescence. *American Naturalist, 124*, 600–603.

Charlesworth, B. (1994). *Evolution in age-structured populations*. Cambridge: Cambridge University Press.

Corder, E. H., et al. (1996). Attenuation of apolipoprotein E epsilon 4 allele gene dose in late age. *Lancet, 347*, 542.

Cummins, J. (1999). Evolutionary forces behind human infertility. *Nature, 39*, 557–558.

Elman, J. L., Bates, E. A., Johnson, M. H., Karmiloff-Smith, A., Parisi, D., & Plunkett, K. (1996). *Rethinking innateness: A connectionist perspective on development*. Cambridge, MA: MIT Press.

Finch, C. E., & Kirkwood, T. B. L. (2000). *Chance, development and aging*. New York: Oxford University Press.

Finch, C. E., & Tanzi, R. (1997). The genetics of aging. *Science, 278*, 407–411.

Gatz, M., et al. (1997). Heritability for Alzheimer's disease: The study of dementia in Swedish twins. *Journal of Gerontology: Medical Sciences, 52A*, M117–M125.

Gosden, R. G. (1985). *Biology of the menopause: The causes and consequences of ovarian aging*. London: Academic Press.

Grimes, D. A. (1994). The morbidity and mortality of pregnancy: Still risky business. *American Journal of Obstetrics and Gynecology, 170*, 1489–1494.

Grove, E. A., Kirkwood, T. B. L., & Price, J. (1992). Neuronal precursor cells in the rat hippocampal formation contribute to more than one cytoarchitectonic area. *Neuron, 8*, 217–229.

Hawkes, K., O'Connell, J. F., & Blurton Jones, N. G. (1997). Hazda women's time allocation, offspring provisioning, and the evolution of long postmenopausal life spans. *Current Anthropology, 38*, 551–577.

Hawkes, K., O'Connell, J. F., Jones, N. G. B., Alvarez, H., & Charnov, E. L. (1998). Grandmothering, menopause, and the evolution of human life histories. *Proceedings of the National Academy of Sciences USA, 95*, 1336–1339.

Hill, K., & Hurtado, A. M. (1991). The evolution of premature reproductive senescence and menopause in human females: An evolution of the "grandmother" hypothesis. *Human Nature, 2*, 313–350.

Hill, K., & Hurtado, A. M. (1996). *Ache life history: The ecology and demography of a foraging people.* New York: Aldine de Gruyter.

King, C. M., Gillespie, E. S., McKenna, P. G., & Barnett, Y. A. (1994). An investigation of mutation as a function of age in humans. *Mutation Research, 316*, 79–90.

Kirkwood, T. B. L. (1977). Evolution of aging. *Nature, 270*, 301–304.

Kirkwood, T. B. L. (1977). The origins of human ageing. *Philosophical Transactions of the Royal Society, London B, 352*, 1765–1772.

Kirkwood, T. B. L. (1999). *Time of our lives: The science of human ageing.* London: Weidenfeld & Nicolson.

Kirkwood. T. B. L., & Cremer, T. (1982). Cytogerontology since 1881: A reappraisal of August Weismann and a review of modern progress. *Human Genetics, 60*, 101–121.

Kirkwood, T. B. L., & Holliday, R. (1986). Ageing as a consequence of natural selection. In K. J. Collins & A. H. Bittles (Eds.), The biology of human ageing (pp. 1–16). Cambridge: Cambridge University Press.

Kirkwood, T. B. L., & Rose, M. R. (1991). Evolution of senescence: Late survival sacrificed for reproduction. *Philosophical Transactions of the Royal Society, London, B, 332*, 15–24.

Lycett, J. E., Dunbar, R. I. M., & Voland, E. (2000). Longevity and the costs of reproduction in a historical human population. *Proceedings of the Royal Society London, B, 267*, 31–35.

Martinez, D. E. (1997). Mortality patterns suggest lack of senescence in hydra. *Experimental Gerontology, 33*, 217–225.

McAdams, H. H., & Arkin, A. (1999). It's a noisy business! Genetic regulation at the nanomolar scale. *Trends in Genetics, 15*, 65–69.

Medawar, P. B. (1952). *An unsolved problem of biology.* London: Lewis.

Meyer, M. R., et al. (1998). APOE genotype predicts when—not whether—one is predisposed to develop Alzheimer disease. *Nature Genetics, 19*, 321–322.

O'Connell, J. F., Hawkes, K., & Blurton Jones, N. G. (1999). Grandmothering and the evolution of *Homo erectus. Journal of Human Evolution, 36*, 461–485.

Partridge, L., & Barton, N. H. (1993). Optimality, mutation, and the evolution of ageing. *Nature, 362*, 305–311.

Pavelka, M. S. M., & Fedigan, L. M. (1991). Menopause: A comparative life history perspective. *Yearbook of Physical Anthropology, 34*, 13–38.

Peccei, J. S. (1995). The origin and evolution of menopause: The altriciality-lifespan hypothesis. *Ethology Sociobiology, 16*, 425–449.

Plassman, B. L., et al. (1997). Apolipoprotein E4 allele and hippocampal volume in twins with normal cognition. *Neurology, 48*, 985–989.

Potten, C. S. (1998). Stem cells in gastrointestinal epithelium: Numbers, characteristics and death. *Philosophical Transactions of the Royal Society of London, B, 353*, 821–830.

Rogers, A. R. (1993). Why menopause? *Evolutionary Ecology, 7*, 406–420.

Rose, M. R. (1991). *Evolutionary biology of aging.* New York: Oxford University Press.

Shanley, D. P., & Kirkwood, T. B. L. (2001). *Evolution of the human menopause.* BioEssays, 23:282–287.

Simic, G., Kostovic, I., Winblad, B., & Bogdanovic, N. (1997). Volume and number of neurons of the human hippocampal formation in normal aging and Alzheimer's disease. *Journal of Computational Neurology, 379*, 482–494.

Smith, J. R., & Whitney, R. G. (1980). Intraclonal variation in proliferative potential of human diploid fibroblasts: Stochastic mechanism for cellular aging. *Science, 207*, 82–84.

Vaupel, J. W., Carey, J. R., Christensen, K., Johnson, T. E., Yashin, A. I., Holm, N. V., et al. (1998). Biodemographic trajectories of longevity. *Science, 280*, 855–860.

Vijg, J. (1990). DNA sequence changes in aging: How frequent? how important? *Aging Clinical and Experimental Research, 2*, 105–123.

Walsh, C., & Cepko, C. L. (1992). Widespread dispersion of neuronal cones across functional regions of the cerebral cortex. *Science, 255*, 434–440.

Weismann, A. (1891). *Essays upon heredity and kindred biological problems* (2nd ed., Vol. 1). Oxford: Clarendon Press.

West, M.J. (1993). Regionally specific loss of neurons in the aging human hippocampus. *Neurobiological Aging, 14*, 287–293.

West, M. J., Slimianka, L., & Gundersen, H. J. G. (1991). Unbiased stereological estimation of the total number of neurons in the subdivisions of the rat hippocampus using the optical fractionator. *Anatomical Record, 231*, 482–497.

Westendorp, R. G. J., & Kirkwood, T. B. L. (1998). Human longevity at the cost of reproductive success. *Nature, 396*, 743–746.

Westendorp, R. G. J., & Kirkwood, T. B. L. (1999). Longevity: Does family size matter? *Nature, 399*, 522.

Williams, G. C. (1957). Pleiotropy, natural selection, and the evolution of senescence. *Evolution, 11*, 398–411.

Williams, G. C. (1999). The Tithonus error in modern gerontology. *Quarterly Review of Biology, 74*, 405–415.

Zwaan, B. J., Bijlsma, R., & Hoekstra, R. F. (1995). Direct selection of life span in Drosophila melanogaster. *Evolution, 49*, 649–659.

4 Age Differences in Cultural Efficiency: Secular Trends in Longevity

Heiner Maier and James W. Vaupel

Max Planck Institute for Demographic Research, Rostock, Germany

Abstract

As individuals grow older, they become less well adapted to surviving. A large and steady age-related increase in adult mortality can be observed across different countries and different time periods. Despite these pervasive age-related decrements in people's capability to survive, we argue that mortality is plastic and that it can be affected by cultural changes. Mortality data for various developed countries indicate that death rates at older ages have fallen dramatically during the twentieth century. Mortality improvements have been greater for females than for males, and the pace of improvement has been more rapid in recent than in earlier decades.

Further evidence for the plasticity of mortality is obtained from an examination of old-age survival in unified Germany. From around 1970 onward, mortality decline in the former German Democratic Republic (GDR, East Germany) was slower than in the former Federal Republic of Germany (FRG, West Germany), which resulted in a mortality gap between the two German states. After German unification in 1990 and the ensuing cultural, political, and economic changes in the former GDR, the mortality gap between east and west decreased. From 1990 to 1996 the female mortality difference between eastern and western Germany was reduced by more than half.

Little is yet known about the specific cultural factors that affect old-age mortality and why mortality among the oldest old has been so plastic during the twentieth century. It is known that the chance of reaching advanced old age is better for women than men, for people born in this century rather than earlier, for people born in developed countries, and for people who have some favorable genes. It is likely that individual lifestyle (such as smoking behavior and diet) and societal factors (such as access to and quality of medical care) are additional important determinants of survival. Psychological traits (such as intellectual abilities and conscientiousness) may also have some influence on longevity.

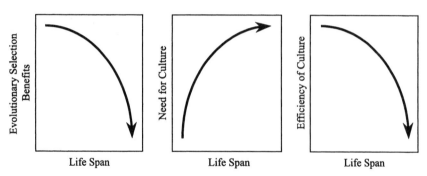

Figure 4.1   Three principles governing the dynamics between biology and culture across the lifespan

Source: Baltes (1997).

Introduction

Baltes (1997) investigated the dynamics of the relationship between culture and biology across the life span. Drawing on evolutionary and ontogenetic perspectives, he outlined a basic architecture of human development. His goal was "to identify the foundational structure that any general theory of human development must have" (p. 366). He argued that any valid theory of human development must be consistent with three basic principles (see Figure 4.1): (1) evolutionary selection benefits decrease with age, (2) there is an age-related increase in the need or demand for culture, and (3) there is an age-related decrease in the effectiveness or efficiency of cultural factors.

In this chapter, we deal with the third principle. It postulates that as individuals get older, culture-based resources become less efficient in offsetting age-related biological decrements. The right panel in Figure 4.1 illustrates the hypothesized lifespan function of cultural effectiveness. We examine the role of cultural factors in the context of human longevity. How effective were and are cultural factors in shaping human longevity? We adopt Baltes's (1997, p. 368) definition and assume that *culture* refers to "the entirety of psychological, social, material, and symbolic (knowledge-based) resources that humans have created over the millennia." It is a major challenge to arrive at one single, valid measure of cultural effectiveness because different aspects of culture may influence human longevity through a variety of pathways. Nevertheless, we offer some observations on how cultural factors might have differentially affected the mortality risk at different ages.

An individual's risk of dying at any given point in time cannot be directly observed. The mortality risk is usually inferred from observing death rates in groups or populations of individuals that share some characteristics such as age or country of residence. To investigate the effects of culture on longevity, we present age-specific death rates and related measures for several developed countries. We emphasize the remarkable improvements in survival that occurred during the last century because they provide a telling example of the profound effects of cultural innovations. We then turn our attention to mortality trajectories in Germany. The fact that East German death rates at the oldest ages fell considerably after German unification highlights the importance of cultural factors that operate late in life. We argue that the marked reduction in mortality at older ages, which was doubtless the result of cultural changes, is in conflict with the hypothesized lifespan function of cultural effectiveness shown in the right panel of Figure 4.1. In a concluding section, we speculate on resources and risk factors at the individual level that may be relevant for determining mortality outcomes.

Secular Trends in Longevity

As illustrated in Figure 4.2, death rates in most countries follow a characteristic age-related pattern. Mortality is high immediately after birth, and then it declines sharply during the first few weeks and months of life. With each year of life in early childhood, the probability of dying in the following year becomes less. At the age of about 10 or 12 years, mortality is lower than at any other time in the entire lifespan. Teenagers

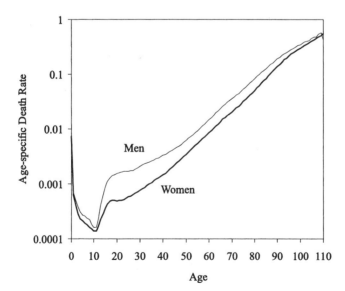

Figure 4.2   Logarithmic plot of the age-specific death rate (probability of not surviving an additional year) in the United States, 1991 to 1995

Source: Berkeley Mortality Database, http://demog.berkeley.edu/wilmoth/mortality/.

and young adults experience a slightly increased level of mortality. From about age 30 until old age, there is an exponential increase in the age-specific death rates. At these adult ages, death rates double about every eight years. At ages above 85 or so, the rate of increase in mortality appears to slow down. Although death rates continue to increase with age, the rate of increase declines at the oldest ages. Thatcher, Kannisto, and Vaupel (1998) investigated death rates above age 80 in 13 low-mortality countries with reliable data. A logistic curve that fitted the data well from age 80 to 105 indicated that death rates might reach a plateau (Thatcher et al., 1998). A quadratic curve fit to the data above age 105 suggested that mortality might even decline after age 110 (Vaupel et al., 1998). It is interesting to note that mortality plateaus at the oldest ages appear to be at variance with evolutionary theory about aging and with Baltes's (1997) first principle (left part of Figure 4.1).

The age-related increase in mortality for most adult ages attests to age-related decrements in biological adaptability. Numerous cross-sectional and longitudinal studies have reported age-dependent decrements in a number of anatomical and physiological factors. As individuals grow older, their biological adaptability decreases, and they are less well adapted to survive. The age-related increase in adult mortality appears to be fairly universal. It can be observed across different countries and regions as well as across different time periods (cf., e.g., Lancaster, 1990). Evolutionary accounts have been used to explain why biological adaptability decreases and the mortality risk increases with age. Most of these accounts rest on the argument that the force of natural selection weakens with increasing adult calendar age and that there is no selection against mutations that are expressed after reproductive activity has ceased (Baltes, 1997; Hamilton, 1966; Medawar, 1952; Williams, 1957; see also Kirkwood, this volume).

Despite these pervasive age-related decrements in people's capability to survive, mortality is plastic, and it has been affected by cultural changes. Evidence for the effects of culture can be obtained by examining mortality trends during the twentieth century (see also Baltes, 1997). A century is a relatively short period of time in the evolution of humans. Evolutionary forces and subsequent changes in the human genome cannot explain mortality changes that occur within the course of a mere century. Mortality changes in the twentieth century are clearly attributable to cultural changes and innovations.

Life expectancy is a synthetic measure of current mortality conditions in a particular year, and it is widely used as a general indicator of mortality. Life expectancy at age x, often denoted by e_x, is the average number of years people have left to live when they celebrate their xth birthday, assuming that death rates remain constant at current levels. Figure 4.3 displays how female life expectancy at ages 0, 60, and 80 increased from 1900 to 1995 in France, Sweden, and the United States. One can see that life expectancy rose dramatically in this time period. Life expectancy at birth increased by 35 years in France, 28 years in Sweden, and 30 years in the United States. Progress in the area of

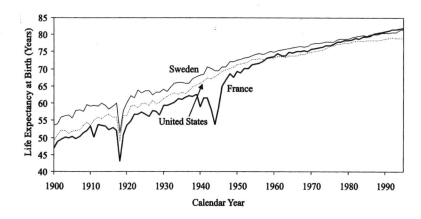

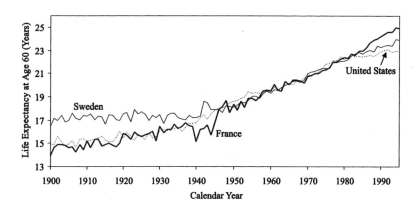

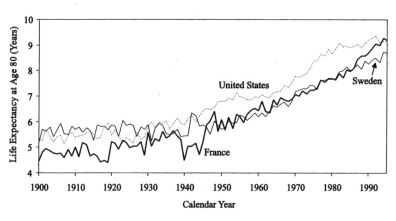

Figure 4.3   Female life expectancy at ages 0, 60, and 80 from 1900 to 1995, separately for France, Sweden, and the United States

Source: Berkeley Mortality Database, http://demog.berkeley.edu/wilmoth/mortality/.

mortality was also evident at older ages, and it was more pronounced in recent decades than in earlier ones. Remaining life expectancy at age 60 rose by 11 years in France and by about 8 years in Sweden and the United States. There were considerable gains even at the oldest ages. Remaining life expectancy at age 80 roughly doubled—from four to five years in 1900 to about eight to nine years in 1995. It seems, then, that cultural factors were rather effective in enhancing survival during the twentieth century.

There were similar but somewhat less pronounced improvements for men. From 1900 to 1995, male life expectancy at birth increased by 30 years in France, 25 years in Sweden, and 26 years in the United States. In these and other developed countries, female life expectancy at birth exceeded that of males throughout the twentieth century, and in some countries the female advantage was dramatic during the two world wars. Sex mortality differences at older ages are less affected by male excess mortality during the two world wars and may be better suited to investigating secular trends. Figure 4.4 shows sex differences in remaining life expectancy at age 60, separately for France, Sweden, and the United States. Figures 4.2 and 4.4, as well as data from many other

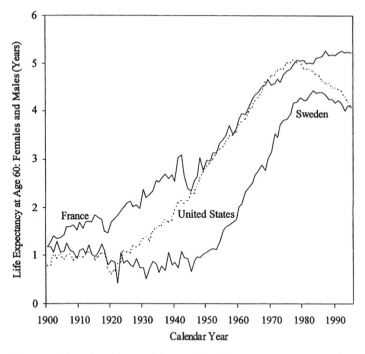

Figure 4.4   Female advantage (in years) in life expectancy at age 60 from 1900 to 1995, separately for France, Sweden, and the United States

Source: Compiled by authors from the Berkeley Mortality Database, http://demog. berkeley.edu/wilmoth/mortality/.

countries (e.g., Trovato & Lalu, 1998; Waldron, 1993), suggest that there exists a persistent female survival advantage.

Biological and social factors contribute to sex differences in mortality. Sex hormones have been identified as making a major contribution to the gender gap. Sex harmones modulate the cholesterol-carrying lipoprotein levels, and women have a healthier lipoprotein pattern (Hazzard, 1986). It has also been suggested that there is a survival advantage to having two X-chromosomes (Christensen et al., 2000; Smith & Warner, 1989). Sexual selection theory, an aspect of evolutionary theory, has been used to explain the origins of sex differences in mortality. Trivers (1972) observed that in humans and some other species, females typically make a greater parental investment in their offspring than do males. For a woman, this investment includes a nine-month gestation period, followed by lactation and much subsequent nurture. Evolutionary psychologists (Daly & Wilson, 1985; Wang & Hertwig, 1999) argue that sex differences in parental investment favor different reproductive strategies for women and men and, consequently, that different traits were selected for in women than in men. The greater female parental investment becomes a resource that males compete for and that limits males' fitness. Wang and Hertwig (1999) argued that reproductive success and personal survival tend to be antagonistic goals in human males because males' design for personal survival is compromised by the requirements for achieving success in intrasexual competition. In contrast, reproductive success and personal survival tend to be interdependent goals in human females because the mother's presence is critical for the survival of the child. This argument suggests that evolution has favored traits that increase reproduction in males and traits that increase survival in females.

Sexual selection theory is consistent with the residual female survival advantage evident in Figures 4.2 and 4.4. However, sexual selection theory alone cannot explain why sex mortality differences increased so noticeably during the twentieth century. From 1900 to 1995, sex differences in life expectancy at age 60 increased from about one year to about four to five years (see Figure 4.4). Cultural and technological innovations contributed to this increase, perhaps in concert with sex-specific behavioral tendencies shaped by evolution. Some of these behavioral factors are reviewed below in the section on survival attributes.

Lower female death rates across the life span translate into a population sex ratio that becomes increasingly unbalanced with age. Among octogenarians in developed countries there are more than twice as many women as men, and among centenarians women outnumber men by a factor of 4 to 6 (cf. Kannisto, 1996, Annex Table 14). Most older people are female, so for simplicity we present only female data in some of the figures of this chapter.

Are there differences in the degree of mortality reduction at different ages? One can determine whether the level of mortality has declined at a given age by considering average annual rates of mortality improvement—that is, percentage reductions in death

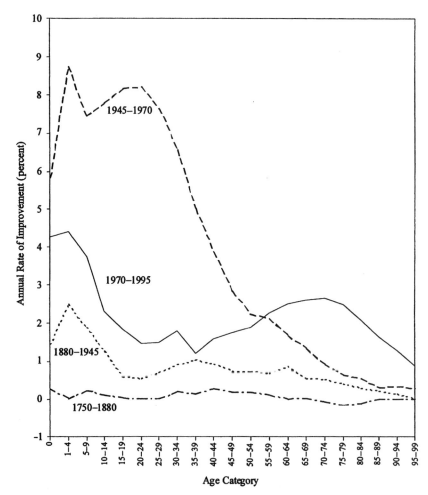

Figure 4.5 Average annual rates of progress (percentage) in reducing Finnish female mortality in various age categories and over four time periods

Source: Kannisto, Turpeinen, and Nieminen (1999). Copyright 1999 by Max-Planck-Gesellschaft. Reprinted with permission.

rates (Kannisto, Lauritsen, Thatcher, & Vaupel, 1994). As illustrated in Figure 4.5, Kannisto, Turpeinen, and Nieminen (1999) documented long-term mortality improvement since 1751 in Finland, a country for which there was no break in the continuity of vital statistics or the population base as a consequence either of wars or territorial changes. They identified four stages of mortality transition in Finland, separated by the years 1880, 1945, and 1970. A pretransition stage (1751–1880) was characterized by constant and often violent fluctuations in death rates caused by famines and wars. The level of death rates remained high and little progress was made regarding mortality at all ages. Sometime around 1880 mortality entered a phase of sustained decline that has continued ever since. However, progress was not uniform for all ages. In a second stage (1880–1945), death rates declined at almost all ages, while progress in the area of infant and child mortality was clearly most pronounced. It was during this stage that advances in prevention diagnosis, in the treatment of diseases, and in sanitary conditions were made. Kannisto et al. (1999) place the onset of the third stage (1945–1970) at the end of World War II, as antibiotics proved effective against a variety of diseases and infections. This third stage was characterized by a sudden acceleration in mortality decline. Progress was enormous in childhood and youth, after which it gradually diminished toward old age. In the latest stage (1970–1995), mortality continued to fall rapidly in infancy and early childhood. Kannisto et al. (1999) termed this stage the "era of delayed aging" because its outstanding feature was the gains in survival at older ages. During the 25 years of this stage, mortality for 70-year-old women declined an average of 2.5% every year. Although the advances were less pronounced for the oldest old, the average annual improvement for women aged 95 was still about 1%.

The trends reported by Kannisto et al. (1999) suggest that there were in fact differences in the degree of mortality reduction at different ages. In the three stages since 1880, cultural factors and innovations were obviously most effective in reducing mortality at the youngest ages. The pattern becomes less clear for adult ages. In stages two (1880–1945) and three (1945–1970), the average annual progress regarding mortality declined with increasing age. However, this was not the case in stage four (1970–1995). Here there was more progress for older individuals than for young and middle-aged adults. It appears that age differences in cultural effectiveness are relative to the particular historical period under observation.

The average annual rate of progress refers to the relative decline in death rates. If mortality is reduced, then the number of lives saved at a given age is proportional to the absolute rather than the relative decline at that age (Vaupel, 1997). For instance, in 1901 to 1905, the probability that a French woman aged 90 would die within one year was 33%. In 1991 to 1995, this probability of death was reduced to 16%. Thus, at the end of the twentieth century 17% more French women aged 90 enjoyed another year of life than at the beginning of the century. Comparing death rates in 1901 to 1905 and in 1991 to 1995, Figure 4.6 shows the absolute reduction in female age-specific death rates (in percent) in France, Sweden, and the United States. Figure 4.6 indicates that the greatest progress occurred at the youngest and the oldest ages. Progress in childhood and at early adult ages was modest, primarily because early in the twentieth century death rates at these ages were already comparatively low. Although the lives saved at the oldest ages are generally not extended for more than a few years, the large absolute reductions in death rates provide further evidence for the plasticity of oldest-old mortality. If the absolute mortality improvements illustrated in Figure 4.6 are chosen as the standard for evaluating the effectiveness of cultural factors during the twentieth century, then it appears that cultural innovations were most effective in enhancing survival at the most

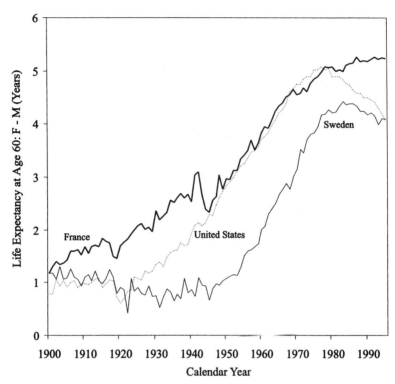

Figure 4.6   Absolute reduction in age-specific female death rates (in per-
                       centages) from 1901–1905 to 1991–1995, separately for France,
                       Sweden, and the United States

Source: Compiled by authors from the Berkeley Mortality Database, http://demog.
berkeley.edu/wilmoth/mortality/.

advanced ages. Note that the empirical functions presented in Figure 4.6 are in stark
contrast to the hypothesized lifespan function of cultural effectiveness shown in the
right part of Figure 4.1.

German Unification and Old-Age Mortality

Further evidence for the plasticity of mortality can be obtained from an examination of
old-age survival in unified Germany. Recent German history offers a unique opportunity
to study the effects of political, economic, and social factors on mortality. Prior to 1945,
East and West Germans shared a cultural and historical background that included the
political system. Between 1949 and 1989, however, Germans lived under different
political and economic systems—a socialist, planned economy (East Germany) versus
a free-market democracy (West Germany). With German unification in 1990, the two
German populations were again integrated into one political and economic system.

From around 1970 onward, mortality trends in East and West Germany diverged. Life expectancy at birth in East Germany increased with a low gradient for both sexes, while life expectancy in West Germany rose more rapidly. Epidemiologists and demographers discussed several possible reasons for the increasing life-expectancy gap in East and West Germany. Less favorable cardiovascular risk-factor profiles were present in East Germany, while West Germany was characterized by a higher average social class, a higher gross national product per capita, and a higher proportion of the gross national product spent on health (Heinemann, Dinkel, & Görtler, 1996). As a consequence of these profiles, in 1988 the east-west gap in life expectancy had reached 2.9 years for women and 2.5 years for men (Dorbritz & Gärtner, 1998). Roughly concurrent with German unification in 1990, life expectancy in East Germany began to increase at an accelerated pace. This improvement in life expectancy was more pronounced for women. German life tables for the years 1995 to 1997 indicate that the east-west differences in life expectancy had been reduced to 1.2 years for women and 2.3 years for men (Statistisches Bundesamt, 1999). This reduction was less impressive for men, but there were improvements for men in both East and West Germany.

A recent study (Gjonça, Brockmann, & Maier, 2000) examined the contribution of different age groups to changes in life expectancy from 1980 to 1996, separately for men and women and for the two German states. Life expectancy at birth for women in East Germany from 1980 to 1996 improved by 5.3 years, and over 71% of this improvement came from ages 60 and over. During that same period, life expectancy for East German men improved by 3.1 years, and 62% of this improvement came from ages 60 and over. It is remarkable that even the oldest age groups contributed substantially to the improvement. For East German women, 31% of the mortality improvement came from ages 80 and above. The corresponding figure for East German men was 17%. Thus, improvement in East German life expectancy was driven by the old age groups, with the oldest old making a substantial contribution.

Were any of the long-term trends in East German oldest-old mortality altered by German unification and the cultural, political, and economic changes associated with it? Mortality data for the oldest old have often been considered to be subject to a large degree of error. The Kannisto-Thatcher oldest-old database was specifically designed to investigate mortality at the oldest ages. It contains data on mortality at age 80 and over in Germany and in many other countries, by sex and single year of age (Kannisto, 1994, 1996; Thatcher, Kannisto, & Vaupel, 1998). Sources of the data are official vital statistics prepared by the authorized agencies in the respective countries. A technique developed by Vincent (1951), the "method of extinct generations," was then applied to arrange data on deaths into cohort mortality histories. Once a cohort is considered extinct, this technique builds up the cohort history (population-at-risk and the number of deaths at each age) by cumulating the deaths, beginning with the oldest. For cohorts that are not yet extinct, the number of survivors was determined by sources such as population registers, population censuses, official estimates, and estimates derived from deaths (Kannisto, 1994). Using data from the Kannisto-Thatcher database, Figure 4.7

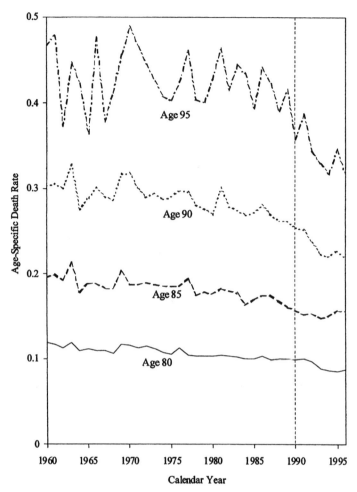

Figure 4.7   Age-specific death rates 1960 to 1996 in East Germany for females
                        at ages 80, 85, 90, and 95 years

Source: Calculated by Gjonça, Brockmann, and Maier (2000) from data in the
Kannisto-Thatcher oldest-old database (Kannisto, 1994, 1996).

shows death rates for the period from 1960 to 1996 for East German women aged
80, 85, 90, and 95. Reduction in oldest-old mortality was minor until the mid-1980s.
Starting in the late 1980s and accelerated with German unification in 1990, oldest-old
death rates declined. Improvement at very old ages (ages 90 and 95 in Figure 4.7) is
striking.

It is informative to examine trajectories of old-age mortality in East Germany in
comparison to mortality trends in West Germany. Figure 4.8 shows the ratios (east/west)
of death rates for East and West German women from 1960 to 1996. Ratios above 1

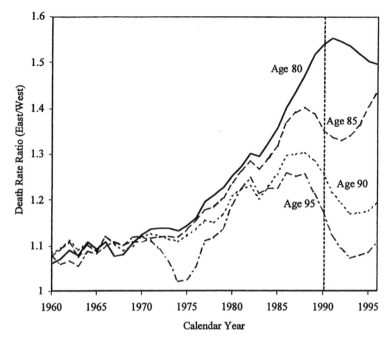

Figure 4.8   Excess mortality in East Germany: Smoothed death rate ratios (East and West Germany) 1960 to 1996 for females at ages 80, 85, 90, and 95 years

Source: Calculated by Gjonça, Brockmann, and Maier (2000) from data in the Kannisto-Thatcher oldest-old database (Kannisto, 1994, 1996).

indicate an excess mortality in East Germany. Figure 4.8 reveals that excess East German mortality was present throughout the period from 1960 to 1996. Despite the slight West German advantage, East and West Germany had similar levels of oldest-old mortality (ratios close to 1.0) until about 1975. After 1975 the mortality gap widened rapidly. In the late 1980s, oldest-old mortality was 20% (age 95) to 50% (age 80) higher in East Germany than in the West. With the collapse of the socialist government in 1989 and German unification a year later, the diverging trends in oldest-old mortality came to a halt. For some ages there even appears to be a reversal in the years since unification, and East and West German death rates have started to converge.

Oldest-old death rates were remarkably sensitive to the cultural, political, and economic changes associated with German unification. It appears that death rates even at the oldest ages responded immediately to the historical drama of unification. Speculation about the specific cultural factors responsible focuses on the health care system and individuals' economic resources (Gjonça, Brockmann, & Maier, 2000). Studies on mortality from conditions amenable to medical interventions confirm that medical resource deficiencies are decisive (Velkova, Wolleswinkel-Van den Bosch, &

Mackenbach, 1997). The financial weakness of the socialist health care system in East Germany could be one reason why improvements in old-age mortality were relatively slow prior to unification. After unification the West German health care system was quickly installed in East Germany, and this could have led to immediate progress in the area of old-age mortality. An alternative argument rests on the extensive literature on socioeconomic differentials in mortality. Individual resource availability increases health chances and, ultimately, survival. With unification, the West German pension scheme was transmitted to East Germany, which made retired persons one of the groups that benefited most from the transformation. Increased individual resources and the opportunities that came with them may have contributed to the accelerated decline in old-age death rates in East Germany.

German unification did not affect death rates equally across all ages. There were even some segments of the population that experienced an increase in mortality. The sudden economic change and the availability of cars resulted in both a rise in vehicle ownership and an increase in the number of inexperienced drivers on roads that were ill suited for the increased traffic. As a consequence, the death rates of East German car owners at ages 18 to 20 increased 11-fold between 1989 and 1991, and for those at ages 21 to 24 years the increase was eightfold (Winston, Rineer, Menon, & Baker, 1999). It appears that a cultural intervention as extensive as German unification can at the same time lead to a reduction of mortality at some ages and to increasing death rates at other ages.

Survival Attributes: Differences Between Individuals

In the preceding sections, we adopted a historical perspective to discuss the effects of cultural factors in their entirety on mortality. There are also many theoretical and empirical contributions in the literature that focus on specific aspects of culture—namely, on social, behavioral, and psychological risk factors affecting mortality and survival. These risk factors are usually conceptualized as survival attributes—that is, as persistent characteristics of individuals, whether innate or acquired.

Research on twins and other populations of related individuals suggests that the length of one's life is moderately heritable. There is a general consensus in studies in behavioral genetics that about 20% to 30% of the total variation in adult human life spans can be attributed to genetic factors (Herskind et al., 1996; Ljungquist, Berg, Lanke, McClearn, & Pedersen, 1998; McGue, Vaupel, Holm, & Harvald, 1993). Another 20% to 30% can be perhaps explained by nongenetic survival attributes that are fixed for individuals by the time they are 30 years old (Vaupel et al., 1998). Among these nongenetic fixed factors are health conditions in early life (Elo & Preston, 1992), socioeconomic conditions in childhood (Davey Smith, Hart, Blane, & Hole, 1998), and the socioeconomic position a person has attained at about age 30 (Kitagawa & Hauser, 1973).

Many studies have addressed the effects of behavioral and lifestyle factors on morbidity and mortality. The detrimental health consequences of smoking are well documented (cf., e.g., Doll, Peto, Wheatley, Gray, & Sutherland, 1994; Jacobs et al., 1999). The association between alcohol consumption and mortality appears to be U-shaped, with a somewhat elevated risk of death for both abstainers and heavy drinkers (Thun et al., 1997). There are also reports that regular physical activity acts as a protective factor against mortality (e.g., Bijnen et al., 1998). With respect to obesity, the risk of death incrases throughout the range of moderate to severe overweight (Calle, Thun, Petrelli, Rodriguez, & Clark, 1999), although there is some debate on whether obesity-related excess mortality declines with age (Bender, Jöckel, Trautner, Spraul, & Berger, 1999).

Psychological traits and dispositions may also have some influence on mortality. Many studies have indicated that intelligence and related constructs are associated with late-life survival (Bosworth, Schaie, & Willis, 1999; Maier & Smith, 1999; Smits, Deeg, Kriegsman, & Schmand, 1999). However, little is known about the mechanisms that generate this association, particularly about the role of physical health. Several chronic diseases are known to affect both cognitive function and mortality, and the association between cognitive function and mortality could be spurious. Lower intellectual functioning could also be indicative of general processes of brain atrophy and system breakdown. At a pragmatic and everyday level, lower intellectual function could also put individuals at risk for other factors that are more direct causes of death.

Do happy people live longer? There is some evidence that this might indeed be the case. Huppert and Whittington (1995) observed that symptoms of psychological distress predicted mortality. Diagnosed major depression increases the risk of dying (Penninx et al., 1999). There is also a large body of studies documenting that favorable self-ratings of health are related to survival above and beyond more objective, externally assessed health measures (Idler & Benyamini, 1997). The relationship between aspects of happiness and satisfaction and survival is not well understood. Unhappiness is probably not the direct cause of an increased mortality risk, but it may reflect potential causes from other life domains (e.g., lack of social ties, clinical and preclinical health conditions). On the other hand, it could be that unhappiness and dissatisfaction can stimulate the release of chemicals that have a negative effect on the immune system (Maier, Watkins, & Fleshner, 1994).

Most psychological research on mortality has focused on the relation between psychological factors measured late in life and survival within a few subsequent years. Only very few studies have examined the effects of psychological factors early in life on late-life survival. Friedman et al. (1995) related childhood personality to vital status 70 years later. The trait of conscientiousness (that is, being responsible, dependable, well organized) was associated with a longer life. Friedman and colleagues explored several pathways that may have led to this finding. There was little evidence that health behavior mediates the relation between conscientiousness and survival. It could be that conscientious persons are better able to cope with life's stresses and are thus less likely to become ill. Although Friedman et al. (1995) is intriguing, the extent to which their results can be generalized is questionable, since only children from the top 1% of the intelligence distribution were eligible for participation.

Danner, Snowdon, and Friesen (2001) studied Catholic nuns, examining the relationship between the emotional content of texts written early in life and survival late in life. Positive emotional content in autobiographies written when these women were a mean age of 22 was strongly related to survival at the ages 75 to 95. Positive emotional content in writings is possibly indicative of a general readiness to express emotion, and these writings may reflect a beneficial response pattern that avoids the adverse effects of suppressing the expression of emotion. Understanding the nature and magnitude of possible lingering effects of early life psychological factors on survival at advanced ages remains an important goal for future research.

Discussion and Conclusion

Psychologists have observed that the relative power of cultural interventions decreases with age. Compared to young adults, older persons need more time, practice, and cognitive support to achieve the same learning gains (Baltes, 1997; Kliegl, Smith, & Baltes, 1989). With respect to peak performance, older adults may never reach the same levels of functioning as younger adults, even after extensive training. This seems to be the case for exceptional performance in the cognitive domain, as well as it clearly is in several other domains (such as sports) (see also Kliegl, Krampe, & Mayr, this volume).

Is there a similar age-related decrease in the effectiveness of cultural interventions when it comes to human mortality? Measures of relative mortality decline (Figure 4.5) suggest that this was true until about 1970. However, the technological and economic innovations introduced in the twentieth century produced unprecedented reductions in death rates, and progress was not confined to younger ages. In more recent decades, it has even been the case that the most striking improvements occurred among older individuals. Survival rates in unified Germany provide an intriguing example for the plasticity of human mortality even at the most advanced ages.

The remarkable improvements in survival at older ages appear to be inconsistent with the proposal that the relative power of cultural innovations wanes with age (right panel of Figure 4.1). This inconsistency can perhaps be resolved if one considers the possibility that the elderly have benefited disproportionately from cultural innovations and from the allocation of societal resources. Differently put, the argument could be made that society has invested more resources in combating mortality at older than at younger ages, which has led to the marked increase in survival at older ages.

How do contemporary societies allocate their resources across ages? The provision of medical care represents a prominent allocation system. Cross-sectional studies suggest that the costs for health care increase with the age of the patient (e.g., Meerding et al., 1998) but with some decreases at advances ages (Lubitz & Riley, 1993; Brockmann, 2000). Furthermore, there is also evidence that proximity to death is a much more important factor than age in determining the costs for acute medical care. Data from the United States (Lubitz & Riley, 1993) and Germany (Brockmann, 2000) indicate that the costs for medical treatment near death decrease with increasing age at death. This may in part be due to the fact that older people suffer from less expensive diseases, but it may also reflect a belief on the part of care providers that aggressive medical interventions are less appropriate for those who are very old and frail.

The provision of health care is only one of many societal allocation systems (see also Behrman, this volume). Lee (1997, 2000) studied a large number of wealth-allocation systems and noted that most familial transfers (such as child costs, costs for higher education, gifts, and bequests) in industrialized societies are downward—that is, from the old to the young. In contrast, most of the wealth transfers through the public sector (such as social security, pensions, and health care) are upward. When the downward transfers through the family are combined with upward transfers through the public sector, the net direction of transfer flows in contemporary industrialized societies is still upward from the young to the old. It seems, then, that there is some indication that older people receive more support. However, it is difficult to draw firm conclusions because both young and old people can also contribute assets and services—such as knowledge, wisdom, experience, or care giving—to society. Quantitative data on these immaterial assets and services and the intergenerational transfer flows thereof are rarely available.

From the data at hand, it can safely be concluded that old-age mortality is not immutable and that cultural factors were quite effective in enhancing late-life survival during the twentieth century. Mortality at older ages is plastic, and we found only little empirical support for the proposal that the plasticity of mortality is reduced in scope with age.

Note

This work was sponsored by the Max Planck Institute for Demographic Research (MPIDR) in Rostock, Germany. We thank P. B. Baltes, K. Brehmer, S. Leek, J. Oeppen, U. M. Staudinger, and two anonymous reviewers. Address correspondence to Heiner Maier, Max Planck Institute for Demographic Research, Doberaner Strasse 114, D-18057 Rostock, Germany. Email: maier@demogr.mpg.de.

References

Baltes, P. B. (1997). On the incomplete architecture of human ontogeny: Selection, optimization, and compensation as foundation of developmental theory. *American Psychologist, 52*, 366–380.

Bender, R., Jöckel, K.-H., Trautner, C., Spraul, M., & Berger, M. (1999). Effect of age on excess mortality in obesity. *Journal of the American Medical Association, 281*, 1498–1504.

Bijnen, F. C. H., Caspersen, C. J., Feskens, E. J. M., Saris, W. H. M., Mosterd, W. L., & Kromhout, D. (1998). Physical activity and 10-year mortality from cardiovascular diseases and all causes. *Archives of Internal Medicine, 158*, 1499–1505.

Bosworth, H. B., Schaie, K. W., & Willis, S. L. (1999). Cognitive and sociodemographic risk factors for mortality in the Seattle Longitudinal Study. *Journal of Gerontology: Psychological Sciences, 54B*, P273–P282.

Brockmann, H. (2000). *Why is health treatment for the elderly less expensive than for the rest of the population? Health care rationing in Germany.* MPIDR Working Paper WP 2000-001. Rostock, Germany: Max Planck Institute for Demographic Research. Retrieved from http://www.demogr.mpg.de/Papers/Working/WP-2000-001.pdf.

Calle, E. E., Thun, M. J., Petrelli, J. M., Rodriguez, M. D., & Clark, C. W. (1999). Body-mass index and mortality in a prospective cohort of U.S. adults. *New England Journal of Medicine, 341*, 1097–1105.

Christensen, K., Kristiansen, M., Hagen-Larsen, H., Skytthe, A., Bathum, L., Jeune, B., Andersen-Ranberg K., Vaupel, J. W., & Ørstavik, K. H. (2000). X-linked genetic factors regulate hematopoietic stem-cell kinetics in females. *Blood, 95*, 2449–2451.

Daly, M., & Wilson, M. (1998). *Homicide.* Hawthorne, NY: Aldine de Gruyter.

Danner, D. D., Snowdon, D. A., & Friesen, W. V. (2001). Positive emotions in early life and longevity: Findings from the Nun Study. *Journal of Personality and Social Psychology, 80*, 804–813.

Davey Smith, G., Hart, C., Blane, D., & Hole, D. (1998). Adverse socioeconomic conditions in childhood and cause specific adult mortality: Prospective observational study. *British Medical Journal, 316*, 1631–1635.

Doll, R., Peto, R., Wheatley, K., Gray, R., & Sutherland, I. (1994). Mortality in relation to smoking: 40 years' observation on male British doctors. *British Medical Journal, 309*, 901–911.

Dorbritz, J., & Gärtner, K. (1998). Bericht 1998 über die demographische Lage in Deutschland mit dem Teil B "Ehescheidungen—Trends in Deutschland und im internationalen Vergleich." *Zeitschrift für Bevölkerungswissenschaft, 23*, 373–458.

Elo, I. T., & Preston, S. H. (1992). Effects of early life conditions on adult mortality: A review. *Population Index, 58*, 186–212.

Friedman, H. S., Tucker, J. S., Schwartz, J. E., Tomlinson-Keasey, C., Martin, L. R., Wingard, D. L., & Criqui, M. H. (1995). Psychosocial and behavioral predictors of longevity: The aging and the death of the Termites. *American Psychologist, 50*, 69–78.

Gjonça, A., Brockmann, H., & Maier, H. (2000). Old-age mortality in Germany prior to and after reunification [On-line]. *Demographic Research, 3.* Retrieved from http://www.demographic-research.org./Volumes/vol3/1.

Hamilton, W. D. (1966). The moulding of senescence by natural selection. *Journal of Theoretical Biology, 12*, 12–45.

Hazzard, W. R. (1986). Biological basis of the sex differential in longevity. *Journal of the American Geriatrics Society, 34*, 455–471.

Heinemann, L., Dinkel, R., & Görtler, E. (1996). Life expectancy in Germany: Possible reasons for the increasing gap between East and West Germany. *Reviews on Environmental Health, 11*, 15–26.

Herskind, A. M., McGue, M., Iachine, I. A., Holm, N., Sorensen T. I. A., Harvald, B., & Vaupel, J. W. (1996). Untangling genetic influences on smoking, body mass index and longevity: A multivariate study of 2,464 Danish twins followed for 28 years. *Human Genetics, 98*, 467–475.

Huppert, F. A., & Whittington, J. C. (1995). Symptoms of psychological distress predict seven-year mortality. *Psychological Medicine, 25*, 1073–1086.

Idler, E. L., & Benyamini, Y. (1997). Self-rated health and mortality: A review of twenty-seven community studies. *Journal of Health and Social Behavior, 38*, 21–37.

Jacobs, D. R., Adachi, H., Mulder, I., Kromhout, D., Menotti, A., Nissinen, A., & Blackburn, H. (1999). Cigarette smoking and mortality risk: 25-year follow-up of the seven countries study. *Archives of Internal Medicine, 159*, 733–740.

Kannisto, V. (1994). Development of oldest-old mortality, 1950–1990. *Odense Monographs on Population Aging, 1.* Odense, Denmark: Odense University Press. Retrieved from http://www.demogr.mpg.de/Papers/Books/Monograph1/OldestOld.htm.

Kannisto, V. (1996). The advancing frontier of survival: Life tables for old age. *Odense Monographs on Population Aging, 3*. Odense, Denmark: Odense University Press. Retrieved from http://www.demogr. mpg.de/Papers/Books/Monograph3/The advancing.htm.

Kannisto, V., Lauritsen, J., Thatcher, A. R., & Vaupel, J. W. (1994). Reductions in mortality at advanced ages: Several decades of evidence from 27 countries. *Population and Development Review, 20*, 793–810.

Kannisto, V., Turpeinen, O., & Nieminen, M. (1999). Finnish life tables since 1751. *Demographic Research* [On-line], 1. Retrieved from http://www.demographic-research.org/Volumes/vol1/1.

Kitagawa, E. M., & Hauser, P. M. (1973). *Differential mortality in the United States: A study in socioeconomic epidemiology*. Cambridge, MA: Harvard University Press.

Kliegl, R., Smith, J., & Baltes, P. B. (1989). Testing-the-limits and the study of age differences in cognitive plasticity of a mnemonic training. *Developmental Psychology, 26*, 894–904.

Lancaster, H. O. (1990). *Expectations of life: A study in the demography, statistics, and history of world mortality*. New York: Springer.

Lee, R. D. (1997). Intergenerational relations and the elderly. In K. W. Wachter & C. E. Finch (Eds.), *Between Zeus and the salmon: The biodemography of longevity* (pp. 212–233). Washington, DC: National Academy Press.

Lee, R. D. (2000). Intergeneral transfer and the economic life cycle: A cross-cultural perspective. In A. Mason & G. Tapinos (Eds.), *Sharing the wealth: Demographic change and economic transfer between generations* (pp. 17–56). Oxford: Oxford University Press.

Ljungquist, B., Berg, S., Lanke, J., McClearn, G. E., & Pedersen, N. L. (1998). The effect of genetic factors for longevity: A comparison of identical and fraternal twins in the Swedish Twin Registry. *Journal of Gerontology: Medical Sciences, 54A*, M441–M446.

Lubitz, J. D., & Riley, G. F. (1993). Trends in Medicare payments in the last year of life. *New England Journal of Medicine, 328*, 1092–1096.

Maier, H., & Smith, J. (1999). Psychological predictors of mortality in old age. *Journal of Gerontology: Psychological Sciences, 54B*, P44–P54.

Maier, S. F., Watkins, L. R., & Fleshner, M. (1994). Psychoneuroimmunology: The interface between behavior, brain, and immunity. *American Psychologist, 49*, 1004–1017.

McGue, M., Vaupel, J. W., Holm, N., & Harvald, B. (1993). Longevity is moderately heritable in a sample of Danish twins born 1870–1880. *Journal of Gerontology: Biological Sciences, 48*, B237–B244.

Medawar, P. B. (1952). *An unsolved problem of biology*. Oxford: Oxford University Press.

Meerding, W. J., Bonneux, L., Polder, J. J., Koopmanschap, M. A., & Van der Maas, P. J. (1998). Demographic and epidemiological determinants of health care costs in Netherlands: Cost of illness study. *British Medical Journal, 317*, 111–115.

Penninx, B. J. W. H., Geerlings, S. W., Deeg, D. J. H., Ejik, J. T. M., Tilburg, W., & Beekman, A. T. F. (1999). Minor and major depression and the risk of death in older persons. *Archives of General Psychiatry, 56*, 889–895.

Smith, D. W. E., & Warner, H. R. (1989). Does genotypic sex have a direct effect on longevity? *Experimental Gerontology, 24*, 277–288.

Smits, C. H. M., Deeg, D. J. H., Kriegsman, D. M. W., & Schmand, B. (1999). Cognitive functioning and health as determinants of mortality in an older population. *American Journal of Epidemiology, 150*, 978–986.

Statistisches Bundesamt. (1999). *Statistisches Jahrbuch 1999 für die Bundesrepublik Deutschland*. Wiesbaden, Germany: Statistisches Bundesamt.

Thatcher, A. R., Kannisto, V., & Vaupel, J. W. (1998). *The force of mortality at ages 80 to 120*. Odense Monographs on Population Aging, 5. Odense, Denmark: Odense University Press. Retrieved from http://www.demogr.mpg.de/Papers/Books/Monograph5/ForMort.htm.

Thun, M. J., Peto, R., Lopez, A. D., Monaco, J. H., Henley, S. J., Heath, C. W., & Doll, R. (1997). Alcohol consumption and mortality among middle-aged and elderly U. S. adults. *New England Journal of Medicine, 337*, 1705–1714.

Trivers, R. L. (1972). Parental investment and sexual selection. In B. G. Campbell (Ed.), *Sexual selection and the descent of man, 1871–1971* (pp. 136–179). Chicago: Aldine.

Trovato, F., & Lalu, N. M. (1998). Contribution of cause-specific mortality to changing sex differences in life expectancy: Seven nations case study. *Social Biology, 45*, 1–20.

Vaupel, J. W. (1997). The remarkable improvements in survival at older ages. *Philosophical Transactions of the Royal Society of London—Series B: Biological Sciences, 352*, 1799–1804.

Vaupel, J. W., Carey, J. R., Christensen, K., Johnson, T. E., Yashin, A. I., Holm, N., et al. (1998). Biodemographic trajectories of longevity. *Science, 280*, 855–860.

Velkova, A., Wolleswinkel-Van den Bosch, J., & Mackenbach, J. (1997). The east-west life expectancy gap: Differences in mortality from conditions amenable to medical intervention. *International Journal of Epidemiology, 26*, 75–84.

Vincent, P. (1951). La mortalité des veillards. *Population, 6*, 181–284.

Waldron, I. (1993). Recent trends in sex mortality ratios for adults in developed countries. *Social Science and Medicine, 36*, 451–462.

Wang, X. T., & Hertwig, R. (1999). How is maternal survival related to reproductive success? *Behavioral and Brain Sciences, 22*, 236–237.

Williams, G. C. (1957). Pleiotrophy, natural selection, and the evolution of senescence. *Evolution, 11*, 398–411.

Winston, F. K., Rineer, C., Menon, R., & Baker, S. P. (1999). The carnage wrought by major economic change: Ecological study of traffic-related mortality and the reunification of Germany. *British Medical Journal, 318*, 1647–1649.

II
Basic Processes of Lifespan Development: Selective Optimization with Compensation (SOC)

5 The Process of Successful Aging: Selection, Optimization, and Compensation

Margret M. Baltes (deceased January 1999)

Free University Berlin, Berlin, Germany

Laura L. Carstensen

Stanford University, Stanford, CA, U.S.A.

Abstract

Although much of the research done by social gerontologists focuses on the decline and loss associated with old age, many older people experience the last stage in life as a satisfying and productive time in life. Especially as the demographics of the world's population change in future decades, it becomes increasingly important to understand the behavioral, cognitive, and motivational processes involved in optimal aging. This chapter—which draws heavily on an earlier article by Baltes and Carstensen (1996)—considers the historical, societal, and philosophical influences that have directed attention away from successful aging and offers the metamodel of selective optimization with compensation (SOC) (Baltes & Baltes, 1990) as a framework for studying adaptive aging. The process of selection—namely, narrowing the array of goals and domains to which resources are directed—is considered to be the cardinal principle of lifespan development and is discussed generally in terms of selective optimization with compensation and specifically within the realm of social behavior in terms of socioemotional selectivity theory (Carstensen, 1993, 1998; Carstensen, Isaacowitz, & Charles, 1999).

Introduction

Since its inception, the primary focus of gerontological research has been on the decline and loss associated with advanced age (Riley, Kahn, & Foner, 1994; Carstensen, Graff, & Lang, 2000). We neither deny nor minimize the importance of research on age-related decline. The plight of old age is very real, embracing losses in physical, cognitive, and social domains. It is not surprising that anticipation of aging is characterized by anxiety and fear both on the part of the individual (fear of loss) and on the part of societies (fears of increased costs and burdens). The plight of aging, however, is only one side of the coin. The other side involves growth, vitality, striving, and contentment.

Discussion of successful aging inevitably raises concerns within and outside the academy. In fact, Cole (1983) contends that positive portrayals of aging are potentially as pernicious as negative ones in that they deny the reality of aging. Cole (1983) and Rosenmayr (1989), for example, believe that unless this "enlightened"view of aging is extended to include the existential challenges of physical and social decline in old age, it may very well have baneful effects. Cole (1983) writes: "The currently fashionable positive mythology of old age shows no more tolerance or respect for the intractable vicissitudes of aging than the old negative mythology" (p. 39).

Such concerns are not without merit. However, even though morbidity and mortality rates do increase with age (Brody, Brock, & Williams, 1987; Manton & Soldo, 1985; see also Maier & Vaupel, this volume), we have reached the point in Western societies where the reduction in infant mortality and the compression of morbidity (Fries, 1990) allow the majority of people to live out their lives in relatively good physical health (Manton, Corder, & Stallard, 1993). Recently, several prominent biological researchers and physicians have argued that successful and positive aging must not be omitted from our conceptions of old age to do justice to its multifaceted nature and vast heterogeneity (Bortz, 1989; Fries, 1990; Rowe & Kahn, 1987). In addition, most older people are satisfied with their lives, even more so than their younger counterparts (Carstensen, Pasupathi, Mayr, & Nesselroade, 2000; Diener & Suh, 1998; Herzog & Rodgers, 1981). Future generations will be in even better health.

Nevertheless, we agree with critics that the focus on theoretically normative psychological outcomes—rooted primarily in middle-class values and, prototypically, in white, male standards—has seriously limited our understanding of successful aging (see also Labouvie-Vief, this volume). The use of normative outcomes pays only minimal attention to the heterogeneity among and within aging people (Maddox, 1987; Thomae, 1981), fails to acknowledge the social construction of old age (Dannefer, 1987), and ignores the potential for multiple outcomes (Schaie, 1983) and diverse standards of success (Boesch, 1954; Yoon, 1996). A person living under objectively poor conditions may strive toward self-actualization; another living in an objectively good situation may experience aging as a tremendous burden. A single individual may be physically ill but psychologically strong, feel despair about family but contentment about work, and experience great dissatisfaction but a profound sense of meaning in life. Furthermore, what is considered successful according to functional norms might not meet with ideal norms or square with statistical norms. Definitions of the meaning of success have changed over historical time and will continue to vary along with changes in societal, cultural, and biological norms. Definition of outcomes, therefore, needs to be multidimensional and multilevel and needs to consider both gains and losses (see also Heckhausen, this volume).

Furthermore, the research question needs to be broadened from a primary focus on outcomes—that is, from: "What is successful aging?" to include "How do people age successfully?" or "What are the processes that allow for mastery of goals in old age?" We suggest that understanding the processes that people use to reach their goals under increasing limitations in resources—whether social, psychological or biological—will lead to additional insights and progress in the field. In this chapter we argue that the metamodel of selective optimization with compensation (P. Baltes & M. Baltes, 1990) offers a suitable framework within which to pose such questions. The proposed model defines success as the attainment of goals that can differ widely among people and can be measured against diverse standards and norms. The three processes identified in the model—namely, selection, compensation, and optimization—in concert provide a way to conceptualize the strategies older people use to age well even in the face of loss. We cannot predict what any given individual's successful aging will look like until we know the domains of functioning and goals that the individual considers important and personally meaningful and in which he or she feels competent.

To provide a context for our argument, we begin by tracing the history of theoretical attempts to define and describe success and successful aging. Next, we examine empirical findings for the most commonly used criteria of successful aging. Last, we introduce the process model of selective optimization with compensation (M. Baltes, 1987; P. Baltes & M. Baltes, 1990), a metamodel of successful aging that incorporates a lifespan view, builds on empirical evidence about gains and losses in old age, permits specification of any desired goal or norm to define success depending on the theoretical perspective embraced, and specifies three processes that facilitate striving toward goals in the face of losses.

Definitions of success have varied throughout history, implying greater or lesser involvement of luck and effort and more or less in the way of evaluative connotations (a fortunate outcome versus any outcome) (Edwards, 1967; Simpson & Weiner, 1989). In modern usage, success typically refers to favorable attainments deriving from one's own behavior and actions. Very often it is measured by economic accomplishments. Because of such materialistic usages, success is considered by some to be a poor choice for describing positive outcomes in old age. Cole (1984), for example, views the current emphasis on successful aging as the capitalist takeover of aging.

Success, however, is not explicitly limited to utilitarian outcomes. Success can refer to the attainment of personal goals of all types, ranging from the maintenance of physical functioning and good health to generativity, ego-integrity, self-actualization, and social connectedness (M. Baltes & Silverberg, 1994; Bellah, Madison, & Sullivan, 1986).

Some critics argue that successful aging is an oxymoron; successful aging means not aging at all. History, as well as our modern youth- and achievement-oriented culture, is replete with tales of the *Jungbrunnen* or "fountain of youth" and consumer products that aim to help people maintain a youthful appearance, increase productivity, and optimize physical health. However, a conceptualization of successful aging founded on denial is ultimately an untenable position. Looking back and seeking to cultivate the still glorious middle years will inevitably lead to despair and eventual defeat (Butler, 1974; Erikson, 1959).

Unlike earlier developmental stages in which goals and success are defined as the acquisition of survival skills, successful aging is intricately interwoven with a sense of meaning and purpose in life and thus invokes existential paradigms or ideals (Cole, 1984; Cole & Gadow, 1986; Rosenmayr, 1983a, 1983b, 1985). Rentsch (1994) observes that aging is the radicalization of the human condition. Aging is described as a dialectic between self-actualization and self-alienation.

Although influenced heavily by the cultural context of the historical era, a deep ambivalence about aging can be traced from ancient to modern times. With the advent of industrial capitalism, human value became equated with productivity, and, at the same time, retirement was institutionalized as a symbol of nonproductivity. Ironically, this more negative view of old people and aging was facilitated by scientific attention to aging. By focusing almost exclusively on problems of elderly people—their isolation, dependence, role loss, and illness—researchers reinforced a very negative portrayal of aging.

The view of aging as a time of decline was further reinforced by well-intentioned advocates and politicians who, to win support for the infirm elderly, portrayed them as sick and needy. The implementation of the Older Americans Act (OAA) and similar policies in the United States and other countries functioned as a double-edged sword by providing protection but also endangering individual autonomy and integrity (Estes & Binney, 1989; Guillemard, 1994).

The last two decades have witnessed several important changes in the views of old age held by the scientific community. Findings in biological, social, and psychological spheres have pointed to unused and latent potentials of elderly adults. Examples are found in the domain of cognitive aging, where it has been shown that elders can improve their cognitive output after improved learning and performance conditions (Baltes & Lindenberger, 1988; Lindenberger & Baltes, 1997; Schaie, 1990; see also Kliegl, Krampe, & Mayr, this volume); in the domain of social behavior, where dependent self-care behavior can be reversed to independent functioning when given prompts, time, and rewards (M. Baltes, 1995; for review, see Mosher-Ashley, 1986–1987); and in the domain of physical functioning, where it has been shown that a great number of physical declines can be postponed and temporarily reversed through proper exercise and diet (M. Baltes & Reichert, 1992; Stones & Kozma, 1985; Whitbourne, 1985). A wealth of empirical findings from both the social and biological sciences have accrued confirming that latent potentials can be activated to compensate for possible losses in old age.

Thus, there appears to be considerable fluidity in old age (Carstensen Graff, & Lang, 2000). Nevertheless, gerontological theories have either focused on decline or growth. None that we know of have considered gains and losses and their potential interactions conjointly. Many early theories of successful aging posited highly idealized human states as the adaptive outcomes of old age. Jung (1931), for example, postulated expansion beyond gender constraints toward full humanity and wisdom as criteria for successful aging. Erikson's (1984) stage model (Erikson, Erickson, & Kivnick, 1986) posited that psychological peace and ego integrity were the criteria for success in old age. Other theorists conceptualized the acceptance of decline as the adaptive task of old age (i.e., Bühler, 1933). The now classic disengagement theory (Cumming & Henry, 1961) characterized success as acceptance of and reconciliation with the loss of power endemic in old age, whereas activity theory (Havighurst & Albrecht, 1953; Maddox, 1965) posited that the maintenance of activity, replacement of lost roles with new ones, and continued psychological involvement in society and interpersonal relationships represented the formula for successful aging.

More recently, Ryff (1982, 1989a, 1989b) proposed an integrative model of successful aging based on developmental, clinical, and mental health perspectives, arguing that multiple aspects of life must be considered when assessing successful aging. Her model includes six dimensions, all referring to positive functioning: self-acceptance, positive relations with others, autonomy, environmental mastery, purpose in life, and personal growth.

In summary, over the past 50 years, a number of theories have been proposed to describe successful aging. The centerpiece of most of these conceptualizations has been the elaboration of focal success outcomes, ranging from disengagement to longevity. No one theory, criterion, or even pattern of criteria has been widely accepted as a cogent prescription or explanation for success in old age. Part of this might be due to the empirical findings on successful aging to which we now turn.

Empirical Findings for Successful Aging Criteria

Physical health, functional autonomy, and longevity have served as indicators of successful aging to biological scientists. Physical health is unquestionably tied to psychological well-being at any age (Bowling & Browne, 1991; Krause, 1990; Rodin, 1986) and psychological variables, like perceived social support and lifestyle, appear to influence morbidity and mortality (Blazer, 1982; House, Landis, & Umberson, 1988; Vaillant 1990; Vaillant, Meyer, Mukamal, & Soldz, 1998).

However, good physical health cannot be a prerequisite in psychological theories of successful aging because, as Wong points out, "even the fittest [eventually] succumb to disabling illness" (1989, p. 518). In addition, the person who has lived the longest, most likely will also have experienced the most losses, whether loss of friends, loss of own health, and so on. The person who strives for autonomy may, at the same time, lose social contacts and experience isolation. Thus, the criteria of functional autonomy and longevity do not necessarily lead to psychological well-being. Successful aging, when studied empirically by psychologists, is most commonly operationalized as life satisfaction, high morale, or the subjective appraisal of well-being. Researchers have used life satisfaction as an index of success in the retirement transition (Parnes, 1981), recovery after widowhood (Wortman & Silver, 1990), and a number of other live events. The voluminous literature about the direct and indirect effects of social structural variables on satisfaction (George, 1990) reveals that statistically significant differences in satisfaction among groups of people do exist. Income, population density, marital status, years of formal education, and other variables do predict life satisfaction but account for very little of the variance in life satisfaction.

Moreover, the vast majority of people report that they are satisfied with their lives regardless of objective indicators (Brim, 1988, 1992; Diener, 1984; George, 1981; Larson, 1978; Lawton, 1983, 1984; Schwarz & Strack, 1989). One possible explanation is that life satisfaction comprises different dimensions in the old versus the young (Ryff, 1989b). Another explanation for preserved life satisfaction in spite of age-related loss is, however, that elderly people adapt to negative changes by using coping strategies such as downward social comparison (Wills, 1991).

Relatively recently, a number of researchers from diverse fields—psychology (Dittmann-Kohli, 1990; Reker, Peacock, & Wong, 1987; Wong, 1989), literature (Weiland, 1989; Woodword & Schwartz, 1986), and history (Cole, 1984)—have shifted their attention to personal meaning in life as an index of successful aging. Wong (1989), following Jung (1931) and Erikson and colleagues (1986), argues that finding personal meaning in life is the major developmental task of old age. Personal meaning has been conceptualized as the interpretation of life (Antonovsky, 1979), the central focus on values (Cole & Gadow, 1986), the cognitive construal of consistency between goals and actions (Rosenmayr, 1985), the acceptance of immutable circumstances and integrative reminiscence (Wong, 1989, 1991; Wong & Watt 1991), self-discovery (Tournier, 1972), future-orientedness and optimism (Schonfield, 1973), and religiosity and spirituality (Cole, 1984).

In closing, we agree with Cole (1984) and Rosenmayr (1985) that a rethinking of successful aging is necessary to avoid a class bias or utopian dream. We disagree, however, that a positive view of the potential of aging necessarily includes a prescription for the outcome or places sole responsibility for successful aging on the individual. Most gerontological theories do not take into account individual or cultural variation in goals and usually apply ideal or statistical norms from within one culture, rarely functional or individual norms. But no one criterion has been found acceptable. Indeed, even ranking the array of success criteria is difficult. Can an old person in excellent physical health but deteriorated mental health be considered a successful ager? Should people who live only to 70 but maintain a highly optimistic view of aging be considered unsuccessful agers? A multicriteria approach is preferred to a monocriterion approach (Ryff, 1989a, 1991). However, unless we accept all criteria as equally important— which would render the numbers of successful aging people extremely small—we are left with the problem of ranking the most important criteria.

A solution to this problem seems to be a flexible definition of success outcomes. Success can be defined by different authorities (such as individual, peer group, society, or scientific theory), by different criteria of assessment (subjective versus objective), and by different norms (functional, statistical, or ideal norm).[1] On the most general level, successful aging implies that people reach personal goals; these might coincide

Table 5.1

Different Norms in Different Domains with Different Goals

	Domains and Goals		
Norm	Physical Health	Social Integration	Psychological Well-Being
Statistical	No major disease	Marriage	No pathology
Ideal	Complete health	Intimacy	Happiness
Functional	Hearing	Communication	Independence

with ideal or statistical norms but may also concur with idiosyncratic goals. Table 5.1 provides an overview and examples of different standards of success.

Allowing variation in goals and norms and identifying the prototypical processes that facilitate successful aging will potentially lead to increasing precision and strength of our theories of successful aging and the construction of environmental conditions and lifestyles conducive to optimal aging. In short, success needs to be redefined such that it is not just associated with normative and ideal goals or outcomes. Success does not and should not be measured against one standard. Any definition of success based exclusively on theoretically normative outcomes and goals will, by its very nature, lack generalizability and longevity. When the question becomes "How is success achieved?," we may find that the processes people use to cope with life and aging are more universal and less dependent on cultural vicissitudes.

The Metamodel of Selective Optimization with Compensation

With this said, a useful model of successful aging must account for the dynamics between gains and losses—that is, on the one hand, for a reduction in reserves and an increasing number of specific losses and challenges in the biological, social, and psychological spheres, and, on the other hand, for potential growth and plasticity in old age. Such a metamodel should be able to harbor a great diversity of outcomes and goals, accommodate different success criteria, and emphasize how elderly people obtain personal goals—that is, age successfully—in the face of simultaneous losses. Moreover, ideally, it should be applicable at the individual level or at the level of the larger collective (M. Baltes & Carstensen, 1999).

In lifespan psychology (P. Baltes, 1987, 1991; P. Baltes, Reese, & Lipsitt, 1980; P. Baltes, Staudinger, & Lindenberger, 1999), the major criterion for successful development is the efficacious functioning of the individual in an identified system (biological, social, psychological), domain (sports, leisure, job, family), or task (self-actualization, cognitive performance, social integration). To augment and enrich one's own reserve capacities and resources, particularly throughout early and middle life, is of the utmost importance since these will also assist successful mastery of developmental tasks in late life. While adherence to the notion of efficacious functioning does not preclude the prescription of developmental goals or outcomes as ideal in successful aging, it does not bank on them, and above all, it allows the operation of diverse norms to evaluate attainment of individually desired goals. Such a model implicitly and explicitly allows for greater variability in successful aging, with the base being heterogeneity and plasticity, two major findings known about aging (P. Baltes & M. Baltes, 1990).

In this sense, the metamodel of selective optimization with compensation (SOC) (P. Baltes & M. Baltes, 1990; M. Baltes, 1987; M. Baltes & Reichert, 1992; M. Baltes, Lang, & Wilms, 1998) defines success as goal attainment and successful aging as minimization of losses and maximization of gains. Using the notion of mastery and adaptation allows diverse specifications of the goals and its evaluation criteria depending on the specific theory tested. Freund, Li, and Baltes (1999) emphasize that the model is intended as a dynamic heuristic (see also Gigerenzer, this volume). Although the three components parts of the model are described as if they refer to static, independent, processes, in practice they are constantly changing. What is considered "selection" at one point in a developmental process (such as pursuing a particular type of expertise) can later become a means to subsequently optimize performance.

The metamodel specifies three processes—selection, compensation, and optimization. If implemented together, use of the processes enables people to master their goals despite, or perhaps even because of, losses and increasing vulnerabilities (see also Brandtstädter & Rothermund, this volume). The three processes embrace a great multitude of psychological mechanisms and strategies. For instance, optimization of one's health may mean for one person to exercise more frequently, for another to diet, and for a third person to reduce stress. According to the model, the same processes are at work even when goals vary over individuals, time, or context. Furthermore, the criteria of goal attainment can vary by type of assessment (objective versus subjective), by the authority (individual, group, family, culture) judging success, and by norms (statistical, ideal, functional).

A real-life example might best illustrate the three processes and their interaction. An old marathon runner can maintain the goal of winning by competing within his own age group and running fewer and easier courses (instances of selection), extending warm-up periods to accommodate a slowed cardiovascular response (compensation), and using a special diet and vitamins to increase fitness (optimization).

The metamodel, thus, is considered prototypical in its genotype of mastery, but it can accommodate wide interindividual differences in its phenotypic manifestation. What and how many domains people choose and the specific strategies they use in striving toward successful aging may differ from person to person. The model is a metamodel that attempts to represent scientific knowledge about the nature of development and aging with the focus on successful adaptation. Although the three processes have theoretical implications for successful development at large (see Marsiske, Lang, Baltes, & Baltes, 1995), we focus here on successful aging.

The order of the descriptions below is not intended to imply the order with which the processes unfold in day-to-day life. The dynamic interplay of these processes and the variability with which they unfold are hallmarks of the model.

Definition of the Three Component Processes and Empirical Evidence Selection

Selection at all levels of behavior (input, processing, output) is a core element of any theory of behavior (see also Brandtstädter & Rothermund, this volume). Selection can be active or passive, internal or external, intentional or automatic. In development including aging, *selection* refers to the increasing restriction of life domains as a consequence or in anticipation of changes in personal and environmental resources. In old age, these changes are often losses. Selection can entail the avoidance of one domain altogether, or it can mean a restriction in tasks and goals within one or more domains. An elderly person whose spouse is suffering from a terminal illness, for example, may give up the domain of sexuality altogether or may restrict some goals and involvements in the social network at large but increase efforts in the domain of leisure activities and family. The adaptive task of the individual is to select high-priority domains, tasks, and goals that involve a convergence between environmental demands, individual motivations, skills, and biological capacity.

Although selection connotes a reduction in the number of high-efficacy domains, tasks, and goals, it is not necessarily limited to a continuation of previous goals and domains, albeit in smaller numbers. Selection can also involve new or transformed domains and goals. Thus, the person who lost a spouse might continue to invest love and care by carrying on the political activities of the spouse, for instance, and maintaining his or her legacy. Selection always entails the readjustment of individual goals. Selection can be proactive or reactive. It can encompass environmental changes (such as relocation), active behavior changes (reducing the number of commitments), or passive adjustment (avoiding climbing stairs or allowing somebody to take responsibility). Proactively, through monitoring current functioning, people predict future changes and losses (death of the spouse) and make efforts to search for tasks and domains that can remain intact even after losses. Selection is reactive when unpredictable or sudden changes force persons to make a selection. If a stroke suddenly severely impairs a person, a decision to remain at home might not be viable, but the person can engage in selection processes about which institution, how much and what kind of self-care, what type of rehabilitation, what activities to engage in, what television program to watch, and when to write a letter or make a telephone call. Other selections (see examples below) represent adjustment to more gradual losses, such as those involving vision.

Empirical Evidence for Selection Processes

Selection is an integral part of any developmental process. Evidence for selection in the form of channeling or canalization can be found in sociology, biology, and psychology. In sociology, selection operates via social structures such as social class (Mayer & Carroll, 1987), race, gender, and ethnicity (Jenks, 1992), social mobility (Beau & Duncan, 1976), as well as via immutable variables such as sex (Mayer, Allmendinger, & Huinink, 1991) and age (Hagestadt, 1990). Dannefer (1987) has called this process *sociogenic differentiation*. The cumulative effect of selection on a structural level has been described by Merton (1968) as the Matthew effect, referring to the self-maintaining properties of particular social paths (see also Mayer, this volume; and for the realm of economics, Behrman, this volume).

In biology, *selection* is the term used to explain canalization and specialization during biological development (Waddington, 1975). Cotman (1985), for instance, argues that specialization on the cellular level involves the loss of alternate courses of cell differentiation. Ontogenetic selection based on the potentials of the genome is a well-known fact that pressures development in specific directions.

In psychology, there is evidence for selection from multiple sources. For Skinner (1966), for instance, selection played a prominent role in the process of shaping. In human development, maturation involves progressive specialization, which involves both gains and losses. Language provides a particularly elegant example of selection. The ability to learn language is far easier early in life than later, and the difficulty in second-language acquisition increases as a function of language development (Kellerman & Smith, 1986).

In personality psychology, findings stemming from self-efficacy theory (Bandura, 1977, 1982, 1991) suggest that agency beliefs guide the search, creation, and acceptance of goals, expectations, and environments. By monitoring competencies and demands via self-efficacy beliefs, a person selects which goals to set, what demands to cope with, when to expend effort, and when to compromise. People with strong self-efficacy beliefs perceive losses as challenge; those with weak ones perceive losses as threats (Bandura & Cervone, 1986; Bandura & Wood, 1989). The strength of self-efficacy beliefs determines which and how often anticipatory scenarios are constructed and imagined, which means of control are activated, and how quickly an activity or domain is abandoned or compromised (Bandura & Jourden, 1991). Self-efficacy may become increasingly important as people age. In a longitudinal study, Seeman, Unger, McAvay, and Mendes de Leon (1999) found that instrumental efficacy beliefs were negatively related to self-reported declines even though they were not related to actual functional ability. The authors argued that because people are more likely to continue to pursue activities that they believe they can do, high efficacy beliefs may help motivate people to maintain autonomy.

Markus and colleagues (Markus & Surf, 1987) have coined the term *multiple selves*, referring to "actual," "feared," and "hoped for" self-schemata that aid and guide the search for new goals. Similarly, the literature on personal control provides yet another body of evidence for selection. *Secondary control* (Heckhausen & Schulz, 1993, 1995; Rothbaum, Weisz, & Snyder, 1982) and *accommodative coping* (Brandtstädter & Renner, 1990) refer essentially to cognitive selection strategies in that they involve the reorganization of goal structures and goal hierarchies so that a fit between personal competence and environmental demands is achieved. Heckhausen (1997) recently reported that age was positively related to the increased use of compensatory secondary control and increased use of striving to avoid losses (see also Heckhausen, this volume). At the same time, age was negatively correlated with strivings for gains.

In social psychology, the social cognitive mechanism of social comparison, which serves to motivate or comfort depending on the reference point, also aids in selection. In the face of difficulties and irreversible losses, downward comparison allows people to adjust and maintain a positive evaluation of the self (Taylor, 1983; Wood, 1989).

The theory of socioemotional selectivity (Carstensen, 1993; Carstensen et al., 1999) considers selection adaptive in the social arena and specifies goal change as the precipitant to selection. The theory contends that emotional goals become increasingly salient with age and that people engage in active efforts to restructure their social worlds such that they maximize emotionally meaningful experiences. In contrast to the most popular traditional views of social aging, which suggest that maintaining earlier levels of social activity is necessary for happiness in old age (Osgoode, 1989), socioemotional selectivity theory proposes that older people prefer contact with emotionally meaningful social partners (Fung, Carstensen, & Lutz, 1999). Presumably, the judicious reduction of social contact in adulthood (and especially in old age) fosters enhanced emotional satisfaction and is, thus, adaptive. Findings reported by Lang and Carstensen (under review) show that adults who perceive their futures as limited and invest primarily in emotionally close social partners experience relatively more social satisfaction and relatively less strain than their counterparts who do not prioritize in this way. Analyses of longitudinal data show that emotional closeness with a select few is maintained or increased from young to middle adulthood even though social contact is reduced during the same time period (Carstensen, 1992). Even in very old age, a time when social networks are notably reduced, emotionally close relationships appear to be maintained while more peripheral social relationships are discarded (Lang & Carstensen, 1994; Lang, Staudinger, & Carstensen, 1998). In a study of old and very old adults followed over a four-year period, Lang (2000) found that close emotional relationships were more stable than peripheral social relationships. Moreover, most social relationships that had been discontinued were terminated largely for voluntary reasons, not because of illness or death. Lansford, Sherman, and Antonucci (1998) recently found that older people reported smaller social networks than younger people but that they also reported greater satisfaction with their networks.

The field of human factors is another research area demonstrating empirical evidence for selection. Studies of driving, for instance, show that the elderly driver is faced with an array of physical and environmental barriers (for a summary, see Committee for the Study on Improving Mobility and Safety for Older Persons, 1988; also Warnes, Rough, & Sixsmith, 1991). Conditions perceived as especially problematic were speed, traffic congestion, complex and confusing signs, unfamiliar streets, and freeway interchanges. Although almost all studies are about the sensorimotoric and cognitive deficiencies of the elderly aggravating driving behavior, there are a few examples for coping strategies. Selections made by elderly people accommodate these deficiencies and environmental barriers. They select to drive during the day (not at dusk, dawn, or night), make only short trips in familiar territory, avoid peak-period driving, reduce risk-taking and aggressive behavior, and drive more defensively.

Compensation

Compensation, the second component factor facilitating mastery of loss in reserves in old age, becomes operative when there are person- or environment-associated changes in means-ends resources—that is, when specific behavioral capacities or skills are lost or reduced below the level required for adequate functioning. Compensation can also become necessary as the result of selection. The organism might have to compensate in domains that are not selected for further enhancement and thus are given less attention and energy. One example is the delegation of certain responsibilities to another person. One also observes compensation in the form of extra attention allocated to important tasks, like walking and balance, even when added efforts detract from performance in another domain, such as memory (Li, Lindenberger, Freund, & Baltes, 2000).

Specifically, *compensation*, whether automatic or planned, refers to the use of alternate means to reach the same goal (to accomplish the same outcome in a specific domain)—that is, previous means-end strategies are reassessed. If a goal within a domain that includes a large number of activities and means is well elaborated, the person will not experience much trouble in counterbalancing or compensating for a specific behavioral deficiency. If the deficiency is large in scope or if the domains and goals are defined by one or very few activities, compensatory efforts will be more difficult. If, for instance, a master musician defines her expertise only as a soloist, it will be difficult for her to compensate for an incurring impairment, such as hearing loss or arthritis, that cuts short her career as a soloist. If, however, she defines her domain of expertise by a number of additional activities aside from playing as a soloist, she may compensate for the impairment by becoming a music teacher, a music critic, or a composer.

Compensation can involve existing behaviors or the acquisition of new skills or construction of new means not yet in ones repertoire. Compensation thus differs from selection in that the goal is maintained, but new means are enlisted to compensate for a behavioral deficiency to maintain or optimize prior functioning. The element of compensation involves aspects of both the mind and technology. Psychological compensatory efforts include, for example, the use of new mnemonic strategies or external memory aids when internal memory mechanics or strategies prove insufficient. The use of a hearing aid is an example of compensation by means of technology. The world of the handicapped is full of technical means that compensate for impairments and make a more or less independent and successful life possible. An avid reader of literature who becomes blind might learn Braille to continue reading or might divert to listening to books on tape. Not only technical means but human means are often needed to compensate. The assistance of a hand or arm when walking, a hired worker who cooks meals, or a companion who does writing may provide the compensatory means that enable elderly people to pursue their lives as fully as possible.

Empirical Evidence for Compensation

Compensation is a multifaceted term that has found its way into biology as well as psychology (Bäckman & Dixon, 1992). In both fields, compensation is possible because of neural or behavioral plasticity, which is available to the organism when equilibrium is disturbed (see also Singer, this volume). In biology, compensatory efforts follow brain injury and sensory handicaps. In the case of neural plasticity, compensatory efforts are seen as the source for recovery (Bach-y-Rita, 1990).

In the area of psychopathology, the vulnerability model of schizophrenia argues for self-healing attempts as compensatory efforts on the part of vulnerable persons to stabilize their psychic equilibrium. Boker et al. (1984) demonstrated that persons at high risk for schizophrenia show relatively more attempts than people who are at lower risk to compensate due to heightened vulnerability.

In cognitive psychology, the pragmatics of intelligence are considered to have compensatory power to alleviate deficits in the mechanics of intelligence (P. Baltes, 1991; Berg & Sternberg, 1985; Salthouse, 1984). In personality psychology, findings from self-efficacy theory suggest that by delegating control to others, proxy control serves a compensatory function (Bandura, 1982). In contrast to selection, proxy control allows the elderly person to maintain earlier goals through the assistance of others. Paradoxically, delegating control to others can be a powerful mechanism for optimizing domains that might otherwise decline. Baltes and her colleagues demonstrated, for example, that dependency can secure and optimize social contact (for reviews, see M. Baltes, 1995; M. Baltes & Wahl, 1991).

Socioemotional selectivity theory posits that social selection of long-term friends and loved ones (as opposed to acquaintances) helps to compensate for losses in areas such as sensory function or memory impairment (Carstensen, 1993). In the case of hearing loss, for example, a familiar social partner is more likely to speak clearly or speak into the good ear than someone unfamiliar with special losses. Gould, Trevithick, and Dixon (1991) showed positive effects of social collaboration in an oral recall task, clearly a process that benefits most from exchanges with familiar others.

Human factors research is replete with empirical findings suggesting compensation (for a summary, see Committee for the Study on Improving Mobility and Safety for Older Persons, 1988; also Warnes et al., 1991). Here too, driving behavior in the elderly may serve as an illustration. Elderly drivers compensate, for instance, for decreased reaction time by driving more slowly and by using interchanges with lights instead of stop signs only; they compensate for loss in peripheral vision by turning their head when changing lanes. Driving can be facilitated by improvements in transportation technology that would tailor more to the elderly driver, such as improvements in the readibility of signs, changes in traffic distribution, and improvements in certain vehicle design features—in short by compensatory means introduced by the environment and not by the elderly person.

In sum, whether the losses are sensory, cognitive, or interpersonal, compensation occurs when a certain behavior (or neural process) is evoked that narrows the gap between actual competence level and environmental demands.

Optimization

Optimization, the third component factor of SOC, refers to the enrichment and augmentation of reserves or resources and, thus, the enhancement of functioning and adaptive fitness in selected life domains. Optimization may occur in existing domains (such as generativity) or involve investment in new domains and goals consonant with developmental tasks of old age (such as acceptance of one's own mortality). How much selection and compensation must be invested to secure maintenance and stimulate optimization is an empirical question. Recent literature in gerontology suggests that many elderly people, in principle, have the necessary resources and reserves to optimize functions but face restrictive or overprotective environments that inhibit optimization (M. Baltes & Wahl, 1991). There is no doubt that the process of optimization will be contingent to a large extent on stimulating and enhancing environmental conditions. Thus, society plays a central role in providing environments that facilitate optimization. In fact, the success of relatively simple interventions (noted below) suggest that elderly adults often live in a world of underdemand rather than overdemand. Optimization is dependent on available possibilities and opportunities, unless older people actively and individually forge new terrain and frontiers (Rosenmayr 1983a, 1983b).

Empirical Evidence for Optimization

The psychological literature is replete with evidence for optimization processes. Improving performance in selected domains is of great interest in education, sport psychology, and cognitive expertise (see Ericsson, Krampe, & Tesch-Romer, 1993, for review). Within gerontology, there is empirical evidence that sensorimotor, cognitive, and psychosocial resources enable people to engage in processes associated with compensation and optimization and subsequently ensure high levels of everyday competence (M. Baltes & Lang, 1997; M. Baltes, Maas, Wilms, Borchelt, & Little, 1999; Lang, Rieckmann, & M. Baltes, 2000; Marsiske, Klumb, & M. Baltes, 1997). There is also ample evidence for optimization from intervention studies. This literature evinces plasticity and growth possibilities into very old age. When environmental conditions encourage practice, training, and exercise and when attention and motivation are stimulated, declines—long considered to be intractable—can be reversed and improved. This has been demonstrated clearly in the domains of cognition, social behavior, and biology. Freund and Baltes (1988) reported findings in which the use of SOC processes was related to indicators of successful aging.

A diverse array of intervention studies demonstrates that old people can profit from "optimizing" environments (see Stern & Carstensen, 2000). Physical exercise improves biological functioning such as pulmonary and cardiovascular functions (for a review, see Bortz 1989; Whitbourne 1985); cognitive intervention can increase memory performance (P. Baltes & Lindenberger, 1988; Lindenberger & P. Baltes, 1997) and can even help to ameliorate the impact of dementia on daily living (Wiedl, Schottke, & Gediga, 1987); behavioral interventions can reverse chronic dependent behaviors and increase autonomy (M. Baltes, 1995).

On a macro level, studies of control-enhancing interventions (Langer & Rodin, 1976; Rodin & Langer, 1977) have become classics. Despite criticisms concerning the underlying change agents, these studies have demonstrated substantial improvements in activity level, health, and life satisfaction following relatively minor institutional modifications. M. Baltes, Neumann, and Zank (1994) demonstrated an increase in independent behaviors (autonomy) of institutionalized elderly people following an intervention aimed at changing the institutional context from one that overprotects to one that enhances autonomy and independence. By implementing a training program for caregivers directed at creating greater sensitivity concerning the need for balance between dependency and autonomy (see also Parmelee & Lawton, 1990), caregivers of elderly adults relinquished their inadvertent tendency to foster dependency and shifted support toward reinforcing independent behavior. Results confirm the malleability of social environmental conditions responsible for dependency in elderly people.

In addition to micro- and macro-level intervention studies, indirect evidence for optimization in late life can be found in empirical tests of socioemotional selectivity theory. Not only are older couples happier than younger couples (which could be explained by selective attrition), but studies of emotion regulation in intimate relationships in old age suggest that, compared to middle-aged couples, older couples display more efforts to quell emotional conflict (express more affection to their partner while voicing concerns) (Carstensen, Gottman, & Levenson, 1995), report greater enjoyment from discussions about children, grandchildren, dreams, vacations, and doing things together, and report less conflict surrounding money, religion, recreation, and children (Levenson, Carstensen, & Gottman, 1993).

Summary and Conclusions

The aim of this chapter is to advocate a process-oriented approach to successful aging. We argue that the search for normative success outcomes in old age—whether longevity, ego integrity, or life satisfaction—will ultimately hold limited benefits due to the vast heterogeneity inherent in human aging. Theoretically derived ideals of what old age and old people should be like have been debated and challenged over the years. Multicriterial approaches have been offered, and yet the focal thrust of this work remains on measuring success or the lack thereof according to normative standards.

We feel that a process-oriented approach has three advantages. First, by accepting personal goals as success outcomes, whatever they may be, a process-oriented approach avoids the problem of imposing universal values and standards. It both acknowledges the heterogeneity of aging people and avoids the inevitable lack of precision inherent in applying global constructs across diverse groups of people.

Second, a process-oriented approach directs attention to the strategies that people use to master specific personal goals. This type of approach accentuates the functional properties of behaviors and strategies. Even behaviors that initially may appear maladaptive, such as limiting social contact, are revealed as adaptive once their function is examined. Consider also a request for assistance walking to the music room. When made by an individual whose primary goal is to continue playing the piano, such a request may be considered compensatory and adaptive. Yet if the individual's goal is to maintain muscular strength, the same behavioral profile may be viewed as maladaptive. In short, a process-oriented approach to the classification of goals and strategies rather than outcomes alone becomes the focus.

Third, the process-oriented approach we advocate considers the interplay of gains and losses inherent in old age. Rather than deny the inevitable losses that all old people experience in advanced age, the selective optimization with compensation model implies that old age holds the potential to be a time when the accumulated knowledge and expertise of a lifetime is invested in the realization of a distilled set of highly meaningful domains and goals. In this view, even losses may lead to gains in some highly valued areas of life.

Clearly, more research is needed before the merits of a process-oriented approach will be known. Findings from the Berlin Aging Study (P. Baltes & Mayer, 1999; P. Baltes & Smith, 1997), however, are highly encouraging. Evidence for the three processes are found, for instance, in the domain of everyday competence (M. Baltes & Horgas, 1997; P. Baltes et al., 1999; Marsiske, Lang, & Baltes, 1994) and in the area of self and personality (Staudinger, Freund, Linden, & Maas, 1999). Although there is ample evidence of each individual component process of the model, there has been virtually no research on the manner in which the components work together. Whether there is a hierarchy among the three component processes remains an empirical question. For example, it may be that compensation is always attempted first and that only when it fails do selections occur.

We suspect that all three components are activated more easily and readily when there is a rich array of resources available from which to draw. When resources become depleted, an increasingly fine-tuned and subtle interplay among the three components is necessary. The interplay between sensory functioning and everyday competence may be complex and indirect (Marsiske et al., 1997). We contend, however, that even very frail people can select, compensate, and optimize to maximize goal attainment. Given overwhelming evidence that increased loss is associated with aging, we also suspect that selection and compensation are necessary precursors to optimization. The time and energy invested in optimizing one domain, task, or goal will necessarily influence one's involvements in other domains. The longitudinal extension of the Berlin Aging Study promises some answers to these questions (P. Baltes & Mayer, 1999).

The model of selective optimization with compensation also suggests new approaches to research. Experimental manipulation of losses could be simulated to study whether, when, and how selective, compensatory, and optimizing processes are implemented and to provide precision and strength to predictions about the interplay among processes and goals across people. Li and colleagues, for example, manipulated task difficulty in a dual-task paradigm involving walking and memory. This line of research allows for specification of tradeoffs between the two tasks and further allows for assessment of attentional capacity involved in walking and balance (Li et al., 2000).

In conclusion, the model proposed in this chapter represents a qualitative departure from the traditional social science approach to successful aging, moving away from a focus on prescribed outcomes and ideal or statistical norms to an analysis in which the primary focus is on the processes people use to obtain desired goals. Skinner (1983), in an account of his own aging, gave eloquent advice on intellectual management to preserve and continue high productivity in light of failing reserves. It was clear from his writings that the intellectual domain was of high priority and that his life was designed around maximizing function in this selected domain as opposed to others. We argue that this type of selective optimization with compensation may be the most important tool for successful aging.

Acknowledgment

This chapter is an updated version of an article originally published in 1996 in *Aging and Society* (Cambridge University Press). It was written in 1995 when Margret M. Baltes was visiting Stanford University. Baltes died on January 28, 1999, so Laura L. Carstensen takes full responsibility for changes made from the original. The essential ideas remain the same and reflect the culmination of a lengthy collaboration from which Carstensen benefitted enormously. Many thanks to Quinn Kennedy for her review of the recent literature.

Note

1. *Statistical norm* means the level of performance—the level of goal attainment that is reached, on average, by a group of people. *Ideal norm* means the highest goal or possible level of achievement towards that goal, as defined by scientific theory, ideology, or social values. *Functional norm* means the level of achievement necessary for effective functioning in whatever domain.

References

Antonovsky, A. (1979). *Health, stress, and coping*. San Francisco: Jossey Bass.

Bach-y-Rita, P. (1990). Brain plasticity as a basis for recovery of function in humans. *Neuropsychologia, 28*, 547–554.

Backman, L., & Dixon, R. (1992). Psychological compensation: A theoretical framework. *Psychological Bulletin, 112*, 259–283.

Baltes, M. M. (1987). Erfolgreiches Altern als Ausdruck von Verhaltenskompetenz und Umweltqualität [Successful aging as a product of behavioral competence and environmental quality]. In C. Niemitz (Ed.), *Der Mensch im Zusammenspiel von Anlage und Umwelt* [Man as product of heredity and environment] (pp. 353–376). Frankfurt: Suhrkamp.

Baltes, M. M. (1995). Dependency in old age: Gains and losses. *Current Directions in Psychological Science, 4*, 14–19.

Baltes, M. M., & Carstensen, L. L. (1999). Social-psychological theories and their applications to aging: From individual to collective. In V. L. Bengtson & K. Warner Schaie (Eds.), *Handbook of theories of aging* (pp. 209–226). New York: Springer.

Baltes, M. M., & Carstensen, L. L. (1996). The process of successful ageing. *Ageing and Society, 16*, 1996, 397–422.

Baltes, M. M., & Horgas, A. (1997). Long-term care institutions and the maintenance of competence. In S. L. Willis, K. W. Schaie, & M. Hayward (Eds.), *Societal mechanisms for maintaining competence in old age*. New York: Springer.

Baltes, M. M., & Lang, F. R. (1997). Everyday functioning and successful aging: The impact of resources. *Psychology and Aging, 12*, 433–443.

Baltes, M. M., Lang, F. R., & Wilms, H.-U. (1998). [Selective Optimization with Compensation: Successful aging in everyday life.] Selektive Optimierung mit Kompensation: Erfolgreiches Altern in der Alltagsgestaltung. In A. Kruse (Ed.), [Psychosocial gerontology] *Psychosoziale Gerontologie*. Vol. 1, *Grundlagen. Jahrbuch der medizinischen Psychologie* (pp. 188–202). Göttingen: Hogrefe.

Baltes, M. M., Maas, I., Wilms, H., Borchelt, M., & Little, T. D. (1999). Everyday competence in old and very old age: Theoretical considerations and empirical findings. In P. B. Baltes & K. U. Mayer (Eds.), *The Berlin Aging Study: Aging from 70 to 100* (pp. 384–402). Cambridge: Cambridge University Press.

Baltes, M. M., Neumann, E.-M., & Zank, S. (1994). Maintenance and rehabilitation of independence in old age: An intervention program for staff. *Psychology and Aging, 9*, 179–188.

Baltes, M. M., & Reichert, M. (1992). Successful aging: The product of biological factors, environmental quality, and behavioral competence. In S. Ebrahim (Ed.), *Health care for older women* (pp. 236–256). Oxford: Oxford University Press.

Baltes, M. M., & Silverberg, S. B. (1994). The dynamics between dependency and autonomy across the life-span. In D. Featherman, R. Lerner, & M. Perlmutter (Eds.), *Life-span development and behavior* (pp. 41–90). Hillsdale, NJ: Lawrence Erlbaum.

Baltes, M. M., & Wahl, H.-W. (1991). The behavior system of dependency in the elderly: Interaction with the social environment. In M. Ory, R. P. Abeles, & P. D. Lipman (Eds.), *Aging, health and behavior* (pp. 83–106). Beverly Hills, CA: Sage.

Baltes, P. B. (1987). Theoretical propositions of life-span developmental psychology: On the dynamics between growth and decline. *Developmental Psychology, 23*, 611–626.

Baltes, P. B. (1991). The many faces of human aging: Toward a psychological culture of old age. *Psychological Medicine, 21*, 837–854.

Baltes, P. B., & Baltes, M. M. (1990). Psychological perspectives on successful aging: The model of selective optimization with compensation. In P. B. Baltes & M. M. Baltes (Eds.), *Successful aging: Perspectives from the behavioral sciences* (pp. 1–34). New York: Cambridge University Press.

Baltes, P. B., & Lindenberger, U. (1988). On the range of cognitive plasticity in old age as a function of experience: 15 years of intervention research. *Behavior Therapy, 19*, 283–300.

Baltes, P. B., & Mayer, K. U. (Eds.). (1999). *The Berlin Aging Study: Aging from 70 to 100*. Cambridge: Cambridge University Press.

Baltes, P. B., Reese, H. W., & Lipsitt, L. P. (1980). Life-span developmental psychology. *Annual Review of Psychology, 31*, 65–110.

Baltes, P. B., & Smith, J. (1997). A systemic-wholistic view of psychological functioning in very old age: Introduction to a collection of articles from the Berlin Aging Study. *Psychology and Aging, 12*, 395–409.

Baltes, P. B., Staudinger, U. M., & Lindenberger, U. (1999). Lifespan psychology: Theory and application to intellectual functioning. *Annual Review of Psychology, 50*, 471–507.

Bandura, A. (1977). Self-efficacy: Toward a unifying theory of behavioral change. *Psychological Review, 84*, 191–215.

Bandura, A. (1982). Self-efficacy mechanisms in human agency. *American Psychologist, 37*, 122–147.

Bandura, A. (1991). Self-regulation of motivation through anticipatory and self-reactive mechanisms. In R. A. Dienstbier (Ed.), *Nebraska symposium on motivation*, 1990 (pp. 69–164). Lincoln: University of Nebraska Press.

Bandura, A., & Cervone, D. (1986). Differential engagement of self-reactive influences in cognitive motivation. *Organizational Behavior and Human Decision Processes, 38*, 92–113.

Bandura, A., & Jourden, F. J. (1991). Self-regulatory mechanisms governing social comparison effects on complex decision making. *Journal of Personality and Social Psychology, 60*, 941–951.

Bandura, A., & Wood, R. (1989). Effect of perceived controllability and performance standards on self-regulation of complex decision making. *Journal of Personality and Social Psychology, 56*, 805–815.

Beau, P. M., & Duncan, O. D. (1976). *The American occupational structure*. New York: Wiley.

Bellah, R. N., Madison, R., & Sullivan, W. K. (Eds.). (1986). *Habits of the heart: Individualism and commitment in American life*. Berkeley: University of California Press.

Berg, C. A., & Sternberg, R. J. (1985). A triarchic theory of intellectual development during adulthood. *Developmental Review, 5*, 334–370.

Blazer, D. (1982). Social support and mortality in an elderly community population. *American Journal of Epidemiology, 115*, 684–694.

Boesch, E. (1954). Über die klinische Methode in der psychologischen Persönlichkeitsforschung. *Zeitschrift für diagnostische Psychologie, 2*, 275–292.

Boker, W., Brenner, H. D., Gerstner, G., Keller, F., Muller, J., & Spichtig, L. (1984). Self-healing strategies among schizophrenics: Attempts at compensation for basic disorders. *Acta Psychiatrica Scandinavia, 69*, 373–378.

Bortz, W. M. (1989). Redefining human aging. *Journal of the American Geriatrics Society, 37*, 1092–1096.

Bowling, A., & Browne, P. D. (1991). Social networks, health, and emotional well-being among the oldest old in London. *Journal of Gerontology, 46*, 20–32.

Brandtstädter, J., & Renner, G. (1990). Tenacious goal pursuit and flexible goal adjustment: Explication and age-related analysis of assimiliative and accommodative strategies of coping. *Psychology and Aging, 5*, 58–67.

Brim, O. G. (1988). Losing and winning: The nature of ambition in everyday life. *Psychology Today, 9*, 48–52.

Brim, O. G. (1992). *Ambition*. New York: Basic Books.

Brody, J. A., Brock, D. B., & Williams, T. F. (1987). Trends in the health of the elderly population. *Annual Review of Public Health, 8*, 211–234.

Bühler, C. (1933). *Der menschliche Lebenslauf als psychologisches Problem* [The human life course as psychological problem]. Leipzig: Hirzel.

Butler, R. N. (1974). Successful aging and the role of the life review. *Journal of the American Geriatrics Society, 22*, 529–535.

Carstensen, L. L. (1998). A life-span approach to social motivation. In S. Heckhausent & C. Dweek (Eds.). Motivation and self-regulation across the life-span (pp. 341–364). New York, Cambridge University Press.

Carstensen, L. L. (1991). Socioemotional selectivity theory: Social activity in life-span context. *Annual Review of Gerontology and Geriatrics, 195–217.*

Carstensen, L. L. (1992). Social and emotional patterns in adulthood: Support for socioemotional selectivity theory. *Psychology and Aging, 7,* 331–338.

Carstensen, L. L. (1993). Motivation for social contact across the life span. A theory of socioemotional selectivity. In J. Jacobs (Ed.), *Nebraska symposium on motivation: Developmental perspectives on motivation* (pp. 209–254). Lincoln: University of Nebraska Press.

Carstensen, L. L., Gottman, J. M., & Levenson, R. W. (1995). Emotional behavior in long-term marriage. *Psychology and Aging, 10,* 140–149.

Carstensen, L. L., Graff, J., & Lang, F. (2000). Psychology's contributions to gerontology. In J. E. Clair (Ed.), *The gerontological prism: Developing interdisciplinary bridges* (pp. 29–48). Amityville, NY: Baywood.

Carstensen, L. L., Isaacowitz, D. M., Charles, S. T. (1999). Taking time seriously: A theory of socioemotional selectivity. *American Psychologist, 54,* 165–181.

Carstensen, L. L., Pasupathi, M., Mayr, U., & Nesselroade, J. (2000). Emotional experience in everyday life across the adult life span. *Journal of Personality and Social Psychology, 79,* 644–655.

Cole, T. R. (1983). The "enlightened" view of aging: Victorian morality in a new key. *Hastings Center Report, 113,* 34–40.

Cole, T. R. (1984). Aging, meaning, and well-being: Musings of a cultural historian. *International Journal of Aging and Human Development, 19,* 329–336.

Cole, T. R., & Gadow, S. D. (Eds.). (1986). *What does it mean to grow old?* Durham, NC: Duke University Press.

Committee for the Study on Improving Mobility and Safety for Older Persons (Eds.). (1988). *Transportation in an aging society: Improving mobility and safety for older persons, Special Report 218.* Washington, DC: National Research Council.

Cotman, C. W. (Ed.). (1985). *Synaptic plasticity.* New York: Guilford.

Cumming, E., & Henry, W. E. (1961). *Growing old: The process of disengagement.* New York: Basic Books.

Dannefer, D. (1987). Aging as intracohort differentiation: Accentuation, the Matthew effect, and the life course. *Sociological Forum, 2,* 211–236.

Diener, E. (1984). Subjective well-being. *Psychological Bulletin, 95,* 542–575.

Diener, E., & Suh, E. M. (1998). Subjective well-being and age: An international analysis. *Annual Review of Gerontology and Geriatrics, 17,* 304–324.

Dittmann-Kohli, F. (1990). The construction of meaning in old age: Possibilities and constraints. *Aging and Society, 10,* 279–294.

Edwards, P. (1967). Life, meaning and value of. In P. Edwards (Ed.), *The encyclopedia of philosophy* (pp. 467–476). New York: MacMillan.

Ericsson, K. A., Krampe, R. T., & Tesch-Romer, C. (1993). The role of deliberate practice in the acquisition of expert performance. *Psychological Review, 100,* 363–406.

Erikson, E. H. (1959). The problem of ego identity. *Psychological Issues, 1,* 101–164.

Erikson, E. H. (1984). Reflection on the last stage—and the first. *Psychoanalytic Study of the Child, 39,* 155–165.

Erikson, E. H., Erikson, J., & Kivnick, H. (1986). *Vital involvement in old age.* New York: Norton.

Estes, C. L., & Binney, E. A. (1989). The biomedicalization of aging. *Gerontologist, 29,* 587–596.

Freund, A., & Baltes, P. B. (1998). Selection, optimization and compensation as strategies of life management: Correlations with subjective indicators of successful aging. *Psychology and Aging, 13,* 531–543.

Freund, A. M., Li, K., & Baltes, P. B. (1999). Successful development and aging: The role of selection, optimization, and compensation. In J. Brandtstädter & R. M. Lerner (Eds.), *Action and self-development: Theory and research through the life span* (pp. 401–434). Thousand Oaks, CA: Sage.

Fries, J. F. (1990). Medical perspectives upon successful aging. In P. B. Baltes & M. M. Baltes (Eds.), *Successful aging: Perspectives from the behavioral sciences* (pp. 35–49). New York: Cambridge University Press.

Fung, H., Carstensen, L. L., & Lutz, A. (1999). The influence of time on social preferences: Implications for life-span development. *Psychology and Aging, 14*, 595–604.

George, L. K. (1981). Subjective well-being: Conceptual and methodological issues. *Annual Review of Gerontology and Geriatrics, 2*, 345–382.

George, L. K. (1990). Social structure, social processes, and social-psychological states. In R. H. Bitstock & L. K. George (Eds.), *Handbook of aging and the social sciences* (pp. 186–204). New York: Academic Press.

Gould, O. N., Trevithick, L., & Dixon, R. A. (1991). Adult age differences in elaborations produced during prose recall. *Psychology and Aging, 6*, 93–99.

Guillemard, A. M. (1994). Europäische Perspektiven der Alternspolitik [European perspectives on aging policies]. In P. B. Baltes, J. Mittelstrass, & U. M. Staudinger (Eds.), [Old age and Aging: An interdisciplinary reader in gerontology] *Alter und Altern: Ein interdisziplinärer Studientext zur Gerontologie* (pp. 614–639). Berlin: De Gruyter.

Hagestad, G. O. (1990). Social perspectives on the life course. In R. Bitstock & L. George (Eds.), *Handbook of aging and the social sciences* (3rd ed., pp. 151–168). New York: Academic Press.

Havighurst, R. J., & Albrecht, R. (1953). *Older people.* New York: Longmans.

Heckhausen, J. (1997). Developmental regulation across adulthood: Primary and secondary control of age-related challenges. *Developmental Psychology, 33*, 176–187.

Heckhausen, J., & Schulz, R. (1993). Optimization by selection and compensation: Balancing primary and secondary control in life span development. *International Journal of Behavioral Development, 16*, 287–303.

Heckhausen, J., & Schulz, R. (1995). A life-span theory of control. *Psychological Review, 102*, 284–304.

Herzog, A. R., & Rodgers, W. L. (1981). Age and satisfaction: Data from several large surveys. *Research on Aging, 3*, 142–165.

House, J. S., Landis, K. R., & Umberson, D. (1988). Social relationships and health. *Science, 241*, 540–545.

Jencks, C. (1992). *Rethinking social policy: Race, poverty and the underclass.* Cambridge, MA: Harvard University Press.

Jung, C. G. (1931). Die Lebenswende [Life's turning point]. In C. G. Jung, *Seelenprobleme der Gegenwart* [Psychological problems of today] (pp. 248–274). Zurich: Rascher.

Kellerman, E., & Smith, M. S. (1986). *Cross-linguistic influence in second language acquisition.* Oxford: Pergamon Press.

Krause, N. F. (1990). Perceived health problems, formal/informal support, and life satisfaction among older adults. *Journal of Gerontology: Social Sciences, 45*, 193–205.

Lang, F. R. (2000). Endings and continuity of social relationships: Maximizing intrinsic benefits within personal networks when feeling near to death? *Journal of Social and Personal Relationships, 17*, 157–184.

Lang, F. R., & Carstensen, L. L. (2002). Time counts: Future time perspective, goals and social relationships. *Psychology and Aging, 17*, 125–139.

Lang, F. R., & Carstensen, L. L. (1994). Close emotional relationships in late life: Further support for proactive aging in the social domain. *Psychology and Aging, 9*, 315–324.

Lang, F. R., Rieckmann, N., & Baltes, M. M. (in press). Adapting to aging losses: Do resources facilitate strategies of selection, compensation, and optimization in everyday functioning? *Journal of Gerontology: Psychological Sciences.*

Lang, F., Staudinger, U., & Carstensen, L. L. (1998). Socioemotional selectivity in late life: How personality and social context do (and do not) make a difference. *Journal of Gerontology: Psychological Sciences, 53*, 21–30.

Langer, E. J., & Rodin, J. (1976). The effects of choice and enhanced personal responsibility for the aged: A field experiment in an institutional setting. *Journal of Personality and Social Psychology, 34*, 191–198.

Lansford, J. E., Sherman, A. M., & Antonucci, T. C. (1998). Satisfaction with social networks: An examination of socioemotional selectivity theory across cohorts. *Psychology and Aging, 13*, 544–552.

Larson, R. (1978). 30 years of research on the subjective well-being of older Americans. *Journal of Gerontology, 33*, 109–125.

Lawton, M. P. (1983). The varieties of well-being. *Experimental Aging Research, 9*, 65–72.

Lawton, M. P. (1984). The variables of well-being. In C. Z. Malatesta & C. E. Izard (Eds.), *Emotion in adult development* (pp. 67–84). Beverly Hills, CA: Sage.

Levenson, R. W., Carstensen, L. L., & Gottman, J. M. (1993). Long-term marriage: Age, gender, and satisfaction. *Psychology and Aging, 8*, 301–313.

Li, K. Z. H., Lindenberger, U., Freund, A., & Baltes, P. B. (2000). *Walking while memorizing: Age differences in external aid use and task priority as compensation during concurrent task performance.* Paper presented at the seventh Biennial Cognitive Aging Conference, Atlanta, GA.

Lindenberger, U., & Baltes, P. (1997). Intellectual functioning in old and very old age: Cross-sectional results from the Berlin Aging Study. *Psychological Aging, 12*, 410–432.

Lundin-Olsson, L., Nyberg, L., & Gustafson, Y. (1997). "Stops walking when talking" as a predictor of falls in elderly people. *Lancet, 349*, 617.

Maddox, G. L. (1965). Fact and artifact: Evidence bearing on disengagement theory from the Duke Geriatrics Project. *Human Development, 8*, 117–130.

Maddox, G. L. (1987). Aging differently. *Gerontologist, 27*, 557–564.

Manton, K. G., Corder, L. S., & Stallard, E. (1993). Estimates of change in chronic disability and institutional incidence and prevalence rates in the U.S. elderly population from the 1982, 1984, and 1989 National Long-Term Care Survey. *Journal of Gerontology: Social Sciences, 48*, 153–166.

Manton, K. G., & Soldo, B. J. (1985). Dynamics of health changes in the oldest-old: New perspectives and evidence. *Milbank Memorial Fund Quarterly, 63*, 206–285.

Markus, H., & Nurius, P. (1986). Possible selves. *American Psychologist, 41*, 954–969.

Markus, H., & Surf, E. (1987). The dynamic of self concept: A social psychological perspective. *Annual Review of Psychology, 38*, 299–337.

Marsiske, M. M., Klumb, P., & Baltes, M. M. (1997). Everyday activity patterns and sensory functioning in old age. *Psychology and Aging, 12*, 444–457.

Marsiske, M. M., Lang, F. R., & Baltes, M. M. (1994). *Beyond routine: Competence and social support in the daily lives of older adults.* Paper presented at the thirteenth Biennial Meeting of the International Society for the Study of Behavioral Development, Amsterdam, Netherlands, June–July 1994.

Marsiske, M. M., Lang, F. R., Baltes, P. B., & Baltes, M. M. (1995). Selective optimization with compensation: Life-span perspectives on successful development. In R. A. Dixon & L. Backman (Eds.), *Compensation for psychological defects and declines: Managing losses and promoting gains* (pp. 35–79). Hillsdale, NJ: Erlbaum.

Mayer, K. U., Allmendinger, J., & Huinink, J. (1991). *Vom Regen in die Traufe: Frauen zwischen Beruf uns Familie* [Out of the frying-pan into the fire: Women between job and family]. Frankfurt: Campus.

Mayer, K. U., & Carroll, G. R. (1987). Jobs and classes: Structural constraints on career mobility. *European Sociological Review, 3*, 14–38.

Merton, R. K. (1968). The Matthew effect in science: The reward and communication system of science. *Science, 199*, 55–63.

Mosher-Ashley, P. M. (1986–1987). Procedural and methodological parameters in behavioral-gerontological research: A review. *International Journal of Aging and Human Development, 24*, 189–229.

Osgood, N. J. (1989). Theory and research in social gerontology. In N. J. Osgood & H. A. Sontz (Eds.), *The science and practice of gerontology* (pp. 55–87). New York: Greenwood Press.

Parmelee, P. A., & Lawton, M. P. (1990). The design of special environments for the aged. In J. E. Birren & K. W. Schaie (Eds.), *Handbook of the psychology of aging* (pp. 464–488). New York: Academic Press.

Parnes, H. (Ed). (1981). *Work and retirement: A Longitudinal study of men.* Cambridge, MA: MIT Press.

Reker, G. T., Peacock, E. J., & Wong, P. T. P. (1987). Meaning and purpose in life and well-being: A life-span perspective. *Journal of Gerontology, 42,* 44–49.

Rentsch, T. (1994). Philosophische Anthropologie und Ethik der späten Lebenszeit [Philosophical anthropology and ethics of late life]. In P. B. Baltes, J. Mittelstrass, & U. M. Staudinger (Eds.), *Alter und Altern: Ein interdisziplinärer Studientext zur Gerontologie.* [Old age and aging: An interdisciplinary Rader in gerontology] Berlin: de Gruyter.

Riley, M W., Kahn, R. L., & Foner, A. (Eds.). (1994). *Age and structural lag.* New York: Wiley.

Rodin, J. (1986). Health, control, and aging. In M. M. Baltes & P. B. Baltes (Eds.), *The psychology of control and aging* (pp. 139–165). Hillsdale, NJ: Erlbaum.

Rodin, J., & Langer, E. (1977). Long-term effects of a control-relevant intervention with the institutionalized aged. *Journal of Personality and Social Psychology, 35,* 897–902.

Rosenmayr, L. (1983a). *Das Alter—ein Stück bewusst gelebten Lebens* [Old age: A time of conscious living]. Berlin: Severin & Siedler.

Rosenmayr, L. (1983b). *Die späte Freiheit* [The late freedom]. Berlin: Severin & Siedler.

Rosenmayr, L. (1985). Changing values and positions of aging in Western culture. In J. E. Birren & K. W. Schaie (Eds.), *Handbook of the psychology of aging* (pp. 190–215). New York: Van Nostrand Reinhold.

Rosenmayr, L. (1989). Wandlungen der gesellschaftlichen Sicht und Bewertung des Alters [Changes in society's perspective toward and evaluation of aging]. In M. M. Baltes, M. Kohli, & K. Sames (Eds.), *Erfolgreiches Altern: Bedingungen und Variationen* [Successful aging: Conditions and variations] (pp. 96–101). Bern: Huber.

Rothbaum, F., Weisz, J. R., & Snyder, S. S. (1982). Changing the world and changing the self: A two-process model of perceived control. *Journal of Personality and Social Psychology, 42,* 5–37.

Rowe, J. W., & Kahn, R. L. (1987). Human aging: Usual and successful. *Science, 237,* 143–149.

Ryff, C. D. (1982). Successful aging: A developmental approach. *Gerontologist, 22,* 209–214.

Ryff, C. D. (1989a). Beyond Ponce de Leon and life satisfaction: New directions in quest of successful aging. *International Journal of Behavioral Development, 12,* 35–55.

Ryff, C. D. (1989b). In the eye of the beholder: Views of psychological well-being among middle-aged and older adults. *Psychology and Aging, 4,* 195–210.

Ryff, C. D. (1991). Possible selves in adulthood and old age: A tale of shifting horizons. *Psychology and Aging, 6,* 286–295.

Salthouse, T. A. (1984). Effects of age and skill in typing. *Journal of Experimental Psychology: General, 113,* 345–371.

Schaie, K. W. (Ed.). (1983). *Longitudinal studies of adult psychological development.* New York: Guilford Press.

Schaie, K. W. (1990). The optimization of cognitive functioning in old age: Predictions based on cohort-sequential and longitudinal data. In P. B. Baltes & M. M. Baltes (Eds.), *Successful aging: Perspectives from the behavioral sciences* (pp. 94–117). New York: Cambridge University Press.

Schonfield, D. (1973). Future commitments and successful aging. I: The random sample. *Journal of Gerontology, 28,* 189–196.

Schwarz, N., & Strack, F. (1989). Evaluating one's life: A judgment model of subjective well-being. In K. Strack, M. Argyle, & N. Schwarz (Eds.), *The social psychology of well-being.* London: Pergamon.

Seeman, T. E., Unger, J. B., McAvay, G., & Mendes de Leon, C. F. (1999). Self-efficacy beliefs and perceived declines in functional ability: MacArthur studies of successful aging. *Journal of Gerontology: Psychological Sciences and Social Sciences, 54,* 214–222.

Simpson, J., & Weiner, E. (Eds.). (1989). *The Oxford English Dictionary* (2nd ed. Vol. 17, pp. 92–93). Oxford: Clarendon.

Skinner, B. F. (1983). Intellectual self-management in old age. *American Psychologist, 38,* 239–244.

Skinner, B. F. (1966). The phylogeny and ontogeny of behavior. *Science, 153,* 1205–1213.

Staudinger, U., Freund, A., Linden, A., & Maas, I. (1999). Self, personality and life regulation: Facets of psychological resilience in old age. In K. U. Mayer & P. B. Baltes (Eds.), *The Berlin Aging Study* (pp. 302–328). Cambridge: Cambridge University Press.

Stones, M. J., & Kozma, A. (1985). Physical performance. In N. Charness (Ed.), *Aging and human performance* (pp. 261–291). New York: Wiley.

Stern, P., & Carstensen, L. L. (Eds.). (2000). *The aging mind: Opportunities in cognitive aging.* Washington, DC: National Academies Press.

Taylor, S. E. (1983). Adjustment to threatening events: A theory of cognitive adaptation. *American Psychologist, 38,* 1161–1173.

Thomae, H. (1981). The Bonn Longitudinal Study of Aging (BOLSA): An approach to differential gerontology. In A. E. Baert (Eds.), *Prospective longitudinal research* (pp. 165–197). Oxford: University Press.

Tournier, P. (1972). *Learning to grow old.* London: SCM Press.

Vaillant, G. E. (1990). Avoiding negative life outcomes: Evidence from a forty-five year study. In P. B. Baltes & M. M. Baltes (Eds.), *Successful aging: Perspectives from the behavioral sciences* (pp. 332–358). New York: Cambridge University Press.

Vaillant, G. E., Meyer, S. E., Mukamal, K., & Soldz, S. (1998). Are social supports in late midlife a cause or a result of successful physical aging? *Psychological Medicine, 28,* 1159–1168.

Waddington, C. H. (1975). *The evolution of an evolutionist.* Edinburgh: Edinburgh University Press.

Warnes, A., Rough, B., & Sixsmith, J. (1991). *Elderly drivers and new technology.* Project Report 6, Commission of the European Communities.

Weiland, S. (1989). Aging according to biography. *Gerontologist, 29,* 191–194.

Whitbourne, S. K. (1985). *The aging body.* New York: Springer.

Wiedl, K., Schottke, H., & Gediga, G. (1987). Reserven geistiger Leistungsfähigkeit bei geriatrischen Psychiatriepatienten und altenheimbewohnern [Reserves of mental functioning in old psychiatric patients and nursing home residents]. *Zeitschrift für klinische Psychologie, 16,* 29–42.

Wills, T. A. (1991). Similarity and self-esteem in downward comparison. In J. Suls & T. A. Wills (Eds.), *Social comparison: Contemporary theory and research.* Hillsdale, NJ: Erlbaum.

Wong, P. T. P. (1989). Personal meaning and successful aging. *Canadian Psychology, 30,* 516–525.

Wong, P. T. P. (1991). Existential versus causal attributions: The social perceiver as philosopher. In S. Zelen (Ed.), *Extensions of attribution theory.* New York: Springer.

Wong, T. P., & Watt, L. M. (1991). What types of reminiscence are associated with successful aging? *Psychology and Aging, 6,* 272–279.

Wood, J. V. (1989). Theory and research concerning social comparisons of personal attributes. *Psychological Bulletin, 106,* 231–248.

Woodward, K., & Schwartz, M. M. (Eds.), (1986). *Memory and desire: Aging, Literature, Psychoanalysis.* Bloomington: Indiana University Press.

Wortman, C., & Silver, C. R. (1990). Successful mastery of bereavement and widowhood: A life-course perspective. In P. B. Baltes & M. M. Baltes (Eds.), *Successful aging: Perspectives from the behavioral sciences* (pp. 225–264). New York: Cambridge University Press.

Yoon, G. (1996). Psychosocial factors for successful aging. *Australian Journal of Aging, 15,* 69–72.

6 Intentionality and Time in Human Development and Aging: Compensation and Goal Adjustment in Changing Developmental Contexts

Jochen Brandtstädter and Klaus Rothermund

University of Trier, Trier, Germany

Abstract

Time is both an action resource and a source of meaning in human development over the life span. The fading of residual life time in old age thus poses particular adaptive challenges that call for selective, compensatory, and optimizing activities. Such activities depend not only on the causal implications of aging, but likewise on the practical conclusions that people draw from having a given age and a given position in the life cycle. The present chapter addresses the different ways in which time, as perceived or personalized time, affects the negotiation of gains and losses as well as the construal of meaning in later life. The main theoretical focus is on the adaptive interplay between between self-regulatory and compensatory activities and mechanisms through which personal goals are adjusted to changes in action resources that are linked to both ontogenetic and historical dimensions of time.

Developmental processes begin, unfold, and end in time. In developmental research, the time axis traditionally serves as an ordering device. Age-graded ontogenetic changes as well as age-linked developmental tasks are ordered along a biographical time dimension, whereas cultural changes, which affect members of different age cohorts at different points of their lifecycle, are charted on a historical time dimension. It is commonly assumed that age and time have no intrinsic explanatory power; when moving from description toward explanation, researchers try to identify causal factors that, on biographical and historical dimensions, are linked to the flow of time (such as age-graded changes in bodily maturation or socialization or history-graded changes in political or economic conditions of society).

Human development, however, is linked to time not only by a causal-physical nexus; it is the joint product of causality *and* intentionality. Intentionality, as it is expressed in life planning and the pursuit of goals over the life course, is intrinsically related to phenomenological, personalized time. In retrospect, personalized time is filled with changes and events that are more or less consistent with the person's current preferences; in prospect, it constitutes an action space filled with risks, potentialities, and more or less attractive possible selves (Brandtstädter, 2001; Heckhausen, this volume; Roberts & Caspi, this volume).

The importance of time perspectives in action, motivation, and life planning has been recognized for a long time (e.g., Lewin, 1953; Nuttin, 1964). Time, and the coordination of physical and perceived time, is needed not only to pursue goals but also to orchestrate and harmonize our strivings: goals that are logically or practically incompatible when simultaneously pursued may become feasible when arranged in a temporal sequence. Gains and losses emerge in time, and their weight in personal planning and decision making underlies a temporal discounting. Furthermore, time is a compensatory resource: we need time to cope with loss, and even slow runners (or learners) may reach the goal when they are granted enough time. Our projects and life activities gain meaningful valence from intended future goals, and they may lose sense and meaning when these intentional links are disrupted (e.g., Klinger, 1977).

Time is thus both an *action resource* and a *source of meaning*. Temporal resources, however, are limited. Most important, our lifetime itself is limited; some of our goals and projects become unfeasible as we move through historical and ontogenetic time. In preventive and compensatory efforts, we invest time to expand our temporal resources or make more efficient use of them (M. Baltes & Carstensen, this volume; Baltes & Baltes, 1990). Social representations of "optimal development" or "successful aging," ethical and religious systems, as well as philosophical teachings of wisdom often advance rules and recommendations as to how and for which purposes scarce lifetime resources should be used. Seneca's treatise, *On the Shortness of Life* (*De brevitate vitae*) is a classical example. The fading of life time affects the construction of meaning; evaluating actions in terms of future personal consequences becomes questionable when no personal future remains. An individual's life, as a singular, temporally closed biographical gestalt, can apparently be evaluated only with reference to values and meanings that transcend the limited horizon of one's personal biography.

Centering on the notion of time, these introductory arguments indicate how causal and intentional aspects are intertwined in development and aging. The causal dynamics of development unfold in physical time; perceived temporal resources structure the ways that developing subjects shape and plan their personal development and aging within the constraints of causal contingencies. Development creates and shapes intentionality and intentional strivings, and developing intentionality in turn shapes the course of personal development: in that particular sense, human ontogeny is a self-referential process (Brandtstädter, 1998; Brandtstädter & Lerner, 1999).

These arguments also apply to the process of aging in its physical, social, and psychological aspects. Our behavior and development—as well as the selective, compensatory, and optimizing activities through which we try to adjust our behavior and development to normative projections (Baltes, 1997; Baltes & Baltes, 1990)—is shaped not only by the causal implications of having a particular age and a particular biographical history but also by the *practical conclusions* that we draw from having a given age, a given position in the life cycle, and particular physical and temporal resources. The processes of aging destroy action resources through time-contingent causal processes (such as functional losses due to changes in the processing speed and reliability of the neural network, in endocrine regulations, in functional reserves); death as a biological phenomenon occurs where these changes exceed critical margins. The adaptive challenges of age and aging, however, essentially arise from projecting these changes into temporally structured intentional spheres and relating them to strivings and desired developmental outcomes. When we ask, for example, why (or why not) some people become depressed in later life, we have to consider these projections and links.

In the following, we present theoretical arguments and research findings that bear on these issues. The theoretical approach that has guided our research focuses on the interplay of two processes—first, on intentional activities through which people shape their development in accordance with their goals and maintain desired self-attributes and, second, on mechanisms that coadjust personal goals and self-definitions to a changing field of resources and constraints (see also Brandtstädter & Greve, 1994; Brandtstädter, Wentura, & Rothermund, 1999).

Coadjusting Personal Goals and Resources Across the Life Span: The Dual-Process Model

Action regulation in nonstationary and partially opaque environments has to reconcile two opposed adaptive tasks—the task of maintaining goals in the face of difficulties and distractions and the task of adjusting one's goals, and a chosen course of action, to irreversible constraints and losses. This *continuity-flexibility dilemma* (see also Bak & Brandtstädter, 1998) also emerges in the sphere of life planning and intentional self-development. Throughout life, we try to achieve self-projects to maintain desired standards of life and functioning and preserve personal continuity, but at the same time we have to adjust goals, plans, and self-definitions to events and changes that occur in historical as well as ontogenetic-biographical time. The dilemmatic tension between these two adaptive tasks reaches its highest levels when the pursuit of goals or maintenance of desired states is rendered impossible by severe resource limitations.

As intimated above, the self-system handles the recurring dilemma between maintaining continuity and adjusting to change through the interplay of two basic types of processes—first, through intentional activities by which the actual state and course of development is brought into congruence with personal goals and self-projections and, second, by mechanisms that adjust goals and self-projects to given circumstances. We denote these two modes as *assimilative* and *accommodative*, respectively (Brandtstädter & Renner, 1990; Brandtstädter & Rothermund, 2002b). Both types of adaptive processes reduce discrepancies between actual and intended self-states, but they achieve this aim in opposite ways.

Assimilative and accommodative processes, as defined above, are antagonistically related; people will not disengage from goals and downgrade ambitions as long as their resources seem sufficient to attain them (for goals of high centrality and importance, even low action-outcome expectancies may suffice to stay in the assimilative mode). Nonetheless, the two modes complement each other in various ways. First, losses and critical life transitions such as chronic illness, bereavement, or unemployment usually form a compound of problems and adaptive tasks that to different degrees may call for assimilative persistence and accommodative flexibility. Second, disengagement from particular goals may be functional to maintain or successfully achieve others; this is particularly true under scarce resources (see also M. Baltes & Carstensen, this volume; Baltes, this volume). Furthermore, flexibility at the level of instrumental goals often serves to maintain other goals. Finally, accommodative processes do not terminate assimilative activities altogether; rather, they redefine reference standards for assimilative efforts and channel available resources to feasible goals, thus overriding a tendency to persevere in, and ruminate about, barren projects that can become maladaptive when individuals are confronted with irreversible losses and constraints (Rothermund & Brandtstädter, 1997a).

In the dual-process model, these basic theoretical assumptions have been elaborated with respect to differential conditions, underlying general mechanisms or microprocesses, and developmental implications (Brandtstädter & Greve, 1994; Brandtstädter & Rothermund, 2002b; Brandtstädter et al., 1999):

• *Differential conditions.* Factors such as perceived control, efficacy, self-complexity, and substitutability of goals differentially enhance or inhibit a tendency of adhering to or disengaging from barren goals and attachments. These factors vary across situations and persons. Together with contextual resources, they constitute a changing field of forces in which assimilative and accommodative processes are negotiated. On the dispositional level, there are stable individual differences in the tendency to use assimilative or accommodative modes of coping. These differences express themselves in characteristic styles and patterns of coping that may be differently suited for different types of critical events (Rothermund, Dillmann, & Brandtstädter, 1994). In empirical applications, dispositional differences in assimilative persistence and accommodative flexibility have been assessed by two scales: Tenacious Goal Pursuit (TGP) and Flexible Goal Adjustment (FGA) (Brandtstädter & Renner, 1990). These scales do not form a single, bipolar dimension but represent orthogonal facets of coping competence that are both positively related to indicators of optimism, satisfaction, and well-being (with FGA, however, usually showing slightly higher relationships to the latter domain) (see also Becker, 1995). As an interesting aside, findings from twin studies indicate that dispositional differences in FGA and TGP have a substantial heritability (Geppert, 1997).

- *Underlying mechanisms and microprocesses.*   Assimilative and accommodative modes engage particular cognitive sets and tendencies. In the assimilative mode, the cognitive system is tuned toward the successful implementation of goals; attention is focalized on the goal, and task-unrelated, distractive stimuli are warded off. This "implementative mind set" (Gollwitzer, 1990; see also Kuhl, 1987) involves an increased availability of cognitions that enhance goal pursuit and maintain an intended course of action against obstacles, which may even involve particular types of biases, such as overpredicting one's control over the goal (Taylor & Gollwitzer, 1995) or overestimating the duration of positive or negative emotions after success and failure, respectively ("durability bias") (Gilbert, Pinel, Wilson, Blumberg, & Wheatley, 1998). As the system shifts toward the accommodative mode, this cognitive set is inhibited and inverted; the field of attention opens again; and responsiveness to information that has been warded off in the assimilative phase increases. Information processing shifts toward a defocused, divergent mode, which also involves an increased availability of content that reduces the attractiveness of the blocked goal in relation to the given situation. The system now becomes susceptible and even biased toward cognitions that mitigate the aversive emotional states that result from the blocking of goals or developmental paths (for experimental evidence, see, e.g., Brandtstädter & Rothermund, 2002a; Rothermund, 1998; Wentura, 1995). As indicated above, the shift from an assimilative to an accommodative cognitive set may be differentially enhanced or impeded by differential and situational factors such as control beliefs, dispositional differences in coping style, or self-complexity.
- *Developmental implications.*   The processes of assimilation and accommodation, as defined above, are basic to intentional self-development across the whole life span (cf. Brandtstädter, 1998); they constitute mechanisms through which self-systems express, perpetuate, and maintain themselves in action and development and within changing contextual conditions. Thus, these processes are not limited to any particular phase of development. The intentional focus of assimilative activities, however, may change over the life span. With advancing age, the focus gradually shifts from an emphasis on growth and expansion of resources toward an emphasis on maintenance and prevention of loss (cf. Baltes, this volume; Ogilvie & Rose, 1995). Empirical applications of the model have largely focused on later life; due to the particular adaptive challenges already mentioned, the transition to old age constitutes a paradigm domain. The results of this research indicate that adaptive resilience, well-being, and efficacy in later life basically hinge on the interplay between assimilative and accommodative processes; consistent with theoretical expectations, our findings point to the particular importance of accommodative flexibility for coping with irreversible loss (e.g., Brandtstädter, Rothermund, & Schmitz, 1997).

In the following, we discuss some selected observations that bear more specifically on issues of time, time resources, and adaptive resiliency, as they were raised in the introductory section. These observations come from an ongoing research project that investigates sources and mechanisms of adaptive resilience in later life (ARS project).[1] The project combines cross-sectional and longitudinal assessments on a sample of 896 participants in the initial age range of 54 to 78 years; the longitudinal assessments span an eight-year-interval (1991 to 1999).

Drawing on data from the ARS panel, the following analyses address (1) the shift from compensatory to accommodative modes in approaching resource limits, (2) time discounting effects in the construal of gains and losses, (3) changes in temporal and meaning perspectives in later life, and (4) possible limitations of adaptive resources in the terminal phases of life. The concluding section reflects on tensions between the decreasing of time in old age and the acceleration of life in developmental settings of modernity.

Negotiating Loss and Gain: From Compensation to Accommodation

From a personal point of view, developmental change involves gains and losses; central to an action perspective of development is the assumption that people continually try to optimize this balance. In later life, the balance of gains and loss tends to tip to the negative, and the question of how scarce resources can be maintained and optimally used becomes a focal concern. The SOC model advanced by P. Baltes and M. Baltes (1990) (see also M. Baltes & Carstensen, this volume; P. Baltes, this volume; Lerner, Dowling, & Roth, this volume) centers on these selective and compensatory processes; the dual-process model shares this focus but puts particular emphasis on the role that the adjustment of goals and ambitions plays in maintaining a positive view of self and personal development.

Developmental changes take on positive or negative valence only when related to systems of values and personal goals; the emotional impact of gains and losses primarily depends on whether the individual expects to be able to maintain his or her prior goals and standards. When goals drift outside the individual's span of control due to, for example, increasing task complexity or the fading of temporal or physical resources, the dual-process model predicts a typical sequence of regulations that ranges from reactant increases of effort over compensatory activities to accommodative readjustments of preferences.

From this theoretical perspective, the activation of compensatory intentions marks a late phase of assimilation where the individual still adheres to the goal; as far as accommodative tendencies already appear, they remain largely restricted to instrumental aspects. Although compensatory activities may aim at a more efficient use of resources, compensation itself uses resources and involves costs. Such costs may already occur on symbolic levels: the use of compensatory devices often functions as an attributive marker that in social contexts symbolizes loss and infirmity. This may partly explain, for instance, why many elderly people are reluctant to use prothetic devices such as hearing aids and canes (e.g., Rothermund & Brandtstädter, 1997b). Although assimilative and compensatory efforts aim at maintaining efficiency (or at least an appearance of efficiency), they often require—somewhat ironically—an accommodation of, or disengagement from, self-definitions of youthful efficiency.

Compensatory efforts are subject to a principle of diminishing returns; when they approach resource limits, cost-benefit ratios become increasingly unfavorable (e.g., Brandtstädter & Wentura, 1995). Age-related decreases in athletic performance exemplify the dilemma (e.g., Ericsson, 1990): to counteract loss, the athlete has to intensify his or her training effort, so that less and less time may eventually remain for other worthwhile pursuits. With the fading of time reserves, opportunity costs of compensation are potentiated by two factors. As discussed above, an increasing amount of time and effort is needed to maintain desired performance levels; in addition, a given span of time also tends to become more valuable since it constitutes an increasingly larger portion of residual life time. Furthermore, it may not be rational to invest increasing compensatory effort to raise one's efficiency for reaching future goals if the remaining time span during which one could benefit from these efforts becomes smaller and smaller (see also Behrman, this volume). It is, of course, true that compensatory activities, particularly when related to health and fitness goals, often aim at extending one's life span, so that temporal investments are traded for increases in residual life time. However, the scope of such compensatory efforts seems to be limited, too. Although average life expectancy has dramatically increased in recent history, mortality statistics indicate that it asymptotically approaches a maximum at about 85 years (Fries, 1990; see also Maier & Vaupel, this volume; Kirkwood, this volume). Insofar as death and dying are negatively valued and count as losses, these limiting phenomena of life also point to "limits in efficiency of culture" (Baltes, 1997, p. 369).

According to received theoretical views, a situation where losses cannot be prevented or goals no longer be achieved should be conducive to alienation and depression. The dual-process model goes beyond these views in assuming that the loss of control over personally valued goals sets into operation accommodative processes that deconstrue the incentive value of barren goals and open the field of attention for alternative options (for experimental evidence, see also Brandtstädter & Rothermund, 2002a; Rothermund, 1998; Wentura, 1995).

According to this theoretical perspective, assimilative and compensatory efforts should be most strongly expressed when losses become clearly perceptible but still appear amenable to corrective intervention. This suggests that compensatory efforts in many domains may show a curvilinear, inverted *u*-shape relation to the age variable. Furthermore, the decrease in assimilative and compensatory efforts should be accompanied by an increase in accommodative tendencies.

Cross-sectional and longitudinal findings from the ARS panel study conform with this expected pattern (Brandtstädter & Rothermund, 2002a). Compensatory activities were assessed in the ARS panel with respect to four different domains of functioning—physical fitness, bodily appearance, memory and mental efficiency, and everyday competence. Measures were taken on two occasions (1995, 1999), yielding a longitudinal interval of four years. In cross-sectional comparisons, the predicted

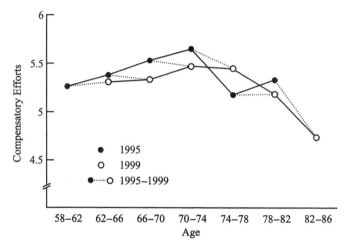

Figure 6.1   Compensatory Efforts and Age (sequential data, ARS project).

inverted *u*-shape relation of compensatory activities emerges for both waves. In the longitudinal picture, four-year longitudinal changes are negatively related to chronological age; longitudinal decreases in compensatory effects are most clear-cut in the oldest cohort. Figure 6.1 illustrates the findings (ratings of compensatory effort were aggregated across functional domains).

Supplementary analyses lend further theoretical substance to these findings. As argued above, compensatory efforts should cease when perceived costs of compensation exceed expected benefits. In line with this argument, moderator analyses reveal that in the younger cohorts, longitudinal increases in compensatory effort are negatively related to developmental losses in the functional domains considered, whereas an inverse relationship obtains for the oldest cohorts. According to our theoretical argument, accommodation of ambitions should dampen the negative emotional impact of perceived functional loss: In line with this argument, the degree to which perceived losses in the considered domains affected satisfaction with actual performance levels was moderated by the participants' motivation to maintain previous levels of performance and to keep up with younger people (see also Brandtstädter & Rothermund, 2002a). Furthermore, maintenance motivation in a given functional domain was found to depend on perceived control within that domain; this contingency was most strongly expressed among participants scoring high in accommodative flexibility as measured by the FGA scale.

Time Discounting and the Construction of Gain and Loss

Decisions in contexts of action and life planning depend on outcome expectancies and on the value of expected outcomes. Time plays a crucial role in this tradeoff: as a rule, the weight of expected outcomes inversely depends on their time delay. These time-discounting effects may of course vary intra- and interindividually; for example, individuals differ in their capacity and readiness to reflect on the future or to create a vivid image of expected outcomes (e.g., Prelec & Loewenstein, 1997).

In social expectations as well as in self-reports, aging is usually associated with an increasingly unfavorable balance of desirable and undesirable changes (e.g., Heckhausen, Dixon, & Baltes, 1989). Notions of time discounting raise the question of how the tradeoff of gains and losses is affected by the subject's construal of time and in particular by the perceived amount of remaining life time. Two different lines of argument may be considered here.

On the one hand, it can be argued that low residual life expectancy should dampen the emotional impact of events because they would affect a shorter time span. This argument receives some support from scattered findings indicating a reduced amplitude of positive or negative emotions in later life (see Turk-Charles & Carstensen, 1999, for a critical review). A similar rationale might account for an increased readiness for altruistic sacrifices that is observed among elderly people. From a philosophical point of view, Nozick (1989) sees old age as the appropriate time to accept risky tradeoffs— even vital risks, perhaps—for altruistic, ego-transcending purposes. In a similar vein, Marquard (1999) has argued that with advancing age, seeking risky challenges may actually involve less risks since in case of failure, "an increasingly smaller amount of personal future would be ruined" (p. 49, our translation). This type of argument seems to provide a partial explanation for the resilience of older people in the face of loss and adversity that has been noted by researchers in the field of aging (see, e.g., Staudinger, Marsiske, & Baltes, 1995).

On the other side, time is needed to cope with negative events or to mitigate their consequences through increased compensatory effort. Although the time span that would be affected by a loss is shorter in later life, it constitutes a larger portion of the time yet to be lived. Whereas the younger person has temporal scope for hope and compensation, a loss may ruin the rest of life for the old person because stories tend to be judged by their final outcome (see also Kahneman, Fredrickson, Schreiber, & Redelmeier, 1993).

Considering the impact of losses and negative events in later life, these two lines of argument lead to opposed predictions. The former argument suggests that chronological age should have a palliative, buffering effect (Hypothesis I), whereas the latter argument would imply an aggravating, counterpalliative effect (Hypothesis II).

We have tested these hypotheses with data from the ARS panel mentioned earlier (Rothermund & Brandtstädter, 1998). As indicators of developmental loss, distances from personal goals as well as changes in perceived goal distance were assessed over a longitudinal interval of four years. Distance ratings were aggregated across a list of 23 goals.[2] The Life Satisfaction Index (LSI) (Neugarten, Havighurst, & Tobin, 1961) and the Geriatric Depression Scale (GDS) (Sheik & Yesavage, 1986) were used as measures of well-being; as both scales are highly correlated in our sample, we combined them to form a global index of subjective life quality. As part of the assessment procedure, participants were also asked to give an estimate of the age they would expect to achieve;

the difference between this estimate and actual age provides a measure of residual life expectancy (RLE).

Effects of age on the relationship between perceived losses and well-being were analyzed in a moderated multiple regression format (Cohen & Cohen, 1983). At first glance, the results seem to support Hypothesis I: the moderating effects obtained indicate that goal deficits as well as changes in perceived goal deficits over the longitudinal interval have a slightly weaker impact on well-being in the higher age groups.

The picture changes in important respects, however, when the measure of residual life expectancy is included. Note that Hypothesis I was based on the assumption that the emotional impact of losses in later life is dampened due to the shorter period of remaining life time. Contrary to this assumption, however, moderating effects indicate that the negative impact of perceived losses on well-being becomes stronger with decreasing RLE. Considering the high negative correlation between age and RLE (−.60), the fact that similar buffering effects obtain for both variables is particularly noteworthy. The palliative effects of (high) RLE become even more pronounced when controlling for age.

Taken together, these findings support Hypothesis II: residual life time appears to function as a resource in coping with losses; perceived losses have a stronger negative impact on subjective life quality when life draws to a close. Hypothesis I, on the other hand, can be maintained only with substantial modification: the palliative effects of chronological age are apparently not due to the smaller span of remaining life time and related discounting effects but must be attributed to coping resources that *increase* with age.

Accommodation theory proposes that the readiness and capacity to adjust goals and preferences to irreversible losses and constraints and to disengage from goals that have become unfeasible under given temporal and developmental reserves may compensate for the loss of resources in other functional domains.

Converging with this assumption, second-order moderation effects indicate that the counterpalliative effect of a fading residual life time is less strongly expressed for participants scoring high in FGA. Figure 6.2 illustrates this effect (chronological age was partialled from RLE to bring out the interaction effect more clearly).

Time Perspectives and Sources of Meaning: The Role of Age and Residual Life Time

Goals and plans that extend into the future lend motivation and meaning to life. Thus, the fading of life time and the loss of personal future destroys not only action resources but sources of meaning as well. How does the shrinking of temporal resources affect time perspectives and future meaning? The assessment procedure of the ARS panel study comprised several measures that addressed this question (Brandtstädter & Wentura, 1994). Participants were asked to rate their future perspectives with regard to perceived *openness (F-OPEN), concreteness (F-CONC), control (F-CONT),* and

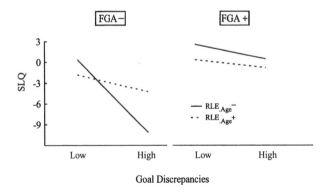

Figure 6.2   Accommodative Flexibility (FGA) as a Protective Resource. While low residual life expectancy (RLE) tends to boost the negative impact of perceived losses and discrepancies (goal deficits) on subjective life quality (SLQ), this effect is mitigated by high flexibility.

affective valence (F-VAL). Besides changes in time perspectives, feelings of *obsolescence* were assessed *(OBS)*.[3] Cross-sectional comparisons and longitudinal gradients over an eight-year-interval reveal a consistent pattern (Brandtstädter, Wentura, & Schmitz, 1997). With advancing age, the personal future tends to be perceived as less open, less concrete, and less controllable; at the same time, future prospects tend to lose their positive valence. These changes are furthermore accompanied by growing feelings of obsolescence. Figure 6.3 illustrates these findings. Longitudinal effects were significant for all measures. Female participants across all age groups scored lower in *F-CONC, F-VAL,* and *F-CONT*; interactions involving the gender factor, however, remained insignificant throughout, suggesting that the overall pattern of changes holds for both sexes.

Effects of chronological age are always mediated by factors that, at least in principle, can also vary within age-homogeneous groups. For example, the age effects shown in Figure 6.3 above could plausibly be mediated by age-related changes in health status. In the present study, the Seriousness of Illness Rating Scale (SIRS) (Wyler, Masuda, & Holmes, 1968) was used to assess differences and changes in health status. As expected, chronological age and SIRS are positively related, and time scales showed similar relationships to both variables. Nonetheless, age effects remain significant even after controlling for differences in health.

As indicated above, effects of chronological age involve two different but highly related components that, however, are not easily disentangled—effects related to the increase of lived time and effects related to the shrinking of time yet to be lived. Our findings indicate that the observed shifts in temporal perspectives primarily reflect the latter type of effects. The changes in temporal perspectives depicted in Figure 6.3 are even more marked when residual life expectancy (RLE) instead of chronological age is taken as a reference (RLE was measured as described in the previous section).

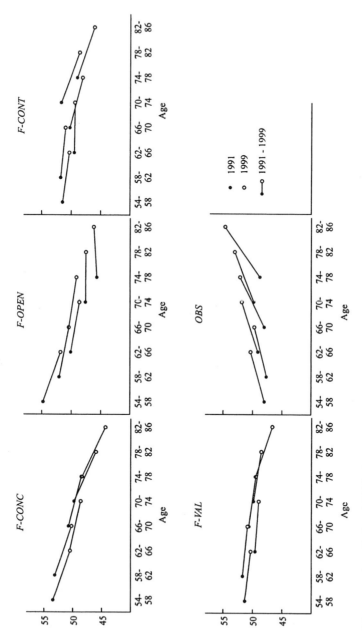

Figure 6.3 Age-Related Shifts in Time Perspectives. Concreteness, openness, perceived controllability, and affective valence of future prospects tend to decrease with advancing age, while feelings of obsolescence increase (sequential data, ARS project).

Losses in "future meaning" (Reker, Peacock, & Wong, 1987) tend to negatively affect well-being and self-esteem in later life. Accommodation theory suggests that these effects may be counteracted by a shift in meaning perspectives and sources of satisfaction. With the closing of action paths in later life, the personal past becomes increasingly important as a source of continuity and self-esteem (cf. Brandtstädter & Greve, 1994; Staudinger & Dittmann-Kohli, 1992). Consistent with this argument, findings from the ARS panel indicate that preoccupation with the past is less indicative of depression in older groups than among younger people (Brandtstädter et al., 1997). Beyond an increased emphasis on the past, we expect a growing orientation toward sources of meaning that transcend the limited time horizon of life. Such "timeless" sources of meaning may be found in values (such as aesthetic, moral, or religious values) that cannot be expressed in terms of time-linked instrumental utilities and that, in that sense, provide strong and timeless criteria for evaluating one's life and action. In line with this argument, findings by Rosenblatt, Greenberg, Solomon, Pyszczynski, and Lyon (1989) suggest that when people are brought to reflect on the finitude of their life, they tend to show an increasing commitment to cultural norms and values. The authors assume that this reaction serves to dampen insecurity and fear. In terms of the dual-process model, however, the shift toward "timeless" values rather appears as an accommodative process that compensates for the loss of future meaning.

Resources and Terminal Limits: The Compression of Depression

We have identified assimilative and accommodative processes as the key mechanisms through which the self-system maintains integrity and continuity across ontogenetic and historical change. At the same time, the interplay of these mechanisms helps to keep the system of personal goals and self-definitions flexible enough so that it can be adjusted to changing resources and constraints within the person's developmental ecology.

Although the self-system of the aging individual is highly resilient, and although it apparently owes much of its resilience to compensatory and accommodative processes, it is not invulnerable in any absolute sense. When there is no substitute for destroyed goals and sources of satisfaction, readjustment would involve a radical paradigm shift in one's life design and self-image. Where basic assumptions about self and the world are shattered, it may take a very long time to restore integrity and to find a new equilibrium (cf. Janoff-Bulman, 1992).

While the impact of critical events generally depends on the relation between situational demands and personal resources, there are challenges and crises that overtax even the most resilient system. Mechanisms of time discounting that mitigate temporally distant threats lose their palliative effects to the degree that the threatening events draw nearer and become current concerns. Such critical situations apparently tend to cumulate and to occur in increasing temporal density in terminal life phases.

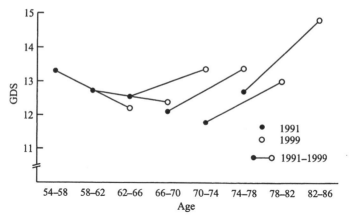

Figure 6.4   Depression and Age. Although the transition toward later life, in the
                      overall picture, is characterized by considerable resiliency and sta-
                      bility, a downward trend toward lower well-being begins to emerge
                      when participants reach their eighth decade (Geriatric Depression
                      Scale, GDS; sequential data, ARS project).

Age-related changes such as chronic health problems, the loss of partners and friends,
and social marginalization and isolation tend to destroy developmental niches and
meaning spheres that have provided security, intimacy, recognition, and physical comfort (e.g., Steverink, Lindenberg, & Ormel, 1998), so that older people are left "alone
with the bad present" (Gutmann, 1998, p. 291). At the same time, temporal resources
and adaptive reserves that would be necessary to transform a negative into a positive
future are running out. Although emotional strain resulting from developmental loss
is buffered by accommodative readjustments in goals and meaning systems, adaptive
systems, almost by definition, cannot easily disengage from goals and valuations on
which their integrity and continuity critically depends.

Comparable to the "compression of morbidity" mentioned earlier, we would thus
expect a *compression of depression* into the terminal phases of life. Cross-sequential
findings from the ARS panel converge with that assumption (Rothermund &
Brandtstädter, in press). Although the transition toward age, in the overall picture,
is characterized by high resilience and stability, a downward trend toward lower well-
being and life quality begins to emerge in the longitudinal as well as in the cross-
sectional pattern when participants approach the age of 70 to 75 years; this trend
appears most strongly in the oldest cohort—that is, at an age level that corresponds to
the average statistical life expectancy. A similar increase in the incidence of depressive
symptoms in this age group was also observed in a number of cross-sectional studies
(e.g., Kessler, Foster, Webster, & House, 1992; Mirowsky & Ross, 1992; Valvanne,
Juva, Erkinjuntti, & Tilvis, 1996).

As these findings suggest, late-onset depression marks a critical point where assimilative and accommodative coping resources, due to the joint influence of cumulating developmental losses and fading temporal resources, may approach a limit. To explore differential factors that mediate this insidious trend, selected reference variables were included as covariates in the cross-sequential analysis. The effects depicted in Figure 6.4 above turned out to be quite robust; even after controlling for longitudinal change in potentially important mediating variables such as health status, personal control over development, or social support, the older cohorts still show a significant increase in GDS (Rothermund & Brandtstädter, in press). In the ANCOVA procedure, only two variables neutralized this effect: the trend toward higher depression in the older cohort disappeared when controlling for changes in residual life expectancy (RLE) and in feelings of obsolescence (*OBS* measure, see above). Apparently, changes in time perspective and the personal construal of future are particularly important as mediators of late-onset depression.

The Acceleration of Time in Modernity: Implications for Aging

In the previous sections, we have reflected on various adaptive challenges that result from the dissipation of temporal resources in later life and have considered mechanisms by which the aging self copes with these challenges. We conclude this essay by pointing out some intriguing analogies that exist between the problems of maintaining a sense of worth and continuity in later life and the adaptive problems that are caused by the "acceleration of time" in modernity (for a fuller discussion, see Brandtstädter, in press).

In developmental settings of high modernity, which are characterized by accelerated cultural change, growing interconnectedness (globalization), and pluralization of life forms, it becomes increasingly difficult to meet both demands of adaptive flexibility and personal continuity. Three overaching trends are salient. First, the temporal range across which skills and experiences can be transferred to the future is narrowing down; the future has become increasingly opaque. Second, the necessity to adjust life policies to rapidly changing role structures and task environments has lead to a blurring of normative "timetables" that traditionally have served as guiding frameworks for organizing one's life and environment. Third, a growing emphasis on lean modes of management and production imposes increasing demands for a planful and maximally efficient use of time and temporal resources across the life span (see also Sennett, 1998). An emphasis on optimization appears to be part of the cognitive-theoretical milieu that characterizes modernity and its use of human and cultural resources. Some caveats should be observed, however, when it comes to elaborate notions of optimality in contexts of development and aging. In particular, we would argue that a comprehensive view of optimization should go beyond notions of self-efficiency to encompass aspects of *self-cultivation* as well (e.g., Brandtstädter & Lerner, 1999). Such a more comprehensive view would take into account the limitations not only of the human design but also of life in itself and would acknowledge that the projects that we pursue during the limited span of our life are basically incomplete (cf. Marquard, 1999; see also Baltes, this volume; M. Baltes & Carstensen, this volume; cf. Kirkwood, this volume).

Incompleteness calls for compensation, and compensation is a hallmark of culture. Anthropological theories have characterized the human species as "homo compensator" (Marquard, 1984, p. 256): humans have created cultural institutions and symbolic spheres as exosomatic means which help them to compensate their "natural" limitations (e.g., Bruner, 1990; Geertz, 1973; Gehlen, 1988). With regard to functional limitations and losses of old age, Baltes (1977) argues in a similar vein that cultural scaffolds and means of compensation become increasingly important and indispensible in later life.

In regard to this important argument, two reservations seem in place. First, we should note that the adaptive capacities for self-cultivation and for the construal of compensatory cultural scaffolds are rooted in the evolved architecture of the human mind (cf. Brandtstädter, 1998; Tooby & Cosmides, 1992), which appears as "incomplete" but which also affords the *competence to compensate for incompetence*. Second, the processes of cultural evolution are to a considerable extent driven by the need to cope with untoward side effects of problem solutions in the past; the same, of course, applies to development and aging within cultural contexts. Cultural change creates, and at the same time permanently destroys, spheres of meaning and adaptive niches. The "discontents of modernity" (Berger, Berger, & Kellner, 1967) essentially stem from the fact that cycles of de- and reconstruction turn at increasing speed.

What are the implications for the present and the future of aging? On the backdrop of cultural ideals of fitness and efficiency, age-related losses in action resources become increasingly charged with negative valence. In the wake of cultural acceleration, feelings of obsolescence, of being unable to keep pace with the processes of change are experienced by growing parts of the population at increasingly earlier points in the life cycle. Subsequent age cohorts share an increasingly smaller portion of their meanings and experiences, which tends to erode empathy and mutual respect between generations (cf. Sennett, 1998). By the same token, it becomes more and more difficult to maintain personal continuity and to extrapolate experiences into the future. Although life experience may endow the older person with some adaptive "elasticity" (Mannheim, 1964, p. 541), experience and expertise are devalued when acquired life forms and problem solutions can no longer be generalized and transferred to the future. While high modernity tends to define "successful aging," somewhat paradoxically, in terms of maintaining the habitus of youthful competence as long as possible, the acceleration of cultural change renders this task more and more difficult. Under these conditions, a need for compensatory intervention into old age is increasingly felt; at the same time, however, limits of compensation tend to become increasingly salient.

The adaptive tasks of preserving personal continuity and adjusting to change become particularly difficult in late life; the historical trends discussed above have increased the dilemmatic tension between these tasks. Thus, if time threatens our identity (cf. Mittelstrass, 1992, p. 405), this seems particularly true for aging in developmental settings of modernity. Well-being and personal continuity under these conditions essentially depend on creating or finding spheres of meaning from where no further displacement seems possible. Within the framework of the dual-process model, we have argued that assimilative and accommodative mechanisms are central adaptive resources that the phylogenetically evolved architecture of mind provides in that regard. On cultural as well as on personal levels, these mechanisms not only fuel and shape activities of optimization and compensation but also adjust normative expectations and goals when such activities reach limits or yield diminishing returns. In that sense, assimilative and accommodative processes undergird the formation of knowledge and expertise about life—of knowledge about developmental options and constraints, of expertise as to which options may be desirable for achieving a positive balance of gain and loss across life, and perhaps also of the wisdom not to "build our luck too near to forces on which we have no influence" (Bloch, 1969, p. 358).

Acknowledgment

Parts of this chapter were prepared while Jochen Brandtstädter was a fellow at the Center for Advanced Study in the Behavioral Sciences (1998–1999). He gratefully acknowledges support by the German-American Academic Council.

Notes

1. The ARS project (Adaptive Resources of the Aging Self) is supported by a grant from the German Research Foundation (DFG) to the senior author.
2. Examples: health, satisfying friendships, intellectual efficiency, social recognition, personal independence.
3. Sample items: "There are always new and fascinating perspectives in my life" (*F-OPEN*); "I have clear goals and expectations for my future" (*F-CONC*); "What the future will bring depends primarily on myself" (*F-CONT*); "I look forward to what lies ahead in my life" (*F-VAL*); "I feel that I cannot keep pace with the modern way of living" (*OBS*).

References

Bak, P. M., & Brandtstädter, J. (1998). Flexible Zielanpassung und hartnäckige Zielverfolgung als Bewältigungsressourcen: Hinweise auf ein Regulationsdilemma. *Zeitschrift für Psychologie, 206*, 235–249.

Baltes, P. B. (1997). On the incomplete architecture of human ontogeny: Selection, optimization, and compensation as a foundation of developmental theory. *American Psychologist, 52*, 366–380.

Baltes, P. B., & Baltes, M. M. (1990). Psychological perspectives on successful aging: The model of selective optimization with compensation. In P. B. Baltes & M. M. Baltes (Eds.), *Successful aging: Perspectives from the behavioral sciences* (pp. 1–34). New York: Cambridge University Press.

Becker, P. (1995). *Seelische Gesundheit und Verhaltenskontrolle*. Göttingen: Hogrefe.

Berger, P. L., Berger, B., & Kellner, H. (1967). *The homeless mind: Modernization and unconsciousness.* New York: Random House.

Bloch, E. (1969). *Philosophische Aufsätze zur objektiven Phantasie* (Gesamtausgabe, Vol. 10). Frankfurt am Main: Suhrkamp.

Brandtstädter, J. (1989). Personal self-regulation of development: Cross-sequential analyses of development-related control beliefs and emotions. *Developmental Psychology, 25,* 96–108.

Brandtstädter, J. (1998). Action perspectives on human development. In R. M. Lerner (Ed.), *Theoretical models of human development,* Vol. 1, *Handbook of child psychology* (5th ed., pp. 807–863). New York: Wiley.

Brandtstädter, J. (2001). *Entwicklung, Intentionalität, Handeln.* Stuttgart: Kohlhammer.

Brandtstädter, J. (in press). Agency in developmental settings of modernity: The dialectics of commitment and disengagement. *American Behavioral Scientist.*

Brandtstädter, J., & Greve, W. (1994). The aging self: Stabilizing and protective processes. *Developmental Review, 14,* 52–80.

Brandtstädter J., & Lerner, R. M. (Eds.). (1999). *Action and self-development: Theory and research through the life span.* Thousand Oaks, CA: Sage.

Brandtstädter, J., & Renner, G. (1990). Tenacious goal pursuit and flexible goal adjustment: Explication and age-related analysis of assimilative and accommodative strategies of coping. *Psychology and Aging, 5,* 58–67.

Brandtstädter, J., & Rothermund, K. (2002a). Intentional self-development: Exploring the interfaces between development, intentionality, and the self. In L. J. Crockett (Ed.), *Agency, motivation, and the life course* (Nebraska Symposium on Motivation, Vol. 48, pp. 31–75). Lincoln, NE: University of Nebraska Press.

Brandtstädter, J., & Rothermund, K. (2002b). The life-course dynamics of goal pursuit and goal adjustment: A two-process framework. *Developmental Review, 22,* 117–150.

Brandtstädter, J., Rothermund, K., & Schmitz, U. (1997). Coping resources in later life. *European Review of Applied Psychology, 47,* 107–114.

Brandtstädter, J., & Wentura, D. (1994). Veränderungen der Zeit- und Zukunftsperspektive im Übergang zum höheren Erwachsenenalter: entwicklungspsychologische und differentielle Aspekte. *Zeitschrift für Entwicklungspsychologie and Pädagogische Psychologie, 26,* 2–21.

Brandtstädter, J., & Wentura, D. (1995). Adjustment to shifting possibility frontiers in later life: Complementary adaptive modes. In R. A. Dixon & L. Bäckman (Eds.), *Compensating for psychological deficits and declines: Managing losses and promoting gains* (pp. 83–106). Mahwah, NJ: Erlbaum.

Brandtstädter, J., Wentura, D., & Rothermund, K. (1999). Intentional self-development through adulthood and later life: Tenacious pursuit and flexible adjustment of goals. In J. Brandtstädter & R. M. Lerner (Eds.), *Action and self-development: Theory and research through the life-span* (pp. 373–400). Thousand Oaks, CA: Sage.

Brandtstädter, J., Wentura, D., & Schmitz, U. (1997). Veränderungen der Zeit- und Zukunftsperspektive im Übergang zum höheren Alter: quer- und längsschnittliche Befunde. *Zeitschrift für Psychologie, 205,* 377–395.

Bruner, J. S. (1990). Culture and human development: A new look. *Human Development, 33,* 344–355.

Cohen, J., & Cohen, P. (1983). *Applied multiple regression/correlation analysis for the behavioral sciences* (2nd ed.). Hillsdale, NJ: Erlbaum.

Ericsson, K. A. (1990). Peak performance and age: An examination of peak performance in sports. In P. B. Baltes & M. M. Baltes (Eds.), *Successful aging: Perspectives from the behavioral sciences* (pp. 154–196). New York: Cambridge University Press.

Fries, J. F. (1990). Medical perspectives upon successful aging. In P. B. Baltes & M. M. Baltes (Eds.), *Successful aging: Perspectives from the behavioral sciences* (pp. 35–49). New York: Cambridge University Press.

Geertz, C. (1973). *The interpretation of cultures. Selected essays.* New York: Basic Books.

Gehlen, A. (1988). *Man, his nature and place in the world.* New York: Columbia University Press.

Geppert, U. (1997). Persönlichkeit, Motive, soziale Kognition. In Max-Planck-Institut für psychologische Forschung (Hrsg.), *Forschungsbericht 1995–1997* (S. 26–31). Munich: Max Planck Institute for Human Development.

Gilbert, D. T., Pinel, E. C., Wilson, T. D., Blumberg, S. J., & Wheatley, T. P. (1998). Immune neglect: A source of durability bias in affective forecasting. *Journal of Personality and Social Psychology, 75,* 617–638.

Gollwitzer, P. M. (1990). Action phases and mind-sets. In E. T. Higgins & R. M. Sorrentino (Eds.), *Handbook of motivation and cognition: Foundations of social behavior* (Vol. 2, pp. 53–92). New York: Guilford Press.

Gutmann, D. (1998). The psychoimmune system in later life. The problem of late-onset disorders. In J. Lomranz (Ed.), *Handbook of aging and mental health: An integrative approach* (pp. 281–295). New York: Plenum.

Heckhausen, J., Dixon, R. A., & Baltes, P. B. (1989). Gains and losses in development throughout adulthood as perceived by different adult age groups. *Developmental Psychology, 25,* 109–121.

Janoff-Bulman, R. (1992). *Shattered assumptions: Towards a new psychology of trauma.* New York: Free Press.

Kahneman, D., Fredrickson, B. L., Schreiber, C. A., & Redelmeier, D. A. (1993). When more pain is preferred to less: Adding a better end. *Psychological Science, 4,* 401–405.

Kessler, R. C., Foster, C., Webster, P. S., & House, J. S. (1992). The relationship between age and depressive symptoms in two national surveys. *Psychology and Aging, 7,* 119–126.

Klinger, E. (1977). *Meaning and void: Inner experience and the incentives in people's lives.* Minneapolis: University of Minnesota Press.

Kuhl, J. (1987). Action control: The maintenance of motivational states. In F. Halisch & J. Kuhl (Eds.), *Motivation, intention and volition* (pp. 279–291). Berlin: Springer.

Lewin, K. (1953). Zeitperspektive und Moral. In G. W. Lewin (Ed.), *Die Lösung sozialer Konflikte* (pp. 152–180). Bad Nauheim: Christian-Verlag.

Mannheim, K. (1964). Das Problem der Generationen. In K. H. Wolff (Ed.), *Mannheim, Karl: Wissenssoziologie. Auswahl aus dem Werk* (pp. 509–565). Neuwied: Luchterhand.

Marquard, O. (1984). Entlastungen. Theodizeemotive in der neuzeitlichen Philosophie. In P. Wapnewski (Hrsg.), *Wissenschaftskolleg. Jahrbuch 1982/93* (pp. 245–258). Berlin: Siedler.

Marquard, O. (1999). Am Ende, nicht am Ziel. *Frankfurter Allgemeine Zeitung, 273,* 49.

Mirowsky, J., & Ross, C. E. (1992). Age and depression. *Journal of Health and Social Behavior, 33,* 187–205.

Mittelstrass, J. (1992). Zeitformen des Lebens: Philosophische Unterscheidungen. In P. B. Baltes & J. Mittelstrass (Eds.), *Zukunft des Alterns und gesellschaftliche Entwicklung* (pp. 386–407). Berlin: de Gruyter.

Neugarten, B. L., Havighurst, R. J., & Tobin, S. S. (1961). The measurement of life satisfaction. *Journal of Gerontology, 16,* 134–143.

Nozick, R. (1989). *The examined life. Philosophical meditations.* New York: Simon & Schuster.

Nuttin, J. R. (1964). The future time perspective in human motivation and learning. *Acta Psychologica, 23,* 60–82.

Ogilvie, D. M., & Rose, K. M. (1995). Self-with-other representations and a taxonomy of motives: Two approaches to studying persons. *Journal of Personality, 63,* 643–679.

Prelec, D., & Loewenstein, G. (1997). Beyond time discounting. *Marketing Letters, 8,* 97–108.

Reker, G. T., Peacock, E. J., & Wong, P. T. (1987). Meaning and the purpose in life and well-being: A life-span perspective. *Journal of Gerontology, 42,* 44–49.

Rosenblatt, A., Greenberg, J., Solomon, S., Pyszczynski, T., & Lyon, D. (1989). Evidence for terror management theory: I. The effects of mortality salience on reactions to those who violate or uphold cultural values. *Journal of Personality and Social Psychology, 62,* 681–690.

Rothermund, K. (1998). *Persistenz und Neuorientierung: Mechanismen der Aufrechterhaltung und Auflösung zielbezogener kognitiver Einstellungen.* Doctoral dissertation, University of Trier, Trier, Germany.

Rothermund, K., & Brandtstädter, J. (1997a). Entwicklung und Bewältigung: Festhalten und Preisgeben von Zielen als Formen der Bewältigung von Entwicklungszielen. In C. Tesch-Römer, C. Salewski, & G. Schwarz (Eds.), *Psychologie der Bewältigung* (pp. 120–133). Weinheim: Psychologie Verlags Union.

Rothermund, K., & Brandtstädter, J. (1997b). Zum Verständnis der Assimilations-Akkommodations-Theorie. In C. Tesch-Römer, C. Salewski, & G. Schwarz (Eds.), *Psychologie der Bewältigung* (pp. 162–171). Weinheim: Psychologie Verlags Union.

Rothermund, K., & Brandtstädter, J. (1998). Auswirkungen von Belastungen und Verlusten auf die Lebensqualität: Alters- und lebenszeitgebundene Moderationseffekte. *Zeitschrift für Klinische Psychologie, 27,* 86–92.

Rothermund, K., & Brandtstädter, J. (in press). Depression in later life: Cross-sequential patterns and possible determinants. *Psychology and Aging.*

Rothermund, K., Dillmann, U., & Brandtstädter, J. (1994). Belastende Lebenssituationen im mittleren und höheren Erwachsenenalter: Zur differentiellen Wirksamkeit assimilativer und akkommodativer Bewältigung. *Zeitschrift für Gesundheitspsychologie, 2,* 245–268.

Sennett, R. (1998). *The corrosion of character.* New York: Norton.

Shiek, J. I., & Yesavage, J. A. (1986). Geriatric depression scale (GDS): Recent evidence and development of a shorter version. *Clinical Gerontology, 5,* 165–173.

Staudinger, U. M., & Dittmann-Kohli, F. (1992). Lebenserfahrung und Lebenssinn. In P. B. Baltes & J. Mittelstrass (Eds.), *Zukunft des Alterns und gesellschaftliche Entwicklung* (pp. 408–436). Berlin: de Gruyter.

Staudinger, U. M., Marsiske, M., & Baltes, P. B. (1995). Resilience and reserve capacity in later adulthood: Potentials and limits of development across the life span. In D. Cicchetti & D. J. Cohen (Eds.), *Developmental psychopathology,* Vol. 2, *Risk, disorder, and adaptation* (pp. 801–847). New York: Wiley.

Steverink, N., Lindenberg, S., & Ormel, J. (1998). Towards understanding successful ageing: Patterned change in resources and goals. *Ageing and Society, 18,* 441–467.

Taylor, S. E., & Gollwitzer, P. M. (1995). Effects of mindset on positive illusions. *Journal of Personality and Social Psychology, 69,* 213–226.

Tooby, J., & Cosmides, L. (1992). The psychological foundations of culture. In J. H. Barkow, L. Cosmides, & J. Tooby (Eds.), *The adapted mind: Evolutionary psychology and the generation of culture* (pp. 19–136). New York: Oxford University Press.

Turk-Charles, S., & Carstensen, L. L. (1999). The role of time in the setting of social goals across the life span. In T. M. Hess & F. Blanchard-Fields (Eds.), *Social cognition and aging* (pp. 319–339). San Diego: Academic Press.

Valvanne, J., Juva, K., Erkinjuntti, T., & Tilvis, R. (1996). Major depression in the elderly: A population study in Helsinki. *International Psychogeriatrics, 8,* 437–443.

Wentura, D. (1995). *Verfügbarkeit entlastender Kognitionen. Zur Verarbeitung negativer Lebenssituationen.* Weinheim: Psychologie Verlags Union.

Wyler, A. R., Masuda, M., & Holmes, T. H. (1968). Seriousness of illness rating scale. *Journal of Psychosomatic Research, 11,* 363–374.

7 An Economic Perspective on Selection, Optimization, and Compensation (SOC)

Jere R. Behrman

University of Pennsylvania, Philadelphia, PA, U.S.A.

Abstract

This chapter first presents and summarizes the standard economic model of individual human development and resource management. In this model, human development is viewed as a sequence of dynamic optimizing decisions under uncertainty that maximize the welfare of the decision maker period by period subject to the basic resource constraints (including outcomes of previous periods that were affected in part by the decision maker and resources that are given from the point of view of the decision maker including genetic endowments and the nature of the larger environment in which the decision maker operates), prices broadly defined (past, present, and expected), the distribution of future shocks including those related to health and mortality as well as to resource availability, and other aspects of the market, cultural, social, and policy environments in which the individual operates. Some attention is paid to important aspects of this formulation, such as whether individual preferences are assumed to be given or determined in these processes, how individual preferences are aggregated within collectives such as households, lifecycle aspects of such development including changes in the relevant decision makers who affect an individual (such as parents when children are very young, collective decisions between parents and children as the children age, primarily the adult children when they are prime-age adults, and their children and the broader society as they become elderly), information problems, when stochastic processes are resolved, and the role of characteristics such as risk aversion. The chapter then considers selection, compensation, and optimization with regard to three basic questions: (1) How do these concepts relate to the standard economic approach to lifespan human developmental processes and resource management? (2) Do these concepts raise questions regarding the formulation of the standard economic approach to lifespan human developmental processes and resource management? (3) Does the standard economic approach to lifespan human developmental processes and resource management raise questions about usefully modifying the use of these concepts?

Introduction

Economists long have been concerned with what determines investments in individuals and in physical and financial assets. These concerns have varied in importance since the early classical economists in the eighteenth century but were reinvigorated in the early decades of the second half of the twentieth century by the seminal studies on human capital of Becker (1967, 1991, 1993), Mincer (1974), and Schultz (1961, 1963). Investments require *current* resources but have returns in the future. One such investment is building a dam this year by using current labor and other resources that will increase hydroelectric power after it is completed in three years and continue for three decades. Learning a new computer skill this year—by paying tuition for a special course and spending time studying rather than earning a current wage—that will increase your productivity over the next decade also is such an investment.

But not all such investments are profitable to undertake. Building the dam is more likely to be profitable when few current resources need to be used, the future addition of hydroelectric generating power is great, and the increased hydroelectric power becomes available sooner. If the current resources needed are very large, the additional hydroelectric generating power very small, or the additional hydroelectric power available only in the distant future, the dam may not be worth building. Similarly, if the tuition and time needed to learn a new computer skill are large, the impact on future productivity is small, and the period during which that gain in future prductivity is very short, it may not be worth learning the new computer skill.

The standard economic model of human capital or human development systematizes these concerns and gives insight into what factors determine whether such investments in individual development are undertaken. As is reflected in the example of learning a new computer skill, this approach may suggest that such investments are less likely with age because the costs of learning may increase if there is less plasticity of learning capacities as humans age and the expected gains may be less if there is greater uncertainty with age about being healthy or even alive in order that the higher productivity can be realized. On the other hand, there may be other factors that make such an investment more attractive with age, such as greater experience with learning how to learn and easier access to resources for investment if individuals have accumulated resources through working many years. Such implications in some ways may be complementary and in other ways different from those in the "lifespan architecture" and related concepts that motivate this book.

This chapter first presents and summarizes the standard economic model of individual human development and resource management and then turns to the implications of this framework for empirical observations about human development and for policies that might affect human development. It then considers how the basic elements of the lifespan architecture and the concepts of selection, optimization, and compensation (SOC) as articulated in Part I of this book relate to the standard economic approach to lifespan human developmental processes and resource management. It concludes with some fundamental questions and challenges for the lifespan architecture and SOC literature.

Standard Economic Model of Human Development and Implications for Interpretations of Empirical Observations and for Policies

Economic Analytical Frameworks for Considering the Determinants of and the Impact of Investments in Human Development

Economists view the use of current resources as being either for current consumption or for investment, which is defined to be those uses that affect future outcomes. Resources devoted to human development are considered to be basically human resource investments.[1] Good theories about the determinants of and the impact of human-resource investments abstract the essence of complex empirical phenomena in ways that lead to testable empirical propositions about behavior and policy choices in the presence of imperfect information. I begin this section with production functions that are embodied in these theories. These production functions illustrate the direct effects of human-resource investments and the ways that the direct effects may depend on other inputs into the production processes. I then turn to micro theories that underlie some dimensions of the behaviors determining investments in human resources, the returns to those investments, and related policy considerations.

Direct Production-Function Impact of Human-Resource Investments   Human development, in addition to being of interest in itself, also may be of interest because it has a "production-function" impact on other outcomes, such as education, health, wages, and productivities in various activities. The new computer skills used as an illustration in the introduction, for example, may be an input into work productivity. The total direct impact of human development can be considered to be the sum of all such effects, each weighted by its appropriate price (where *price* is used here to mean a conversion factor that permits translation of different benefits and costs into comparable units).[2]

A firm production function, for example, can illustrate the impact of human development, other characteristics of workers, and other production inputs (such as machinery and equipment) on firm production. A production function is a technological relation that gives the maximum output that can be produced with a given set of inputs by a firm (or by other production units). The production function in itself does not say anything about whether the inputs actually used are the best combination of inputs, given the firm's objectives. But production functions are essential parts of models of behaviors related to human-resource investments within the larger contexts of objectives that a individual or family has, markets that they face, and assets that they have at the time that decisions related to human development are made.

I write the production function for firm f to highlight the role of some attributes of worker i in firm f—including innate characteristics (G_{if}), human capital that reflects previous human-resource investments such as learning new computer skills (H_{if}), work effort (E_{if}) of worker i in the production of the firm's output (Q_f) given similar attributes of other workers in the firm (L_f), capital stock of the firm (K_f), firm management capabilities and organization (M_f), and technological knowledge (T_f):

$$Q_f = Q(G_{if}, H_{if}, E_{if}, L_f, K_f, M_f, T_f). \tag{7.1}$$

All these variables can be vectors with multiple elements. Human capital, for example, includes education (whether from formal schooling, training, work experience, or lessons from day-to-day life), physical health, personality, psychological states, and so on. It is important for a number of questions about human development to know the impact of earlier human-resource investments in worker i on firm's f's production. For example, to evaluate the rate of return to increasing resources devoted to human development, it is necessary to have some notion of what effects better human development has on economic productivity and on other outcomes, for which there are similar production functions.

There are a number of important questions about this production process beyond what is the impact of human development on productivity: What are the interactions between human development and other factors that enter into production? Is the marginal product of human development affected by other individual, family, or institutional attributes? Are resources devoted to human development more effective if the individual has better innate abilities? Comes from a better family background? Has access to better social-sector services, including schools and preventative and curative health care? How do these effects change over the life cycle?

If analysts had good information on all of the inputs and outcomes of all the relevant production processes, considerable light could be shed on answers to such questions by estimating critical parameters in these production processes. But there are some basic problems in undertaking such estimates:

- Some critical variables are not likely to be observed by analysts. Examples for relation (7.1) include worker's innate endowments G_{if}, worker's effort E_{if}, and the firm's management capabilities M_i. The lack of observations on such variables not only means that it is very difficult to assess their impact. It also means that it is difficult to assess the impact of observed variables. If individuals with more ability are likely to receive more human-development resources and their abilities are not controlled in estimates of production relations such as (7.1), for example, the impact of human development on productivity is likely to be overestimated because it is in part proxying for unobserved abilities.

• Some critical variables are likely to be observed only very poorly by analysts. Resources devoted to human development itself are a central example. Therefore, most empirical studies represent human development very crudely, by such measures as duration of participation in formal related programs such as schooling, by imperfect test scores, or by family characteristics. If the observed indicator of human development that is used for analysis is a noisy representation of true human development with the noise random, this aspect of the data is not controlled in the estimation results in underestimates of the true effects of human development. If measurement error in the observed indicator of human development is systematically related to other variables in the production function, the result is a multiplicity of biases in the estimates of the production technology in relation (7.1), depending on exactly what is the nature of relation between the observed indicator and the true extent of human development.

• Though relation (7.1) is written for simplicity without reference to time, production processes are dynamic, so longitudinal data on all the relevant variables may be required before the production processes can be understood. Moreover, important aspects of the production process, such as interaction between genetic endowments and human-resource investments, may change over time or over the life cycle of workers. But often data are available only at a point in time or for very limited time periods. This may result in omitted variable biases that lead to misleading estimates of the nature of the production processes (see below).

• Production-function estimates, even if they are not subject to other biases, refer to only the direct effects of human development on the outcome considered. But human-resource investments may affect other inputs into the production process, such as worker effort. Workers who have invested in new computer skills, to continue with the above example, may take pride in their use and put forth more effort. If so, the total effects of human-resource investments include such indirect effects in addition to the direct effects that are captured by production-function estimates.

• To assess all of the impacts of a particular human-resource investment, good production-function estimates for all the relevant production processes are required. But human-resource investments may have impacts on many outcomes, some of which may be very hard to measure empirically, such as the state of an individual's mental health.

Family or Individual Demands for Human-Resource Investments   Resources devoted to human development may have current consumption benefits for individuals and families and may have future investment effects through production processes such as just discussed. Because the proximate determinants of such investments often are families, many economists have emphasized family (or household) models of the determination of human-resource investments.[3] Becker's (1967) Woytinsky lecture provides a simple but very useful and widely used framework with which to think about investments in human capital from the perspective of families or individuals at a particular point of time.[4] These considerations relate to how private resource management and societal resource management interact to determine private human-resource investments and the returns to those investments.

Human-resource investments in an individual over time can be viewed to be a sequence of such decisions, with those at any point in time reflecting not only factors at that point of time and expectations regarding the future but the outcomes of past decisions. The investment decision whether to continue in postsecondary schooling, for example, is determined by the child's innate capabilities, all past investments in a child's human resources (and thus the child's current stock of human resources at the time of the postsecondary schooling decisions), current prices (such as the postsecondary schooling tuition and fees and the wage rates that reflect the cost of not working in order to attend school), and epectations relating to the future returns to postsecondary schooling. All such investments are made under uncertainty, but uncertainty is likely to be greater for some investments than for others, particularly for those for which there is relatively little experience on which to base subjective distributions regarding future outcomes.

Within this framework, human-capital investment demands at a point in time reflect the equating of expected present discounted values of marginal (or additional) private benefits and expected present discounted values of marginal (or additional) private costs for human-capital investments in a given individual, as is represented by the solid lines in Figure 7.1A. Discounting makes possible the comparison of two streams of costs and benefits over time, each defined in terms of constant prices by converting them into their present or current values. Discounting is critical for comparing investments in which there are different lags between the investments and the payoffs. A gain of one dollar in 15 years, for example, is worth only $0.47 now if the appropriate discount rate is 5% and only $0.22 if the appropriate discount rate is 10%.[5] The failure to discount for comparing events that happen at very different points in time can lead to quite misleading results (e.g., overstating considerably the present value of more distant future gains due to current human-resource investments in comparison with gains that will be realized with lesser lags). For simplicity, in what follows I refer to *marginal benefits* and *marginal costs* without always qualifying explicitly by the phrase *present discounted value*, but it should be kept in mind that making events that occur across time comparable is essential for analyzing investments in human resources (as well as other investments).

The marginal private benefits and costs reflect the objective (welfare, preference) function of the investor, the assets of the investor, the markets that the investor faces, and the policy regimes that the investor faces. The marginal private benefit curve depends,

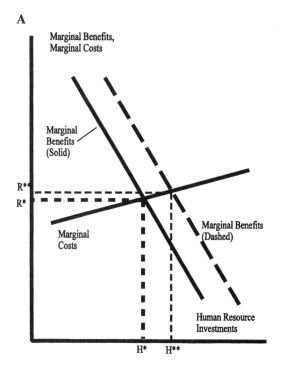

Figure 7.1A   Private Marginal Benefits and Private Marginal Costs of Human Resource Investments, with Higher (Dashed) and Lower (Solid) Marginal Benefits.

inter alia, on the expected private gains in productivities (economic or in terms of whatever productivities are valued by the investor) due to human-capital investments. These benefits depend on the marginal impact of the human-capital investment on productivities such as in relation (7.1) and on the marginal rewards that accrue to the investor because of that impact. The marginal private benefit curve is downward-sloping because of diminishing returns to human-capital investments (given genetic and other endowments that are determined in part by past decisions, including the mating decisions of an individual's parents that affect the individual's genetic endowments and aspects of the environment experienced earlier by the individual). The marginal private cost may increase with human-capital investments because of increasing marginal private costs of borrowing on financial markets or because of increasing marginal costs of time devoted to such investments rather than working.

The best human-capital investment for this individual is H^*, where the two curves intersect, with both the marginal private benefit and the marginal private cost equal to R^*. This illustrates that it is the marginal or additional benefits and costs that count, *not* the total benefits and costs. For higher human-resource investments than H^*, the marginal costs exceed the marginal benefits, so there is pressure to reduce the investments to the H^* level because that increases the gains over costs. For lower human-resource investments than H^*, the marginal costs are less than the marginal benefits, so further gains can be made by increasing investments to the H^* level. This focus on the marginal benefits and marginal costs is typical for economic analyses of maximizing decisions. Whatever the total costs and benefits, generally the benefits net of costs can be increased by moving to the point at which the marginal benefits equal the marginal costs, as illustrated above. The assumption is not that individuals always are involved in complicated optimizing marginal calculations but that there are pressures to behave as if they were because to do so increases the attainment of their objectives. This equilibrium human capital investment at H^* is associated with an equilibrium rate of return i^* that equates the present discounted value of expected marginal private benefits with the present discounted value of expected marginal private costs. By comparing this rate of return with those on other investments, the investor can decide whether this investment should be undertaken.

If the marginal private-benefit curve is higher for every level of human-capital investment as for the dashed line in Figure 7.1A, all else equal, the equilibrium human-capital investment (H^{**}) and the equilibrium marginal private benefit (R^{**}) both are greater. The marginal private-benefit curve may be higher at a point of time for one of two otherwise identical individuals except for the difference noted below because one individual (or whomever is investing in that individual)[6,7]

1. Has greater genetic endowments that are complementary with resources devoted to human capital investments;
2. Has lower discount rates so that the future benefits of human-capital investments have greater value at the time of the investment decision;
3. Is younger so that the post-investment period in which to reap the returns from the investment is longer;[8]
4. Has better health and a longer expected life due to complementary investments, so that the post-investment period in which that individual reaps the returns to the investment in human development is greater and therefore the expected returns greater;
5. Has human-capital investments options of higher quality (such as access to higher-quality public human-development programs or services) so that the marginal private benefits for a given level of private investments are higher and the equilibrium investments greater;[9]
6. Has greater marginal private benefits to a given level of such investments because of discrimination that favors that individual due to gender, race, language, family, village, or ethnic group;
7. Has returns to human-resources investments that are obtained more by the investor or the relevant decision maker (for example, if traditional gender roles dictate that individuals of one sex but not the other provide old-age support for their parents,

parental incentives may be greater to invest in individuals who are likely to provide such support);[10]

8. Has greater marginal private benefits to a given level of investment because of being in a more dynamic economy in which the returns to such investments are greater;

9. Has greater marginal private benefits to a given level of such investments because of greater externalities from the human capital investments of others in the same economy; or

10. Lives in a more stable economy so that the discount rate for future returns is lower (because risk is less) and thus the marginal private benefit of future returns greater.

If the marginal private cost is lower for every level of human-capital investment (see the dashed line in Figure 7.1B), all else equal, the equilibrium human-capital investment (H^{***}) is greater, with the marginal private benefit (R^{***}) lower at the higher investment level. The marginal private cost might be lower for numerous reasons. Compare two otherwise identical individuals at the same point of time except that one

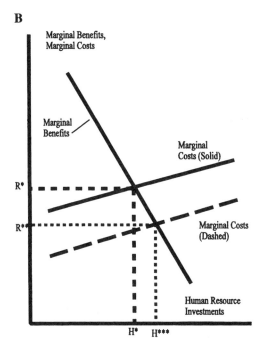

Figure 7.1B   Private Marginal Benefits and Private Marginal Costs of Human Resource Investments, with Higher (Solid) and Lower (Dashed) Marginal Costs.

individual (1) has lower private-cost access to human-development programs related to such investments because of closer proximity to such services or lesser user charges, (2) has fewer opportunity costs for time used for such investments (for example, such costs may have as an important component the costs of time, and such costs may vary among individuals due to differing labor market wages), (3) is from a family with greater access to credit (or less need for credit) for financing such investments because of greater wealth or status or better connections, or (4) is from a group that is favored for such investments because of discrimination or policies.

This maximization process leads to demands for human-development and other human-capital investments in individual *i* that depend on all relevant prices P, on all relevant resources R, on all the parameters of the relevant production functions (including those for the production of human resources), and on preferences:

$$H_i = H(P, R \mid \text{production parameter, preference parameters}). \tag{7.2}$$

The prices include all prices that enter into the investor's decision-making process, including the prices paid for human-development-related services, basic education, and other consumption and investment purposes and for transferring resources over time (that is, the interest rate) and for insuring against uncertainty. At the time that any human-resource investment decision is made, these prices include all past and current prices for these goods and services (perhaps embodied in current stocks of human capital), as well as expected future prices (including expected future returns to human-capital investments). These prices are not just monetary costs but are all costs, including time costs. The resources include all resources of the individual, family, educational institutions, and community that affect family decisions. These resources include human resources that reflect past investments and related decisions, financial resources, physical resources, genetic endowments, and general learning environments.

This simple framework systematizes five critical, commonsense points for investigating dimensions of the determinants and the effects of human-capital investments:

- The marginal benefits and marginal costs of human-capital investments in a particular individual differ depending on the point of view from which they are evaluated. (1) There may be externalities (effects on others that are not transferred through markets, such as the knowledge externalities mentioned below) or capital- and insurance-market imperfections so that the social returns differ from the private returns (see below), and (2) there may be a difference between who makes the investment decision (parents for children, children or other relatives for elderly adults) and the individuals in whom the investment is made that may result, for example, in gender (or birth-order) differentials in incentives for investments in individuals given traditional gender (birth-order) roles in old-age care for parents.

- Human-capital investments are *determined* by a number of actual and potential individual, family, community, market, and policy characteristics, only a subset of which are observed in social science data sets that are available to analyze human-development determinants and effects. To identify the impact of the observed characteristics on human-capital investments, it is important to control for the correlated unobserved characteristics. For example, children with higher-income parents may tend to have greater innate abilities of the types that increase economic success, may grow up in more supportive environments, and may attend higher-quality schools. If so, and if only family incomes and parental schooling are observed and if the children's abilities and the community and school characteristics are not observed in the data, then the impact of family background on such investments is likely to be overestimated with usual procedures.

- To identify the *impact* of human-capital investments, it also is important to control for individual, family, and community characteristics that determine the human-capital investments and also have direct effects on outcomes of interest. Otherwise, the estimated effect includes not only the impact of the human-capital investments but also the effects of individual, family, and community characteristics that directly affect the outcomes of interest and are correlated with the human-capital investment because they partly determine those investments. For example, if innate ability affects both investments in human development and wages directly due to the impact of ability on production in relation (7.1) (in addition to any indirect effect through human development) and if there is no control for innate ability in estimates of the impact of human development on wages, the estimated effects are likely to be biased because the representation of human development in the wage-production relation is partly proxying for innate ability.

- Empirically estimated determinants of and effects of human-development investments are for a given macroeconomic market, policy, societal, and regulatory environment. The actual returns may change substantially with changes in that environment, such as those associated with, for example, improving markets, opening up an economy more to international markets, eliminating regulations on migration, or lessening discrimination in labor markets. As a result, evaluation of human-development programs and other policies from historical data is difficult unless the stable parameters in underlying structural relations determining behavior (such as production functions or preferences) can be obtained in such analysis. Reduced-form relations such as the demand functions in (7.2) that combine production and preference parameter responses to current and expected future market and other changes are less likely to be stable given such changes, which has implications for evaluation of human-development-related policies.

- The impacts of changes in policies may be hard to predict by policymakers and outside analysts. If families face a policy change, they can adjust *all* of their behaviors in response, with cross-effects on other outcomes, not only on the outcome to which the policy is directed. Provision of subsidized mental health services, for example, effectively is an income subsidy to the family, which the family can divert in part at least to whatever use it wishes by cutting back on family funding for the same services, in addition to a price subsidy that makes the use of such services relatively cheaper.

What are the implications of such considerations for the concerns emphasized in the lifespan architecture literature and the related concepts of selection, compensation, and optimization that motivate this book? It is useful to consider, for example, investments in lifelong learning during the latter parts of adulthood and old age. The human-capital-investment approach suggests a number of reasons why the marginal benefits of such investments may be lower and the marginal costs of such investments higher than similar investments when the person is younger. The marginal benefits are likely to be lower because of shorter remaining expected healthy life time in which to gain the benefits of such investments and greater uncertainty regarding to what extent the benefits will be realized rather than cut short by debilitating illness or death. The marginal costs may be higher because of less plasticity and learning capacity. While there may be effects working in the opposite direction,[11] both of these effects are likely to be important in many cases and suggest that optimal human-resource investments occur largely when persons are younger than seems to be suggested by some of the literature covered elsewhere in this book (see Wellman, this volume; Salthouse, this volume).

Estimation of demands for human-capital investments in relation (7.2) that is sensitive to these considerations can be informative for addressing a number of relevant questions. For example, how responsive are family human-development decisions to the prices of resources or programs for human development? How important are incomplete markets, particularly for capital and insurance, in human-development decisions? Do imperfections in such markets mean that individuals from poorer backgrounds face relatively severe constraints on human development because their families have very limited resources for self-financing human-development investments and cannot readily finance them through capital markets? What role do information imperfections play in the family human-development decisions? Are potential family and individual investors in human development well informed about the potential returns to human development? How do these relations change as individuals age?

Estimation Issues in Ascertaining the Determinants of and the Impact of Investments in Human Resources

Estimation of the determinants of human development by family behaviors and of the impact of human development is central to understanding the magnitude of these effects. These concerns are central to this book because of the importance of empirical inference regarding what we know or what we think we know about human-capital investments and how they relate to lifespan architecture and related concepts. Therefore, this section considers different types of relations that might be informative based on the analytical framework presented above, some estimation problems, and, very briefly, some possible resolutions of these problems. Only by having some sensitivity to these estimation problems can good judgments be made to assess empirical studies regarding what we know and where there are lacunae in our knowledge. Before turning to this discussion, it is useful to emphasize that any empirical interpretations of causality depend (though too often implicitly rather than explicitly) on some underlying model (see Brandtstädter & Rothermund, this volume; Mittelstrass, this volume). It is not possible just to look at the data and see what they say about causal effects that determine human development, the impact of human development, or other behaviors of interest, though it is possible to show correlations. Therefore, to clarify what we really know about causality, it is desirable to be as explicit as possible about the assumptions regarding the underlying models of behavior.

Estimated Relations Related to Human Development   The frameworks presented above imply that for investigating the *determinants* of family behaviors related to human development, one can estimate (1) the underlying structural relations that determine human development (such as human-development production functions analogous to relation (7.1) with human development as the outcome and the production inputs into human development as inputs) and (2) demand relations for human development or for inputs used to produce human development (such as expressions that are analogous to relation (7.2)). The *impact* of these human resources can be evaluated by estimating (1) the underlying production functions in which human development is an input directly or indirectly (relation (7.1)) and (2) output "demand" relations (relation (7.2)), perhaps conditional on human development and on other production stocks at the start of the period of interest as well as on what is known about the distributions of variables the actual values of which will be revealed in the future.

Structural Relations—Production Functions: Structural relations are the basic underlying relations in the models of family and firm behaviors. The most commonly estimated structural relations are production functions. A linear approximation to a general production function of the type discussed above can be represented with firm output (Q_f) produced by two categories of variables relating to the ith worker in the fth firm (XI) and to the fth firm (XF) and by an explicit stochastic disturbance term (U_f).[12]

$$Q_f = a_{XI}XI + a_{XF}XF + U_f, \qquad\qquad (7.1A)$$

where the a's are parameters to be estimated that indicate the respective effects on Q_f of changing the respective inputs. The stochastic term captures random effects that are not correlated with any of the other predetermined right-side variables such as weather fluctuations or other chance events. While this production function is written for firms, there also are production functions that are analogous in form, which pose the same estimation problems for each of the outcomes affected by human development and for the production of the aspects of human development that depend on various inputs.

The distinction among four different subgroups of variables each for XI and XF is useful for discussion of estimation issues. The superscripts o and u refer to "observed in the data used" and "unobserved in the data used"; the superscript b refers to variables that are behaviorally determined within the model used; and the superscript p refers to variables that are predetermined within the model used. With these distinctions, the variable list in the general production function relation is XI^{ob}, XI^{ub}, XI^{op}, XI^{up}, XF^{ob}, XF^{ub}, XF^{op}, XF^{up}, U_f. If these were substituted into (7.1A), each would have its own coefficient a to indicate its impact on Q_f. The distinctions among these different variables are important because some of the most important and most pervasive estimation problems arise from unobserved variables or behaviorally determined variables. Of course, exactly into which categories various variables fall in a particular case depends on both the underlying model of behavior (which determines what is behaviorally- determined and what is predetermined within the model)[13] and on the data in the particular data set used (which determines what is observed and what is unobserved).

The parameters (a's) in the production function give the direct impact of the right-side variables—some of which may reflect directly policies—on Q_f. With good estimates of the appropriate production functions, the direct determinants of many outcomes determined by family behaviors and the direct impacts of many human-capital investments could be evaluated with considerable confidence. Such estimates can help to answer many of the questions raised above.

Reduced-Form "Demand" Relations: A second set of relations that can be estimated to explore the determinants of and the impact of family and firm behaviors and of policies related to human development are "demand" relations. These relations give some behavioral outcome as dependent on all predetermined (from the point of view of the entity—family, or whatever—making the decisions) prices and resources and on the parameters in the underlying production functions and preferences. The outcome may be the demand for some good or service (such as the family demand for human development or firm demand for trained workers) or may be the supply of some good or service (such as the supply of an individual's time for work or for learning), for which reason I put "demand" in parentheses in the start of this paragraph. These are the relations that most commonly are estimated. These demand functions in principle are derived explicitly from the constrained maximization behaviors of families (and of firms). As such, they incorporate all of the underlying structural (such as production function) parameters that are involved in that process. But all of the choice variables during the period of interest are substituted out, so the demand functions are not underlying structural relations such as production functions but are so-called reduced-form relations because the maximizing behavior that determines such variables has been combined and "reduced" to the relations that give the behavioral outcomes as a function of purely predetermined and expected prices and resources.[14]

On a general level, demand functions can be written with a vector of behavioral outcomes (Z) dependent on a vector of prices broadly defined (P) and a vector of resources (R)—with the relevant prices and resources depending for what entity is the demand function. If there are uncertainties regarding relevant future prices, policies, and shocks, then the characteristics known at the time of the decision of interest regarding the distributions of those outcomes should be included instead of their realized values. A linear approximation to the demand function for a family (or firm) facing prices PF and with resources RF and a vector of stochastic terms (V_f) is

$$Z_f = b_{PF}PF + b_{RF}RF + V_f, \tag{7.2A}$$

where the b's are the parameters to be estimated and indicate the impact of the variables for which they are coefficients on the demands for Z_f. The stochastic term in each relation includes all the effects of all the stochastic terms in all of the production activities in which the family is engaged (that is, all of the elements of the vector U_f), plus perhaps other chance events. Both prices and resources may be observed or unobserved in the data, so it is useful to indicate that distinction here as above in the discussion of production-function inputs. For example, years of formal schooling prior to the time period under consideration are resources that usually are observed in social science data sets, but genetic endowments are resources that are not likely to be observed in such data sets. There is one such demand relation (or one element in the vector Z_f) for every behavioral outcome of the family (and similarly for other entities), including all human-resource investments and all behavioral inputs that affect human-resource investments through production relations such as (7.1A). Each of these demand relations conceptually includes the same identical right-side predetermined variables, reflecting that there may be important cross-effects (for example, the nature of food markets may affect demand for mental-health services). That means that any predetermined variable that affects any one behavioral outcome may affect any or all other behavioral outcomes. Estimation of such demand relations could help answer some of the questions raised above, such as how the price of a certain type of human development input affects a whole set of behavioral decisions.

Estimation Problems in Attempting to Ascertain the Determinants of and the Impact of Human-Resource Investments   There are a number of possible problems in obtaining good estimates of the determinants of and the impact of human development. Therefore, what are presented as estimates of relations may be biased: the true determinants of human development and the true impact of human development are *not* revealed because of estimation problems. These estimation problems all share a common characteristic: the disturbance term in the relation actually estimated is *not* simply an element in U_f or V_f that is distributed independently of all the right-side variables in the relation being estimated but instead is correlated with right-side variables (for example, because it is a compound disturbance term that includes unobserved variables as well as U_f or V_f or because of the way that U_f and V_f are defined for the sample used in the estimates). In this section, some of these estimation problems are discussed very briefly to attempt to give some flavor of their impact in order to indicate the limitations in what we think we know about empirical realities relating to the determinants and the impact of human-resource investments. Interested readers are referred to standard econometric texts for extensive discussions of these and of other related estimation issues.

Measurement Error: Measurement error may contaminate any of the observed variables. Random measurement error occurs if what is observed is not the true human-development variable but the true variable plus a random error.[15] Random measurement error in the dependent variable merely adds to the stochastic disturbance term but does not bias the coefficient estimates of right-side variables. Therefore, random measurement in measures of an aspect of human development does not cause biases in the estimates of the determinants of that aspect of human development. Random measurement error in a right-side variable causes bias in the coefficient estimates of interest. Consider, for example, the case in which human development is a right-side variable that is posited to affect learning. Intuitively, because observed human development is a noisy measure of true human development, the true dependence of productivity on human development is masked, and the result is an underestimate of the human-development effect. The bias is greater the larger is the variance in the measurement error relative to the variance in the true value.

Omitted Variables: In both production-function estimates and demand-function estimates, there may be variables that should be included among the right-side variables but that are not observed and therefore not included. For the production-function estimates, for example, there may be unobserved inputs such as innate genetic endowments related to ability and personality traits. In terms of relation (7.1A) with the subcategories of variables, the basic estimation problem is that the observed right-side variables $(XI^{ob}, XI^{op}, XF^{ob}, XF^{op})$ may be correlated with the unobserved variables $(XI^{ub}, XI^{up}, XF^{ub}, XF^{up})$ that are included in the compound disturbance term with U_f. Therefore, the estimates of the impact of the observed variables include not only their true effects but also part of the effects of any correlated unobserved variables. As a result, standard estimates of their effects are likely to be biased, with the bias either up or down depending on the exact model and magnitudes. For the demand relations (7.2A), the compound disturbance term includes, in addition to V_f, the other unobserved variables (PF^u, RF^u). If any of the observed variables on the right side of relation (7.2A) are correlated with any of the unobserved variables, their coefficient estimates are biased because, in addition to their own effects, they are representing in part the effect(s) of the correlated unobserved variable(s). The sign and magnitude of omitted variable bias depends on the effect of the omitted variable(s) and on its correlation with included variables. If, for example, decisions determining years of schooling respond positively to innate ability and both years of schooling and ability have impact on some outcome in either a production function such as relation (7.1A) or a demand relation such as (7.2A) and if there is no control for ability, the estimated coefficient of years of schooling includes the effect of schooling plus the effect of ability adjusted for the extent to which ability and years of schooling are correlated.

Simultaneity: Simultaneity bias occurs when a variable that is determined in the current period within the model appears as a right-side variable in some other relation. For example, consider the production function in relation (7.1A) in which human development is one of the inputs, and assume that some dimensions of human development depend on current consumption and income of individuals. In this case, these aspects of human development (and any other right-side variable that is behaviorally determined within the period) are correlated with the disturbance term in this relation. This is the case because for the elements of human development that are affected by current consumption (such as current nutrition or health status), there is a demand function of the form of relation (7.2A). Included on the right side of that relation is a stochastic term (V_f) that includes the stochastic terms from all of the production-function relations in the model—including economic production that relates to income for the individual concerned. This results in a correlation between aspects of human development determined in the current period and the stochastic term in the production function that causes biases in the estimated impact of such aspects of human development on production. The sign and the magnitude of the bias depend on the exact structure of the model.

Selectivity: Selectivity bias may result if observations are available only for a selected subset of the sample (see also Nesselroade & Ghisletta, this volume). Such selectivity may occur for any of the relations (7.1A) or (7.2A) discussed above. For instance, suppose that tests of aspects of human development are administered to individuals in hospitals but that, of course, not all individuals of the eligible age range are hospitalized. If it were desirable to know the impact of hospital-program quality on these test outcomes, a function of the general form of relation (7.2A) could be estimated. But this relation can be estimated only for those individuals hospitalized because only for those individuals are there test scores. The problem is that this subsample is not randomly selected. The subsample selection procedure, with its systematic relation between the disturbance term in the true relation and hospital quality, creates a correlation between the disturbance term and hospital program quality for the subsample for which estimates of the desired relation can be made. As a result, if this relation is estimated using only this subsample, a biased estimate is obtained of the true relation between the test scores and hospital program qualities.

Possible Resolutions for Estimation Problems: The resolutions for these statistical problems are either (1) to obtain more and better data or (2) to use statistical methods to control for them. More and better data includes better measurements of variables that currently tend to be included in data sets, the addition of variables that currently tend not to be observed in data, twins data for controlling for endowments at the time of conception,[16] longitudinal data for following behaviors and their impacts over time, and data from experiments. Statistical methods include, for example, using instrumental variables to control for random measurement error and for simultaneity of behaviors, using fixed effects to control for unobserved factors, and incorporating into the estimated model the processes that generated the data and relevant subsamples. All of these resolutions have costs in terms of resources and assumptions. Important advances in our understanding have resulted from both better data and new statistical techniques, but space constraints preclude further discussion here.

Framework for Policy Choices Related to Human Development

Policies determine in important part the context in which individuals or families make decisions regarding human-resource investments and the extent to which the rest of society provides net positive (negative) resources for such investments for particular individuals and the prices that individuals face for such investments. Policies, thus, play an important role in what Baltes (1997) refers to as "culture," and policy changes can alter significantly the context in which individuals make human-resource investments. Standard economic rationale for policies include concerns about efficiency and productivity and about the distribution of resources among members of society.

Economic Efficiency: A situation is efficient if no one person could be made better off without making someone else worse off.[17] This refers to different individuals at the same point of time or at different points of time. Or, to make the statement in reverse, if there is inefficiency, everyone could be made better off with the same resources without making anyone worse off. It would seem from such statements that inefficiency, all else equal, is clearly not socially desirable. Inefficiency may arise from "market failures" such as externalities (effects of one unit that are external to that unit in ways that are not transferred through market prices), increasing returns to scale over the relevant output range (so that prices do not reflect the true marginal social costs), and public goods (in which case, the marginal cost of providing marginal benefits is zero, so pricing at marginal costs cannot provide revenues to cover total costs). Inefficiency also may arise from "policy failures" such as restrictions on prices (including wages) so that they do not reflect marginal costs and restrictions on entry and exit so that sellers or buyers can affect the prices that they face (and therefore have incentives to set prices different from marginal costs).

Distribution: Distribution is a major policy motive distinct from efficiency. A very efficient economy might have a very undesirable distribution of command over resources. Society well might want to ensure, for example, that everyone has basic education, employment skills, and human-development levels even at some cost in terms of efficiency and productivity (see also Mayer, this volume).

Choosing Among Policies　There are a number of reasons why private decisions relating to human-resource investments may not be efficient within a particular market and policy environment. Explicit examples are discussed below. There also are concerns about distribution—most commonly, the command over resources of the poorer members of society—that often have been among the motives for policies related to human development.

If all other markets in the economy are operating efficiently and there are differences between marginal private and social incentives in the human-capital investment market for human development so that private incentives are to invest at levels other than the efficient levels, policies that changed the human-capital investment to the socially efficient levels would increase efficiency.[18] But that still does not indicate what policies would be best to induce human-capital investments at desirable levels. There is a large range of possibilities, including governmental fiats and regulations, governmental provision of human-development services, price incentives in the market for human-capital investments, price incentives in other markets, and changing institutional arrangements in various markets.

Three important considerations should guide choices among alternative policy changes:

First, policies have costs—not only the direct costs of implementation and monitoring but also the distortionary costs introduced by policies that may encourage socially inefficient behavior. These include the distortionary costs of raising revenues to finance fiscal expenditures that are necessary for policy formulation and imlementation, which in some cases are estimated to be considerable (e.g., Devarajan, Squire, & Suthiwart-Narueput, 1997). In fact, the costs may be sufficiently large that it is not desirable to attempt to offset some market failures by policies. But if it is desirable to do so, there is a case generally for making policy changes that are directed as specifically as possible to the distortion of concern (or as high as possible in a policy hierarchy defined by increasing distortion costs) because that lessens the distortion costs introduced by the policy. The less focused are policies, the more widespread and more substantial are likely to be the distortion costs of the policies themselves, in addition to any distortion costs from raising revenues to finance the policies.

Second, there are tremendous information problems regarding exactly what effects policies have, particularly in a rapidly changing world. This is an argument in favor of policies that are as transparent as possible, which probably generally means higher in the policy hierarchy with regard to distortion costs because more direct policies are likely to be more transparent. The information problems further often are an argument for price policies (taxes or subsidies) because if there are shifts in the underlying relations, they are likely to be more visible in a more timely fashion if they have impact on governmental resources than if they only change the distortions faced by private entities, as tends to happen with quantitative policies. Furthermore, there is a strong argument for society, through governments, to subsidize the collection and provision of more information about human development more generally because information is not likely to be provided optimally otherwise by private providers. Information has "public-goods" characteristics in the technical sense of that term so that the marginal cost of providing more information is near zero and possibly declining; as a result, private providers cannot cover their costs of provision except by restricting the quantities provided and charging a price above the low marginal social costs.[19]

Third, as noted above, distribution is a concern separate from efficiency. Moreover, there well may be tradeoffs between policies that increase efficiency and distributional ends. If increasing human development for the persons for whom the rates of return in terms of productivity is highest is efficient, and if there are positive complementarities between aspects of human development and income-generating capacity as is often claimed, then there is a tradeoff between increasing human development for persons for whom the productivity effects are greatest and increasing human development for the persons who are poorest.[20] Society might have the objective of assuring that everyone have basic access to human-development resources, as noted at the start of this section. But presumably it is desirable to ensure that everyone has this basic access at as little cost in terms of productivity as possible. Therefore, rather than ignoring efficiency considerations in pursuit of distributional goals, it is desirable to choose policies as high as possible in the efficiency policy hierarchy and still ensure that the basic access targets are met.

Specific Examples of Possible Inefficiencies in Human-Resource-Related Markets, Empirical Evidence, and Policy Options   Most readers are likely to understand intuitively what are distributional motives for policies, such as ensuring that every member of society has access to basic services. But intuitions are likely to be less developed with regard to the efficiency motive, so it is useful to consider some explicit respects in which human-development service-related markets might be inefficient in the absence of policy changes.

The private incentives for investments in human resources are largely those that are given by markets that individual units—families and firms—engage in (though there also may be some important incentives other than market incentives, such as those within units such as family or firms that could lead to inefficiency).[21] Under standard assumptions regarding production technologies, if prices are "right" in the sense that they reflect the true social marginal benefits and costs, an entity (family, family farm, family enterprise, factory, trading firm, or whatever) that is maximizing its own revenue net of costs chooses the efficient combination of inputs for each product, efficient quantities and qualities of all inputs, and efficient quantities and qualities of all outputs. Such entities behave efficiently by following the marginal conditions discussed above, given that from their individual perspectives prices are fixed by markets. Likewise, if prices are right in the above sense, families that maximize their objective functions by satisfying the marginal condition that marginal welfare for the last dollar (peso or whatever) spent on all goods is the same, choose efficient consumption and investment bundles. Inefficiencies thus usually are deemed to reflect "market failures" in the sense that market prices fail to incorporate all social marginal benefits and costs or "policy failures" if the reasons that prices do not reflect social marginal benefits lies not in production technicalities but in policies.

Figure 7.1 can be reinterpreted to consider the question of whether investments in human capital are efficient (under the assumption that all other allocations are efficient). If the private incentives for such investments are the same as the social incentives, the solid curves in Figure 7.1A represent both the marginal private and the marginal social incentives and H^* is the privately optimal and the socially optimal (efficient) level of human-capital investment. In this case, the private and the social rates of return to this investment are the same. Also in this case, even if this rate of return is quite high, there is no efficiency reason for public resources to be devoted to human development. Private behaviors result in just the right investments from a social perspective regarding efficiency.

Now consider what happens if the private and social incentives differ for human-capital investments, first with respect to the marginal benefits and then with respect to the marginal costs. Note that in each of these cases the social rates of return for this investment differ from the private rates of return, which suggests an efficiency argument for a policy change.

Let the dashed line in Figure 7.1A represent the marginal social benefits for human-capital investments that are drawn to be greater than the marginal private benefits.[22] In this case, the private incentives are to invest in H^*, which is less than the socially optimal (efficient) level of human-capital investment H^{**}. Therefore, there is an efficiency argument to consider policies to induce or to require private investments of H^{**} instead of H^*. Why might marginal social benefits exceed marginal private benefits for human-capital investments? Among the most frequent answers to this question are some that primarily reflect market failures (e.g., examples 1 to 5 below) and others that reflect policy failures (e.g., example 6 below):

1. Private investors underestimate the true private and therefore social returns from such investments.
2. More investment in human development, in addition to the direct eventual impact on the individual's own benefits, may increase the productivity of others with whom the individual interacts through effects that are spread other than through markets (and thus are externalities as defined above and are not reflected in the individual's or firm's investment returns).
3. Individuals with higher than average unobserved motivation and unobserved abilities, given their characteristics that will be observed by potential employers, are not able to self-finance such human-capital investments because they can not borrow for such investments.
4. Uncertainty in combination with families wanting to avoid risk and imperfect or costly insurance options means that the private incentives are to underinvest in human capital from a social point of view because on the social (aggregate) level such risks are reduced by pooling them across members of society.

5. There are social gains beyond the private gains to human-capital investments because basic human resources reduce the probabilities of illnesses and unemployment, both of which have social benefits beyond the distributional ones through reducing respectively the stress on public-health systems and the probability of illegal activities.

6. Policies limit price flexibility (such as administratively set prices for human-development-related services), labor-market flexibility (such as mandatory termination payments, health insurance, and pensions tied to a particular employer), and human-development programs (such as limiting subsidies to public human-development programs) that distort the incentives for human development.

Now let the dashed line in Figure 7.1B represent the marginal social costs for human-capital investments that are drawn to be less than the marginal private costs.[23] In this case, the private incentives are to invest in H^*, which is less than the socially optimal (efficient) level of human-capital investment H^{***}. Therefore, there is an efficiency argument to consider policies to induce or to require private investments of H^{***} instead of H^*. Why might marginal social costs be less than marginal private costs for human-capital investments? Among the most frequent answers to this question, one points primarily to a market failure, and one points primarily to a policy failure: (1) there are capital- and insurance-market imperfections, more so for human-capital investments than other investments (in part because human capital is not recognized as collateral), so that the marginal private costs for such investments exceed the true marginal social costs, particularly for those from poorer families who cannot relatively easily self-finance and self-insure such investments; (2) the sectors that provide services related to human-capital investments, such as health systems and schools, produce inefficiently in part because they are heavily regulated by governments and organized not to be very responsive to scarcities and to clients' demands.

How Does the Economic Approach to Human Development Relate to the Considerations in Part I of this Book?

The considerations in Part I of this book relate to the essence of the architecture of lifespan development as synthesized, for example, by Baltes (1997). This "architecture" or reputedly robust frame of constraints, "contains three elements: First, evolution neglected old age, and therefore, biological potential wanes with age. Second, for development to extend into progressively later portions of the life span, more and more culture is required. Third, because of the age-linked weakening of biological potential, the efficiency of culture decreases with age" (p. 377). Based on this frame of reference, a general metatheory of adaptive human development is proposed—selective optimization with compensation (SOC). These considerations raise three basic questions, to which I turn in this section.[24]

How do the Elements of the Architecture of Lifespan Development and the SOC Concepts Relate to the Standard Economic Approach to Lifespan Human-Development Processes and Resource Management?

The standard economic approach to lifespan human-development processes and re-source management assumes sequential optimization over the life cycle, subject to a number of market, societal (policy), and resource constraints. This approach implies that, all else equal, the more private resources are devoted to human-resource invest-ments, then the (1) the greater the marginal private gains from those investments, (2) the lower are the marginal private costs of those investments, (3) the less that future gains are discounted to the present to obtain their present discounted value, (4) the more that an individual already has complementary assets (including genetic endowments and those from previous human-resource investments), and (5) the less uncertainty there is about future gains (assuming risk aversion). The application of this framework to human-resource investments that start to have returns shortly after the investment—which includes many human-resource investments such as schooling and learning on the job—is likely to lead to larger investments in the earlier parts of the life cycle. The economic literature has tended to focus on such human-resource investments. But the logic of this framework also suggests that if there are investments that have returns that are, for example, age-dependent and appear only late in the life cycle, then it is likely to be optimal to delay the investments until late in the life cycle.

This approach seems on a general level to be quite related to selective optimiza-tion with compensation. Human-resource investments have costs as well as benefits. Resource-management decisions are made sequentially, as if individuals are optimizing the expected attainment of their objectives subject to the constraints that they face. This results in selection of different human-resource investment strategies depending on the particular constraints that an individual, or whoever is making the human-resource investment in that individual, faces at that time. These constraints are likely to differ across individuals and, for each individual, over the life cycle. Depending on the ex-tent of substitution possible in the production of whatever is of interest in the relevant objective function and the nature of markets for the inputs into such production, it may be optimal to compensate for factors in short supply through using other inputs.

The second two elements of the architecture of lifespan development—that more and more culture (by which I mean social resources) are required to maintain given levels of functioning with greater aging and that the effectiveness of those resources declines on average with aging—also is consistent with standard economic approaches to human-resource investments and depreciation of capital stocks, given fixed genetic endowments that include some components that are likely to manifest themselves only later in the life cycle.

The standard economic approach to empirical analysis of lifespan human-develop-ment processes and resource management has focused on the earlier part of the life cycle, but with aging populations it has shifted increasingly toward analysis of older individuals. This shift also seems parallel to some of the concerns that are discussed in Part I of this book. While most empirical economic analysis proceeds with no attention to the possible important role of genetic endowments, there is a substantial literature that does explore the role of genetic and other unobserved factors and that tends to claim that these roles are important and that controlling for them affects our understanding of observed factors—all of which seems consistent with the emphasis in Part I of this book.

The standard economic approach to societal (cultural) support for human development focuses on two basic policy motivations and implies that, all else equal, more social resources should be devoted to human-resource investments in an individual the more such resource transfers (1) increase efficiency or (2) facilitate obtaining society's distributional goals. On a general level, again, this recognition of the possible important role of the broader society in individual human development seems to resonate with some of the major themes in Part I above (see also Mayer, this volume).

Do the Elements of the Architecture of Lifespan Development and the SOC Concepts Raise Questions Regarding the Formulation of the Standard Economic Approach to Lifespan Human-Development Processes and Resource Management?

The first element in the architecture—that "evolution neglected old age"—raises questions about (1) the interactions of genetic endowments with economic allocations to human-resource development, (2) the stability over time of the impact of genetic endowments, and (3) the probably increased uncertainty regarding the impact of genetic endowments in the latter stage of the lifespan. As noted, economic analysis of human-resource investments has focused on earlier life-cycle stages. But the shifting age structure of human populations has shifted attention increasingly to economic issues related to resources allocated to aging.

These questions have important implications for empirical analysis as conducted by economists and other social scientists. First of all, if economists and other social scientists are attempting to estimate structural processes such as in relation (7.1), how human development over the life cycle enters into such processes needs to be included in the analysis, or there may be misinterpretations of the effects of variables such as schooling on which there has been considerable attention. But typically no or very little attention has been paid to many aspects of human development in empirical economic analysis. Second, while there is an increasing tendency for social scientists to be concerned with the impact of unobserved genetic (and other) endowments on empirical estimates, there has been little effort to deal with the difficult estimation problems that are raised if those endowments interact with observed variables or if their impact changes over the life cycle. Yet those are precisely the type of issues that are raised for empirical work by the first element of the lifespan architecture as summarized above based on Baltes (1997). Third, for human development to be incorporated into economic and other social-science analysis, data sets must include good measures of the important aspects of human development. But often, even if they have some coverage, it is limited and partial.

The major themes of Part I of this book also may have important implications for public policy regarding dealing with information imperfections and insurance. In particular, the increasing uncertainties for every larger shares of aging populations and the possibilities of technological developments to compensate in part for developments among the aging raise challenges for deciding on desirable public-resource allocations.

Does the Standard Economic Approach to Lifespan Human Development Raise Questions about Usefully Modifying Elements of the Architecture of Lifespan Development and the SOC Concepts?

The economic approach to optimization emphasizes that optimization, selection (at least in terms of behavioral choices) and compensation are not separate concerns. To the contrary, optimization requires selective choices and possibly compensation. This suggests that the three elements of the metatheory described at least in Baltes (1997) are not independent in any real sense but are integrated aspects of a unified approach to private optimization.[25]

The economics approach also provides insight into the nuances of optimization and when behavioral selection and compensation occur. In particular, it emphasizes the nature of the underlying production technology (such as, to what extent is substitution possible) and market and policy options, in addition to the nature of differing implications of genetic endowments over the life cycle.

The economic approach also raises questions as to whether the lifespan human-development literature indeed is considering optimization. The lifespan human-development literature tends to emphasize balancing off costs versus benefits, which is in the spirit of optimization. But conceptually, at least given smooth production technologies with diminishing returns, optimization involves equating *marginal* benefits and *marginal* costs, *not* total or average benefits and costs. Indeed, comparing total benefits and costs as seems to be suggested in the lifespan development literature in general does *not* lead to optimization.[25]

The economic literature also addresses more directly the decision of how private decisions might be made to optimize at different points in the life cycle by addressing the timing question directly through discounting the future benefits and costs (see also Gigerenzer, this volume). While the literature covered in Part I of the book is very cognizant of differences over the lifespan (in fact, that is one of its central tenets) and it also emphasizes that there are costs to different human-development strategies, it does not seem to provide guidance regarding how even in principle (even if difficult in fact) benefits and costs at different points in time (different stages of the life cycle) can be compared usefully.

The economic approach moreover emphasizes what determines individual behaviors that may affect human-resource investments or that may be affected by the state of human development and how such behaviors are affected by production technologies, markets, policies, and resources of the individual. This appears to be a broader view of what determines human behaviors in which important aspects of institutions such as markets and policy environments are incorporated explicitly into the analytical framework. This broader view may be essential for confident empirical inferences about the determinants of and the impact of human-resource investments that are not contaminated by missing variable biases, simultaneity biases, statistical selectivity, and other estimation problems.

Another important aspect of the economic approach to empirical estimates pertains to obtaining unbiased parameters estimates by controlling for problems such as measurement error, omitted variable bias, simultaneity, and selectivity (see also Nesselroade and Ghisletta, this volume). This approach recognizes that there are likely to be many estimation problems using behavioral data or even most experimental data and that these can be understood better and controlled better by incorporating into the analysis the behaviors that generated the data—such as the determinants of who is in a sample being analyzed.

With regard to empirical work, finally, there seems to be symmetry in two important respects. First, the empirical psychological literature often has ignored what economists would think of as important economic factors, such as prices—just as economists often have ignored important aspects of human development as seen by psychologists. Second, when psychologists do consider economic factors, they appear very partial and crude to economists—just as the reverse is true for psychological indicators.

The economic approach to policy motivations provides guidance about how society's policies, including the transfer of resources among individuals, should evolve in light of changing age distributions and, at least initially, increasing uncertainty associated with the impact of genetic endowments on aging populations. This contrasts with the second element of the architecture—that more and more resources are "required" by proving a framework to assess when society should and should not provide such resources. To what extent should society provide more support for aging individuals because of efficiency concerns and distributional concerns?[27] What means of providing such support are likely to be most effective? Efforts to reduce that uncertainty through gathering information and to improve prospects for aging through research directed at technological change, moreover, can be viewed as investment decisions just as are the human-resource investment decisions. But for these activities, there are thought to be substantial market failures because they are public goods (or near public goods) in the sense that the marginal costs of developing new information or new technology for one additional user is virtually zero. Therefore, private optimizing behavior is likely to restrict supply in order to be able to charge prices that cover costs, with the result that marginal private costs of users is likely to exceed the social marginal costs—thus implying an efficiency argument for use of social resources for the production of new information and new technology. The economics policy paradigm is likely to be helpful in elucidating under what conditions, to what extent, and in what form are such social (cultural) subsidies likely to be justified.

Thus, the economic approach to human-resource development raises some fundamental questions for the architecture of lifespan development and the SOC concepts. Is there a useful sense in which the SOC concepts are independent, or are they all really just integrated aspects of optimization? What are the roles of production technologies, markets, and policy options in determining when behavioral selection and compensation occur? Is the lifespan human-development literature really considering optimization, though it tends to ignore, or at least underplay, the importance of marginal decisions? How can the lifespan development literature incorporate the importance of different timing of benefits and costs? How can markets and institutions be incorporated into the analytical framework? How can confident empirical inferences be made regarding key relationships for the lifespan development literature? What are the efficiency (in the economics sense) and distributional bases for claims regarding policies and what culture should provide? Such questions pose serious challenges for the literature on the architecture of lifespan development and the SOC concepts.

Acknowledgment

This research was supported in part with funds from NIA R01 AG11725-01A1 and NSF SBR95-11955. The author thanks two anonymous referees and the editors for useful comments on earlier drafts, but only he is responsible for the contents of this chapter.

Notes

1. As noted in the introduction, Becker (1975, 1993), Mincer (1974), and Schultz (1961, 1963) generally are considered to have been seminal in emphasizing human-resource investments within economic frameworks.
2. Monetary prices often are used for this purpose. Some monetary prices may be easy to observe, such as wages. Others may be difficult to impute, such as the price of happiness. For comparisons over time or space, constant prices for identical goods and services must be used to avoid confounding price differences with quantity differences. For comparisons over time, further, the timing must be incorporated into the analysis by using present discounted values, which are discussed in the next section.
3. Models have been proposed by economists for how families allocate resources across generations (e.g., Becker, 1991, 1993; Behrman, Pollak, & Taubman, 1982, 1995) and among family members (e.g., Chiappori, 1988, 1992; Lundberg & Pollak, 1993; Manser & Brown, 1980; McElroy & Horney, 1981).
4. The investor may vary depending on the particular situation and the life-cycle stage of the individual in whom the investment is made. In some cases, for example, the individual may be the investor, but in other cases it may be a family. In still other cases, there may be implicit or explicit bargaining among family members—between spouses or between children and their parents—regarding investments in human resources. If there is such bargaining, the fall-back or "threat point" of the individuals involved may be critical because their bargaining power may depend on what their options are if they opt out of

the family. Space precludes developing the implications of these bargaining possibilities in this chapter, but see Behrman (1997), Haddad, Hoddinott, and Alderman (1996), and Lundberg and Pollak (1996) and the references therein for more extensive discussion. To avoid awkward terminology in the text of this chapter, I refer to the investor as the family of the individual, but I try to be clear when it makes a difference who the investor is.

5. If the interest rate is r per year, the present discounted value of a dollar received next year is $1/(1 + r)$ dollars because if one had that much currently, one could obtain an interest payment at rate r at the end of the year and have 1 dollar next year. More generally, the present discounted value of a dollar received or paid in n years is $1/(1 + r)n$.

6. For the last three of these comparisons, the otherwise identical individuals would have to live in different economies or at different times. Some of these examples, both on the marginal benefit and the marginal cost side, depend on their being imperfect capital and insurance markets. For example, if insurance markets are perfect and insurance is costless, risk does not affect families differentially. But it is widely perceived that capital and insurance markets for human-resource investments are quite imperfect.

7. Some of these examples, both on the marginal benefit and the marginal cost side, depend on their being imperfect capital and insurance markets. For example, if insurance markets are perfect and insurance is costless, risk does not affect families differentially. But it is widely perceived that capital and insurance markets for human resource investments are quite imperfect.

8. For this reason, investments in schooling and training tend to be made relatively early in the life cycle. The economics literature has tended to focus on such investments. But investments also have costs, so if certain investments do not have returns until later in the life cycle, there also are incentives to put off these investments (and their costs) into the future closer to the time at which the returns might be realized.

9. If the investor must pay for greater human-resource-service-related quality, however, investment does not necessarily increase with a higher-quality option. What happens to the equilibrium investment depends on where the marginal private-cost curve for the higher-quality option is in addition to the location of the marginal private-benefit curve.

10. This tendency may be offset if, for example, human capital substitutes sufficiently for financial and physical transfers in marriage markets (e.g., Rao, 1993: Behrman, Foster, Rosenzweig, & Vashishtha, 1999).

11. An example of an effect that may work in the opposite direction is the impact of capital-market imperfections, which are thought widely to limit human-resource investments. Such contraints are likely to be particularly severe when individuals are younger, before they have accumulated many resources. Once they have accumulated resources, they can more easily self-finance human-resource investments even if capital markets do not permit financing such investments. Of course, as they grow older still, this effect may be reduced or reversed because they may deplete their resources through dissavings to finance consumption and medical expenditures.

12. I use linear approximations in this section because they are the simplest forms, but they still permit characterization of various estimation issues. Long-linear forms in which all of the variables are replaced by the logarithms of their values (which implies interactions among all the right-side variables) are identical in representation once the variables are redefined. In empirical studies, linear and log-linear specifications are very common, but other functional forms also are used. For other functional forms, the essence of the estimation issues is the same. If the functional form that is used is not a good approximation to the true functional form, there is misspecification error that is akin to omitted variable bias discussed below (with the unobserved variable being the variable that would have to be added to transform the assumed specification to the true functional form).

13. For example, all community characteristics usually are assumed to be predetermined. But families, individuals, and firms can change community characteristics by migrating, which is incorporated into some modeling (e.g., Rosenzweig & Wolpin, 1988).

14. In some empirical studies, the underlying structural parameters can be identified from estimation of the demand relations. In most cases, however, demand functions are just posited to result from constrained

maximization, and the underlying structural parameters are not identified in the estimates, though the demand parameters still are some combinations of these parameters. In such cases, demand functions permit the estimation of the total effects of predetermined variables on the behavioral variables of concern, but not estimation of the exact mechanisms through which preferences and technical production functions affect the behavioral outcomes. As noted above, this means that demand-function parameters may be unstable if there are changes in markets or policies or expectations.

15. Random measurement error is what usually is emphasized and is what I discuss here. Measurement error also may be systematically related to the true variable, with implications that depend on the nature of the systematic relation.

16. While economists—as have a number of psychologists—have made some use of twins data to esti-mate models of heritability, the primary use as been to use monozygotic twins to control for genetic endowments at conception (dating back at least to Behrman & Taubman, 1976, which is elaborated in Behrman, Hrubec, Taubman, & Wales, 1980, but with a number of more recent visible studies, including Ashenfelter & Krueger, 1994, and Behrman, Rosenzweig, & Taubman, 1994). Some use also has been made of combined monozygotic and dizygotic twins to identify whether families reinforce or compensate for genetic endowment differentials in their children and to identify whether marriage market sorting is positive or negative on unobserved characteristics relating to earnings in labor markets (e.g., Behrman, Rosenzweig, & Taubman, 1994).

17. Note that this is not the same as engineering or scientific efficiency. An engine that is very efficient in the engineering sense, for example, may be very inefficient economically because it uses inputs that have better uses elsewhere.

18. If all other markets in the economy are *not* operating efficiently, policies that narrow the differences between private and social marginal incentives in the human-capital investment market or in some segment of that market do not necessarily increase efficiency and productivity. And clearly in the real world there are many market failures, so some distortions may be counterbalancing others. But in the absence of specific information to the contrary (such as on the existence of two counterbalancing distortions), a safe operating presumption is that lessening any one distortion between social and private incentives is likely to increase efficiency.

19. The relevant information includes *not* only information about the functioning of human-resource markets and possible market failures but also serious evaluations of governmental policies that are related to human development and possible policy failures. Policies are the result of behaviors and are subject to the estimation problems that are discussed above.

20. The available studies on the positive relations between productivity (or wage) gains and human-development and education interactions, however, may overstate the causal effect because of the failure to control for the selectivity of human development in the presence of important unobserved (by analysts) attributes such as ability and motivation.

21. Udry (1996) provides a recent empirical study of inefficiencies within African families with regard to the allocation of productive resources, including labor time, between men and women. I review other such studies in Behrman (1999).

22. The marginal social benefits also could be lower than the marginal private benefits, in which case the marginal social-benefits curve would be below the marginal private-benefits curve, and policies to attain efficiency would have to reduce the private incentives to the social levels. The basic analysis would be the same, but with the opposite sign on the differences between the marginal private and social benefits and therefore on the appropriate policies. To keep the presentation as simple as possible in the text, I consider only the case in which the marginal social benefits exceed the marginal private benefits, which is the case usually emphasized in the literature on human resources.

23. The marginal social costs also could be higher than the marginal private costs, so a comment parallel to that in the previous note also applies here.

24. But first I state the obvious caveat that what I can say about the considerations in Part I depends on my understanding of them, which probably is limited. One of the goals of this book is to encourage

interdisciplinary interaction on these topics in hopes that it will lead to fruitful new understandings. And such interdisciplinary interactions may lead to new understandings through clarification of errors that occur when a person from another discipline attempts to use and comment on concepts in a particular discipline, as well as through insights that are gained from correct cross-disciplinary understanding. So with this caveat, I proceed.

25. This critique is *not* weakened, as suggested by one referee, by the realization that because of information imperfections and transaction costs individuals may "satisfize" through some pragmatic algorithm such as choosing first one category out of all possibilities and then choosing within that category. Even with such sequential algorithms that lead to a series of decisions rather than one globally optimal decision, at each decision juncture optimizing (in the sense used by economists) subject to the information and transaction costs determines selection and compensation, they are not separate actions.

    The editors have suggested to me that, as elaborated in Baltes, Lindenberger, and Staudinger (1998), optimization is used in two ways in SOC theory: (1) as a class of psychological processes that aim at improving performance in a domain in the absence of loss, which, as such, is independent of, and distinguishable from, selection and compensation, and (2) as the joint outcome of selection, optimization as just defined, and compensation, which in SOC theory generally is called successful development. The latter appears to be closely related to the constrained optimization on which attention is focused in economics. But despite this clarification from the editors, it remains unclear to me what the value of unconstrained optimization (if that is what "absence of loss" means) is for guiding understanding of behaviors.

26. There is some ambiguity in the SOC theory on this point. Baltes, Lindenberger, and Staudinger (1998), for example, stress the need to be locally adaptive and optimize sequentially given the options available to an individual at each point in time and space. In the limit as this process reduces to a sequence of very small decisions, it approaches using the marginal calculus to make optimal decisions. But the presentation of SOC theory still generally appears to be in terms of total, not marginal, costs and benefits.

27. The notion of efficiency as used by economists, moreover, is different that the use of the term *efficiency* in the above summary of the second element in the lifespan architecture. In that summary, this term is used to refer to how effective or productive societal and cultural resources are, and the claim is made that they decline with age. The important point here is not terminology, which may be idiosyncratic across academic disciplines. The important point is that the marginal productivity of using social and cultural resources indeed may decline with age but that that possibility in itself does not say anything about whether resources devoted to aging individuals are used efficiently in the economics sense defined above. What happens to efficiency in the way that economists use the term would seem to be the more interesting question regarding how society wants to use its resources and to what extent is it desirable to provide subsidies from society as a whole to aging persons.

References

Ashenfelter, O., & Krueger, A. (1994). Estimates of the economic return to schooling from a new sample of twins. *American Economic Review, 84*, 1157–1174.

Baltes, P. B. (1997). On the incomplete architecture of human ontogeny: Selection, optimization, and compensation as foundation of development theory. *American Psychologist, 32*, 366–380.

Baltes, P. B., Lindenberger, U., & Staudinger, U. M. (1998). Life-span theory in developmental psychology. In R. M. Lerner (Ed.), *Handbook of child psychology*, Vol. 1, *Theoretical Models of Human Development* (5th ed., pp. 1029–1143). New York: Wiley.

Becker, G. S. (1967). *Human capital and the personal distribution of income: An analytical approach.* Ann Arbor: University of Michigan, Woytinsky Lecture. Republished in G. S. Becker, *Human capital* (2nd ed., pp. 94–117). (New York: NBER, 1975).

Becker, G. S. (1975). *Human capital* (2nd ed.). New York: National Bureau of Economic Research.

Becker, G. S. (1991). *A treatise on the family* (2nd ed.). Cambridge, MA: Harvard University Press.

Becker, G. S. (1993). Nobel lecture: The economic way of looking at behavior. *Journal of Political Economy, 101*, 385–409.

Behrman, J. R. (1997). Intrahousehold distribution and the family. In M. R. Rosenzweig & O. Stark (Eds.), *Handbook of population and family economics* (pp. 107–168). Amsterdam: North-Holland.

Behrman, J. R. (1999). Labor markets in developing countries. In O. Ashenfelter & D. Card (Eds.), *Handbook of labor economics* (Vol. 3, pp. 2859–2939). Amsterdam: North-Holland.

Behrman, J. R., Foster, A., Rosenzweig, M. R., & Vashishtha, P. (1999). Women's schooling, home teaching, and economic growth. *Journal of Political Economy, 107*, 682–714.

Behrman, J. R., Hrubec, Z., Taubman, P., & Wales, T. J. (1980). *Socioeconomic success: A study of the effects of genetic endowments, family environment, and schooling*. Amsterdam: North-Holland.

Behrman, J. R., Pollak, R. A., & Taubman, P. (1982). Parental preferences and provision for progeny. *Journal of Political Economy, 90*, 52–73.

Behrman, J. R., Pollak, R. A., & Taubman, P. (1995). The wealth model: Efficiency in education and equity in the family. In J. R. Behrman, R. A. Pollak, & P. Taubman (Eds.), *From parent to child: Intrahousehold allocations and intergenerational relations in the United States*. Chicago: University of Chicago Press.

Behrman, J. R., Rosenzweig, M. R., & Taubman, P. (1994). Endowments and the allocation of schooling in the family and in the marriage market: The twins experiment. *Journal of Political Economy, 102*, 1131–1174.

Behrman, J. R., & Taubman, P. (1976). Intergenerational transmission of income and wealth. *American Economic Review, 66*, 436–440.

Chiappori, P.-A. (1988). Rational household labor supply. *Econometrica, 56*, 63–89.

Chiappori, P.-A. (1992). Collective labor supply and welfare. *Journal of Political Economy, 100*, 437–467.

Devarajan, S., Squire L., & Suthiwart-Narueput, S. (1997). Beyond rate of return: Reorienting project appraisal. *World Bank Research Observer, 12*, 35–46.

Haddad, L., Hoddinott, J., & Alderman, H. (Eds.). (1996). *Intrahousehold resource allocation: Methods, models, and policy*. Baltimore, MD: Johns Hopkins University Press for the International Food Policy Research Institute.

Lundberg, S., & Pollak, R. A. (1993). Separate spheres bargaining and the marriage market. *Journal of Political Economy, 6*, 988–1010.

Lundberg, S., & Pollak, R. A. (1996). Bargaining and distribution in marriage. *Journal of Economic Perspectives, 10*, 139–158.

Manser, M., & Brown, M. (1980). Marriage and household decision-making: A bargaining analysis. *International Economic Review, 21*, 31–44.

McElroy, M. B., & Horney, M. J. (1981). Nash-bargained household decisions: Toward a generalization of the theory of demand. *International Economic Review, 22*, 333–347.

Mincer, J. B. (1974). *Schooling, experience, and earnings*. New York: National Bureau of Economic Research.

Rao, V. (1993). The rising price of husbands: A hedonic analysis of dowry increases in rural India. *Journal of Political Economy, 101*, 666–677.

Rosenzweig, M. R., & Wolpin, K. J. (1986). Evaluating the effects of optimally distributed public programs. *American Economic Review, 76*, 470–487.

Rosenzweig, M. R., & Wolpin, K. J. (1988). Migration selectivity and the effects of public programs. *Journal of Public Economics, 37*, 265–289.

Schultz, T. W. (1961). Investment in human capital. *American Economic Review, 51*, 1–17.

Schultz, T. W. (1963). *The economic value of education*. New York: Columbia University Press.

Udry, C. (1996). Gender, agricultural production and the theory of the household. *Journal of Political Economy, 104*, 1010–1046.

III
A Lifespan View of Self
and Personality

8 Completing the Psychobiological Architecture of Human Personality Development: Temperament, Character, and Coherence

C. Robert Cloninger

Washington University School of Medicine, St. Louis, MO, U.S.A.

Abstract

Three models of personality and its development are described in terms of their psychobiological mechanisms. Personality is the organization within the individual of the psychobiological processes by which we adapt to experience. Personality as temperament involves individual differences in heritable traits that influence the salience of stimuli to which we attend selectively. Temperament is superseded by a model of self that includes temperament and character. The organization of self is described by three character dimensions, which correspond to executive, legislative, and judicial functions. The development of these higher cortical functions is experience-dependent and influenced by social and cultural learning. Temperament and character together can account for some of the self-organizing characteristics of personality development but are incomplete models of human personality and intellectual development. They cannot explain uniquely human characteristics, such as creativity, freedom of will, or spirituality, which involve individual differences in personality coherence. Personality coherence refers to mind as a complex adaptive system functioning as a unified whole, much like the quantum coherence of superfluids. This hierarchy of models is discussed in relation to Baltes's (1997) hypothesis about the incompleteness of human ontogeny when limited to its first two levels.

Paul Baltes (1997) has observed that genetic and social-cultural influences on human intellectual development do not complete the task of maintaining a positive balance of gains over losses across the lifespan. As we age, gene-environment interactions cause decreased flexibility, plasticity, and learning efficiency, as well as problems in the brain mechanics of basic information processing that cannot be effectively overcome by greater social-cultural compensation. Many people become intellectually impaired, forgetful, or even demented, and everyone eventually dies.

Baltes has carefully distinguished between two main components of intellectual function—the fluid mechanics and the crystallized pragmatics. The fluid cognitive mechanics refers to the basic "hardware" or brain mechanisms that are largely content-free, universal, biological, and susceptible to genetic differences in inheritance and development. The crystallized pragmatics are largely content-rich, culture-dependent, and experience-based "software" by which the hardware is directed and organized.

Accordingly, Baltes's dual-process model of intellectual development is directly comparable to my own work on personality development in which I have distinguished between temperament and character. I have defined temperament in terms of heritable individual differences in basic information processing of emotional responses to simple stimuli, which is comparable to fluid mechanics of intelligence. Differences in temperament are heritable, developmentally stable throughout life, and little influenced by social and cultural influences. In contrast, character is what individuals make of themselves intentionally in terms of goals and values. Character development is experience-dependent, influenced by social and cultural influences, and can initially increase with age, particularly from puberty to early adulthood and little thereafter under commonplace conditions (Cloninger et al., 1993, 1997). Hence temperament and character are comparable to fluid and crystallized intelligence, respectively. This suggestion is supported by the work of Staudinger and Pasupathi (2000) to extend the dual-process model of intelligence to understand wisdom by incorporating information about personality, emotion, and motivation as well as experiential contexts.

The incompleteness of character is revealed in the difficulty of treating patients with character disorders. Despite strenuous efforts with pharmacological and psychotherapeutic interventions, the results of therapy for character disorders often show little benefit. This underscores the incompleteness of the theory underlying cognitive-behavioral therapy because it shows that cognitive schemas are rarely changed in therapy in a fundamental way. Individual differences in character can also be described as individual differences in the schemas or initial perspectives by which we organize our responses to experience. Most therapy for personality disorders does not efficiently change measures of character traits or cognitive schemas. Patients are usually left to struggle throughout their lifespan in an effort to balance emotional conflicts in such a way that personal and social gains will exceed losses (Beck, 1996).

Recent experimental and clinical findings regarding the importance of intuitive aspects of cognitive function suggest that this incompleteness is a consequence of limiting awareness only to temperament and character. Specifically, in the domain in which intellect and personality merge, Baltes and his colleagues (Baltes, 1997; Baltes & Smith, 1990) have studied measures of wisdom and have found that Baltes's measures do not increase with age. However, Baltes has measured wisdom as an advanced form of crystallized intelligence within his dual-process model. As a consequence, wisdom involves a form of intellectual expertise for Baltes (Chandler & Holliday, 1990), whereas others have noted that wisdom has an intuitive, holistic, integrative mechanism that is distinct from the algorithmic logic of crystallized intelligence (Labouvie-Vief, 1990; Sternberg, 1990; see also Labouvie-Vief, this volume). Furthermore, experimental studies have shown that algorithmic models of crystallized intelligence, which involve verbatim statements in memory, provide an inadequate description of cognitive growth and development (Bjorklund, 1997). They do not account well for the facts of cognitive growth, such as how children learn intuitively in play, how forgetting and reminiscence occur, or how true memories are distinguished from false memories (see also Wellman, this volume). This has led to the dissociation of intuitive learning of the gist of things from the rational learning of verbatim memories (Reyna & Brainerd, 1998).

Likewise, in the personality domain, there is a third level of personality integrative function that is uniquely human and involves the nonalgorithmic, intuitive processing that underlies human creativity, inventiveness, and integrative spirituality. It is my suggestion that this integrative function, which I will call *personality coherence*, completes the architecture of human ontogeny. Personality coherence refers to mind as a complex adaptive system that functions as a unified whole without separate or conflicting parts. The importance of personality coherence in adaptation across the lifespan has been recognized in social cognitive research on personality for many years (Cervone & Shoda, 1999). Well-adapted people can maintain an integrated sense of continuity throughout their life despite changing demands in different contexts across the lifespan. In fact, the unique power and direction of personality coherence emerges especially in the face of adversity, illness, and imminent death, which are so prominent in old age. Furthermore, such suffering serves the crucial function of bringing the limitations of algorithmic processes and the incompleteness of the individual self into conscious awareness. This point of awareness can provide a useful link between Baltes's findings about the incompleteness of genetic and cultural determinants of human ontogeny and other research regarding the role of intuitive learning in the cognitive development of personality coherence.

My own research on the understanding of personality development has gone through three major phases. I will refer to these three phases in terms of models of personality as *temperament*, as *self*, and as *coherence*. Nevertheless, these phases serve to illustrate a hierarchy of paradigms, each of which exists to some extent in other current and past theories in the philosophy of mind and in the psychobiology of cognition and personality. They are truly a hierarchy of nested hypotheses about personality in which the model of coherence includes that of self as a special case and the model of self includes temperament as a special case. I have been forced to develop more comprehensive models by experimental observations that could not be satisfied by the more restricted cases. Here I will only sketch this succession of paradigms in sufficient detail to reveal the major conceptual and experimental issues that I have confronted in order to spare the reader from adopting inadequate paradigms, which are unfortunately all too commonplace. The third phase is still under development and consequently is less well supported by empirical data. Interested readers can consult other cited sources for additional details and documentation, as well as comparisons to other models of human personality (Cloninger, Przybeck, Svrakic, & Wetzel, 1994). Alternative models of personality, such as those derived by linear factor analysis, do not distinguish temperament and character and so confound relevant developmental phenomena in which these domains differ (see also Roberts & Caspi, this volume).

Human Personality as Temperament

Individual Differences in Temperament

My initial approach to describing human personality was to provide a description of individual differences in temperament. Temperament has usually been defined as those components of personality that are heritable, developmentally stable, emotion-based, or uninfluenced by sociocultural learning (Cloninger, 1994). I initially assumed that if temperament could be properly measured, then other aspects of personality could be predicted as developments from these basic predispositions. Accordingly, I sought to describe the underlying neurogenetic basis of human personality in terms of multiple dimensions of temperament, which I defined as the automatic associative responses to simple emotional stimuli that determine differences in habits and emotional responses, such as fear, anger, and disgust.

I initially distinguished three quantitative dimensions of temperament based on prior research on genetic structure of personality in humans, neurobiological studies in humans and other animals, phylogenetic analyses, and behavioral conditioning (Cloninger, 1986, 1987). These three dimensions were called *harm avoidance* (anxiety-proneness versus outgoing vigor and risk-taking), novelty seeking (exploratory impulsiveness versus stoical frugality), and reward dependence (social attachment versus aloofness). I then developed reliable clinical measures of these dimensions, including a self-report questionnaire called the Tridimensional Personality Questionnaire (TPQ) and related rating procedures for clinicians and observers. Factor analytic studies confirmed that these three dimensions were nearly uncorrelated with one another and highly internally consistent except that *persistence* (industry versus underachievement) emerged as an independent fourth temperament dimension. Persistence had originally been a subscale of reward dependence, but it proved empirically to be independently heritable in large-scale twin studies in the United States and Australia (Heath, Cloninger, & Martin, 1994; Stallings, Hewitt, Cloninger, Heath, & Eaves, 1996). The descriptors of high and low scorers on each of these four dimensions are summarized in Table 8.1.

These dimensions have been extensively studied in clinical, neurobiological, and genetic research, as reviewed in detail elsewhere (Cloninger, 1998, 1999, 2000; Cloninger & Svrakic, 2000). These four temperament dimensions are each about 50%

Table 8.1

Descriptors of Individuals Who Score High and Low on
the Four Temperament Dimensions

Temperament Dimension	Descriptors of Extreme Variants	
	High	Low
Harm avoidance	Pessimistic	Optimistic
	Fearful	Daring
	Shy	Outgoing
	Fatigable	Vigorous
Novelty seeking	Exploratory	Reserved
	Impulsive	Rigid
	Extravagant	Frugal
	Irritable	Stoical
Reward dependence	Sentimental	Critical
	Open	Aloof
	Warm	Detached
	Sympathetic	Independent
Persistence	Industrious	Apathetic
	Determined	Spoiled
	Ambitious	Underachiever
	Perfectionist	Pragmatist

heritable according to twin studies, and each is influenced by multiple specific genes according to linkage and association studies (Cloninger, 2000; Comings et al., 2000).

Clinical studies have confirmed my original hypothesis (Cloninger, 1987) that these temperament dimensions distinguish subtypes of personality disorders. Specific subtypes of personality disorder are associated with a specific configuration of temperament features, as depicted in Figure 8.1. For example, antisocial personality disorder is associated with high scores in novelty seeking and low scores in harm avoidance and reward dependence. More generally, individuals with anxious personality disorders (called cluster C in DSM-IV) are high in harm avoidance, impulsive personality disorders (cluster B in DSM-IV) are high in novelty seeking, and aloof personality disorders (cluster A in DSM-IV) are low in reward dependence. If a four-cluster system is used, obsessional patients are higher in persistence. These results have been confirmed by independent investigators in many countries throughout the world, showing the cross-cultural generality of this temperament model (reviewed in Cloninger & Svrakic, 2000). However, as will be discussed in more detail later, clinical studies have also shown that there are other aspects of personality besides these temperament dimensions that are needed to specify the degree of maturity of particular individuals or whether they have a personality disorder. Degree of maturity was quantified by the sum of scores on two character traits (self-directedness and cooperativeness), which distinguish individuals with and without personality disorders (Cloninger, Svrakic, & Przybeck, 1993).

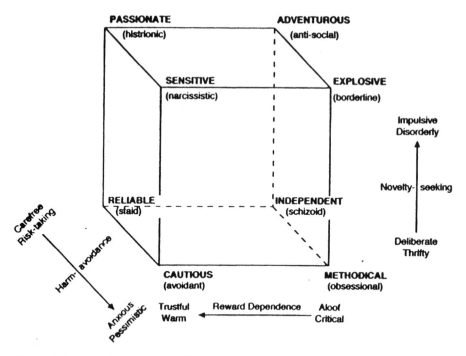

Figure 8.1   Temperament Cube.

In brief, temperament has been shown to describe differences between individuals in what they consciously experience and report to be emotionally salient. In other words, temperament describes what grabs our attention and how intensely we respond. Furthermore, the self-report measures agree strongly with clinical ratings by expert observers and also correlate with objective laboratory tests, such as individual differences in startle and regional brain activity (Cloninger, 1998, 2000; Sugiura et al., 2000; see also Singer, this volume). This indicates strong correspondences between subjective experience, objective performance, and self-reported knowledge of temperament.

The Role of Temperament in Personality Development

I had begun my work on temperament expecting that interactions among multiple temperament dimensions would predict patterns of personality development. In fact, we found that temperament dimensions were developmentally stable: they change little with increasing age, with psychotherapy, or with pharmacotherapy! We can measure the same temperament dimensions in preschoolers (3 to 5 years old), children (ages 9 to 14), and adults regardless of age with age-appropriate questions that correspond to consistent psychological concepts. Among a large sample of adults varying in age, we find little correlation between temperament scores and age. Results are summarized in Table 8.2 for temperament in a cross-sectional sample of 1,800 individuals of

Table 8.2
Relative Risk of Immaturity (Mild and Severe Personality Disorder) as a Function of
Temperament Type in a Sample from the General Community (Cloninger et al., 1994)

Temperament Type	Configuration	N	Percent Immature
High risk:			
Explosive	NHr	39	72%
Methodical	nHr	44	59%
Adventurous	Nhr	25	48%
Sensitive	NHR	30	40%
Average		15	33%
Low risk:			
Cautious	nHR	30	17%
Independent	nhr	31	16%
Passionate	NhR	50	12%
Reliable	nhR	36	6%
Total		300	33%

Table 8.3
Temperament and Age: Proportions of Items Endorsed on TCI Scales of
Temperament by Age in a Cross-Sectional Sample of 1,800 Individuals Older
Than 17 Years from the General Population

Age	NS	HA	RD	PS
<21	0.51	0.42	0.72	0.59
21–30	0.51	0.37	0.66	0.61
31–40	0.46	0.39	0.67	0.63
41–50	0.43	0.40	0.68	0.60
51–60	0.43	0.37	0.67	0.62
61–70	0.39	0.39	0.67	0.57
71+	0.35	0.43	0.66	0.53

varying age. Novelty seeking does decrease with age, but the other dimensions show
no consistent pattern change.

We found that temperament configuration did vary in the probability with which
they were associated with immaturity. The relationship is moderately strong, as summarized in Table 8.3. Thus individuals with an explosive configuration (high harm
avoidance and novelty seeking, low reward dependence) has a high probability of
being immature in character. However, the probability is not a certainty, so that temperament alone does not determine whether a person is mature or immature. In more
clinical terms, temperament does not determine whether an individual has a personality
disorder, is average in maturity, or is unusually well integrated.

Both the high and the low extremes of each temperament dimension have advantages and disadvantages depending on the context. Accordingly, no genetic engineering or other manipulation can devise the optimal temperament for all circumstances. Adaptability lies in diversity within the whole population, which is based on conflicting drives within individuals. Consequently temperament can never provide a complete solution to individual integration.

Critique of Personality as Temperament

Temperament can be reliably measured and studied by self-report and by observations at many levels of organization from genetic, chemical, anatomical, and physiological to behavioral. Temperament provides a useful account of individual differences in processes of selective attention and emotional salience but does not stand alone. It provides no account of the self-organizing property of human personality, which gives it properties of executive control or empathic cooperation as observed in primates generally (see also Lerner, Dowling, & Roth, this volume). It also provides no account of intuition or subjective awareness that underlies uniquely human characteristics, such as creativity, symbolic invention, or the drive for coherence and integration itself.

Human Personality as Self

Individual Differences in Character

When I observed that variation in temperament alone did not account for individual differences in degree of maturity or whether an individual had a personality disorder, I examined what aspects of personality were omitted in my model of personality. I compared the traits measured by the TPQ with other personality measurement systems, as well as the descriptions of human character in humanistic and transpersonal psychology and psychodynamic psychiatry. Since the traits I had originally measured in the TPQ had been demonstrated to be heritable, developmentally stable, and emotion-based, I designated them as temperament traits. In contrast, character has long been defined as what people make of themselves intentionally. In other words, character is the reflection of our goals and values. Accordingly, character traits can be specified in terms of our concept of our self, our concept of our relations with others, and our concept of our participation in the world as a whole.

To measure this, I extended the TPQ by developing reliable measures of three traits called self-directedness (self concept), cooperativeness (concept of relations with others), and self-transcendence (concept of our participation in the world as a whole) (Cloninger et al., 1993). The descriptors of high and low scores on these three character traits are presented in Table 8.4. The Temperament and Character Inventory (TCI) measures the four temperament dimensions (same as in the TPQ) and the three character

Table 8.4

Descriptors of Individuals Who Score High and Low on
the Three Character Dimensions

Character Dimension	Descriptors of Extreme Variants	
	High	Low
Self-directedness	Responsible	Blaming
	Purposeful	Aimless
	Resourceful	Inept
	Self-accepting	Vain
	Generative	Unproductive
Cooperative	Reasonable	Prejudiced
	Empathic	Insensitive
	Helpful	Hostile
	Compassionate	Revengeful
	Principled	Opportunistic
Self-transcendent	Judicious	Undiscerning
	Intuitive	Empirical
	Inventive	Unimaginative
	Transpersonal	Dualistic
	Spiritual	Practical

traits of self-directedness, cooperativeness, and self-transcendence. Thus the TCI provides a dual-aspect description of self as the marriage of temperament and character.

The TCI is applicable in samples from the general population as well as in patients with psychiatric disorders. The factor structure is the same, but mean values are generally lower for the character traits in psychiatric patients (Svrakic, Whitehead, Przybeck, & Cloninger, 1993; Bayon, Hill, Svrakic, Przybeck, & Cloninger, 1996). Most important, the TCI character traits distinguish individuals with no personality disorder from those with personality disorders diagnosed by others by expert clinicians using structured interviews (Svrakic et al., 1993). In fact, personality disorders are not discrete diseases but differ only quantitatively in degree of maturity from others. Accordingly, there is more information about maturity preserved by simply quantifying the character configuration of people using the TCI.

A useful indicator of maturity overall is simply the sum of scores in TCI self-directedness and cooperativeness. However, the three-dimensional character configuration provides additional information. Descriptors of traits associated with the possible configurations of the TCI character dimensions are shown in Figure 8.2.

The psychobiology of these character dimensions is now being actively investigated, but less is known about them than for temperament because the measures became available only in 1993. Initially, character was expected to be less heritable than temperament, but genetic studies now contradict this. Each of the character dimensions show moderate heritability and associations with multiple candidate genes (Comings et al., 2000).

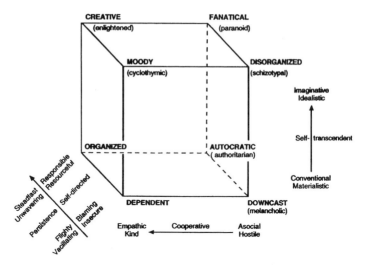

Figure 8.2   Character Cube.

In psychophysiological studies, self-directedness has been correlated with the evoked potential P300, which is an indicator of individual differences in emotional relief from updating of expectancies. Furthermore, only self-directedness and no other temperament or character trait is correlated with P300 (Vedeniapin, Anokhin, Sirevaag, Rohrbaugh, & Cloninger, 2001). This finding has been confirmed independently (M. Hansenne, personal communication, 2000). Cooperativeness and self-transcendence are related to measures of contingent negative variation (Cloninger, 1998). These results are especially important because they show that temperament and character traits are functionally dissociated and that individual differences in character are related to executive brain function and the updating of expectancies and working memory.

Character Development

Initially, my colleagues and I observed that character traits increased with age, particularly during the transition from adolescence to early adulthood (Cloninger et al., 1993). The increase in levels of character traits are summarized in Table 8.5 based on cross-sectional studies of studies of 1,800 individuals varying in age. There are some increases with age, particularly for cooperativeness from adolescence into early adulthood. However, the amounts of increase in character with age are small on average and negligible after middle age (see also Roberts & Caspi, this volume).

The different possible configurations of character are described in Figure 8.2. For example, individuals high in all three character traits are labeled as creative, and those who are low in self-directedness but high in the other two are labelled as

Table 8.5

Character and Age: Proportions of Items Endorsed on TCI Scales of Temperament by Age in a Cross-Sectional Sample of 1,800 Individuals Older Than 17 Years from the General Population

Age	SD	C	ST
<21	0.64	0.80	0.50
21–30	0.71	0.79	0.51
31–40	0.74	0.83	0.51
41–50	0.74	0.84	0.50
51–60	0.76	0.86	0.53
61–70	0.77	0.86	0.52
71+	0.77	0.84	0.53

cyclothymic. We observed that there are nonlinear relations among temperament and character configurations (Cloninger, Svrakic, & Svrakic, 1997). Specifically, different temperament configurations are associated with the same character configuration (that is, show equifinality), and the same temperament configuration can lead to different character configurations (that is, show multifinality). Using the labels for temperament configurations given in Figure 8.1, we can describe the correspondences between temperament and character configurations. For example, individuals with histrionic and reliable temperaments account for 29% and 20% of individuals with a creative character configuration (that is, high in all three character dimensions); this is an example of equifinality, different temperaments leading to the same character. However, these same temperament configurations can also result in other character configurations besides the creative character; the histrionic temperament also often leads to a cyclothymic character, whereas the reliable temperament also often leads to an organized character. Such multifinality is another indication of the nonlinearity of relations among temperament and character; if the relations were linear, there would be one-to-one relations among temperament and character. Furthermore, predictions about the nonlinear dynamics of personality development were confirmed in longitudinal data about 593 individuals followed over a period of one year (Cloninger et al., 1997).

Next we examined the pattern of character development in more depth by studying the sequence of changes in subscales of the three characters. Each character dimension has multiple subscales, which may each represent a distinct step in development. In fact, we observed that increases in subscale scores tended to follow a characteristic temporal sequence. This typical or canonical sequence is summarized and compared with the sequences described by Piaget, Freud, and Erikson in Table 8.6. There is sufficient correspondence to suggest that what we are calling character development is what others have observed as cognitive maturation, psychosexual development, or ego development (see also Labouvie-Vief, this volume). This is also supported by findings that character traits are strongly related to maturity of ego defenses assessed by the Defense Style Questionnaire (Mulder, Joyce, Sellman, & Cloninger, 1996).

Table 8.6

Comparison of Different Descriptions of Personality Development

TCI Developmental Step		Piaget	Freud	Erikson
[1] co1	Trust	Sensorimotor (reflexive)	Oral (passive)	Trust
[2] sd1	Responsible	Sensorimotor (enactive)	Anal (negativistic)	Autonomy
[3] st1	Intuitive	Self-object differentiation		Early phallic
[4] sd2	Purposefulness	Intuitive	Late phallic (exploratory)	Initiative
[5] co2	Empathy	Operational (concrete)	Latency (conforming)	
[6] st2	Conscientious	Operational (abstract)	Early genital (conscientious work)	Identity
[7] sd3	Resourcefulness			
[8] co3	Helpful		Later genital (social maturity)	Intimacy
[9] st3	Spirituality			
[10] sd4	Humility			
[11] co4	Compassion			Generativity
[12] st4	Enlightened			
[13] sd5	Creative			Integrity
[14] co5	Freely loving			
[15] st5	Aware			

Another crucial aspect of character development is the possibility of improvement in response to treatment. The hope of therapy is that treatment leads to fundamental improvement in personality, particularly in character. Empirically, what is found in therapeutic interventions is that the level of self-directedness at the beginning of therapy predicts the degree of improvement. This has been observed with cognitive-behavioral therapy for bulimea and depression, as well as in treatment of depression with antidepressants (Cloninger & Svrakic, 2000). There are often some benefits from cognitive-behavioral therapy, but most patients with personality disorders do not make fundamental changes in their character. That is, stable change in their cognitive schemas or what can be called their initial perspective is infrequent. Patients are most likely to return to their usual or best prior level of adjustment prior to the crisis that brought them to therapy. What is accepted as a good outcome of therapy is for a patient with personality disorder to become their own self-directed therapist for their persistent cognitive distortions (Beck, 1996). Such limited benefits underscore the need for better understanding the mechanisms of character development.

Critique of Personality as Self

In the model of personality as self, individual differences in human personality are described in terms of temperament and character. This description provides a useful account of selective attention in terms of attention and higher cognitive functions in terms of character, such as executive functions (self-directedness), legislative functions (cooperativeness), and judicial functions (self-transcendence). These traits together provide a rich account of normal personality and its disorders. Rather than characterizing only pathology, we can begin to understand how disorders can arise and be maintained despite leading to much suffering.

Much more needs to be learned about the neurobiology of character. Recent brain imaging results indicate that quantification of character can allow us to relate individual differences in regional brain activity to differences in character configurations. Past lesion studies and psychosurgical results also support this: dorsolateral and medial prefrontal lesions cause deficits in self-directedness, whereas right-sided or bilateral orbito-frontal lesions cause deficits in social judgment and cooperation (Freeman & Watts, 1942; Stuss & Benson, 1986). Also lesions of the frontal pole (Brodmann area 10) cause deficits in intuition or self-transcendence, such as loss of creativity, abstract fantasy, and flexibility (Freeman & Watts, 1942). The frontal poles are the brain region that is last to myelinate in man and are considered to be the most recent phylogenetic development in human cognitive ability, which is creativity and spirituality. Nevertheless, much more needs to be learned about the psychological mechanisms involved in character change. There are observable patterns of character development over time, and these can be predicted in terms of nonlinear dynamics (see also Lerner, Dowlings & Roth, this volume). However, the amount of character development with age is small on average, and almost nonexistent after 40 years of age (see Roberts & Caspi, this volume). Furthermore, current treatment methods produce only limited results inefficiently over many years.

The model of character does provide an account of human personality with higher cognitive functions at an intellectual level. These higher cognitive processes can supervise the drives of temperament but always involve executive, legislative, and judicial decisions based on finite information in an ever-changing environment. Consequently, character alone cannot ensure stable integration of human behavior.

Human Personality as Coherence

Intuitive Approaches to Integration and Well-Being

After the model of temperament and character was developed in 1993, I gradually became aware that these dimensions could not adequately explain the phenomena that are uniquely human—creativity, freedom of will, and intuitive awareness. First, I observed that individuals who were high in all three character dimensions were described as being exceptionally creative, inventive, flexible, judicious, and intuitive (Cloninger, 1999). We noted that such individuals were characterized by exceptionally integrated lifestyles. In psychoanalytic terms, they viewed life with positive anticipation, altruism, and sublimation (Cloninger, 1998, 1999). In more spiritual terms, they viewed life with the theological virtues of hope, charity, and faith. Second, we observed that creative or integrated characters were not only emotionally stable and well organized but also were more cheerful and happy than any other character configuration (Cloninger, 1998; Coward, 1995). For them life was easy, satisfying, fresh, and wonderful with little tension or conflict. Third, empirical measures of the degree of integration, sublimation, or self-transcendence were found to predict those who do best when treated for serious illnesses like cancer (Coward, 1995). Fourth, interventions that were designed to foster such an integrative spirit improve mental and physical outcomes in cancer patients and patients with severe character disorders (Linehan, Armstrong, & Suarez, 1991).

From the perspective of a creative character, suffering is actually not bad or even inappropriate. When we do not understand a situation in its full reality, then some suffering is likely. Furthermore, such suffering is useful to the human being because it is the way by which the self becomes aware of its limitations as an individual with finite knowledge and capacities. Thus suffering makes us aware that our finite individual being participates in an infinite universal unity of being. Every human being has a natural drive for coherence and happiness. This is our spontaneity, which gives our being its humanity.

Consequently, I developed an approach to psychotherpy designed to foster the creative perspective in a paradoxical manner without emotional tension or intellectual judgment. This approach is called *coherence therapy* and focuses on the use of paradoxical intention to facilitate cognitive development toward personal well-being along a path of nonresistance, as summarized in Table 8.7. Paradoxically, letting go of effortful struggle leads to a free flow of creative change. Likewise, working to help others leads to mutual sharing of love. Also, awareness without intellectual judgment leads to serenity and happiness. Anecdotally, I have found that use of these principles has greatly improved my psychotherapeutic effectiveness, confirming the reports of controlled therapeutic interventions designed to operate according to similar principles (Linehan et al., 1991). However, available controlled trials use methods that are multifaceted, and it is unclear which procedures are actually essential for the therapeutic benefits. More generally, it remains unclear what are actually the necessary and sufficient conditions for therapeutic change with *any* form of therapy for mental illness, which are all associated with substantial unpredictability of response. This uncertainty suggests that unmeasured and possibly hidden variables are influencing therapeutic responses for mental disorders in general. Consequently, I have been tried to develop a more fundamental understanding of the mechanisms influencing personality development before doing therapeutic trials.

Table 8.7
Principles of Coherence Therapy: The Path of Nonresistance

---

1. Letting go
   - No struggles with self or others
   - Being what you are and following truth without any effort to become what are not
   - Hopeful calmness with anticipation that reality is unfolding in a way that is really good even if you cannot understand it
2. Working at service of others
   - Spontaneous acts of kindness and cooperation
   - Altruism, unconditional compassion
   - Forgiveness of those who are aggressive
3. Awareness
   - Simply being light and listening to our intuitive sensitivity
   - Sublimation
   - Intuitions that have quality of certainty and clarity
4. Knowledge of the processes of thought
   - Initial perspective makes us strong or weak.
   - Words of judgment can lead to untrue ideas.
   - Automatic reactions can amplify our errors of judgment.

Searching for the Mechanism of Spirit

My observations about creative character structures are similar to observations made about creativity and wisdom in work on mental self-government. Creativity and wisdom are more than intelligence or maturity of character (Sternberg, 1988, 1990). Likewise, personality coherence is well recognized as a fundamental phenomenon of the operation of complex adaptive systems as a whole. Personality coherence cannot be explained by observations about separate psychological mechanisms in social cognitive research (Cervone & Shoda, 1999). Likewise, personality development remains highly unpredictable in particular individuals, and the results of therapeutic interventions with personality disorders are highly incomplete despite extensive efforts with pharmacological, cognitive-behavioral, psychodynamic approaches (Beck, 1996; Cloninger, 1999).

In order to understand personality coherence and its therapeutics, it seems important to have a fuller understanding of the basic psychobiological mechanisms influencing human development. Specifically, a creative character can be reliably described as being inventive, intuitive, flexible, and judicious, but what explains the unique properties of the phenomena themselves? The features of creativity and wisdom have attracted substantial interest in psychology (Vernon, 1970; Sternberg, 1988, 1990), paleontology (Mithen, 1996), and neuroscience (Eccles, 1989), but little has been done to specify a general model of their underlying mechanisms and functional properties. These features of adaptability emerged only about 60,000 years ago in modern man, even though the brain size and structure of modern man had changed little from that of early man (Eccles, 1989; Mithen, 1996). Are there biophysical mechanisms that could explain the evolution of the human consciousness in the coherent manner predicted by the paleontologist Teilhard de Chardin (1959)?

More objectively, experimental studies have shown that theories of crystallized intelligence and of the self, such as Piaget's model of epigenetic construction or algorithmic models of information-processing involving verbatim statements in memory, are inadequate descriptions of cognitive growth and development (Bjorklund, 1997). They do not account well for the facts of cognitive growth. For example, they do not account for how children learn intuitively in play (Bjorklund, 1997), how forgetting and reminiscence occur (Brainerd, Reyna, Howe, Kingma, 1990), how true memories are distinguished from false memories (Brainerd, Reyna, Mojardin, 1999; Reyna & Brainerd, 1998; Miller & Bjorklund, 1998), how misinformation affects judgments of identity and similarity (Brainerd & Reyna, 1998), or how gist learning is dissociable from processes of reasoning, emotionality, and intentionality (Ackerman, 1998; Brainerd & Reyna, 1993). This has led to fuzzy-trace models of learning and memory based on the dissociation of intuitive learning of the gist of things from the rational learning of verbatim memories (Reyna & Brainerd, 1998). When we are functioning creatively like a gifted child, our initial perspective is preverbal and intuitive, whereas models of self, character, and the schemas of cognitive psychology are expressed in words. In contrast, we learn "the gist of things" prior to the production of words, just as children acquire language and cognitive schemas by immersion in the actuality of what is given in direct experience like a gift without personal effort, analysis, or tension.

I am only beginning to develop partial insights into the mysteries of creativity and intuitive learning. A small insight that I have found helpful is that the answers require that we recognize the fundamental nature of the distributed coherence in the cognition of modern man in terms of both its psychology and physics. The answer, I suggest, is unlikely to be in the gross physical characteristics of the brain of modern man, which differs little from that of early men who were not creative, artistic, or spiritual. It is unlikely to be in the gross physical characteristics of the brains of individuals with and without personality disorders, which differ little from one another in most cases. Rather, the difference between the suffering of beings with personality disorders and others who are creative is in the degree to which they have awareness and coherence of their entire being. Such awareness is intuitive and preverbal, just as giftedness is undeniably preverbal and intuitive (Winner, 1996). Intuitive awareness is what makes us a truly sapient human being.

Another useful insight has been that the psychological properties of personality coherence and intuitive information processing show a remarkable correspondence to the properties observed in physics at the quantum level. It is probably not surprising that the subtlest aspects of human cognition may be based on the subtlest aspects of laws known to physics. The mechanical view of human psychobiology advocated by materialists is simply inadequate to account for the properties of the most sophisticated human abilities, such as coherence, subjectivity, creativity, and intuition. The correspondences

Table 8.8
Properties of Human Beings and Analogous Quantum
Phenomena

Property of Human Beings	Analogous Quantum Phenomenon
Creativity	Noncausality
Freedom of will	Uncertainty principle
Serenity and fluidity	Distributed coherence
Intuitive awareness	Nonlocality
Sense of unity of being	Universality of Higgs field

between uniquely human cognition and quantum processes, summarized in Table 8.8, are strong.

First, let us consider the properties of human will. The psychological concepts of a creative and free will are incompatible with classical Newtonian physics, which would require that nature behave as a machine whose function is necessarily determined by initial conditions (Walker, 2000). Classical views of mechanics are inadequate to explain human personality development. Creativity in humans involves more than clever application of what has been done before; it involves productions without precedent, which could not have been predicted from what had previously occurred. Such psychological creativity corresponds to nonalgorithmic processes in quantum physics, such as noncausality. Noncausality is demonstrated by physical events that are unpredictable, underdetermined, or underconstrained by all information about initial conditions. Freedom of will is a closely related psychological phenomenon, corresponding to the uncertainty principle of Heisenberg: there is a finite limit to the precision with which events in space-time can be specified from initial conditions. In other words, there are aspects of the future that are unpredictable, underconstrained, or free because we can have only limited knowledge about their initial conditions. Furthermore, this freedom is somehow entangled with subjective awareness of the observer because there is a choice of the degree of constraint placed on different parameters (Bell, 1993, p. 40–43).

Next, let us consider the properties of intuitive awareness and understanding. Certain states of awareness have been described as moments of optimal experience, peak performance, states of fluidity, or flow states and are associated with creative insight, happiness, and fluid mental and physical performance (Csikszentmihalyi, 1990). Such awareness carries with it a qualities of certainty and serenity; in fact, intuition is sometimes called the inner eye of certainty (Bayrak, 1993). The understanding also inspires what to do like a spontaneously received gift without deliberation, tension, or effort and is regularly experienced by gifted children when they function intuitively (Winner, 1996). It is also called "choiceless awareness" because of its spontaneity and accompanying qualities of timelessness and certainty (Krishnamurti, 1973; Krishnamurti & Bohm, 1985). These states of personality coherence and psychological fluidity are analogous to macroscopic quantum manifestations of distributed coherence similar to superfluidity. In other words, personality coherence corresponds to quantum coherence in that both are complex systems functioning as a unified whole.

The intuitive and subjective aspects of human awareness involves what Schrodinger (1967) referred to ambiguously as the "singularity" of consciousness. Ordinary states of human consciousness involve temporal "binding" so that past-present-future can all be experienced as a continuity in a stream of consciousness, which is regarded as a unique capacity of modern human beings (Eccles, 1989). Such "binding" is crucial to the subjective sense of identity, which is different from the function of intuition, as will be described more fully in the following section. The singularity of information in intuition is more analogous to the quantum phenomenon of nonlocality (also called *inseparability*). The term *nonlocality* is used because entangled quantum entities share information simultaneously regardless of distance, as if the same thing is in more than one place at the same time (Bohm, 1980; Bell, 1993).

Finally, in intuitive states of awareness, there is often a sense of participation in a unity of being. According to quantum field theory, space is a universal field of infinite energy. In other words, space is a plenum of energy, which is the beginning and end of all physical phenomena in space-time or, more broadly, the unity of all being. This concept has been confirmed repeatedly by experimental high-energy physics, which regularly encounters phenomena that can be explained only by quanta emerging from space or returning into space. This movement in space-time indicates a direction of all physical developments to and from its source.

Physics is lacking a general theory of the nature of space and the space-energy field. However, a consensus has emerged that a universal field, called a Higgs field, pervades all space. The Higgs field has been used to develop a unified field theory incorporating all the fundamental interactions of matter. Experimental support for the field has been indicated in recent particle discoveries, but not all predicted particles have yet been observed.

Such phenomena as noncausality and nonlocality were so contrary to everyday experience that physicists, including Einstein, were forced to undergo a revolution in their thinking during the past century (Bell, 1993). Now these phenomena are firmly established experimentally in physics (Tittel, Brendel, Zbinden, & Gisen, 1998; Bouweester et al., 1997; Zeilinger, 2000). Nevertheless, most psychologists, neuroscientists, and philosophers of mind continue to think in terms of classical physics (Rey, 1997). Fortunately, other leaders in the same fields have begun to consider quantum phenomena in relation to human cognition seriously (Penrose, 1989; Eccles, 1989; Chalmers, 1996; Stapp, 1999; Walker, 2000).

Critique of Personality as Coherence

Excellent experimental work distinguishing intuitive learning from algorithmic verbatim learning has already been carried out in children (see also Gigerenzer, this volume). Now more such experimental work is needed across the lifespan in order to evaluate possible changes in the efficiency of intuitive learning in middle age, young-old age (60 to 79), and old-old age (80+). The intuitive acquisition of language is certainly reduced in old age compared to children, but the relative efficiency of intuitive and verbatim learning is unclear. Such information would be useful in evaluating the completeness of a tripartite model of personality (temperament, character, and coherence) as proposed here.

The incompleteness of the self and its limited ability to integrate conflict has been appreciated as long as humans have felt incomplete as individuals who need relationship to others and the universe as a whole. What is most remarkable about integrated characters who operate with hope, love, and faith is their sense of serenity and certainty. Such serenity and positive well-being clearly provide an exceptional adaptive capacity and freedom in dealing with adversity, illness, and imminent death (Coward, 1995). However, little is known about the measurement of parameters of personality coherence like personal flexibility or free will. Until this can be done in a reliable manner, it will not be possible to determine the mechanisms involved in human development that depend on such variables. Elsewhere I have described an initial clinical approach to personality description in terms of measures of coherence— including creativity, free will, serenity, wisdom, and integration—and applied this to the differential diagnosis of high adaptive functioning and mental disorders (Cloninger, 2002).

It is clear that at least three components or levels of personality and consciousness must be distinguished. The first aspect of human consciousness is selective attention and memory of existence. "I exist" is a certainty, as noted by Augustine originally in the fourth century (Augustine, 1991). If anyone expresses doubt about this, even this doubt *is* something that exists. This is the level of temperament, fluid intelligence, associative conditioning of emotions and habits, and procedural learning of skills. Furthermore, there is a second certainty of human consciousness: "I exist and I know I exist." (Augustine, 1991). In the words of Descartes, "I think, therefore I am." This is the level of self-consciousness, subject-object differentiation, rationality, crystallized intelligence, declarative memory, and personal subjectivity beyond material existence. Finally, there is a third certainty of human consciousness, as was also noted by Augustine: "I will (and love) to be and to know." Furthermore, Augustine also emphasizes the incompleteness of the self and thereby the will for coherence and relatedness, which in his case is relatedness to God understood as the origin and end of all things: "I am not complete until I am at one with Thee." This is the level of personality coherence, indivisibility of being, creativity, noesis (rational intuition—that is, integration of reason and intuition), freedom of will, spirit, and awakening of understanding. In the words of quantum physics, "The observer is the observed" (Krishnamurti, 1973; Bohm, 1980). At this level of quantum phenomena, a person is in the world but not of the world (noncausality), adapts with flexibility and no resistance to change (coherence), has awareness beyond space-time (nonlocality), and has unity of being (universality). Hence psychological phenomena that were once treated metaphysically or mystically are becoming approachable in a rigorous scientific manner (see Mittelstrass, this volume).

This general model provides an explicit picture of what makes us uniquely human, as well as what aspects of our personality we share with subhuman animals. It is a model consistent with both the phylogeny and ontogeny of learning and personality. However, such a model is only the beginning of the opening of doors to what is truly an inexhaustible set of mysteries.

General Conclusions

My studies of temperament and character have confirmed the incompleteness of genetic and cultural processes as determinants of human ontogeny. Likewise, Baltes (1997) has found that fluid and crystallized intelligence are limited in their ability to maintain a positive balance of gains over losses with increasing age. Recent experimental work on learning indicates that intuitive learning is dissociable from verbal learning and has crucial roles in both intellectual and personality development throughout the lifespan. Such intuitive learning appears to underlie those aspects of development that are uniquely human, such as creativity, freedom of will, and spirituality. Such intuitive information processes merit further study across the lifespan to help us understand the incompleteness of algorithmic intellectual processes and of the individual self. Further study is also needed to understand the fundamental quantum-like nature of the intuitive processes underlying personality coherence that complete human ontogeny. Recognition of the incompleteness of the individual self points the way to personality coherence through a path of nonresistance that completes the integration of character by means of self-transcendence and sublimation of individual conflicts.

References

Ackerman, B. (1998). Children's false memories: A test of the dissociability of cognitive and social processes. *Journal of Experimental Child Psychology, 71*, 178–183.

Augustine. (1991). *The Trinity* (E. Hill, Trans.). Brooklyn, NY: New City Press.

Baltes, P. B. (1997). On the incomplete architecture of human ontogeny. *American Psychologist, 52*, 366–380.

Baltes, P. B., & Smith, J. (1990). Toward a psychology of wisdom and its ontogenesis. In R. J. Sternberg (Ed.), *Wisdom: Its nature, origins, and development* (pp. 87–120). New York: Cambridge University Press.

Bayon, C., Hill, K., Svrakic, D. M., Przybeck, T. R., & Cloninger, C. R. (1996). Dimensional assessment of personality in an outpatient sample: Relations of the systems of Millon and Cloninger. *Journal of Psychiatric Research, 30*, 341–352.

Bayrak, T. (1993). *Ibn 'Arabi's divine governance of the human kingdom* (pp. 411–430). Louisville, KY: Fons Vitae.

Beck, J. S. (1996). Cognitive therapy of personality disorders. In P. M. Salkovskis (Ed.), *Frontiers of cognitive therapy* (pp. 165–181). New York: Guilford Press.

Bell, J. S. (1993). *Speakable and unspeakable in quantum mechanics* (pp. 40–43). New York: Cambridge University Press.

Bjorklund, D. F. (1997). In search of a metatheory for cognitive development (or, Piaget is dead and I don't feel so good myself). *Child Development, 68,* 144–148.

Bohm, D. (1980). *Wholeness and the implicate order.* London: Routledge.

Bouwmeester, D., Pan, J. W., Mattle, K., Eibl, M., Weinfurter, H., & Zeilinger, A. (1997). Experimental quantum teleportation. *Nature, 390,* 575–579.

Brainer, C. J., & Reyna, V. F. (1993). Memory independence and memory interference in cognitive development. *Psychological Review, 100,* 42–67.

Brainerd, C. J., & Reyna, V. F. (1998). Fuzzy-trace theory and children's false memories. *Journal of Experimental Child Psychology, 71,* 81–129.

Brainerd, C. J., Reyna, V. F., Howe, M. L., & Kingma, J. (1990). The development of forgetting and reminiscence. *Monographs of the Society for Research in Child Development, 5,* 1–93.

Brainerd, C. J., Reyna, V. F., & Mojardin, A. H. (1999). Conjoint recognition. *Psychological Review, 106,* 160–179.

Cervone, D., & Shoda, Y. (1999). *The coherence of personality: Social-cognitive bases of consistency, variability, and organization.* New York: Guildford Press.

Chalmers, D. J. (1996). *The conscious mind: In search of a fundamental theory.* New York: Oxford University Press.

Chandler, M. J. with Holliday, D. (1990). Wisdom in a postapocalyptic age. In Sternberg, R. J. (ed.): Wisdom: Its nature, origins, and development. New York: Cambridge University Press, pp. 121–141.

Cloninger, C. R. (1986). A unified biosocial theory of personality and its role in the development of anxiety states. *Psychiatric Developments, 3,* 167–226.

Cloninger, C. R. (1987). A systematic method for clinical description and classification of personality variants: A proposal. *Archives of General Psychiatry, 44,* 573–587.

Cloninger, C. R. (1994). Temperament and personality. *Current Opinion in Neurobiology, 4,* 266–273.

Cloninger, C. R. (1998). The genetics and psychobiology of the seven-factor model of personality. In K. R. Silk (Ed.), *The biology of personality disorders* (pp. 63–84). Washington, DC: American Psychiatric Press.

Cloninger, C. R. (1999). *Personality and psychopathology.* Washington, DC: American Psychiatric Press.

Cloninger, C. R. (2000). Biology of personality dimensions. *Current Opinion in Psychiatry, 13,* 611–616.

Cloninger, C. R. (2002). Implications of comorbidity for the classification of mental disorders: The need for a psychobiology of coherence. In M. Maj (Ed.), *psychiatric diagnosis and classification.* Chichester, West Sussex, UK: John Wiley & Sons, pp. 79–106.

Cloninger, C. R., Przybeck, T. R., Svrakic, D. M., & Wetzel, R. D. (1994). *The temperament and character inventory (TCI): A guide to its development and use.* St. Louis, MO: Washington University Center for Psychobiology of Personality.

Cloninger, C. R., & Svrakic, D. M. (2000). Personality disorders. In B. J. Sadock & V. A. Sadock (Eds.), *Comprehensive textbook of psychiatry* (7th ed., pp. 1723–1764). New York: Lippincott Williams & Wilkins.

Cloninger, C. R., Svrakic, D. M., & Przybeck, T. R. (1993). A psychobiological model of temperament and character. *Archives of General Psychiatry, 50,* 975–990.

Cloninger, C. R., Svrakic, N. M., & Svrakic, D. M. (1997). Role of personality self-organization in development of mental order and disorder. *Development and Psychopathology, 9,* 681–906.

Comings, D. E., Gade-Andavolu, R., Gonzalez, N., Wu, S., Muhleman, D., Blake, H., et al. (2000). A multivariate analysis of 59 candidate genes in personality traits: The Temperament and Character Inventory. *Clinical Genetics 58,* 375–385.

Coward, D. D. (1995). The lived experience of Self-transcendence in women with AIDS. Journal of Obstetrics, Gynecologic, and Neonatal Nursing, 24, 314–318.

Csikszentmihalyi, M. (1990). *Flow: The psychology of optimal experience*. New York: Harper Collins.

Eccles, J. (1989). *Evolution of the brain: Creation of the self*. London: Routledge.

Freeman, W., & Watts, J. W. (1942). *Psychosurgery: Intelligence, emotion, and social behavior following prefrontal lobotomy for mental disorders*. Springfield, IL: Thomas.

Heath, A. C., Cloninger, C. R., & Martin, N. G. (1994). Testing a model for the genetic structure of personality: A comparison of the personality systems of Cloninger and Eysenck. *Journal of Personality and Social Psychology, 66*, 762–775.

Krishnamurti, J. (1973). *The awakening of intelligence*. San Francisco: Harper.

Krishnamurti, J., & Bohm, D. (1985). *The ending of time*. San Francisco: Harper.

Labouvie-Vief, G. (1990). Wisdom as integrated thought: Historical and developmental perspectives. In R. J. Sternberg (Ed.), *Wisdom: Its nature, origins and development* (pp. 52–86). New York: Cambridge University Press.

Linehan, M. M., Armstrong, H. E., & Suarez, A. (1991). Cognitive-behavioral treatment of chronically pararsuicidal borderline patients. *Archives of General Psychiatry, 39*, 795–799.

Miller, P. H., & Bjorklund, D. F. (1998). Contemplating fuzzy-trace theory: The gist of it. *Journal of Experimental Child Psychology, 71*, 184–193.

Mithen, S. (1996). *The prehistory of the mind: The cognitive origins of art, religion, and science*. London: Thames and Hudson.

Mulder, R. T., Joyce, P. R., Sellman, J. F., & Cloninger, C. R. (1996). Towards an understanding of defense style in terms of temperament and character. *Acta Psychiatrica Scandinavica, 93*, 99–104.

Penrose, R. (1989). *The emperor's new mind: Concerning computers, minds, and the laws of physics*. New York: Oxford University Press.

Rey, G. (1997). *Contemporary philosophy of mind*. Oxford: Blackwell.

Reyna, V. F., & Brainerd, C. J. (1998). Fuzzy-trace theory and false memory: New frontiers. *Journal of Experimental Child Psychology, 71*, 194–209.

Schrodinger, E. (1967). *What is life?* New York: Cambridge University Press.

Stallings, M. C., Hewitt, J. K., Cloninger, C. R., Heath, A. C., & Eaves, L. J. (1996). Genetic and environmental structure of the Tridimensional Personality Questionnaire: Three or four temperament dimensions? *Journal of Personality and Social Psychology, 70*, 127–140.

Stapp, H. (1999). Attention, intention, and will in quantum physics. *Journal of Conscious Studies: The Volitional Brain, 6*, 143–164.

Staudinger, U. M., & Pasupathi, M. (2000). Life-span perspectives on self, personality, and social cognition. In T. Salthouse & F. Craik (Eds.), *Handbook of cognition and aging* (pp. 633–688). Hillsdale, NJ: Erlbaum.

Sternberg, R. J. (1988). *The nature of creativity*. New York: Cambridge University Press.

Sternberg, R. J. (1990). *Wisdom: Its nature, origins, and development*. New York: Cambridge University Press.

Stuss, D. T., & Benson, D. F. (1986). Personality and emotion. In D. T. Stuss & D. F. Benson (Eds), *The frontal lobes* (pp. 121–140). New York: Raven Press.

Sugiura, M., Kawashima, R., Nakagawa, M., Okada, K., Sato, T., & Goto, R. (2000). Correlation between human personality and neural activity in cerebral cortex. *NeuroImage, 11*, 541–546.

Svrakic, D. M., Whitehead, C., Przybeck, T. R., & Cloninger, C. R. (1993). Differential diagnosis of personality disorders by the seven factor model of temperament and character. *Archives of General Psychiatry, 50*, 991–999.

Teilhard de Chardin (1959). The Phenomenon of Man. New York: Harper & Row.

Tittel, W., Brendel, J., Zbinden, H., & Gisen, N. (1998). Violation of Bell inequalities by photons more than 10 km apart. *Physical Review Letters, 81*, 3563–3566.

Vedeniapin, A. B., Anokhin, A. A., Sirevaag, E., Rohrbaugh, J. W., & Cloninger, C. R. (2001). Visual P300 and the self-directedness scale of the temperament-character inventory. *Psychiatry Research, 101*, 145–156.

Vernon, P. E. (1970). *Creativity: Selected readings*. Baltimore, MD: Penguin Books.

Walker, E. H. (2000). *The physics of consciousness: Quantum minds and the meaning of life* (pp. 257–266). Cambridge, MA: Perseus Books.

Weihs, G., Jennewein, T., Simon, C., Weinfurter, H., & Zeilinger, A. (1998). Violation of Bell's inequality under strict Einstein locality conditions. *Physical Review Letters, 81*, 5039–5043.

Winner, E. (1996). *Gifted children: Myths and realities*. New York: Basic Books.

Zeilinger, A. (2000). Quantum teleportation. *Scientific American, 282*, 50–59.

9 The Cumulative Continuity Model of Personality Development: Striking a Balance Between Continuity and Change in Personality Traits Across the Life Course

Brent W. Roberts

University of Illinois at Urbana–Champaign, IL, U.S.A.

Avshalom Caspi

Institute of Psychiatry, University of London,
London, U.K., and University of Wisconsin, Madison, WI, U.S.A.

Abstract

Research has shown that personality-trait consistency is more common than personality-trait change and that when personality-trait change occurs, it is seldom dramatic. This finding results in a theoretical dilemma, for trait theories provide no explanation for personality change. Alternatively, most theories of adult developmental focus on change but not change in personality traits. To address this theoretical oversight, we first describe the mechanisms that promote personality continuity, such as the environment, genetic factors, psychological functioning, and person-environment transactions. Then we describe the counterpart to continuity, the mechanisms that facilitate personality change, such as responding to contingencies, observational learning, learning generalization, and learning from others' descriptions of ourselves. We argue that identity processes can explain both the mechanisms of continuity and change and form the basis for a theory that explains the empirical findings on personality-trait development over the life course. Specifically, we make the case that the development of a strong identity and certain facets of identity structure, such as identity achievement and certainty, are positively related to many of the mechanisms that promote personality continuity. Furthermore, we argue that one unintentional consequence of identity development is to put oneself into contexts that promote personality change, such as new roles or a different circle of friends.

Over the last several decades, the topic of personality-trait development has led a quixotic existence that paralleled the fortunes of the field of personality psychology in general. With Mischel's (1968) behaviorist critique of traits, the study of personality-trait development was left focused on social and environmental causes of both consistency and change. It was common in the late 1960s and early 1970s for authors to assume that traits were not consistent and, if they were, to attribute all of the consistency to environmental consistency (e.g., Nesselroade & Baltes, 1974). In the ensuing years, numerous longitudinal studies of personality yielded impressive evidence for the continuity of personality, and the field moved rapidly past the moderate position that there is both continuity and change in traits in adulthood (e.g., Kogan, 1990), to the extreme position that personality traits become "fixed" in young adulthood and remain unchanging thereafter (McCrae & Costa, 1994). This "strong stability" position precludes the idea that personality traits continue to develop in adulthood and, if accepted, effectively preempts the study of adult personality-trait development altogether.

Neither the extreme environmental argument nor the strong stability argument is justified given the empirical evidence. For example, despite the impression given by Mischel's (1968) critique of personality traits and the ensuing person-situation debate (Kenrick & Funder, 1988), the evidence for the consistency of personality traits across time was always compelling. As long ago as 1941, Crook compiled data from six longitudinal studies showing that trait consistency averaged above .80 over several weeks and dropped to around .50 after six and a half years. Subsequent reviews using anywhere from 20 to 152 longitudinal studies of personality consistency have replicated Crook's findings (Conley, 1984; Roberts & DelVecchio, 2000; Schuerger, Zarrella, & Hotz, 1989). Studies of the longitudinal consistency of traits also have shown that one of the most profound moderators of consistency is the age of the sample being studied (Caspi & Roberts, 1999; Finn, 1986; Roberts, Helson, & Klohnen, 2002). For example, in a review of 152 longitudinal studies, Roberts and DelVecchio (2000) showed that estimates of personality consistency (unadjusted for measurement error) increased from .31 in childhood, to .54 during the college-age period, to .64 at age 30, and then reached a plateau near .74 between ages 50 and 70 (over an average span of seven years).

Complementing the robust evidence for the relatively enduring nature of personality traits is the evidence for change in personality continuing well past young adulthood. Studies that examine change in personality traits find an increase or decrease in mean levels across most age periods (Dudek & Hall, 1991; Field & Millsap, 1991; Finn, 1986; Helson & Moane, 1987; Leon, Gillum, Gillum, & Gouze, 1979; Nilsson & Persson, 1984; Roberts, Helson, & Klohnen, 2002; Stevens & Truss, 1985). Furthermore, individual differences in personality-trait change exist at most ages (Jones & Meredith, 1996) and are related to life experiences in young adulthood (Pals, 1999), midlife (Roberts, 1997; Roberts & Chapman, 2000), and old age (Tower & Kasl, 1996). It should be noted that the effect sizes associated with trait consistency usually exceed .50, while the effect sizes for mean-level change and individual differences in change are much smaller in magnitude.

The picture that emerges from the longitudinal evidence for personality development leads to several conclusions. First, personality traits are highly consistent compared to other psychological constructs and are exceeded in consistency only by measures of cognitive ability (e.g., Conley, 1984). Second, personality consistency increases with age and yet may never reach a level high enough to indicate that personality traits stop changing. Third, according to mean-level and individual-difference approaches, personality change can and does occur even into old age. The picture one draws from the empirical data seems eminently reasonable: personality traits increase in consistency as people age, reaching levels that are quite high but not so high as to rule out the possibility or reality of meaningful shifts in traits over time.

Unfortunately, this temperate perspective on personality-trait development across the life course is not captured well in the existing theories of personality and adult development. In his review of personality and aging, Kogan (1990) highlighted three theoretical approaches to personality development. The first model is the *classical psychometric theory* or *trait model* of personality development (see also Conley, 1985). According to this perspective, traits remain so stable in adulthood that they are essentially "temperaments" and are impervious to the influence of the environment (e.g., McCrae & Costa, 1994; McCrae et al., 2000). The second model, termed the *contextual model* (Lewis, 1999), reflects the perspective that personality traits are shaped by environmental contingencies often contained within social roles (Brim, 1965). This perspective emphasizes the flux and change of personality and can only assume that personality consistency results from the consistency of social environments—a relatively weak and primarily untested argument. The third model is centered on the *stage theories* of Erikson (1950) and Levinson (1986), both of whom emphasize the change and emergence of specific life tasks and associated crises at different ages. This perspective essentially ignores personality-trait development. Taken separately, each of these three perspectives on personality development is lacking in some fundamental way. Classical psychometric trait theories beg the question of developmental process by defining personality as only that component of human nature that does not change—in our opinion a small and possibly uninteresting portion of human nature. Contextual models choose to ignore the genetic and psychological mechanisms that promote continuity and provide often overly optimistic perspectives on the mutability of personality (see also Cloninger, this volume). The stage models of adult development focus on important topics—the development of social roles and identity—but fail to incorporate these ideas with the prevailing evidence that differences in personality exist and are stable despite or because of development of social roles and identity structures.

We would add the *lifespan development approach* as a fourth model, which proposes a dialectic between consistency and change over the life course. The lifespan perspective comes closest to approximating the empirical picture of personality-trait development in that it specifies quite clearly that people are open systems and that they exhibit both continuity and change in personality throughout the life course (see also Lerner, Dowling, & Roth, this volume). Furthermore, according to the lifespan model, the effects of psychological, social, and cultural factors diminish as people grow older, often as a result of selection, optimization, and compensation processes (Baltes, Lindenberger, & Staudinger, 1999; see also Smith, this volume).

In the present chapter, we seek to expand on the lifespan model and set down the central tenets of the *cumulative continuity model* of personality development. Unlike previous conceptualizations of personality development, the cumulative continuity model attempts to integrate the findings of empirical research on the development of personality traits with the theoretical and empirical models derived from identity research in an attempt to explain the patterns of personality-trait continuity and change across the life course. In this effort, we attempt to integrate personality-trait development and identity development with perspectives derived from lifespan models (Baltes, Lindenberger, & Staudinger, 1999; Brandtstädter & Greve, 1994).

We begin our argument under the assumption that the empirical data to date are accurate. That is, personality traits increase in consistency with age, are mostly consistent in adulthood, and yet retain the capacity for change throughout the adult life course. If one accepts these data, several questions arise: First, why are personality traits consistent? We can no longer simply assume, as is done in the classical psychometric model, that personality traits are stable and that stability needs no explanation (Nesselroade & Featherman, 1997). In the first section below, we address the mechanisms that promote continuity in personality traits. The second question that arises is, What are the mechanisms that facilitate personality-trait change in adulthood? We address this question in the second section. Third, why do personality traits change less as people age and yet still retain some plasticity? In the last section, we answer this question by putting forward the argument that identity development and structures of identity mediate between personality traits and the mechanisms of change and continuity and that the mediating role of identity helps to explain, in part, the patterns of continuity and change in personality traits across the life course.

How Is Continuity Achieved? Mechanisms of Continuity Across the Life Course

There is a surprising consensus concerning the mechanisms that facilitate continuity in personality. For example, research from personality psychology (Buss, 1987), social psychology (Ickes, Snyder, & Garcia, 1997; Snyder & Ickes, 1985), and lifespan development (Baltes, 1997) have concluded that the way people select environments contributes to personality continuity. Furthermore, the function of assimilation strategies in personality continuity has been emphasized in both developmental (Block, 1982) and lifespan developmental psychology (Brandtstädter & Greve, 1994). In this section, we examine a parsimonious set of mechanisms that we feel subsume the majority of factors thought to affect continuity in personality traits across the lifespan.

Environmental Influences

One continuity-promoting mechanism is so mundane that it is often overlooked: personality characteristics may show continuity across the life course because the environment remains stable. To the extent that parental demands, teacher expectancies, and peer and partner influences remain stable over time, we could expect such environmental stability to promote personality continuity (Cairns & Hood, 1983). Sameroff (1995) has coined the term *environtype* to underscore that, like genotypes, stable environmental factors can shape and influence the course of phenotypic expressions over time.

Several longitudinal studies have shown that there is a good deal of continuity in the "psychological press" of children's and adults' socialization environments. Significant continuities have been found in observational studies, as well as in parents' reports of child-rearing practices from childhood to adolescence (e.g., Hanson, 1975; McNally, Eisenberg, & Harris, 1991; Patterson & Bank, 1989; Pianta, Sroufe, & Egeland, 1989; Roberts, Block, & Block, 1984). In addition, the socioenvironmental conditions of adult life that impinge on material, physical, and psychological well-being also show remarkable intragenerational persistence (Warren & Hauser, 1997). These longitudinal "environmental correlations" are about the same magnitude as longitudinal "personality correlations." For example, Roberts (1997) reported that the status level of a person's job was just as consistent as the personality trait of agency over a 16-year period (e.g., .55 versus .42). If the environments that people inhabit are as stable as these data suggest, then continuities observed in personality measures may simply reflect the cumulative and enduring continuities of those environments (Sameroff, Seifer, Baldwin, & Baldwin, 1993). What is needed is a formal test of the possibility that environmental continuities actually account for observed personality continuities.

Genetic Influences

Quantitative methods that are used to estimate genetic and environmental components of phenotypic variance at a given point in time can be extended to estimate genetic contributions to continuity across time (Plomin & Caspi, 1999). Genetic influences on personality continuity may be explored in twin studies by analyzing cross-twin correlations—that is, by fitting behavior-genetic models to the correlation between Twin A's score at time 1 and Twin B's score at time 2. Few studies have explored genetic contributions to temporal continuity by analyzing cross-twin correlations. In adulthood, at least two longitudinal studies have examined the genetic and environmental etiology of age-to-age continuity. McGue, Bacon, and Lykken (1993) administered the Multidimensional Personality Questionnaire to a sample of twins on two occasions, 10 years apart. The results showed that the MZ cross-twin correlations were consistently and significantly larger than the DZ cross-twin correlations. The authors estimate that approximately 80% of phenotypic stability may be associated with genetic factors.

Similarly, Pederson and Reynolds (1998) reported that genetic factors contribute to 50% of phenotypic stability (see also Pedersen, 1993).

Although the data suggest that genetic factors can influence the continuity of personality, they do not address the mechanisms by which they do so. One possibility is to examine physiological mechanisms. This is illustrated by research on shyness or "inhibition to the unfamiliar." Individual differences in behavioral inhibition are heritable and stable, and, at least in early childhood, their phenotypic stability appears to be influenced by genetic factors (Plomin et al., 1993). Kagan (1997) has suggested that inherited variations in threshold of arousal in selected limbic sites may contribute to longitudinal consistencies in this behavioral style. Another possibility is that genetic factors exert their influence on phenotypic stability through gene-environment correlations; thus, personality continuity across the life course may be the result of transactional processes that are, in part, genetically influenced.

Person-Environment Transactions Across the Life Course

In a third set of perspectives described as person-environment transactions, both the environment and existing individual differences play a role in promoting continuity of personality traits. There are many kinds of transactions, but three play particularly important roles in promoting the continuity of personality across the life course and in controlling the trajectory of the life course itself. Reactive transactions occur when different individuals exposed to the same environment experience it, interpret it, and react to it differently. Evocative transactions occur when an individual's personality evokes distinctive responses from others. Proactive transactions occur when individuals select or create environments of their own.

Reactive Person-Environment Transactions   Each individual extracts a subjective psychological environment from the objective surroundings, and it is that subjective environment that shapes subsequent personality development. This is the basic tenet of the phenomenological approach historically favored by social psychology and embodied in the famous dictum that if people "define situations as real, they are real in their consequences" (Thomas & Thomas, 1928). It also is the assumption connecting several prominent theories of personality development—Epstein's (1991) writings on the development of self-theories of reality, Tomkins's (1979) description of scripts about the self and interpersonal interactions, and Bowlby's (1973) analysis of working models.

All three theories assert that people continually revise their "self-theories," "scripts," and "working models" as a function of experience. But if these function as filters for social information, the question also is raised about how much revision actually occurs (Gurin & Brim, 1984). The answer is provided, in part, by cognitive social psychologists whose research suggests that once self-schemata—psychological constructs of the self—become well organized, a host of cognitive processes makes individuals selectively responsive to information that is congruent with their expectations and self-views (Fiske & Taylor, 1991). Presistent ways of perceiving, thinking, and behaving are preserved, in part, by features of the cognitive system, and because of these features the course of personality is likely to be quite conservative and resistant to change (Westen, 1991).

The role of cognitive factors in promoting the continuity of individual differences in personality and psychopathology has been detailed by Crick and Dodge (1994), whose social information-processing model of children's social adjustment includes five steps: (1) to encode information about the event, (2) to interpret the cues and arrive at some decision about their meaning and significance, (3) to search for possible responses to the situation, (4) to consider the consequences of each potential response and to select a response from the generated alternatives, and (5) to carry out the selected response. Research has identified individual differences in processing social information at all of these steps (Quiggle, Garber, Panak, & Dodge, 1992).

A basic assumption of this and other social information processing models is that early temperamental characteristics in combination with early social experiences can set up anticipatory attitudes that lead the individual to project particular interpretations onto new social relationships and situations (Rusting, 1998). That is, people are prone to assimilate experience that is consistent with their self-perceptions (Block, 1982; Brandtstädter & Greve, 1994). This is accomplished through a variety of informational processes in which the person interprets new events in a manner that is consistent with his or her experientially established understanding of self and others. Individuals are thus hypothesized to elicit and selectively attend to information that confirms rather than disconfirms their self-conceptions (Snyder & Ickes, 1985). This promotes the stability of the self-concept, which, in turn, promotes the continuity of behavioral patterns that are congruent with that self-concept (Graziano, Jensen-Campbell, & Hair, 1996).

Individual differences in social information processing also may reflect unconscious mental processes; individual differences play a more important role in automatic rather than in controlled processing of social information (e.g., Rabiner, Lenhart, & Lochman, 1990). Indeed, psychoanalytic concepts (such as transference) are implicit in cognitive perspectives on personality development. For example, methodologically sophisticated N = 1 studies and experimental studies using the tools of research in social cognition have shown how recurring emotional states organize experience and how individuals transfer affective responses developed in the context of previous relationships to new relationships (e.g., Andersen & Baum, 1994; Horowitz et al., 1994). However, persistent ways of perceiving, thinking, and behaving are not preserved simply by psychic forces, nor are they entirely attributable to features of the cognitive system; they also are maintained by the consequences of everyday action (Trachtenberg & Viken, 1994).

A second set of consistency generating reactive person-environment transactions may come into play when a person's existing cognitive and emotional schemas surrounding their personality are threatened. This second set of mechanisms, which we refer to as *strategic information-processing mechanisms*, subsumes a wide range of conscious and unconscious information-processing factors. These mechanisms share one thing in common; they all act to reconfigure the meaning of experience, not experience itself.

The first mechanism drawn from lifespan developmental theory is ironically termed *accommodative* strategies (Brandtstädter & Greve, 1994) and refers to the adjustments one makes in goals or self-evaluative standards in order to maintain consistent self-views (see also Heckhausen, this volume). Brandtstädter (1992) showed that people increase the use of flexible goal adjustment with age and simultaneously diminish their tenacious goal pursuit. Thus, with age people recalibrate their goals rather than persist in attempting to achieve specific outcomes (for example, earning enough for retirement rather than earning enough to become rich). By recalibrating goals, people can maintain consistent self-views (I am successful). One of the most effective means with which people can maintain consistent views of themselves is to renorm their self-evaluative standards. For example, with age individuals inevitably face decreasing physical and cognitive abilities, especially in comparison with young people. Rather than norming themselves against young people or people in general, older individuals can maintain the perception that they are active and sharp by renorming their evaluative standards exclusively against older people.

Similarly, the optimization and compensation strategies from the SOC model (Baltes & Baltes, 1990) can be seen as continuity-promoting mechanisms. *Optimization* refers to emphasizing goals and activities that reflect a person's strengths rather than emphasizing something new or untested (such as selection). *Compensation* reflects the inevitable tailoring of goals and activities to make up for the natural degradation of abilities in old age. So, for example, one can both emphasize and come to depend on crystallized knowledge more than fluid intelligence because of the diminishing speed with which information is processed in old age. Both of these mechanisms entail emphasizing, if not fostering, existing characteristics or skills. Applied to the sphere of personality, one can easily see that the successful utilization of optimization and compensation strategies would facilitate the maintenance of personality traits. For example, despite decreasing expenditure of energy at work (such as a propensity to work hard), a person's impression that he or she is conscientious may be maintained if the person can emphasize other facets of conscientiousness, such as their organization skills or ability to be efficient. With time and decreasing energy, a person may be forced to fall back on organizational skills to compensate for a lack of energy and efficiency.

Brandtstädter and Greve (1994) described a fourth information-processing factor, *immunization*, which is defined as processes that protect the self from self-discrepant evidence. These mechanisms include deemphasizing the personal relevance of an experience, searching for and finding an alternative interpretation, and questioning the credibility of the source of information. In relation to personality consistency, one may imagine a person receiving feedback from a friend or acquaintance that he or she is neurotic. If this person feels that he or she is not neurotic, then immunizing mechanisms may be employed to discount the friend's opinion. To maintain a consistent self-perception, this person may attempt to trivialize the importance of the relationship, attribute the feedback to the friend's own issues (alternative interpretation), or question the friend's ability to make such interpretations (question credibility). All of these strategies would serve to maintain the person's self-perception that he or she is not neurotic or at least not as neurotic as the friend claims.

Accommodation, optimization, compensation, and immunization mechanisms are assumed to be cognitive schemas that can be accessed in conscious awareness. *Defense mechanisms*, a fifth strategic information-processing factor, are assumed to perform similar functions to the conscious information-processing mechanisms identified above but to do so unconsciously (Norem, 1998). Contemporary perspectives define defense mechanisms as unconscious mental operations that function to protect the individual from experiencing excessive anxiety (Cramer, 1998). Defense mechanisms are seen not only in the classical psychoanalytic sense as acting to filter unacceptable internal thoughts, impulses, or wishes but also in the contemporary sense as filtering out experiences and information that threaten one's self-esteem or self-integration (Cramer, 1998).

If we assume that, in part, personality change results from experiencing events that contradict closely held views of the self or from receiving feedback from others that we are different than originally expected (see below), then defense mechanisms should contribute to continuity in personality. We suspect that receiving feedback that contradicts one's self-perceptions is anxiety provoking. The anxiety, whether conscious or not, that is experienced in these situations should by its very nature invoke the use of defense mechanisms. Take, for example, the incident described above where a person receives feedback that he or she is neurotic. Rather than consciously reshaping the nature of the information, an alternative would be to unconsciously project back the information on the person delivering the feedback. The person providing feedback is now considered neurotic and needs the attention, if not sympathy, of the person originally deemed to be neurotic. Alternatively, the person could conveniently forget (repress) that the he or she was described as neurotic or "isolate" the event from other cognitions and emotions (Baumeister, Dale, & Sommer, 1998), so that it is quickly forgotten or deemed to be of little importance. Needless to say, personality continuity should be maintained to the extent that defense mechanisms can transform or inoculate disconfirming experience or feedback.

We refer to accommodation, optimization, compensation, immunization, and defense mechanisms as "strategic" information processing because we see each as serving the agenda of maintaining continuity in self-perceptions and continuity in self-integrity, which should both coincide with elevated levels of personality continuity. These strategic information-processing mechanisms act in conscious awareness and the unconscious. Unfortunately, to our knowledge, the continuity-promoting nature of these mechanisms has not been tested in longitudinal studies of personality development.

When the two sets of reactive person-environment transactions are combined, we see two compelling reasons for why people maintain consistent self-perceptions over time. First, people automatically filter incoming information so that it conforms to pre-existing self-perceptions. Second, when confronted with information that contradicts or threatens conscious or unconscious self-perceptions, people can use a variety of strategic information-processing mechanisms to inoculate the threatening information and render it benign. Thus it is seldom the case that humans are simple, passive recipients of experience, which is often the assumption behind interventions intended to improve people in some fashion. Rather, people will be intrinsically prone to gather self-affirming experience and discount or defend against experience that demands change. People are prone to remain consistent and not to react unwittingly to their environment.

Evocative Person-Environment Transactions   Individuals evoke distinctive reactions from others on the basis of their unique personality characteristics. The person acts; the environment reacts; and the person reacts back in mutually interlocking evocative transaction. Such transactions continue throughout the life course and promote the continuity of personality.

Already very early in life, children evoke consistent responses from their social environment that affect their subsequent interactions with adults and peers (Bell & Chapman, 1986). It also is through evocative transactions that phenomenological interpretations of situations—the products of reactive interaction—are transformed into situations that are "real in their consequences." Expectations can lead an individual to project particular interpretations onto new situations and relationships and then to behave in ways that corroborate those expectations (Wachtel, 1994).

The process through which evocative person-environment transactions can sustain individual differences has been explored in social-interactional and experimental analyses of aggressive behavior where children's coercive behaviors have been shown to shape the responses of adults to them (Lytton, 1990; Patterson & Bank, 1989). This is not, however, substituting one "main-effects" model (parental influence) with another such model (child influence). A transactional model recognizes that partners react back and forth in mutually reciprocally related evocative transactions and contribute to the continuity of dispositional characteristics by evoking congruent responses from each other. Increasingly, behavioral genetic designs will help to untangle whether evocative effects are the product of genetic differences or represent true environmental effects (O'Connor, Deater-Deckard, Fulker, Rutter, & Plomin, 1998; see also McClearn, this volume), and new statistical techniques for analyzing interaction data may help to decompose how different individuals and relationships in the family conspire to maintian behavioral continuity (Cook, Kenny, & Goldstein, 1991).

Individuals also manifest their personalities in expressive behavior (Borkenau & Liebler, 1995). Facial expressions of emotion are especially important in evocative person-environment transactional processes for they convey information to others what the individual is feeling and about how the individual is likely to act. The finding that personality traits are registered in facial expressions suggests that personality-related expressions of emotion may influence the course of social development by evoking congruent and reciprocal responses from other persons in the social environment (Keltner, 1996).

Proactive Person-Environment Transactions

One of the primary tenets of Baltes (1997) SOC model is the idea that persons select goals and tasks that shape their developmental contexts for a long period of time. These goals, which Roberts and Robins (2000a) described as major life goals, affect the primary structures of the life course, including the type of work people pursue and the types of relationship partners people seek out. Arguably, the most consequential environments for personality development are interpersonal environments, and the personality-sustaining effects of proactive transactions are most apparent in friendship formation and mate selection (Asendorpf & Wilpers, 1998; Kandel, Davies, & Baydar, 1990). Personality effects on social relationships serve to maintain and elaborate intitial personality differences between people and proactive transactions may account for the age-related increase in the magnitude of stability coefficients across the lifespan.

Friends tend to resemble each other in physical characteristics, values, attitudes, and behaviors (e.g., Dishion, Patterson, Stoolmiller, & Skinner, 1991). Whereas popular wisdom holds that members of peer groups are similar because peers influence their friends to behave in similar ways, empirical studies suggest that members of peer groups are similar because individuals selectively choose to affiliate with similar others (e.g., Ennett & Bauman, 1994). Cairns and Cairns (1994) suggest that affiliations with similar others may serve as guides for norm formation and the consolidation of behavior patterns over time. Continuities in social networks may thus contribute to behavioral continuity because the demands of the social environment remain relatively stable over time. Moreover, consistency in how members of the social network relate to the individual may contribute to behavioral continuity because it affects how individuals view and define themselves.

Research on marriage similarly indicates that partners tend to resemble each other in physical characteristics, cognitive abilities, values and attitudes, and personality traits (Epstein & Guttman, 1984). Assortative mating has genetic and social consequences, and it also may have implications for the course of personality development because similarities between spouses create an environment that reinforces initial tendencies (Buss, 1984). This proactive transactional process is documented in a 50-year longitudinal study of political attitudes. The political liberalism acquired by women while in college in the 1930s was sustained across their life course in part because they selected liberal friends and husbands who continued to support their politically liberal attitudes (Alwin, Cohen, & Newcomb, 1991). In a 10-year longitudinal study of couples, Caspi and Herbener (1990) found that persons who married a partner similar to themselves were subsequently more likely to show personality continuity over time. It may be that through assortative mating, individuals set in motion processes of social interchange that help to sustain their dispositions, for in selecting marriage partners individuals also select the environments they will inhabit and the reinforcements to which they will be subject for many years (Buss, 1987).

Dispositional Mechanisms

A fourth category of factors that may contribute to personality trait consistency has to do with a person's psychological makeup. That is, certain personality traits tend to facilitate consistency across the life course. Several psychological factors associated with increased consistency cluster around the concept of maturity. Roberts, Caspi, and Moffitt (2000) defined maturity in terms of the Big Five as a combination of agree-ableness, conscientiousness, and emotional stability (see also Allport, 1961; Hogan & Roberts, in press). That is people who are mature have the capacity for warm interper-sonal relationships, are responsible and dependable, and don't fall to pieces under stress. The latter component of maturity, adjustment, has been shown to correlate with person-ality consistency in a number of studies. For example, Asendorpf and Van Aken (1991) found that ego resiliency, which is, in part, related to emotional adjustment (Klohnen, 1996), predicted personality consistency over time in a longitudinal sample of chil-dren. More specifically, children who were more resilient tended to be more consistent over time. Similarly, Schuerger, Zarrella, and Hotz (1989) found that clinical samples, which we can assume are less emotionally stable, were less consistent than nonclini-cal samples. Also consistent with the Roberts et al. (2000) maturity hypothesis is the proposal by Clausen (1993) that the trait of planful competence predicts higher levels of personality consistency in adulthood. People who are planfully competent tend to be more self-confident, dependable, and intellectually invested. Finally, Roberts, et al. (2000) demonstrated strong empirical support for the maturity hypothesis. In an eight-year longitudinal study, they found that men and women who were more controlled, less neurotic, and more prosocially oriented demonstrated less change in personal-ity traits and greater profile consistency across personality traits over an eight-year period.

How Does Change Come About? Mechanisms of Change Across the Life Course

We now focus on the empirical and theoretical mechanisms that promote personality change. Most of the theoretical writings on what causes personality change come from nonpsychological domains (such as sociology) or rely on behavioral models or role the-ories that have not been updated in relation to personality development in over 30 years. In reviewing the disparate literature on personality change, we identified four primary mechanisms of change—responding to contingencies, watching ourselves, watching others, and listening to others (Caspi & Roberts, 1999). We review each of these in turn.

Responding to Contingencies

One of the most simplistic and yet powerful theories of change is the notion that people respond to reinforcers and punishers and that by doing so change their behavior. That is, they accommodate to an environmental press that calls for them to act differently than they have done in the past (Block, 1982; Brandstädter & Greve, 1994). The contingencies that people respond to can be either explicit or implicit. Explicit contingencies come in the form of concrete contingencies applied to a person's behavior where that person is aware of the agenda. Implicit contingencies are more subtle and come in the form of unspoken expectations and demands that often come with the acquisition of new social roles (Sarbin, 1964).

The most direct form of explict contingency is a parent's attempt to shape a child's behavior. For example, Kagan's (1994) work on behavioral inhibition demonstrates the interplay between parental attempts to shape a child's personality and the child's biologically and genetically based temperament. Behaviorally inhibited children experience greater levels of distress at lower thresholds when confronted with novel situations. Although childhood behavioral inhibition has been related to possessing traits of shyness, introversion, and neuroticism in adulthood, not all inhibited children become shy adults. Several parental interventions on the part of inhibited children can shape whether an inhibited child becomes an introverted adult. Parents who expose their inhibited children to novelty, provide firm and consistent limits, and do not overprotect their children from novel situations may help children overcome behavioral inhibition (Kagan, 1994). In contrast, many parents respond to their child's distress in novel situations by rewarding the child for avoiding these situations in the future. The reinforcement of these avoidance behaviors inadvertently promotes continued behavioral inhibition (Gerlsma, Emmelkamp, & Arrindell, 1990) and may increase the likelihood that the child grows up to become an inhibited adult. Likewise, different parenting socialization practices interact with childhood temperament in the development of conscientiousness (Kochanska, 1991). Fearful children are more likely to internalize regulators of conduct when mothers use subtle, gentle, psychological discipline. Fearless children, in contrast, do not respond well to increased socialization pressures; rather they tend to develop stronger internalization in response to a mutually positive and cooperative orientation between themselves and their parents (Kochanska, 1997).

Implicit contingencies are often communicated through the acquisition of roles or positions in a group, community, or society. Implicit contingencies are thought to shape behavior, and thus personality, by defining the appropriate way to play a role (Sarbin, 1964). Roles such as being a leader or follower come with specific expectations and demands for appropriate behavior that is known to the person assuming the role and to the people interacting with that person. For example, Sarbin and Jones (1955) asked respondents to describe their expectations for the manager role. Across several groups, the respondents agreed that managers should act industrious, serious, stable, intelligent, fair-minded, tactful, and reasonable. Thus, a person who is impulsive by nature would be expected to set aside his or her predilection to make snap decisions if he or she assumes the role of manager in an organization. Exposure to these implicit role demands over a long period of time may be one factor contributing to personality change (e.g., Roberts, 1997).

Behaviorist notions of shaping personality directly through parenting styles or role pressures can be overly simplistic. Nonetheless, behavioral models of change are still the most elegant and powerful factors that influence change in a person's behavior and subsequent change in personality. The factors most often missing from behaviorally derived socialization models have to do with the cognitive and volitional aspects of personality. A discussion of these factors follows.

Watching Ourselves

In addition to the press of the environment on behavior, one of the critical moderators of change is whether people have the opportunity to reflect on their own actions. For example, many efforts aimed at changing patients in a therapeutic situation focus on promoting insight into maladaptive behaviors. Psychodynamically oriented therapists establish a level of transference in which the patient's unconscious proclivities then arise. Once the maladaptive unconscious drives are identified, a therapist may then attempt to make the patient aware of these patterns in order to strengthen the person's capacity for more adaptive alternatives. Likewise, cognitively oriented therapists attempt to identify problematic thoughts and replace them through cognitive reeducation with more adaptive schemas, scripts, or interpretations of day-to-day events (see Messer & Warren, 1990, for a review). In essence, much of what goes on in therapy is an attempt to shift people's focus to watch themselves more closely in their daily lives. By gaining insight into their behavior, clients can then direct their efforts toward acting differently in future situations.

Change also is thought to come about through watching ourselves act differently in new situations or in response to new contingencies. Thus, change comes about through a combination of environmental contingencies and self-insight. The most intensively studied model consistent with this position in Kohn and Schooler's (1983) learning-generalization model. Like the socialization models, the first key position of the learning-generalization model is that our psychological makeup changes in response to the specific pressures and demands of roles such as work and parenting. Where the learning-generalization approach goes beyond simple behaviorism is in detailing the process through which contingencies are shaped by cognition. Personality is thought to be shaped by role experiences through the internalization of role demands into one's self-concept (Deci & Ryan, 1990). This introjection process is facilitated when people draw conclusions about themselves by watching their own actions. For example, if taking on a supervisory role entails less personal connection to coworkers and subordinates, then supervisors may see themselves acting less friendly with subordinates, which they then interpret as a lack of interpersonal connection and diminished sociability (Howard & Bray, 1989).

Invariably, introjected experiences that happen in specific contexts are generalized to other domains of life. For example, if a woman becomes more self-directed at work, she will become more self-directed in her marriage and her leisure activities. Kohn and Schooler (1983) report evidence to support the generalization effect, showing that men in intellectually demanding careers increased their engagement in intellectually stimulating leisure-time activities.

Watching Others

Another significant source of information and learning comes through watching others, such as parents, teachers, coaches, and mentors. This approach to change is consistent with a social-learning perspective—that multiple information-processing mechanisms are involved in the acquisition of new behavior (Bandura, 1986). Bandura's (1965) Bobo doll experiments constitute some of the most elegant studies illustrating the human capacity to acquire behavioral potential through simply watching others, especially role models, and further illustrate the importance of combining observation with implicit or explicit reward structures for the behavior to be expressed (see also Bandura, 1986).

The most likely sources of observational learning are parents and significant role models. For example, the child's opportunity to watch his or her parent's work and how they approach their job may influence the child's own choice of career. Research on vocational interests appears to support this claim, showing that a child's vocational interests are related to the values that parents hold (Holland, 1962). Fathers who valued curiosity in their sons had sons who peaked on the investigative and artistic scales of Holland's vocational model (Holland, 1996). Of course, these covariations between parent and child values could be explained in part by the heritability of vocational interests (Bouchard, 1995).

In work contexts, observational learning is afforded through relationships with mentors (Chao, 1997). Mentorship reflects an intense work relationship between senior and junior members of an organization (Kram, 1985). One of the major functions of mentors is to demonstrate role appropriate behaviors and to show how to behave effectively in an organizational setting. Although there are few longitudinal studies showing that change comes about because of the mentor relationship, outcome studies that compare mentored versus nonmentored workers show some of the potential socializing effects of observing a role model. Riley and Wrench (1985) found that mentored women reported higher levels of career success and satisfaction than nonmentored women. Chao, Walz, and Gardner (1992) found that mentored engineers and managers experienced more job satisfaction, greater understanding of organizational norms and goals, and higher salaries.

Listening to Others

A critical source of information about ourselves (and subsequently a potential source of change) is the people with whom we interact, as well as the feedback they provide to us. This is the primary thesis of symbolic interactionism (Blumer, 1969) and identity theory (Stryker, 1987). Symbolic interactionism emphasizes the meanings that individuals attribute to experience. These meanings are thought to be derived primarily through social interaction (Blumer, 1969).

Identity theory translates the sociological system of symbolic interactionism from the level of society to the level of the individual. According to identity theory, people develop meanings about themselves through receiving feedback from other individuals (Stryker & Statham, 1985). This feedback, described as *reflected appraisals*, can be either congruent or incongruent with a person's self-perceptions (Kiecolt, 1994). Burke (1991) proposed that when reflected appraisals are incongruent with people's self-perceptions, they change their behavior in order to change the reflected appraisals. Thus, when people receive new feedback concerning their personality, either through the changes in their friends' or spouses' opinions or through exposure to new social groups, people will be more likely to change.

Unfortunately, the empirical database showing that listening to others contributes to change is lacking. Rather, the most provocative research in this area, provided by Swann (1987), shows that people tend not to listen to others if it means changing their self-perceptions. In an ingenious series of studies, Swann has shown that (1) people search out feedback that confirms their preexisting self-perceptions, (2) people prefer to associate with others who confirm their self-perceptions, and (3) this process is relatively independent of the evaluative nature of the feedback. That is, people with negative self-perceptions prefer to hear from others that they are seen as neurotic and depressed than to hear that they are seen as happy and upbeat (see also Swann, Stein-Seroussi, & McNulty, 1992). Most of Swann's research has been cross-sectional. We still do not know the long-term effects of being given feedback by significant people in our lives, such as spouses or respected coworkers, that contradicts our closely held self-views. It may be that persistence on the part of spouses, friends, and coworkers may lead to some personality change.

Why Does Personality Continuity Increase with Age?

The challenge that confronts us now is to integrate mechanisms of consistency and change with the picture of personality development provided by the data accrued over the last several decades. In the process, we describe an organizing system that can explain how consistency and change mechanisms cooccur in an individual and explain the gradual increase in consistency over the life course, combined with the capacity for change that is apparently never eliminated. We propose that this puzzle is solved by linking consistency and change in personality traits to the concept and facets of what is termed "identity" and more specifically to the development of identity and aspects of identity structure.

Our argument is based on two assumptions. First, we argue that the process of developing, committing to, and maintaining an identity leads to processes that facilitate both continuity and change in personality traits (e.g., see Helson & Srivastava, 2001). Second, the process of identity development does not end in adolescence, as originally conceived (Erikson, 1950), but continues throughout adulthood (Stewart & Ostrove, 1998). Therefore, personality change should continue well into adulthood, and the increase in personality consistency should correspond to the strengthening of commitments to identity that occur with age (e.g., Waterman & Archer, 1990).

Identity has multiple meanings depending on the source of the definition. From an Eriksonian perspective, to have an identity reflects, in part, coming to terms with how one will relate to society as an adult, especially through one's career (Erikson, 1950). Alternatively, Marcia (1980) defined identity as "a self-structure—an internal, self-constructed, dynamic organization of drives, abilities, beliefs, and individual history" (p. 159). Similarly, Waterman (1984) described identity as a "clearly delineated self-definition comprising the goals, values, and beliefs to which the person is unequivocally committed" (p. 331).

From the perspective of sociologists and social psychologists, the definition of identity is broader in scope. Burke (1991) defined identity as "a set of 'meanings' applied to the self in a social role or situation defining what it means to be who one is"(p. 837). Waterman and Archer (1990) also differentiated subnorms of identity that reflect the fact that people can develop identities in specific domains, such as work, politics, and religion. With time and age, these identity domains are thought to become increasingly integrated into a coherent overall identity. Baumeister (1997) argued that identity consists of the definitions that are created for and superimposed on the self. People make choices and take actions to fulfill a vision of how they are in the present and how they want to be in the future. The imposition of an identity reflects the fact that as social beings, we are often assigned qualities by others based on factors beyond our control, such as our sex and race or the class and religion into which we were born.

These definitions share commonalities important to our argument. First, each maintains that an identity is developed in relation to society, most likely through a role such as work, marriage, friendships, a specific leisure-time activity, or a combination of any or all of these. Second, the process of creating an identity requires making choices and commitments and entails taking actions on the part of an individual to maintain the identity throughout adulthood. Third, a sense of identity provides the perception of continuity. Fourth, identities may be forced on us despite our best wishes.

How Do Identity development and Identity Structure Explain Personality-Trait Consistency?

Intrinsic to the identity-development process is the search for an identity that fits with one's values, abilities, and predispositions. Adolescence, which is the primary period of identity development, is a time "during which the young adult through free role experimentation may find a niche in some section of his society, a niche which is firmly defined and yet seems to be uniquely made for him" (Erikson, 1968, p. 156). Thus, one of the overriding concerns of adolescence and young adulthood is selecting and building an identity that fits with one's characteristics. We see in this process the manifestation of the selection process identified by Baltes and Baltes (1990) and others (Buss, 1987; Ickes, Snyder, & Garcia, 1997; Snyder & Ickes, 1985) that presumably contributes to personality consistency, if one chooses an identity well. Supporting the contention that building one's niche facilitates personality continuity is recent longitudinal research showing that elevated levels of person-environment fit predicted higher levels of personality consistency over time (Roberts & Robins, 2000b).

Identity development also facilitates personality consistency through providing clear reference points for making life decisions (proactive person-environment effects). Erikson (1950) highlighted the role identity plays in maintaining continuity, arguing that a sense of identity provides the ability to experience one's self as something that has continuity and sameness, and to act accordingly. Likewise, Burke (1991) argued that identity provides a set of meanings that serve as a standard or reference for who one is. People who have committed to an identity can make more informed decisions about what job to take or which person to marry because they have a clearer perception of their own attributes and goals. Choosing an identity that fits better with one's characteristics should lead to consistency through one's attributes being rewarded in these new environments. Put another way, having a strong identity should permit a person to enter into situations in which assimilation takes precedence over accommodation (Whitbourne, 1996).

In addition to simply having an identity, several features of identity, such as clarity and certainty, may enhance the proactive selection process. Clarity should lead to choosing environments that are more consistent with one's identity. Choosing and interacting in environments that are consistent with one's identity will make experiences easier to assimilate (e.g., Block, 1982; Brandtstädter & Greve, 1994). Conversely, research has shown that failure to express one's traits leads to anxiety (Wiggins & Trobst, 1997). Choosing friends, partners, and coworkers who are similar to ourselves brings about more opportunities to express our traits and to be reinforced for who we are (Cairns & Cairns, 1994; Caspi & Herbener, 1990; Pfeffer, 1995).

Identity clarity and certainty also should facilitate optimization and compensation processes. Individuals with clearer, more certain identities will know their strengths and weaknesses better and therefore be able to emphasize their strengths more efficiently (optimization) and understand how to make amends for their weaknesses (compensation). Conversely, persons who are unclear or uncertain about their identity should be less able to choose situations that capitalize on their attributes and may be essentially unaware of the relevance of new situations to their identity (Baumgardner, 1990).

Being committed to an identity also may promote other personality-consistency mechanisms. Strong identities may serve as a filter of information and life experiences (reactive person-environment transaction) and lead each individual to interpret new events in ways that are consistent with their indentities. Berzonsky (1993; Berzonsky & Neimeyer, 1994) found that different identity styles were associated with different patterns of information processing. For example, the foreclosed identity status was associated with processing social information on a normative basis, whereas the moratorium identity status was associated with a more informational search orientation. To the extent that having a clear, well-defined identity overlaps with concepts such as self-schema (the importance of self-relevant information), evidence would support the notion that identity serves as a filter of self-relevant information. Indeed, studies have shown that self-schemas affect our judgments of other persons (Hochwaelder, 1996), speed processing of information consistent with the self (Fekken & Holden, 1992), and promote the recall of self-relevant information (Bruch, Kaflowitz, & Berger, 1988). Dodge and Tomlin (1987) even showed that self-schemas are imposed on situations that are ambiguous, leading to interpretations that are consistent with one's self-concept. Likewise, to the extent that a person's identity becomes known to others in the form of a reputation (Hogan & Roberts, 2000), other people may react to a person in a way that is consistent with his or her personality (evocative person-environment transaction). For example, if a person has a reputation of being outgoing, other people may invite him or her to social engagements more often. Or if a person has a reputation for being domineering, others may avoid that person or act submissive in his or her presence, which in turn engenders more domineering behavior.

If one accepts that a person's overall identity is really an integration of multiple role identities and their components (Roberts & Donahue, 1994; Rosenberg & Gara, 1985), then the ways in which identities and their components are structured should also affect personality consistency. For example, role identities, which represent the characteristics that a person ascribes to himself or herself in a particular role, are often organized hierarchically (Stryker & Statham, 1985). This hierarchy is structured around whether a person sees the role identity as important, satisfying, and worth investing in. This notion of a role-identity hierarchy is similar to the notion of a cardinal trait (Allport, 1961). There are certain attributes that are more central to a person's identity than other attributes. We suspect that features of more central role identities will be less likely to change as people will be more invested and committed to maintaining consistency in their cardinal dispositions. Conversely, characteristics that are not central may be less consistent because they are less relevant to a person's overall identity.

An additional feature of identity structure that may affect personality consistency is the extent to which a person's identity is complex or differentiated. This feature of identity structure reflects the number of different characteristics and their distinctiveness within a person's identity (Rosenberg & Gara, 1985). For example, if people see their "work identity" as a place in which both achievement and affiliation actions arise and their "friend identity" as a place only for affiliative actions, then the latter is less complex than the work-role identity. Likewise, if a person has many role identities, then their overall identity is more differentiated. Complexity can facilitate personality consistency by permitting multiple outlets for the enactment of the same trait. For example, the experience of a setback at work that threatens a person's self-perception that he or she is hard working and achievement oriented may be ameliorated if this person has other role identities in which achievement-oriented behavior can be enacted, such as in a "leisure identity" dominated by competitive activities. Conversely, if a person does not have a well-elaborated identity structure, then setbacks that threaten primary features of a role identity may be more likely to result in change in personality because there are no ways to compensate for the negative feedback.

Aspects of identity achievement, certainty, and consolidation also are related to dispositional factors linked to personality consistency. For example, having an achieved identity was found to be related to higher levels of psychological well-being (Helson, Stewart, & Ostrove, 1995). Vandewater, Ostrove, and Stewart (1997) showed that having an achieved identity was directly related to higher family and work-role quality and indirectly to life satisfaction and psychological well-being. Ronka and Pulkkinen (1995) found that having a clear career line, akin to the notion of an achieved identity, was related to fewer problems in social functioning in adulthood. Identity achievement also has been shown to be related to higher levels of self-esteem, autonomy, and moral reasoning and lower levels of anxiety (see Marcia, 1980). Likewise, self-certainty is related to an increased sense of control over future situations (Trope & Ben-Yair, 1982), clarity of the self-concept is associated with higher levels of self-esteem (Campbell, 1990), and identity consolidation is related to less marital tension, positive feelings about mothering, work satisfaction, and personality variables such as self-confidence, positive well-being, competence, affiliation, and independence (Pals, 1999). Therefore, identity and aspects of identity such as achievement, certainty, clarity, and consolidation are linked to higher levels of psychological well-being and adjustment—aspects of maturity that in turn are related to higher levels of personality-trait consistency.

In sum, both empirical evidence and logical analysis point to the potential role that identity and aspects of identity play in facilitating personality-trait consistency. Having a strong identity may promote personality-linked life choices, create more powerful filtering effects on self-relevant experience and information, and elicit reactions from the environment that are consistent with one's identity.

How Do Identity Development and Identity Structure Explain Personality Change?

The link between identity processes and mechanisms of change is less clearly supported by empirical research, and therefore we must rely more on conceptual and logical arguments. It is clear that choosing and consolidating identities often entails exposure to new situations and roles. Inevitably, people will select environments that bring with them contingencies that reward certain behaviors and punish other behaviors. To the extent that a person selects an identity that is consistent with his or her abilities and proclivities, the new identity should reinforce his or her personality. For example, if a meticulous person has the good fortune to enter a profession that reinforces his or her behavior, such as accounting, he or she should find ample rewards for continuing a detailed approach to work. This example highlights one of the most likely ways in which identity selection and consolidation may lead to personality-trait change. It may enhance and deepen personality characteristics that already exist. Therefore, over time, our accountant may become even more meticulous and painstaking in his or her approach to work, and this may generalize to other life domains (e.g., see Kohn & Schooler, 1978).

Of course, new identities, and the roles in which they are played out, will inevitably bring contingencies that do not match one's personality: "Adults must come to terms with what they have discovered to be the negative as well as the positive aspects of their identity commitments" (Waterman & Archer, 1990, p. 41). The contingencies that do not fit an individual's personality lead to negative affect, which may press the individual to accommodate and change (e.g., Clore, Schartz, & Conway, 1994). One example of this phenomenon comes from a series of studies examining the factors that contribute to criminals desisting from crime. Sampson and Laub (1990) argue that the establishment of strong social bonds leads to a decrease in antisocial and delinquent behavior in criminals. Social bonds are investments made in social institutions such as work and marriage that are reflected in becoming committed to a job or developing a strong attachment to a spouse. These social investments are thought to exact a form of social control through the role demands embedded in these contexts that call on individuals to act with more responsibility and probity—that is, to change their personality. Sampson and Laub (1990) found that job stability and a strong emotional attachment to one's spouse significantly reduced delinquent and criminal activity in men (see also Laub, Nagin, & Sampson, 1998). Viewed from the lens of identity formation, one could assume that being a criminal and being married were both components of the identities of these men. For these men, to commit successfully to and consolidate their marriage identity entailed a reduction in their criminal behavior. That is, they had to let go of those aspects of themselves subsumed in their criminal identity, the result of which was for these men to act more responsibly as they aged.

Another example of the role of identity in the personality-change process comes from the classic longitudinal study of the career progression, or lack thereof, of AT&T managers (Howard & Bray, 1989). As the AT&T managers increased in managerial level, they became more ambitious and achievement oriented and less affiliative than managers who did not increase in position. One interpretation of this profile of change is that it resulted from the acquisition of power and responsibility that came with the leader role. With increasing status and commensurate increases in power, the AT&T

managers were given the responsibilities to make important decisions such as whom to hire and fire. The acquisition of power would inevitably reinforce self-perceptions of ambitiousness and achievement. More important, acquiring power over subordinates, something that comes only with the acquisition of a role (Hogan & Roberts, 2000), would thwart affiliative motives. After being forced to fire, demote, or pass over employees, it would become clear that being close to one's subordinates may result in emotional distress at their departure. We can assume that maintaining the identity of being a "successful manager" entailed a reduction in sociability if that identity was to be maintained in a consistent fashion. It is unlikely that becoming less sociable was part of their identity of a successful executive, and yet it was still the result of successfully enacting the identity.

Just as new roles and identities bring contingencies that may shape personality, they also afford opportunities to see ourselves doing things that are novel. For example, a new father who learns the responsibilities of changing diapers or the joys of making a son or daughter smile is, in turn, given the opportunity to see himself act in ways that he may not have envisioned. To the extent that the father did not envision his behavior, seeing his new skills develop may shift his self-perception and result in personality change. Likewise, new identities and developing identities will bring with them other people to watch, such as mentors or friends. Selecting and consolidating one's identity may affect this in two ways. First, entering into an identity narrows and specifies new social comparisons (Waterman & Archer, 1990). Social comparisons may provide important information about one's personality, such as clarification of one's self-perceptions. Second, establishing an identity will make it clear whom one wants to observe and learn from. Examples of this process are provided by research on life-turning points in settings such as the military, which afford recruits wider social comparisons and more role models (e.g., Elder, 1985; Sampson & Laub, 1990).

Selecting and consolidating an identity also provides opportunities for receiving feedback. At the crudest level, people become aware of their success relative to others. Beyond global evaluations of success and failure, new identities may provide rich feedback on one's specific attributes, such as work style, relationship habits, or parenting idiosyncrasies. As one consolidates an identity, others may provide feedback directly, such as through a performance-review process at work, or indirectly, through watching others perform the same role. Many social institutions are specifically equipped to provide feedback. For example, most large organizations provide training in areas such as customer service, leadership, and team building that involve an evaluation of one's skills and an attempt to enhance them. Similarly, many couples engage in some form of therapy or counseling that also provides structured insights into relationship style.

Finally, sometimes we select new identities in order to change (Snyder & Ickes, 1985). People may choose a different career or partner to try a different life path or attempt to fulfill a vision of an ideal or possible self (e.g., Markus & Nurius, 1986). Religious systems may be shifted to enhance spirituality. Graduate school may be entertained as a way of enhancing expertise and critical acumen. New hobbies may be adopted in old age for the purpose of providing challenge and personal growth (Whitbourne, 1996).

In summary, it is clear that identity-selection and -consolidation processes provide opportunities for personality-trait change. Currently, there is little direct research demonstrating the link (cf. Pals, 1999). What is needed are longitudinal studies that follow both the identity-selection and -consolidation process, the mechanisms of change entailed in those processes, and personality-trait development over time.

How Do Identity Development and Identity Structure Explain the Increase in Personality Consistency with Age?

To be useful, our link between identity and personality-trait development must also account for the increase in consistency with age and the higher levels of instability in young adulthood. The ability of the identity-development and personality-trait-development connection to explain the gradual increase in consistency rests on the assumption that identity development does not stop in adolescence. Rather, choosing, establishing, and consolidating a strong identity should take longer than originally hypothesized and extend well into adulthood.

We contend that identity development continues well into what is considered adulthood and that identity consolidation may continue further still. For example, the timeline for what is considered adolescence or the identity-formation period has been stetching significantly over the last 100 years. Before 1920, fewer than 16% of the populace completed high school, and most people left school by age 16 to start a career (Modell, 1989). Earlier in the twentieth century, many people were entering their careers in their late teens and early twenties and by age 30 were in their career for 14 years and most likely married and with children (Modell, 1989). Furthermore, life expectancy at this time was approximately 55. The combination of life-context factors and life-expectancy limitations during this earlier period in history meant that age 30 may have corresponded to middle age. In contrast, the generations that followed increasingly acquired more schooling, delayed their careers, and delayed their development of a strong identity (Littwin, 1986). With the increasing effectiveness of public-health interventions, the lifespan steadily increased. Current generations now confront a life course in which childhood and adolescence can stretch into the twenties, and identity-related decisions about work, marriage, and children can be delayed well into the thirties (Arnett, 2000; Modell, 1989). Arnett (2000) refers to the period between ages 15 and 30 as "emerging adulthood" in a tacit acknowledgement that adulthood is now forestalled both demographically and psychologically until after age 30.

Findings from three studies of identity development support the assumption that identity development and identity processes continue well beyond adolescence and sometimes into middle age. First, Pals (1999) showed that identity consolidation, the process of refining and enhancing the identity choices made in late adolescence, continued well into young adulthood and possibly early middle age. Second, Pulkkinen and Kokko (2000) examined patterns of continuity and change in overall identity and domain-specific identities in a sample of men and women from age 27 to age 36. They found that men and women continued to show identity development in this age period and furthermore that the preponderance of change was in the direction of greater commitment. People more often moved into achieved and foreclosed identities than into moratorium or diffuse identities. Third, in an ongoing investigation of identity in middle age, Stewart, Ostrove, and Helson (2001) developed scales assessing identity certainty that tapped a person's sense of having a strong and clear identity. They found that identity certainty was rated higher in middle age (ages 40 and 50) than in young adulthood (age 30). The combination of changing life-course demographics, the evidence for continued change in identity in adulthood, and the verification that identity consolidation continues to take place after identities are committed to provides preliminary support for the argument that identity development continues well into middle age.

If the development of an identity and identity certainty continue into middle age, this could explain, in part, why personality consistency tends to increase until after age 50 (Roberts & DelVecchio, 2000). Stronger and clearer identities should facilitate the process of selecting roles and environments that are consistent with one's personality. Furthermore, a strong identity should facilitate optimization and compensation processes by providing a clearer picture of what should be emphasized in one's repertoire of skills and abilities (optimization) and knowledge of what personal characteristics could be relied on in stressful situations (compensation). The increasing complexity and differentiation of identity that come with age and experience (e.g., Labouvie-Vief, Chidod, Goguen, Diehl, & Orwoll, 1995) should provide additional buffering of a person's personality from experiences that may invalidate closely held assumptions about oneself (see Labouvie-Vief, this volume). In addition, the social interface of identity should serve an important continuity promoting function, such that renorming one's self-referencing group (for example, "compared to older people ... ") in middle and old age can serve to maintain consistent self views and in turn personality continuity (Brandtstädter & Greve, 1994). Conversely, the lack of a strong identity or commitment to an identity in young adulthood could help explain the lower levels of consistency reported for people in adolescence and young adulthood. People at this time may be switching identities more readily or holding identities in moratorium until they feel comfortable making a commitment to these identities. Those without strong identities miss out on the consolidating effects of having a reference point for making clear decisions about new roles.

In summary, we believe the nexus of evidence is compelling that the link between identity and personality-trait development helps to explain patterns of personality-trait continuity and change in the adult life course. For our theory to hold up, several empirical relations between identity and age need to be clarified. For example, what is the relation between age and identity achievement and consolidation? Is it true that a large majority of individuals continue to consolidate their identity well into middle age? Do changes in identity diminish with age? More direct links between identity development and personality development also need to be tested. First, individuals who have yet to settle on an overall identity or on a set of subidentities should be less consistent in their behavior and self-perceptions. Second, before a person has consolidated his or her identity, life experiences may not translate clearly into personality change. That is, if a person is not committed to an identity, then experiences in that identity may not be seen as self-relevant (cf. Roberts, 1997). Furthermore, the experiences may be relevant to the development of an identity but not to personality change. For example, performing less well in school or work may not translate into lowered perceptions of ability but may inform a decision to choose a different major or job because one finds the previous areas "uninteresting."

Summary

We were drawn to the idea of identity as the mediating structure between trait continuity and change because the development and resolution of identity effectively integrates the consistency and change mechanisms that contribute to personality development. On one hand, we choose identities based on our self-perceptions and motives in an attempt to find a niche in the adult world. Furthermore, we use our identities to evaluate whether relationships, work, and other roles fit with our picture of ourselves. These functions of identity are consonant with many of the mechanisms of personality-trait consistency we outlined above. On the other hand, some aspects of our identity are forced on us from others, as when we are attributed characteristics associated with stereotypes of the young or old, males or females, and minorities or majorities. We also cannot foresee all of the aspects of our future identities. Therefore, it is unlikely that any given identity will fit perfectly. The resulting disparity between the idealized identity and the actual identity means that identities will come with a set of demands, some of which will not mesh well with our personality traits (see Laub et al., 1998). These incongruities may result in an environmental press that facilitates personality change.

In outlining some of the tenets of the cumulative continuity model of personality development, we have made three basic points. First, we argued that the picture developing from the longitudinal database of personality development shows that personality traits increase in consistency with age and yet retain some plasticity throughout life. This pattern of development is not accounted for adequately by current theories of personality development. Second, we reviewed mechanisms that are related to maintaining personality consistency and mechanisms that facilitate personality change. Third, we argued that identity development and structure could account, in part, for the mechanisms of consistency, the mechanisms of change, and the pattern of personality-trait consistency and change demonstrated in the empirical database. We hope that these ideas can now move the empirical tests of personality development beyond gross questions of whether and when personality traits change to questions about why and how continuity and change occur.

Acknowledgment

Preparation of this chapter was supported by a grant from the University of Illinois Research Board and a grant from the National Institute of Mental Health (MH49414).

References

Allport, G. W. (1961). *Pattern and growth in personality*. New York: Holt, Rinehart & Winston.

Alwin, D. F., Cohen, R. L., & Newcomb, T. M. (1991). *Political attitudes over the life span: The Bennington women after fifty years*. Madison: University of Wisconsin Press.

Andersen, S. M., & Baum, A. (1994). Transference in interpersonal relations: Inferences and affect based on significant-other representations. *Journal of Personality, 62*, 459–497.

Arnett, J. J. (2000). Emerging adulthood: A theory of development from the late teens through the twenties. *American Psychologist, 55*, 469–480.

Asendorpf, J. B., & Van Aken, M. A. G. (1991). Correlates of the temporal consistency of personality patterns in childhood. *Journal of Personality, 59*, 689–703.

Asendorpf, J. B., & Wilpers, S. (1998). Personality effects on social relationships. *Journal of Personality and Social Psychology, 74*, 1531–1544.

Baltes, P. B. (1997). On the incomplete architecture of human ontogeny. *American Psychologist, 52*, 366–380.

Baltes, P. B., & Baltes, M. M. (1990). Psychological perspectives on successful aging: The model of selective optimisation with compensation. In P. B. Baltes & M. M. Baltes (Eds.), *Successful aging: Perspectives from the behavioural sciences* (pp. 1–34). New York: Cambridge University Press.

Baltes, P. B., Lindenberger, U., & Staudinger, U. M. (1999). Life-span theory in developmental psychology. In W. Damon & R. M. Lerner (Eds.), *Handbook of child psychology* (5th ed., Vol. 1, pp. 1029–1143). New York: Wiley.

Bandura, A. (1965). Influence of models' reinforcement contingencies on the acquisition of imitative response. *Journal of Personality and Social Psychology, 1*, 589–595.

Bandura, A. (1986). *Social foundations of thought and action*. Englewood Cliffs, NJ: Prentice-Hall.

Baumeister, R. F. (1997). Identity, self-concept, and self-esteem: The self lost and found. In R. Hogan, J. Johnson, & S. Briggs (Eds.), *Handbook of personality psychology* (pp. 681–711). San Diego: Academic Press.

Baumeister, R. F., Dale, K., & Sommer, K. L. (1998). Freudian defense mechanisms and empirical findings in modern social psychology: Reaction formation, projection, displacement, undoing, isolation, sublimation, and denial. *Journal of Personality, 66*, 1081–1124.

Baumgardner, A. (1990). To know oneself is to like oneself: Self-certainty and self-affect. *Journal of Personality and Social Psychology, 58*, 1062–1072.

Bell, R. Q., & Chapman, M. (1986). Child effects in studies using experimental or brief longitudinal approaches to socialization. *Developmental Psychology, 22*, 595–603.

Berzonsky, M. D. (1993). Identity style, gender, and social-cognitive reasoning. *Journal of Adolescent Research, 8*, 289–296.

Berzonsky, M. D., & Neimeyer, G. J. (1994). Ego identity status and identity processing orientation: The moderating role of commitment. *Journal of Research in Personality, 28*, 425–435.

Block, J. (1982). Assimilation, accommodation, and the dynamics of personality development. *Child Development, 53*, 281–295.

Blumer, H. (1969). *Symbolic interactionism: Perspective and method*. Englewood Cliffs, NJ: Prentice-Hall (pp. 282–299). Reprinted by permission.

Borkenau, P., & Liebler, A. (1995). Observable attributes as manifestations and cues of personality and intelligence. *Journal of Personality, 63*, 1–25.

Bouchard, T. J., Jr. (1995). Longitudinal studies of personality and intelligence: A behavior genetic and evolutionary psychology perspective. In D. Saklofske & M. Zaidner (Eds.), *International handbook of personality and intelligence.* New York: Plenum.

Bowlby, J. (1973). *Attachment and loss.* New York: Basic Books.

Brandtstädter, J. (1992). Person control over development: Some developmental implications of self-efficacy. In R. Schwarzer (Ed.), *Self-efficacy: Thought control of action* (pp. 127–145). Washington, DC: Hemisphere.

Brandtstädter, J., & Greve, W. (1994). The aging self: Stabilizing and protective processes. *Developmental Review, 14,* 52–80.

Brim, O. G. (1965). Adult socialization. In J. A. Clausen (Ed.), *Socialization and society* (pp. 182–226). Boston: Little Brown.

Bruch, M. A., Kaflowitz, N. G., & Berger, P. L. (1988). Self-schema for assertiveness: Extending the validity of the self-schema construct. *Journal of Research in Personality, 22,* 424–444.

Burke, P. J. (1991). Identity processes and social stress. *American Sociological Review, 56,* 836–849.

Buss, D. M. (1984). Toward a psychology of person-environment correspondence: The role of spouse selection. *Journal of Personality and Social Psychology, 47,* 361–377.

Buss, D. M. (1987). Selection, evocation, and manipulation. *Journal of Personality and Social Psychology, 53,* 1214–1221.

Cairns, R. B., & Cairns, B. D. (1994). *Lifelines and risks: Pathways of youth in our time.* Cambridge: Cambridge University Press.

Cairns, R. B., & Hood, K. E. (1983). Continuity in social development: A comparative perspective on individual difference prediction. In P. B. Baltes & O. G. Brim Jr. (Eds.), *Life-span development and behavior* (pp. 301–358). New York: Academic Press.

Campbell, J. D. (1990). Self-esteem and clarity of the self-concept. *Journal of Personality and Social Psychology, 59,* 538–549.

Caspi, A., & Herbener, E. S. (1990). Continuity and change: Assortative marriage and the consistency of personality in adulthood. *Journal of Personality and Social Psychology, 58,* 250–258.

Caspi, A., & Roberts, B. W. (1999). Personality change and continuity across the life course. In L. A. Pervin & O. P. John (Eds.), *Handbook of personality theory and research* (Vol. 2, pp. 300–326). New York: Guilford Press.

Chao, G. T. (1997). Organizational socialization: Mentoring phases and outcomes. *Journal of Vocational Behavior, 51,* 15–28.

Chao, G. T., Walz, M., & Gardner, D. (1992). Formal and informal mentorships: A comparison on mentoring functions and contrast with non-mentored counterparts. *Personnel Psychology, 45,* 619–636.

Clausen, J. A. (1993). *American lives: Looking back at the children of the Great Depression.* New York: Free Press.

Clore, G. L., Schwartz, N., & Conway, M. (1994). Affective causes and consequences of social information processing. In R. S. Wyer & T. K. Srull (Eds.), *Handbook of social cognition* (2nd ed., Vol. 1, pp. 323–417). Hillsdale, NJ: LEA.

Conley, J. J. (1984). The hierarchy of consistency: A review and model of longitudinal findings on adult individual differences in intelligence, personality, and self-opinion. *Personality and Individual Differences, 5,* 11–26.

Conley, J. J. (1985). A personality theory of adulthood and aging. In R. T. Hogan (Ed.), *Perspectives in personality* (Vol. 1, pp. 81–115). Greenwich Conn: JAI Press.

Cook, W. L., Kenny, D. A., & Goldstein, M. J. (1991). Parental affective style risk and the family system: A social relations model analysis. *Journal of Personality and Social Psychology, 100,* 492–501.

Cramer, P. (1998). Defensiveness and defense mechanisms. *Journal of Personality, 66,* 879–894.

Crick, N. R., & Dodge, K. A. (1994). A review and reformation of social information-processing mechanisms in children's social adjustment. *Psychological Bulletin, 115,* 74–101.

Crook, M. N. (1941). Retest correlations in neuroticism. *Journal of General Psychology, 24,* 173–182.

Deci, E. L., & Ryan, R. M. (1990). A motivational approach to self: Integration in personality. In R. A. Dienstbier (Ed.), *Perspectives on motivation: Nebraska Symposium on Motivation* (pp. 237–288). Lincoln: University of Nebraska Press.

Dishion, T. J., Patterson, G. R., Stoolmiller, M., & Skinner, M. L. (1991). Family, school, and behavioral antecedents to early adolescent involvement with antisocial peers. *Developmental Psychology, 27*, 172–180.

Dodge, K. A., & Tomlin, A. M. (1987). Utilization of self-schemas as mechanisms of interpretational bias in aggressive children. *Social Cognition, 5*, 280–300.

Dudek, S. Z., & Hall, W. B. (1991). Personality consistency: Eminent architects 25 years later. *Creativity Research Journal, 4*, 213–231.

Elder, G. H. (1985). Perspectives on the life course. In G. Elder Jr. (Ed.), *Life course dynamics* (pp. 23–49). Ithaca, NY: Cornell University Press.

Ennett, S. T., & Bauman, K. E. (1994). The contribution of influence and selection to adolescent peer group homogeneity: The case of adolescent cigarette smoking. *Journal of Personality and Social Psychology, 67*, 653–663.

Epstein, S. (1991). Cognitive-experiential self theory: Implications for developmental psychology. In M. R. Gunnar & L. A. Sroufe (Eds.), *Self processes and development: The Minnesota symposia on child development* (pp. 79–123). Hillsdale, NJ: Erlbaum.

Epstein, E., & Guttman, R. (1984). Mate selection in man: Evidence, theory and outcome. *Social Biology, 31*, 243–278.

Erikson, E. H. (1950). *Childhood and society.* New York: Norton.

Erikson, E. H. (1968). *Identity youth and crisis.* New York: Norton.

Farmer, R., & Nelson-Gray, R. O. (1990). Personality disorders and depression: Hypothetical relations, empirical findings and methodological considerations. *Clinical Psychology Review, 10*, 453–476.

Fekken, C. G., & Holden, R. R. (1992). Response latency evidence for viewing personality traits as schema indicators. *Journal of Research in Personality, 26*, 103–120.

Field, D., & Millsap, R. E. (1991). Personality in advanced old age: Continuity or change? *Journal of Gerontology: Psychological Sciences, 46*, 299–308.

Finn, S. E. (1986). Stability of personality self-ratings over 30 years: Evidence for an age/cohort interaction. *Journal of Personality and Social Psychology, 50*, 813–818.

Fiske, S. T., & Taylor, S. E. (1991). *Social cognition.* New York: McGraw-Hill.

Gerlsma, C., Emmelkamp, P. M., & Arrindell, W. A. (1990). Anxiety, depression, and perception of early parenting: A meta-analysis. *Clinical Psychology Review, 10*, 251–277.

Graziano, W. G., Jensen-Campbell, L. A., & Hair, E. C. (1996). Perceiving interpersonal conflict and reacting to it: The case for agreeableness. *Journal of Personality and Social Psychology, 70*, 820–835.

Gurin, P., & Brim, O. G. (1984). Change in self in adulthood: The example of sense of control. In P. B. Baltes & O. G. Brim (Eds.), *Lifespan development and behavior* (Vol. 6, pp. 282–334). New York: Academic Press.

Hanson, R. A. (1975). Consistency and stability of home environmental measures related to IQ. *Child Development, 46*, 470–480.

Helson, R., & Moane, G. (1987). Personality change in women from college to midlife. *Journal of Personality and Social Psychology, 53*, 176–186.

Helson, R., & Srivastava, S. (2001). Three paths of adult development: Conservers, seekers, and achievers. *Journal of Personality and Social Psychology, 80*, 995–1010.

Helson, R., Stewart, A. J., & Ostrove, J. (1995). Identity in three cohorts of midlife women. *Journal of Personality and Social Psychology, 69*, 544–557.

Hochwaelder, J. (1996). Effects of self-schema on assumptions about and processing of schema-consistent traits of other persons. *Perceptual and Motor Skills, 82*, 1267–1278.

Hogan, R. T. & Roberts, B. W. (2000). A socioanalytic perspective on person/environment interaction. In W. B. Walsh, K. H. Craik, & R. H. Price (Eds.), *New directions in person-environment psychology* (pp. 1–24). Mahway, NJ: Erlbaum.

Hogan, R., & Roberts, B. W. (in press). A socioanalytic model of maturity. *Journal of Career Assessment*.

Holland, J. L. (1962). Some explorations of a theory of vocational choice: I. One- and two-year longitudinal studies. *Psychological Monographs, 76*.

Holland, J. L. (1996). *Making vocational choices*. Odessa, FL: PAR.

Horowitz, M. J., Milbrath, C., Jordan, D. S., Stinson, C. H., Ewert, M., Redington, D. J., et al. (1994). Expressive and defensive behavior during discourse on unresolved topics: A single case study of pathological grief. *Journal of Personality, 62*, 527–563.

Howard, A., & Bray, D. (1989). *Managerial lives in transition*. New York: Guildford Press.

Ickes, W., Snyder, M. S. & Garcia, S. (1997). Personality influences on the choice of situations. In R. Hogan, J. Johnson, & S. Briggs (Eds.), *Handbook of personality psychology* (pp. 165–195). San Diego: Academic Press.

Jones, C. J., & Meredith, W. (1996). Patterns of personality change across the life span. *Psychology and Aging, 11*, 57–65.

Kagan, J. (1994). *Galen's prophecy: Temperament in human nature*. New York: Basic Books.

Kagan, J. (1997). Biology and the child. In W. Damon & N. Eisenberg (Eds.), *Handbook of child psychology*. New York: Wiley.

Kandel, D. B., Davies, M., & Baydar, N. (1990). The creation of interpersonal contexts: Homophily in dyadic relationships in adolescence and young adulthood. In L. N. Robins & M. R. Rutter (Eds.), *Straight and devious pathways to adulthood* (pp. 221–241). New York: Cambridge University Press.

Keltner, D. (1996). Facial expressions of emotion and personality. In C. Magai & S. H. McFadden (Eds.), *Handbook of emotion, adult development, and aging* (pp. 385–401). San Diego: Academic Press.

Kenrick, D. T., & Funder, D. C. (1988). Profiting from controversy: Lessons from the person-situation debate. *American Psychologist, 43*, 23–34.

Kiecolt, K. J. (1994). Stress and the decision to change oneself: A theoretical model. *Social Psychology Quarterly, 57*, 49–63.

Klohnen, E. C. (1996). Conceptual analysis and measurement of the construct of ego-resiliency. *Journal of Personality and Social Psychology, 70*, 1067–1079.

Kochanska, G. (1991). Socialization and temperament in the development of guilt and conscience. *Child Development, 62*, 1379–1392.

Kochanska, G. (1997). Multiple pathways to conscience for children with different temperaments: From toddlerhood to age five. *Developmental Psychology, 33*, 228–240.

Kogan, N. (1990). Personality and aging. In J. E. Birren & S. W. Schaie (Eds.), *Handbook of the psychology of aging* (pp. 330–346). San Diego: Academic Press.

Kohn, M. L., & Schooler, C. (1978). The reciprocal effects of the substantive complexity of work and intellectual flexibility: A longitudinal assessment. *American Journal of Sociology, 84*, 24–52.

Kohn, M. L., & Schooler, C. (1983). *Work and personality: An inquiry into social stratification*. Norwood, NJ: Ablex.

Kram, K. E. (1985). Mentoring alternatives: The role of peer relationships in career development. *Academy of Management Journal, 28*, 110–132.

Labouvie-Vief, G., Chiodo, L. M., Goguen, L. A., Diehl, M., & Orwoll, L. (1995). Representations of self across the life span. *Psychology and Aging, 10*, 404–415.

Laub, J. H., Nagin, D. S., & Sampson, R. J. (1998). Trajectories of change in criminal offending: Good marriages and the desistance process. *American Sociological Review, 63*, 225–238.

Leon, G. R., Gillum, B., Gillum, R., & Gouze, M. (1979). Personality stability and change over a 30-year period: Middle age to old age. *Journal of Consulting and Clinical Psychology, 47*, 517–524.

Levinson, D. J. (1986). A conception of adult development. *American Psychologist, 41*, 3–13.

Lewis, M. (1999). On the development of personality. In L. A. Pervin & O. P. John (Eds.), *Handbook of personality: Theory and research* (2nd ed., pp. 327–346).

Littwin, S. (1986). *The postponed generation: Why America's grown-up kids are growing up later*. New York: Morrow.

Lytton, H. (1990). Child and parent effects in boys' conduct disorder: A reinterpretation. *Developmental Psychology, 26*, 683–697.

Marcia, J. E. (1980). Identity in adolescence. In J. Adelson (Ed.), *Handbook of adolescent psychology* (pp. 159–187). New York: Wiley.

Markus, H., & Nurius, P. (1986). Possible selves. *American Psychologist, 41*, 954–969.

McCrae, R. R., & Costa, P. T. (1994). The stability of personality: Observation and evaluations. *Current Directions in Psychological Science, 3*, 173–175.

McCrae, R. R, Costa, P. T., Jr, Ostendorf, F., Angleitner, A., Hrebickova, M., Avia, M. D., et al. (2000). Nature over nurture: Temperament, personality, and life span development. *Journal of Personality and Social Psychology, 78*, 173–186.

McGue, M., Bacon, S., & Lykken, D. T. (1993). Personality stability and change in early adulthood: A behavioral genetic analysis. *Developmental Psychology, 29*, 96–109.

McNally, S., Eisenberg, S., & Harris, J. (1991). Consistency and change in maternal child-rearing practices and values: A longitudinal study. *Child Development, 62*, 190–198.

Messer, S. B., & Warren, S. (1990). Personality change and psychotherapy. In L. Pervin (Ed.), *Handbook of personality theory and research*. New York: Guildford Press.

Mischel, W. (1968). *Personality and assessment*. New York: Wiley.

Modell, J. (1989). *Into one's own: From youth to adulthood in the United States 1920–1975*. Berkeley: University of California Press.

Nesselroade, J. R., & Baltes, P. B. (1974). Adolescent personality development and historical change: 1970–1972. *Monographs of the Society for Research in Child Development, 39*, 1–74.

Nesselroade, J. R., & Featherman, D. L. (1997) Establishing a reference frame against which to chart age-related changes. In M. A. Hardy (Ed.), *Studying aging and social change: Conceptual and methodological issues*. Thousand Oaks, CA: Sage.

Nillson, L. V., & Persson, B. (1984). Personality changes in the aged. *Acta Psychiatrica Scandanavia, 69*, 182–189.

Norem, J. K. (1998). Why should we lower our defenses about defense mechanisms? *Journal of Personality, 66*, 895–917.

O'Connor, T. G., Deater-Deckard, K., Fulker, D., Rutter, M., & Plomin, R. (1998). Genotype-environment correlations in late childhood and early adolescence: Antisocial behavioral problems in coercive parenting. *Developmental Psychology, 34*, 970–981.

Pals, J. L. (1999). Identity consolidation in early adulthood: Relations with ego-resiliency, the context of marriage, and personality change. *Journal of Personality, 67*, 295–329.

Patterson, G. R., & Bank, L. (1989). Some amplifying mechanisms for pathologic processes in families. In M. R. Gunnar & E. Thelen (Eds.), *Systems and development: The Minnesota Symposia on Child Psychology* (Vol. 22, pp. 167–209). Hillsdale, NJ: Erlbaum.

Pedersen, N. L. (1993). Genetic and environmental continuity and change in personality. In T. J. Bouchard Jr. & P. Propping (Eds.), *Twins as a tool of behavioural genetics* (pp. 147–162). New York: Wiley.

Pedersen, N. L., & Reynolds, C. A. (1998). Stability and change in adult personality: Genetic and environmental components. *European Journal of Personality, 12*, 365–386.

Pfeffer, J. (1995). A political perspective on careers: Interests, networks, and environments. In M. B. Arthur, D. T. Hall, & B. S. Lawrence (Eds.), *Handbook of career theory*. Cambridge: Cambridge University Press.

Pianta, R. C., Sroufe, L. A., & Egeland, B. (1989). Continuity and discontinuity in maternal sensitivity at 6, 24, and 42 months in a high-risk sample. *Child Development, 60*, 481–487.

Plomin, R., & Caspi, A. (1999). Behavioral genetics and personality. In L. A. Pervin & O. P. John (Ed.), *Handbook of personality theory and research* (Vol. 2, pp. 251–276). New York: Guilford Press.

Plomin, R., Kagan, J., Emde, R. N., Reznick, J. S., Braugart, J. M., Robinson, J., et al. (1993). Genetic change and continuity from 14 to 20 months: The MacArthur Longitudinal Twin Study. *Child Development, 64*, 1354–1376.

Pulkkinen, L., & Kokko, K. (2000). Identity development in adulthood: A longitudinal study. *Journal of Research in Personality, 34*, 445–470.

Quiggle, N. L., Garber, J., Panak, W. F., & Dodge, K. A. (1992). Social information processing in aggressive and depressed children. *Child Development, 63*, 1305–1320.

Rabiner, D. L., Lenhart, L., & Lochman, J. E. (1990). Automatic versus reflective social problem solving in relation to children's sociometric status. *Developmental Psychology, 26*, 1010–1016.

Riley, S., & Wrench, D. (1985). Mentoring among women lawyers. *Journal of Applied Social Psychology, 15*, 374–386.

Roberts, B. W. (1997). Plaster or plasticity: Are work experiences associated with personality change in women? *Journal of Personality, 65*, 205–232.

Roberts, B. W., Caspi, A, & Moffitt, T. (2000). *The kids are alright: Growth and stability in personality development from adolescence to adulthood*. Manuscript, University of Illinois, Urbana-Champaign.

Roberts, B. W., & Chapman, C. (2000). Change in dispositional well-being and its relation to role quality: A 30-year longitudinal study. *Journal of Research in Personality, 34*, 26–41.

Roberts, B. W., & DelVecchio, W. F. (2000). The rank-order consistency of personality from childhood to old age: A quantitative review of longitudinal studies. *Psychological Bulletin, 126*, 3–25.

Roberts, B. W., & Donahue, E. M. (1994). One personality, multiple selves: Integrating personality and social roles. *Journal of Personality. 62*, 201–218.

Roberts, B. W., Helson, R., & Klohnen, E. C. (2002). Personality development and growth in women across 30 years: Three perspectives. *Journal of Personality, 70*, 79–102.

Roberts, B. W., & Robins, R. W. (2000a). Broad dispositions, broad aspirations: The intersection of the Big Five dimensions and major life goals. *Personality and Social Psychology Bulletin, 26*, 1284–1296.

Roberts, B. W., & Robins, R. W. (2000b). *A longitudinal study of person-environment fit and personality development*. Manuscript, University of Illinois, Urbana-Champaign.

Roberts, G. C., Block, J. H., & Block, J. (1984). Continuity and change in parents' child rearing practices. *Child Development, 55*, 586–597.

Ronka, A., & Pulkkinen, L. (1995). Accumulation of problems in social functioning in young adulthood: A developmental approach. *Journal of Personality and Social Psychology, 69*, 381–391.

Rosenberg, S., & Gara, M. A. (1985). The multiplicity of personal identity. In P. Shaver (Ed.), *Self situations, and social behavior: Review of personality and social psychology* (Vol. 6, pp. 87–113). Beverly Hills, CA: Sage.

Rusting, C. L. (1998). Personality, mood, and cognitive processing of emotional information: Three conceptual frameworks. *Psychological Bulletin, 124*, 165–196.

Sameroff, A. J. (1995). General systems theories and developmental psychopathology. In D. Cicchetti & D. J. Cohen (Eds.), *Developmental psychopathology* (pp. 659–695). New York: Wiley.

Sameroff, A. J., Seifer, R., Baldwin, A., & Baldwin, C. (1993). Stability of intelligence from preschool to adolescence: The influence of social and family risk factors. *Child Development, 64*, 80–97.

Sampson, R. J., & Laub, J. H. (1990). Crime and deviance over the life course: The salience of adult social bonds. *American Sociological Review, 55*, 609–627.

Sarbin, T. R. (1964). Role theoretical interpretation of psychological change. In P. Worchel & D. Byrne (Eds.), *Personality change* (pp. 176–219). New York: Wiley.

Sarbin, T. R., & Jones, D. S. (1955). The assessment of role expectations in the selection of supervisory personnel. *Educational and Psychological Measurement, 15*, 236–239.

Schuerger, J. M, Zarrella, K. L., & Hotz, A. S. (1989). Factors that influence the temporal stability of personality by questionnaire. *Journal of Personality and Social Psychology, 56*, 777–783.

Snyder, M. S. & Ickes, W. (1985). Personality and social behavior. In E. Aronson & G. Lindzey (Eds.), *Handbook of social psychology* (pp. 248–305). New York: Random House.

Stevens, D. P., & Truss, C. V. (1985). Stability and change in adult personality over 12 and 20 years. *Developmental Psychology, 21*, 568–584.

Stewart, A. J., & Ostrove, J. M. (1998). Women's personality in middle age: Gender, history, and midcourse corrections. *American Psychologist, 53*, 1185–1194.

Stewart, A. J., Ostrove, J. M., & Helson, R. (2001). Middle aging in women: Patterns of personality change from the thirties to the fifties. *Journal of Adult Development, 8*, 23–37.

Stryker, S. (1987). Identity theory: Developments and extensions. In K. Yardley & T. Honess (Eds.), *Self and identity: Psychosocial perspectives* (pp. 89–103). Chichester, UK: Wiley.

Stryker, S., & Statham, A. (1985). Symbolic interaction role theory. In G. Lindzey & E. Aronson (Eds.), *Handbook of social psychology* (pp. 311–378). Hillsdale, NJ: Erlbaum.

Swann, W. B., Stein-Seroussi, A., & McNulty, S. E. (1992). Outcasts in a white-lie society: The enigmatic worlds of people with negative self-conceptions. *Journal of Personality and Social Psychology, 62*, 618–624.

Swann, W. B., Jr. (1987). Identity negotiation: Where two roads meet. *Journal of Personality and Social Psychology, 53*, 1038–1051.

Thomas, W. I., & Thomas, D. (1928). *The child in America*. New York: Knopf.

Tomkins, S. S. (1979). Script theory: Differential magnification of affects. In H. E. Howe Jr. & R. A. Dienstbier (Eds.), *Nebraska Symposium on Motivation* (pp. 201–236). Lincoln: University of Nebraska Press.

Tower, R. B., & Kasl, S. V. (1996). Depressive symptoms across older spouses: Longitudinal influences. *Psychology and Aging, 11*, 683–697.

Trachtenberg, S., & Viken, R. J. (1994). Aggressive boys in the classroom: Biased attributions or shared perceptions? *Child Development, 65*, 829–835.

Trope, Y., & Ben-Yair, E. (1982). Task construction and persistence as a means for self-assessment of abilities. *Journal of Personality and Social Psychology, 42*, 637–645.

Vandewater, E. A., Ostrove, J. M., & Stewart, A. J. (1997). Predicting women's well-being in midlife: The importance of personality development and social role involvements. *Journal of Personality and Social Psychology, 72*, 1147–1160.

Wachtel, P. L. (1994). Cyclical processes in personality and psychopathology. *Journal of Abnormal Psychology, 103*, 51–54.

Warren, J. R., & Hauser, R. M. (1997). Social stratification across three generations: New evidence from the Wisconsin Longitudinal Study. *American Sociological Review, 62*, 561–572.

Waterman, A. S. (1984). Identity formation: Discovery or creation? *Journal of Early Adolescence, 4*, 329–341.

Waterman, A. S., & Archer, S. L. (1990). A life-span perspective on identity formation: Developments in form, function, and process. In P. B. Baltes, D. L. Featherman, & R. M. Lerner (Eds.), *Life-span development and behavior* (Vol. 10, pp. 30–59). Hillsdale, NJ: LEA.

Westen, D. (1991). Social cognition and object relations. *Psychological Bulletin, 109*, 429–455.

Whitbourne, S. K. (1996). Psychosocial perspectives on emotions: The role of identity in the aging process. In C. Magai & S. H. McFadden (Eds.), *Handbook of emotion, adult development and aging* San Diego: Academic Press.

Wiggins, J. S., & Trobst, K. K. (1997). When is a circumplex an "interpersonal cirumplex"? The case of supportive actions. In R. Plutchik & R. H. Conte (Eds.), *Circumplex models of personality and emotions* (pp. 57–80). Washington, DC: APA.

10 The Gain-Loss Dynamic in Lifespan Development: Implications for Change in Self and Personality During Old and Very Old Age

Jacqui Smith

Max Planck Institute for Human Development, Berlin, Germany

Abstract

This chapter explores the utility of the gain-loss proposition of lifespan psychology (P. Baltes, 1987) as an explanatory heuristic for change in various aspects of self and personality in adulthold and old age. Underlying the gain-loss proposition is the suggestion that developmental change is not only one of growth (gain) but also always involves some loss of functional efficacy. Although widely accepted as a useful metalevel developmental concept, empirical work specifically devised to examine the gain-loss dynamic is less prevalent. Most studies of self and personality functioning in adulthood and old age focus on a single dimension of change (gain, maintenance, or loss). The Baltes proposition, however, points to the advantages of taking a broad systemic approach whereby the dialectics among dimensions of gain, maintenance, and loss are considered. The final section of this chapter focuses on such a systemic approach. It examines the idea that the transition from the third to the fourth age is characterized by the breakdown of systems that contribute to a positive ratio of gain over loss.

Are aspects of self-related and personality functioning expected to change in late adulthood and very old age? If so, how might we best characterize the nature of age-related changes in these life phases: Do they represent growth or decline, gains or losses? Furthermore, what criteria and standards could be used for this judgment?

P. Baltes (1987) proposed that rather than describing development as unidimensional, it is best considered as involving *both* gains and losses. Underlying his gain-loss proposition was the suggestion that developmental change at all ages entails elements of gain (growth) and elements of loss. As he argued in 1987 (p. 613), the process of human development from childhood to old age is considered to be an age-related change in adaptive capacity in which there is a "joint occurrence of growth (gains) and decline (losses)." Ontogenetic development, according to him, should be viewed not as a monolithic process of progression and growth but as an ongoing, changing, and interacting system of gains and losses in adaptive capacity. Later publications (e.g., P. Baltes, Lindenberger, & Staudinger, 1998, p. 1043) advanced the more radical view that there is "no gain in development without loss, and no loss without gain." This view was based on the assumption that development always involves selection and therefore a tradeoff between alternative pathways and success-failure constellations. This later proposal, however, opens up many questions not only about the definition of gains and losses in a developmental context but also, as discussed below, about possible causal and reciprocal contingent relationships between gains and losses, together with their antecedents, correlates, and consequences.

The application of propositions about gains and losses appears on first glance to be especially useful for models of self-related and personality functioning (for application to cognitive functioning, see Salthouse, this volume; Wellman, this volume). In part, this is because the propositions refer to processes of adaptation and to adaptive capacity, topics that are at the core of self and personality concepts. Many authors, indeed, have proposed, adapted, or integrated ideas about gains and loss into their models of the self in adulthood and old age (e.g., Brandtstädter & Wentura, 1995; Carstensen, Isaacowitz, & Charles, 1999; Higgins, 1997; Schulz & Heckhausen, 1996; Staudinger & Pasupathi, 2000).

In contrast, one might question whether the Baltes gain-loss proposals apply well to research on old age. Historically, the period of old age has been associated primarily with functional decline and loss. To address potential questioners on this front, P. Baltes (1997) added three supplementary concepts to his propositions about the dynamics of gain and loss that apply especially to this life phase. First, the observation that, with regard to the ratio of gains to losses, successful aging involves the *relative* maximization of gains and minimization of losses. The gains observed in late life may not be as great (in absolute terms) or as significant as those in early life, but relative to the normative functional profile of an older adult, instances of gain are important. Second, he proposed that in old age there is a shift in the relative allocation of resources associated with development. This shift is away from functions associated with growth and instead toward those associated with *maintenance* (that is, sustaining or recovering normal levels of functioning in the face of a new contextual challenge or a loss in potential) and the *regulation of loss* when maintenance or recovery is no longer possible (P. Baltes, 1997; see also Featherman, Smith, & Peterson, 1990; Staudinger, Marsiske, & Baltes, 1995). Finally, P. Baltes (1997) offered a reason why the general tenets of his gain-loss propositions may have less predictive power in very old age. Findings that in old age losses begin to outnumber gains, he suggested, indicate the apparent breakdown of systems that contribute to the positive ratio of gains over losses. Baltes argued that this occurs because the architectural design of human development is by definition "incomplete."

These three supplementary proposals from P. Baltes (1987, 1997; P. Baltes et al., 1998) about the nature of functioning and change in old age, together with earlier proposals that positive characteristics like wisdom and a sense of personal integrity might be achieved in old age (see also Birren, 1980; Erikson, Erikson, & Kivnick, 1989), represented exceptions to the traditional primarily negative loss-based focus on old age and spurred much research in the 1990s. There are still many open questions, however, regarding the potential for areas of growth (and indeed maintenance of functioning) in late adulthood and about the relative balance of gains and losses during very old age. Indeed, there has been surprisingly little empirical work *specifically* devised to examine ideas about a gain-loss dynamic. Most studies of self and personality functioning in adulthood and old age, for example, focus on a single outcome variable and interpret this outcome as indicative of either gain, maintenance, or loss. The Baltes propositions, however, point to the advantages of taking a broad systemic approach whereby the dialectics and interdependencies among multiple outcomes and multiple directions of change are considered. To date there is also little research on the idea that a shift occurs in late adulthood in the allocation of developmental resources. When this shift occurs on a systemic versus domain-specific level and what factors modify this proposed qualitative change in the organization of development represent open research questions that will advance the field.

This chapter explores the utility of the P. Baltes (1987, 1997) gain-loss propositions as an explanatory heuristic for interpreting findings about functioning and change in various aspects of self and personality during old and very old age. To begin, I briefly review concepts and metaphors of gain and loss and then discuss associated definitional and theoretical issues in relation to self-related and personality functioning in late adulthood. The final section of the chapter focuses on findings about very old age from the Berlin Aging Study (BASE; P. Baltes & Mayer, 1999). The central question addressed here is whether the fourth age is a period of life in which the potential for gain (growth) is limited to such an extent that loss prevails. Work in the Berlin Aging Study suggests that an overall negative gain-loss balance may in fact be a defining characteristic of transition to the fourth age (e.g., Smith & P. Baltes, 1997). These findings are in accord with Baltes's proposals about the negative consequences of the incomplete architecture of ontogeny for development at the end of life.

Concepts of Gain and Loss: Theoretical Issues

The terms *gain* and *loss* have a multitude of meanings and connotations (*Oxford English Dictionary*, 2001). *Gain*, for example, can mean (1) to achieve (or acquire, access, attain, acquaint) possession or ownership of something, (2) to increase (accrue, accumulate, benefit) possession or advantage of any kind consequent on some action or change of conditions, or (3) to accelerate toward or reach a position. Loss, on the other hand, implies failure to keep possession of something, diminution of an individual's possessions or advantages, or the disadvantage involved in being deprived. Whereas some connotations of gain assume that there has to be prerequisite resources or means available to lead to a gain, others leave the prior status open (a gain may emerge, for example). For a loss to occur, however, a prior higher or more desirable status must have existed.

In general, both gains and losses have to do with change, both quantitative and qualitative. When used as nouns, the terms refer to a status alteration or modification, and when used as verbs, they refer to a process that contributes to some different state.

Psychological usage of the concepts of gains and losses primarily address these different aspects of change. They describe the goal states, outcomes, or *endpoints of change* (as growth or decline), the *direction of regulative processes of change* (functional versus dysfunctional adaptation), and *subjective evaluations of change* (positive and desirable or negative and undesirable). These three central analogs of gains and losses that were applied to lifespan development by P. Baltes (1987, 1997) are summarized in Table 10.1. As outlined in the next section, the growth-decline analog is most often used in theories about change trajectories across the lifespan. Ideas about the functional regulation of gains and losses play a particular role in explanations at the process level, whereas hedonistic models of perceived gains and losses come to the fore in research about life-related decisions and evaluation (such as developmental goals and subjective well-being).

The majority of psychological researchers avoid a precise definition of what constitutes a gain or a loss, in part because our discipline, unlike psychiatry and medicine, has rarely established absolute cutoff points or criteria as thresholds (see also Behrman, this volume; Heckhausen, this volume). For the most part, lifespan psychologists use relative scales, status comparisons among subgroups, or comparisons of individuals over time. Dimensions in which relative gains and losses are examined are specified (see some examples in Table 10.1), but specific scores on these dimensions or amounts of change are usually not defined as indicative of a developmental gain or a loss. Furthermore, the nature of what is considered a gain or a loss itself is considered to change with the age period and context examined. It involves objective in addition to subjective criteria and is conditioned by theoretical predilection, standards of comparison, cultural and historical context, and criteria of functional fitness or adaptivity (for reviews, see P. Baltes et al., 1998; Hobfoll, 1989; Schulz & Heckhausen, 1996; Staudinger & Pasupathi, 2000; Uttal & Perlmutter, 1989).

Together the three analogs of gain and loss outlined in Table 10.1 (growth versus decline, functional versus dysfunctional, and desirable versus less desirable) make a package in the Baltes framework. Furthermore, as also indicated in Table 10.1, this package is linked to three overarching metaphors about preferred directions of change and to theoretical proposals about gain-loss dynamics over the lifespan (refer also to P. Baltes, 1997).

The first metaphor addresses developmental status and specifies that *the preference is for gain*: growth, functional adaptation, and positive outcomes are preferred over decline, dysfunction, and negative outcomes. A key assumption in many developmental theories of self and personality is that individuals strive to obtain and retain a positive (desired) status and that perceived threats to doing this activate a host of protective

Table 10.1

Analogs of Gain and Loss in Relation to Change: Central Psychological Concepts, Metaphors, and Propositions (following P. Baltes, 1987, 1997)

Central Concepts		
Gain-Loss Analog	Focus	Examples of Changes
Growth versus decline	Outcome status	Performance or resource level Means (strategies) Size (capacity) Complexity Structure (differentiation) Stability or plasticity Maturity (entrophy)
Functional versus dysfunctional	Regulation process	Adaptivity Efficiency Effectiveness
Desirable versus less desirable	Subjective evaluation	Positive versus negative value Perceived costs and benefits Success or failure

Overarching Metaphors
1. Preference for gain 2. Maximization of gains and minimization of losses 3. No gain in development without loss and no loss without gain

Propositions About Gain-Loss Dynamics
1. In old age, the balance between gains and losses becomes less positive, if not negative. 2. Conditions of loss or limitations can provide a context for new forms of mastery or innovation. 3. There is a systematic change in the relative allocation of resources to growth, maintenance, and loss regulation across the lifespan: in early life resources focus on growth; during adulthood and old age resources are directed to maintenance and loss management.

regulative processes (e.g., Brandtstädter, 1998; Brandtstädter & Lerner, 1999; see also Brandtstädter & Rothermund, this volume). Furthermore, in line with the first metaphor, are the demonstrations of Tversky and Kahneman (1981) that humans have a strong cognitive bias to overestimate the threat and risk of loss.

The second and third metaphors outline the dynamics and relationships between gains and losses. On the one hand, *the central goal of developmental regulation is to maximize gains and minimize losses,* and, on the other hand, *there is no gain in development without loss and no loss without gain.* There is much literature in support of these two metaphors in the area of self and personality. For example, the self and personality system is considered to be geared to minimize losses or negative events (see reviews by Solomon & Corbit, 1974; Taylor, 1991). Furthermore, motivation and emotion theorists have long observed that the removal of aversive conditions (associated with the experience of loss, anger, fear, or anxiety) is often associated with an offsetting positive experience (such as relief, relaxation, or a positive affect). Taylor (1991) commented, however, that she was not able to find comparable research to show that experiences of intense positive emotions were offset by an intense negative emotional experience (such as anger, sadness, or depression—that is, an instance of gain-to-loss). In development, however, there may be instances where a positive event (gain) in one domain could only occur through a process (such as selection) that in the long term contributed to a loss (as a function of nonselection) in another. It is in this sense that P. Baltes (1997) explained his symmetric gain-loss metaphor.

Permanency of Gains and Losses: Growth and Decline

When thinking about development, theoretical questions arise about the permanency of gains and losses across the lifespan and possibilities for modification. If the effects of a gain or a loss are considered permanent (in a developmental sense), for example, the phenomena are described as instances of growth or decline. Theorists ask whether gains accumulate to build a qualitatively higher level of functioning or whether accumulated losses contribute to a qualitatively lower level. Another central question concerns the extent to which the effects of a gain or loss can be modified: if modification is possible, then intervention studies might be developed, for example, to convert the effect of a loss into a gain or perhaps modify a gain so that it becomes a better platform for subsequent gains.

In general, many theorists have defined development in early life in terms of the cumulative effects of gains and consider changes in late life as a counterpart reflecting the cumulative effects of losses (Birren, 1988; Kagan, 1980; Uttal & Perlmutter, 1989). Idealized developmental functions for early life were represented as temporal sequences of *growth-related change* (gains) that are normative, appear in all or most individuals, and generalize over cohorts (Charles, 1970; Overton, 1998; Wohlwill, 1973). Stage studies of development often define specific sets of gains as the prerequisite building blocks for movement to higher stages of development. Theorists of aging also assume to some degree the cumulative and permanent effects of loss and map *decline- or loss-related change* (Birren, 1959; Charles, 1970). As Birren (1988) recalled, the initial purpose of theorists of aging was to explain how behavior is organized over the adult years and then disorganized in old age. The idealized function of aging was seen as beginning with a phase of stability of functioning in midlife followed by progressive decline.

These conceptions of the permanency of gains and losses in the context of developmental trajectories across the lifespan appear in theories about changes in performance level and status as well as in theories of change in domain structure, complexity, and stability (Baltes, 1987). In some models, componential gains have to be integrated coherently to be of overall benefit to the psychological system. During early life, for example, theorists suggest that the structures of intelligence and personality are transformed and become more differentiated, complex, and stable and that this process contributes to more effective and efficiently functioning systems (e.g., P. Baltes, 1987;

Caspi & Roberts, 2001; Costa & McCrae, 1992; Kagan, 1980). In late life, there are suggestions that these structures may show dedifferentiation and lability (P. Baltes et al., 1998; Nesselroade, 1989, 1991; Reinert, 1970; Uttal & Perlmutter, 1989), especially in conjunction with pathological disorders (Agronon & Maletta, 2000).

Personality dispositions, especially neuroticism, extraversion, and openness, are thought to show much structural and interindividual stability (continuity) at least into the late seventies (Costa & McCrae, 1980; McCrae & Costa, 1990; Roberts & DelVecchio, 2000). McCrae and Costa (1996) have argued that personality traits are endogenous dispositions whose maturation is minimally affected by environmental influences and that personality structure and rank-order individual differences stabilize around age 30. An extensive review and meta-analysis of research on rank-order personality consistency confirmed proposals about structural continuity but suggested that rank-order consistency may not plateau until ages 50 to 70 (Roberts & DelVecchio, 2000; see also Roberts & Caspi, this volume). In addition, Roberts and DelVecchio (2000) reported that stability coefficients tend to increase as the age of study participants increases and that they tend to decrease as the time interval between observations increases.

The possibility that there may be age-related differences in the mean-level expression of various personality traits and individual differences in intraindividual change have recently become the focus of interest among personality researchers (e.g., P. Baltes et al., 1998; Staudinger & Pasupathi, 2000). McCrae (2001) and colleagues, for example, reported that different personality traits may show different aging trajectories and that there is substantial variation in intraindividual change over time that needs to be explained. In their analyses of large national cross-sectional and longitudinal samples of individuals between the ages of 35 and 84 years, for example, linear declines were found with age. The magnitude of the age correlations were small, ranging from $-.12$ to $-.19$ (Costa et al., 1986). Cross-national comparisons of scores on the Big Five personality factors (NEO and CPI scales) from samples that include adults in the age range 18 to 50+ years have also indicated dimension-specific age trajectories (McCrae et al., 1999; Yang, McCrae, & Costa, 1998). Age gradients for extraversion, neuroticism, and openness are generally negative, those for agreeableness and conscientiousness are positive. The median estimate of absolute change across the five personality factors in five cultures was one to seven T-score points per decade from age 20 to 50+ (McCrae, 2001). Whether this rate of change is stable or increases in late adulthood is an open question.

Longitudinal analyses over a 30- to 40-year time span of Q-Sort data from the Berkeley Intergenerational Studies have revealed consistent group patterns of change from ages 18 to 60 and large interindividual differences in direction of change on dimensions of self-confidence, cognitive commitment, outgoingness, and dependability (Jones & Meredith, 1996). The longitudinal findings of Jones and Meredith, however, suggest adult trajectories that differ somewhat from those indicated by McCrae, Costa et al. (1999). Whereas Jones and Meredith found average increases during adulthood for self-confidence, outgoingness (both facets of extraversion), and cognitive commitment (openness), McCrae and Costa found negative age gradients for extraversion and openness. McCrae and Costa found that agreeableness increased with age, but Jones and Meredith were unable to fit normative curves to this dimension (interindividual differences in intraindividual change were very large). Both sets of researchers reported increases in dependability (conscientiousness) during adult years.

In a developmental and functional context, it becomes important to define with more precision when age differences and change are trivial versus significant both for gains and losses (Abelson, 1985; see also Smith & M. Baltes, 1998). McCrae (2001), for example, pointed out that the cross-sectional age comparisons suggested that it might take 60 years for extraversion to decrease by one standard deviation (a substantial change at a statistical level). At the same time, he acknowledged that we may deplore (at a functional level) the findings about declines in extraversion and openness. Small differences at a statistical level may nevertheless have important functional consequences. This is especially the case if the gains and losses have a permanent character. In general, gains and losses that do have a permanent effect on the psychological system, even if small, play a significant role in regulating development in general.

The Functionality Analog: Gains and Losses in Adaptive Potential

Theories of self and personality are an important source of ideas with regard to functionality (gains and losses imply changes in adaptive potential) and to functional versus dysfunctional behavior and outcomes. Change, in this context, is viewed as adaptation and is often seen as being goal-directed and regulated by fundamental processes that afford effective, efficient, and functional movement toward goals (e.g., P. Baltes et al., 1998; Pervin, 1989). Processes of change and adaptation are most often time-dependent (require a certain length of time to occur) rather than age-dependent (covary with other factors that are age-related). Time is required to adjust to a challenge or to make a decision about a new personal project, for example. In some instances, time-dependent change processes may also interact with age (differences in adaptation or recovery phases for young and older adults illustrate this point). It is the latter instance that is of most interest to developmental researchers.

Considerations of the functional analog of gains and losses often address the second and third overarching metaphors mentioned in Table 10.1 and especially the idea that regulation processes are more adaptive and functional if they are directed toward maximizing gains and minimizing losses. Effective regulation is described as the tendency to realize one's own potential (self-actualization) but also to maintain self-images and self-efficacy, preserve resources, and counteract losses (e.g., Brandtstädter, 1998; Carver & Scheier, 1990; Staudinger et al., 1995). Brandtstädter and Lerner (1999), for example, proposed that individuals "strive to expand their action resources and developmental potentials, to defend themselves against losses and constraints, and to economize the use of resources so that there remain reserves to enrich their developmental prospects" (p. xiii).

Several writers have addressed the first metaphor in Table 10.1, the notion that individuals strive for environments and contexts that afford personal "gain." Rawls (1971), for example, proposed that, in line with the Aristotelian principle of motivation, "humans take more pleasure in doing something as they become more proficient at it, and of two activities they do equally well, they prefer the one calling on a larger repertoire of more intricate and subtle discriminations" (Rawls, 1971, p. 426). Bandura (1989) and Brim (1992) followed up on this proposal. Brim (1992), for example, posited three things that underlie individuals' thoughts and plans about their life direction: (1) a basic drive for growth and mastery, (2) the preference to live in a way that is characterized as a level of just manageable difficulties (not too hard and not too easy), and (3) strategies involved in managing to achieve this level by adjusting to successes and failures. Planning for the achievement of a balance between winning and losing, Brim contended, is one of the main sources of happiness and a sense of personal well-being.

Many social and personality theories have suggested that people generally select their actions and their orientations to maintain a positive self-evaluation and self-image and regulate emotions (e.g., Brandtstädter, 1998; Brandtstädter & Lerner, 1999; Carstensen, 1993; Carver & Scheier, 1990; Freund & P. Baltes, 1998; Taylor & Brown, 1988). This is the same as saying that people attempt to anticipate and prevent (minimize) discrepancies from arising at the highest level between desired self and present perceptions of self by taking steps to create certain concrete perceived realities at the lower level (e.g., Taylor, 1991). These general self-regulatory tendencies are interrupted when obstacles to goal attainment (either momentary or prolonged) are encountered or anticipated. In such situations, regulatory processes are first mobilized to adjust and evaluate the new conditions and subsequently engaged to minimize (or neutralize) any negative consequences (e.g., Carver & Scheier, 1990 Taylor, 1991).

Is old age associated with stabilty or loss in adaptive potential? Various dimensions of the self are thought to show differential aging trajectories and perhaps qualitative (structural) change (Bengtson, Reedy & Gordon, 1985; Brim, 1992; Freund & Smith, 1999; Neugarten, 1969; Smith & Baltes, 1999b; Staudinger, Freund, Linden, & Maas, 1999). Personal goals and values, future and ideal self-concepts (possible selves), coping styles, control beliefs, and feelings of loneliness for example, have been nominated as probable sites for differentiated change, gains, and losses (Brandtstädter & Greve, 1994; Filipp & Klauer, 1986; Lachman, 1986; Markus & Herzog, 1991; Ryff & Essex, 1992; Smith & Freund, in press). Possible differences in the individual contexts and time-scales for such changes, however, present considerable measurement problems. So, for example, evidence for change may be observed only when specific rather than global contexts of self-functioning are examined (such as specific control beliefs about health conditions versus global control beliefs about life in general). In addition, little is known about the time-scale of change: Do the processes of change take decades, or are they swift? Is the likelihood of observing change minimal in the majority of study designs? Given the preponderance of theories suggesting change-associated and adaptive processes designed to maintain and protect the self in old age (e.g., P. Baltes & M. Baltes, 1990; Brandtstädter & Greve, 1994; Schulz & Heckhausen, 1996; Markus & Nurius, 1986), it will be important in future work to gain initial insights into both the different contexts and time-scales of the change proposed.

The Desirability Metaphor: Judgments of Success and Failure

The third analog introduced in Table 10.1 concerns the extent to which gains and losses are subjectively evaluated as positive or negative, as indicating success or failure, or as desirable or not. This aspect is clearly related to both the growth-decline and functional-dysfunctional analogs and is central to the definition of what represents a gain or a loss. Research suggests that the answer is complex as well as being context and characteristic specific (e.g., Heckhausen, Dixon, & Baltes, 1989; Kahneman, Diener, & Schwarz, 1999).

Kahneman and Tversky (1984, see also 2000) have long shown in work associated with their Prospect Theory that in situations of selection and choice, people evaluate things not by the expectation of their absolute outcomes but rather by the expectation of subjective value of these outcomes and the subjective evaluation of the experiences linked with change involved. Not all gains are evaluated positively, and not all losses negatively. Something else goes into the equation—namely, a strong preference not only to strive for gains as suggested in action theoretical models but to avoid the risk of loss. They proposed that the attractiveness of the possible gain is not nearly sufficient to compensate for the aversiveness of the possible loss. However, tendencies to focus on and regulate behavior in the direction of risk aversion or risk seeking vary depending on the perceived probability of a gain or loss. Moderate and high probabilities are generally underweighted in a choice selection contributing to (1) people being risk adverse when approaching a gain situation by reducing the attractiveness of the positive outcome and (2) people being risk seeking in avoiding losses by attenuating the aversiveness of negative outcomes. Low probabilities, on the other hand, are overweighted resulting in the reverse pattern. In such contexts, the positive value of improbable gains is enhanced, and the aversiveness of unlikely severe losses is amplified.

Tversky and Griffin (2000) added a further dimension to predicting the positive and negative values associated with present gains and losses—namely, past experiences with similar change and outcomes. Taking somewhat of a developmental view (at least in the sense that they included a time dimension and long-term memory), they acknowledged that experience of an event produces a direct "endowment" effect in the sense that it contributes to a sense of emotional well-being and, in addition, produces an indirect "contrast" effect on the evaluation of subsequent events (positive events that follow a positive event might be seen as less exciting and negative events following a negative event as less bad. Their model offers a strategy for maximizing gains. According to Tversky and Griffin, the way to maximize happiness (gain) is to find ways to treat positive experiences in the past as different from those in the present (in order to avoid a letdown effect) and to compare present conditions to worse situations in the past (to enjoy the benefits of the positive contrast).

Schwarz and Strack (1999) point out, however, that comparison strategies, even when applied to one's own life, are strongly influenced by transient context effects. Subjective judgments about the desirability of gains and losses and the extent to which they represent success or failure are likely to shift depending on instructions, interview context, information accessibility, and an individual's mood.

The Nature of the Dynamic Relationship Between Gains and Losses

Central to Baltes's use of gain-loss metaphors are his propositions about the dynamics of gains and losses. The metaphors listed in Table 10.1, on the one hand, provide general outlines of these dynamics and, on the other hand, open up a range of questions about the nature of the relationships (see also Labouvie-Vief, this volume). For example, do some gains necessarily entail losses? Do losses trigger gains? Are the processes underlying gains and losses within a domain independent? Are there causal relationships across dimensions of functioning such that a loss in one area enables or can be compensated for by a gain in another?

Uttal and Perlmutter (1989), although generally in agreement with the Baltes framework on the dynamics of gains and losses, pointed out that researchers need to pay more attention to specifying their assumptions about the nature of dynamic relationships between gains and losses. They argued that there was a tendency for lifespan researchers to search for causal relationships and, furthermore, that the search in early life is primarily for examples of *gains that cause losses* (it is assumed that losses are the by-products of gains), whereas the search in later life is for *losses that cause gains* (to assume that gains are the by-products of compensation for losses). Uttal and Perlmutter cautioned that gains and losses need not necessarily be causally related: they may also simply be phenomena that occur simultaneously and perhaps follow the occurrence of other independent factors.

The idea that losses might trigger or lead to some gains is certainly of great interest to researchers of old age who would like to portray this life phase as one that is not simply characterized by loss. For a developmental loss to occur or be perceived to have occurred, a higher status must have existed previously. The idea that a condition of loss, limitation, or deficit could serve a catalytic role for positive change introduced a new script for considering lifespan development (P. Baltes, 1987; Uttal & Perlmutter, 1989). The loss-triggers-gain concept had also been the basis of earlier hedonistic theory and models of self-related functioning (e.g., Helson, 1964; Solomon & Corbit, 1974). Taylor (1991, p. 67), for example, noted that much research on the consequences of negative events indicates that losses may first serve to mobilize physiological, affective, and cognitive resources, to stimulate behavioral activity, and then eventually to initiate gain-oriented processes that "reverse, minimize, or undue" the negative conditions.

Research in line with this and other loss-triggers-gain concepts was initiated in the 1990s, in particular with regard to psychological compensation (e.g., Bäckman & Dixon, 1992; Dixon & Bäckman, 1995), immunizing and protective strategies (Brandtstädter & Greve, 1994), and life-management strategies (such as selection, compensation, and optimization; e.g., Freund & Baltes, 1998). The Socioemotional Selectivity Theory proposed by Carstensen (1993) also implies that loss might trigger gain. This theory suggests, for example, that "losses" in old age with regard to the absolute size of the personal network of social contacts may be balanced or compensated by a "gain" in the amount of time and energy that can be invested in emotional contact with close partners and significant others. Another example comes from M. Baltes (1996), who showed that some loss-related behavior observed in older adults (such as dependency and expressed need for support) may allow personal resources to be freed up for use in other domains "selected" for personal efficacy and growth.

The idea that losses or deficits may be catalysts for gain is also implied in Baltes's proposals about the architecture of ontogeny, especially regarding the possible future evolution of culture (Smith & P. Baltes, 1999a). The loss and decline phenomena of old age observed at the present time are not viewed as being fixed or immutable. On the contrary, the cultural context of aging and a "culture of old age" is evolving (e.g., Manton, Stallard, & Corder, 1997; Olshansky, Carnes, & Grahn, 1998; see also Maier & Vaupel, this volume). What, then, might be possible in terms of positive growth and maintenance of high levels of functioning into very old age if cultural conditions were to be further optimized and innovative cultural factors and resources were introduced? It may be possible, for example, to identify cultural factors already available to small subgroups of the population that could to be made more widely accessible and foster the general "good" of older persons in the population. Learning more about the long-term consequences of specific lifestyles and preventative health measures is one example of such research (e.g., Vita, Terry, Hubert, & Fries, 1998).

One purpose of the propositions about the dynamics of gain and loss (P. Baltes, 1987, 1997) was to facilitate speculation and to provide a research impulse in the directions illustrated above. Nevertheless, more work is needed to tease out the conceptual value of the propositions. In particular, future research should focus on the nature of the causal relationships or reciprocal contingent relationships together with their antecedents, correlates, and consequences. Further work is also needed on the extent to which tradeoffs between gains and losses can be activated over time and across domains of functioning.

The Negative Gain-Loss Balance in the Fourth Age: Findings from the Berlin Aging Study

Whereas self-related and personality functioning in the third age may be characterized by stability and opportunities for successful functioning (P. Baltes, 1997; Rowe & Kahn, 1997; Staudinger & Pasupathi, 2000), the fourth age presents a different picture

(M. Baltes, 1998; P. Baltes, 1997; P. Baltes & Smith, in press; Smith & P. Baltes, 1997). This life period appears to be one in which the normally robust regulative psychological systems of self and personality are especially at risk for dysfunctionality and ultimate breakdown in a form that could be characterized as *psychological mortality* (Smith, 2002, 2001a). The section below focuses on findings from the Berlin Aging Study (BASE: P. Baltes & Mayer, 1999) to illustrate the proposal that the fourth age is a period of life in which the potential for gain (growth) is limited to such an extent that loss prevails.

Trajectories of Change in Personality Dimensions

Cross-sectional age gradients (age 70 to 100+ years) found in the Berlin Aging Study for the personality traits extraversion, openness, and neuroticism, measured using items from the NEO scale, were in line with those found by McCrae, Costa et al. (1999). In very old age, extraversion and openness appear to have small but significant negative aging trajectories (age correlations were $r = -.19$ and $-.20$, respectively), while neuroticism showed no relation to age (Smith & P. Baltes, 1999b). Initial longitudinal analyses of these dimensions have revealed similar change patterns (estimated average T-score changes over 30 years in SD units are as follows: extraversion, -1.2 SD; openness, -0.9 SD) (Smith, Freund, & P. Baltes, in prep.). These estimated rates of change appear to be faster than found in younger ages (-0.5 SD) (McCrae, 2001). On average, neuroticism appears to increase (estimated 4.2 T-score units over 10 years). This increase is explained by individual differences in changes in functional health and distance from death rather than by age per se.

The Very Old Self: Is Adaptive Potential Maintained?

Dynamics of Self-Images   Data collected in the Berlin Aging Study provided a broad picture of possible differences in changes among dimensions of the self in very old age. For example, we have found small negative age differences in the content of self-definitions obtained using the "Who am?" task (Freund & Smith, 1999) but few age differences in scenarios about possible selves (Smith & P. Baltes, 1999b). Longitudinal analyses of the dynamics of hopes and fears about the future self revealed that this motivational system is intact in old age (Smith & Freund, in press). Surprisingly, BASE participants were found to focus more on achieving new aspects of hoped-for selves than on maintaining present ones: 72% added new hopes about personal projects over a four-year period, and 27% added highly elaborated possible self-images (images that included matched hopes and fears). The majority of possible selves were related to personal characteristics, followed by health.

Trajectories of Control Beliefs   Beliefs about personal control are the most focal and pervasive of the mechanisms of agency and sense of control (M. Baltes & P. Baltes, 1986; Bandura, 1989; Lachman, 1986). They influence how people think, feel, and act.

In particular, it is considered that the belief that one's own efforts can influence a gain-associated outcome (a belief in internal control over a desirable outcome) increases the likelihood of selecting goals to act upon, the amount of time and energy invested on these goals selected, and the likelihood of experiencing positive emotional well-being in association with the outcome of one's efforts.

A scale assessing general beliefs about control over the good and bad things in life (gains and losses) was included within BASE. Three strong factors were found characterizing beliefs about internal control over desirable events, internal control over less desirable events, and external-powerful others' control. These three dimensions of control beliefs showed different age gradients (Smith & P. Baltes, 1999b). Whereas beliefs about personal (internal) control over positive and negative events did not differ with age (see also Heckhausen, this volume), the belief that others play a significant role in determining the events in one's life (external control) increased significantly with age ($r = .33$) (see also Kunzmann, Little, & Smith, in press). Furthermore, beliefs about internal and external locus of control were not exclusive. For instance, 27% of the BASE sample tended toward a shared-responsibility model, in that they believed that the locus of control lay both with themselves (internal) *and* with others (external).

Age-Related Trends in Desirable and Less Desirable Personality Attributes

As reviewed above, dimensions of self and personality appear to show different age trajectories. Some show no correlation to age, while others show a small negative age correlation. Whereas in the domain of intellectual functioning there is a long-standing theoretical and psychometric tradition of comparing classes of trajectories (fluid-mechanics versus pragmatic intelligence), an analogous system of specifying classes of self and personality dimensions is not prominent in the literature on aging.

In the Berlin Aging Study, we laid the groundwork for such a theoretical categorization (Smith & P. Baltes, 1997, 1999b). Our goal was in effect to examine whether a gain- (stability) or loss-related decline model could be used to summarize the diverse findings in relation to age for aspects of self and personality. Personality characteristics were grouped in terms of social and psychological desirability. *Desirable characteristics* were defined as those that researchers have found to positively influence the process of dealing with life problems—for example, interest in being with others (extraversion), openness to new ideas and experiences (openness), frequent experience of positive emotions (positive affect), and feelings of being in control of one's life (internal control). Psychologically *less desirable characteristics* are those that are known to signal elements of dysfunctionality, such as neuroticism, negative affect, and the belief that one's life is controlled by others (external control).

This categorization of variables as more or less socially desirable reflects a general consensus in the psychological research literature about what "on average" is functional

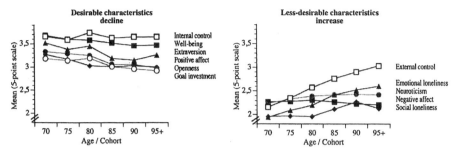

Figure 10.1   Age-Gradients in Desirable and Less Desirable Personality Characteristics. Considered together, the small but negative age differences
in desirable characteristics and the positive age differences in less
desirable characteristics suggest something like a chronic stress reaction in the self in old age. Such a picture supports theses regarding
generalized loss-related decline (Smith & P. Baltes, 1999a;b).

versus dysfunctional. The categorization is open to debate, however (e.g., Aldwin,
1991; Pearlin & Mullan, 1992; Snyder & Forsythe, 1991). We acknowledge that the
functionality (desirability) of personality characteristics can also be context specific.
For some goals and contexts, characteristics typically thought to be dysfunctional may
actually be adaptive. "Dysfunctional" attributes, such as anger and loneliness, may
actually be adaptive in particular contexts if they signalize the necessity for change.
Likewise, it might be adaptive (and helpful) for very ill persons to believe that others
will care for their well-being (external control). Nevertheless, in the long term, such
less desirable personality characteristics may indeed be dysfunctional, especially if
they become chronic behavior.

The findings illustrated in Figure 10.1 indicate some negative changes in dimensions that psychologists consider to be central to a sense of personal well-being. There
were age-related decreases in some but not all of the desirable characteristics and increases in some undesirable ones. Specifically, as to desirable characteristics, older
participants in BASE reported less extraversion, openness, positive affect, and subjective life investment compared to participants aged 70 to 84 years. Conversely, as to
less desirable attributes, older participants felt that their lives were more controlled by
others (external control) and reported that they experienced more emotional loneliness.
Age correlations were relatively small and, in general, mean differences amounted to
less than 0.5 SD.

These "negative" age trends in constructs of self and personality are much smaller
in magnitude than those observed for intellectual abilities (compare to Lindenberger &
Baltes, 1997; see also Smith & P. Baltes, 1999b). As a whole, however, these trends
toward increased overall dysfunction could be interpreted as type of chronic stress
reaction to cumulative losses. The cumulative losses and declines in health, autonomy,

and social contact in very old age may result in eventual decline (or rather a decrease in adaptivity and flexibility) of the self-regulation systems of most individuals (Smith, 2002).

Trajectories of Well-Being: Losses in the Positive Side of Life

There are conflicting proposals regarding expected levels of reported well-being in the period of very old age (e.g., Campbell, Converse, & Rodgers, 1976; Diener, Suh, Lucas, & Smith, 1999; Kunzmann, Little, & Smith, 2000; Smith, 2001b; Smith, Fleeson, Geiselmann, Settersten, & Kunzmann, 1999). One set of proposals argues for lower levels (cf. Atchley, 1991). It is suggested that the losses and declines associated with the period of very old age overwhelm individuals to such a degree that they moderate their expression of well-being. Another set of proposals about expected levels of reported well-being in the period of very old age argues that, just as in earlier parts of the life course, large numbers of individuals should report high well-being (e.g., P. Baltes, 1991; Brandtstädter & Greve, 1994; Brim, 1992; Herzog, Rodgers, & Woodworth, 1982; Lawton, 1991; Staudinger et al., 1999). These researchers suggest that individual changes in evaluative standards used to judge satisfaction and the operation of self-protective mechanisms that minimize losses contribute to the maintenance of reported positive well-being even in very old age.

Overall 63% of BASE participants reported that they were satisfied or very satisfied with their life at present, 83% reported that they were satisfied or very satisfied when they looked back over their life, and 63% expected to be satisfied in the future (Smith, 2001b Smith et al., 1999). They also reported experiencing positive affect more often than negative affect.

Within the cross-sectional BASE sample, there was some indication that overall subjective well-being (PGCMS), expected future life satisfaction, and especially the experience of positive emotions including happiness may decrease from age 70 to over 100. Each of these measures showed significant but small negative age correlations.

Subsequent analyses of longitudinal follow-ups of the BASE sample have indicated that these small age-related negative correlations for the positive side of well-being do represent age-related change (Smith, 2001b; Smith, Borchelt, Maier, & Jopp, in press). Our analyses to date reveal trajectories of decline from 70 to 100+ years in some aspects of subjective well-being and stability in others. Decline was evident in the positive side of well-being, aging satisfaction, life satisfaction, and positive affect. For aging satisfaction, the total estimated decline from 70 to 100+ years was equivalent to 1.1 SD, for life satisfaction, 0.8 SD, and positive affect 0.7 SD. Negative affect was characterized by stability: there was neither decline nor increase in very old age. There were large individual differences in average level on each component of subjective well-being, but no significant interindividual differences in intraindividual change (regardless of level, individuals changed at approximately the same rate). The number of chronic strains (across six domains) recorded at the first measurement occasion has proved to be a significant predictor of individual differences in average level of functioning over time (Smith, 2001b). Models testing whether stability was the best estimate for the seventies and decline for the eighties were found to fit well for aging satisfaction and positive affect. These findings suggest that the period of transition from the third age (young old) to the fourth age (oldest old) may be critical for these two aspects of positive well-being.

In this context, we have also found that dissatisfaction with aging, as measured by the subscale of the PGCMS (Lawton, 1975; Liang & Bollen, 1983), is a predictor for distance from death after both the control for age, socioeconomic status, health, and intellectual functioning (Maier & Smith, 1999). Few other studies have investigated this aspect of perceived well-being in relation to mortality, although there is an extensive literature concerning the predictive links between subjective health and mortality (e.g., Idler, 1993). We suspected that these evaluations might reflect quite accurate summary perceptions about individuals' present status with respect to functioning in a variety of domains. Negative evaluations of the effects and outcomes of aging themselves are probably not the cause for an increased mortality risk (Smith, 2001a), but they rather reflect potential causes from other domains of functioning (such as intellectual, health, or biological functioning). A temporal sequence of steps—involving first a decline in health and intellectual functioning, next a decline in subjective well-being, and finally death—is consistent with our findings (Maier & Smith, 1999).

Rather than setting our own criteria for what constitutes "a good life," we accepted the BASE participants' own reports of their personal sense of emotional well-being and life satisfaction. The majority reported being satisfied and contented. However, we have found strong evidence that, during old age, the positive side of well-being decreases (less life satisfaction, less satisfaction with the way one is aging, less frequent experience of positive affect). The transition from the third age to the fourth age and the accumulated chronic strain of dealing with the effects of multiple physical illnesses, frailty, functional impairment, and social losses that characterize the fourth age appear to test the limits of adaptive self-related processes (Smith, 2001b). Whereas the majority of the young old may enjoy a sense of well-being, the capacity to maintain positive well-being in the face of loss and chronic life strain is reduced in the oldest old. It is important to note that so far we have found *no* evidence that the negative side of well-being increases during old age: frequency of negative affect, depressivity (assessed by observer ratings), and prevalence of diagnosed major depression were not related to age.

Desirable and Less Desirable Profiles of Functioning: Loss in the Fourth Age

So far in this chapter, I have presented information about age-related differences and change in separate psychological domains. In this section, I summarize findings about subgroup differences in profiles of functioning *across* the domains of intelligence, self and personality, and social relationships (Smith & P. Baltes, 1997, 1999b; Smith & M. Baltes, 1998).

To date, relatively little is known about the nature of the structural and systemic relationships among the domains of psychological functioning in old and very old (Baltes, 1997; P. Baltes & Smith, 1997; Birren & Schroots, 1996; Magnusson, 1995). One assumption behind the search for differences in profiles of functioning across domains is that (like physical and mental health) these represent both the outcomes of differential aging and potential sources for continued differentiation. As in general models of dynamic systems and complexity, the idea is that there is some order and common processes underlying the interdependencies between the constructs considered in a profile but that variations in the overall systemic composition and operation have arisen at some point in the lives of individuals (e.g., Bateson, 1996; Finch, 1996; Magnusson & Stattin, 1998). Once established, the variations in the systemic profile likely have consequences for how individuals age and adapt to illness and environmental changes. Models of self-organizing criticality, for example, would suggest that different sets of factors might contribute to the breakdown, reorganization, or maintenance of each profile (e.g., Bak, Tang, & Wiesenfeld, 1988).

Cross-sectional data allow inferences to be made only about the various pathways that might have led to the formation of identifiable "clusters" of individuals who have similar profiles. Members of each cluster are more similar to each other (in a multivariate space of interrelated variables) than they are to individuals in other subgroup clusters. The conditions that gave rise to this clustering of individuals on a set of variables are a matter of theoretical debate.

In this sense, then, the identification and description of cluster membership and profiles of functioning *serve as a* heuristic for the further development of theories about the ratio of gains and losses in old age and the systemic nature of gain-loss dynamics. This was a prime motivation behind various efforts to describe clusters of individuals within BASE participants (Smith & M. Baltes, 1998; Smith & P. Baltes, 1997, 1999b).

Along with this prime motivation, our work in BASE with regard to profiles of functioning had three main goals. To begin, we wondered how many subgroups would be revealed in the BASE data by cluster analysis and how the psychological profiles of these groups would differ in terms of overall level and shape (pattern of high and low scores across the domains). Two sets of cluster analyses were undertaken. The first set, described here, was restricted to 12 constructs selected to broadly represent the central psychological dimensions considered in the research literature on old age—namely, perceptual speed, memory, knowledge, neuroticism, extraversion, life investment, internal and external control, social and emotional loneliness, reported number of close confidants, and perceived support (Smith & P. Baltes, 1997, 1999b).

A second goal was to characterize the nature of the profiles. As a first step to do this, we decided to rank order the profile of construct scores on a dimension of desirability or functional status. Previous researchers have distinguished aged lifestyles characterized by *activity* versus *disengagement* (e.g., Neugarten, Havighurst, & Tobin, 1968; Maddox,

1994), individuals who maintain intellectual functioning and those who show early decline (Riegel & Riegel, 1972; Schaie, 1989), and profiles of successful versus less successful aging (e.g., P. Baltes & M. Baltes, 1990; Garfein & Herzog, 1995; Williams & Wirths, 1965). We decided instead to focus on a categorization of desirability, both in terms of social acceptance and effective function. The idea underlying this decision was that many different profiles may be functionally effective given particular life contexts and yet not necessarily be the best possible or most successful profile.

The evaluation of profiles in terms of desirability (functional status) involved two steps (see Smith & P. Baltes, 1997). To begin, based on the gerontological literature, we categorized scores on each of the constructs examined as either desirable (functional) or less desirable in old age (see also the discussion above). Less desirable characteristics included, for example, impaired cognitive performance, high neuroticism, high loneliness, low well-being, poor physical mobility, minimal financial resources, and few living kin. On the basis of this categorization, an overall mean level of desirability for the subgroup profiles obtained from the cluster analysis was calculated, and this overall score was used to rank order the cluster subgroups.

Having extracted the cluster subgroups and described their overall functional desirability, a third goal of the work in BASE was to examine whether the subgroups obtained differed in age and gender composition. Further, we wondered whether composition differences also indicated age- and gender-related differences along a dimension of functional status (desirability). Underlying this goal was the desire to gain a first impression of the balance of desirable and less-desirable psychological profiles in the old and the oldest old and for men and women in BASE. Are younger age groups (70 to 84 years) more likely to be represented in the subgroups showing desirable profiles, and the oldest old in profile subgroups with less desirable attributes? Is there evidence that, compared to older men, proportionately more older women exhibit less desirable psychological profiles?

Table 10.2 provides an overview of the nine clusters revealed from the first set of BASE analyses of 12 psychological constructs (N = 516) (for details, refer to Smith & P. Baltes, 1997). As can be seen, there was one rather large group containing 119 persons (23% of the sample) and two comparatively small groups (N = 29 and 32), each reflecting about 6% of the sample. The cluster profiles were separately interpreted in terms of their overall desirability, level (mean), and defining peaks (where dimensions were scored over 0.5 SD higher or lower than the sample mean). To simplify presentation, the groups are listed in the order of their desirability score, from the more positive (rank 1) to the more negative (rank 9). Table 10.2 also includes information about the average age of each group and the relative involvement of men and women.

It is interesting to note that there are different variations of general profiles that in terms of level and desirability are generally positive, average, and negative. The first three groups listed in Table 10.2 (47% of the sample) reflected various patterns of desirable attributes (positive to average functional status) and what could be called "successful aging." In each group, positive attributes predominated, though the groups

Table 10.2

The Subgroups Extracted from a Cluster Analysis of 12 Psychology Constructs
(adapted from Smith & P. Baltes, 1997). The groups are listed in their rank order
on an overall score of desirability (functional status)

Rank	Subgroup Label/Desirable Status	N	Percent	Age	Percent Female/Male
1	Cognitively very fit, vitally involved	50	9.8%	77.9	48%/52%
2	Socially oriented and engaged	29	5.7%	82.5	45%/55%
3	Cognitively fit, well-balanced, easing through life	119	23.3%	81.1	37%/63%
4	Cognitively fit, reserved loner	42	8.2%	81.1	55%/45%
5	Fearful, lonely, but supported	75	14.7%	88.0	68%/32%
6	Anxious, lonely, holding on to control	44	8.6%	84.7	50%/50%
7	Dependent but well-balanced	64	12.5%	91.2	53%/47%
8	Cognitively impaired, disengaged, but content	55	10.7%	88.5	36%/64%
9	Cognitive impairment, withdrawn, in despair	32	6.2%	91.2	69%/31%

differed in the set of dimensions that defined the peaks of their profile and in the size
and location of the peaks (see Smith & P. Baltes, 1997).

There were definite differences in the age and gender composition of the clusters
characterized as desirable and less desirable (Smith & P. Baltes, 1997, 1999b). Among
the 70- to 84-year-olds in BASE, 69% were included in the high functional status
(desirability) groups and 31% in the less desirable profile groups. Among individuals
aged 85 years and older, only 25% were in the desirable groups, and 75% were in
the less desirable groups. The relative risk of membership in the less desirable profile
subgroup was 2.5 times higher for the oldest old (age 85 to 103) than for people between
the ages of 70 and 84 years.

Whereas 53% of the men in BASE were members of desirable profile groups, only
41% of the women were. These differences between men and women were apparent
in the old (76% men versus 63% women in desirable groups) and the oldest old (30%
versus 19%). No subgroup exclusively consisted of men or women. However, the sexes
were not equally represented in four clusters. Two subgroups consisted of twice as
many men as women (groups 3 and 8), and two included twice as many women as men
(groups 5 and 9). Overall, the relative risk of being a member of a less desirable profile
group was 1.3 times higher for women compared to men.

The outcome is clear. Risk of membership in the less desirable clusters was larger
for the oldest old compared with the young old. These are dramatic age differences
in risk ratios. While further analyses—including longitudinal, cohort-sequential, and
interventive ones—need to be conducted to substantiate this pattern of results, the

central outcome is unlikely to change. The oldest old, and especially older women, are at a much higher risk for dysfunctionality than the young old. Whereas women live longer than men, their functional status is less desirable, and this disadvantage increases with age. This pattern of a major increase in risk for the fourth age is even more remarkable because the sole focus was on psychological measures such as intelligence, the self, personality, and social behavior. Psychologically speaking, advanced old age appears to be a situation of great challenge and a period characterized by chronic stress. Advanced old age, the fourth age, is a kind of testing-the-limits situation for psychological resilience (Smith, 2002).

In subsequent analyses, we have examined the long-term consequences of these profiles of psychological functioning in terms of survival. Cluster membership indeed predicted survival over eight years (Smith & P. Baltes, 2001). At the mid-2000 mortality update, 25% of the 516 sample was registered as alive. Cox proportional-hazards models and survival-curve analyses indicated that the nine clusters showed different survival curves that reflect our classification as desirable or less desirable. Whereas 60% of participants with desirable profiles of functioning survived, the large majority of members of less desirable profile groups had died. A unique effect for cluster categorization remained after controls are added to the analyses for age, gender, socioeconomic status, physical health, and functional capacity. Among individuals over 85 years (where fewer than 15% survived to mid-2000), the finding was highly significant: on average, individuals over 85 years in the desirable clusters lived at least two years longer than individuals in the less desirable clusters. The maintenance of even a limited positive balance of gains over losses in very old age appears to have some survival advantages.

Outlook

Lifespan conceptions about the multidirectional (multidimensional) and dynamic aspects of the gains and losses associated with change are important because they furnish the investigator with a strong mental schema that serves to counterbalance the pervasive "everyday" stereotype that early life involves only positive aspects and growth whereas late life is associated with negative aspects and decline. So much research has focused on documenting and understanding negative change and pathological functioning in old age that we often forget to ask about the range of normal functioning or about the potential to change in a positive direction.

In the fourth age, the individual may not have sufficient capacity to achieve "gains" without the intervention of outside support and the context of a culture of aging. Indeed, in very old age, it might be better to talk about "nonloss" than gain and also to develop metaphors related to "satisficing" rather than "maximizing." Even though there are solid methodological and theoretical reasons for this limited definition of aging, its disadvantage is that it reifies a decline and deficit conception of aging, thereby perhaps preventing us from discovering whatever potential for growth remains (see also Rowe & Kahn, 1997). The lifespan conceptions about multidimensional and dynamic aspects of change outlined above at least "open up" questions about possible gains and losses at all ages and motivate the use of methods that assess the potential for change as well as the limits.

References

Abelson, R. P. (1985). A variance explanation paradox: When a little is a lot. *Psychological Bulletin, 97,* 129–133.

Agronon, M. E., & Maletta, G. (2000). Personality disorders in later life: Understanding the gap in research. *American Journal of Geriatric Psychiatry, 8,* 4–18.

Aldwin, C. M. (1991). Does age affect the stress and coping process? Implications of age differences in perceived control. *Journal of Gerontology: Psychological Sciences, 46,* P174–P180.

Atchley, R. C. (1991). The influence of aging or frailty on perceptions and expressions of the self: Theoretical and methodological issues. In J. E. Birren, J. E. Lubben, J. C. Rowe, & D. E. Deutchman (Eds.), *The concept and measurement of quality of life in the frail elderly* (pp. 207–225). San Diego: Academic Press.

Bäckman, L., & Dixon, R. A. (1992). Psychological compensation: A theoretical framework. *Psychological Bulletin, 112,* 259–283.

Bak, P., Tang, C., & Wiesenfeld, K. (1988). Self-organized criticality. *Physical Review A (General Physics), 38,* 364–374.

Baltes, M. M. (1996). *The many faces of dependency in old age.* New York: Cambridge University Press.

Baltes, M. M. (1998). The psychology of the oldest old: The fourth age. *Current Opinion in Psychiatry, 11,* 411–415.

Baltes, M. M., & Baltes, P. B. (Eds.). (1986). *The psychology of control and aging.* Hillsdale, NJ: Erlbaum.

Baltes, P. B. (1987). Theoretical propositions of lifespan developmental psychology: On the dynamics between growth and decline. *Developmental Psychology, 23,* 611–626.

Baltes, P. B. (1991). The many faces of human aging: Toward a psychological culture of old age. *Psychological Medicine, 21,* 837–854.

Baltes, P. B. (1997). On the incomplete architecture of human ontogenesis: Selection, optimization, and compensation as foundation of developmental theory. *American Psychologist, 52,* 366–381.

Baltes, P. B., & Baltes, M. M. (1990). Psychological perspectives on successful aging: The model of selective optimization with compensation. In P. B. Baltes & M. M. Baltes (Eds.), *Successful aging: Perspectives from the behavioral sciences* (pp. 1–34). New York: Cambridge University Press.

Baltes, P. B., Lindenberger, U. & Staudinger, U. M. (1998). Lifespan theory in developmental psychology. In R. M. Lerner (Ed.), *Handbook of child psychology,* Vol. 1, *Theoretical models of human development* (5th ed., pp. 1029–1143). New York: Wiley.

Baltes, P. B., & Mayer, K. U. (1999). *The Berlin Aging Study: Aging from 70 to 100.* New York: Cambridge University Press.

Baltes, P. B., & Smith, J. (1997). A systemic-wholistic view of psychological functioning in very old age: Introduction to a collection of articles from the Berlin Aging Study. *Psychology and Aging, 12,* 395–409.

Baltes, P. B,. & Smith, J. (in press). New frontiers in the future of aging: From successful aging of the young old to the dilemmas of the Fourth Age. *Gerontology.*

Bandura, A. (1989). Self-regulation of motivation and action through internal standards and goal systems. In L. A. Pervin (Ed.), *Goal concepts in personality and social psychology* (pp. 19–85). Hillsdale, NJ: Erlbaum.

Bateson, P. (1996). Design for a life. In D. Magnusson (Ed.), *The life-span development of individuals:*

Behavioral, neurobiological, and psychosocial perspectives—A synthesis (pp. 1–20). Cambridge: Cambridge University Press.

Bengtson, V. L., Reedy, M. N., & Gordon, C. (1985). Aging and self-conceptions: Personality processes and social contexts. In J. E. Birren & K. W. Schaie (Eds.), *Handbook of the psychology of aging* (2nd ed., pp. 544–593). New York: Van Nostrand Reinhold.

Birren, J. E. (1959). Principles of research on aging. In J. E. Birren (Ed.), *Handbook of aging and the individual: Psychological and biological aspects* (pp. 3–42). Chicago: University of Chicago Press.

Birren, J. E. (1980). Age and decision strategies. In A. T. Welford & J. E. Birren (Eds.), *Decision making and age* (pp. 23–26). New York: Arno Press.

Birren, J. E. (1988). A contribution to the theory of the psychology of aging: As a counterpart of development. In J. E. Birren & V. L. Bengtson (Eds.), *Emergent theories of aging* (pp. 153–176). New York: Springer.

Birren, J. E., & Schroots, J. J. F. (1996). History, concepts, and theory in the psychology of aging. In J. E. Birren & K. W. Schaie (Eds.), *Handbook of the psychology of aging* (4th ed., pp. 3–23). San Diego: Academic Press.

Brandtstädter, J. (1998). Action perspectives on human development. In R. M. Lerner (Ed.), *Handbook of child psychology*, Vol. 1, *Theoretical models of human development* (5th ed., pp. 807–863). New York: Wiley.

Brandtstädter, J., & Greve, W. (1994). The aging self: Stabilizing and protective processes. *Developmental Review, 14*, 52–80.

Brandtstädter, J., & Lerner, R. (Eds.) (1999). *Action and self-development: Theory and research through the life span.* Thousand Oaks, CA: Sage.

Brandtstädter, J., & Wentura, D. (1995). Adjustment to shifting possibility frontiers in later life: Complementary adaptive modes. In R. A. Dixon & L. Bäckman (Eds.), *Compensating for psychological deficits and declines: Managing losses and promoting gains* (pp. 83–106). Hillsdale, NJ: Erlbaum.

Brim, O. G. (1992). *Ambition: How we manage success and failure throughout our lives.* New York: Basic Books.

Campbell, A., Converse, P. E., & Rodgers, W. L. (1976). *The quality of American life: Perceptions, evaluations, and satisfactions.* New York: Russell Sage Foundation.

Carstensen, L. L. (1993). Motivation for social contact across the life span: A theory of socioemotional selectivity. *Nebraska Symposium on Motivation, 40*, 209–254.

Carstensen, L. L., Isaacowitz, D. M., & Charles, S. T. (1999). Taking time seriously: A theory of socioemotional selectivity. *American Psychologist, 54*, 165–181.

Carver, C. S., & Scheier, M. F. (1990). Origins and functions of positive and negative affect: A control process view. *Psychological Review, 97*, 19–35.

Caspi, A., & Roberts, B. W. (2001). Personality development across the life course: The argument for change and continuity. *Psychological Inquiry, 12*, 49–66.

Charles, D. C. (1970). Historical antecedents of life-span developmental psychology. In L. R. Goulet and P. B. Baltes (Eds.), *Life-span developmental psychology: Research and theory* (pp. 24–53). New York: Academic Press.

Costa, P. T., Jr., & McCrae, R. R. (1980). Influence of extraversion and neuroticism on subjective well-being: Happy and unhappy people. *Journal of Personality and Social Psychology, 38*, 668–678.

Costa, P. T., & McCrae, R. R. (1992). Trait psychology comes of age. In T. B. Sonderegger (Ed.), *Nebraska Symposium on Motivation 1991: Psychology and aging* (Vol. 39, pp. 169–204). Lincoln: University of Nebraska Press.

Costa, P. T., Jr., McCrae, R. R., Zonderman, A. B., Barbano, H. E., Lebowitz, B., & Larson, D. M. (1986). Cross-sectional studies of personality in a national sample: 2. Stability in neuroticism, extraversion, and openness. *Psychology and Aging, 1*, 144–149.

Diener, E., Suh, E. M., Lucas, R. E., & Smith, H. L. (1999). Subjective well-being: Three decades of progress. *Psychological Bulletin, 125*, 276–302.

Dixon, R. A., & Bäckman, L. (Eds.). (1995). *Compensating for psychological deficits and declines: Managing losses and promoting gains.* Mahwah, NJ: Erlbaum.

Erikson, E. H., Erikson, J. M., & Kivnick, H. Q. (1989). *Vital involvement in old age: The experience of old age in our time.* New York: Norton

Featherman, D. L., Smith, J., & Peterson, J. (1990). Successful aging in a post-retired society. In P. B. Baltes & M. M. Baltes (Eds.), *Successful aging: Perspectives from the behavioral sciences* (pp. 50–93). New York: Cambridge University Press.

Filipp, S.-H., & Klauer, T. (1986). Conceptions of self over the life span: Reflections on the dialectics of change. In M. M. Baltes & P. B. Baltes (Eds.), *The psychology of control and aging* (pp. 167–205). Hillsdale, NJ: Erlbaum.

Finch, C. E. (1996). Biological bases for plasticity during aging of individual life histories. In D. Magnusson (Ed.), *The life-span development of individuals: Behavioral, neurobiological, and psychosocial perspectives—A synthesis* (pp. 488–511). Cambridge: Cambridge University Press.

Freund, A. M., & Baltes, P. B. (1998). Selection, optimization, and compensation as strategies of life-management: Correlations with subjective indicators of successful aging. *Psychology and Aging, 13,* 531–543.

Freund, A. M., & Smith, J. (1999). Content and function of the self-definition in old and very old age. *Journal of Gerontology: Psychological Sciences, 54B,* 55–67.

Garfein, A. J., & Herzog, A. R. (1995). Robust aging among the young-old, old-old, and oldest-old. *Journal of Gerontology: Social Sciences, 50B,* S77–S87.

Heckhausen, J., Dixon, R. A., & Baltes, P. B. (1989). Gains and losses in development throughout adulthood as perceived by different adult age groups. *Developmental Psychology, 25,* 109–121.

Helson, H. (1964). *Adaptation-level theory.* New York: Harper & Row.

Herzog, A. R., Rodgers, W. L., & Woodworth, J. (1982). *Subjective well-being among different age groups (Research Report Series).* Ann Arbor: University of Michigan, Institute for Social Research, Survey Research Center.

Higgins, E. T. (1997). Beyond pleasure and pain. *American Psychologist, 52,* 1280–1300.

Hobfoll, S. E. (1989). Conservation of resources: A new attempt at conceptualizing stress. *American Psychologist, 44,* 513–524.

Idler, E. L. (1993). Age differences in self-assessments of health: Age changes, cohort differences, or survivorship? *Journal of Gerontology: Social Sciences, 48,* S289–S300.

Jones, C. J., & Meredith, W. (1996). Patterns of personality change across the life span. *Psychology and Aging, 11,* 57–65.

Kagan, J. (1980). Perspective on continuity. In O. G. Brim Jr. & J. Kagan (Eds.), *Constancy and change in human development* (pp. 26–74). Cambridge, MA: Harvard University Press.

Kahneman, D., Diener, E., & Schwarz, N. (Eds.). (1999). *Well-being: The foundations of hedonic psychology.* New York: Russell Sage Foundation.

Kahneman, D., & Tversky, A. (1984). Choices, values, and frames. *American Psychologist, 39,* 160–173.

Kahneman, D., & Tversky, A. (Eds.). (2000). *Choices, values, and frames.* New York: Cambridge University Press and Russell Sage Foundation.

Kunzmann, U., Little, T., & Smith, J. (2000). Is age-related stability of well-being a paradox? Cross-sectional and longitudinal evidence from the Berlin Aging Study. *Psychology and Aging, 15,* 511–526.

Kunzmann, U., Little, T., & Smith, J. (in press). Perceiving control: A double-edged sword in old age. *Journal of Gerontology: Psychological Sciences.*

Lachman, M. E. (1986). Personal control in later life: Stability, change, and cognitive correlates. In M. M. Baltes & P. B. Baltes (Eds.), *The psychology of control and aging* (pp. 207–236). Hillsdale, NJ: Erlbaum.

Lawton, M. P. (1975). The Philadelphia Geriatric Center Morale Scale: A revision. *Journal of Gerontology, 30,* 85–89.

Lawton, M. P. (1991). A multidimensional view of quality of life in frail elders. In J. E. Birren, J. E. Lubben, J. C. Rowe, & D. E. Deutchman (Eds.), *The concept and measurement of quality of life in the frail elderly* (pp. 3–27). San Diego: Academic Press.

Liang, J., & Bollen, K. A. (1983). The structure of the Philadelphia Geriatric Center Morale Scale: A reinterpretation. *Journal of Gerontology, 38*, 181–189.

Lindenberger, U., & Baltes, P. B. (1997). Intellectual functioning in old and very old age: Cross-sectional results from the Berlin Aging Study. *Psychology and Aging, 12*, 410–432.

Maddox, G. L. (1994). Lives through the years revisited. *Gerontologist, 6*, 764–767.

Magnusson, D. (1995). Individual development: A holistic, integrated model. In P. Moen, G. H. Elder Jr., & K. Lüscher (Eds.), *Examining lives in context: Perspectives on the ecology of human development* (pp. 19–60). Washington, DC: American Psychological Association.

Magnusson, D., & Stattin, H. (1998). Person-context interaction theories. In R. M. Lerner (Ed.), *Handbook of child psychology* (Vol. 1, pp. 685–760). New York: Wiley.

Maier, H., & Smith, J. (1999). Psychological predictors of mortality in old age. *Journal of Gerontology: Psychological Sciences, 54B*, 44–54.

Manton, K. G., Stallard, E. & Corder, L. (1997). Changes in age dependence of mortality and disability: Cohort and other determinants. *Demography, 34*, 135–157.

Markus, H. R., & Herzog, A. R. (1991). The role of the self-concept in aging. *Annual Review of Gerontology and Geriatrics, 11*, 110–143.

Markus, H., & Nurius, P. (1986). Possible selves. *American Psychologist, 41*, 954–969.

McCrae, R. R. (2001). Traits through time. *Psychological Inquiry, 12*, 85–87.

McCrae, R. R., Jr., & Costa, P. T., Jr. (1990). *Personality in adulthood*. New York: Guilford Press.

McCrae, R. R., Jr., & Costa, P. T., Jr. (1996). Toward a new generation of personality theories: Theoretical contexts for the five-factor model. In J. S. Wiggins (Ed.), *The five-factor model of personality: Theoretical perspectives* (pp. 51–87). New York: Guilford Press.

McCrae, R. R., Jr., Costa, P. T., Jr., de Lima, M., Simoes, A., Ostendorf, F., Angleitner, A., Marusic, I., Bratko, D., Caprara, G. V., Barbaranelli, C., & Chae, J.-H. (1999). Age differences in personality across the adult life span: Parallels in five cultures. *Developmental Psychology, 35*, 466–477.

Nesselroade, J. R. (1989). Adult personality development: Issues in addressing constancy and change. In A. I. Rabin, R. A. Zucker, R. A. Emmons, & S. Frank (Eds.), *Studying persons and lives* (pp. 41–85). New York: Springer.

Nesselroade, J. R. (1991). Interindividual differences in intraindividual change. In L. M. Collins & J. L. Horn (Eds.), *Best methods for the analysis of change: Recent advances, unanswered questions, future directions* (pp. 92–105). Washington, DC: American Psychological Association.

Neugarten, B. L. (1969). Continuities and discontinuities of psychological issues into adult life. *Human Development, 12*, 121–130.

Neugarten, B. L., Havighurst, R. J., & Tobin, S. S. (1968). Personality and patterns of aging. In B. L. Neugarten (Ed.), *Middle age and aging* (pp. 173–177). Chicago: Chicago University Press.

Olshansky, S. J., Carnes, B. A., & Grahn, D. (1998). Confronting the boundaries of human longevity. *American Scientist, 86*, 52–61.

Overton, W. F. (1998). Developmental psychology: Philosophy, concepts, and methodology. In R. M. Lerner (Ed.), *Handbook of Child Psychology* (Vol. 1, pp. 107–188). New York: Wiley.

Oxford English Dictionary Online. (2001). Oxford University Press. Retrieved from http://dictionary.oed.com.

Pearlin, L. I., & Mullan, J. T. (1992). Loss and stress in aging. In M. L. Wykle, E. Kahana, & J. Kowal (Eds.), *Stress and health among the elderly* (pp. 117–132). New York: Springer.

Pervin, L. A. (Ed.). (1989). *Goal concepts in personality and social psychology* (pp. 19–85). Hillsdale, NJ: Erlbaum.

Rawls, J. (1971). *A theory of justice*. Cambridge, MA: Harvard University Press.

Reinert, G. (1970). Comparative factor analytic studies of intelligence throughout the life span. In L. R.

Goulet & P. B. Baltes (Eds.), *Life-span developmental psychology: Research and theory* (pp. 467–484). New York: Academic Press.

Riegel, K. F., & Riegel, R. M. (1972). Development, drop, and death. *Developmental Psychology, 6*, 306–319.

Roberts, B. W., & DelVecchio, W. F. (2000). The rank-order consistency of personality from childhood to old age: A quantitative review of longitudinal studies. *Psychological Bulletin, 126*, 3–25.

Rowe, J. W., & Kahn, R. L. (1997). Successful aging. *Gerontologist, 37*, 433–440.

Ryff, C. D., & Essex, M. J. (1992). Psychological well-being in adulthood and old age: Descriptive markers and explanatory processes. *Annual Review of Gerontology and Geriatrics, 12*, 144–171.

Schaie, K. W. (1989). The hazards of cognitive aging. *Gerontologist, 29*, 484–493.

Schulz, R., & Heckhausen, J. (1996). A lifespan model of successful aging. *American Psychologist, 51*, 702–714.

Schwarz, N., & Strack, F. (1999). Reports of subjective well-being: Judgmental processes and their method-ological implications. In D. Kahneman, E. Diener, & N. Schwarz (Eds.), *Well-being: The foundations of hedonic psychology*. New York: Russell Sage Foundation.

Smith, J. (2001a). Life experience and longevity: Findings from the Berlin Aging Study. *Zeitschrift für Erziehungswissensschaft, 4*, 577–599.

Smith, J. (2001b). Well-being and health from age 70 to 100 years: Findings from the Berlin Aging Study. *European Review, 9*, 461–477.

Smith, J. (2002). The Fourth Age: A period of psychological mortality. In *Max Planck Forum: Biomolecular aspects of aging: The social and ethical implications, 4*, 75–88.

Smith, J., & Baltes, M. M. (1998). The role of gender in very old age: Profiles of functioning and everyday life patterns. *Psychology and Aging, 13*, 676–695.

Smith, J., & Baltes, P. B. (1997). Profiles of psychological functioning in the old and oldest old. *Psychology and Aging, 12*, 458–472.

Smith, J., & Baltes, P. B. (1999a). Lifespan perspectives on development. In M. H. Bornstein & M. E. Lamb (Eds.), *Developmental psychology: An advanced textbook* (4th ed., pp. 47–72). Hillsdale, NJ: Erlbaum

Smith, J., & Baltes, P. B. (1999b). Trends and profiles of psychological functioning in very old age. In P. B. Baltes & K. U. Mayer (Eds.), *The Berlin Aging Study: Aging from 70 to 100* (pp. 197–228). New York: Cambridge University Press.

Smith, J., & Baltes, P. B. (2001). *Psychological profiles predict survival in old age*. Manuscript, Max Planck Institute for Human Development, Berlin.

Smith, J., Borchelt, M., Maier, H., & Jopp, D. (in press). Health and well-being in old age. *Journal of Social Issues*.

Smith, J., Fleeson, W., Geiselmann, B., Settersten, R. A., & Kunzmann, U. (1999). Sources of well-being in very old age. In P. B. Baltes, & K. U. Mayer (Eds.), *The Berlin Aging Study: Aging from 70 to 100* (pp. 450–471). New York: Cambridge University Press.

Smith, J., & Freund, A. F. (in press). The dynamics of possible selves in old age. *Journal of Gerontology: Psychological Sciences*.

Smith, J., Freund, A. F. & Baltes, P. B. (in prep.). *Changes in personality during old age*. Manuscript, Max Planck Institute for Human Development, Berlin.

Snyder, C. R., & Forsythe, D. R. (Eds.). (1991). *Handbook of social and clinical psychology: The health perspective*. New York: Pergamon Press.

Solomon, R. L., & Corbit, J.. D. (1974). An opponent-process theory of motivation: 1. Temporal dynamics of affect. *Psychological Review, 81*, 119–145.

Staudinger, U. M., Freund, A. M., Linden, M., & Maas, I. (1999). Self, personality, and life regulation: Facets of psychological resilience in old age. In P. B. Baltes & K. U. Mayer (Eds.), *The Berlin Aging Study: Aging from 70 to 100* (pp. 302–328). New York: Cambridge University Press.

Staudinger, U. M., Marsiske, M., & Baltes, P. B. (1995). Resilience and reserve capacity in later adulthood: Potentials and limits of development across the life span. In D. Cicchetti & D. J. Cohen (Eds.), *Developmental psychopathology*, Vol. 2, *Risk, disorder, and adaptation* (pp. 801–847). New York: Wiley.

Staudinger, U. M., & Pasupathi, M. (2000). Life-span perspectives on self, personality, and social cognition. In F. I. M. Craik & T. A. Salthouse (Eds.), *The handbook of aging and cognition* (2nd ed., pp. 633–688). Mahwah, NJ: Erlbaum.

Taylor, S. E. (1991). Asymmetrical effects of positive and negative events: The mobilization-minimization hypothesis. *Psychological Bulletin, 10*, 67–85.

Taylor, S. E., & Brown, J. D. (1988). Illusion and well-being: A social psychological perspective on mental health. *Psychological Bulletin, 103*, 193–210.

Tversky, A., & Griffin, D. (2000). Endowments and contrast judgments of well-being. In D. Kahneman & A. Tversky (Eds.), *Choices, values, and frames* (pp. 709–725). New York: Cambridge University Press and Russell Sage Foundation.

Tversky, A., & Kahneman, D. (1981). The framing of decisions and the psychology of choice. *Science, 24*, 453–458.

Uttal, D. H., & Perlmutter, M. (1989). Toward a broader conceptualization of development: The role of gains and losses across the life span. *Developmental Review, 9*, 101–132.

Vita, A. J., Terry, R. B., Hubert, H. B., & Fries, J. F. (1998). Aging, health risks, and cumulative disability. *New England Journal of Medicine, 338*, 1035–1044.

Williams, R. H., & Wirths, C. G. (1965). *Lives through the years: Styles of life and successful aging.* New York: Atherton Press.

Wohlwill, J. F. (1973). *The study of behavioral development.* New York: Academic Press.

Yang, J., McCrae, R. R., & Costa, P. T., Jr. (1998). Adult age differences in personality traits in the United States and the People's Republic of China. *Journal of Gerontology: Psychological Sciences, 53B*, 6, 375–383.

IV
A Lifespan View of Intelligence
and Cognition

11 Enablement and Constraint

Henry M. Wellman

University of Michigan, Ann Arbor, MI, U.S.A.

Abstract

A general issue for understanding development concerns the interplay between enablement and constraint, gains and losses. Notions of expertise provide one framework commonly used to consider such questions. For example, notions of expertise often underpin Baltes's lifespan metatheory with its emphasis on gains and losses and on the tradeoffs between selection and optimization. Three features often come to the foreground, if one thinks of cognitive development in terms of acquiring expertise: (1) the domain-general character of initial learning processes, (2) a presumed developmental shift from an amassed set of facts and experiences to a derived set of abstract principles, and (3) the expectation that more practice and more experience lead to more knowledge and that more knowledge leads to more powerful learning. All of these expectations are challenged by features of early cognitive development. While early cognitive development does encompass the accumulation of knowledge and skill in ways that meet these expectations, it also profoundly manifests (1) domain-specific inital learning states and mechanisms, (2) abstract frameworks of understanding that precede and shape the accumulation of bodies of more specific knowledge rather than being derived from them, and (3) learning mechanisms and trajectories where less is more. In this chapter, I discuss these features of early development as a way to contribute to a lifespan metatheory that comprehensively encompasses the full scope of cognitive development. I argue, among other things, that a comprehensive understanding of cognitive development may need to be especially informed by developments at both extremes of the life course—early childhood and late life.

> *In limitations he first shows himself the master.*
> *(Goethe, as quoted in Bartlett 1992)*
> —*Goethe (1802)*

A general issue for understanding development concerns the interplay between enablement and constraint, plasticity and fixedness. Conceivably, development could move simply from plasticity to fixity, from potential to accomplishment. At times, scholars and researchers interested in early periods of the lifespan—infancy and childhood—have written and acted as if development was unidirectional in this fashion. But this is simplistic, as Baltes's lifespan proposals make clear. In particular, Baltes's metatheoretical perspectives—especially those on gains and losses and on selective optimization with compensation—emphasize some of the intricate interrelations and balances between enablement and constraint. At the very least, to optimize some performance, capacity, or skill requires selection of a focus for resources and efforts, and since resources are inevitably limited, such selection breeds losses as well as gains. To use an economic metaphor, each developmental advance entails opportunity costs (alternatives not invested in; see Behrman, this volume); to use a poetic metaphor, each developmental path necessitates "a road not taken."

A third perspective that underpins Baltes's writings, including the target article, is that of expertise (see also Salthouse, this volume). Humans acquire knowledge and skill over the lifespan: most contemporary Western adults, for example, acquire considerable, albeit commonplace, expertise in reading or in driving cars. Scientists and engineers, skilled traditional wayfarers or master herbalists, acquire more individualized, specialized expertises. The achievement and maintenance of commonplace and specialized expertise is an ever-present task. Thus, Baltes's example of Arthur Rubenstein focuses not only on selection, optimization, and compensation but on expertise, in this case maintaining expert piano playing. Notions of expertise help frame and articulate relationships between gains, losses, selection, and optimization. One relation between gains, losses, and expertise is alluded to in the epigram by Goethe that begins this chapter; another is parodied in the saying that "an expert is someone who knows more and more about less and less."

How can we conceptualize the interplay between gains, losses, and expertise as knowledge and skill wax and wane over the life course? Baltes's examples and analyses focus on adult cognitive development. Over the last 15 years, researchers interested in early cognitive development have wrestled with parallel issues. One of my aims in this chapter is to focus on early development by way of endorsing a comprehensively lifespan perspective on cognitive development; every person who lives to late life was once a young child. Another aim is to consider more closely the notion of expertise as a metatheoretical construct for thinking about gains and loses, about enablement and constraint. I believe that background assumptions about the acquisition of expertise often shape our theories and discussions of cognitive development, but these expectations can prove misleading for understanding certain crucial aspects of early development. They may also mislead us for understanding development more generally.

Developmental Features of Expertise

Research on expertise (see, e.g., Chi, Glaser, & Farr, 1988; Ericsson & Smith, 1991) classically addresses persons who, for example, have become expertly knowledgeable at chess, baseball statistics, typing, or X-ray diagnostics. In everyday parlance, as well, experts are notably knowledgeable or skillful at some topic or practice—expert mechanics, gardeners, craftsmen. Practice, experience, hours of study and apprenticeship change novices into experts in these and other areas. Children, of course, are typically unexpert, and so novice-expert distinctions provide a contrast used to think about learning and development in early life as well as maturity. In what follows, I focus on three developmental features that are often assumed to characterize acquisition of expertise or of shifts from novice to expert. These features come to us, I believe, from our everyday understandings of what it means to be expert, but they also, implicitly and explicitly, frame many scientific discussions of expertise.

First, the processes that lead to expertise are intriguingly domain general in their view of developmental origins. To be clear, expertise is *not* domain general in terms of developmental outcomes. For outcomes, developing expertise is seen as yielding diverse domains of expert knowledge: chess and X-rays represent different skill domains, and chess masters' knowledge is specific to chess (e.g., Chase & Simon, 1973), not X-rays. But, developmentally, domain-general processes of practice and experience are typical mechanisms seen as yielding expertise. The picture is one of a level conceptual playing field that differentiates according to the dictates of experience and practice. Indeed, how else is it possible for humans to become experts of such contrived subjects as baseball, chess, and the Beatles, or, more mundanely, even to become expert readers? A great many contemporary persons become skilled, expert readers, a process that requires considerable instruction, practice, and experience. It is certainly difficult to argue that humans have some special, evolved aptitude or mental faculty specifically for reading: Paleolithic man evolved in an environment that contained no print, and the historical invention, development, and spread of writing was itself slow, problematic, and extended (e.g., Adams, Treiman, & Pressley, 1998). Yet sufficient practice, exposure, and instruction now yield millions of readers expert in the task of decoding print. General processes of perception, memory, information acquisition, analysis, and inference must be at work to yield fluent readers, chess masters, or expert physicians and so more generally have been emphasized in considering the development of expertise.

Second, the progression from novice to expert is from less to more, from ignorance to knowledge. Within an expertise perspective, this is almost a definitional truism; experts know a lot, and this accumulated knowledge and know-how is exactly why they are experts and not novices. More subtly, increased knowledge not only represents gains in information acquired; it yields gains in the capacity to learn still more. That is, increasing knowledge yields more effective, efficient learning as well. Knowledge effects, or the knowledge-dependent nature of learning, memory, and comprehension, are well demonstrated in research on cognitive functioning and cognitive development (Alexander, 1992; Bjorklund, 1987; Chi, et al., 1989; Keil, 1984). In comparison to those who know less, individuals who know more learn quicker, recall better, distinguish better between peripheral versus central information, and so on. Reading, again, yields a good example, as captured in "Matthew effects" (Stanovich, 1986). In the gospel of Matthew, it is said that "Unto everyone that hath shall be given." Research shows that beginning readers who are more knowledgeable and more skilled go on to become still more advanced over beginning readers with less skill (e.g., Adam, et al., 1989; Stanovich, 1986). More skill means more hours engaged in reading, means more words read per minute, means more appreciation of narrative forms, means more comprehension, and so on in a developmental spiral. In short, more is more: more practice and experience leads to more knowledge, and more knowledge leads to better learning.

Third, and relatedly, acquiring expertise is bottom-up in character. Experts build up and then work from a large store of facts and observations. According to Webster's New Collegiate Dictionary, one meaning of the term *expert* is "experienced." Another is "having, involving, or displaying special skill or knowledge derived from ... experience." Voluminous experience-based knowledge is the infrastructure of expertise. Of course, in the process of acquiring expertise, experts do more than simply learn a lot of facts. They come to appreciate certain integrative frameworks, hone in on abstract principles, and recognize or construct more expansive constructs that help tie together initially unrelated facts and observations into larger scripts, theories, and systems of understanding (e. g., Chi, Hutchinson, & Robin, 1989). These sorts of higher-level understandings, indeed, are part of what account for the knowledge-dependent nature of learning described above: more knowledge leads, in part, to larger, integrative connected systems of concepts that increase understanding, meaningfulness, associative connections and hence result in increased memory and learning as well. The point here is that experts get expert by first learning a lot. Concrete experiences precede abstract conceptions; higher knowledge systems are derived from a database of events, observations, facts, and features amassed in the voluminous practice and experience that builds expertise.

Several key characteristics of early cognitive development fail to fit these background expectations. Indeed, they turn such expectations on their head.

Less Is More

Species adapt to their world in numerous ways. Humans rely heavily, in comparison to other species, on learning and development, mechanisms that allow adjustment within ontogenesis to the environment an individual actually encounters, in addition to adjustment within phylogenesis to specieswide past environmental circumstances. Relatedly, humans have a prolonged period of life before they reach reproductive, physical, and cognitive maturity: each person spends on the order of 15 to 20 years as "immature" infant, child, and youth (see also Lerner, Dowling, & Roth, this volume). From a perspective of expertise, these two features—emphasis on learning and prolonged childhood—seem to go nicely hand in hand: Prolonged childhood means more time for learning; more time spent learning yields more expert knowledge. In this view, the initial status of children as novices reflects their lack of knowledge, which in turn determines their less efficient status as learners. As knowledge builds, learning potential also builds at least up to some point of asymptote or maturity.

Certainly, infants and children are characterized by several features that suggest less efficient learning. Infants have reduced sensory capacities in comparison to older children and adults—poorer visual acuity and poorer intercoordination between senses. Young children have poorer attentional control, slower speed of processing, shorter memory spans, and so on. But increasingly, researchers interested in early development have begun to argue that these features—these deficits of young children's cognitive status—may actually aid some foundational sorts of learning rather than impede them. There is, of course, at least one classic line of argument to this effect, based on an analysis of how infants' limited motor capacities enable them to learn more. In some species, newborn organisms are able to move on their own; this seems like it would enhance learning about the world. But for humans, locomotion (crawling and then walking) emerges only after many months of life. Moreover, locomotion is still notably limited in efficiency and endurance for many childhood years. Nonetheless, early movement limitations have been considered to be cognitively advantageous in that limited movement capacities increase the infant's and young child's dependency on and proximity to their caretakers, resulting not only in safety from predators but in increased opportunities for socially facilitated learning and social information acquisition. Thus, a prolonged period of *lesser* motor capacity fosters *increased* learning.

In an important expansion of this sort of analysis, Turkewitz and Kenny (1982) argued that certain sensory limitations in infancy probably function in a parallel fashion. They suggest that full exposure to the phenomenal world, via the mature sensory capabilities of adults, might overwhelm a young organism designed as a *learning* device with too much, and too complex, input. If so, then sensory limitations in infancy might not just reflect immaturely developed sensory systems; they might help reduce the input to more manageable proportions (for an analogous situation in old age, see Salthouse, this volume; Kliegl, Krampe, & Mayr, this volume). Turkewitz and Kenny (1982) give as an example that young infants' visual focus is limited and inflexible so that only objects 10 to 12 inches away are clearly in focus: "Such limitations reduce the amount of information which the infant must contend with and assimilate. Further, because those stimuli which are close to the infant, i.e. are within reach, are most clearly focused, temporal contiguity between visual and tactile stimulation from an object would be promoted" (p. 362). In short, sensory "deficits" may paradoxically substitute for cognitive facility: "Sensory limitation during infancy may . . . substitute for perceptual organization during infancy by providing an orderly world for the infant" (p. 362).

Newport (1991) has extended this analysis from sensory limitations to cognitive limitations by considering language learning. Research on critical periods of acquiring syntactic competence in one's language suggests that there is a sensitive period in language learning: language learning begun late in life—critically, after age 12 or so—is notably impaired. Empirically, Newport and her colleagues have documented the nature of this sensitive period by researching second-language learning; syntactic competence in a second language by immigrants to a new country is crucially dependent on the age they immigrated more than their number of years of exposure to their second language (Johnson & Newport, 1989). Newport has also researched this sensitive period by researching first-language learning in deaf children learning sign language, by comparing competence in adults first exposed to sign as youths at different ages (Newport, 1990). In both first- and second-language learning, acquisition becomes notably constrained as children mature into adults.

One often discussed possibility underlying these data is that a special learning mechanism for acquiring language is active early in life but then declines with age, so that decreasing effectiveness in language learning in later life coincides with diminished learning processes. This might be seen as a special case of the sort of age-related decline in cognitive capacity that Baltes deals with more generally (Baltes, 1997, this volume). Perhaps for the special case of language learning, a decline in learning capacity just occurs earlier—in childhood—than the late-life declines documented by Baltes. Thus, loss in a key learning mechanism results straightforwardly in loss of performance.

Perhaps. But there is an alternative possibility that Newport terms the "less is more hypothesis." She argues that learning processes and systems actually continue to get better with childhood development but that these improvements in learning capacity actually impede language learning. Conversely, initial less powerful or less mature learning processes aid language learning: less is more: "The idea behind the Less Is More Hypothesis is that perhaps the child succeeds better at language learning precisely because she begins with the ability to extract only limited pieces of the speech stream, with a gradual increase over maturation and learning in the amount of material to be analyzed; in contrast, the more capable adult extracts more of the input but is then faced with a more difficult problem of analyzing everything all at once" (Newport, 1991, p. 126).

Elman (1993) provides a computational demonstration that early cognitive limitations can enhance learning rather than impede it. Elman devised a connectionist network designed to learn an artificial language with humanlike complexity. In particular, the artifical language included the equivalent of syntactically simpler sentences (such as "The girl ran away") as well as more complex sentences including multiple embedded clauses (such as "The girl who the dogs that I chased down the block frightened, ran away"). Elman found that it was not possible to train the network to adequately discriminate acceptable versus unacceptable sentences of the language if it was presented initially with a complete, "adult" set of sentences varying in all the critical features, embeddings, and so on. However, if the input to the system was staged so that initially the network was exposed only to simpler sentences, with more complex sentences gradually introduced later, then the network could learn the language. Incremental, tutorially controlled exposure to the language resulted in mastery. Thus, a complex, competent system coupled with an enhanced (for example, arranged) learning environment could ensure learning.

Given this apparent need for a complex network coupled with a simplified sequence of inputs, a demonstrably less competent, more limited system would not be expected to learn. But Elman next devised a more limited version of the network itself. In essence, the system's memory span was degraded so that initially it would process only three to four words at a time. Then the "memory window" was increased progressively to four to five words, five to six words, six to seven words, and finally no memory degradation at all. This initially less competent, gradually maturing system effectively learned the language. Moreover, the critical result is that this cognitively more limited system learned the language from the original, complete, *un*staged set of input. An initially less powerful learning device in this case achieved better eventual mastery.

Elman (1993) describes in intriguing detail when and how this outcome results. In essence, the shorter memory span filters out some of the enormous complexity inherent in the input language, so that at first the system sees only a subset of the input: "When the network is given a limited temporal window, the data are the full adult language, but the *effective* data are only those sentences, or portions of sentences, which fall within the window. These are simple sentences" (p. 84).

These results seem paradoxical, at least as seen from a traditional set of expectations about development that are consistent with background assumptions about developing expertise: "One might have predicted that the more powerful the network, the greater its ability to learn a complex domain. However, this appears not always to be the case. If the domain is of sufficient complexity, and if there are abundant false solutions, then the opportunities for failure are great. What is required is some way to artificially constrain the solution space to just that region which contains the true solution. The initial memory limitations fill this role; they act as a filter on the input, and focus learning on just that subset of facts which lay the foundation for future success" (Elman, 1993, pp. 84–85).

The possible learning advantages that accrue to a developmentally immature organism might be broader still. Consider, for example, speed of processing limitations. One of the truly lifespan findings of cognitive development is the curvilinear nature of speed of processing in relation to age. Speed of processing for a variety of basic cognitive tasks increases systematically in childhood (e.g., Kail, 1991). Then, during adulthood, speed of processing levels off, followed by measurable declines in later life (e.g., Kail & Salthouse, 1994). Young children's slower processing of information certainly hinders some forms of learning. But a slower speed of processing could also reduce the amount of information available for consideration as the child constructs an initial understanding of phenomena, just as a network's shorter memory span can. Indeed, Bjorklund and Green (1992) argue that three features of young children's cognition that are usually thought of as immaturities impeding learning may actually be of adaptive value for early learning instead: relatively poor metacognitive awareness of one's own cognitive abilities and strategies, relatively high egocentric focus on one's own point of view or perspective (see also Sabbagh & Baldwin, 1997), and relatively slow speed of processing in comparison to older children and adults.

Domain-Specific Initial Knowledge or Constraints

The limitations that may enable developmental learning described thus far are potentially domain-general—memory, speed of processing, attentional focus. But researchers interested in early development have been increasingly interested in domain-specific knowledge and processes. Consider language acquisition again, but in this case word learning. As many have pointed out, uncovering the proper meaning of even a single word poses the language learner with an enormous inductive problem (Markman, 1989; Quine, 1961). To use a standard example, the word *rabbit*, even used by a speaker pointing to a small animal, might have any of an infinite number of referents—the small animal, its long ears, its twitchy nose or frightened expression, invisible internal animal parts, some larger category that this particular instance (whether animal or animal parts) is just an exemplar of, a small herbivorous animal if it is a Monday but a big carnivore if it is a Tuesday, and so on. However, young children regularly acquire vocabularies of 10,000 words or more by four years or so (e.g., McCarthy, 1954). How do they do it? The answer seems to be, in part, that children approach the word-learning task with certain simplifying assumptions and thus severely constrain the sorts of meanings they will entertain. In the realm of object labeling, for example, which has been the focus of almost all of the discussion and research on this issue, young children may well approach the language-learning task assuming that object names refer to single entire objects, that objects receiving the same name will be similar in shape, and more (Markman, 1989; Merriman & Bowman, 1989).

Young children, it now seems to many researchers, also approach the task of learning about other sorts of phenomena with domain-specific initial knowledge or expectations. Two early domain-specific systems of knowledge and learning that have been vigorously researched are knowledge of physical objects and knowledge of persons, or theory of mind. I will concentrate briefly on these, although young children's understanding of biological phenomena—plants, animals, death, germs, inheritance— has also been studied. (For a more complete review of children's reasoning in these three domains, see Wellman & Gelman, 1992, 1998.) A priori, physical, psychological, and biological phenomena and reasoning are arguably separable in some deep sense. Languages and cultures worldwide make various distinctions between animate and inanimate, between subject and object, and between psychological entities, living things, and physical objects (e.g., Wierzabicka, 1992).

First consider children's understanding of physical objects and physical forces. Piaget (1954) concluded that infants had to construct an understanding that the world is composed of solid object-like entities. This was acquired late in infancy, based on the infant's domain-general cognitive developmental mechanisms in conjunction with extensive interactions with objects, especially searching for visible, then invisible, then invisibly moved objects. But in the past 15 years, these conclusions have been systematically overturned (e.g., Baillargeon, 1986; Baillargeon & DeVos, 1991; Spelke, Breinlinger, Macomber, & Jacobson, 1992). For example, Spelke (e.g., 1994) has proposed that very young infants have certain core concepts that constrain their conception and perception of physical objects. In particular, physical objects move on paths that are connected (according to the continuity constraint) and cannot move through physical obstructions (solidity constraint). To illustrate one relevant line of research, in Spelke et al. (1992), four-month-old infants were habituated to a display in which a ball was dropped into a table behind a vertical screen. During habituation, infants were presented trials where they saw the background wall and floor, then a screen covered the display, and finally a hand holding a ball appeared above the screen and dropped the ball behind the screen. The screen was then removed, revealing the ball at the bottom of the display on the table top. After habituation, infants then were presented two types of test events. For all test events, they saw a shelf placed within the display directly in the path of the falling ball and then saw the two contrasting test items, where again the ball fell out of sight behind the screen. For the *consistent* test event, the screen was removed to reveal the ball on the shelf, consistent with the principles of continuity and solidity. For the *inconsistent* test event, the ball was revealed in the old position on the table top at the bottom of the display—as if, to the adult mind, it had passed through the shelf. Four-month-olds looked longer at the inconsistent than the consistent test event, registering enhanced attention if the ball failed to behave in accord with solidity and continuity.

Of course, young children could know a lot about objects without that constituting a special domain of understanding. To address that issue, understanding of objects must be compared to a potentially contrasting domain. The most well-studied contrast concerns naïve understanding of persons—folk psychology as distinct from folk physics. Of course, people are also physical objects, but they are distinctively psychological beings as well. At least to adults, persons are special "objects" with internal, mental entities, states, and causes. This has led to extensive research on young children's "theory of mind" (Astington, 1993; Wellman, 1990; Perner, 1991).

In fact, very young children firmly distinguish between the mental and physical worlds. For example, if told about one person who has a dog and another one who is thinking about a dog, three-year-old children correctly judge which "dog" can be seen, touched, and petted and which cannot because it is "only imagination" (Estes, Wellman, & Woolley, 1989). If asked to consider a thought about a raisin "in the head" versus a swallowed raisin "in the stomach," three-year-olds know which one is literally inside the person and which is only metaphorically "in his mind" (Watson, Gelman, & Wellman, 1998).

Relatedly, even toddlers grasp something of the special subjectivity of mental states. Thus, two-year-olds understand that desires and emotions are subjective in that different people can have different desires or emotions about the exact same objective situation (Bartsch & Wellman, 1995; Wellman, Harris, Banerjee, & Sinclair, 1995). This seems true even of 18-month-olds. For example, Repacholi and Gopnik (1997) had 18-month-old children taste two snacks—broccoli from one small bowl and goldfish crackers from another. Almost all children clearly preferred the crackers. Then an adult, facing the child across the table, tasted each snack, going "Mm" and smiling to one snack and "Eww" and displaying disgust to the other. In a *matched* condition, the adult liked the crackers and disliked the broccoli, matching the child's preference. In a *mismatch* condition, she liked the broccoli instead. After displaying her reaction to each bowl, the adult held her hand halfway between the two bowls and said, "I want some more. Can you give me some more?" In *both* conditions, 18-month-olds overwhelmingly gave the adult more of what she, the adult, had liked. In the mismatch condition, therefore, the children interpreted the adult's nonspecific request ("give me some more") appropriately and subjectively, in terms of her previously displayed desires.

These distinctions between physical and psychological domains seem to rest on infant distinctions between persons and physical objects. Several sorts of information argue that infants recognize "that they are like other human beings as opposed to inanimate stimuli" (Legerstee, 1992). For example, by five to six months, infants distinguish the way in which objects interrelate versus humans interact with objects (e.g., Woodward, 1998) and distinguish physical causes, where one object launches another via contact, versus interpersonal causes, where action without prior physical contact is common (e.g., Spelke, Phillips, & Woodward, 1995). In fact, Meltzoff (e.g., Meltzoff & Moore, 1995) argues that not only do infants understand various differences between physical versus human psychological phenomena but they learn about these domains via different learning mechanisms as well. In particular, even young infants begin to learn about the world of self and others via mechanisms of imitation whereby they imitate and thus further understand other human actors. However, infants imitate other people but not inanimate objects (Meltzoff & Moore, 1995; Legerstee, 1991). Complementarily, Baillargeon (e.g., Baillargeon, Kotovsky, & Needham, 1995) argues that infants' early understanding of physical objects depends on certain domain-specific learning mechanisms (see also Leslie, 1994).

Different authors advance different accounts of how to characterize these domain-specific understandings. In particular, some prefer to think of them as mental modules (Fodor, 1983; Chomsky, 1975; Leslie, 1994), whereas others construe them as naïve theories (Karmiloff-Smith, 1992; Gopnik & Wellman, 1994; Carey, 1985). In my research and writing, I favor thinking about such early knowledge as foundational theories (Wellman & Gelman, 1992, 1998; see also Gopnik & Meltzoff, 1997). At the least, these early understandings seem theory-like in several intriguing fashions. In these domains, children do more than consider surface, evidential phenomena; they utilize theoretical constructs that posit nonobvious, invisible entities or states in order to explain or understand those phenomena. As Premack and Woodruff (1978, p. 515) assert about a "theory of mind": "A system of inferences of this kind is properly viewed as a theory, first, because such states are not directly observable, and second, because the system can be used to make predictions, specifically about the behavior of other organisms." Thus, a person's invisible beliefs and desires are used to understand their observable actions; an object's inferred continuity and solidity are used to understand its movements and effects. In these domains, even young children are interested not just in predictable regularities but in the explanations for those regularities. Like a theory, this early knowledge identifies characteristic entities in a domain (such as solid objects versus mental states) and encompasses characteristic causal devices (for example, the intention and attitudes that cause an actor's acts versus the mechanisms of physical contact that propel an object's movements).

However, to be clear, that children have more and deeper knowledge at a younger age than previously thought or expected does not necessarily challenge an expertise account. Perhaps, instead, research of the sort just reviewed should be seen as describing distinctive domains of early expertise. In these areas, perhaps, children are experts. Indeed, rephrasing the description just offered, in these domains young children seem like experts in that they possess considerable knowledge, they recognize underlying nonobvious constructs, they are able to reason logically, and their initial knowledge facilitates the practice and experience that underwrite additional learning and an enriched knowledge base. Nothing in an expertise account requires that young children be universal novices (although that is sometimes claimed; e.g., Brown & DeLoache, 1978). Instead, to the extent that expertise requires cumulative experience *and* experiences differ by domain, then children would necessarily become expert at some things before others. Arguably, experiences with persons and with physical objects are so ubiquitous, even in the lives of infants, that children might acquire expertise rapidly in especially these domains of knowing. At least some evidence suggests that humans, physical objects, and animals are the kinds of things that parents most often talk about, are the sorts of objects that children most often talk about, and provide the experiences that children find most interesting (e.g., Wellman, Hickling, & Schult, 1997).

Nonetheless, to the extent that core, domain-specific knowledge is evident in infants, who are both inexperienced and preverbal, then it is difficult to envision these knowledge systems as forms of expertise—at least not forms of expertise in the typical sense of the cumulative products of domain-general learning processes.

Frameworks and Abstract Knowledge

A deeper challenge to an expertise perspective on early developing knowledge concerns the bottom-up character of expertise. To reiterate, experts first build up and then work from a large store of specific facts and observations. Abstract knowledge is derived from these amassed observations and facts; thus development necessarily proceeds from concrete to abstract, from observational data to naïve theory. However, at least in several core domains of the sort described above, development seems to proceed as much from abstract to specific as the reverse. How could this be? Again, I find it helpful to think about young children's understanding as theory-like and, in this case in particular, to consider a distinction between framework versus specific theories (Wellman, 1990).

In thinking about scientific theories, philosophers of science have distinguished between specific theories versus framework theories or research traditions. In this analysis, specific theories are detailed scientific formulations about a delimited set of phenomena. To use psychological examples, theories at this level might include the Rescorla-Wagner theory of classical conditioning, Piaget's theory of object permanence, and Freud's theory of the Oedipal complex. On the other hand, there are also more global framework theories. Examples in psychology might include behaviorism or psychodynamics. Philosophers of science have called framework theories *paradigms* (Kuhn, 1962), *research programs* (Lakatos, 1970), or *research traditions* (Laudan, 1977, p. 79):

> A research tradition provides a set of guidelines for the development of specific theories. Part of those guidelines constitute an ontology which specifies, in a general way, the types of fundamental entities which exist in the domain or domains within which the research tradition is embedded. The function of specific theories within the research tradition is to explain all the empirical problems in the domain by "reducing" them to the ontology of the research tradition. ... Moreover, the research tradition outlines the different modes by which these entities can interact. Thus, Cartesian particles can only interact by contact, not by action-at-a-distance. Entities within a Marxist research tradition can only interact by virtue of the economic forces influencing them.

Parenthetically, I believe that in the target article Baltes (this volume) outlines principles that would help articulate a framework theory of lifespan development. He specifies several critical entities such as "gains and losses," "cognitive mechanics versus pragmatics," and "the old-old." A variety of cognitive phenomena are "reduced to" or construed in terms of these entities. Moreover, he outlines certain general causal-explanatory mechanisms, trajectories, and modes of interaction—mechanisms of selection, optimization, and compensation and the changing balance between gains and losses. It is Baltes's explicit hope that his set of metatheoretical principles, which he calls an *architectural frame*, "represents the most general frame within which developmental theory is embedded. Whatever the specific content and form of a given psychological theory of human ontogeny, they need to be consistent with this architectural frame" (Baltes, 1997, p. 369, this volume). This is the job description of a framework theory. In general, a framework theory helps constrain and generate specific theories that flesh out the framework in various particulars for various topics.

If everyday domain-specific knowledge is theory-like, then there might be everyday framework theories as well as everyday specific theories. I believe that there are—or that there are cognitive frameworks very much like them. For example, an everyday belief-desire theory of mind constitutes a framework that provides the "architecture" for individuals' more specific understandings—more specific theories about more limited mental capacities (such as memory) and more specific theories about specific individuals (such as the specific beliefs, desires, traits, and so on that allow one to understand his or her wife or husband).

Assume for the moment that there are such things as everyday framework versus specific theories. From an expertise point of view, specific understandings and specific theories should precede and provide the database needed to construct more abstract framework theories. However, increasingly, researchers of early cognitive development argue that framework theory-like understandings precede specific knowledge in several core domains. What evidence underwrites such claims? Well, if children first acquire framework understandings rather than specific knowledge of concrete phenomena, then we could expect children's understanding and reasoning to appeal to the framework involved even in the absence of specific knowledge. That is, their conceptualization may be sensible and general *before* being accurate and specific. Sensitivity to larger forms of thinking in the absence of detailed information seems evident in much of the research on children's understanding of objects, persons, and biological kinds. For example, three-year-olds, like adults, tend to explain human action by appeal to the mental states of the actor, especially his or her beliefs and desires (Bartsch & Wellman, 1989; Schult & Wellman, 1997). However, their sense of what the actor's beliefs and desires really are is often vague ("she just wanted to"), distorted, or wrong (Bartsch & Wellman, 1989). Children appear to understand the animate-inanimate distinction, in essence, at an early age but often do not know where various entities, such as plants, fall with regard to that distinction (Richards & Siegler, 1986). Three- and four-year-olds appear to know that various objects have invisible insides or nonobvious essences and that such insides and essences function like theoretical constructs to help people reason about objects' identity and function (Gelman, Coley, & Gottfried, 1994). Yet at the same time they are inaccurate or vague about just what those insides are (Gelman, 1987; Gelman & Wellman, 1991). In short, in certain core domains young children often invoke a larger framework of understanding before evidencing accurate or detailed understandings of the specifics of that domain.

Not everyone agrees that a notion of everyday framework theories best captures this developmental phenomena. But there is increasing agreement that in some key instances very young children appreciate certain abstract or global properties, categories, principles, or theories that developmentally shape, rather than derive from, more specific understanding and skills. Hence, Rochel Gelman (1990) argues that "skeletal principles" define domains of cognitive development. Simons and Keil (1995) argue that in some core cases abstract knowledge precedes concrete knowledge rather than the reverse. Mandler (2000) argues on the basis of considerable empirical research that global categories precede basic ones in infants' and toddlers' understandings.

Conclusions

Three expectations often come to the foreground, if one thinks of cognitive development in terms of acquiring expertise: the domain-general character of initial learning processes, a presumed developmental shift from an amassed set of facts and experiences to a derived set of abstract principles, and the belief that more practice and more experience lead to more knowledge and that more knowledge leads to more powerful learning. All of these expectations are challenged by features of early cognitive development. While early cognitive development does encompass the accumulation of knowledge and skill in ways that meet these expectations, it also profoundly manifests domain-specific initial learning states and learning mechanisms, abstract frameworks of understanding that precede and shape accumulating bodies of more specific knowledge, and learning mechanisms and trajectories where less is more.

Young children, then, can seem like strange, perplexing mixtures. They grasp certain basic frameworks but often without knowledge of the facts and particulars that seem to be implicated to adults. They are severely limited but yet are prodigious learners nonetheless. Parents and researchers commonly experience children as precocious yet ignorant, both wise and witless. Apparently contradictory construals of competent infants as well as barely cognizant babies coexist in our research literature and everyday discussions. These apparent paradoxes stem, I believe, from the mismatch between young children's knowledge and learning versus our commonsense expectations of expertise. Expertise expectations mislead us into falsely construing the nature of gains and losses, learning and development as they appear in early childhood.

It is important to emphasize here that the expectations concerning expertise that I have addressed do not fully or faithfully portray scientific research on the acquisition of expertise itself (Beddard & Chi, 1992; Ericsson & Lehman, 1996). Actual investigations of how humans acquire expertise often do not portray such learning as monotonically increasing, bottom-up, or necessarily domain-general. As novice scientists, mathematicians, radiologists, readers, and so on become expert, knowledge proceeds from abstract to specific as well as specific to abstract (probably in cycles) (e.g., Johnson & Mervis, 1988), learning takes advantage of domain-specific processes as well as general ones (e.g., Marchant, Robinson, Anderson, & Schadewold, 1991), and losses as well as gains materialize (e.g., Adelson, 1984). Not only research on early cognition but also investigation of the acquisition of real-life expertise has much to tell us about the complex acquisitional relationships between initial constraints and the time-dependent stages of increasing and decreasing competences.

However, it is important to underline that cognitive development appears to be profoundly age-specific, a feature that Baltes (this volume) emphasizes. That is, the nature, effectiveness, and character of learning differ in some stages of the lifespan over others, dependent on a background of other capacities, limitations, and timetables. Cognitive development encompasses learning, as in the accumulating information prototypic of expertise, but it is more than learning alone. Development, learning, enablement, and constraint ebb, flow, and intercoordinate. Because humans have extended developmental lives and engage in massive learning, the nature of the intercoordination between these factors is extensive, and it shapes gains, losses, trajectories, and outcomes in complex, nonobvious fashions. Everyday expectations about expertise anticipate or privilege only some sorts of developmental patterns—in particular, a curvilinear trajectory from less is less, to more is more, and then to less is less once again as cognitive capacities diminish in old age. However, development encompasses other pattern as well: at the least, in early cognition less is sometimes more.

One hope I have for this chapter is to contribute to a more comprehensive life-course characterization of development and learning. In comparison to other species, humans engage in remarkable life-long learning. Not only do we have a long period of development leading up to maturity—a prolonged period of early learning—but we continue to learn well past maturity, past parenthood, into late life (see also Salt-house, this volume). Indeed, my colleagues and I have argued that human learning in adulthood can be seen as a human neotony (Gopnik & Wellman, 1994). Adult capacities for extensive learnings and change represent a prolongation of developmental openendedness—*incompleteness*, in Baltes's terms—well into the epochs of maturity and of a capacity for learning that in many species is more limited to early epochs.

A comprehensive lifespan metatheory of this extended human cognitive development may need to be especially informed by developments at both extremes of the life course—early childhood and late life. Both these ages are especially incomplete. Baltes (this volume) cogently reviews how cognitive change in the old old, the "fourth age," evidences special features and constraints. I argue here that research on cognitive development in early life indicates that it, too, evidences special features and constraints. Indeed, sensory limitations, slower speeds of processing, limits to independence, and motor limitations are common characteristics of both the start and the ends of our lives. Moreover, in line with Baltes's arguments (this volume), it is worth emphasizing that throughout life cognition and development are sociocultural phenomena—saturated with human social goals, social interactions, social information acquisition, cultural tools, scaffoldings, practices, and meanings. A culturally evolved set of practices and aids (print and large print, trikes and wheel chairs, schools and assisted-living facilities) help us to learn and cope, to change and maintain.

From the point of view of early life, humans invent and profit from cultural support because from the start we are prepared and evolved for cultural learning (Tomasello et al., 1992). Early in life we acquire the infrastructure and practices of learning from others. Teaching is a perfect example. Alone among species (Tomasello & Call, 1997), we may engage in deliberate pedagogy: this requires not only capacities to engage in teaching but capacities to benefit from instruction. Early childhood manifests not just the first increments on a learning curve of life-long extent; it sets an infrastructure for the processes—including sociocultural learnings and proclivities—that allow learning to take place and allow it to continue to take place as adults, older adults, and the old old. From the point of view of late life, every cognitively competent person instantiates a mechanism shaped by earlier experiences, memories, and foundational achievements. The practices of aging, being elderly, and dying that individuals engage in are socio-cultural and historical and provide a scaffolding for late life—one that is profoundly developmental, as well. Of course, on almost all conceivable layers, early childhood and late life are different. For example, the cultural scaffolding that supports learning is rich for childhood and impoverished, underdeveloped, perhaps even ineradicably incomplete for old age. As Baltes (this volume) nicely puts it, old age is new: it has less history and less evolutionary or culturally developed support. Those sociocultural forces and practices that have shaped childhood more completely have not had similar opportunity to shape late life. In these ways, among others, human infants riding the first trickles of a stream of experience versus human elderly with a full river of experience behind them are profoundly different. At the same time, however, it is not too fanciful to suggest that lessons learned in research about early life may have some application to late life, as well. In particular, consider one last time young children's concern with frameworks over details coupled with the "less is more" hypothesis.

As Baltes notes, "What is a gain or a loss in ontogenetic change is a topic of theoretical as well as empirical inquiry" (Baltes, 1997, p. 367, this volume); what is considered a gain or a loss "can change with age," involves subjective in addition to objective criteria, and is "conditioned by . . . cultural and historical context." Loss is a matter of interpretation, and, at least potentially, the challenges of loss in late life provide an opportunity for an important reassertion of the power of "less is more." In this regard, it is worth noting that diverse speculations on spiritual maturity and on the wisdom of elders emphasize a liberating perspective on life itself that focuses on broad, integrative concerns and perspectives and that privileges less over more. Common proverbs such as "knowledge and wisdom are far from one" and "after losses men grow humbler and wiser" capture this sort of perspective. So too do sages and scholars: "Age does not make us childish, as they say; it only finds us true children still" (Goethe, as quoted in Bartlett 1992). "Doors, windows in a house, are used for their emptiness; thus we are helped by what is not" (Lao-tzu, as quoted in Bartlett 1992). Clinicians who work with those facing death or severe illness also comment on a liberating connection to life that can come from the experience of late-life loss itself. Remen (1996) in her book describing some of her lessons from such clinical encounters, titled *Kitchen Table Wisdom*, quotes one patient as representing many in saying, "The more I threw away, the more I seemed to have" (p. 183). And she talks eloquently about individuals coping with severe loss who find an appreciation for "the great simplicity of living" (p. 139).

These perspectives are not meant to diminish the pain of loss, including the pains and losses of late-life limitations, constraints, and declines. But they emphasize that one sort of sociocultural scaffolding that might help complete the incompleteness of old age is not necessarily biomedical and is not necessarily strategically aimed at maintenance in the face of decline. Sociocultural resources aimed at achieving the grace and gains incumbent in loss itself and in aging itself may be needed to fulfill the promise of a fourth age for many individuals (see also Labouvie-Vief, this volume; M. Baltes & Carstensen, this volume). To paraphrase the quote by Goethe that begins this chapter, in limitations we may first, and last, show ourselves to be masters.

References

Adams, M. J., Treiman, R., & Pressley, M. (1998). Reading, writing, and literacy. In W. Damon, I. Sigel, & K. Renninger (Eds.), *Handbook of child psychology*, Vol. 4, *Child psychology in practice*. New York: Wiley.

Adelson, B. (1984). When novices surpass experts: The difficulty of the task may increase with expertise. *Journal of Experimental Psychology: Learning, Memory and Cognition, 10*, 483–495.

Alexander, P. A. (1992). Domain knowledge: Evolving themes and emerging concerns. *Educational Psychology, 27*, 33–51.

Astington, J. W. (1993). *The child's discovery of the mind*. Cambridge, MA: Harvard University Press.

Baillargeon, R. (1986). Representing the existence and the location of hidden objects: Object permanence in six- and eight-month-old infants. *Cognition, 23*, 21–41.

Baillargeon, R., & DeVos, J. (1991). Object permanence in young infants: Further evidence. *Child Development, 62*, 1227–1246.

Baillargeon, R., Kotovsky, L., & Needham, A. (1995). The acquisition of physical knowledge in infancy. In D. Sperber, D. Premack, & A. Premack (Eds.), *Causal cognition: A multi-disciplinary debate* (pp. 79–116). New York: Oxford.

Baltes, P. B. (1997). On the incomplete architecture of human ontogeny: Selection, optimization, and compensation as foundation of developmental theory. *American Psychologist, 52*, 366–380.

Bartlett, J. (1992). *Familiar quotations* (16th edition). London: Little, Brown.

Bartsch, K., & Wellman, H. M. (1989). Young children's attribution of action to beliefs and desires. *Child Development, 60*, 946–964.

Bartsch, K., & Wellman, H. M. (1995). *Children talk about the mind*. New York: Oxford University Press.

Beddard, J., & Chi, M. T. H. (1992). Expertise. *Current Directions in Psychological Research, 1*, 135–139.

Bjorklund, D. F. (1987). How age changes in knowledge base contibute to the development of children's memory. *Developmental Review, 1*, 93–130.

Bjorklund, D. F., & Green, B. L. (1992). The adaptive nature of cognitive immaturity. *American Psychologist, 47*, 46–54.

Brown, A. L., & DeLoache, J. S. (1978). Skills, plans, and self-regulation. In R. S. Siegler (Ed.), *Children's thinking: What develops?* (pp. 3–35). Hillsdale, NJ: Erlbaum.

Carey, S. (1985). *Conceptual Change in Childhood*. Cambridge, MA: MIT Press.

Chase, W. G., & Simon, H. A. (1973). Perception in chess. *Cognitive Psychology, 4*, 55–81.

Chi, M. T. H., Glaser, R. & Farr, M. (Eds.), (1988). *The nature of expertise*. Hillsdale, NJ: Erlbaum.

Chi, M. T. H., Hutchinson, J., & Robin, A. (1989). How inferences about novel domain-related concepts can be constrained by structured knowledge. *Merrill-Palmer Quarterly, 35*, 27–62.

Chomsky, N. (1975). *Reflections on language*. New York: Random House.

Elman, J. L. (1993). Learning and development in neural networks: The importance of starting small. *Cognition, 48*, 71–99.

Ericcson, K. A., & Lehman, A. C. (1996). Expert and exceptional performance. *Annual Review of Psychology, 47*, 273–305.

Ericcson, K. A., & Smith, J. (1991). *Toward a general theory of expertise: Prospects and limits*. Cambridge: Cambridge University Press.

Estes, D., Wellman, H. M., & Woolley, J. D. (1989). Children's understanding of mental phenomena. In H. Reese (Ed.), *Advances in child development and behavior* (pp. 41–87). New York: Academic Press.

Fodor, J. A. (1983). *Modularity of mind*. Cambridge, MA: MIT Press.

Gelman, R. (1987). *Cognitive development: Principles guide learning and contribute to conceptual coherence*. Paper presented at the American Psychological Association Meetings, New York.

Gelman, R. (1990). First principles organize attention to and learning about relevant data: Number and the animate-inanimate distinction as examples. *Cognitive Science, 14*, 79–106.

Gelman, S. A., Coley, J. D., & Gottfried, G. M. (1994). Essentialist beliefs in children: The acquisition of concepts and theories. In L. A. Hirschfeld & S. A. Gelman (Eds.), *Mapping the mind: Domain specificity in cognition and culture* (pp. 341–365). New York: Cambridge University Press.

Gelman, S. A., & Wellman, H. M. (1991). Insides and essences: Early understandings of the non-obvious. *Cognition, 38*, 213–244.

Gopnik, A. & Meltzoff, M. N. (1997). *Words, Thoughts, and Theories*. Cambridge, MA: MIT Press.

Gopnik, A., & Wellman, H. M. (1994). The theory theory. In L. Hirschfeld & S. Gelman (Eds.), *Mapping the mind: Domain specificity in cognition and culture* (pp. 257–293). New York: Cambridge University Press.

Hirschfeld, L. A., & Gelman, S. A. (1994). *Mapping the mind: Domain specificity in cognition and culture.* New York: Cambridge University Press.

Johnson, J., & Newport, E. (1989). Critical period effects in second-language learning. *Cognitive Psychology, 21*, 60–99.

Johnson, K. E., & Mervis, C. B. (1988). Impact of intuitive theories on feature recruitment through the continuum of expertise. *Memory and Cognition, 26*, 383–401.

Kail, R. (1991). Developmental changes in speed of processing during childhood and adolescence. *Psychological Bulletin, 109*, 490–501.

Kail, R., & Salthouse, T. A. (1994). Processing speed as mental capacity. *Acta Psychologica, 86*, 199–225.

Karmiloff-Smith, A. (1992). *Beyond modularity.* Cambridge, MA: MIT Press.

Keil, F. C. (1984). Mechanisms of cognitive development and the structure of knowledge. In R. Sternberg (Ed.), *Mechanisms of cognitive development* (pp. 81–99). New York: Freeman.

Kuhn, T. (1962). *The structure of scientific revolutions.* Chicago: University of Chicago Press.

Lakatos, I. (1970). Falsification and the methodology of scientific research programmes. In I. Lakatos & A. Musgrave (Eds.), *Criticism and the growth of knowledge* (pp. 91–196). Cambridge: Cambridge University Press.

Laudan, L. (1977). *Progress and its problems: Towards a theory of scientific growth.* Berkeley: University of California Press.

Legerstee, M. (1991). The role of person and object in eliciting early imitation. *Journal of Experimental Child Psychology, 51*, 423–433.

Legerstee, M. (1992). A review of the animate-inanimate distinction in infancy. *Early Development and Parenting, 1*, 59–67.

Leslie, A. M. (1994). ToMM, ToBy, and agency: Core architecture and domain specificity in cognition and culture. In L. Hirschfeld & S. Gelman (Eds.), *Mapping the mind: Domain specificity in cognition and culture* (pp. 119–148). New York: Cambridge University Press.

McCarthy, D. (1954). Language development in children. In L. Carmichael (ed.) *Manual of Child Psychology.* (2nd, edition, pp. 492–630) New York: Wiley.

Mandler, J. M. (2000). Perceptual and conceptual processes in infancy. *Journal of Cognition and Development, 1*, 3–36.

Marchant, G., Robinson, J., Anderson, U., & Schadewold, D. (1991). Analogical transfer and expertise in legal reasoning. *Organization Behavior and Human Decision Processing, 48*, 272–290.

Markman, E. M. (1989). *Categorization and naming in children.* Cambridge, MA: MIT Press.

Meltzoff, A. N., & Moore, M. K. (1995). A theory of the role of imitation in the emergence of self. In P. Rochat (Ed.), *The self in infancy.* (pp. 73–93) Geneva: Elsevier.

Newport, E. (1990). Maturational constraints on language learning. *Cognitive Science, 14*, 11–28.

Newport, E. L. (1991). Contrasting concepts of the critical period for language. In S. Carey & R. Gelman (Eds.), *The epigenesis of mind: Essays on biology and cognition* (pp. 111–130). Hillsdale, NJ: Erlbaum.

Perner, J. (1991). *Understanding the representational mind.* Cambridge, MA: MIT Press.

Piaget, J. (1954). *The construction of reality in the child.* New York: Basic Books.

Premack, D., & Woodruff, G. (1978). Does the chimpanzee have a theory of mind. *Behavioral and Brain Sciences, 4*, 515–526.

Quine, W. V. O. (1961). *From a logical point of view.* New York: Harper & Row.

Remen, N. R. (1996). *Kitchen table wisdom.* New York: Riverview Press.

Repacholi, B. M., & Gopnik, A. (1997). Early reasoning about desires: Evidence from 14- and 18-month olds. *Developmental Psychology, 33*, 12–21.

Richards, D. D., & Siegler, R. S. (1986). Children's understandings of the attributes of life. *Journal of Experimental Child Psychology, 42*, 1–22.

Sabbagh, M. A., & Baldwin, D. A. (1997). *Low-cost constraints: What social understanding means for semantic development*. Paper presented at the Society for Research in Child Development, Washington, DC.

Schult, C. A., & Wellman, H. M. (1997). Explaining human movements and actions: Children's understanding of the limits of psychological explanation. *Cognition, 62*, 291–324.

Simons, D. J., & Keil, F. C. (1995). An abstract to concrete shift in the development of biological thought. *Cognition, 56*, 129–163.

Spelke, E. S. (1994). Initial knowledge: Six suggestions. *Cognition, 50*, 431–445.

Spelke, E. S., Breinlinger, K., Macomber, J., & Jacobson, K. (1992). Origins of knowledge. *Psychological Review, 99*, 605–632.

Spelke, E. S., Phillips, A. T., & Woodward, A. L. (1995). Infants' knowledge of object motion and human action. In A. Premack (Ed.), *Causal understanding in cognition and culture*. Oxford: Clarendon Press.

Stanovich, K. E. (1986). Matthew effects in reading: Some consequences of individual differences in the acquisition of literacy. *Reading Research Quarterly, 21*, 360–407.

Tomasello, M., & Call, J. (1997). *Primate cognition*. New York: Oxford University Press.

Tomasello, M., Kruger, A. C. & Ratner, H. H. (1993). Cultural learning. *Behavioral and Brain Sciences, 16*, 639–650.

Turkewitz, G., & Kenny, P. A. (1982). Limitations on input as a basis for neural organization and perceptual development: A preliminary theoretical statement. *Developmental Psychobiology, 15*, 357–368.

Watson, J. K., Gelman, S. A., & Wellman, H. M. (1998). Young children's understanding of the non-physical nature of thoughts and the physical nature of the brain. *British Journal of Developmental Psychology, 16*, 321–335.

Wellman, H. M. (1990). *The child's theory of mind*. Cambridge, MA: MIT Press, a Bradford Book.

Wellman, H. M., & Gelman, S. A. (1992). Cognitive development: Foundational theories of core domains. *Annual Review of Psychology, 43*, 337–375.

Wellman, H. M., & Gelman, S. A. (1998). Knowledge acquisition in foundational domains. In D. Kuhn & R. Siegler (Eds.), *Handbook of child psychology*, Vol. 2, *Cognition, perception and language*, (5th ed, pp. 523–573). New York: Wiley.

Wellman, H. M., Harris, P. L., Banerjee, M., & Sinclair, A. (1995). Early understanding of emotion: Evidence from natural language. *Cognition and Emotion, 9*, 117–149.

Wellman, H. M., Hickling, A. K., & Schult, C. A. (1997). Young children's explanations: Psychological, physical, and biological reasoning. In H. M. Wellman & K. Inagaki (Eds.), *The emergency of core domains of thought: Physical, psychological, and biological thinking*. San Francisco: Jossey Bass.

Wierzabicka, A. (1992). *Semantics, culture and cognition: Universal human concepts in culture-specific configurations*. New York: Oxford University Press.

Woodward, A. (1998). Infants selectively encode the goal object of an actor's reach. *Cognition, 69*, 1–34.

12 Interrelations of Aging, Knowledge, and Cognitive Performance

Timothy A. Salthouse

University of Virginia, Charlottesville, VA, U.S.A.

Abstract
This chapter reviews the research literature concerned with the relation between age and knowledge and with the role of knowledge on the relations between age and cognitive performance. Although it is generally assumed that accumulation of experience with age leads to greater quantity or quality of knowledge, the empirical evidence from large-scale studies with representative samples of research participants suggests that while there appears to be an increase in knowledge from age 18 to about age 40 or 50, the dominant trend in later years of adulthood is one of either stability or decline. Among the hypotheses discussed to account for the lack of continuous growth in knowledge are generational confounds in education, losses offsetting gains, an asymptote on exposure to new information, and increased specialization of one's knowledge. Each hypothesis has some plausibility, but it is concluded that the reasons for the failure to find continuous age-related increases in knowledge are still not well understood. Several conceptual models of the role of knowledge on the relations between age and cognition are discussed, including moderation, mediation, and migration. Because interactions of age and knowledge have been inconsistent, and because statistical control of knowledge tends to increase rather than decrease the negative relations between age and measures of cognitive performance, the available empirical evidence seems to favor the migration interpretation. That is, age-related effects on cognition appear to be reduced among people with high levels of knowledge because people tend to "migrate" into higher knowledge groups with increasing age.

The realization that different cognitive variables have different age trends dates back to the earliest empirical studies on aging. For example, several studies published in the 1920s found larger age-related differences for measures of memory and reasoning than for measures of vocabulary and general information (e.g., Foster & Taylor, 1920; Hollingworth, 1927; Willoughby, 1927). Many labels have been used to characterize

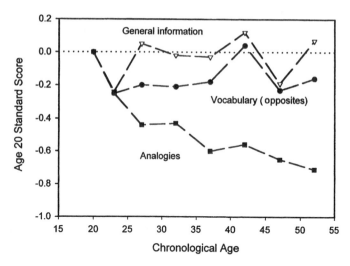

Figure 12.1   Age Relations on Three Different Cognitive Variables in a Sample of 678 adults.

Data from the Jones and Conrad (1933) study.

the two types of cognition (such as new learning versus reliance on stored information, educative versus reproductive abilities, fluid versus crystallized abilities, and mechanics versus pragmatics), but the terms *process* and *product* may be the most descriptive because the first term refers to the efficiency of processing at the time of assessment, and the second term refers to the cumulative products of past processing (see also P. Baltes, this volume; Wellman, this volume).

   The different age trends can be illustrated with data collected by Jones and Conrad (1933) on three subtests from the Army Alpha test battery (see Figure 12.1). (The vertical axis in most of the figures in this chapter represents performance in standard score or *z*-score units to facilitate comparison across variables and studies. Sometimes a sample of young adults will be used as the reference distribution as in this figure, and other times the entire sample will be used as the reference distribution. In either case, the units along the vertical axis are standard deviations of the relevant distribution, and thus the scale is informative about the magnitude of the age difference relative to the distribution of scores in the reference sample.)

   Notice in Figure 12.1 that across the range from 20 to 55 years of age the measures of general information and vocabulary tend to remain stable but that increased age is associated with lower scores on the analogies measure. This same general pattern has been reported many times, and it is now widely accepted that different types of cognitive measures can have quite different age trends.

   There are two major implications of these findings. The first implication is that because the constituent variables exhibit different age relations, no single number will be meaningful as an index of overall cognitive ability across all of adulthood. That is, if cognitive ability is composed of both product and process aspects, then it is not meaningful to refer to a single age trend in cognitive functioning. Jones and Conrad (1933) expressed this point elegantly by stating that the older adult derives more intellectual power from accumulated stocks of information than do young adults.

The second major implication of the different age trends is that there are at least two quite distinct phenomena to explain in the field of cognitive aging—the age-related decline in process aspects of cognition and either stability or increase with age in product aspects of cognition. The majority of cognitive aging research has focused on process aspects of cognition, in part because of an interest in remediating or preventing age-related cognitive decline. However, in this chapter, I focus on two issues concerned with aging and product or knowledge aspects of cognition. The first issue concerns the relation between age and measures of the quantity of knowledge, which might be expected to be positive because knowledge presumably derives from experience and experience is often assumed to increase continuously with advancing age. The second issue is the role played by knowledge on the relations between age and cognitive performance and particularly the ability of greater knowledge to offset the consequences of age-related decline in process aspects of cognition. This issue is particularly relevant to the P. Baltes and M. Baltes (1990) selective optimization with compensation (SOC) framework because of the possibility that optimizing one's knowledge in select domains might compensate for declines that may be occurring in other aspects of cognitive functioning (see also M. Baltes & Carstensen, this volume; P. Baltes, this volume; cf. Lerner, Dowling, & Roth, this volume).

Conceptualizations of the Role of Knowledge on Age-Cognition Relations

Before reviewing the relevant literature, it is important to clarify alternative possibilities for the role of knowledge on age differences in cognitive performance and ways that they might be distinguished. Because there has been relatively little research focusing on the interrelations of age, knowledge, and cognitive performance, most of the conceptualizations to be described were originally discussed in the context of research on the role of experience on age-cognition relations. Five possibilities, or models, all of which assume that there are positive effects of knowledge on cognitive performance, are represented in Figure 12.2. (The three functions in each figure correspond to different levels of knowledge.) The five models and their main characteristics are (A) moderation, interaction between age and knowledge; (B) stability, no age effects; (C) decline, negative age effects; (D) mediation, no age effects but negative relation between age and knowledge; and (E) migration, negative age effects but positive relation between age and knowledge. This classification scheme is not exhaustive because there could be positive age effects, as well as different combinations of relations between age and knowledge with stability or decline. However, the five models portrayed in this figure appear to be the most plausible and theoretically interesting possibilities to account for the role of knowledge on age-cognition relations at the current time.

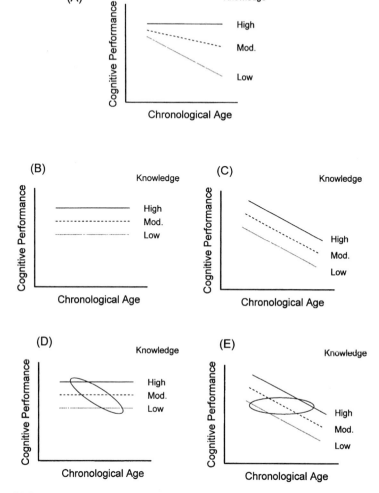

Figure 12.2   Schematic Illustrations of Five Alternative Models of the Joint Effects of Age and Experience or Knowledge on Cognitive Performance.

Panel A represents the *moderation model.* This is the view that knowledge moderates the relations between age and cognitive performance, such that there are large negative age relations among people with little relevant knowledge but small to nonexistent age relations among people with greater amounts of relevant knowledge. Some version of the moderation model is the most frequently mentioned possibility in the research literature concerned with experience, and the search for the predicted age-by-experience (or age-by-knowledge) interaction has been either an explicit or an implicit goal in many studies.

There are some cases, as with certain measures of reading or aspects of language comprehension or production, in which an interaction may occur that is attributable to an absolute or a functional measurement ceiling, in which almost everyone eventually achieves nearly the same high level of proficiency. However, because of the restricted range of assessment, the absence of age differences in these situations may be of only limited interest. That is, if the criterion activity can be mastered by virtually everyone, then there will likely be little or no sensitivity of the performance measures to variables such as age or additional knowledge. As an illustration, consider possible criterion variables reflecting proficiency in aspects of walking or talking. Because these tasks are mastered by most normal people, the range of variability would likely be highly restricted, and consequently it may be unrealistic to expect them to have relations with other variables. The moderation interpretation is more interesting when one can be confident that the interactions are not attributable to measurement artifacts, and yet people with high levels of knowledge still have smaller age-related declines than people with lower levels of knowledge.

Panel B represents positive knowledge effects but no age effects (stability), and Panel C represents positive knowledge effects with negative age effects (decline). In both cases, the age and knowledge effects are additive, and it is assumed that there is no relation between age and amount of knowledge. The same age trends are therefore expected at each level of knowledge.

Panel D represents a *mediation model* in which lack of knowledge is presumed to be responsible for the observed age-related decline. The flat lines signify that there is no relation between age and cognitive performance at any level of knowledge, but the ellipse indicates that increased age is typically associated with lower levels of knowledge within the population. When the emphasis is on experience instead of knowledge, this interpretation is known as the *disuse perspective* because it is frequently postulated that disuse functions as a mediator of age-related decline, as indicated by the admonition to "use it or lose it." The model in Panel D predicts main effects of experience (or knowledge) but no age-by-experience (or age-by-knowledge) interaction and a negative relation between age and experience (or there would be no evidence of disuse). Furthermore, this model implies that if a measure of the amount of experience (or knowledge) is statistically controlled, then the age effects on measures of cognitive performance should be substantially reduced. That is, if there is no disuse (in this case, because of statistical control), then little or no age-related decline would be expected. According to the mediation model, therefore, negative age-cognition relations are attributable to a negative relation between age and amount of relevant experience (or knowledge).

The mediation model differs from the other models under consideration because it asserts that lack of knowledge (or experience) mediates age-related decline observed in certain measures of cognitive performance. However, it should be noted that this interpretation is plausible only if there is a negative relation between age and relevant knowledge (or experience).

Panel (E) represents what can be termed a *migration model*. This model predicts a main effect of knowledge but with no interaction of age and knowledge, implying that the effects of knowledge are similar at all ages (or equivalently, that the age effects are similar across all levels of knowledge). The distinguishing feature of this model is that there is frequently a positive relation between age and knowledge (represented by the ellipse superimposed on the functions for each level of knowledge), as if with advancing age there is a "migration" of many of the individuals from lower to higher levels of knowledge. Because knowledge is positively related to many aspects of cognitive performance, no overall relation may be evident between age and measures of cognitive performance if the benefits of greater knowledge function to counteract the effects of any age-related declines that might have occurred in basic aspects of cognitive functioning. The migration model therefore implies that statistical control of knowledge would result in an increase in negative age differences because the greater knowledge effectively serves to offset any declines in basic processing efficiency that the individuals may be experiencing. In other words, the migration model attributes the absence of strong negative age relations in certain measures of cognitive performance to positive age-knowledge relations. This model may be the closest to what P. Baltes and M. Baltes (1990) refer to as *optimization with compensation* if the migration into higher knowledge levels is viewed as optimization and the greater knowledge is interpreted as compensating for declines in other aspects of cognitive functioning.

The mediation and migration models are similar in that in neither case is an interaction predicted between age and knowledge on cognitive performance, but instead there is either a negative (mediation) or a positive (migration) relation between age and knowledge that serves to alter the age-performance relations. However, the prediction from the migration interpretation is opposite that of the mediation interpretation because the age-knowledge relation is positive rather than negative, and thus control of knowledge should increase, rather than decrease, the magnitude of the negative age differences in measures of cognitive performance. Stated somewhat differently, in mediation the *presence* of a negative age relation is caused by a *lack* of knowledge, whereas in migration the *absence* of a negative age relation is caused by an *abundance* of knowledge.

The moderation and migration models are also similar in that both models predict high levels of cognitive performance among older adults with high levels of relevant knowledge. However, the underlying mechanisms in the two cases are quite different. In the moderation model, knowledge serves as a moderator of the age-cognition relations because the interaction indicates that people with high levels of knowledge exhibit smaller age-related declines in cognitive performance than people with low levels of knowledge. This model therefore implies that the impact of aging on certain aspects of cognitive functioning can be altered as a function of the amount of relevant knowledge. In contrast, the migration model attributes high cognitive functioning in certain samples of older adults to their higher levels of knowledge offsetting the consequences of declines in basic abilities. Unlike the moderation model, in the migration model knowledge does not have a moderating or interactive role on the age-cognition relations, but rather age and knowledge are "confounded" such that increased age tends to be associated with higher levels of knowledge.

To summarize, the key features of the five perspectives, all of which assume positive effects of knowledge on measures of cognitive performance, are as follows: (A) moderation—interaction of age and knowledge, smaller age relations at high levels of knowledge; (B) stability—no age effects, no age-knowledge relation; (C) decline—negative age effects, no age-knowledge relation; (D) mediation—negative age-experience (age-knowledge) relations, control of experience (knowledge) reduces negative age differences; and (E) migration—positive age-knowledge relations, control of knowledge increases negative age differences.

In all except the moderation model, the effects of age and knowledge on cognitive performance are additive, and therefore to account for the age relations on measures of cognitive performance it is only necessary to explain the main effects of age and knowledge and any relation that might exist between age and knowledge. However, if the evidence were to support the moderation model, it would also be necessary to explain why the age-related effects differ as a function of amount of knowledge.

Age-Knowledge Relations

Before examining the research results concerning age and knowledge, it is useful to briefly describe how knowledge has been assessed in studies of aging and cognition. The most common method is by various tests of word knowledge, or vocabulary, in which the examinee is required to either produce or select an appropriate definition of a target word such as *pontificate* or *virulent*. When the questions refer to different types of information, the tests are assumed to assess general information. A number of specialized knowledge tests have also been used in which the questions refer to particular domains of knowledge, such as science, social science, or humanities. Examples of questions in these specialized tests are "What is the function of the kidney?" "What is a regressive tax?" and "Who was the composer of the Brandenburg Concertos?"

Many studies investigating age-related effects in cognition have administered some type of vocabulary test in small convenience samples. The typical finding in these studies is that the older adults in the sample tend to have higher vocabulary scores than the young adults. Although it is tempting to infer from these results that knowledge increases continuously with age, this conclusion may not be warranted because the samples in these studies are usually small and may not be representative of the general population because they often include only young college students and highly motivated older adults.

Problems of unrepresentative samples also plague studies involving age comparisons with other measures of knowledge. For example, Stanovich, West, and Harrison

(1995) reported that older adults were higher in measures of general knowledge (based on tests involving the recognition of authors, magazine titles, and so on) than college students. However, 73% of the older adults in their sample had college degrees, and 45% had advanced graduate degrees, and thus the two groups were almost certainly not equally representative of their respective age cohorts.

In a recent report, Ackerman and Rolfhus (1999) compared college students and adults between 30 and 59 years of age on several specially constructed knowledge tests. The adults had higher knowledge scores than the students, but within the adult sample the age correlations for the tests ranged from −.13 to .19 with a median of −.015. Their results thus provide no evidence of greater knowledge with increased age among the nonstudent adults in the sample. A small positive correlation of .19 between age and a composite measure of knowledge based on these same tests was reported in a later study by Ackerman (2000). However, the sample in that study was relatively young (mean age of 34.2 years) and unrepresentative of the population with respect to education (all participants had acquired a bachelor's degree, and 25% had also received advanced degrees).

One project with relatively large samples is Schaie's (1996) Seattle Longitudinal Study. Results from two vocabulary measures administered to new cross-sectional samples in the 1984 and 1991 waves of that project revealed an increase in the average score from the twenties to the forties, then a period of stability, and a decrease around age 70.

The most informative data on age relations are those derived from nationally representative samples, typically stratified on age, gender, ethnic group, educational attainment, and geographical region. The normative samples for standardized tests of cognitive ability possess these characteristics, and therefore they are particularly valuable for determining true age trends in relevant variables.

Figure 12.3 illustrates the age relations for the information and vocabulary subtest scores from the normative samples in the 1955, 1981, and 1997 revisions of the Wechsler battery. Notice that the mean scores increase from age 20 to about age 40 or 50 and decrease beyond age 50. The Kaufman Adolescent and Adult Intelligence Test (Kaufman & Horn, 1996) is another standardized test with norms from a large nationally representative sample. Figure 12.4 portrays the age trends on two measures of vocabulary from that test battery, double meanings and definitions. Once again, there is a slight increase to about age 50 followed by a decline. Finally, the Woodcock-Johnson Psycho-Educational Battery–Revised (1989, 1990) is unique because it includes three tests of specialized knowledge (in the topics of science, social science, and humanities). Figure 12.5 portrays the age trends for the three measures of knowledge in the normative sample for this battery.

The mean scores in all of these data sets exhibit a similar pattern—namely, an increase from the twenties to the forties or fifties, followed by a gradual decline totaling between one-half and one standard deviation from about age 50 to 80. Although not represented in these data, results from studies focusing on adults above the age of 70 indicate that there may be an acceleration in the decline of measures of vocabulary

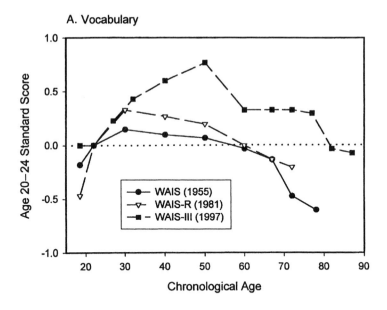

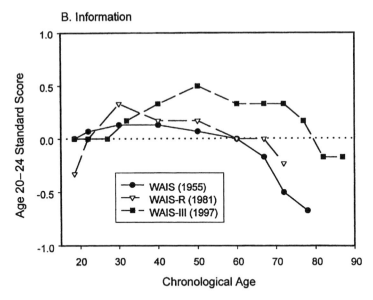

Figure 12.3 Age Relations on the Vocabulary (A) and Information (B) Variables from the Normative Samples in Three Versions of the Wechsler Battery.

Data from Wechsler (1955, 1981, 1997)

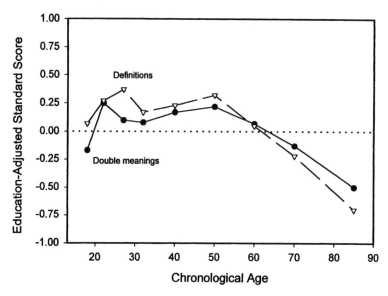

Figure 12.4 Age relations on Variables Assessing Word Knowledge from the Normative Sample (N = 1,500) in the Kaufman Adult Intelligence Test.

Data from Kaufman and Horn (1996).

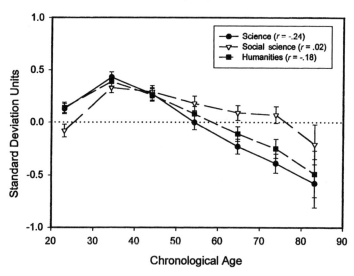

Figure 12.5 Age Relations on Three Tests of Specialized Knowledge for 1,184 Individuals with More Than Nine Years of Education from the Normative Sample in the Woodcock-Johnson Test of Cognitive Abilities.

Bars around each point are standard errors. Data from Salthouse (1998).

and knowledge at older ages (e.g., Hultsch, Hertzog, Dixon, & Small, 1998; Lindenberger & Reischies, 1999).

Assessments of other types of knowledge reveal broadly similar patterns. For example, Demming and Pressey (1957) developed three tests of what they termed *practical knowledge*. The tests, and sample questions in each, were as follows.

- *Yellow pages* Where in the yellow pages of the telephone directory would you look if you wanted to buy an Airedale—under heating equipment, kennels, shoe stores, real estate, dairy equipment?
- *Legal terms* A document controlling disposition of one's property at death is called a bond, title, contract, will, equity.
- *Occupations* The person to baptize a baby is a naturalist, notary public, nurseryman, magistrate, clergyman.

These tests were administered to two nonrepresentative samples—namely, inmates in a penitentiary and students attending evening classes. In both samples, the average scores increased to about age 40, but very few adults in either sample were above the age of 50, and thus there was no information in this study about the trend at older ages. However, a later study by Gardner and Monge (1977) found that the age functions for scores on specially constructed tests of knowledge of transportation, finance, and disease peaked in the fifties and then declined, which is the same pattern found with measures of vocabulary and general information.

Tacit knowledge relevant to management was recently assessed by Colonia-Willner (1998) in a unique sample of 157 midlevel bank managers between 24 and 56 years of age. The measures of tacit knowledge in this study were based on ratings of the desirability of alternative responses to various scenarios, which were scored in terms of how closely an individual's ratings resembled the ratings of "experts." Because the scores were deviations, lower values correspond to better performance (smaller deviations represent ratings that are closer to the expert ratings). All correlations between the tacit knowledge measures and age were positive, with a .28 correlation between age and the overall tacit knowledge score, indicating that increased age was associated with less tacit knowledge (a larger discrepancy from the experts).

A third example of a specialized type of knowledge concerns the concept of wisdom, which is often assumed to be a domain in which older adults have an advantage over young adults. Unfortunately, this assumption has been difficult to evaluate because of a lack of consensus about how wisdom might be assessed. One approach to the assessment of wisdom-related knowledge has involved tests of the comprehension or interpretation of proverbs because they are often considered to reflect fundamental principles of human existence. However, research on proverb interpretation has revealed either a pattern of stability across the adult years (e.g., Sorenson, 1938) or a pattern of age-related declines (e.g., Aftanas & Royce, 1969; Albert, Duffy, & Naeser, 1987; Bromley, 1957; Hamsher & Benton, 1978). Baltes and his colleagues adopted another approach to the assessment of wisdom by proposing that an individual's level of wisdom could be assessed by his or her responses to selected life dilemmas, scored according to several theoretically determined criteria. This method of assessment has been used in a number of independent studies, and in none of them have there been significant age differences favoring older adults (Baltes, Staudinger, Maercker, & Smith, 1995; Smith & Baltes, 1990; Staudinger, 1999).

To many researchers working in the area of aging and cognition, a discovery of stability across most of the adult years is a welcome finding, particularly when contrasted with the widespread declines found in variables reflecting process aspects of cognition. Nevertheless, the absence of more dramatic and sustained increases in knowledge is puzzling because increased age is presumably associated with greater cumulative exposure and opportunities to acquire information, and thus one might expect knowledge to increase continuously across most, if not all, of the adult years.[1]

Several hypotheses have been proposed to account for the lack of continuous age-related increases in knowledge, but it should be recognized at the outset that they are probably not mutually exclusive and almost certainly are not exhaustive of the possible explanations for this phenomenon.

One interpretation of the failure to find age-related increases in knowledge is that there have been generational shifts in the average amount of education, and amount of education is usually positively correlated with knowledge. It has therefore been argued that age trends in knowledge might be altered if adjustments were made for the age differences in either the quantity or quality of education. There are two issues to consider when evaluating this interpretation—what is actually achieved by control of education, and the empirical consequences on age-knowledge relations of controlling amount of education. With respect to the first issue, there are at least three possibilities for how education might be related to level of knowledge across adulthood. One is that education has a direct influence on amount of knowledge by the increased opportunities to acquire knowledge during the period of formal schooling. A second possibility is that education has an indirect effect on level of knowledge by stimulating knowledge-seeking activities at later periods in one's life. Finally, it is also possible that amount of education is a proxy for general intellectual ability in that greater amounts of intellectual ability are presumably needed to gain access to higher levels of education. To the extent that this latter possibility is valid, then the results of controlling for amount of education may not be readily interpretable because education may actually be a surrogate measure of the efficiency with which knowledge can be acquired. At the current time, there is little relevant evidence that would allow these possibilities to be unequivocally distinguished, and it is likely that several of them are operating simultaneously.

Fortunately, at least some empirical results suggest that difficulties of interpretation may not be serious because control of education often has little effect on the relations between age and knowledge. For example, this is true in the nationally representative sample used in the norms for the Woodcock-Johnson Psycho-Educational Battery, even though the correlations between amount of education and the measures of knowledge were in the .4 to .5 range. That is, the education-partialed correlations between age and knowledge were nearly identical to the unpartialed correlations (science, partial, $r = -.26$, original $r = -.24$; social science, partial $r = .02$, original $r = .03$; and humanities, partial $r = -.18$, original $r = -.19$).

A second interpretation of the lack of consistent age-related increases in knowledge is that losses offset gains, in the sense that the acquisition of new information may be accompanied by the forgetting of old information. The combination of the two opposing processes could lead to stability in measures of overall knowledge if the effects of the two processes are close to equilibrium. Unfortunately, this interpretation is difficult to investigate without detailed assessments over time of the same types of information in the same individuals.

A third interpretation is that after a certain point, increased age may be associated with progressively more restricted exposure to new and different experiences. This view suggests that there may be something analogous to an asymptote, perhaps around the period of middle adulthood, on opportunities to acquire new information. That is, some time after formal schooling is completed, there may be a decrease in the diversity of one's experiences, and consequently exposure to new types of information may become progressively more limited. This interpretation therefore implies that the reason for the lack of continuous increases in knowledge with advancing age is not because of any factors operating within the individual but rather because of a gradual constriction in the range of novel experiences as people grow older. It should be possible to investigate this interpretation by attempting to relate measures of the diversity or novelty of information exposure to measures of available knowledge, but research of this type has apparently not yet been conducted. Perhaps the closest research is the Kohn and Schooler project (e.g., Kohn & Schooler, 1983; Schooler, Mulatu, & Oates, 1999), in which relations between substantive complexity of work and measures of cognitive functioning were examined, but their assessments did not include measures of knowledge.

A fourth interpretation of the lack of continuous age-related increases in knowledge is based on the idea that one's knowledge becomes progressively more specialized with age and experience. That is, tests designed for the general population are necessarily broad and relatively superficial rather than highly specific and detailed, or else they would have very limited applicability. However, when an individual pursues vocational and avocational interests, much of his or her knowledge is likely to become increasingly more specialized, and these broad tests would probably fail to detect any increases in specialized knowledge that may be occurring. The idea that it may not be possible for a single test to assess all facets of one's knowledge because of its specialized and idiosyncratic nature has been recognized by several writers, including recently by Ackerman (1996) and Cattell (1972, 1998).

The specialized-knowledge interpretation is challenging to investigate because on the one hand, it is assumed that if tests could be specialized to the individual, then they might exhibit increases with age, but on the other hand, if the tests are too highly specialized, then it may be impossible to make any across-person comparisons.

Nevertheless, two types of evidence seem relevant to the selective specialization interpretation. The first consists of the examination of relations between age and specialized knowledge tests among high performers, or experts, within a given domain. That is, in some studies, the individuals were selected specifically because they had considerable experience with the relevant activity, and consequently they can be considered experts in that domain.

There are only a few studies of this type, and the samples are typically small, but the results are nevertheless informative. In an early study of 20 bridge players, Charness (1979) found a small positive correlation between age and score on a bridge knowledge test ($r = .16$), but in a later study (Charness, 1983) with 45 bridge players ranging from 21 to 71 years of age, the age-knowledge correlation was $-.40$. Pfau and Murphy (1988) reported a correlation of $-.12$ between age (across a range from 17 to 75) and chess knowledge in a sample of 59 chess players. Finally, Meinz and Salthouse (1998) administered a test of musical notation knowledge to 128 individuals who varied in amount of musical experience and found a correlation of $-.17$ between age and musical knowledge. The correlations between age and the measures of knowledge are therefore small and are more often negative than positive. Furthermore, it is important to point out that the failure to find strong positive correlations is not because the knowledge tests were not valid in the domains because the correlations between the knowledge scores and measures of skill or performance in the domain were quite high, ranging from .63 to .86.

The apparent implication of these results is that high levels of specialization can be achieved in a domain without evidence of age-related increases in relevant knowledge. This is surprising because one of the factors that might have been presumed to contribute to the older adults' expertise and high performance in the domain in greater knowledge.

A second method of investigating the specialized-knowledge interpretation consists of examining knowledge in topics grouped according to the individual's self-rated interest. The rationale is that if as people grow older they tend to specialize in a relatively small number of topics, then the relations between age and knowledge would be expected to be more positive for topics that the individuals rate as high in interest.

This prediction was examined in two recent studies in my laboratory (Study 3 in Hambrick, Salthouse, & Meinz, 1999, and an unpublished study). Individuals in both studies were recruited to participate in a project investigating determinants of crossword-puzzle skill, and the quantity of knowledge in different topic areas was hypothesized to be one potential determinant of puzzle-solving ability. The participants in the studies were first asked to rate (on a five-point scale) their levels of interest in 10 different topics (American history, American literature, art, geography, music, mythology, science, sports, world history, and world literature), and then their level of knowledge in each area was assessed with both multiple-choice and short-answer recall questions.

If selective specialization is operating, then we would expect main effects of interest (higher levels of interest associated with greater amounts of knowledge), and, most important, an interaction of age and interest in the direction of larger age-related increases in knowledge for high-interest topics.

The first study involved 195 adults between 18 and 87 years of age. Figure 12.6 portrays the age relations in this study, with the different panels containing data from the different topics. The three lines in each panel correspond to the average age function across the entire sample, and separate lines represent the functions for the subsets of individuals rating their self-interest in the topic as high or as low. It is apparent that despite main effects of interest in each topic (higher interest associated with greater knowledge), the three sets of age relations were nearly parallel. Furthermore, regression analyses in which age and interest were both treated as continuous variables revealed that none of the cross-product interactions between age and self-rated interest were statistically significant. The results of this study are therefore inconsistent with the selective specialization interpretation because they suggest that the relation between age and knowledge was the same regardless of the level of self-reported interest.

The second study involved 206 adults between 18 and 84 years of age. This was a replication of the previous study except that now the participants were also asked to rate their interests in the 10 topics for each decade of their life from age 15 to the current time. We hypothesized that there might be a different outcome with measures of cumulative or peak interest instead of current interest, but in fact the patterns for each type of interest measure were actually quite similar and nearly identical to that found in the first study. Scores on the knowledge tests were greater when self-rated interest was high, but there were no interactions of age and self-rated interest. Once again, then, there was no trend for greater age-related increases in knowledge for topics in which the individual reports the highest levels of interest.

The results of these two studies, along with those from the studies involving people with specific types of experience, are obviously not consistent with the specialized knowledge interpretation of the lack of continuous age-related increases in knowledge. Because the differential education interpretation does not appear plausible and there is no evidence relevant to the gain-loss equilibrium and the restricted exposure interpretations, there is not yet a convincing resolution of the puzzle of why knowledge does not increase continuously with advancing age.

Role of Knowledge on Cognitive Functioning

Although the evidence is mixed with respect to a positive relation between age and knowledge, there are several reasons for expecting positive relations between knowledge and cognitive performance. That is, prior research suggests at least five possible consequences of greater knowledge on aspects of cognitive performance: (1) enhanced memory and other cognitive processes through richer and more elaborate encoding and more effective retrieval cues because of the presence of an organizational structure and

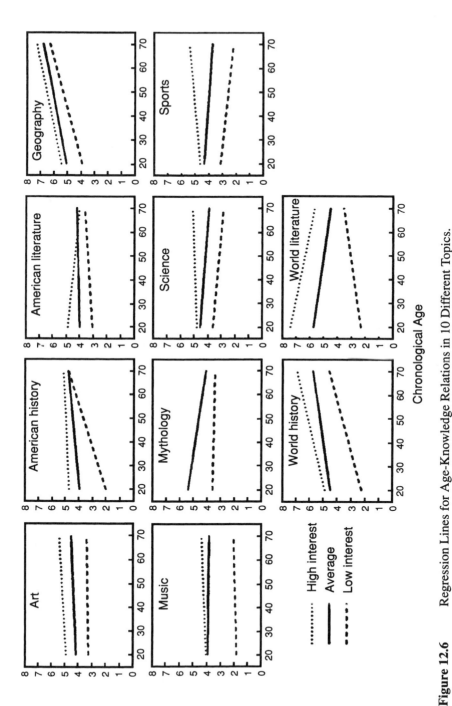

Figure 12.6   Regression Lines for Age-Knowledge Relations in 10 Different Topics.

Data from Study 3 from Hambrick, Salthouse, and Meinz (1999). The solid line is the regression line for all participants, and the other two lines represent only the participants with high or low self-rated interest in the topic. Note that the statistical analyses were conducted on the original data in which age and knowledge were both treated as continuous variables.

the ability to chunk information in terms of familiar groupings; (2) facilitated solutions of problems by quicker access to relevant information (such as pattern recognition) and better organized representations of the problem, which may allow a greater amount of information to be considered when making decisions; (3) more accurate prediction of future outcomes by capitalizing on expectations about events that generally occur; (4) more efficient modes of functioning, such as reliance on knowledge-based direct retrieval or compiled algorithms instead of slow, controlled processes; and (5) reduced processing requirements (such as attention and working memory) when prior solutions for familiar problems can be easily accessed and the need for resource-intensive computation can be minimized. Moreover, in some cases, a greater amount of knowledge has been found to be associated with performance in cognitive tasks that is equivalent to (Walker, 1987) or even greater than (Chi, 1987) that of individuals with higher levels of basic cognitive abilities.

In light of the expected positive relations between knowledge and measures of cognitive performance, it is meaningful to consider the role of knowledge on age-cognition relations. Relevant research from my laboratory will therefore be discussed to attempt to determine which of the possibilities portrayed in Figure 12.2 is most plausible.

I refer to the first study, an unpublished study conducted with a former graduate student, Elizabeth Meinz, as the City Memory Study. In this study, we tested memory with names of streets, shopping districts, residential areas, and other information relevant to one of two cities. Two memory lists were presented, each containing eight items from Atlanta, the city of residence, and eight items from St. Louis, which was presumably unfamiliar to most of the participants. The items were presented sequentially and were followed immediately by written recall.

The sample in this study consisted of 125 adults ranging from 18 to 83 years of age. The participants had lived in Atlanta between 0 and 68 years, with an average of 19 years. No test of knowledge was administered, but we assumed that there was greater knowledge for items from the more familiar city and possibly more so with increased age because of a correlation of .38 between age and the number of years the individual reported having lived in Atlanta.

As expected, more items were correctly recalled from the familiar city (mean 59% correct) than from the unfamiliar city (mean 23% correct). If knowledge contributes to the preservation of memory performance across adulthood, an age-by-familiarity interaction might have been predicted in the direction of smaller age-related declines for familiar items. However, this was not found, and instead there were nearly parallel age-related decreases for familiar (age correlation = −.25) and unfamiliar (age correlation = −.24) items. In other words, the results indicate that although familiarity was beneficial (because of the main effect of the city on memory performance), it was not differentially so for older adults.

These findings are obviously inconsistent with the moderation hypothesis because there was no interaction of age and familiarity or knowledge, and the age-related decline was similar for the high-knowledge and low-knowledge materials. Because no direct measure of knowledge was available, it was not possible to examine the age-knowledge relation or the effects of statistical control of knowledge on the age relations, and consequently the results may or may not be consistent with the migration interpretation.

A second study, also conducted with Elizabeth Meinz (Meinz & Salthouse, 1998), involved two comparisons of the role of knowledge on the relations between age and memory. The participants in this study were recruited to represent considerable variation in musical experience, and the amount of experience ranged from none to many years as a professional musician. One comparison in this study consisted of a contrast between memory for musical material (notes from a melody on a staff) and for non-musical material (symbols on concentric circles). The assumption was that most of the participants would be very familiar with the musical stimuli but would have little or no familiarity with the nonmusical stimuli. Following the same rationale as in the City Memory Study, therefore, it was predicted that the age-related declines might be much smaller for the more familiar material. However, this prediction was not confirmed because the age trends were similar for the music stimuli ($r = -.31$) and for the nonmusic stimuli ($r = -.35$).

The second comparison in the Meinz and Salthouse (1998) study consisted of contrasting the age relations for the music stimuli among people with different amounts of musical knowledge. Level of musical knowledge was assessed by a test of musical notation information that was administered to all participants in the study. Although there were main effects of age (negative) and of knowledge (positive) on the measure of music memory performance, there was no interaction of age and knowledge. Instead, the age relations were similar for the high-knowledge ($r = -.67$), medium-knowledge ($r = -.38$) and low-knowledge ($r = -.52$) individuals. The lack of an interaction is clearly inconsistent with the moderation view. However, there was also little evidence for the migration interpretation in this study because even though there was a high positive correlation ($r = .81$) between the knowledge score and the measure of music memory performance, the relation between age and knowledge was actually slightly negative ($r = -.17$) rather than positive. At least in this study, therefore, there was no evidence for a migration to higher levels of domain-specific knowledge with increased age.

The next set of studies involved a variety of verbal fluency tasks in which the individual was allowed a limited time to generate as many words as possible that satisfied specific criteria, such as beginning with a particular letter or being a member of a particular category. Because the items in these tasks are words, relevant knowledge can be assessed with a test of vocabulary.

The outcomes of particular interest in these comparisons were the age-by-knowledge interaction (as predicted by the moderation hypothesis) and the amount of increase in the negative age relation after control of the measure of knowledge (as predicted by the migration hypothesis). Data were available from four separate study and task combinations involving different fluency tasks or samples of research participants. In each case, the samples consisted of between 120 and 250 adults spanning a wide range of ages.

Table 12.1

Proportions of Variance Associated with the Interaction of Age and Knowledge, and with Age Before and After Control of Knowledge

Study Variable	Proportion of Variance		
	Age* Knowledge	Age	Age.Knowledge
Salthouse, Fristoe, and Rheo (1996), N = 259			
Letter fluency	.002	.038	.100
Salthouse, Toth, Hancock, and Woodard (1997), N = 124			
Letter fluency	.004	.016	.067
Category Fluency	.002	.018	.072
Hambrick, Salthouse, and Meinz (1999), Study 1, N = 201			
Letter fluency	.000	.058	.204
Salthouse (1993)			
Study 1, N = 100 young, 100 old			
Nouns	.020	.067	.112
S-words	.000	.080	.145
Anagrams	.000	.025	.080
Word switch	.000	.316	.412
Study 2, N = 77 young, 77 old			
Word beginnings	.001	.120	.175
Word endings	.011	.213	.283
Make words	.006	.265	.343
Scrabble	.040	.055	.094

The top portion of Table 12.1 summarizes the proportions of variance associated with the age-by-knowledge interaction and the age-related variance before and after control of the measure of knowledge. The absence of any interactions of age and knowledge is clearly·inconsistent with the moderation hypothesis. It can also be seen that in each case statistical control of the knowledge measures increased the magnitude of the age-related variance by making the age relations more negative. This result, together with the finding that in these samples increased age was associated with greater knowledge, is consistent with the migration interpretation. In other words, these findings suggest that knowledge does not appear to moderate the negative relations between age and various measures of cognitive performance but rather that the negative effects associated with increasing age can be attenuated when increased age is associated with greater amounts of relevant knowledge.

The same types of analyses were also conducted on data from eight different verbal tasks investigated in two studies in a project by Salthouse (1993). There were 100 young adults and 100 older adults in Study 1 and 77 young adults and 77 older adults in Study 2. The results of these studies are reported in the bottom portion of Table 12.1 in the same manner as with the fluency variables. As can be seen, these variables exhibited the same pattern as the fluency variables. Only one of the eight possible interactions between age and knowledge was statistically significant (the Scrabble variable in Study 2), and therefore the results are inconsistent with the moderation hypothesis. In contrast, the relation between age and knowledge was positive in each study, and the negative effects of age on the performance variables increased after control of knowledge, both findings consistent with the predictions from the migration hypothesis.

Another type of analysis is also relevant to the role of knowledge on age-cognition relations. This analysis examines two possibilities for how knowledge might contribute to age-related effects on cognitive performance. First, older adults could have a higher quantity of knowledge than young adults but have the same pattern of utilization of knowledge. And second, compared to young adults, older adults might exhibit a greater reliance on knowledge relative to other determinants of performance.

The distinction between these two alternatives can be expressed in terms of a regression equation,

$$P = a(K) + b(A),$$

where P is performance on the criterion task, K is knowledge, and A is general abilities (or process aspects of cognition).

The interesting question within this framework is, Where are the age effects? The level of relevant abilities, A, is likely to be lower for older adults because it reflects process aspects of cognition, whereas K may be higher for older adults because of the evidence of increases in vocabulary knowledge, at least from the twenties to the fifties. Finally, age differences may be evident on a and b, which would indicate differential reliance on the performance determinants, as though there is a shift with age in the method used to perform the task. In particular, older adults might have lower values of b (reflecting reduced reliance on process abilities) but higher values of a (reflecting greater reliance on knowledge).

How can these possibilities be investigated? If measures of P, K, and A are available, then regression equations can be constructed, and the resulting parameters can be compared across individuals of different ages. Ideally, analyses of this type would be carried out at the level of individuals. However, this would not only require that each individual perform several different criterion tasks, but different sets of predictors for each task would also be needed to ensure variation in both predictors and criteria such that regression analyses could be conducted. Data such as these at the level of individuals are not yet available, but relevant data at the group level are contained in the two studies in the Salthouse (1993) project. Knowledge can be assessed with tests of vocabulary, other types of ability can be assessed with measures of perceptual speed, and scores on the simple verbal tasks can serve as the criterion variables.

The analyses revealed a slight advantage of older adults in knowledge (older adults were superior to young adults in K), a large advantage of young adults in perceptual speed (young adults were superior to older adults in A), and relatively small age differences in the criterion tasks (the two groups were nearly equivalent in P). Of greatest interest were the regression coefficients. No significant differences were apparent in the regression parameters across the two age groups. In other words, although there were significant age differences in the level of knowledge and in the level of speed, there was no age difference in the relation of these variables to the criterion measures. The findings therefore imply that there was a similar weighting, or "importance," of knowledge and ability in the samples of young and old adults.

These results led to the conclusion that "Age differences are reduced in tasks with moderate to large knowledge involvement not because of changes in the predictive value of different factors at different ages but because the average level of one performance determinant (knowledge) tends to increase with age at the same time that the average level of the other performance determinant (speed) tends to decrease" (Salthouse, 1993, p. 35). This conclusion is obviously more consistent with the migration interpretation than with the moderation interpretation. It therefore appears that greater knowledge does not alter the relation between age and relevant measures of cognitive performance when people of different ages have similar levels of knowledge but rather that the consequences of age-related declines in other cognitive abilities can be minimized when increased age is associated with greater amounts of knowledge. Knowledge might therefore function as an attenuating factor in age-cognition relations, but only when it is positively correlated (or confounded) with increased age (see also Staudinger & Lindenberger, this volume).

Summary

I will finish with two simple conclusions. First, although most research concerned with aging and cognition has focused on process aspects of cognition, I believe I have shown that there are many important and interesting issues related to product aspects of cognition. And second, although it is still not clear why it has been difficult to find evidence of continuous age-related increases in knowledge in moderately large representative samples, there is evidence that when older adults have high levels of knowledge, their performance in tasks where that knowledge is relevant can equal or possibly even surpass the performance of young adults.

Note

1. As an aside, it is interesting to note that the relation of cumulative experience to tests of knowledge has been recognized for decades. In fact, Conrad (1930, p. 594) suggested that because of greater exposure opportunities with advancing age, stability of performance on most knowledge tests actually implied the presence of decline. Furthermore, because of the presumed confounding of age and experience, Conrad recommended against the inclusion of knowledge tests in cognitive assessments. However, this proposal was countered by Sorenson (1933), who claimed that information and knowledge tests should not only be included in cognitive test batteries but in fact should be emphasized. His argument was that knowledge tests were actually fairer to older adults than other types of cognitive tests because they did not introduce a penalty for disuse, as he suggested was the case for other types of tests.

References

Ackerman, P. L. (1996). A theory of adult intellectual development: Process, personality, interests, and knowledge. *Intelligence, 22*, 227–257.

Ackerman, P. L. (2000). Domain-specific knowledge as the "dark matter" of adult intelligence: Gf/Gc, personality, and interest correlates. *Journal of Gerontology: Psychological Sciences, 55B*, P69–P84.

Ackerman, P. L., & Rolfhus, E. L. (1999). The locus of adult intelligence: Knowledge, abilities, and nonability traits. *Psychology and Aging, 14*, 314–330.

Aftanas, M. S., & Royce, J. R. (1969). Analysis of brain damage tests administered to normal subjects with factor score comparisons across ages. *Multivariate Behavioral Research, 4*, 459–481.

Albert, M. S., Duffy, F. H., & Naeser, M. (1987). Nonlinear changes in cognition with age and their neuropsychologic correlates. *Canadian Journal of Psychology, 41*, 141–157.

Baltes, P. B., & Baltes, M. M. (1990). Psychological perspectives on successful aging: The model of selective optimization with compensation. In P. B. Baltes & M. M. Baltes (Eds.), *Successful aging: Perspectives from the behavioral sciences* (pp. 1–34). Cambridge: Cambridge University Press.

Baltes, P. B., Staudinger, U. M., Maercker, A., & Smith, J. (1995). People nominated as wise: A comparative study of wisdom-related knowledge. *Psychology and Aging, 10*, 155–166.

Bromley, D. B. (1975). Some effects of age on the quality of intellectual output. *Journal of Gerontology, 12*, 318–323.

Cattell, R. B. (1972). *Abilities: Their structure, growth and action*. Boston: Houghton-Mifflin.

Cattell, R. B. (1998). Where is intelligence? Some answers from the triadic theory. In J. J. McArdle & R. W. Woodcock (Eds.), *Human cognitive abilities in theory and practice*. (pp. 29–38). Mahwah, NJ: Erlbaum.

Charness, N. (1979). Components of skill in bridge. *Canadian Journal of Psychology, 33*, 1–16.

Charness, N. (1983). Age, skill, and bridge bidding: A chronometric analysis. *Journal of Verbal Learning and Verbal Behavior, 22*, 406–416.

Chi, M. T. H. (1978). Knowledge structures and memory development. In R. Siegler (Ed.), *Children's thinking: What develops?* (pp. 73–96). Hillsdale, NJ: Erlbaum.

Colonia-Willner, R. (1998). Practical intelligence at work: Relationship between aging and cognitive efficiency among managers in a bank environment. *Psychology and Aging, 13*, 45–57.

Conrad, H. S. (1930). General information, intelligence, and the decline of intelligence. *Journal of Applied Psychology, 14*, 592–599.

Demming, J. A., & Pressey, S. L. (1957). Tests indigenous to the adult and older years. *Journal of Counseling Psychology, 4*, 144–148.

Foster, J. C., & Taylor, G. A. (1920). The applicability of mental tests to persons over 50. *Journal of Applied Psychology, 4*, 39–58.

Gardner, E. F., & Monge, R. H. (1977). Adult age differences in cognitive abilities and educational background. *Experimental Aging Research, 3*, 337–383.

Hambrick, D. Z., Salthouse, T. A., & Meinz, E. J. (1999). Predictors of crossword puzzle proficiency and moderators of age-cognition relations. *Journal of Experimental Psychology: General, 128*, 131–164.

Hamsher, K. S., & Benton, A. L. (1978). Interactive effects of age and cerebral disease on cognitive performance. *Journal of Neurology, 217*, 195–200.

Hollingworth, H. L. (1927). *Mental growth and decline*. New York: Appleton.

Hultsch, D. F., Hertzog, C., Dixon, R. A., & Small, B. J. (1998). *Memory change in the aged*. New York: Cambridge University Press.

Jones, H. E., & Conrad, H. (1933). The growth and decline of intelligence: A study of a homogeneous group between the ages of 10 and 60. *Genetic Psychological Monographs, 13*, 223–298.

Kaufman, A. S., & Horn, J. L. (1996). Age changes on tests of fluid and crystallized ability for women and men on the Kaufman Adolescent and Adult Intelligence Test (KAIT) at ages 17–94. *Archives of Clinical Neuropsychology, 11*, 97–121.

Kohn, M. L., & Schooler, C. (1983). *Work and personality.* Norwood, NJ: Ablex.

Lindenberger, U., & Reisches, F. M. (1999). Limits and potentials of intellectual functioning in old age. In P. B. Baltes & K. U. Mayer (Eds.), *The Berlin Aging Study: Aging from 70 to 100.* New York: Cambridge University Press.

Meinz, E. J., & Salthouse, T. A. (1998). The effects of age and experience on memory for visually presented music. *Journal of Gerontology: Psychological Sciences, 53B,* P60–P69.

Pfau, H. D., & Murphy, M. D. (1998). Role of verbal knowledge in chess skill. *American Journal of Psychology, 101,* 73–86.

Salthouse, T. A. (1993). Speed and knowledge as determinants of adult age differences in verbal tasks. *Journal of Gerontology: Psychological Sciences, 48,* P29–P36.

Salthouse, T. A. (1998). Independence of age-related influences on cognitive abilities across the life span. *Developmental Psychology, 34,* 851–864.

Salthouse, T. A., Fristoe, N., & Rhee, S. H. (1996). How localized are age-related effects on neuropsychological measures? *Neuropsychology, 10,* 272–285.

Salthouse, T. A., Toth, J. P., Hancock, H. E., & Woodard, J. L. (1997). Controlled and automatic forms of memory and attention: Process purity and the uniqueness of age-related influences. *Journal of Gerontology: Psychological Sciences, 52B,* P216–P228.

Schaie, K. W. (1996). *Intellectual development in adulthood: The Seattle Longitudinal Study.* New York: Cambridge University Press.

Schooler, C., Mulatu, M. S., & Oates, G. (1999). The continuing effects of substantively complex work on the intellectual functioning of older workers. *Psychology and Aging, 14,* 483–506.

Smith, J., & Baltes, P. B. (1990). Wisdom-related knowledge: Age/cohort differences in response to life-planning problems. *Developmental Psychology, 26,* 494–505.

Sorenson, H. (1933). Mental ability over a wide range of adult ages. *Journal of Applied Psychology, 17,* 729–741.

Sorenson, H. (1938). *Adult abilities.* Minneapolis: University of Minnesota Press.

Stanovich, K. E., West, R. F., & Harrison, M. R. (1995). Knowledge growth and maintenance across the life span: The role of print exposure. *Developmental Psychology, 31,* 811–826.

Staudinger, U. M. (1999). Older and wiser? Integrating results on the relationship between age and wisdom-related performance. *International Journal of Behavioral Development, 23,* 641–664.

Walker, C. H. (1987). Relative importance of domain knowledge and overall aptitude on acquisition of domain-related information. *Cognition and Instruction, 4,* 25–42.

Wechsler, D. (1955). *Manual for the Wechsler Adult Intelligence Scale.* New York: Psychological Corporation.

Wechsler, D. (1981). *WAIS-R Manual: Wechsler Adult Intelligence Scale–Revised.* New York: Psychological Corporation.

Wechsler, D. (1997). *WAIS-III: Wechsler Adult Intelligence Scale, Third Edition. Administration and Scoring Manual.* San Antonio: Psychological Corporation.

Willoughby, R. R. (1927). Family similarities in mental test abilities (with a note on the growth and decline of these abilities). *Genetic Psychological Monograph, 2,* 235–277.

Woodcock, R. W., & Johnson, M. B. (1989, 1990). *Woodcock-Johnson Psycho-Educational Battery–Revised.* Allen, TX: DLM.

13 Formal Models of Age Differences in Task-Complexity Effects

Reinhold Kliegl

University of Potsdam, Potsdam, Germany

Ralf T. Krampe

Max Planck Institute for Human Development, Berlin, Germany

Ulrich Mayr

University of Oregon, Eugene, U.S.A.

Abstract

Sometimes, older adults perform just as well and even just as fast as younger adults—even in relatively complex cognitive tasks tapping the "mechanics of cognition" (Baltes, 1997, this volume). This chapter attempts to unravel the possible reasons for this astonishing phenomenon. In particular, we argue that theoretically predicted age invariance under speeded task conditions constitutes the optimal baseline for delineating domains of functioning according to the severity of associated age differences. In the first part of this chapter, we address the general issue of how process-specific effects can be delineated from general effects of aging in cognitive functions. The critical observation here is that very often an age difference is already present in an experimental condition meant to serve as a baseline for the assessment of an age difference in a cognitive process in a more complex condition. We propose experimental control techniques that may eliminate the interpretational ambiguity associated with such ordinal interactions. In the second and third parts, we illustrate this approach for research on movement timing and semantic memory access to demonstrate a clear delineation of processing domains with different degrees of age sensitivity. Although our research examples are from the field of cognitive aging, the proposal to eliminate baseline differences between quasi-experimental groups by means of experimental control should be useful as well for age contrasts in other segments of the lifespan (such as child development; cf. Wellman, this volume) and for comparative work involving other quasi-experimental variables (groups differing in health, social status, attitudes, and so on). A better understanding of basic constraints of the cognitive system will contribute to theoretical accounts of selection, optimization, and compensation, processes that have to operate within these constraints (Baltes & Baltes, 1990; M. Baltes & Carstensen, this volume). Therefore, in the final section, we discuss the implications of age-related functional dissociations for an understanding of adaptive processes that operate throughout the lifespan.

Experimental Control Techniques

Models of cognitive aging aim at the specification of age differences in information-processing parameters that generalize as much as possible across levels of difficulty within cognitive tasks and ideally across a large variety of cognitive tasks. A number of mathematical models have been developed with this general approach during the last 20 years. We briefly review this approach in the next section and then focus on how the same goal can be reached with experimental control techniques.

Mathematical Models Derived from Ordinal Interactions of Age and Task Complexity

One of the most solid and methodologically troublesome results of cognitive aging research is the fact that age differences in cognitive tasks often increase monotonically as a function of task complexity or difficulty as reflected in young adults' performance. For example, as young adults' reaction times increase with the number of alternatives in a choice-reaction task, the associated absolute age differences increase as well, yielding significant ordinal interactions between age and the number of choices. The difficulty of inferring a complexity-specific age deficit from such interactions has long been recognized (e.g., Bogartz, 1976; Loftus, 1978). For example, age differences across manipulations of task complexity are typically much less pronounced or even absent after logarithmic transformation of the latencies—that is, when they are expressed in proportions (as the ratio of old and young response latencies).

Moreover, metaanalyses of experimental age-comparative research covering a wide spectrum of reaction-time tasks uncovered a high degree of regularity when old adults' mean performance in experimental conditions is plotted over corresponding ones of young adults in so-called Brinley plots. Based on these results, it was argued that the overadditive age x task interaction in the traditional ANOVA (that is, a significant age difference in absolute performance differences between task conditions) constitutes insufficient evidence for a specific age deficit in the complex experimental condition (that is, the condition involving the cognitive process for which a specific age deficit is hypothesized) if an age difference is already present in the baseline condition. As they appeared to generalize across specific cognitive tasks, the linear and sometimes curvilinear Brinley functions spawned theoretical proposals of a deficiency in a hypothetical generic information processing step due to, for example, slowing (Salthouse, 1985a, 1985b), organizational overhead (Cerella, 1985, 1990), or information loss (Myerson, Hale, Wagstaff, Poon, & Smith, 1990; but see Mayr & Kliegl, 1993, for an early criticism). On the assumption that young and old adults carry out the same sequence of information processing in cognitive tasks (the correspondence assumption; Cerella, 1990), cognitive content of a task is virtually immaterial for the explanation of age differences, and all that matters is the scaling or theoretical specification of the hypothetical information-processing step.

More recently, this approach has been expanded to generate predictions not only for the relation between mean performances of young and old adults but also for the relation of young and old adults' response latency distributions. The most comprehensive account appears to be the one by Faust, Balota, Spieler, and Ferraro (1999), who proposed a rate-amount model according to which differences and standard deviations of response latencies are derived from a multiplicative relation of amount of information to be processed and individual processing rates. The amount of information processed represents contributions from task and individual differences (which are separable in principle); individual processing rates are assumed to be constant across task conditions. This model implies linear relations for (1) condition means of a particular individual as a function of the overall group means for the same conditions (individual Brinley function), (2) condition means for a particular group as a function of the condition means of another group (group Brinley function), (3) individuals condition means as a function of the individuals' overall means, (4) standard deviations across conditions and overall means for individuals, and (5) standard deviations across individuals and overall means for conditions. These predictions had been reported in isolation before and were shown to hold reasonably well for a comparison of young and old adults who were tested on a large and diverse set of response time tasks with young adults' latencies in the range of 500 to 2000 ms. Thus, the rate-amount model provides an elegant framework for a large number of empirical linear regularities.

Such models of age differences in generic information processing have served very well as conservative baselines for the delineation of broader processing domains. However, it has become increasingly clear that an age difference in a single parameter (such as "general" slowing) will not account for the diversity of cognitive performances across domains. For example, even for latency-based tasks, different proportional age differences were found for lexical and nonlexical tasks (e.g., Hale, Lima, & Myerson, 1991; Lima, Hale, & Myerson, 1991) and for working memory tasks that do and do not require the simultaneous storage and processing of intermediate results (e.g., Mayr & Kliegl, 1993). Consequently, these models no longer sustain claims of a "general" explanatory power with respect to cognitive aging but continue to be useful as safeguards against a proliferation of specific accounts or "issue isolationism" (Salthouse, 1985b). In line with the goals of these mathematical models, we propose an approach based on experimental control techniques that also aims at the delineation of broad processing domains that are differentially susceptible to effects of age. Moreover, we want to show that with this approach we can test empirically two central assumptions of the mathematical models discussed above—namely, (1) that there always is an age difference in tasks that are carried out under time constraints (a speed factor) and (2) that age differences in tasks are monotonically related to young adults' levels of performance. We introduce this approach under the headings of age simulation and time-accuracy functions.

Age Simulation

The major assumption underlying the idea of age simulation is that "it is possible to produce the behavioral changes in a short period of time that are indicative of and/or identical with long-term ontogenetic changes as they occur in nature" (Baltes & Goulet, 1971, p. 154). Baltes, Reese, and Nesselroade (1977) specified the following five steps: (1) definition of the developmental phenomenon (the age-related function) to be explained, (2) formulation of a set of hypotheses about age-associated variables that might produce the phenomenon, (3) experimental manipulation of these variables, (4) test of the data obtained through simulation against the target phenomenon (isomorphy check), and (5) examination of external validity as well as search for alternative causal mechanisms. In a recent application of this approach, age simulation was used to equate young and old adults' accuracies by experimentally manipulating reading time per word in a psycholinguistic experiment with an orthogonal manipulation of a large number factors relating to syntactic complexity (Kliegl, Fanselow, Junker, Schlesewsky, & Oberauer, 2000). An age simulation is successful if the manipulation of a single variable (for example, shortening reading time per word for young adults) eliminates age differences in a large number of experimental conditions. Given the success of slowing models reviewed above, it would be of little interest that age differences would disappear if young adults are given half the presentation time of old adults. Note, however, that there may well be some conditions for which this would not work. A definitely nontrivial contribution to an understanding of task- or domain-specific age differences would be implied if a disordinal pattern of interactions were taken as the starting point for an age simulation. Figure 13.1 shows the interaction of age with three manipulations of syntactic complexity reported by Kliegl et al. (2000). Prior to age simulation (top panel), as expected, age differences are larger for the difficult condition on the first factor. Notably, there is age invariance on the second factor and a larger age difference in the simple condition on the third factor. There is no monotonic function that transforms old adults' means in the three panels into those of young adults.

In contrast, given an elimination of the global age difference by reduction of presentation time for young adults, it is a purely empirical question whether the interactions are accentuated, reduced, or eliminated. Indeed, Kliegl et al. (2000) reported that age simulation that amounted to cutting presentation time of young adults from 750 ms to 310 ms eliminated the disordinal pattern of age differences in Figure 13.1 (bottom panel) and 27 other experimental conditions; there was one significant interaction

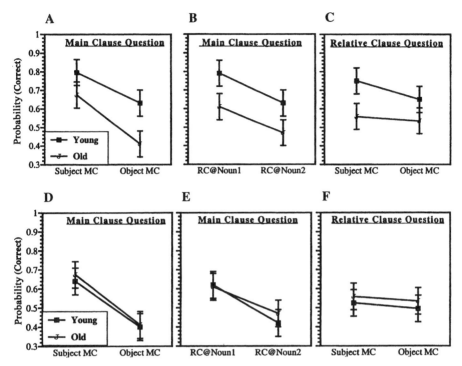

Figure 13.1 Interaction of Age with Three Manipulations of Syntactic Complexity. Top panels: Effects of age and associated interactions with three syntactic complexity effects: (A) subject-object initiality of main clause given a main clause question, (B) position of relative clause after first or second noun of main clause, (C) subject-object initiality of main clause given a relative clause question (top panels). Bottom panels: Effects of reducing presentation times for young adults on age *x* syntactic complexity interactions for comprehension accuracy. From Kliegl et al. (2000).

involving age that did not replicate and was most likely spurious. Kliegl et al. interpret the old-young presentation-time ratio as an example of a *domain-general age difference* because within the domain of syntactic complexity manipulations examined, a single parameter could be used to reproduce a complex age-differential pattern of means. We call it *domain-general* and not *general* because the precise ratio is larger than that associated with traditional response-time tasks (1.5) and is even larger than ratios associated with lexical processing—a different language-related domain. Alternatively, the age simulation could have led to a simple parallel downward shift of young adults, suggesting a complex pattern of *condition-specific age differences* or a *delineation of condition-specific against domain-general effects*, if most but not all age-differential effects had disappeared. The credibility of a successful age simulation depends on the number of experimental conditions involved—the larger the number, the more powerful the test of the invariance between young and old adults over all conditions. Age simulation via manipulations of presentation time can in principle be applied to numerous other experimental pardadigms, such as visual search, figural reasoning, working, and episodic memory tasks. Moreover, rather than presentation time, other performance-limiting processing resources might be manipulated depending on the nature of the task or the theoretical concept at issue. For example, target luminance was used to this end in a study examining age differences in processing speed in a backward masking task (Gilmore, Morrison, Behi, & Koss, 2000). The choice of the manipulation should be guided as much as possible by theoretical reasoning about the cause of the age difference. Alternatively, of course, one can test whether the results of age simulations are invariant with respect to the type of manipulation employed. Indeed, different outcomes for different manipulations may be the most diagnostic information in this respect.

Time-Accuracy Functions (TAFs)

Age simulation equates young and old adults in task performance at a specific level of accuracy in a specific experimental condition (or for the overall mean level). The most general experimental control technique is to determine the complete function between chance and perfect performance as a function of a critical processing resource (such as presentation time) for all experimental conditions of an experiment at the individual level (Kliegl, Mayr, & Krampe, 1994). As an example, consider the functions in Figure 13.2 taken from a mental arithmetic study (Verhaeghen, Kliegl, & Mayr, 1997). Participants were presented strings of arithmetic tasks as displayed in the figure; computation results were restricted to the range of 1 to 9 (that is, the task was very simple). For each condition, the amount of presentation time required to achieve several different levels of correct responses was determined. From these data, a three-parameter exponential function could be estimated; parameters specified (1) the time needed to rise from chance performance, (2) the rate at which the asymptote is approached, and (3) the asymptotic accuracy. Age group x condition curves based on the parameter means are displayed in the figure. There were no age differences when the solution could be determined by updating a single digit—that is, in conditions that did not involve the intermediate storage and retrieval of computational results induced by the presence of parentheses. This is particularly interesting because there were no age differences in accuracy despite the fact that the task was carried out under time limits. Moreover, the age invariance held across the entire range of performance between chance and asymptotic levels. Therefore, the age differences observed in the context of coordination demands (with respect to intermediate processing steps) point to a specific age deficit relative to the age invariance in processing speed as assessed in the simple condition. In terms of parameters of the exponential function, age differences were restricted to the intercept and the asymptote of the exponential functions.

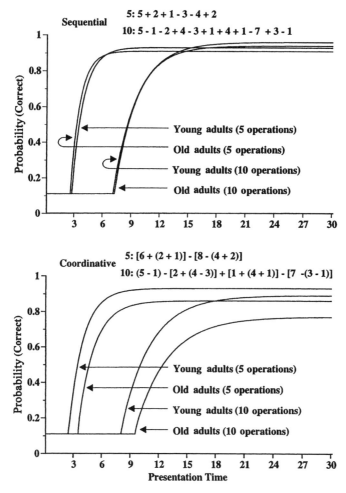

Figure 13.2   Time-Accuracy Functions for Sequentially and Coordinatively Complex Mental Arithmetic Tasks for Young and Old Adults. There are no age differences in sequentially complex conditions. Age differences in coordinatively complex conditions are restricted to intercepts and asymptotes of functions. Data from Verhaeghen et al. (1997).

The more typical pattern, of course, is that age groups differ in the simple condition and the complex condition—for example, in figural search versus figural search with storage and retrieval demands (Kliegl et al., 1994; Mayr, Kliegl, & Krampe, 1996). In this case, there still is the possibility to test whether age differences in processing speed differ proportionally (whether they map onto different group Brinley functions). Specifically, if there are no age differences in TAF asymptotes, a significant interaction between age and condition for the slope of exponential TAFs translates into linear Brinley functions with different slopes (see also Kliegl, Mayr, & Oberauer, 2000). In summary, the statistical and mathematical techniques and experimental control techniques presented in this section show that there are efficient ways for dealing with ordinal age x complexity interactions. Moreover, the extensive mapping of age differences across a wide spectrum of task difficulty as it is required for the determination of time-accuracy functions suggested that there are experimental conditions or even entire processing domains within which there are no age differences. Rather than concluding that this allows us to abandon the techniques, we argue on the basis of the following two demonstrations that mapping out performance across task difficulty in the presence of age-invariant conditions will provide a close to optimal scenario for a window on compensatory processes under conditions of limiting constraints in basic information processing.

Age Differences in Movement Timing

In many respects, repetitive movement timing is an ideal area of investigating global and specific processing deficits as they might occur in later adulthood. The strategic advantages can be summarized along four aspects: (1) a large variety of human motor behaviors presumably involves the same central timing mechanism; (2) there exists a sizeable body of empirical evidence revealing negative age effects in cognitive-motor tasks; (3) movement timing tasks are amenable to experimental control techniques that establish a large variation of age-unrelated task difficulty and complexity; and (4) elaborate mathematical models exist that permit estimation of such difficulty and complexity effects.

As to the first point, several studies have demonstrated that timing control in a variety of different motor tasks relies to a large degree on the same central mechanism. Keele and Ivry (Ivry, 1996; Ivry & Keele, 1989; Keele & Ivry, 1991), among others, have strongly argued for the cerebellum as such a multipurpose device that is called on whenever temporal processing is a requirement of the task. The central timing device has been dubbed the *central clock* or internal clock in the literature. *Central timing capacity* refers to the accuracy or speed (temporal resolution) of this hypothetical clock device.

Consistent with research in other domains of cognitive functioning, several studies have demonstrated age-related declines in speeded cognitive-motor tasks as diverse as finger tapping (Salthouse, 1985a), reaching (Stelmach, Amrhein, & Goggin, 1988), bimanual coordination (Krampe & Ericsson, 1996), tracking pursuit (Jagacinski, Liao, & Fayyad, 1995), and handwriting (Dixon, Kurzman, & Friesen, 1993). Typically, age effects in these studies increased as a function of task complexity. This empirical research could be interpreted as yet another example of age-related decline or slowing in central or multipurpose mechanisms that could also produce age x complexity interactions.

The idea of general age-related slowing affecting the central clock or timer has been discussed in the recent literature (Block, Zakay, & Hancock, 1998; Craik & Hay, 1999).

The third advantage in investigating age-differences in movement timing is that related tasks naturally lend themselves to experimental control techniques that provide an extensive description of individual and condition-specific performances (that is, performance-resource functions that can be understood as a generalization of TAF). In most movement timing experiments, the critical measure of performance is not maximum speed but variability of repeated production of the same behavior (such as the production of a specific target interval). A central finding in related studies is that variability systematically increases as a function of target duration (Wing, 1980). Individual performance-resource functions can be obtained by systematically varying the required tempo for a certain movement-production task. A second source of timing variability (inaccuracy) is the rhythmic complexity of the temporal pattern to be produced. Our basic approach is to test participants with timing tasks differing in their rhythmic complexities and to vary the experimentally induced performance tempo systematically. By this approach, we can make use of sophisticated mathematical models that permit the estimation of person-specific and process-specific parameters (see also Molenaar, Huizenga, & Nesselroade, this volume). In the introduction, we argued that for statistical reasons estimating these parameters over large ranges of individual performance spectra is critical to demonstrating global deficits as well as process-specific dissociations. The theoretical notion behind this approach to movement timing and aging is that the two sources of variability described above (1) reflect different processes, (2) reveal themselves by different relations between overall tempo and variability, and (3) show differential sensitivities to age-related declines.

The remainder of this section is organized into three parts. We first describe the performance constraints involved in repetitive-movement production tasks. Then we review the empirical evidence for age differences in central timing capacity. In the third part, we describe a theoretical framework, the rhythm program hypothesis (Vorberg & Wing, 1996), that we used to model age differences in component processes of movement timing. We illustrate how central timing processes that show relative age-graded stability can be dissociated from age-sensitive executive control processes that are highly sensitive to age-related decline.

Performance Constraints in Repetitive Movement Timing

The temporal coordination of actions with respect to internal constraints (such as the availability of mental schemata or the stable representation of an intended tempo or duration) and environmental constraints (such as the timing of external events) is part of the adaptive nature of human behavior. By *temporal coordination*, we mean the proper sequencing of a series of actions as well as their execution at optimal points in time. These ubiquitous aspects of human action are referred to as the problems of *serial order* and *timing control.*

A. Isochronous tapping

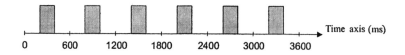

B. Timing of a simple rhythmic pattern (two target intervals)

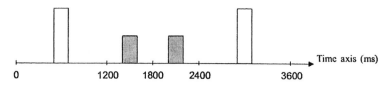

C. Timing of a complex rhythmic pattern (three target intervals)

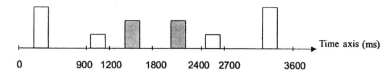

Figure 13.3   Illustration of Ideal Timing Patterns in Three Movement Production Tasks. Panel A shows an isochronous tapping task in which participants repetitively produce the same target duration of 600 ms. Panels B and C are examples of a rhythm tasks with cycle periods of 3600 ms. The simple rhythm task (B) consists of two targets durations forming a sequence of long, short, long. The complex rhythm consists of three target durations and a sequence of long, short, medium, medium, short, long intervals. The height of the columns visualizes the target duration to be produced as indicated in the *x*-axis. Gray columns refer to identical target durations in the three tasks.

Figure 13.3 depicts three different movement timing tasks of the type we used in our experiments. In such tasks, participants typically generate the depicted sequences by repetitive keypresses or taps. The standard procedure follows the *continuation paradigm* (Wing & Kristofferson, 1973b): participants hear a pacing signal that follows the exact timing pattern and they synchronize with the signal for a specified number of taps. After that, the signal ceases, and participants continue to produce the pattern without external pacing. The critical measures are the variabilities of observed intervals with respect to their mean values.

The top panel (A) in Figure 13.3 shows a simple repetitive tapping task. Panels B and C in Figure 13.3 show two rhythmic patterns with a cycle period of 3600 ms. The rhythmic pattern in panel B consists of a sequence of long, short, short, long intervals. The rhythm depicted in panel C is more complex in terms of its sequencing demands and the scaling relations formed by three different target intervals. Figure 13.3 illustrates our methodological approach: the darkened bars in each panel refer to exactly the same target duration; however, this interval must be produced in different contexts. By assessing performance accuracy (observed variability) at tempos varied systematically across tasks, we can contrast the effects of the hypothesized movement control processes.

Simple tapping tasks like the one depicted in panel A have no sequencing requirements because the same target interval is produced over and over again. For this very reason, this kind of task has been used in several studies to assess central timing capacity in its purest form. Wing and Kristofferson (1973a, 1973b) proposed a *two-level model of movement timing* that distinguishes between a central timekeeper or clock and peripheral motor implementation. The central clock delineates delays after which the motor system implements the triggered movement with a specific effector. Peripheral implementation causes another (motor) delay. So conceived the central clock is a multipurpose device that controls movement timing for different effectors and also guarantees temporal coordination in multilimb (such as bimanual) movements. According to the two-level timing model, both the central clock and motor implementation process produce variability. Wing and Kristofferson developed a method to obtain separate variance estimates for the two component processes based on the autocovariance function of a time series observed in a tapping task like the one in Figure 13.3. Among the strongest evidence in support of the two-level timing model is the demonstration of a dissociation between central clock and motor delay variances when tapping variability is assessed at multiple performance tempos: Wing and Kristofferson (1973b) showed that the increase in observed variance at slower tempos could be exclusively attributed to the central clock. Motor-delay variances remain relatively constant when tapping tempo decreases. Mathematical explorations of the effects of central clock speed show that a slowed central clock leads to a larger variability for a given interval duration (Fetterman & Killeen, 1992; Gibbon, Church, & Meck, 1984; Krampe, Engbert, & Kliegl, 2001). Moreover, a slower clock produces a steeper increase in the function relating mean interval duration and variability.

In principle the rhythmic patterns shown in Figure 13.3 (panels B and C) could be produced by a central clock or timekeeper if we assume that the clock can be arbitrarily calibrated to successive target intervals. Alternatively, we might assume that rhythmic timing is controlled by hierarchical representations in which target durations for the different intervals are prespecified on the basis of an internal representation of the overall cycle period. This assumption was most elegantly developed in the rhythm programming framework proposed by Dirk Vorberg and Alan Wing (1996). We use their framework to provide evidence for our central claims regarding age differences in movement timing: central timing capacity reflects processes that show relative age-graded stability until late adulthood. In contrast, higher-level executive-control functions involved in maintaining or changing such hierarchical representations as rhythm programs suffer from considerable age-related decline. Before we turn to the rhythm programming framework, we review earlier studies that investigated age differences in central timing capacity.

Evidence for Age-Related Changes in Central Timing Capacities

Maximum tapping rate has for some time been considered a relatively good proxy of central timing capacity (Keele & Hawkins, 1982), and negative correlations between age and single-finger tapping speed have indeed been considered as evidence for more general age-related slowing (Salthouse, 1985a). More recent studies in which maximum rate was measured through multiple assessment studies (Krampe and Ericsson, 1996; Krampe, Mayr, & Kliegl, 2002) suggest that this measure is not a good predictor of complex movement coordination but more likely reflects disuse or biomechanical constraints that are external to central timing capacity.

Few age-comparative studies have used repetitive movement production tasks to directly test the implications of the Wing-Kristofferson two-level timing model. Woodruff-Pak and Jaeger (1998) assessed variability in timed tapping for an interval of 550 ms duration in individuals with ages ranging from 20 to 89 years. Using the Wing-Kristofferson method to decompose clock and motor components, they found significant age-related increases in clock variability. Variability of the motor component remained relatively stable with age. Duchek, Balota, and Ferraro (1994) also used the Wing-Kristofferson method and the same pacing tempo in their study with older individuals with mild senile dementia (Alzheimer type) and age-matched, healthy adults. They found that individuals with mild dementia showed a breakdown in central time-keeping mechanisms but not in motor implementation. Healthy older adults above and below the age of 80 showed the same efficiency of timing control for both central timekeeping and peripheral implementation mechanisms as young college students. Likewise Greene and Williams (1993) and also Krampe, Engbert, and Kliegl (2001) found relative age-graded stability for central timing capacity.

Mathematical Modeling of Age-Related Changes Based on the Rhythm-Programming Framework

At the core of the rhythm-program hypothesis (Vorberg & Wing, 1996) is the distinction between a *parameter specification* process and the actual control of different intervals within a rhythmic pattern by another process called *timekeeper execution*. Timekeepers are temporary representations of certain interval durations. Parameter specification refers to the programming of the target durations for the different timekeepers as specified in the underlying *rhythm program*. The idea that timing control in complex movements is based on hierarchical representations (motor programs) as opposed to

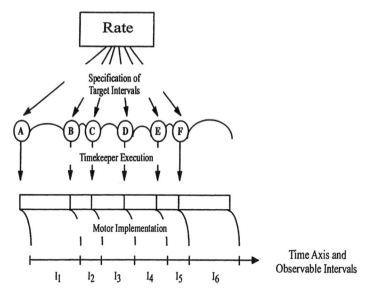

Figure 13.4   Schematic Illustration of the Stages in the Hypothetical Rhythm-Program Process Underlying the Production of the Complex Rhythm Task Depicted in Figure 13.3C.

local transitions between successive responses dates back to Lashley's (1951) seminal work. Similar to the concept of motor programs, a rhythm program is an abstract representation of the serial order of events in an action sequence that translates into a hierarchy of adjustable timekeepers when implemented at the time of performance.

Figure 13.4 depicts a hypothetical rhythm-programming process underlying the production of the rhythmic pattern in Figure 13.3C. This specific model was adapted from the Vorberg and Wing framework. The overall cycle period for this rhythm is (ideally) 3600 ms. The rhythm-program hypothesis maintains that individuals have a higher-level representation of this overall period (or the mean tempo or rate). This rate parameter is used to specify target durations for the lower-level timekeepers (A–F in Figure 13.4). For this specific rhythm the six timekeepers are being programmed to realize delays of 1/4, 1/12, 1/6, 1/6, 1/12, and 1/4 of the cycle period at the time of execution. According to the model, this programming takes place prior to each initiation of the next cycle. While these frequent updating processes may appear costly from a processing point of view, they permit the flexibility typical of human movement timing: the overall tempo (the cycle period) can be changed without the rhythm program becoming obsolete. Krampe et al. (2002) have argued that these updating processes are examples of executive control processes. Once the target durations are specified, timekeepers can be executed (produce their specific delays) without further intervention of higher-level control processes. Conceptually, the timekeeper execution level in the rhythm-program hypothesis corresponds to the central timing level in the Wing-Kristofferson model described earlier. This is to say that timekeepers are cognitive representations that are updated and are updated by even higher-level cognitive processes, the target specification operations described above. The final stage in the rhythm programming framework is also identical to the two-level timing model: after executing its specific delay each timekeeper triggers a movement that is then implemented with a certain motor delay.

According to the rhythm-program hypothesis, the variability of the produced intervals is the sum of the variances contributed by target specification, timekeeper execution, and motor implementation processes. Moreover, the model permits these components to be estimated separately from the variance-covariance matrices obtained from the observed time series. Two recent studies (Krampe et al., 2001; Krampe, Kliegl, Mayr, Engbert, & Vorberg, 2000) successfully applied the rhythm program hypothesis to pianists' timing performances in rhythm-production tasks. In one of the studies, Krampe et al. (2001) compared young and older amateur pianists with two tasks differing in rhythmic complexity. The goal of the study was to determine age differences in the three component processes. This was possible because participants performed the tasks at 10 different tempos such that the component processes could be disentangled on the basis of their differential relation to the overall tempo. Krampe et al. (2001) found no age effects for motor implementation and timekeeper execution components. At the same time, considerable age-related deficits emerged at the central programming stage for different target intervals.

More recently, we (Krampe et al., 2002) conducted an extensive study (14 sessions) on young and older adults who performed different timing tasks including the three tasks depicted in Figure 13.3. Our goal was to experimentally dissociate central timing capacity and higher-level programming processes. By systematically varying the performance tempo for each of the three tasks, we were able to compare the variabilities for a given target interval in different task contexts (see Figure 13.3). The simple tapping task with its isochronous (same interval between all taps) structure served as a baseline reflecting central timing capacity, and we observed no age effects in this regard. As predicted by the rhythm-program hypothesis, we found that variability for a given target interval increases over and above the central timing baseline when programming demands increase from simple (task in Figure 13.3B) to complex (task in Figure 13.3C). Most important, this relative increase was more pronounced in older adults and magnified at even slower durations. We argue that this demonstrates a dissociation of central timing capacity and higher-level programming processes that can not be reduced to a single general slowing factor.

Age Differences in Semantic Fluency

Cognitive tasks represent a mixture of processes of which usually some capture a more or less interesting age decrement (such as processes related to response execution or sensory factors). Such a process mixture is involved in tasks requiring access of semantic memory. The difficult part of the strategy suggested here, then, is to find the adequate no-age-difference baseline condition with which the condition representing the potentially age-sensitive process can be compared. However, there is a potentially productive, if challenging, way of proceeding in such situations—namely, to switch from the level of tasks to the level of processes. An age-invariant processing component that may serve as the baseline for other age-sensitive processes can sometimes be isolated with the adequate combination of experimental conditions and analytic technique. Such an approach comes at the cost of requiring theoretical assumptions about how the processes under scrutiny can be isolated. Also, we again need to keep in mind that credibility of a hypothetical age-invariant component can be established best by demonstrating that critical processing demands can be manipulated substantially without producing negative age effects.

Mayr and Kliegl (2000) recently applied such a strategy in the context of a semantic fluency task. This task requires participants to name as quickly as possible members of a specified semantic category. Age differences in this task are usually obtained, but they are smaller than in speeded tasks that do not rely on semantic memory. The theoretically interesting aspect about semantic-fluency tasks is that performance probably relies on two different component processes that may vary in terms of their age sensitivity (e.g., Moscovitch & Winocur, 1992).

First, fluency tasks are usually regarded as sensitive indicators for executive control deficits. Executive demands are probably invoked by the problem of maintaining an adequate search criterion across the recall phase that is appropriately updated after each retrieval act. Given our findings of specific age-related executive-control deficits (e.g., Mayr et al., 1996; Verhaeghen et al., 1997), we hypothesized that this executive component may also be the primary source of the age difference in semantic-fluency tasks.

As a second component, semantic fluency obviously requires access to semantic memory. There is an unresolved controversy in the literature whether or not access to semantic memory per se is affected by aging (e.g., Laver & Burke, 1993; Lima et al., 1991). In particular, proponents of the generalized slowing account claim that semantic-memory retrieval is affected by general decline in processing speed, only to a somewhat lesser degree than other cognitive domains. In contrast, proponents of more modular views of aging maintain that the moderate age differences in semantic tasks may reflect age-insensitive semantic components and age-sensitive (executive control) components. If this scenario were correct and if there was a way of dissociating these two components, a particular striking example of a contrast between an age-insensitive and an age-sensitive processing component could be established. The reason that this could be a particularly striking example is that the semantic-retrieval component within a semantic-fluency task should have a relatively large contribution to overall performance that can take up to several seconds for each act of retrieval. Generalized-slowing accounts would predict particularly large absolute (but constant proportional) age differences for such time-consuming operations. In contrast, our modular model makes exactly the opposite prediction—namely, that absolute age differences should stay constant and proportional age differences should actually decrease as more semantic processing is required.

How can we distill the age-sensitive executive and the age-insensitive semantic component from semantic-fluency data? The main assumption underlying our procedure is that each retrieval latency reflects executive and semantic processes in an additive manner. A second assumption is that semantic difficulty of each retrieval process increases with the position of the word in the retrieval sequence. The second assumption rests on two arguments. First, retrieval is nonrandom, with more prototypical category members being earlier in the sequence than more remote members. Second, with increasing retrieval position, the probability of resampling an already retrieved word increases so that additional semantic processing would be needed to find a remaining category member. Thus, we assume that the increase of retrieval latencies across retrieval positions reflects largely semantic retrieval efficiency. In contrast, we claim that the role of executive processes during semantic retrieval is to create and update an adequate search set for every single retrieval process. Thus, different than the semantic component, the executive component should be *not* affected by retrieval position. With the additional, simplifying assumption that semantic difficulty should increase in an approximately linear manner as a function of retrieval position, this leads to a very simple linear model of retrieval latencies as a function of retrieval position. The slope of the linear function should represent semantic efficiency, whereas the constant of this function should reflect the executive component.

Figure 13.5 presents as a test of this model young and old adults' retrieval latencies across the first nine retrieval positions of a semantic fluency protocol and as a function of three different semantic difficulty levels of the categories (such as clothes versus criminal acts). As a first important result, we found linear functions to provide an excellent fit of retrieval latencies as a function of retrieval position. In fact, this fit was better than that of traditionally reported hyperbolic or quadratic functions (e.g., Fitzgerald, 1983). Second, the semantic-difficulty manipulation selectively affected the slopes of the retrieval function in young adults, which is exactly what we should expect if the function slope reflects primarily semantic processing. Even more important: Consistent with the prediction that semantic processing is not affected by aging, old adults did not exhibit larger search slopes than young adults. However, old adults did exhibit an increase in the intercept of the retrieval-position functions. This is consistent with the assumption that old adults need a constant amount of additional time for each act of retrieval, which we interpret as a selective slowing of executive processes. The only not-predicted effect was that for old adults there was also a difficult to interpret, additional increase in the intercept for the most difficult categories (for further discussion of the details of this data pattern, see Mayr and Kliegl, 2000).

Particularly important in this example is that with the retrieval-position factor we could actually establish a large variation in non-age-related complexity. This can be readily appreciated when viewing the above data in terms of old-young plots.

A. Young adults

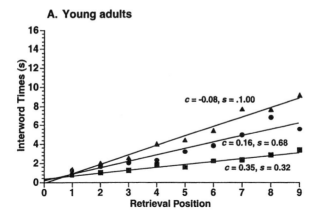

B. Old adults

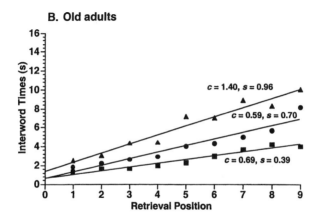

Figure 13.5   Young and Old Adults' IWTs as a Function of Retrieval Position and Difficulty Level for No-Switch Trials. Easy = squares, medium = circles, difficult = triangles. Also shown is the best-fitting linear regression line and corresponding model parameters. Data from Mayr and Kliegl (2000).

Inconsistent with generalized slowing models, the relative age difference actually becomes the smaller the more complex the task (the larger the retrieval position).

Using this pattern of results as a starting point, we can now proceed to make further, nontrivial predictions about the relative contributions between executive and semantic processing demands to age differences in semantic fluency. Imagine a situation in which participants do not only have to produce members of a single semantic category but have to alternate between two semantic categories. On first sight, it seems that such a situation would increase executive demands considerably. In fact, there is actually one model of age differences in semantic fluency that attributes the age-sensitive executive demand to requirements of switching between semantic fields during the recall process (Troyer, Moscovitch, & Winocur, 1997). On the basis of this model, age effects in the switching situation should be particularly large. In contrast, in its most straightforward formulation, our model attributes the age-sensitive executive component to each single retrieval process, simply because updating of the search set needs to occur after each act of retrieval, no matter whether a switch in category is required or not. The additional processing demands that are invoked by the category-switching requirements may actually be semantic in nature because going from one category to the next will afford a search in long-term memory (see also Mayr & Kliegl, 2000b). Thus, in terms of semantic processing, switching may require simply more of the same processes required in the traditional semantic-fluency task.

The results confirmed these predictions in a surprisingly clear manner. Overall age differences were not larger in switching than in nonswitching conditions even though the switch factor had a very strong general effect (the only exception was, again, a subtle age difference in the condition with the most difficult categories). The hypothesis that switching is primarily a long-term memory-retrieval process received additional support through the finding that the switch effect increased as a function of category difficulty. This sensitivity to a semantic-difficulty manipulation would be expected if access to a particular category of long-term memory takes longer for difficult than for easy categories.

Overall, these results show that a processing component that is very complex when judged in terms of overall time demands can nevertheless be age invariant. In the context of this absence of an age effect across a large variation of complexity, the established age difference in what we believe is the executive component is particularly striking. This pattern constitutes a strong violation of generalized slowing models and seems to suggest at least some degree of modularity of the aging mind.

Discussion

Adaptive Processes in Task Performance and Development

Different from theories focusing the negative consequences of age-related general loss or slowing, the SOC framework (P. Baltes, 1997; P. Baltes & M. Baltes, 1990; M. Baltes & Carstensen, this volume) motivates the investigation of adaptive processes on (at least) two conceptual levels—namely, the level of individual development and the level of an individual's behavior in a specific task context. Adaptive processes at the level of an individual's development necessarily occur at a larger time scale. Throughout this chapter, we have argued that component processes in cognitive-motor functioning differ considerably in their sensitivities for age-related decline. The question arises as to whether individuals can adapt to or even moderate these long-term changes through their own behavior. The study of young and older pianists by Krampe and Ericsson (1996) provides some preliminary answers. Older concert pianists (mean age of 60 years) showed the typical age-related decline in measures of fluid intelligence (digit-symbol, two-choice reaction-time task). However, their performance in speeded expertise-related tasks was almost as good as in a young expert-control group. Moreover, the degree to which older experts were able to maintain a level close to young-expert performance depended on the amounts of deliberate practice (Ericsson, Krampe, & Tesch-Römer, 1993) that older experts had invested during the later years of adulthood. Detailed diaries from pianists in the Krampe and Ericsson (1996) study revealed that older professional pianists dedicated less than half the amount of weekly time to deliberate practice activities compared to young expert pianists and also relative to what they had invested at younger ages. The total amount of time that older experts spent on activities that directly related to their profession (deliberate solitary practice plus teaching, organizing concerts, music-related administration, and so on) even surpassed that of young experts, pointing to a progressive shift in the relative focus of skill-related time investment. Older professional pianists also showed a significant reduction in leisure time compared to their young counterparts. Krampe and Ericsson (1996) argued that older experts were highly motivated to *selectively* maintain those cognitive-motor functions relevant to their skill at a level appropriate for meeting their professional requirements. From the perspective of the SOC model, the described reduction in leisure time can be interpreted as old experts' priority selection (deliberate practice over leisure) compensating for increased time demands through professional activities that do not lead to an improvement of their pianist skills.

From the Basic-Level Mechanics to the Pragmatics of Real-World Problem Solving

The picture of the aging mind that emerges from our work is one of different levels of proportional age differences. First, there are domains of processing that seem to be basically age invariant. Probably most important, this includes the fluent access to the overlearned knowledge base in long-term memory (e.g., Mayr & Kliegl, 2000; Verhaeghen et al., 1997; see also Laver & Burke, 1993). However, there are other, less knowledge-based processing components that also seem to survive the aging process in a relatively unaffected manner, such as low-level timing processes (e.g., Krampe et al., 2001).

Second, there is a domain of processes that seems best represented by typical choice response-time tasks. In a broader functional context, the processes implied by such tasks can be characterized as involving a simple "readout" of the environment for stimuli that fit prepared, simple actions. No new information is being generated here; no changes of preset paths are required. Aging seems to take a moderate but nevertheless quite noticeable toll here. Estimates from metaanalyses on response-time tasks and also from our own work typically provide slowing factors ranging between 1.5 and 2.0.

Finally, there seems to be a third level of age differences that comes into play when selection of action is not determined by a fixed, prepared set of simple actions. Rather, coordinatively complex tasks but also episodic memory tasks typically require online changes to a given path of action, the formation of novel links, and thus, in the end, the generation of new knowledge. Here we find the most dramatic age differences with slowing factors of around 3.0 to 4.0.

Of course, this picture is a crude oversimplification. For example, recent work seems to suggest that verbal and nonverbal processing may be differentially affected by aging over and above the effect of semantic knowledge, a differentiation that may very well introduce an additional factor that is orthogonal to the distinctions we propose here (Jenkins, Myerson, Joerding, & Hale, 2000). Also, at this point we are not so much concerned with the theoretically important question to what degree of such a pattern of dissociations necessarily implies a distinct set of aging processes. Instead, the question we would like to discuss in the final section of this chapter is what such a multilevel pattern of age differences with different slowing factors for different domains may imply for the "pragmatics of cognitive functioning" when it comes to real-world demands. As we will argue, in this context the issue of whether different functions are associated with different proportional slowing functions is far more than an academic question (Heckhausen & Mayr, 1998).

The basic-component efficiency that we and others have been looking at does not translate into the cognitive system's overall problem-solving ability in a one-to-one manner. From the perspective of the to-be-solved problem, basic cognitive processes are "distal factors," and their ultimate effect on a problem solution is modulated by more "proximal" rules that ultimately determine the cognitive system's output. Thus, it is important to consider the contribution of these proximal rules.

A critical aspect in this respect is that real-world problems usually have more than one solution and often more than one path to any given solution. To illustrate, think of a professor who is asked by one of his students for help with a difficult but interesting problem. One prototypical way of dealing with this situation could be for the professor to rely on her knowledge of the relevant literature and give the student some hints about which further readings may be helpful. However, another way could be to sit down with the student and think the issue through with the hope of coming up with a potentially new and interesting solution. The question in such situations then is: What determines the path of action that is taken?

A framework that may be useful for thinking about this issue is that of a race between different strategies of problem solution (cf. Gigerenzer, this volume). The critical assumption is that every query to the cognitive system starts a race among various processes for coming up with an answer to the query. This concept has been applied successfully in a number of domains, such as skill acquisition (Logan, 1988) and children's' development of proficiency with mental arithmetic (Lemaire & Siegler, 1995).

What matters in a race is speed. Processes that are fast in providing a solution will dominate over slower processes in determining the cognitive system's final output. Here it is where the issue of proportional slowing factors becomes important. Consider what happens if aging would lead to a uniform slowing across all domains of processing. Aside from the fact that problem solutions would take somewhat longer, the overall structure of problem solutions would stay invariant across the lifespan because the win/ loss ratios do not change. In contrast, when the various processes taking part in the race slow differentially, the entire configuration of problem solutions changes. Specifically, on the basis of the three-level picture of proportional age differences, we predict that across the adult lifespan the frequency of problem solutions based on overlearned knowledge should increase. However solutions that would require building novel links or the change of preexisting settings should become very rare. In other words, the closer that the professor from the above example is to retirement, the smaller the probability that the advice is based on an online-generated, new thought process rather than on overlearned knowledge.

This is what we would predict as a consequence from the multilevel pattern of age deficits in basic processes for real-world problem solving, *all other things being equal*. However, from a perspective that takes the potential for optimization and compensation serious, these "other things" become critical. Processes of optimization and compensation can be viewed as an interface between basic-process efficiency and the actual problem-solving efficiency. One way in which a developing individual can influence efficiency is by selective practice and maintenance of an "aging-endangered skill" as discussed in the preceding section (e.g., Krampe and Ericsson, 1996).

A second possible optimization strategy is suggested by findings that we have obtained when assessing time-accuracy functions in coordinatively demanding tasks. Old adults succeeded in attaining the same asymptotic accuracy as young adults, albeit with much larger time demands (e.g., Kliegl et al., 1994; Mayr et al., 1996). In other words, in many cases even the highly age-sensitive third-level processes can be performed by old adults as well as by young adults if given sufficient time. Extrapolating from this result to real-world problem situations, we suggest that innovative, newly generated problem solutions should be within the range of possible "cognitive products" for many older adults. Thus, whether to be satisfied with a possibly suboptimal problem offered by a relatively fast-acting process or whether to wait for the potentially better solutions offered by slow reasoning is a real choice, even at older ages. However, there are probably two conditions that have to be met for reasoning-based problem solutions to occur. First, one needs sufficient motivation for accepting the large time costs involved in ad-hoc reasoning. Given that the time costs increase overproportionally with age, also the strain on the motivational system would be much larger in old than in young adults (see also Brandtstädter & Rothermund, this volume; Heckhausen, this volume). Second, additional compensatory processes are probably necessary that have the purpose of protecting the time-sensitive reasoning processes from time pressure. For example, the aging professor who becomes interested in the student's problem could ask him to come back the next day to find the time for thinking through the problem without the external time pressure that easily arises in interactive situations.

In this context, an interesting area of future research should be the time-management strategies that may be used by high-performing older adults to selectively optimize their cognitive products and compensate for age-related losses. Specifically, we would expect that these are directed (1) toward a highly selective use of the costly third-level processes (when the potential gains clearly outweigh the costs), (2) toward protecting these processes from time pressure and external interference, and (3) placing them into those times of the day in which cognitive efficiency is highest (e.g., Hasher, Zacks, & May, 1999).

Acknowledgment

The research described in this chapter was carried out while the three authors were at the Department of Psychology at the University of Potsdam. It was supported by three projects in the Innovationskolleg "Formale Modelle kognitiver Komplexität" (INK 12; Deutsche Forschungsgemeinschaft).

References

Baltes, P. B. (1997). On the incomplete architecture of human ontogeny: Selection, optimization, and compensation as foundation of developmental theory. *American Psychologist, 52*, 366–380.

Baltes, P. B., & Baltes, M. M. (1990). Psychological perspectives on successful aging: The model of selective optimization with compensation. In P. B. Baltes & M. M. Baltes (Eds.), *Successful aging: Perspectives from the behavioral sciences* (pp. 1–34). Cambridge: Cambridge University Press.

Baltes, P. B., & Goulet, L. R. (1971). Exploration of developmental variables by manipulation and simulation of age differences in behavior. *Human Development, 14*, 149–170.

Baltes, P. B., Reese, H. W., & Nesselroade, J. R. (1977). *Life-span developmental psychology: Introduction to research methods.* Monterey, CA: Brooks Cole.

Block, R. A., Zakay, D., & Hancock, P. A. (1998). Human aging and duration judgments: A meta-analytic review. *Psychology and Aging, 13*, 584–596.

Bogartz, R. S. (1976). On the meaning of statistical interaction. *Journal of Experimental Child Psychology, 22*, 178–183.

Cerella, J. (1985). Information processing rates in the elderly. *Psychological Bulletin, 98*, 67–83.

Cerella, J. (1990). Aging and information processing rates in the elderly. In J. E. Birren & K. W. Schaie (Eds.), *Handbook of the psychology of aging* (3rd ed., pp. 201–221). New York: Academic Press.

Craik, F. I. M., & Hay, J. F. (1999). Aging and judgments of duration: Effects of task complexity and method of estimation. *Perception and Psychophysics, 61*(3), 549–560.

Dixon, R. A., Kurzman, D., & Friesen, I. C. (1993). Handwriting performance in younger and older adults: Age, familiarity, and practice effects. *Psychology and Aging, 8*, 360–370.

Duchek, J. M., Balota, D. A., & Ferraro, F. R. (1994). Component analysis of a rhythmic finger-tapping task in individuals with senile dementia of the Alzheimer's type and in individuals with Parkinson's disease. *Neuropsychology, 8*, 218–226.

Ericsson, K. A., Krampe, R. T., & Tesch-Römer, C. (1993). The role of deliberate practice in the acquisition of expert performance. *Psychological Review, 100*, 363–406.

Faust, M. E., Balota, D. A., Spieler, D. H., & Ferraro, F. R. (1999). Individual differences information-processing rate and amount: Implications for group differences in response latency. *Psychological Bulletin, 125*, 777–799.

Fetterman, J. G., & Killeen, P. R. (1992). Time discrimination in *Colombia livia* and *Homo sapiens. Journal of Experimental Psychology: Animal Behavior Processes, 18*(1), 80–94.

Fitzgerald, J. M. (1983). A developmental study of recall from natural categories. *Developmental Psychology, 19*, 9–14.

Gibbon, J., Church, R. M., & Meck, W. H. (1984). Scalar timing in memory. In L. Allan & J. Gibbon (Eds.), *Timing and time perception* (Vol. 423, pp. 52–77). New York: Annals of the New York Academy of Science.

Gilmore, G. C., Morrison, S. R., Behi, N. L., & Koss, E. (2000). *Information processing speed is the same for healthy adults and Alzheimer's disease patients when proximal stimulus strength is equated.* Paper presented at Cognitive Aging Conference, Atlanta.

Greene, L. S., & Williams, H. G. (1993). Age-related differences in timing control of repetitive movement: Application of the Wing-Kristofferson model. *Research Quarterly for Exercise and Sport, 64*, 32–38.

Hale, S., Lima, S. D., & Myerson, J. (1991). General cognitive slowing in the nonlexical domain: An experimental validation. *Psychology and Aging, 6*, 512–521.

Hasher, L., Zacks, R. T., & May, C. P. (1999). Inhibitory control, circadian arousal, and age. In D. Gopher & A. Koriat (Eds.), *Attention and performance XVII: Cognitive regulation of performance: Interaction of theory and application.* Cambridge, MA: MIT Press.

Heckhausen, J., & Mayr, U. (1998). Entwicklungsregulation und Kontrolle im Erwachsenenalter und Alter: Lebenslaufpsychologische Perspektiven [Developmental regulation and control across adulthood: A lifespan psychological perspective]. In H. Keller (Ed.), *Entwicklungspsychologie* [Developmental Psychology] Bern: Huber.

Ivry, R., & Corcos, D. M. (1993). Slicing the variability pie: Component analysis of coordination and motor dysfunction. In K. Newell & D. M. Corcos (Eds.), *Variability and motor control* (pp. 415–447). Champaign, IL: Human Kinetics.

Ivry, R. B. (1996). The representation of temporal information in perception and motor control. *Current Opinions in Neurobiology, 6*, 851–857.

Ivry, R. B., & Hazeltine, R. E. (1995). Perception and production of temporal intervals across a range of durations: Evidence for a common timing mechanism. *Journal of Experimental Psychology: Human Perception and Performance, 21*, 3–18.

Ivry, R. B., & Keele, S. W. (1989). Timing functions of the cerebellum. *Journal of Cognitive Neuroscience, 1(2)*, 136–152.

Jagacinski, R. J., Liao, M.-J., & Fayyad, E. A. (1995). Generalized slowing in sinusoidal tracking by older adults. *Psychology and Aging, 10*(1), 8–19.

Jenkins, L., Myerson, J., Joerding, J. A., Hale, S. (2000). Converging evidence that visuospatial cognition is more age-sensitive than verbal cognition. *Psychology and Aging, 15*, 157–175.

Keele, S. W., & Hawkins, H. L. (1982). Explorations of individual differences relevant to high level skill. *Journal of Motor Behavior, 14*, 3–23.

Keele, S. W., & Ivry, R. (1991). Does the cerebellum provide a common computation for diverse tasks? In B. M. Boland, J. Cullinan, & L. H. Mehta (Eds.), *Annals of the New York Academy of Science* (Vol. 608, pp. 179–211). New York: New York Academy of Science.

Kliegl, R., Fanselow, G., Junker, M., Schlesewsky, M., & Oberauer, K. (2000). *Age simulation of syntactic complexity effects by control of reading time.*

Kliegl, R., Mayr, U., & Krampe, R. T. (1994). Time-accuracy functions for determining process and person differences: An application to cognitive aging. *Cognitive Psychology, 26*, 134–164.

Kliegl, R., Mayr, U., & Oberauer, K. (2000). Resource limitations and process dissociations in individual differences research. In U. van Hecker, S. Dutke, & G. Sedek (Eds.), *Generative mental processes and cognitive resources: Integrative research on adaptation and control.* (pp. 337–366). Dordrecht, The Netherlands: Kluwer.

Krampe, R. T., Engbert, R., & Kliegl, R. (2001). Age-specific problems in rhythmic timing. *Psychology and Aging, 16*, 12–30.

Krampe, R. T., & Ericsson, K. A. (1996). Maintaining excellence: Deliberate practice and elite performance in young and older pianists. *Journal of Experimental Psychology: General, 125*, 331–359.

Krampe, R. T., Kliegl, R., Mayr, U., Engbert, R., & Vorberg, D. (2000). The fast and the slow of skilled bimanual rhythm production: Parallel vs. integrated timing. *Journal of Experimental Psychology: Human Perception and Performance, 26*, 206–233.

Krampe, R. T., Mayr, U., & Kliegl, R. (2002). *Timing, sequencing, and executive control in repetitive movement production*. Manuscript submitted for publication.

Lashley, K. S. (1951). The problem of serial order in behavior. In L. A. Jeffress (Ed.), *Cerebral mechanisms in behavior* (pp. 112–136). New York: Wiley.

Laver, G. D., & Burke, D. M. (1993). Why do semantic priming effects increase in old age? A meta-analysis. *Psychology and Aging, 8*, 34–43.

Lemaire, P., & Siegler, R. S. (1995). Four aspects of strategic change: Contributions to children's learning of multiplication. *Journal of Experimental Psychology: Genera, 124*, 83–97.

Lima, S. D., Hale, S., & Myerson, J. (1991). How general is general slowing? Evidence from the lexical domain. *Psychology and Aging, 6*, 416–425.

Loftus, G. R. (1978). On interpretation of interactions. *Memory and Cognition, 6*, 312–319.

Logan, G. D. (1988). Toward and instance theory of automatization. *Psychological Review, 95*, 492–527.

Madden, D. J., Pierce, T. W., & Allen, P. A. (1992). Adult age differences in attentional allocation during memory search. *Psychology and Aging, 7*, 594–601.

Maylor, E. A., & Rabbitt, P. M. A. (1994). Applying Brinley plots to individuals: Effects of aging on performance distributions in two speeded tasks. *Psychology and Aging, 9*, 224–230.

Mayr, U. (2001). Age differences in the selection of mental sets: The role of inhibition, stimulus ambiguity, and response set overlap. *Psychology and Aging, 16*, 96–109.

Mayr, U., & Klicgl, R. (1993). Sequential and coordinative complexity: Age-based processing limitations in figural transformations. *Journal of Experimental Psychology: Learning, Memory, and Cognition, 19*, 1297–1320.

Mayr, U., & Kliegl, R. (2000). Complex semantic processing in old age: Does it stay or does it go? *Psychology and Aging, 15*, 29–43

Mayr, U., & Kliegl, R. (2000b). Task-set switching and long-term memory retrieval. *Journal of Experimental Psychology: Learning, Memory, and Cognition 26*, 1124–1140.

Mayr, U., Kliegl, R., & Krampe, R. T. (1996). Sequential and coordinative processing dynamics across the life span. *Cognition, 59*, 61–90.

McClelland, G. H., & Judd, C. M. (1993). Statistical difficulties of detecting interactions and moderator effects. *Psychological Bulletin, 114*, 376–390.

Moscovitch, M., & Winocur, G. (1992). The neuropsychology of memory and aging. In F. I. M. Craik & T. A. Salthouse (Eds.), *The handbook of aging and cognition* (pp. 315–372). Hillsdale, NJ: Erlbaum.

Myerson, J., Hale, S., Wagstaff, D., Poon, L. W., & Smith, G. A. (1990). The information-loss model: A mathematical theory of age-related cognitive slowing. *Psychological Review, 97*, 475–487.

Salthouse, T. A. (1985a). Speed of behavior and its implications for cognition. In J. E. Birren & K. W. Schaie (Eds.), *Handbook of the psychology of aging* (pp. 400–426). New York: Van Nostrand Reinhold.

Salthouse, T. A. (1985b). *A theory of cognitive aging*. Amsterdam: Elsevier.

Salthouse, T. A. (1993). Speed mediation of adult age differences in cognition. *Developmental Psychology, 29*, 722–738.

Salthouse, T. A. (1996). A processing-speed theory of adult age differences in cognition. *Psychological Review, 103*, 403–428.

Salthouse, T. A., & Kersten, A. W. (1993). Decomposing adult age differences in symbol arithmetic. *Memory and Cognition, 21*, 699–710.

Stelmach, G. E., Amrhein, P. C., & Goggin, N. L. (1988). Age differences in bimanual coordination. *Journal of Gerontology: Psychological Sciences, 43*, 18–23.

Troyer, A., Moscovitch, M., & Winocur, G. (1997). Clustering and switching as two components of verbal fluency: Evidence from younger and older healthy adults. *Neuropsychology, 11*, 138–146.

Verhaeghen, P., Kliegl, R., & Mayr, U. (1997). Sequential and coordinative complexity in time-accuracy functions for mental arithmetic. *Psychology and Aging, 12*, 555–564.

Vorberg, D., & Wing, A. M. (1996). Modelling variability and dependence in timing. In H. Heuer & S. W. Keele (Eds.), *Handbook of perception and action*, Vol. 3, *Motor skills* (pp. 181–261). London: Academic Press.

Wing, A. M. (1980). The long and the short of timing in response sequences. In G. E. Stelmach & J. Requin (Eds.), *Tutorials in motor behavior* (pp. 469–486). Amsterdam: North-Holland.

Wing, A. M., & Kristofferson, A. B. (1973a). Response delays and the timing of discrete motor responses. *Perception and Psychophysics, 14*, 5–12.

Wing, A. M., & Kristofferson, A. B. (1973b). The timing of interresponse intervals. *Perception and Psychophysics, 13*, 455–460.

Woodruff-Pak, D. S., & Jaeger, M. E. (1998). Predictors of eyeblink classical conditioning over the adult age span. *Psychology and Aging, 13*, 193–205.

V
At the Frontiers of Lifespan Methodology

14 Structuring and Measuring Change over the Life Span

John R. Nesselroade

The University of Virginia, Charlottesville, VA, U.S.A.

Paolo Ghisletta

University of Geneva, Switzerland

Abstract

The long-standing topic of how to represent and measure change in behavioral sciences is examined. We contend that focusing on change processes such as growth and development intrinsically requires one to operationalize three fundamental and intimately connected concepts—measurement, design, and analysis. In the measurement section, we discuss some historical developments such as initial attempts to obtain "ostensive" characteristics of behavioral abstractions, some controversies surrounding difference scores and regression toward the mean, and the various factor analytic approaches offered by Cattell's (1952) data box. We also examine more recent measurement schemes, such as multivariate representations of change and latent difference scores. In the design section, we stress the importance of a proper selection of occasions of measurement, and we discuss recent advances, such as planned incompleteness of data and the use of minilongitudinal studies to overcome practical difficulties. Finally, in the modeling section, we discuss newer modeling approaches, such as dynamic factor models and dampened linear oscillator models. While not settling any of the historical controversies, we contend that the more recent and promising methodological innovations for studying change discussed here, although not a solution, represent a much needed step toward the fundamental goal of more adequately representing and measuring change.

How to represent and measure quantitative change is a long-standing topic, rich in both history and controversy, in behavioral science (see, e.g., Bohrnstedt, 1969; Burr & Nesselroade, 1990). Oddly, for decades investigators in subdisciplines such as developmental psychology have blithely proceeded with studying their content relatively undeterred by the fact that there was precious little agreement among even the experts on such seemingly fundamental matters as how to measure, represent, and construe quantitative change (e.g., Cronbach & Furby, 1970; Harris, 1963). Proposed solutions to the most basic concerns (such as calculating change scores on psychological and behavioral attributes) have been among the most controversial. A significant amount of the explicit effort to improve the situation has been generated within the lifespan development research and theory tradition. Succeeding generations of methodologically sensitive individuals have revisited the old problems, recognized some new ones, and have both invented their own procedures and adapted those of other fields to improve the representation of measured changes in interesting psychological and behavioral variables (e.g., Boker & Nesselroade, 2000, 2001; Goulet & Baltes, 1970; Meredith & Tisak, 1982; McArdle & Hamagami, 2001; Nesselroade & Reese, 1973; Nesselroade & Baltes, 1979).

We examine some of the relevant historical issues and approaches to the measurement of change to set the stage for a discussion of more recent, promising efforts to better represent and measure quantitative change. Indeed, we believe that some major and fundamental shifts are occurring in the way developmentalists think about change and process. Some currently available methods for measuring and representing changes in quantitative variables will be described and summarized, and some projections will be made concerning future directions of methodological innovation for studying developmental change (see also Molenaar, Huizenga, & Nesselroade, this volume).

The Context for Change Measurement

Without clear and unambiguous concepts of process and change, there cannot be much in the way of a developmental science. For concepts of change to have scientific viability, there must be available practical and valid ways to render change concepts operational. The latter rests heavily on the capacity to represent and measure change. This simple chain of reasoning rather tersely defines the content domain of this chapter.

We believe that to facilitate the study of growth, development, and other kinds of change processes, change measurement has to be defined and made operational simultaneously across three major domains—measurement, design, and modeling or analysis (see Nesselroade, 1991a, 1991b). We examine each of these domains in turn, exploring their particular interfaces with efforts to resolve some of the very old problems in change measurement.

Much of the work reviewed here stems from the classical test-theory tradition (Gulliksen, 1950) and relies on assumptions of interval or ratio scales of measurement. Item Response Theory (IRT) modelers are also attentive to the problems of measuring change (Embretson, 1991; Nesselroade & Schmidt McCollam, 2000). Moreover, a considerable body of work has focused on methods for the analysis of categorical and ordinal measurements, which in turn has lead to nonparametric statistical methods for representing change concepts (Cliff, 1991). We focus on the first set of methodologies and literature. Readers interested in the latter measurement strategies are referred to—for instance, earlier work by Siegel (1956) and Ferguson (1965) as well as more recent advances by Cliff (1996, 1997) and Collins and Horn (1991).

Measurement

There is a long history of concern with issues of measurement in relation to representing behavioral and psychological change (e.g., Cattell, 1966; Collins & Horn, 1991; Cronbach & Furby, 1970; Harris, 1963; Lord, 1956; McNemar, 1958; Nesselroade, 1970; Thorndike, 1924). That history reflects, in part, some fundamental issues of measurement and scaling (see also Kliegl, Krampe, & Mayr, this volume). To a degree, it also reflects what seems to be a genuine "self-consciousness" of behavioral scientists toward the physical sciences regarding change measurement. Nunnally (1967), for example, discussed the advantages of the physical sciences in being able to rely on "ostensive" characteristics (such as length and its derivatives), as contrasted with the necessary operationism in psychology, which adds one or more "layers" between concepts and the primitive data (an issue also raised by Bereiter, 1963). In the latter case, physical renditions of abstractions such as drive strength can be straightforwardly made in terms of functions of length (such as speed of maze travel or pointer displacement of a spring-loaded scale), but more abstract concepts (such as intelligence and extraversion) do not lend themselves to ready translations into length or other ostensive characteristics. These more abstract concepts represent a much more formidable measurement challenge and thereby invite additional problems in representing changes.

In a somewhat similarly pessimistic vein, Humphreys (circa 1960) argued that there was rarely any justification for the use of difference scores and that the available information was contained in the two measures and their interrelationships. One can easily witness the residue of the pessimism of Cronbach, Humphreys, and others both in the reluctance with which change scores are used and then in the elaborate and defensive justification that often accompanies them when they are used.

Regrettably, wishing does not eliminate this class of problems. For example, there are major scaling difficulties for difference scores when the metrical characteristics of the component measurements are dubious (e.g., Cattell, 1966). Other problems have been systematically identified and described. For example, Bereiter (1963) focused on a fundamentally important set of issues that he identified as "some persisting dilemmas in the measurement of change." Exemplary of these problems was what Bereiter called the unreliability-invalidity dilemma. The dilemma describes the situation that the more highly correlated two sets of measurements are, the less reliable will be the difference scores based on them. Conversely, the higher the reliability of the differences, the less highly correlated will be the two sets of measurements comprising those differences. The less highly correlated the two sets of measurements are, the less they can be said to be measuring the same construct and thus appropriately differenced in the first place. This dilemma derives directly from the most literal interpretations of classical test theory (e.g., Gulliksen, 1950), including an implicit assumption of relatively highly stable attributes.

An important set of problems regarding change scores concerns those associated with the phenomenon of regression toward the mean (Campbell & Kenny, 1999; Nesselroade, Stigler, & Baltes, 1980). These issues have been rather thoroughly reviewed by Campbell and Kenny (1999). Suffice it to say that there are explicit expectations regarding the behavior of subsequent scores of individuals who are selected on the basis of their initial scores. The existence of such expectations raises potentially interesting questions regarding the meaning (and causes) of whatever changes are observed.

Efforts to minimize, if not eliminate, the problems identified as endemic to difference or change scores have included, on the one hand, the development of alternative kinds of change scores.[1] In addition to the raw difference score, these include residual change scores, true residual change scores, regression-based models, and base-free measures of change (see, e.g., Tucker, Damarin, & Messick, 1966). On the other hand, other ways altogether have been proposed as more effective for evaluating change (e.g., Cronbach & Furby, 1970).

It was recognized that correlating observed change scores (which are not free of measurement error) with other observed or latent variables underestimates the magnitude of the relationship examined (Bereiter, 1963; Raykov, 1999). Hence, explicit models for evaluating changes across multiple occasions of measurement have been proposed (Rogosa, Brandt, & Zimowski, 1982; Meredith & Tisak, 1990; McArdle, 1986; McArdle & Nesselroade, 1994; Nesselroade & Jones, 1991).

Many such models are based on *multivariate representations* of change. Typically, these approaches involve modeling with latent variables of one sort or another. Multivariate representations can be thought of as taking one of several expressions identified within the context of the data-box heuristic presented by Cattell (1952), a version of which is shown in Figure 14.1. The first of these is identified with the R,Q slice of data representing a sample of individuals measured on a sample of variables. A second is identified with the S,T slice of data, representing a sample of individuals measured on one variable over a sample of occasions. The third is identified with the O,P slice of data, representing one person measured on a sample of variables over a sample of occasions. Not only do the usual concerns regarding cross-validation and generalizability obtain with regard to the two dimensions defining a given "slice" of data, but the representativeness of a given "slice" of data in relation to the other "slices" of the same aspect that might have been selected but weren't must be attended to as well. This feature of generalizability occurs more or less routinely in some designs focused on changes (for example, panel designs and replicated P-technique studies) (Lebo & Nesselroade, 1978; Nesselroade & Molenaar, 1999; Zevon & Tellegen, 1982), but it is not systematically dealt with in others. For instance, researchers often proceed as if observations based on interindividual differences across persons at a given point of time (such as R technique) can be generalized to intraperson changes (such as

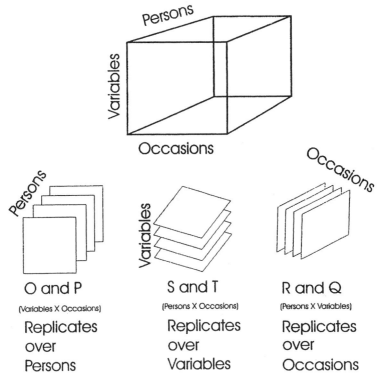

Figure 14.1   A Version of the Data Box.

This version (Cattell, 1952) emphasizes aspects of generalizability and cross-validation.

P technique); a close examination of this assumption is provided in Molenaar, Huizinga, and Nesselroade (this volume).

R,Q Techniques

R,Q data slices include what is typically labeled cross-sectional data. Factor analyzing the interrelations of variables (covaried over people) has been labeled *R technique*. The obverse approach, factoring people covaried over variables, is called *Q technique*. This approach was developed and used to study primarily differences among individuals. However, the measurement process can be repeated (replicated across occasions) on the same individuals to produce *panel data*, a common form of longitudinal information. Largely within the framework of this kind of data there have been several conceptual advances that have greatly facilitated the representation of change. Three important ones are (1) factorial invariance, (2) concepts of quantitative versus qualitative change, and (3) distinction between measurement models and structural models. All three of these conceptual advances intimately involve the notion of latent variables or factors as discussed elsewhere (e.g., Meredith, 1964, 1993; Jöreskog, Sörbom, 1993; Nesselroade, 1970, 1983; Horn & McArdle, 1992).

The premium placed on factorial invariance by the multivariate orientation to representing change has helped to elaborate both its conceptual and operational meanings (Meredith, 1964, 1993). Both strict metric invariance and the less rigorous concept of configural invariance (see, e.g., Horn, McArdle, & Mason, 1983; Thurstone, 1947) have been invoked to legitimize comparative analyses. The concept of factor invariance was central to drawing a clear distinction between quantitative and qualitative changes (e.g., Baltes & Nesselroade, 1970; Nesselroade, 1970).

S,T Techniques

Data derived from this aspect of the data box include multiple persons and multiple occasions of measurements and only one variable. Analyzing the interrelations of persons across occasions is called *S technique*, and analyzing the relations among occasions computed across persons (such as learning curves) is called *T technique*. From the 1950s to the 1980s, realization grew that several occasions of measurement offered a sounder basis for making inferences regarding change than did just two occasions (see, e.g., Rogosa et al., 1982). One approach to analyzing such data involved using repeated measures ANOVA and MANOVA (see, e.g., McCall & Appelbaum, 1973). But these group-oriented approaches essentially assumed similar changes across time for all individuals in the sample, and individual differences in shapes were regarded as error.

Another line of approach (Rao, 1958; Tucker, 1958, 1966) evolved from the principal component and factor-analysis traditions. As presented by Tucker (1966), for example, under the title, *generalized learning-curve* analysis, these methods provided both individualized weights (individual differences information) and generalized reference curves (group information). In Figure 14.2, the basic idea is illustrated with performance curves for five individuals and three generalized reference curves.[2] Individualized linear combinations of the generalized reference curves, where the weights defining the linear combinations are the individual's unique set of weights (as shown in Figure 14.2), can provide close approximations to an entire sample of individual performance curves.

Subsequent work in this area resulted in what is more generally referred to now as *latent growth curve modeling* (LGM) (e.g., Meredith & Tisak, 1984, 1990; McArdle, 1986; Duncan, Duncan, Strycker, Li, & Alpert, 1999). These methods were applied to univariate or multivariate T data of the data-box heuristic (see Figure 14.1). The estimation of latent reference curve parameters via *structural equation modeling* (SEM) techniques soon followed. The synergy of LGM and SEM allows for broader applications and for more powerful ways to model pathways across time. For instance, it is possible to include latent variables as correlates, antecedents, or consequents of change (McArdle & Epstein, 1987). Also, the basis change function underlying the time series may be estimated from the data directly, as opposed to having to prespecify it (McArdle, 1986; Ghisletta & McArdle, 2001). Moreover, the analyses of unbalanced or

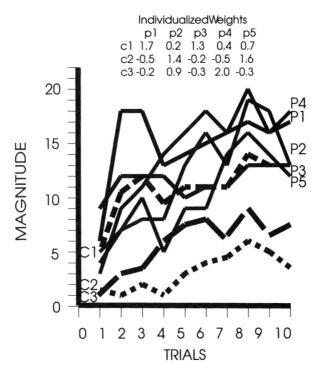

Figure 14.2   Five Individual Curves (P1, P2, P3, P4, and P5) in a Learning Task and Three Generalized Curves (C1, C2, and C3) Representing Them.

Also presented are the individualized weights by which each person's performance curve can be approximated (generally quite well) as a linear combination of the reference curves.

incomplete data sets (Aber & McArdle, 1991; McArdle & Hamagami, 1992; McArdle & Bell, 1999) is possible, as well as the study of multivariate change (McArdle, 1988; McArdle & Anderson, 1990). Similar approaches have evolved in different contexts under the labels *random-effects* models, *hierarchical linear* models, and *multilevel* models (Bryk, Raudenbush, & Congdon, 1996; Rasbash et al., 2000; Littell, Milliken, Stroup, & Wolfinger, 1996; MacCallum, Kim, Malarkey, & Kiecolt-Glyser, 1997; McArdle & Hamagami, 1996).

O,P Techniques

A third class of data is defined by multiple variables measured on one individual (or other experimental unit) over multiple occasions of measurement—that is, multivariate time series data (see also Kliegl, Krampe, & Mayr, this volume). Often, the time series are relatively short, numbering in the tens of occasions rather than the hundreds.

The most common multivariate representation of change in this case is illustrated by P-technique factor analysis (Cattell, 1963) and its derivatives (chain-P and dynamic factor analysis) (Browne & Nesselroade, in prep.; Cattell & Scheier, 1961; Molenaar, 1985; Nesselroade & Molenaar, 1999; Nesselroade, McArdle, Aggen, & Meyers, 2001). In P technique, the interrelationships among variables computed across occasions are the focus of analysis. In O technique, the obverse relationships are examined.

The individual case approach can include simultaneous replications as a way to deal with questions of generalizability (Lebo & Nesselroade, 1978; Nesselroade & Ford, 1985; Zevon & Tellegen, 1982). In part to deal with the generalizability question head on, Nesselroade and Molenaar (1999) presented a rationale and test for evaluating the homogeneity of the lagged covariance matrices of multiple individuals so that informed choices could be made regarding the pooling of change and process information across multiple individuals. Where such pooling proves to be warranted, the "functional" number of observations can be greatly increased, thus providing a more stable basis for estimating a set of model parameters (e.g., Nesselroade & Molenaar, 1999).

Data of the O,P aspect of the data box provide a useful, springboard from the more or less traditional *static* and *kinematic* models of change to the more dynamic ones (Nesselroade & Schmidt McCollam, 2000; Nesselroade, 2000). This distinction is elaborated on in a subsequent section on analysis and modeling issues.

Design Issues

As was noted above, issues of measurement help to frame questions regarding change. An important role in these questions of change is also played by features of research design (Nesselroade, 1970, 1991a, 1991b). For example, which variables will be measured? How many times? At what intervals? These are design questions, but the answers have direct impact on the representation of change.

Elsewhere, pertinent questions of design have been discussed as matters of selection and selection effects (e.g., Nesselroade, 1991a, 1991b). Those considerations hinged on three kinds of selection: (1) person selection, which involves such traditional statistical issues as power and sampling bias; (2) variable selection, which includes matters of construct measurement and heterogeneity versus homogeneity at the variables level; and (3) occasion selection, which includes the length of intervals between occasions and the number of occasions of measurement.

Person selection has long been a consideration of traditional sampling and statistical approaches. Variable selection concerns have appeared in many guises (see, e.g., Little, Lindenberger, & Nesselroade, 1999), although some fundamentally critical issues have not received nearly the attention they deserve. For our purposes here, however, in examining the representation of change, the occasion-selection aspect warrants the lion's share of attention.

Determining the appropriate interval between measurements is critical (e.g., Boker & Nesselroade, 2001, 2002; Nesselroade & Boker, 1994; McArdle & Woodcock, 1997). A measurement interval that is too short with respect to the rate of change of the intrinsic dynamic can produce data that are problematically sensitive to measurement error. Most likely, in this case, the intrinsic dynamic will remain undetected. A measurement interval that is too long with respect to the rate of change of the intrinsic dynamic can produce data that will very likely underestimate any temporal organization in the process and thereby produce an outcome that is an oversimplification of the true intrinsic dynamic. This oversimplification may be such that again, the intrinsic dynamic remains undetected. When the intrinsic dynamic is oscillatory, selecting the appropriate interval is especially devilish. One can produce positive, negative, or zero test and retest correlations simply by measuring the same oscillatory process using different intervals between measurements. Thus, the measurement interval problem appears to be a major source of the confusion and conflict that has plagued empirical attempts at change measurement (Boker & Nesselroade, 2001, 2002). Simulations reported by Boker and Nesselroade indicate that under some conditions an optimal measurement interval can be empirically determined and that given such a measurement interval, parameters for dynamical systems can be accurately estimated, even in the presence of considerable measurement error.

A strong focus on intraindividual variability and change has led to the proposal of designing longitudinal studies around bursts of measurement—mini-longitudinal studies embedded within traditional longitudinal measurement protocols (Nesselroade, 1991a). Here the focus is on assessing the nature of short-term, intraindividual variability at each of several, more separated occasions of measurement.

Another occasion-related idea was first proposed by Bell (1953, 1954) as the *convergence* approach, whereby overlapping short-term individual segments are analyzed to draw inferences about a longer-term group curve. The assumption that the individual trajectories belong to the same longitudinal curve is not always sensible but is testable (Aber & McArdle, 1991; Duncan, Duncan, & Hops, 1996). This data-collection strategy is the basis for cross-sequential designs (Baltes, 1968; Schaie, 1965). The substitution of longitudinal designs with cross-sequential designs leads to several gains: (1) the duration of the study can be considerably shortened; (2) the costs involved (e.g., monetary, organizational, personnel-related) can be reduced drastically; and (3) attrition can be dramatically lessened. Of course, there are costs involved, the biggest being that the parameter estimates result in less precision (bigger standard errors). A necessary but probably often untenable assumption is that the data are missing at random (Rubin, 1976).

The convergence approach is one example of a more general scheme of "planned incompleteness of data" (McArdle, 1994), arrangements that illustrate dramatically how change measurement and research design interface. Following this strategy, the researcher no longer administers all tests to all people at all times. Rather, the tests are administered selectively with respect to people and to occasions. For instance, inferences regarding a process occurring between ages 60 and 90 can be based on subsets of 60-, 70-, and 80-year-olds measured annually for 12 years each. This design allows the different, shorter longitudinal segments to be calibrated on their overlapping occasions and concatenated into one longer longitudinal curve. The analysis is based on yearly measurements collected over 12 years instead of 30 years. Advanced statistical strategies are needed to analyze such data. Prime among these are the maximum-likelihood estimation methods (Anderson, 1957; Rubin, 1974) and data-imputation methods (Buck, 1960; Little & Rubin, 1987). A recent, popular variation of maximum-likelihood estimation methods is the "factorization of the likelihood" or "raw likelihood estimation" method (McArdle, 1994; McArdle & Hamagami, 1992, 1996; Arbuckle, 1996).

Considerably advantageous over its predecessor—single-imputation—is the multiple-imputation strategy. Here any incomplete datum is imputed not once but more times (typically, three to 10) by a deterministic and a coupled stochastic component. The deterministic components of the imputed data are based on the same imputation method, while the stochastic components are represented by different "draws" from an error distribution. This will lead to several complete data sets, differing with respect to the stochastic component of the imputed data, thus incorporating uncertainty due to the missing data mechanism (Rubin, 1978; Rubin & Schenker, 1991; Lavori, Dawson, & Shera, 1995).

There is a wealth of design matters that become pertinent when a researcher's focus is on representing and measuring change. Accepting this means that the intricacies of research design, which have sometimes not been attended to carefully enough, cannot be safely ignored when a concerted effort to study change in some phenomenon is being planned. For instance, a key design issue that is beginning to be clarified within the context of developmental psychology has to do with the interchangeability of intraindividual change and interindividual differences information. To what extent, for example, can one trade off occasions for subjects, and *vice versa*, in designing developmental studies? Do the differences among individuals reflect the nature of the changes that occur within individuals over time? This matter has been raised but not fully answered in the past (e.g., Bereiter, 1963; Cattell, 1966). In the present volume, the chapter by Molenaar, Huizinga, and Nesselroade examines this matter in considerable detail under the topic of *ergodicity*.

Analysis and Modeling Issues

Given that proper heed has been paid to the necessary measurement and design concerns in trying to build a representation of change, there remains a number of knotty modeling and analysis issues with which one must deal. Some of these were alluded to earlier when, for example, the many options for computing change scores and the analysis of "planned missingness" were mentioned. In earlier discussions (e.g., Nesselroade,

1970), it was useful to draw a distinction between structuring change and measuring change. The label *structuring change* was used to connote applying multivariate models to data in order to build a framework within which one could justifiably examine and *measure* change. For example, using the concept of factorial invariance to build the case for measuring quantitative change illustrates the point (Baltes & Nesselroade, 1970; Nesselroade, 1970).

Once the change situation has been properly structured, some of the difficulties of measuring change can be straightforwardly answered (e.g., McArdle & Nesselroade, 1994). Other matters remain more difficult to resolve, however. To illustrate the point, consider the difference score. The difficulties of dealing directly with raw difference scores were mentioned in earlier sections of this chapter. One way of surmounting some of these problems is to render the difference score a latent variable (e.g., McArdle & Nesselroade, 1994; Raykov, 1999). In theory, at least, this separates the differences from errors of measurement and eases some of the problems associated, for instance, with the unreliability-invalidity dilemma described by (Bereiter, 1963).

Data from the O,P slices of the data box (Figure 14.1), which, in general, represent time series, have considerable promise not only for capturing change processes from a conventional point of view but also for offering transparently direct links to a variety of dynamical models.[3] In Figures 14.3, 14.4, and 14.5, some illustrative examples described by Nesselroade et al. (2001) are given. Figure 14.3 illustrates the basic P-technique model introduced by Cattell, Cattell, and Rhymer (1947). This model serves to illustrate the historical move to more dynamical models.

In the basic P-technique model (Figure 14.3), one set of relationship between latent variables (factors) and manifest variables serves the entire time series. There are no carry-over effects across lags in the structure of the variable/factor relationships.[4] The white-noise factor score (WNFS) and the direct autoregressive factor score (DAFS) models (see Figures 14.4 and 14.5, respectively), illustrate the elaboration of the basic P-technique model by introducing parameters that vary as a function of length of lag (for example, occasion t to occasion $t + 1$ is a lag of 1; occasion t to occasion $t + 2$ is a lag of 2, and so on). The WNFS and DAFS models are related to models described earlier by for example, Engle & Watson (1981); Geweke & Singleton (1981).

Static and Kinematic Functions over Time

It seems worth considerable effort to try to get developmentalists to come to grips with the fact that many of the traditional ways with which change has been modeled are not really very adaptive. For example, plots of mean changes over time, as might be produced following a repeated measures ANOVA or MANOVA strategy, may actually say very little about intraindividual change and even less regarding interindividual differences in intraindividual change, which has been argued to be a central focus of lifespan developmental research (Baltes, Reese, & Nesselroade, 1977). Even so-called growth

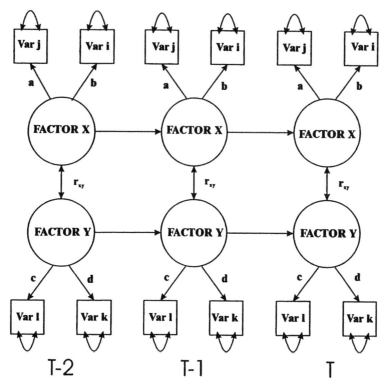

Figure 14.3   P-technique Factor-Analysis Model.

One person's scores on variables *i*, *j*, *k*, and *l* are interrelated in a static model. The very same model is presumed to hold across all occasions of measurements, exemplified here by T-2, T-1, and T. The factor loadings are invariant across time, and only concurrent factor-variables relationships are allowed, thus ignoring any potential time-lagged effects.

curves (see Figure 14.2) suffer from similar limitations. Either explicitly (Tucker, 1966) or implicitly (Meredith & Tisak, 1990), these models assign a single score (weights in Figure 14.2) per curve to an individual that remains the same across time. McArdle (1988) recognized this problem in making the distinction between *curves of factors* and *factors of curves*. McArdle and Hamagami (2001) also extended the growth-curve approach in the dual change score by including a dynamic parameter of proportionality between one's previous score and one's current latent-change score.

Dynamic Functions over Time

The alternative to static and kinematic models are models that have parameters whose values are keyed to some index of time (such as lags), as are the models depicted, for example, in Figures 14.4 and 14.5. More generically, autoregressive and

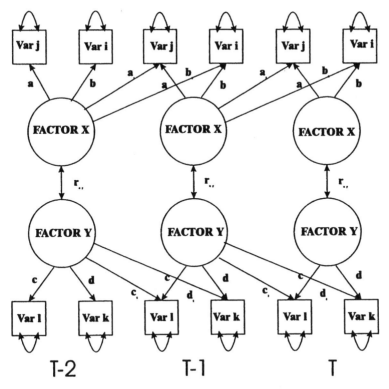

Figure 14.4   The White-Noise Factor Score (WNFS) Model.

The dynamic-factor analysis model specification presented by Molennar (1985). This model expands the P-technique model to allow for time-lagged relationships such that factor scores at previous time points can directly affect variables' scores at later time points.

moving-average models (ARMA models) (see, e.g., Browne & Nesselroade, 2003) offer a basis for building notions of process as a way to represent changes.

Some dynamical systems models go well beyond variations on time-series models such as those discussed above. For example, differential equations models such as the dampened, linear oscillator have been used by Boker and Graham (1998) and Boker and Nesselroade (2001, 2002), to represent change processes. These models can be specified and estimated using conventional SEM tools, which makes them quite accessible to developmental researchers.

Figure 14.6 illustrates the specification of a dampened linear oscillator as a structural equation model. The input data for fitting this model include estimates of the first and second derivatives. Two of the parameters being estimated (η and ζ) are related to the frequency of oscillation and the damping, respectively. Boker and Nesselroade (2001, 2002) give more details on implementing these procedures. A further step in the search for more dynamic representations of processes of change is the use of dampened

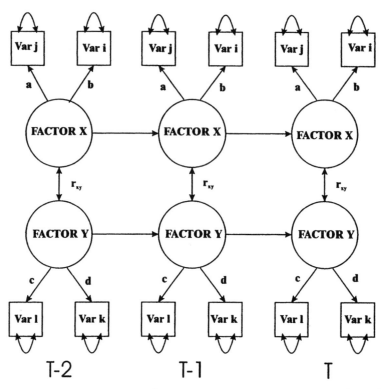

Figure 14.5   The Direct Autoregressive Factor Score (DAFS) Model.

The dynamic-factor analysis model specification presented by McArdle (1982). This model expands the P-technique model to allow for time-lagged relationships such that factor scores at previous time points influence factor scores at later time points (thus affecting indirectly scores on manifest variables at later time points).

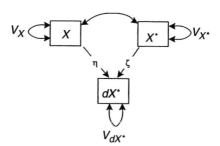

Figure 14.6   SEM Representation of a Dampened Linear Oscillator.

Multiple-regression model with location and velocity (first derivative) as predictors of acceleration (second derivative). From Boker and Nesselroade (2001).

linear oscillators with coupling (see, e.g., Boker & Graham, 1998; Boker & Nesselroade, 2001, 2002). Such models can be used to represent a wide variety of intraindividual change patterns, ranging from short-term, intraindividual variability to those reminiscent of the course of ability change across the life span (see, e.g., Nesselroade & Boker, 1994). Coupling parameters represent the influence of one system or subsystem on another. Figure 14.7 illustrates two dampened linear oscillators interrelated by the two coupling parameters γ_1 and γ_2. The values of these coupling parameters can either be tested against 0.0 (are they significantly greater than chance values) or against each other (is the dynamic influence of X on Y greater than the dynamic influence of Y on X?).

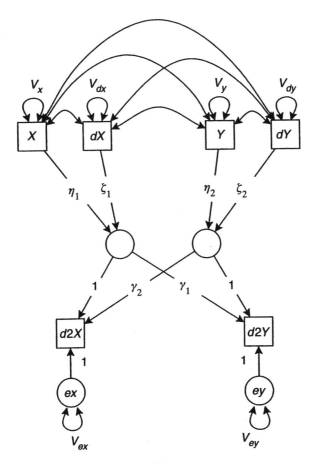

Figure 14.7   SEM Representation of Coupled Linear Oscillators.

The dampened linear oscillator model is fitted to two variables, related by the coupling parameters gamma1 and gamma2, which assess the intervariable dynamic effects. From Boker, Postolache, Naim, and Lebenluft (1998).

Similarly, the so-called bivariate dual change models by McArdle and Hamagami (2001) allow for relational-dynamic questions. These models are extensions of multivariate LGM, in which the relational questions are addressed by the correlations between the level and slope scores of more variables (McArdle & Hamagami, 1996; MacCallum et al., 1997). With the multivariate approach, questions such as "Does the change in *A* influence the score of *A*?" can be expanded to "Does the change in *A* influence the score of *B*?" Certainly, more powerful questions can be addressed with these examples of recent advances in the study of change.

The additional information gained with this bivariate dual-change model over the static correlations of the variables' latent level and slope scores concerns the potential direct effect that one variable expresses on itself and on the other variable. The effect examined is the regression path of a variable's status at time *t* to the difference in status of that variable between time *t* and time $t + i$ ($i = 1,2$, etc.), all exempt of error or systematic unrelated variance. The same effect can be tested across variables, such that the interest lies in quantifying the effect of status in variable *A* at time *t* on change in status of variable *B* between times *t* and $t + i$. Dynamic relations identifying lead-lag kinds of associations between two (or more) variables can therefore be explicitly formalized and tested. Applications in the realm of lifespan cognition include the relationships between crystallized and fluid cognitive abilities expressed in the investment theory and the speed hypothesis (McArdle, Hamagami, Meredith, & Bradway, 2000). In this application, the lead-lag relationships of *Gf* and *Gc* are examined to assess if one component of cognitive abilities has a stronger dynamic effect on the other within the system of abilities considered. The interest lies thus in identifying the more potent variable within a closed system with respect to time.

Conclusion

There is no question that the representation and measurement of change remains a number one priority for the study of development over the lifespan—and rightly so. Without proper, efficient ways to represent change, there cannot be an effective developmental science. Nearly a century of trying to solve the problems of measuring psychological change has not yet resulted in an agreed-upon set of methods and procedures. Recommendations are qualified, and controversies still abound, even though developmentalists have no more important business than to represent process and change well.

In line with predictions regarding the course of maturation in a scientific discipline (West, 1985), we believe that there is an irrevocable effort to move toward more dynamical models for representing developmental change. The signs are there (e.g., Nesselroade & Schmidt McCollam, 2000; Thelen & Smith, 1994), even if they are still somewhat inconsistent and nonuniform.

As the field moves more rigorously in a process-oriented direction, reaching out to other disciplines, we believe that it is important that change be conceptualized as a natural, inseparable part of process. Baltes (1987, 1997, this volume) has pointed to the many facets that must be captured if a comprehensive account of developmental change across the lifespan is to be realized. Merely keeping abreast of the field will necessitate learning about newer, more complex measurement, design, and analytical techniques. To make significant research contributions, we believe that these techniques will have to be mastered. It is imperative that younger scientists accept this and commit themselves to meeting and overcoming the challenges presented by applying well these new methods. As our younger colleagues do this, they will help to breathe new life into the lifespan orientation to the study of individual development.

Acknowledgment

This work was supported by the Institute for Developmental and Health Research Methodology at the University of Virginia, Charlottesville, Virginia, and the Max Planck Institute for Human Development, Berlin, Germany.

Notes

1. For a review of various derived scores and recommendations concerning their use, see Hummel-Rossi and Weinberg (1975).
2. These data represent a subset of the scores presented by Tucker (1966).
3. Panel data, too, provide a basis for fitting dynamical models to empirical data (e.g., Boker & Graham, 1998; Boker & Nesselroade, 2001).
4. Carry-over effects may reside in the implied factor scores, but, as is well-known, factor scores often cannot be estimated convincingly.

References

Aber, M. S., & McArdle, J. J. (1991). Latent growth curve approaches to modeling the development of competence. In M. Chandler & M. Chapman (Eds.), *Criteria for competence: Controversies in the conceptualization and assessment of children's abilities* (pp. 231–258). Hillsdale, NJ: Erlbaum.

Anderson, T. W. (1957). Maximum likelihood estimation for the multivariate normal distribution when some observations are missing. *Journal of the American Statistical Association, 52,* 200–203.

Arbuckle, J. L. (1996). Full information estimation in the presence of incomplete data. In G. A. Marcoulides & R. E. Schumacker (Eds.), *Advanced structural equation modeling: Issues and techniques* (pp. 243–277). Mahwah, NJ: Erlbaum.

Baltes, P. B. (1968). Longitudinal and cross-sectional sequences in the study of age and generation effects. *Human Development, 11,* 145–171.

Baltes, P. B. (1987). Theoretical propositions of life-span developmental psychology: On the dynamics between growth and decline. *Developmental Psychology, 23,* 611–626.

Baltes, P. B. (1997). On the incomplete architecture of human ontogeny: Selection, optimization, and compensation as foundation of developmental theory. *American Psychologist, 52,* 366–380.

Baltes, P. B., & Nesselroade, J. R. (1970). Multivariate longitudinal and cross-sectional sequences for analyzing ontogenetic and generational change: A methodological note. *Developmental Psychology, 2,* 163–168.

Baltes, P. B., Reese, H. W., & Nesselroade, J. R. (1977). *Life span developmental psychology: Introduction to research methods.* Monterrey, CA: Brooks/Cole.

Bell, R. (1953). Convergence: An accelerated longitudinal approach. *Child Development, 24,* 145–152.

Bell, R. (1954). An experimental test of the accelerated longitudinal approach. *Child Development,* 381–386.

Bereiter, C. (1963). Some persisting dilemmas in the measurement of change. In C. W. Harris (Ed.), *Problems in measuring change.* Madison: University of Wisconsin Press.

Bohrnstedt, G. W. (1969). Observations on the measurement of change. In E. Borgatta (Ed.), *Sociological methodology.* San Francisco: Jossey-Bass.

Boker, S. M., & Graham, J. (1998). A dynamical systems analysis of adolescence substance abuse. *Multivariate Behavioral Research, 33,* 479–507.

Boker, S. M., & Nesselroade, J. R. (2001, 2002). A method for modeling the intrinsic dynamics of intraindividual variability: Recovering the parameters of simulated oscillators in multi-wave data. *Multivariate Behavioral Research.*

Boker, S. M., Postolache, T., Naim, S., & Lebenluft, E. (1998). *Mood oscillations and coupling between mood and weather in patients with rapid cycling bipolar disorder.* Manuscript, Department of Psychology, University of Notre Dame.

Browne, M. W., & Nesselroade, J. R. (2003.). *Representing psychological processes with dynamic factor models: Some promising uses and extensions of ARMA time series models.*

Bryk, A. S., Raudenbush, S. W., & Congdon, R. (1996). *Hml: Hierarchical linear and nonlinear modeling with hlm/21 and hlm/31 programs.* Chicago: Scientific Software International.

Buck, S. F. (1960). A method of estimation of missing values in multivariate data suitable for use with an electronic computer. *Journal of the Royal Statistical Society, Series B, Methodological, 22,* 302–306.

Burr, J., & Nesselroade, J. R. (1990). Change measurement. In A. van Eye (Ed.), *Statistical methods in longitudinal research* (Vol. 1, pp. 3–34). New York: Academic Press.

Campbell, D. T., & Kenny, D. A. (1999). *A primer on regression artifacts.* New York: Guilford Press.

Cattell, R. B. (1952). The three basic factor-analytic research designs: Their interrelations and derivatives. *Psychological Bulletin, 49,* 499–520.

Cattell, R. B. (1963). The structuring of change by P-technique and incremental R-technique. In C. W. Harris (Ed.), *Problems in measuring change* (pp. 167–198). Madison: University of Wisconsin Press.

Cattell, R. B. (1966). Patterns of change: Measurement in relation to state dimension, trait change, lability, and process concepts. In R. B. Cattell (Ed.), *Handbook of multivariate experimental psychology* (pp. 355–402). Chicago: Rand McNally.

Cattell, R. B., Cattell, A. K. S., & Rhymer, R. M. (1947). P-technique demonstrated in determining psychophysical source traits in a normal individual. *Psychometrika, 12,* 267–288.

Cattell, R. B., & Scheier, I. H. (1961). *The meaning and measurement of neuroticism and anxiety.* New York: Ronald Press.

Cliff, N. (1991). Ordinal methods in the assessment of change. *In Best methods for the analysis of change: Recent advances, unanswered questions, future directions* (pp. 34–46). Washington, DC: American Psychological Association.

Cliff, N. (1996). Answering ordinal questions with ordinal data using ordinal statistics. *Multivariate Behavioral Research, 31,* 331–350.

Cliff, N. (1997). *Ordinal methods for behavioral data analysis.* Mahwah, NJ: Erlbaum.

Collins, L. M., & Horn, J. L. (Eds.). (1991). *Best methods for the analysis of change.* Washington, DC: American Psychological Association.

Cronbach, L. J., & Furby, L. (1970). How should we measure "change"—or should we? *Psychological Bulletin, 74,* 68–80.

Duncan, S. C., Duncan, T. E., & Hops, H. (1996). Analysis of longitudinal data within accelerated longitudinal designs. *Psychological Methods, 1,* 236–248.

Duncan, T. E., Duncan, S. C., Strycker, L. A., Li, F., & Alpert, A. (1999). *An introduction to latent variable growth curve modeling: Concepts, issues, and applications.* Mahwah, NJ: Erlbaum.

Embretson, S. E. (1991). A multidimensional latent trait model for measuring learning and change. *Psychometrika, 56*, 495–516.

Engle, R., & Watson, M. (1981). A one-factor multivariate time series model of metropolitan wage rates. *Journal of the American Statistical Association, 76*, 774–781.

Ferguson, G. A. (Ed.). (1965). *Nonparametric trend analysis.* Montreal: McGill University Press.

Geweke, J. F., & Singleton, K. J. (1981). Maximum likelihood "confirmatory" factor analysis of economic time series. *International Economic Review, 22*, 37–54.

Ghisletta, P., & McArdle, J. J. (2001). Latent growth curve analyses of the development of height. *Structural Equation Modeling, 8*, 531–555.

Goulet, L. R., & Baltes, P. B. (Eds.). (1970). *Life-span developmental psychology: Research and theory.* New York: Academic Press.

Gulliksen, H. (1950). *Theory of mental tests.* New York: Wiley.

Harris, C. W. (Ed.). (1963). *Problems in measuring change.* Madison: University of Wisconsin Press.

Horn, J. L., & McArdle, J. J. (1992). A practical and theoretical guide to measurement invariance in aging research. *Experimental Aging Research, 18*, 117–144.

Horn, J., McArdle, J. J., & Mason, R. (1983). When invariance is not invariant: A practical scientist's view of the ethereal concept of factorial invariance. *Southern Psychologist, 1*, 179–188.

Hummel-Rossi, B., & Weinberg, S. L. (1975). Practical guidelines in applying current theories to the measurement of change. Part I: Problems in measuring change and recommended procedures. Part II: Numerical illustrations of research designs concerned with measuring change. *Abstracted in the Journal Supplement Abstract Service (JSAS) Catalog of Selected Documents in Psychology, 5*, 226.

Humphreys, L. G. (circa 1960). *Derived scores. Manuscript,* Department of Psychology, University of Illinois.

Jöreskog, K. G., & Sörbom, D. (1993). *LISREL 8 user's reference guide.* Chicago: Scientific Software International.

Lavori, P. W., Dawson, R., & Shera, D. (1995). A multiple imputation strategy for clinical trials with truncation of patient data. *Statistics in Medicine, 14*, 1913–1925.

Lebo, M. A., & Nesselroade, J. R. (1978). Intraindividual differences dimensions of mood change during pregnancy identified in five P-technique factor analyses. *Journal of Research in Personality, 12*, 205–224.

Littell, R. C., Milliken, G. A., Stroup, W. W., & Wolfinger, R. D. (1996). *SAS system for mixed models.* Cary, NC: SAS Institute.

Little, R. J. A., & Rubin, D. B. (1987). *Statistical analysis with missing data.* New York, N.Y.: Wiley.

Little, T., Lindenberger, U., & Nesselroade, J. R. (1999). On selecting indicators for multivariate measurement and modeling with latent variables. *Psychological Methods, 4*, 192–211.

Lord, F. M. (1956). The measurement of growth. *Educational and Psychological Measurement, 16*, 421–437.

MacCallum, R. C., Kim, C., Malarkey, W. B., & Kiecolt-Glaser, J. K. (1997). Studying multivariate change using multilevel models and latent curve models. *Multivariate Behavioral Research, 32*, 215–253.

McArdle, J. J. (1986). Latent growth within behavior genetic models. *Behavior Genetics, 16*, 163–200.

McArdle, J. J. (1988). Dynamic but structural equation modeling of repeated measures data. In J. R. Nesselroade & R. B. Cattell (Eds.), *Handbook of multivariate experimental psychology* (2nd ed., pp. 561–614). New York: Plenum Press.

McArdle, J. J. (1994). Structural factor analysis experiments with incomplete data. *Multivariate Behavioral Research, 29*, 409–454.

McArdle, J. J., & Anderson, E. (1990). The age variable in structural equation modeling. In J. E. Birren & K. W. Schaie (Eds.), *Handbook of the psychology of aging* (3rd ed., pp. 21–43). San Diego: Academic Press.

McArdle, J. J., & Bell, R. Q. (1999). An introduction to latent growth models for developmental data analysis. In T. D. Little, K. U. Schnabel, & J. Baumert (Eds.), *Modeling longitudinal and multilevel data: Practical issues, applied approaches, and specific examples* (pp. 69–107). Mahwah, NJ: Erlbaum.

McArdle, J. J., & Epstein, D. B. (1987). Latent growth curves within developmental structural equation models. *Child Development, 58,* 110–133.

McArdle, J. J., & Hamagami, F. (1992). Modeling incomplete longitudinal and cross-sectional data using latent growth structural models. *Experimental Aging Research, 18,* 145–166.

McArdle, J. J., & Hamagami, F. (1996). Multilevel models from a multiple group structural equation perspective. In G. A. Marcoulides & R. E. Schumaker (Eds.), *Advanced structural equation modeling: Issues and techniques* (pp. 89–124). Mahwah, NJ: Erlbaum.

McArdle, J. J., & Hamagami, F. (2001). Latent difference score structural models for linear dynamic analysis with incomplete longitudinal data. In L. Collins & A. Sayer (Eds.), *New methods for the analysis of change* (pp. 139–175). Washington, DC: American Psychological Association.

McArdle, J. J., Hamagami, F., Meredith, W., & Bradway, K. P. (2000). Modeling the dynamic hypotheses of gf-gc theory using longitudinal life-span data. *Learning and Individual Differences, 12,* 53–79.

McArdle, J. J., & Nesselroade, J. R. (1994). Using multivariate data to structure developmental change. In S. H. Cohen & H. W. Reese (Eds.), *Life span developmental psychology: Methodological contributions* (pp. 223–267). Hillsdale, NJ: Erlbaum.

McArdle, J. J., & Woodcock, R. W. (1997). Expanding test-retest design to include developmental time-lag components. *Psychological Methods, 2,* 403–435.

McCall, R. B., & Appelbaum, M. I. (1973). Bias in the analysis of repeated-measures designs: Some alternative approaches. *Child Development, 44,* 401–415.

McNemar, Q. (1958). On growth measurement. *Educational and Psychological Measurement, 18,* 47–55.

Meredith, W. (1964). Notes on factorial invariance. *Psychometrika, 29,* 177–185.

Meredith, W. (1993). Measurement invariance, factor analysis and factor invariance. *Psychometrika, 58,* 525–543.

Meredith, W., & Tisak, J. (1982). Canonical analysis of longitudinal and repeated measures data with stationary weights. *Psychometrika, 47,* 47–67.

Meredith, W., & Tisak, J. (1984). *"Tuckerizing" curves.* Paper presented at the annual meeting of the Psychometric Society, Santa Barbara, CA.

Meredith, W., & Tisak, J. (1990). Latent curve analysis. *Psychometrika, 55,* 107–122.

Molenaar, P. C. M. (1985). A dynamic factor model for the analysis of multivariate time series. *Psychometrika, 50,* 181–202.

Nesselroade, J. R. (1970). Application of multivariate strategies to problems of measuring and structuring long-term change. In L. R. Goulet & P. B. Baltes (Eds.), *Life-span developmental psychology: Research and theory* (pp. 193–207). New York: Academic Press.

Nesselroade, J. R. (1983). Temporal selection and factor invariance in the study of development and change. In P. B. Baltes & O. G. Brim (Eds.), *Life-span development and behavior* (Vol. 5, pp. 59–87). New York: Academic Press.

Nesselroade, J. R. (1991a). Interindividual differences in intraindividual changes. In L. M. Collins & J. L. Horn (Eds.), *Best methods for the analysis of change: Recent advances, unanswered questions, future directions* (pp. 92–105). Washington, DC: American Psychological Association.

Nesselroade, J. R. (1991b). The warp and woof of the developmental fabric. In R. Downs, L. Liben, & D. Palermo (Eds.), *Visions of development, the environment, and aesthetics: The legacy of Joachim F. Wohlwill* (pp. 213–240). Hillsdale, NJ: Erlbaum.

Nesselroade, J. R. (2000). *Elaborating the different in differential psychology or wishing SMEP a mid-life crisis—and the sooner the better!* Presidential address given at the annual meeting of the Society of Multivariate Experimental Psychology, Saratoga Springs, NY, October.

Nesselroade, J. R., & Baltes, P. B. (Eds.). (1979). *Longitudinal research in the study of behavior and development.* New York: Academic Press.

Nesselroade, J. R., & Boker, S. M. (1994). Assessing constancy and change. In T. Heatherton & J. Weinberger (Eds.), *Can personality change?* Washington, DC: American Psychological Association.

Nesselroade, J. R., & Ford, D. H. (1985). P-technique comes of age: Multivariate, replicated, single-subject designs for research on older adults. *Research on Aging, 7,* 46–80.

Nesselroade, J. R., & Jones, C. J. (1991). Multi-modal selection effects in the study of adult development: A perspective on multivariate, replicated, single-subject, repeated measures. *Experimental Aging Research, 11*, 21–27.

Nesselroade, J. R., McArdle, J. J., Aggen, S. H., & Meyers, J. M. (2001). Alternative dynamic factor models for multivariate time-series analyses. In D. M. Moskowitz & S. L. Hershberger (Eds.), *Modeling intraindividual variability with repeated measures data: Advances and techniques*. Mahwah, NJ: Erlbaum.

Nesselroade, J. R., & Molenaar, P. C. M. (1999). Pooling lagged covariance structures based on short, multivariate time-series for dynamic factor analysis. In R. H. Hoyle (Ed.), *Statistical strategies for small sample research*. Newbury Park, CA: Sage.

Nesselroade, J. R., & Reese, H. W. (Eds.), (1973). *Life-span developmental psychology: Methodological issues*. New York: Academic Press.

Nesselroade, J. R., & Schmidt McCollam, K. M. (2000). Putting the process in developmental processes. *International Journal of Behavioral Development, 24*, 295–300.

Nesselroade, J. R., Stigler, S. M., & Baltes, P. B. (1980). Regression toward the mean and the study of change. *Psychological Bulletin, 88*, 622–637.

Nunnally, J. C. (1967). *Psychometric theory*. New York: McGraw-Hill.

Rao, C. R. (1958). Some statistical methods for the comparison of growth curves. *Biometrics, 14*, 1–17.

Rasbash, J., Browne, W., Goldstein, H., Yang, M., Plewis, I., Healy, M., et al. (2000). *A user's guide to mlwin*. London: Institute of Education.

Raykov, T. (1999). Are simple change scores obsolete? An approach to studying correlates and predictors of change. *Applied Psychological Measurements, 23*, 120–126.

Rogosa, D. R., Brandt, D., & Zimowski, M. (1982). A growth curve approach to the measurement of change. *Psychological Bulletin, 92*, 726–748.

Rubin, D. (1974). Characterizing the estimation of parameters. *Journal of the American Statistical Association, 69*, 467–474.

Rubin, D. (1976). Inference and missing data. *Biometrika, 63*, 581–592.

Rubin, D. B. (1978). Multiple imputations in sample surveys: A phenomenological Bayesian approach to nonresponse. *Proceedings of the Survey Research Methods Section of the American Statistical Association*, 20–34.

Rubin, D. B., & Schenker, N. (1991). Multiple imputation in health-care databases: An overview and some applications. *Statistics in Medicine, 10*, 585–598.

Schaie, K. W. (1965). A general model for the study of developmental problems. *Psychological Bulletin, 64*, 92–107.

Siegel, S. (1956). *Nonparametric statistics for the behavioral sciences*. New York: McGraw-Hill.

Thelen, E., & Smith, L. B. (1994). *A dynamic systems approach to the development of cognition and action*. Cambridge, MA: MIT Press.

Thorndike, E. L. (1924). The influence of chance imperfections of measures upon the relation of initial scores to gain or loss. *Journal of Experimental Psychology, 7*, 225–232.

Thurstone, L. L. (1947). *Multiple factor analysis*. Chicago: University of Chicago Press.

Tucker, L. R. (1958). Determination of parameters of a functional relation by factor analysis. *Psychometrika, 23*, 19–23.

Tucker, L. R. (1966). Learning theory and multivariate experiment: Illustration by determination of generalized learning curves. In R. B. Cattell (Ed.), *Handbook of multivariate experimental psychology* (pp. 476–501). Chicago: Rand McNally.

Tucker, L. R., Damarin, F., & Messick, S. (1966). A base-free measure of change. *Psychometrika, 31*, 457–473.

West, B. (1985). *An essay on the importance of being nonlinear*. Berlin: Springer-Verlag.

Zevon, M., & Tellegen, A. (1982). The structure of mood change: Idiographic/nomothetic analysis. *Journal of Personality and Social Psychology, 43*, 111–122.

15 The Relationship Between the Structure of Interindividual and Intraindividual Variability: A Theoretical and Empirical Vindication of Developmental Systems Theory

Peter C. M. Molenaar

University of Amsterdam, Amsterdam, The Netherlands

Hilde M. Huizenga

University of Amsterdam, Amsterdam, The Netherlands

John R. Nesselroade

University of Virginia, Charlottesville, VA, U.S.A.

Abstract

Proponents of the developmental systems theory (DST), like Gottlieb and Lerner, have questioned the relevance of behavior genetics for the study of developmental processes. In this chapter, the criticism of DST will be reformulated in a way that is consistent with Wohlwill's thesis that the study of developmental processes requires analysis of intraindividual differences, not interindividual differences. The reasoning is straight-forward: (1) behavior genetics is a branch of applied multivariate statistics, conjoined with simple and uncontroversial Mendelian laws of inheritance; (2) standard multi-variate statistics, including (developmental) behavior genetics, is based on analysis of interindividual differences; (3) the results of an analysis of interindividual differences of a given phenotype may not be related at all to the structure of intraindividual differences of the same phenotype; (4) developmental processes give rise to intraindividual variation and also interindividual heterogeneity. From the above reasoning, the reformulated conclusion of DST follows.

In this chapter 1 and 2 above will be taken to be self-evident. As to 4, a concise appeal to the mathematical statistical literature will suffice to show that developmental processes constitute a subset of the class of dynamical systems, where the standard definition of a dynamical system is given in terms of a collection of time-dependent distribution functions characterizing the structure of within-system (that is, intraindividual) variation over time. This leaves open the possibility of introducing additional specifications concerning between-system (interindividual) variation of the time-dependent within-system structure. The main part of the chapter will be devoted to a defense of 3—namely, that the results of an analysis of interindividual differences may not be related at all to the structure of intraindividual differences.

The hypothesis that an analysis of interindividual variation yields qualitatively the same results as an analysis of intraindividual variation of the same measures is known in mathematical statistics as the *ergodicity hypothesis*. The classical theorems about ergodicity show that it holds only in case a process is strictly stationary—that is, the collection of time-dependent distribution functions characterizing the process has moments that are constant in time. This implies that developmental processes, which almost by definition have at least some moments that vary in time, are nonergodic and that for these developmental processes there is no relationship between analyses of inter- and intraindividual variation.

In a simulation study, it will be shown that behavior genetical factor analysis of interindividual variation can yield results that are entirely unrelated to the structure of intraindividual variation of each of the subjects making up the sample. The psychometrical and practical consequences of this finding are discussed at some length.

In the final part of this chapter, it will be indicated how a more valid analysis of nonergodic intraindividual variation by means of time-series analysis techniques like dynamic factor analysis can be carried out. A simple inductive methodology, new in the behavioral sciences, will be sketched with which lawful relationships generalizing over genuinely homogeneous populations of subjects can be derived.

Introduction

From a very general perspective, developmental psychology can be conceived of as the study of ontogenetic trajectories across the lifespan, including their similarities and their differences (Baltes, Reese, & Nesselroade, 1977; Nesselroade & Ghisletta, this volume). The life history of each individual is thus depicted as a path in a high-dimensional behavioral space, while a population of subjects defines an ensemble of such age-dependent paths. Although this is a rather abstract picture of the domain of developmental psychology, it has the merit of bringing into focus a longstanding theoretical debate about the proper way to study developmental processes. This theoretical debate concerns the question of whether the pattern of interindividual variation within an ensemble of life histories at some point in time contains sufficient information to arrive at valid causal explanations of the pattern of intraindividual variation characterizing the time course of each individual life history.

Said another way, do the differences among individuals at a given time reflect how those individuals change over time? Cattell (1966), for example, opined that "we should be very surprised if the growth pattern in a trait bore no relation to its absolute pattern, as an individual differences structure" (p. 358). As will be seen, however, it is overly optimistic to believe that the resemblance between the two kinds of patterns is sufficiently strong to warrant blithely drawing inferences regarding the course of individual development from differences existing among individuals at a given point in time.

To argue for the lack of relevance of studies of interindividual differences with respect to causal explanations of ontogenetic trajectories is one of the basic tenets of Wohlwill's (1973) important monograph on the study of behavioral development. According to Wohlwill, the proper way to understand developmental processes is based on the study of so-called developmental functions describing the intraindividual, age-dependent variation of a behavioral system. Wohlwill's theoretical point of view is shared, at least in large part, by others. Baltes and Nesselroade (1979), in presenting a live point rationale for the conduct of longitudinal research, argued that the analysis of causes (determinants) of interindividual change and the analysis of causes (determinants) of interindividual differences in intraindividual change were two distinct reasons for repeated measurements research designs. Gottlieb (1992, cf. also Burgess & Molenaar, 1995) not only stressed the primacy of the study of individual developmental trajectories but also drew the important conclusion that therefore standard quantitative genetical methods are largely irrelevant to developmental psychology. Much in what follows will be devoted to a detailed scrutinization of Gottlieb's conjecture concerning this lack of relevance of quantitative genetics.

The common core of the theoretical points of view expressed by Baltes, Nesselroade, Wohlwill, Gottlieb, and others is that causal explanations of developmental processes have to be based on studies of intraindividual variation of behavioral systems. In what follows, we denote this theoretical core as *developmental systems theory* (DST). We acknowledge from the outset that the definition of DST we will enunciate abstracts from several additional aspects of the developmental theories put forward by Wohlwill as well as by Gottlieb. Furthermore, the specific phrasing of our definition of DST is not found in the published works of these theorists. Yet this definition seems to capture their essential insights concerning the proper study of developmental systems. In fact, the views of several other developmental psychological theorists are compatible with DST as we define it (e.g., Ford, 1987; Ford & Lerner, 1992; Magnusson, 1995; cf. Lerner, Dowling, & Roth, this volume). Moreover, as is shown in the remainder of this chapter, by means of formal arguments and numerical simulations, our definition of DST yields definitive conclusions about the acceptability of DST. Indeed, we will present the precise conditions under which the basic claims of DST hold.

Intra- and Interindividual Differences

Our first task is to provide clear definitions of interindividual variation and of intraindividual variation. In doing so, we will use the qualifications *age-dependent* and
time-dependent interchangeably. There is a logical difference between age and time,
having to do with the definition of the zero point, but for our purposes this difference
can be neglected.

In terms of the general characterization of the domain of developmental psychology
presented in the previous section, intraindividual variation pertains to age-dependent
differences of the ontogenetic trajectory of a single given behavioral system. Stated
otherwise, intraindividual variation is associated with age-dependent differences across
the life history of a single given subject. What is important in this definition is that the
behavioral system or the subject is fixed (given), whereas the time course of its ontogenetic trajectory or life history is considered to be stochastic. *Stochastic* means only that
the actual ontogenetic trajectory or life history is a particular realization of a random
age-dependent function; it does not imply that the values of this random function at
consecutive points in time are mutually uncorrelated. The domain of generalization
of results obtained in an analysis of intraindividual variation is the time domain (for
example, prediction, retrodiction, and interpolation). That is, these results generalize to
the past and future development of the given system or subject but in their basic form
do not generalize to a population of individuals or an ensemble of systems.

In contrast, interindividual variation pertains to differences among the ontogenetic
trajectories of an ensemble of behavioral systems at a fixed number of time points one or
more. Stated otherwise, interindividual variation is associated with differences in the life
histories of an ensemble of subjects at a given set of time points. The important aspect
of this definition is that the behavioral systems or subjects are considered to be random,
whereas the set of time points is given (fixed). Hence the domain of generalization of
results of an analysis of interindividual variation is basically the population of subjects
or systems, not the time domain.

There can be interindividual variation without intraindividual variation, and vice
versa. Consider an example of interindividual variation without intraindividual variation: the speed of conduction in peripheral nerves as well as the speed of basic information processing appears to be constant in each human being across a large portion of
the lifespan, whereas these constant intraindividual levels differ considerably between
different subjects (Anderson, 1992). Intraindividual variation without interindividual
variation is exemplified by the entrainment of circadian rhythms of human beings living
in the same environment: their daily variation of body temperature, for instance, is time
locked to (synchronized with) the common day-night cycle.

The distinction between interindividual variation and intraindividual variation can
be further clarified at a more operational level by reference to the well-known data
box of (Cattell, 1952; for a more detailed exposition, see Nesselroade & Ghisletta,
this volume). This data box has three general dimensions—persons, variables, and

occasions. Cattell specified six possible kinds of covariation that can be determined from this data box according to a general recipe involving three steps:

1. Take one or more fixed values along one dimension,
2. Select a subset of instances along another dimension, and
3. Estimate covariances between these instances over cases drawn from the remaining dimension.

For instance, Cattell's so called R technique (traditional cross-sectional analysis) consists of the following choices in this recipe:

1. Fix one or more occasions,
2. Select a subset of variables, and
3. Estimate covariances between variables over a sample of persons.

Clearly, R technique pertains to interindividual variation. In contrast, Cattell's so-called P technique consists of these choices:

1. Fix one or more persons,
2. Select a subset of variables, and
3. Estimate covariances between these variables over a sample of occasions.

Hence P technique pertains to intraindividual variation.

Concluding this section, we hope to have made clear that intra- and interindividual variation differ in a number of important respects—namely, in a logical sense (one can occur without the other), in an operational sense (P technique versus R technique), and in terms of domains of generalization (time domain versus population of subjects). In the next section, we will address differences between the statistical analysis of these two kinds of variation.

The Statistical Analysis of Intra- and Interindividual Variation

Applied statistical analysis consists of a wide range of specialized approaches, including regression analysis, factor analysis, cluster analysis, and analysis of variance. Within the confines of this chapter, it is impossible to discuss all the different ways in which these specialized approaches can be used to study inter- versus intraindividual variation. We therefore choose a particular approach—namely, factor analysis—in order to highlight the communalities and differences concerned. Hence, in what follows, references to the structure of inter- and intraindividual variation should be understood in the more restricted sense of the covariance structure of inter- and intraindividual variation. In Molenaar (1999), it is shown that almost all such statistical approaches can be regarded as special cases based on a single canonical model; hence, in this sense, a focus on factor analysis would not seem to limit the generality of our conclusions (cf. Elliott, Aggoun, & Moore, 1995). Yet it remains for further studies to determine the actual relationships between analyses of intra- versus interindividual variation within each of the other specialized analytic methods.

The statistical analysis of intraindividual variation (the analysis of time-dependent variation of the multidimensional trajectory of a single subject or system) is called *time-series analysis*. Dimension reduction, factor analysis, or structural equation modeling of such a trajectory is called *dynamic factor analysis* (Molenaar, 1985, 1994; Nesselroade, McArdle, Aggen, & Meyers, 2000; Priestley, 1988). The statistical analysis of interindividual variation (the variation of the values of multidimensional trajectories at one or more given time points across an ensemble of subjects) is called *multivariate (statistical) analysis*. Dimension reduction, factor analysis, or structural equation modeling of such data will be referred to as *standard factor analysis* (e.g., Morrison, 1990). If more than one time point is involved, then we have (standard) *longitudinal factor analysis*.

Time-series analysis and its close analog, *signal analysis*, constitute a field of research that appears to evolve more or less independently from multivariate analysis. There exists a voluminous literature on time-series and signal analysis in the engineering sciences (e.g., Goodwin & Sin, 1984) and econometrics (e.g., Hamilton, 1994) that is almost completely neglected in psychology. Below we consider possible reasons for this neglect. A quick glance in modern textbooks on time-series and signal analysis may convey the impression that it is quite distinct from multivariate analysis. And, indeed, there are important differences that largely have to do with the respective domains of generalization. The domain of generalization of multivariate analysis (Cattell's R technique) is a population of subjects who are not ordered with respect to each other, whereas the domain of generalization associated with time-series analysis is the time domain consisting of ordered time points.

The ordering of the elements comprising the time domain in combination with the sequential dependencies characterizing intraindividual variation indeed gives rise to distinct features of the models and methods used in time-series and signal analysis. For instance, the dynamic factor model for multivariate time series not only has factor loadings expressing the instantaneous effects of the common factors on the manifest series but also lagged factor loadings expressing the delayed effects of these factors (Molenaar, 1985). The particular value of a factor at time t may affect the manifest series instantaneously not only at t but also at later times $t + 1, t + 2, \dots$, before its influence has waned. Also the sequential dependencies that are characteristic of time-series data require the use of adapted statistical methods (e.g., Molenaar & Nesselroade, 1998).

Despite the distinct features of time-series analysis in comparison with standard multivariate analysis, it can be shown that the two kinds of statistical analysis are basically equivalent. A uniform estimation technique for time-series models and standard multivariate models is presented, with several illustrations, in Molenaar (1999). The similarity between the statistical analysis of dynamic factor models of intraindividual variation and longitudinal factor models of interindividual variation can be made clear even more directly by recognizing that both kinds of analysis can be executed by means of the same structural equation modeling software (cf. Molenaar, 1997; Jöreskog & Sörbom, 1993). We therefore conclude that the statistical analysis of intraindividual variation differs in detail, but not in principle, from the statistical analysis of interindividual variation.

The Basic Question

It was indicated above that intraindividual variation and interindividual variation constitute two qualitatively distinct types of variation. We saw that, despite this qualitative difference, the statistical models and methods to analyze both types of variation are fundamentally the same. The latter, mathematical-statistical equivalence between time-series analysis and standard multivariate analysis allows for a direct comparison of the results of their application to, respectively, intra- and interindividual variation. We therefore are ready to pose our basic question: Under which circumstances is the structure of interindividual variation the same as the structure of intraindividual variation?

Before elaborating this question further, let us first consider the implications of one possible answer to it. Suppose (rather counterfactually, as we show below) that the structures of intra- and interindividual variation observed under identical background conditions are the same. This would imply that standard multivariate analysis of interindividual variation would yield results that also apply to intraindividual variation. More specifically, it then would follow that standard multivariate analysis is appropriate to study developmental processes. Consequently, it would follow that the claims of DST have to be rejected. Hence it will be clear that an answer to our basic question also provides a definite test of DST.

As we restrict our attention to factor analysis, the basic question can be stated more specifically: Under which circumstances does dynamic factor analysis of intraindividual variation yield the same results as longitudinal factor analysis of interindividual variation? Of course, to provide a definitive answer, the same set of manifest variables should figure in both dynamic factor analysis and longitudinal factor analysis. Also the background conditions should be the same. The typical situation we have in mind is the following: the same battery of tests is repeatedly administered to a sample of subjects, yielding an ensemble of multivariate time series of test scores. Then dynamic factor analysis is applied to the multivariate time series of test scores of a given single subject. Also longitudinal factor analysis is applied to the ensemble of multivariate test scores at a given set of measurement occasions (time points). The question now is under what circumstances the results thus obtained are the same.

In a nondevelopmental context, the study of emotion and affect has exemplified many of these same issues (Lebo & Nesselroade, 1978). Emotion and affect are, by definition, intraindividual variability concerns. Yet much of the early scale construction work rested primarily on cross-sectional data. Nevertheless, the scales were then used as appropriate measures of intraindividual variability concepts. The hazards of confounding intra- and intervariability conceptions will no doubt differ across domains, but given no other information, they cannot be assumed to be negligible.

Ergodicity

We deliberately introduced some new labels, particularly *ensemble* and *ontogenetic trajectory*, for concepts that already have well-established terminology in psychometrics (respectively, *population* and *dependent variable*). The reasons for doing so have to do with capitalizing on the geometrical intuitions so vividly conveyed by these new denotations and also relate to a mathematical-statistical theory—*ergodicity theory*—that is of direct relevance to the subject matter of this chapter. It so happens that this so-called ergodicity theory provides a fundamental answer to our basic question.

Ergodicity is a basic concept in statistical mechanics and equilibrium thermodynamics (e.g., Petersen, 1983). To grasp the concept's essential meaning, consider a closed domain containing a pure gas, where each gas molecule traverses a path or trajectory according to standard dynamical laws. The totality of these time-dependent trajectories of all gas molecules within the domain constitutes an ensemble. The dynamics of this ensemble is called *ergodic* if statistics like the mean velocity computed by following a single molecule in time is (asymptotically) the same as the mean velocity computed by averaging across all molecules at a given interval in time. Notice that this closely parallels the basic issue of this chapter: a process is ergodic if the structure of its intraindividual variation is the same as the structure of its interindividual variation. In contrast, if a process is nonergodic, then the two structures are not the same. Extending this notion to ontogenetic development, the claims of DST are valid for nonergodic processes but do not hold for ergodic processes. Hence if we can determine whether a process is or is not ergodic, we also can determine unambiguously whether standard longitudinal factor analysis yields valid results concerning the structure of individual development.

The mathematical-statistical theory of ergodicity gives explicit criteria for identifying ergodic processes. Unfortunately, however, these criteria are quite complex and difficult, both in formal and application-oriented senses. A heuristic characterization of ergodicity that covers most cases is that the means, variances, and covariances associated with an ergodic process are invariant in time. It then is immediately apparent that developmental processes—which almost by definition have time-varying means, variances, or covariances—are nonergodic. In our view, this is a quite noteworthy mathematical-statistical result with important consequences.

We should stress that our heuristic definition of an ergodic process is rightly regarded as providing only an initial impression of what actually constitutes an ergodic process. This, however, suffices for our immediate purpose, which is to make clear that ergodic processes lack some of the features that are characteristic of developmental processes. Genuine developmental processes often have time-varying mean levels—such as increasing mean trends characterizing growth, maturation, and learning and decreasing mean trends characterizing decay and loss. In general, these are the multi-directional patterns of gains and losses described by Baltes (1987, 1997, this volume; cf. Kirkwood, this volume; Singer, this volume) as characteristic of the human life-span. The variance of developmental processes is often time-varying also, sometimes in coordination with the mean trend (such as so-called fan-spread patterns). The same can be said of dependencies between components of a multivariate developmental process (Baltes & Nesselroade, 1973; Baltes, Nesselroade, & Cornelius, 1978), the structure of which can be time-varying in many intricate ways. Well-known examples are structural differentiation, the emergence or disappearance of communalities (as indexed, for instance, by the number of common factors), and time-varying complexity due to increased hierarchical organization (see, e.g., Olsson & Bergman, 1977). Last but not least, developmental processes can undergo sudden qualitative changes that mark the transition to an entirely new type of dynamical organization (van der Maas & Molenaar, 1992). Contrast this with the characteristics of ergodic processes, which have a constant mean level, a constant variance, invariant structural dependencies, and invariant dynamical organization. From this perspective, it is apparent that developmental processes are in general nonergodic.

Some Consequences of Nonergodicity

In the previous section, we arrived at the important conclusion that developmental processes are in general nonergodic. This implies that a longitudinal analysis of interindividual variation of a developmental process can be expected to yield results that are different from a time-series analysis of intraindividual variation of the same process. In this section, we discuss some practical and theoretical consequences of this implication in the context of factor analysis.

Standard (longitudinal) factor analysis is a classical tool for the construction of psychological tests (Lord & Novick, 1968). A large number of psychological tests have been constructed in this way. Now suppose that it has been concluded in a longitudinal factor analysis that a particular psychological test obeys a one-factor model at each measurement occasion, that the factor loadings stay invariant across measurement occasions, and that the intercorrelations of factor scores between measurement occasions are high. Hence the structure of interindividual variation of the scores on this test is simple: it stays qualitatively the same across measurement occasions and is character-ized by a high stability. In fact, it obeys the criteria for a trait factor as defined by Baltes and Nesselroade (1973; see also Nesselroade & Bartsch, 1977). If this particular test then is used in a clinical or counseling setting to predict the scores of a single subject belonging to the population from which the longitudinal sample was drawn, can we be sure that this simple structure also characterizes this subject's intraindividual variation?

More specifically, can we expect to find in a dynamic factor analysis of this single subject's scores also a one-dimensional dynamic factor that stays qualitatively invariant in time and has high stability? If the test is measuring a developmental process, then, in general, the answer will be negative.

An illustration of this situation is given in Molenaar, Rovine, and Corneal (1997). The same psychological test measuring emotional disposition was repeatedly applied to each of a small number of stepsons. The intraindividual variation of each stepson's time series was analyzed by means of dynamic factor analysis. It was found that the time series of each stepson obeyed a different dynamic factor model (different numbers of common dynamic factors, different loading patterns, and so on). Moreover, the factorial composition of the multivariate time series of scores of none of these stepsons corresponded with the normative factor structure obtained in a standard factor analysis of this test.

Apparently, prediction of an individual's course of development based on psychological tests that have been constructed by means of standard factor analytical methods may yield quite unreliable results. If the course of emotional disposition of each of the stepsons in the study of Molenaar et al. (1997) would be predicted by means of the normative factor structure, then the predictions would be poor because the structure of intraindividual variation of each of these stepsons differs in important respects from the normative pattern.

At a more theoretical level, the consequences of nonergodicity can be clearly observed in classical test theory. Lord and Novick (1968) defined the basic concept of *true score* as the mean of the intraindividual distribution of scores of a fixed subject. Lord and Novick (1968) went on to remark: "The true and error scores defined above are not those primarily considered in test theory. They are, however, those that would be of interest to a theory that deals with individuals rather than with groups (counseling rather than selection)" (p. 32). Next, instead of defining true and error scores for a single fixed person tested an arbitrarily large number of times, true and error scores are defined for an arbitrarily large number of persons tested at one or more fixed times. Hence instead of focusing on intraindividual variation as stipulated by the initial definition of true score, classical test theory is based on interindividual variation. The quote by Lord and Novick given above clearly indicates the restricted nature of results thus obtained in classical test theory. Similar substitutions are found in the scaling literature (e.g., Torgerson, 1958), where, for instance, collecting data to implement Thurstone's law of categorical judgment is accomplished by having many judges react to a set of stimuli once rather than having one judge react to the set many times.

Nonergodicity and Heterogeneity

In a previous section, a nonergodic process was heuristically defined as having time-varying statistical characteristics. To reiterate, this definition is imprecise and incomplete in several respects and gives only a very rough first indication of what nonergodicity is.

The mathematical-statistical literature on ergodicity is enormous and very demanding, combining topological dynamics, abstract measurement theory, information theory, and many more high-level, technical subjects (cf. Guttmann, 1999, for a delightful, non-technical introduction). Notwithstanding its complexity, ergodicity theory provides us with a definite formal vindication of the claims of DST in that it specifies the restrictive stationarity conditions under which an analysis of interindividual variation yields results that also bear on the structure of intraindividual variation. These stationarity conditions are in general incompatible with developmental processes.

A developmental process is basically an intraindividual process (Baltes et al., 1977). Insofar as this process is nonergodic, the proper way to investigate its dynamical structure is by analysis of intraindividual variation. One cannot expect to obtain valid information about the dynamic structure of a nonergodic developmental process in an analysis of interindividual variation. This leads to the conclusion that the principled way to study developmental processes is by means of time-series analysis. In the typical time-series analysis situation, this implies that each subject is investigated individually (so-called N = 1 design).

If a nonergodic and nonstationary developmental process is investigated in a replicated time-series design in which a number of subjects is studied individually under identical conditions (same design, measurement scales, and so on), then one can expect to find different outcomes for each subject. For instance, in the replicated dynamic factor analysis of Molenaar et al. (1997) alluded to earlier, different numbers of dynamic factors and different patterns of factor loadings were found for each stepson. Nesselroade and Molenaar (1999) also found substantial interindividual differences between the structures of intraindividual variation in a replicated dynamic factor analysis of multivariate cognitive and biomedical time series obtained with elderly persons. Ongoing dynamic factor-analytical studies of personality and learning yield similar results involving interindividual heterogeneity.

In a logical sense, the distinctness of nonergodicity, nonstationarity, and interindividual heterogeneity implies that all kinds of combinations of the three can occur. Yet it is evident that not all possible combinations will occur equally often. Nonergodicity together with nonstationarity will be a potentially powerful source of interindividual heterogeneity, as is confirmed in the empirical dynamic factor-analytic studies mentioned above. In the next section, we present additional theoretical and empirical evidence for the association of nonergodicity/nonstationarity and interindividual heterogeneity. Presently, however, it is noted that such an association raises a new, intriguing question: If developmental processes are in general nonergodic and if nonergodicity usually is associated with interindividual heterogeneity, then why has this heterogeneity not been observed in standard multivariate analyses?

To elaborate this new question somewhat further, it is first noted that standard multivariate analysis is based on the assumption that the population of subjects is homogeneous with respect to the relevant aspects. Taking standard factor analysis as an example, this homogeneity assumption implies that all subjects in a given population obey exactly the same factor model. That is, under the rules of standard factor analysis, the factor model is invariant across subjects regarding the number of factors and the numerical values of the factor loadings, factor variances and covariances, and the measurement error variances. How can these strict invariance constraints underlying standard factor analysis be met in cases where a substantial amount of interindividual heterogeneity in the structure of intraindividual variation is present (such as varying numbers of factors and patterns of factor loadings across subjects)? Of course, standard (longitudinal) factor analysis is an analysis of the structure of interindividual variation, not intraindividual variation. But can the difference between the interindividual and intraindividual structures of variation really be that large? And is the presence of substantial heterogeneity in the structure of intraindividual variation really compatible with the strict homogeneity assumptions underlying standard factor analysis? Stating the latter question in terms of Cattell's data-box metamodel: Can the test scores of a sample of subjects, which each obey different P-technique models, meet the homogeneity assumptions underlying R technique?

The same question can be asked in terms of the general characterization of the domain of developmental psychology given in the first section. Suppose we have an ensemble of multivariate ontogenetic trajectories, where each trajectory obeys a different dynamic factor model. If we now consider this ensemble at one or more fixed time points, can the values of the ontogenetic trajectories at these time points still be assumed to meet the homogeneity assumptions underlying standard (longitudinal) factor analysis?

From the standpoint of modeling developmental phenomena, the questions just raised are rather pressing. One quick, possible way to answer is to refer to our earlier discussion of the logical distinctness of intra- and interindividual variation. If these two types of variation are logically distinct, then it would seem to follow that heterogeneity in the one is compatible with homogeneity in the other. But perhaps this is pushing the distinction too far. Both types of variation concern the same ensemble of ontogenetic trajectories, one characterizing single trajectories or life histories and the other characterizing the values of all trajectories at a single time point. Because of their common grounding in the same ensemble of ontogenetic trajectories, there will be general constraints on the possible configurations of intra- and interindividual variation. Although there do not appear to be available any formal proofs in this respect, it is plausible to expect that in most cases where a substantial amount of heterogeneity is present in the structures of intraindividual variation characterizing individual life histories, the homogeneity assumptions underlying standard multivariate analysis of interindividual variation cannot be met.

We close this section by summarizing its main conclusions. We argued the plausibility of expecting nonergodicity and nonstationarity to be accompanied by interindividual heterogeneity in the structure of intraindividual variation. We also argued that it is plausible to expect that such heterogeneity is in general incompatible with the homogeneity assumptions underlying standard multivariate analysis. Admittedly, our arguments lack a definite formula proof (filling this need will figure predominantly in our future research agendas), but they agree with common sense and coincide with the empirical evidence now available. There is, however, a more direct way to guide the search for answers to this cluster of questions—namely, simulation studies. It is to this topic that we now turn.

Simulation Studies of Population Heterogeneity

The conclusion reached in the previous section is that developmental processes can generate interindividual heterogeneity that is incompatible with the homogeneity assumptions underlying standard multivariate analysis.[1] This raises the question: Why hasn't the presence of such heterogeneity been detected in standard multivariate analysis? In this section, we provide an answer to this question based on simulation studies.

In Molenaar (1997), the following simulation study is described. Ontogenetic trajectories are generated for an ensemble of N subjects, where the multivariate trajectory of each subject obeys a different dynamic factor model. Subjects can differ in the number of dynamic factors, in the patterns and numerical values of the lagged factor loadings, and the values of the measurement-error variances. The ensemble thus obtained has profound interindividual heterogeneity in the structure of intraindividual variation. Next, the values of the multivariate trajectories at a fixed time point are subjected to standard factor analysis. It then is found that a standard one-factor model yields a satisfactory fit to these data. This is a remarkable finding because the obtained standard one-factor model conforms to almost none of the dynamic factor models used to generate the individual trajectories. The dynamic factor models of most subjects have more than one dynamic factor (up to four factors), while those subjects whose simulated trajectories obey a dynamic one-factor model have factor loadings and measurement error variances that differ substantially from those in the fitted standard one-factor model. It appears that standard factor analysis is quite insensitive to the presence of substantial heterogeneity in the structure of intraindividual variation.

To show more clearly some of the implications of this finding, another simulation study was performed along similar lines (Molenaar, 1999). This time a longitudinal factor analysis was carried out, and the longitudinal factor scores for each subject were compared with the corresponding dynamic factor scores used to simulate the data. Again a heterogeneous ensemble was created in which the multivariate, ontogenetic trajectory of each subject obeyed a different dynamic factor model. Now the values of the trajectories at two fixed time points were subjected to standard longitudinal factor analysis, yielding a satisfactorily fitting longitudinal one-factor model. Finally, the longitudinal factor scores based on this model were determined for each subject and correlated with the corresponding factor scores in the dynamic factor model. The correlations thus obtained were very low and sometimes even negative.

The latter finding has disturbing implications for applied psychology. If the simulated ensemble corresponded to real data used for test construction, then it would be concluded that the test measures a unidimensional construct. In reality, however, the test scores of most subjects in the longitudinal sample obeyed intraindividual structures that were not unidimensional at all. Individual assessments and predictions based on the longitudinal one-factor model would in general be expected to be poor and sometimes even completely off the mark (as indicated by the negative correlations between longitudinal and dynamic factor scores obtained in the simulation study).

It is concluded from the simulation studies mentioned above that standard (longitudinal) factor analysis is insensitive to the presence of extreme heterogeneity of the structures of intraindividual variation. This may explain why such heterogeneity never is found in standard analyses of interindividual variation, even in cases where nonergodic and nonstationary developmental processes are at stake.

Heterogeneity in Quantitative Genetics

We now turn to the more specific claim of DST concerning the lack of relevance of quantitative genetical (including behavior genetical) analyses of developmental processes (Gottlieb, 1995, cf. also Burgess & Molenaar, 1995). From a mathematical-statistical perspective, quantitative genetics is simply a particular variant of standard multivariate analysis. The only extra pieces of *a priori* information that are added to the standard multivariate models of quantitative genetics hardly transcend simple consequences of Mendel's indisputable laws of heritability. Examples of this are the fixing of the correlation between additive genetical factors of members of MZ or DZ twin pairs at, respectively, 1.0 and 0.5. Hence we will conceive of quantitative genetics as an exercise in applied multivariate analysis. In doing so, we completely neglect the political, social, and emotional connotations of quantitative genetics.

The results of the simulation studies mentioned in the previous section also would seem to apply to quantitative genetics because the latter is based on the same type of standard factor model. Yet there are some reasons to pay special attention to the effects of heterogeneity in quantitative genetics. To begin with, the standard factor models used in quantitative genetics are considered to be more robust than their counterparts in general multivariate analysis. For instance, in the commonly employed twin design, the intercorrelation of additive genetical factors of MZ twins is known to be 1.0, while it also is known that the intercorrelation of genetical dominance factors in DZ twins is 0.25. Such *a priori* information about the patterns of intercorrelation between the latent common factors in a quantitative genetical model is considered to lead to increased precision in their estimation. Consequently, the presence of heterogeneity may be detected more easily in quantitative genetical analyses than in standard factor analyses.

Another reason to pay special attention to the effects of heterogeneity on quantitative (behavior) genetics concerns the ways in which information in the genetic code is transformed into behavioral variation. Genes code for proteins and not for the complex behaviors like intelligence, personality, and emotion that are typically studied in quantitative genetical applications. This raises the question of how genes can affect behavior. There has to be postulated some developmental process leading from gene production under genetical control to overt behavioral variation. Although this still is largely *terra incognito*, one plausible scenario is that gene control of protein production directly affects the growth of neural networks underlying overt behavior. According to this scenario, genetical influences as detected in behavior genetics are an indirect manifestation of gene control of brain maturation.

It was argued in Molenaar, Boomsma, and Dolan (1993), based on a concise overview of relevant studies in quantitative genetics, that the developmental (such as embryogenetical) processes explaining genetical effects on the growth of neural networks will have to be self-organizing and perhaps chaotic (cf. Molenaar & Raijmakers, 1999). Without intending to enter here into the details of this argument, it is noted only that a particular side-effect of such self-organizing chaotic processes is the creation of endogeneous variation that is independent of variation due to genetical or environmental influences (cf. Roberts & Caspi, this volume; Singer, this volume). Stated in more colorful terms: epigenetic processes constitute a third source of variation alongside genetical and environmental influences. This intrinsic endogenous variation, due to epigenetic processes making up the pathway from gene control to neural growth, will add up to heterogeneity in the structure of intraindividual variation and, according to the same line of argument used in earlier sections, also to heterogeneity in interindividual variation. We therefore expect this heterogeneity to be present, especially in the context of quantitative (behavior) genetical studies.

In the next section, we present the results of a simulation study of the effects of heterogeneity on one of the most often used behavior genetical models. This *genetical factor model* of Martin and Eaves (cf. Boomsma & Molenaar, 1986) is a special case of the standard factor model. It will be investigated in the context of the popular MZ and DZ twin design. Special attention is given to the estimation of individual genetic factor scores, the possibility of which was introduced in Molenaar and Boomsma (1987). The genetic factor score for each subject can be estimated and compared with the corresponding true factor score of the same subject used in the data simulation. We are especially interested in the effects of heterogeneity on estimated genetical factor scores because the technique of individual genetical factor score estimation is employed for example, in biomedical applications.

A Simulation Study of Heterogeneity in Quantitative Genetics

We first outline the particular instance of the Martin-Eaves genetical factor model used to generate the data. Suppose we have the usual MZ and DZ twin design and a four-variate, vector-valued phenotype is measured for each subject. Let i refer to the ith twin pair, $i = 1, :::, N$; let j refer to the jth member of a twin pair, $j = 1, 2$; let $k = 1$ refer to MZ pairs; and let $k = 2$ refer to DZ pairs. Let G denote a common additive genetical factor, and let E denote a common specific environmental factor. Then the model used to generate the data can be represented as

$$y_{1ijk} = a_1 G_{ijk} + b_1 E_{ijk} + e_{1ijk}$$
$$y_{2ijk} = a_2 G_{ijk} + b_2 E_{ijk} + e_{2ijk}$$
$$y_{3ijk} = a_3 G_{ijk} + b_3 E_{ijk} + e_{3ijk}$$
$$y_{4ijk} = a_4 G_{ijk} + b_4 E_{ijk} + e_{4ijk},$$

where $r_{Gi11,Gi21} = 1.0$ (additive genetical factor scores are identical for MZ twin pairs), $r_{Gi12,Gi22} = 0.5$ (the correlation between additive genetical factor scores is 0.5 for DZ twin pairs), and $r_{Ei1k;Ei2k} = 0.0$ (specific environmental factor scores are uncorrelated for both MZ and DZ twin pairs). The term e_{1ijk} denotes independent (measurement error) influences on y_{1ijk}, which are uncorrelated with all other measurement errors for different univariate components of the phenotype-different i, j, and k.

To generate data according to the above model, we assigned numerical values to the fixed parameters. To begin with, the variances of G and E were fixed at 1.0. The variances of the measurement errors were fixed at $\text{var}[e_{1ijk}] = \text{var}[e_{2ijk}] = \text{var}[e_{3ijk}] = \text{var}[e_{4ijk}] = 4.0$. Assignment of numerical values to the factor loadings was somewhat more complicated. Remember that we want to study the effects of heterogeneity on quantitative genetical analyses. Our quantitative genetical model is the particular version of the Martin-Eaves genetical factor model given above. In view of the discussion at the end of the previous section, it would seem plausible to interpret the factor loadings in the Martin-Eaves model as proxies for the endogenous structure laid down during epigenesis. We should stress that this interpretation does not at all affect the generality of conclusions obtained in this simulation study; it only gives possible substance to an otherwise formal exercise. Following (part of) the design of earlier simulation studies of the effects of heterogeneity (Molenaar, 1997; Molenaar & Raijmakers, 1999), we therefore defined the factor loadings as quantities that could vary between subjects. More specifically, the factor loadings were allowed to be random variables in the population of subjects. This implies that under some conditions of the simulation experiment, each subject has its own set of numerical values for these factor loadings.

A practically convenient way to assign numerical values to the factor loadings in the Martin-Eaves genetical model is as follows. Let $\sim$ denote "is distributed as," and let $N(m,s)$ denote the normal distribution with mean m and standard deviation s. Then the factor loadings are assigned numerical values according to the following rules:

- Genetical factor loadings

$$a_1 \sim N(2, s), a_2 \sim N(3, s), a_3 \sim N(3, s), a_4 \sim N(2, s)$$

- Environmental factor loadings

$$b_1 \sim N(2, s), b_2 \sim N(1, s), b_3 \sim N(1, s), b_4 \sim N(2, s)$$

Notice that each of these factor loadings should have general subscripts i, j, and k but that to avoid notational clutter these have been omitted. It should be understood throughout this section that irrespective of type or membership of twin pair, each subject is allowed to have its own realizations of factor scores defined as random variables over single subjects. We generated data according to the model thus defined under five conditions. In the first (baseline) condition, s was assigned the value $s = 0$. This yielded data that met the standard homogeneity conditions of quantitative genetical modeling. In particular, all subjects within and between twin pairs had exactly the same numerical pattern of factor loadings. In the second condition, s was assigned the value $s = 0.5$. From this, we obtained data displaying a mild form of heterogeneity in that each subject within and between twin pairs had different numerical values for the factor loadings. In the third, fourth, and fifth conditions, s was assigned the numerical values $s = 1.0$, $s = 1.5$, and $s = 2.0$, respectively. Notice that in the fifth condition, which yielded data displaying the most severe form of heterogeneity, factor loadings could vary substantially between subjects. For instance, in this condition the first genetical factor loading was distributed as $a_{1i} \sim N(2,2)$, implying that for about 95% of the subjects the numerical values of this factor loading could vary between, roughly, $-2 < a_{1i} < 6$. In each condition we generated data for 1,000 MZ twin pairs and 1,000 DZ twin pairs. The data thus obtained were analyzed according to the standard Martin-Eaves model given above (under the assumption that factor loadings are invariant within and between twin pairs). Details of the Lisrel model-fitting procedure can be found in Boomsma and Molenaar (1986). Within each of the five conditions defined above, the genetical factor scores were estimated for each first member of a twin pair (in total 2,000 subjects). Factor scores were estimated according to the regression method and the Bartlett method (cf. Lawley & Maxwell, 1971). The estimated genetical factor scores then were compared with the true genetical factor scores of these subjects used in generating the data. To quantify the fidelity of estimated genetical factor scores under each of the five conditions, the percentage of variance shared by estimated and true scores is reported.

We first present some details about the fits of the standard model in the five conditions. The chi-squared goodness-of-fit statistic is not significant in any of the five conditions. Under the assumption that this statistic is chi-squared distributed (with 60 degrees of freedom), its p values range from .82 in condition 1 ($s = 0$; homogeneous baseline condition in which all true factor loadings are invariant across subjects) to $p = .10$ in condition 5 ($s = 2$; maximally heterogeneous true factor loadings across subjects). Of course, the data become increasingly nonnormally distributed for increasing values of s. This nonnormality, however, is confined to the kurtosis, and therefore the estimation procedure and model selection can be corrected rather straightforwardly by using techniques described in Bentler and Dudgeon (1996). The estimated factor loadings in condition 1 are all well within the 95% confidence intervals about their true values. In contrast to condition 1, in conditions 2 to 5 each true factor loading is varying between subjects, whereas in each condition only a single estimate is obtained in the standard quantitative genetical analysis. The estimated factor loadings obtained in conditions 2 to 5 are all within 95% confidence intervals about their true mean values. To give an example, the true genetical factor loading a_1 of the first phenotypical variable y_1 on G is defined in condition 5 as a normally distributed variable with mean 2 and standard deviation 2: $a_1 \sim N(2,2)$. Its estimated value in condition 5 is est-$a_1 =$ 1.96, and the associated estimated standard error is .10. Hence this estimated factor loading is well within the 95% confidence interval about its true mean value: 2.16 > est-a_1 > 1.76.

Summarizing the results reported thus far, it appears that quantitative genetical analysis based on the Martin-Eaves model is insensitive to the presence of increasing amounts of heterogeneity in the population of subjects. The fit of the Martin-Eaves model in each of the five conditions is satisfactory according to the usual criteria (chi-squared goodness-of-fit statistic, standardized residuals, and so on). No flags are waving in conditions 2 to 5 to indicate that the data do not conform to the homogeneity assumptions underlying the standard quantitative genetical analysis. If these had not been simulated data, which we know do not meet the assumption of invariant factor loadings across subjects but, instead had been real data, nothing in the standard quantitative genetical analysis would have warned us about the presence of substantial heterogeneity.

We now turn to the estimation of genetical factor scores based on the fitted Martin-Eaves model in each condition. For reasons given in the previous section, there is special interest in studying the fidelity of estimated genetical factor scores. The situation in each of the five conditions is the same: we have a satisfactorily fitting genetical factor model, we have the raw (generated) data, and also (this is the benefit of simulated data) we have available the true individual genetical (and environmental) factor scores. The procedure that was followed to assess the fidelity of estimated factor scores is quite straightforward. In each condition, we first estimated the individual genetical factor scores based on the Martin-Eaves model fitted to the data. More specifically, two different factor score estimators are used—the regression estimator and the Bartlett estimator (cf. Lawley & Maxwell, 1971, for details). Next, we determined the degree to which the estimated genetical factor scores matched their true values. This was accomplished by computing the squared correlation between true and estimated genetical factor scores. The comparison between estimated and true genetical factor scores was carried out for each individual subject. In order not to complicate the results thus obtained, only the first member of each MZ and DZ twin pair was considered. This avoided possible confounding effects due to the differential dependencies existing within MZ and DZ twin pairs. Hence each squared correlation between true and estimated genetical factor scores within each condition was based on 2000 subjects. The results are shown in Table 15.1.

The effect of increasing heterogeneity (increasing values of s) on the fidelity of the Bartlett factor-score estimator is much larger than on the fidelity of the regression estimator. Yet for the regression estimator, the squared correlation between estimated and true genetical factor scores also decreases substantially with increasing heterogeneity. This squared correlation for the regression estimator in the homogeneous condition 1 is

Table 15.1

Squared Correlations Between Estimated and True
Genetical Factors

Condition	Factor Scores	
	Regression Estimates	Bartlett Estimates
1 ($s = 0.0$)	.761	.624
2 ($s = 0.5$)	.743	.586
3 ($s = 1.0$)	.700	.509
4 ($s = 1.5$)	.646	.419
5 ($s = 2.0$)	.585	.336

about 3/4, but it decreases to about 1/2 in the most heterogeneous condition, 5. Had the data in condition 5 been real, one would have expected on the basis of simulation studies of the standard genetical model that the estimated genetical factor scores would predict about 75% of the true genetical factor-score variation (Boomsma & Molenaar, 1986). (Notice that in our example the average heritability h^2 is rather low: h^2 is about .5). In reality, however, only 50% of this variation would be shared by estimated and true genetical factor scores.

Discussion and Conclusion

The results of the small-scale simulation study of the effects of heterogeneity on quantitative genetical analysis are entirely in line with analogous simulation studies of the effects of heterogeneity on standard (longitudinal) factor analysis (Molenaar, 1997; Molenaar & Raijmakers, 1999). They show that standard factor analysis of interindividual variation is more or less insensitive to substantial heterogeneity, although one basic assumption of the standard factor model is that the model structure is invariant across subjects. In fact, in the previous simulation studies with standard (longitudinal) factor models, the heterogeneity concerned was much more severe in that different subjects also could have different numbers of common factors or different specific error variances. Still, satisfactorily fitting standard (longitudinal) factor models with only a few (one or two) common factors were obtained with these heterogeneous data. It is concluded that the Martin-Eaves genetical factor model does not appear to be substantially more robust with respect to heterogeneity than standard factor models in general.

Apart from convergence with previous studies, it is noted that the present simulation study is preliminary and leaves most issues open until a larger-scale simulation experiment can be done to provide more definitive answers. Some of the issues concerned are alternative ways to operationalize heterogeneity, alternative statistical techniques to accommodate nonnormality, different estimators of factor scores, longitudinal genetical factor models, and, most important, different model types such as regression models, variance component models, and so on. Also, following the suggestion of an anonymous reviewer, one could investigate whether it is possible to embed nonergodic, intraindividual processes within a larger ergodic model.

The results regarding the effects of heterogeneity are only indirectly related to the ergodicity issue concerning the relationship between the structures of intraindividual variation and interindividual variation. Yet we have given arguments to indicate that it is plausible to expect the presence of nonergodicity and nonstationarity to be associated with the presence of heterogeneity. Also the empirical evidence obtained thus far consistently points in this direction.

In view of these remarks, it appears that the basic claims of DST are vidicated in both a formal (ergodicity theory) and empirical (heterogeneity studies) way. More specifically, it appears that applying standard multivariate methods to analyze interindividual variation is an invalid approach to the study the intraindividual structure of (nonergodic) developmental processes (a paper giving a mathematical-statistical proof of this assertion is in preparation). The conclusion, then, is that developmental processes should be studied by means of time-series analysis techniques. That is, standard (longitudinal) factor analysis should be replaced by dynamic factor analysis. Only if there is no heterogeneity or nonergodicity in the ensemble of ontogenetic trajectories can standard (longitudinal) factor analysis yield valid results about the developmental processes concerned. We realize that this may be a rather unwelcome conclusion for those psychologists who associate scientific psychology with generalization across some homogeneous population of subjects (as in Cattell's R technique). Results obtained in dynamic factor analysis (as in Cattell's P technique) do not generalize directly across subjects. These conclusions were presaged nearly 40 years ago by Bereiter (1963) when he argued that it was "when correlations between measures over persons bore correspondence to correlations between measures for the same or randomly equivalent individuals over varying occasions . . . [that] the study of individual differences may be justified as an expedient substitute for the more difficult P-technique" (p. 15).

We admit that taking this message of DST seriously requires the use of new designs and techniques. This is not the proper place to elaborate further on the implementation of paradigms that are valid for the study of intraindividual variation. We would, however, like to refer the interested reader to Nesselroade and Molenaar (1999) for the presentation of a replicated dynamic factor-analysis design that allows for the detection of homogeneous subgroups of intraindividual structure. Such subgroups, which manifestly are homogeneous with respect to the structure of intraindividual variation, constitute the starting point for more principled ways to approaching the matter of generalizability according to the aforementioned ideal of a scientific psychology.

Note

1. Sociological researchers also have long recognized this as a problem—the problem of unobserved or unmeasured heterogeneity.

References

Anderson, M (1992). Intelligence and development: A cognitive theory. Oxford: Blackwell Publishers.

Baltes, P. B. (1987). Theoretical propositions of life-span developmental psychology: On the dynamics between growth and decline. *Developmental Psychology, 23*, 611–626.

Baltes, P. B. (1997). On the incomplete architecture of human ontogeny: Selection, optimization, and compensation as foundation of developmental theory. *American Psychologist, 52*, 366–380.

Baltes, P. B., & Nesselroade, J. R. (1973). The developmental analysis of individual differences on multiple measures. In J. R. Nesselroade & H. W. Reese (Eds.), *Lifespan developmental psychology: Methodological issues* (pp. 219–249). New York: Academic Press.

Baltes, P. B., & Nesselroade, J. R. (1979). History and rationale of longitudinal research. In J. R. Nesselroade & P. B. Baltes (Eds.), *Longitudinal research in the study of behavior and development* (pp. 1–39). New York: Academic Press.

Baltes, P. B. Nesselroade, J. R., & Cornelius, S. W. (1978). Multivariate antecedents of structural change in development: A simulation of cumulative environmental patterns. *Multivariate Behavioral Research, 13*, 127–152.

Baltes, P. B., Reese, H. W., & Nesselroade, J. R. (1977). *Life-span developmental psychology: Introduction to research methods.* Monterrey, CA: Brooks/Cole.

Bentler, P. M., & Dudgeon, P. (1996). Covariance structure analysis: Statistical practice, theory, and directions. *Annual Review of Psychology, 47*, 563–592.

Bereiter, C. (1963). Some persisting dilemmas in the measurement of change. In C. W. Harris (Ed.), *Problems in measuring change.* Madison: University of Wisconsin Press.

Boomsma, D. I., & Molenaar, P. C. M. (1986). Using LISREL to analyze genetic and environmental covariance structure. *Behavior Genetics, 16*, 237–250.

Burgess, R. L., & Molenaar, P. C. M. (1995). Commentary. *Human Development, 38*, 159–164.

Cattell, R. B. (1952). The three basic factor-analytic research designs: Their interrelations and derivatives. *Psychological Bulletin, 49*, 499–520.

Cattell, R. B. (1966). Patterns of change: Measurement in relation to state dimension, trait change, lability, and process concepts. In R. B. Cattell (Ed.), *Handbook of multivariate experimental psychology* (pp. 355–402). Chicago: Rand McNally.

Elliott, R. J., Aggoun, L., & Moore, J. (1995). *Hidden Markov Models: Estimation and control.* New York: Springer.

Ford, D. H. (1987). *Humans as self-constructing living systems.* Hillsdale, NJ: Erlbaum.

Ford, D. H., & Lerner, R. M. (1992). *Developmental systems theory: An integrative approach.* Newbury Park, CA: Sage.

Goodwin, G. C., & Sin, K. S. (1984). *Adaptive filtering, prediction and control.* Englewood Cliffs, NJ: Prentice Hall.

Gottlieb, G. (1992). *Individual development and evolution: The genesis of novel behavior.* New York: Oxford University Press.

Gottlieb, G. (1995). Some conceptual deficiencies in developmental behavior genetics. *Human Development, 38*, 131–141.

Guttmann, Y. M. (1999). *The concept of probability in statistical physics.* Cambridge: Cambridge University Press.

Hamilton, J. D. (1994). *Time series analysis.* Princeton, NJ: Princeton University Press.

Jöreskog, K. G., & Sörbom, D. (1993). *LISREL 8 user's reference guide.* Chicago: Scientific Software International.

Lawley, D. N., & Maxwell, M. A. (1971). *Factor analysis as a statistical method* (2nd ed.). London: Butterworths.

Lebo, M. A., & Nesselroade, J. R. (1978). Intraindividual differences dimensions of mood change during pregnancy identified in five P-technique factor analyses. *Journal of Research in Personality, 12*, 205–224.

Lord, F. M., & Novick, M. R. (1968). *Statistical theories of mental test scores*. Reading, MA: Addison-Wesley.

Magnusson, D. (1995). Individual development: A holistic, integrated model. In P. Moen, G. H. Elder Jr., & K. Lüscher (Eds.), *Examining lives in context: Perspectives on the ecology of human development* (pp. 19–60). Washington, DC: American Psychological Association.

Molenaar, P. C. M. (1985). A dynamic factor model for the analysis of multivariate time series. *Psychometrika, 50*, 181–202.

Molenaar, P. C. M. (1994). Dynamic latent variable models in developmental psychology. In A. von Eye & C. C. Clogg (Eds.), *Latent variables analysis: Applications for developmental research* (pp. 155–180). Newbury Park, CA: Sage.

Molenaar, P. C. M. (1997). Time-series analysis and its relationship with longitudinal analysis. *International Journal of Sports Medicine, 18*, 232–237.

Molenaar, P. C. M. (1999). Longitudinal analysis. In H. J. Ader & G. J. Mellenbergh (Eds.), *Research methodology in the social, behavioural and life sciences* (pp. 143–167). London: Sage.

Molenaar, P. C. M., & Boomsma, D. I. (1987). Application of nonlinear factor analysis to genotype-environment interaction. *Behavior Genetics, 17*, 71–80.

Molenaar, P. C. M., Boomsma, D. I., & Dolan, C. V. (1993). A third source of developmental differences. *Behavior Genetics, 23*, 519–524.

Molenaar, P. C. M., & Nesselroade, J. R. (1998). A comparison of pseudo-maximum likelihood and asymptotically distribution-free dynamic factor analysis parameter estimation in fitting covariance-structure models to block-Toeplitz matrices representing single-subject multivariate time series. *Multivariate Behavioral Research, 33*, 313–342.

Molenaar, P. C. M., & Raijmakers, M. E. J. (1999). Additional aspects of third source variation for the genetic analysis of human development and behaviour: A commentary on Eaves et al. *Twin Research, 2*, 49–52.

Molenaar, P. C. M., Rovine, M. J., & Corneal, S. E. (1997). Dynamic factor analysis of emotional dispositions of adolescent stepsons towards their stepfathers. In R. K. Silbereisen & A. von Eye (Eds.), *Growing up in times of social change* (pp. 287–318). Berlin: De Gruyter.

Morrison, D. F. (1990). *Multivariate statistical methods* (3rd ed.). New York: McGraw-Hill.

Nesselroade, J. R., & Bartsch, T. W. (1977). Multivariate perspectives on the construct validity of the trait-state distinction. In R. B. Cattell & R. M. Dreger (Eds.), *Handbook of modern personality theory* (pp. 221–238). Baton Rouge, LA: Hemisphere.

Nesselroade, J. R., McArdle, J. J., Aggen, S. H., & Meyers, J. M. (2000). Alternative dynamic factor models for multivariate time-series analyses. In D. M. Moskowitz & S. L. Hershberger (Eds.), *Modeling intraindividual variability with repeated measures data: Advances and techniques*. Mahwah, NJ: Erlbaum.

Nesselroade, J. R., & Molenaar, P. C. M. (1999). Pooling lagged covariance structures based on short, multivariate time-series for dynamic factor analysis. In R. H. Hoyle (Ed.), *Statistical strategies for small sample research*. Newbury Park, CA: Sage.

Olsson, U., & Bergman, L. R. (1977). A longitudinal factor model for studying change in ability structure. *Multivariate Behavioral Research, 12*, 221–242.

Petersen, K. (1983). *Ergodic theory*. New York: Cambridge University Press.

Priestley, M. B. (1988). *Nonlinear and nonstationary time-series analysis*. London: Academic Press.

Torgerson, W. J. (1958). *Theory and methods of scaling*. New York: Wiley.

van der Maas, H. L., & Molenaar, P. C. M. (1992). Stagewise cognitive development: An application of catastrophe theory. *Psychological Review, 99*, 395–417.

Wohlwill, J. F. (1973). *The study of behavioral development*. New York: Academic Press.

16 Combining Molecular and Quantitative Genetics: Decomposing the Architecture of Lifespan Development

Gerald E. McClearn

The Pennsylvania State University, University Park, PA, U.S.A.

Abstract

The pertinent genetic model for analysis of continuously distributed phenotypes is that of quantitative genetics, which considers both environmental and genetic sources of influence on the measured characteristic. These sources may be anonymous, and the typical analytical outcome is a decomposition of the observed variance into components attributable to these two broad domains, to various definable subsets of them, and to interactions within and between them. Further, developmental analyses permit description of changes in the relative contributions of these components over time. Recent advances in molecular genetics are making possible the examination of the influence of individual genetic loci in the hitherto anonymous polygenic sets of quantitative investigations. These advances offer unprecedented opportunities both for enhanced reductionist approaches that elucidate the molecular basis of the genetic influence and for integrationist approaches that explore the dynamics of individuated genetic and environmental factors in complex developing systems.

At the turn of the twentieth century, one of the greatest persisting mysteries of biological science concerned the transmission of characteristics from parent to offspring. There were two fundamental questions: what is transmitted from the adult parent to the offspring, and how does the fertilized egg ultimately develop into an adult? In 1900, the discoveries and interpretations of Mendel provided the beginnings of an answer to the first question. Mendel's brilliant deduction that the hereditary system comprised paired elements and his description of the basic rules by which they operated had languished unnoticed for about 35 years. When rediscovered, they motivated an intense burst of research in exploring the generality of these rules. The focus of the study of heredity (soon to be named *genetics*) was on the transmission of the Mendelian elements (soon to be named *genes*); the matter of the developmental processes by which they eventuated in a mature organism became the concern of another discipline— *embryology* (Keller, 1994).

Within genetics, two paradigms soon became distinguishable. On the one hand, the Mendelian enthusiasts were demonstrating Mendelian phenomena in a burgeoning array of categorical traits (or *phenotypes*). On the other hand, a biometrical approach, sometimes called *Galtonian* (Murphy & Trojak, 1983), doubted that the Mendelian processes were pertinent to the inheritance of phenotypes that were distributed continuously rather than in a categorical fashion. A lively controversy endured for nearly two decades until Fisher (1918) demonstrated that the statistical results of the biometricians could be rationalized as the consequence of the cumulative or collective effects of a number of genes of relatively small influence, unlike the genes with major effect that were the objects of Mendelian research. From this model, the quantitative genetic theory has been elegantly elaborated (see, for example, Falconer & Mackay, 1996). This theory has been applied with very considerable explanatory and predictive success to a wide variety of biological and behavioral characteristics. Its usefulness has furthermore been demonstrated with resounding clarity in the pragmatic arena of agriculture, where the plenitude of food in the developed nations is to a substantial degree the consequence of successful application of quantitative genetic theories and methods.

The Fisherian insight resolved the issue of whether there were different mechanisms of inheritance—one for the major Mendelian genes that gave rise to categorical differences among individuals, and another that applied to the continuous distributions of "normal" variability. The conclusion was that the difference was in the number and effect sizes of the genes involved but that the system of transmission was basically the same for both classes of phenotypes. The case of the major gene effect can be viewed as the limiting case of the polygenic system. However, because of differing empirical and analytical methods required for the study of the categorical and continuous phenotypes, two more or less distinct bodies of literature—the *single gene* and the *quantitative*— exist. Both of these subdisciplines of genetics have provided information pertinent to the origins of individuality in development and aging.

There have been several recent reviews of this age-relevant literature (Finch & Tanzi, 1997; Jazwinski, 1996; Johnson, 1997; Martin, 1996; Miller, 1999; Shmookler-Reis & Ebert, 1996). A comprehensive overview of this literature is beyond the scope of the present chapter. The present objective is to provide a general broad-stroke perspective on aging-related genetic architecture illustrated by selected examples from diverse areas—some old, some new, some human, some animal—to give a sense of the breadth and variety of evidence that relates to that perspective.

In the mid-twentieth century, the intellectual explosion of molecular genetics began. With incredible speed, the biochemical nature of Mendel's hypothetical elements was discovered, and the mechanisms through which they functioned were described. The targets of molecular genetics research have principally been major genes. Recently, with the genome projects mapping the chromosomes of human beings and those of various model species, it has become possible to identify chromosomal locations containing the more robust of the polygenes, and the gleaming prospect arises of combining the quantitative and molecular approaches in a comprehensive approach to developmental individuality.

The Conventional Quantitative Genetic Model

For later terminological convenience and clarity, we may distinguish two concepts associated with the term *gene*. Sometimes the referent is a location on one of the chromosomes, a *locus*. Many loci can be occupied by (really, constituted of) one of two or more variant forms, called *alleles*. These loci, described as *polymorphic*, are the genetic basis of individual differences among members of the species. When we refer to the influence of a gene, we are thus most often referring to the consequences of allelic differences: individuals with one allelic constitution differ from individuals with other allelic constitutions. For each locus on *autosomes* (chromosomes other than the sex chromosomes), each individual has two alleles, one from each parent. Individuals with two like alleles are called *homozygotes*; those with different alleles are *heterozygotes*. For the sex chromosome, individuals of one sex (males in human beings and many other species) have only one copy, obtained from the mother, and are termed *hemizygotes*.

The conceptual model of quantitative genetics concerns interindividual differences in phenotypes. Two domains of influence are identified—the genotype and the environment. For binomial convenience, it is often assumed that the effect sizes of the many relevant loci are not only small but equally small. Fisher's work (1918) showed how the measures of variances and correlations among relatives of different degree are interpretable in terms of this summated action of many genes. A standard result from a quantitative genetic analysis is decomposition of the variance of the phenotype into components attributable to individual differences in the relevant genes and to individual differences in relevant environments. The impact of the environment is, in general, estimated by the residual term—the variance not accounted for by the genetic factors. As a consequence, the definition of the environment is enormously broad and inclusive, ranging from physical influences on cellular mechanisms to social effects of peer groups. Different study designs permit the further compartmentalization of environmental effects, for example, into family-shared components and individually unique components or into long-term and short-term influences. (Measurement error may also be included in the environmental component.)

It is important to emphasize that these variance components are descriptive statistics, estimating the respective influences for that particular population under its particular range of environmental circumstances. *Heritability* (the proportion of phenotypic variance due to genetic differences) and *environmentality* (the proportion due to environmental factors) are not fixed parameters for all time and all places. Even a heritability of 1.0, signifying no detectable environmental influence, would not mean that no conceivable environment could influence the phenotype. It would mean that within the particular array of environments to which the study population was exposed, there did not exist a powerful environmental influence or that if such an influence was present, it was not sufficiently widespread to affect the variance in the study population sufficiently to be recognized. Thus, some newly devised intervention (pharmacological, educational, nutritional) or new risk factors (such as environmental pollution, famine, epidemics, war) could completely change the picture.

The Individuation of the Genetic Elements

Quantitative genetic analyses can proceed in complete ignorance of the specific elements included within either the genetic or environmental domains. However, inevitably, as Mendelian research proliferated, genes came to be identified that had major effects on phenotypes that are continuously distributed. For example, various major genes such as *midget* (see Fowler & Edwards, 1961) have dramatic effects on body size in mice, a classical continuously distributed phenotype. It is reasonable to presume that there exist other alleles at those loci that might contribute to the normal range of variation.

But the pace of identifying presumed specific loci within the polygenic system was necessarily slow and very incomplete because only genes that had allelic forms with relatively large effect could be found. However, doubts had long been expressed about the assumption that polygenes had equally small effects, and it came to be accepted that there might be a distribution of effect sizes—with a few of near-major gene proportions, many of more modest influence, and many more of truly tiny contributions. The Human Genome Project, with its systematic mapping of the human genome and that of several model species, has made it possible to seek evidence of the chromosomal location of some of these polygenes that have effect sizes too small to be detected by conventional Mendelian methods but are large enough to be identified with the help of the detailed chromosomal markers now available (McClearn, Plomin, Gora-Maslak, & Crabbe, 1991). The basic evidence produced by this type of research is that a gene with some effect on the phenotype is somewhere in the neighborhood of a chromosomal marker. Such a gene is called a *quantitative trait locus* or QTL. The neighborhood specified is usually extensive, containing very many genes, but identification of the QTL is a step toward more molecular characterization of the effective gene. Furthermore, even in advance of such detail, QTL methodology can powerfully supplement and complement other approaches to the understanding of the mechanisms of gene action and of interactions among genes and between genes and environments in complex systems.

The Mechanisms of Gene Action

In the case of major genes, it is possible to compare individuals of the different phenotypic categories with respect to other attributes and thus test hypotheses concerning the causal pathways through which the gene exerts its influence. One of the most dramatic early successes of this approach was the condition of phenylketonuria (PKU), in which homozygosity for a particular allele resulted in profound mental retardation. A correlated feature was a distinctive odor of the urine of affected individuals. In investigating the origin of the odor, Fölling (1934) found an excess of phenylpyruvic acid and thus opened the way to the characterization of a defective enzyme, the metabolic consequences of which included a toxic influence on the developing nervous system and ultimately led to a rational nutritional intervention (see Lyman, 1963, for a history of this scientific saga).

From this and many other studies, even before the molecular nature of genes was discovered, evidence accumulated that genes operate through basic anatomical structure and physiological, biochemical, immunological, endocrinological, and neurochemical processes. Thus, whereas the immediate action of genes remained mysterious, it became increasingly clear that somewhere downstream, the mechanism operated through the basic biological processes concerning which whole disciplines have provided enormous amounts of information. That is to say, huge parts of the machinery of gene influence have already been illuminated by the other life sciences. Molecular genetics provided the link from the genes to these biological processes. Briefly, the genetic information is coded as sequences of base pairs in deoxyribonucleic acid (DNA), which, with other constituents, comprises the chromosomes within the nucleus of each cell. The DNA information is transcribed as ribonucleic acid (RNA) that, in the cell cytoplasm, participates in processes that eventuate in the production of structural, transport, or catalytic proteins and impinge on physiology, biochemistry, and so on.

Figure 16.1 provides a schema that summarizes many of the above points. The system displays genetic and environmental inputs, represented by an elongated oval and rectangle, respectively. The individuated elements (some of which may or may not be known in the case of any specific phenotype) within each category are represented by small ovals and rectangles. The causal field (Mackie, 1974) is represented by the large oval, with the elements of the causal machinery including and downstream from the enzymic gene product and the phenotypes influenced by this causal field represented by small squares.

This representation, showing that genes and environments work through the same systems, makes clear the intellectual bankruptcy of any conception that pits nature *versus* nurture or represents them as opposing, contending forces. It also indicates that the search for genetic influences and for their mechanisms of influence is not a narrowly parochial activity. As seen in the PKU example above, insights into mechanism downstream from the gene paved the way for an *environmental* intervention.

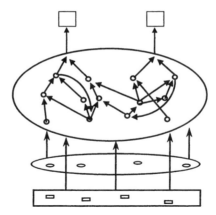

Figure 16.1   Schema Depicting Genetic and Environmental Influences on a Common Causal Field Affecting a Pair of Phenotypes.
Figure Adapted from McClearn, & Vogler (2001)

Some of the salient features of causal fields are suggested in the representation of parallel, redundant, multiple-element pathways, with feedback systems, and with converging and diverging pathways. In such a field, notions of linear, unidirectional causality become limited (Sattler, 1986) and can capture only part of the information in the system. Circular and network causality considerations are necessary, and attribution of effects of any causal elements within such a field must be context dependent (Kacser & Burns, 1979). Specifically, the causal field constitutes the arena in which interactions between and among genetic and environmental factors occur (cf. Molenaar, Huizenga, & Nesselroade, this volume).

It must be said that whereas the pathways from genes to some particular diseases are reasonably well characterized, there are no exhaustive descriptions of the causal field for complex polygenic systems. Nonetheless, significant features of the causal field have been identified for many such systems. Molecular studies of the route from DNA to primary gene product open the way to characterizing the metabolic route on which the gene product impinges. Such research has generated and is generating a wealth of basic and biomedically relevant data. Strategies derived from quantitative genetics are also useful for exploring the causal field.

Quantitative Genetics and the Search for Mechanism

Application of methods derived from (or rationalized by) the quantitative genetic model can generate powerful opportunities for the testing of hypotheses about the anatomical, biochemical, endocrinological, biochemical, and neurological mechanisms differing between or among genetically defined groups and, by inference, identify at least part of the causal mechanism through which the influence of the genes is mediated.

Among the principal tools available for animal model work in quantitative genetics is the extant assortment of inbred strains of rats, and, especially, of mice. As a consequence of repeated generations of sibling mating, a condition is achieved in which the animals are genetically uniform (that is to say, such strains asymptotically approach homozygosity at all loci). In essence, the researcher has available an unlimited pool of identical twins. Inbreeding is not directional with respect to any particular phenotype, and the successful exploitation of inbred strains depends on discovering strains with the requisite levels of the phenotype under investigation. The uniformity of genotypes of inbred strains offers many interpretational advantages, but there are limitations as well (McClearn & Hofer, 1999; Miller et al., 1999).

In any case, it is not necessary to depend on the fortuities of strain differences for use in a particular domain. Selective breeding permits the assembly of model systems to specification. In selective breeding, animals from a genetically heterogeneous population that display high levels of some phenotype are mated together (and similarly for low levels of the phenotype). Over successive generations, this procedure directs all of the alleles available in the population gene pool that influence the phenotype in the "increasing" direction into one line and the "decreasing" alleles into another line. In effect, the complex polygenic determinants have been segregated into maximally contrasting sets, providing a powerful research resource. This selective breeding strategy is one of the most powerful at the disposal of researchers into complex, continuously distributed traits. Among the many physiological and biomedical domains to utilize selectively bred lines in research on mechanism, pharmacogenetics has found them of particular value. To illustrate the point, Deitrich (2000) has recorded more than 300 studies that have utilized lines of mice selectively bred for differences in sensitivity to a hypnotic dose of alcohol (McClearn & Kakihana, 1981). Among the key words describing these studies are *membrane structure, neuromuscular junctions, fertility, norepinephrine, nicotinic receptors, chloride channels, Purkinje neurons, tyrosine, cerebellar phospholipids, teratogenesis, acetaldehyde, neurotensin, activity, hippocampus, taste aversion, hepatic microsomes, alcohol consumption, thyroid status, locomotion, hyperglycemia, thermoregulation, protein kinase C, serotonin.* From this list it can be seen that many features of a genetically influenced causal field can be illuminated without any knowledge of specific genes in the consortium of genes influencing the phenotype.

There are special considerations in application of selective breeding to gerontological issues, of course. For many aging-related variables, the animals are not capable of reproducing after their gerontologically relevant phenotype has been assessed (see also Kirkwood, this volume). Nonetheless, selective breeding for life-course variables, such as age of reproductive maturity, has provided prime gerontological material in *Drosophila* (see Arking, 1991; Rose, 1991), and programs to exploit the strategy in mammalian systems are in progress (Harrison & Roderick, 1997).

Interactions

The general picture of genetic and environmental agencies influencing a common causal field provides plentiful scope for interactions of genes with environments, genes with genes, and environments with environments. The latter is beyond the scope of this presentation, but examples of the other two types can be cited to contribute to the picture of the architecture of development.

Interactions Between and Among Genes

Early in the history of Mendelian genetic research, there were observations that the effects of allelic differences at some loci were dependent on the allelic condition at another locus or loci. The classical example is that of albinism, in which homozygosity for one particular allele at the relevant locus overrides all of the other loci that ordinarily have an influence on coat color of animals. Two examples can illustrate the modifying effects of polygenic background genotype on the expression of a particular gene.

Fowler and Edwards (1961) were able to examine the effect of the *midget* allele, mentioned earlier, when it was on different genetic backgrounds. The phenotype was less severe in a line of mice different from the line in which the gene was first found, revealing a moderating influence of the new polygenic background. In addition, the clear Mendelian properties (yielding the expected number of normal and affected offspring in different mating combinations) that were displayed in the original line were greatly distorted in another line.

Coleman and Hummel (1975) provide a similar example. Homozygosity for a particular allele at the *diabetes* locus in mice produces a syndrome with features of the medical condition in human beings, but, in different inbred strains, the consequences differ hugely in respect to glucose level, body weight, and pathophysiology, revealing the effects of the different polygenic backgrounds, and, presumably, of the redundant, interacting pathways through the causal field.

A third example involves two specific, identified, genetic loci. The role of the $\varepsilon 4$ allele of the *ApoE* locus in the etiology of late-onset Alzheimer's disease is a matter of intense research effort. An allelic dose-response has been reported overall, with elevated risk due to possession of a single $\varepsilon 4$ allele, and with additional risk for those possessing two copies. Kamboh, Sanghera, Ferrell, and Dekosky (1995), however, have reported an interaction with the *ACT* locus. Two alleles at this locus are labeled *A* and *T*. For homozygous *TT* individuals, possession of two $\varepsilon 4$ alleles does not constitute a greater risk than does possession of one; for AA individuals the $\varepsilon 4$ risk is elevated, the risk is $\varepsilon 4$ dose-related, and the risk is especially high for those homozygous $\varepsilon 4/\varepsilon 4$ and *AA/AA*.

Interactions Between Genes and Environment

In the context of contradictory evidence of the importance of aluminum as a risk factor in Alzheimer's disease, Fosmire, Focht, and McClearn (1993) explored the possibility that genetic factors might affect individuality in response to elevated dietary aluminum levels in mice. Comparison of control animals of five inbred strains with those given food containing high levels of aluminum revealed large strain differences in brain aluminum concentrations. Three strains showed no effect at all, one showed a slight elevation, and one showed a threefold increase. Although not directly addressing the issue of Alzheimer's risk, these results are instructive in illustrating genetically based individual differences in sensitivity to environmental risk factors—or, the equivalent, environmental influences on the effect of genetic differences.

In a similar vein, Bouchard and colleagues have explored the possibility of genetic influence on differential response to experimental overfeeding (Bouchard et al., 1990) of young human male monozygotic twins. Comparison of the between-pair to the within-pair variance in weight gain and fat distribution led to the conclusion that genetic factors contributed to the wide range of individuality in response to this manipulation of the nutritional environment.

As a final example, the now-classic research of Cooper and Zubek (1958) may be cited. These investigators reared rats of two lines, selectively bred respectively for good and poor learning performance in a maze, under three environmental conditions— standard, restricted, and enriched. The environmental circumstances had a clear effect, as did the genotypic difference. A major interaction occurred, however, in that the enriched condition improved the maze-dull rats greatly but affected the maze-bright animals relatively little. Similarly, the restricted condition had relatively little effect on the dull animals but worsened the performance of the bright animals substantially.

Collectively, these results provide a valuable heuristic message concerning the extent to which susceptibility to health risk factors and also amenability to therapeutic or preventive interventions can be dependent on genotype (see McClearn, Vogler, & Hofer, 2001).

Temporal Heterogeneity of Genetic and Environmental Influences

In midcentury, vigorous efforts were being made to merge Mendelian and quantitative genetics with embryology (see, for example, Grüneberg, 1952; Waddington, 1957; see also Singer, this volume). At the same time, the revolutionary new insights into gene action provided a new and enormously powerful conceptual tool for addressing the genetics of developmental processes. Among early avenues of molecular research was the regulation of gene expression—the turning on and turning off of genes. The phenomena associated with the molecular genetics of development are a central focus of current research, with enormous potential for uniting (or reuniting) genetics and the developmental sciences in a lifespan perspective.

Illustrative of this potential are the dramatic lifespan changes in gene expression that have emerged from studies of "heat-shock proteins" in *Drosophila*. These proteins are synthesized massively in response to exposure to heat stress or to other stressor agents. Some of them have also been found to change levels developmentally. For example, King and Tower (1999) showed that the RNA of a gene identified as *hsp22* is present throughout the body of *Drosophila*. Between days 6 and 30, this RNA level increased 60-fold in the head and 16-fold in the abdomen. In the thorax, *hsp22* RNA is abundant throughout but increases only 2.5-fold over the age span studied. A separate study revealed a 150-fold increase in the *hsp-22* protein between young and old flies. Other *hsp* genes displayed smaller age-related increase in transcription; *hsp23*, for example showed an approximate 5-fold induction in thorax.

Age-relevance was emphasized in observations on two cohorts of flies reared at different temperatures—25° and 29°C. This environmental difference resulted in median survival times of 52 and 32 days, respectively. *hsp22* protein was not detected until 40 days in the longer-lived cohort but was present already at 12 days in the shorter-lived. The authors note that the onset of *hsp22* protein induction approximately coincides with the beginning of the "dying phase" of the survival curve for the population.

On the basis of these and other results, Kurapati, Passananti, Rose, and Tower (2000) hypothesized that the induction of *hsp* genes during aging promotes extension of the functional life span of the flies. They tested this proposition by comparing the RNA levels of *hsp22* and *hsp23* in five lines of flies selectively bred for increased longevity and in five matched control lines. The hypothesis was resoundingly supported: RNAs of both *hsp* genes were significantly higher in the head and thorax (and possibly in the abdomen) of the more longevous lines. The largest difference was for *hsp22* RNA, which was 2-fold to 10-fold higher in the selected lines.

These heat-shock studies clearly illustrate the power of molecular genetic methods in elucidating the architecture of development.

The field of skeletal genetics offers several examples of chronological changes in gene effects in human beings. The major gene for the vitamin D receptor (*VDR*), for example, has a demonstrable effect on bone mass in prepubertal girls but not during postpubertal adolescence (Ferrari, Rizzoli, Slosman, & Bonjour, 1998). Polygenic examples are provided by Dequeker, Verstraeten, Guesens, and Gevers (1987) and Smith, Nance, Kang, Christian, and Johnston (1973), who have suggested genetic influence on appendicular cortical bone mass in adults but not in children and on axial trabecular bone mass in children but not in adults.

A pertinent example showing the utility of still (molecularly) uncharacterized quantitative trait loci is the dramatic change in QTLs related to growth in mice (Cheverud et al., 1996). Two distinct sets of QTLs were found, one affecting early growth with diminishing influence by about six weeks of age and another with effects first appearing during the interval from three to six weeks. The notion of different teams of genes coming into play during different developmental epochs is a useful heuristic image.

Analyses of change in genetic architecture are not restricted to the phenotypes affected by major genes but may also be undertaken with polygenic systems. Snieder, van Doornen, and Boomsma (1997) provide an example analysis of age dependency of gene expression for total cholesterol, low-density lipoprotein, high-density lipoprotein,

Table 16.1

Variance Components of Selected Health-Related Phenotypes in Older (65 and Older) and Younger (Less Than 65) Cohorts of SATSA Twins

Phenotype	"Younger" Cohort			"Older" Cohort		
	Genetic	Es	Ens	Genetic	Es	Ens
Cholesterol	.63	.18	.19	.32	.36	.31
Triglycerides	.73	0	.28	.28	0	.72
Diastolic BP	.22	.27	.51	.26	.08	.65
Systolic BP	.62	.07*	.31	.12	.24*	.64
FEV	.57	0	.43	.85	0	.15
Vital capacity	.57	0	.43	.27	.21	.52

Note: In this analysis, a common environmental component (Ec) was also estimated. Here, the E and Ec estimates are combined.

triglycerides, apolipoprotein A1, apolipoprotein B, and lipoprotein(a). Subjects were middle-aged parents (35 to 65 years) and their adolescent twin offspring and a separate sample of middle-aged twins (34 to 63 years). Heritability estimates ranged from substantial to high in both the young (.47 to .98) and middle-aged groups (.58 to .73). Evidence for a shared environmental influence was found only for ApoB. The results indicated further that partly different gene sets were involved in childhood and in adulthood for the lipids and lipoproteins but that the same genes influenced the apolipoproteins and lipoprotein (a) at both ages.

Further polygenic examples concerning strongly health-related phenotypes are provided by results from the Swedish Adoption/Twin Study of Aging (SATSA) (See Table 16.1). This study includes a number of twin pairs reared apart as well as those reared conventionally. This feature provides an enhanced power to distinguish environmental influences shared (Es) by twin pair members from nonshared (Ens) environmental influences. By dividing the study population into two groups, one older and one younger than 65 years, stability or changes in components of variance over age can be examined.

There is a generally held and not unreasonable proposition that with advancing age, there is an accumulation of effects of environment, with a consequent decline in the relative influence of genes. Some of these results are in accord with this expectation—the heritability of cholesterol, triglycerides (Heller, de Faire, Pedersen, Dahlén, & McClearn, 1993), systolic blood pressure (Hong, de Faire, Heller, McClearn, & Pedersen, 1994), and vital capacity (McClearn, Svartengren, Pedersen, Heller, & Plomin, 1994) all show decline in the genetic component in the older cohort relative to the younger cohort. This is not an invariant outcome, however. For forced expiratory volume, the heritability remains high in both age groups (McClearn et al., 1994), and diastolic blood pressure has a modest heritability in both. The pattern of environmental influences is also variable. In general, the Es estimates are lower than the Ens estimates. It is particularly interesting that for several phenotypes, the influence of the early shared rearing environment is greater in the older than in the younger cohort. Analyses of this sort may well be of great value in guiding the search for relevant environmental influences on these health-related variable.

Interactions in Development

Most any example of genotype X environment interaction implies a developmental process. Some examples with explicit developmental features may also be cited. A particularly clear case is provided by Rogina and Helfand (1995), who studied expression of a particular gene in the antennae of *Drosophila* that previously had been shown (Helfand et al., 1995) to vary with chronological age. Rate of aging of the flies was manipulated by temperature and by utilizing two other genes known to shorten life span. In all cases, the pattern of expression of the target gene was scaled proportionately to the life span rather than to chronological age. The authors note the compatibility of these observations with the "rate of living" hypothesis.

An example describing the influence of anonymous polygenes on susceptibility to intrauterine teratogens is that of Fraser and Fainstat (1951), who showed inbred strain differences in susceptibility to the cleft-palate-producing effects of cortisone injected to the mothers during pregnancy. Subsequently, Bonner and Slavkin (1975) provided evidence that the histocompatibility gene complex was a major factor in the strain difference of this susceptibility phenotype.

Postnatal environments were explored by Blizard and Randt (1974), who manipulated the rearing circumstances of mice of the two inbred strains along two dimensions. There were three environmental rearing conditions: "normal" rearing in opaque plastic cages with wire cage tops; "restricted" rearing in which opaque cage covers eliminated outside visual stimulation; and "enriched" rearing in a large clear lucite box containing a variety of manipulanda. Nutrition was also varied, with both a "normal" diet and a "reduced casein" diet. The various combinations of these conditions were imposed from 21 to 42 days of age, whereupon all animals were returned to normal laboratory conditions until measured on a test of activity and a "novel-object" test between 90 and 124 days of age. Complicated strain-condition interactions were observed. As a brief summary, animals of one strain revealed sensitivity to the effects of rearing condition on five of the seven measures that were derived from the test situations. Animals of the other strain, on the other hand, showed effects in only one aspect of the activity test situation. In sharp contrast, animals of the latter strain showed some effects of undernutrition, whereas the former were totally unaffected.

A summary example of gene-gene and gene-environment interaction with special pertinence to gerontology is provided by Vieira and colleagues (2000), who combined quantitative genetic and QTL perspectives in a study of longevity in *Drosophila*. The flies were reared in five different environments—standard culture, higher-than-standard temperature, lower-than-standard temperature, heat shock, and starvation stress. Seventeen quantitative trait loci were examined, and all displayed either sex or environment specificity or both. In a quantitative analysis, *all* of the significant genetic variation appeared in the genotype × sex and genotype × environment interaction terms. This work is a strong alerting signal that interactions may be of much greater significance than is usually appreciated when linear models are deployed.

The Fluctuation of Phenotypes

The focus of most gerontological research is on phenotypes that display a change in mean value as a function of chronological age. If individual differences appear in the rate of change of such a phenotype, then we must expect ordinal relationships among individuals to differ from occasion to occasion, given a developmentally significant time between occasions. Trans-occasion stabilities are of very considerable importance to any developmental science, imposing as they do a limit on predictability from one age to another. A case in point is the study of Heller and McClearn (1992), who measured tail tendon fiber break time, a putative biomarker of age, in mice of two inbred strains and their F_1 at 50, 150, 300, and 450 days of age. Because four fibers were measured from each mouse, coefficient alpha reliabilities could be computed (genotypes combined); these were above 0.93 for all occasions. Nonetheless, the correlation between 50 and 150 days was only 0.39. This particular system appears to become more stable phenotypically later in life, however, with the 150- to 300-day and the 300- to 450-day correlations being 0.60 and 076, respectively.

With shorter intervals between measurement occasions, the interoccasion stability (or lack thereof) is often taken as a reflection of measurement error, interpreted as being normally distributed around a "true" value. An example of fluctuation of a repeatedly measured phenotype may be taken from observations on voluntary alcohol consumption of mice of the BALB/c strain (see Figure 16.2). Both intraindividual variability and interindividual variability in that intraindividual variability are evident. Any single measure would obviously have limited value in characterizing an individual mouse on this phenotype.

As error theory informs us, a single measurement value must be regarded as only one sample from a distribution of values that could have been obtained for that organism at (about) the same time.

Nesselroade (1991) has expanded the conceptualization of intraindividual variability to include fluctuations due not to error but to dynamic processes (see also Molenaar, Huizenga, & Nesselroade, this volume; Nesselroade & Ghisletta, this volume). One model that addresses this source of variability is that of the negative feedback control system, features of which are descriptive of many homeostatic processes (Murphy & Trojak, 1983). Basically, the model concerns labile variables. A homing value or set point is posited to exist, together with a comparator that assesses departure of the variable from its set point and a mechanism for returning a deviant variable to that point. Variables considered over a time span must therefore be regarded as moving targets.

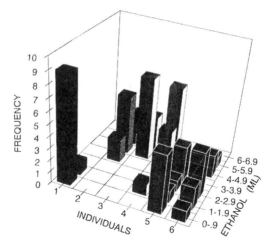

Figure 16.2   Frequency Distributions of 10 Consecutive Daily Alcohol Consumption Measurements from Six Individual Mice.

Some are moving more rapidly and more extensively than others. Body mass or skeletal dimensions, for example, in addition to genuine error, can display departures from the set point (and recovery to it) due to some environmental effect over days, weeks, or months. Other variables, such as blood pressure or locomotor activity, as examples, may respond in seconds or minutes.

For some variables, the displacing forces may be rare events; for others the system may be in a nearly constant state of displacement and recovery. Individual differences in magnitude of displacement, lag time in onset of recovery process, rate of recovery process, degree of damping, steady-state error, and other parameters of the control system may provide information of much greater value to the understanding of aging processes than the single measures that are commonly used (Murphy & Trojak, 1983).

It is also important to note that the notion of set point is applicable for a limited period in a lifespan trajectory. For lifespan developmental purposes, it is important to extend the basic concept of homeostasis to accommodate change processes. Thus, the terms *homeorhesis* (Waddington, 1957) and *rheostasis* (Mrosovsky, 1990) refer to "set points" changing dynamically either in response to an intrinsic program or to environmental stimuli.

Genetics and Fluctuation

Phenotypic fluctuation—its existence, causes, and assessment—has obviously significant implications for research design and for analytical procedures. From the present perspective, the relevant issue is the extent of genetic influence on the phenotypic fluctuability. Berg (1987), for example, has discussed the implications of the existence of "variability" genes, and Murphy and Trojak (1986) have discussed genetics and "laxity" of phenotypes in quantitative homeostasis. In a recent work of specific relevance to gerontology, de Haan, Gelman, Watson, Yunis, and Van Zant (1998) have identified quantitative trait loci affecting variability in longevity within the uniform genotypes of different recombinant inbred strains of mice.

An example of genetic influence on a intermediate-term recovery process is provided by Ross (1985), who evaluated catch-up growth in two inbred mouse strains and in derived F_1 and F_2 generations. Animals were maintained by food restriction approximately at their 21-day weight until 42 days of age, at which time they were given unlimited access to food. Body weights following realimentation were compared to the means of normally reared animals from each of the genotypic groups, which provided an estimate of the respective set points. There was strong evidence of inbreeding depression in the slow and incomplete growth of the inbred animals of both strains. By comparison, the F_1 animals displayed an accelerated growth almost precisely to the level of their controls, and the F_2 animals were only slightly less efficient than that. The explanation of the superiority of the heterogeneous mice in catch-up growth would appear to reside in the well-known phenomenon of hybrid vigor arising from heterozygosity.

Yet another contribution to the homeostatic fuzziness (Nesselroade's "hum") of a single measure of some phenotypes is their intrinsic cyclicity. Phenotypes well known to be subject to periodic variation include locomotor activity, sleep and waking, eating, hormone levels, and many others, and good experimental practice typically limits the assessment of such variables to relatively narrow temporal intervals.

There are two genetic perspectives on such cyclicity—the role of genes in establishing the cyclical pattern and the actual changes in gene expression during the cycles. Examples of the former include alleles of a gene named period (*per*) (Konopka & Benzer, 1971) that disrupt the biological clock that influences pupal eclosion time and locomotor activity in *Drosophila*. One mutant form of the gene reduces and one lengthens the normally diurnal pattern, and another provides an arrhythmic pattern.

A particular type of gene-environment interaction is that in which gene expression is altered as a consequence of environmental influences. One example involves the behavioral stress of immobilization in Sprague-Dawley rats (McMahon et al., 1992). Immobilization for two hours per day for seven consecutive days resulted in elevation of levels of the mRNAs of the genes that specify tyrosine hydroxylase and dopamine β-hydroxylase in the adrenal glands. A single immobilization elevated only the tyrosine hydroxylase mRNA. Thus, the temporal scale for this alteration in gene expression is on the order of days or a week.

As a brief summary, then, the genetic and environmental architecture of developmental processes can be regarded as kaleidoscopic. Some of the genes may be turned on early (perhaps from fertilization) and stay on; some may swing into action during a specific developmental epoch according to developmental schedule and stay on; some may oscillate, either in a circannual, circadian, or some other cyclic pattern; others may be called into play in response to environmental slings and arrows (or, to include as well positive environmental influences, we might use the companion Shakespearean notion of "buffets and rewards"). Thus, in considering the genetic influence on any given phenotype at any given time, the notion of "momentary effective genotype" (modified from Hullian learning theory of the 1950s) conveys an appropriate sense of the dynamism of the genotype.

In general, the various alterations in the effective genotype can be considered in terms of frequency or rate of change. The standard quantitative genetic model appears to be most powerful in addressing phenotypes that are relatively stable and slow-changing. Estimation of the "true" values or set points of phenotypes that are subject to rapid, high-frequency fluctuations may be problematic (unless multiple measurements are possible), with one possible result being an inflation of the estimate of the unshared environmental component. Such situations may best be approached by characterization of the parameters of the system (Murphy & Trojak, 1983; see also Molenaar, Huizenga, & Nesselroade, this volume).

No one of these genetic perspectives alone provides the whole story of inheritance in complex situations such as those of aging processes. There is increasing realization that the incredibly powerful reductionist tools of molecular genetics must be complemented by an integrationist perspective (see, for example, Maddox, 1998) and that this blend must be informed by considerations from the "sciences of complexity." Of particular relevance to the present topic are the observations of Molenaar, Boomsma, and Dolan (1993), Molenaar, Huizenga, and Nesselroade (this volume), and Nesselroade and Ghisletta (this volume), who emphasize that nonlinear epigenetic processes may account for much of the "nonshared" environmental variance component in quantitative genetic analyses. Similarly, Finch and Kirkwood (2000) have explored chance and random events and stochastic processes in the context of genes and environment in aging (see also Baltes, this volume; Kirkwood, this volume). Jazwinski (1996) and Yates, Marsh, and Iberall (1972) have been especially persuasive about the relevance of systems concepts to the phenomena of aging. Such a comprehensive view—embracing the language, concepts, and methods of parallel pathways, network causality, hierarchical organization, catastrophes, bifurcations in chaotic systems, feedback loops—is just emerging and will undoubtedly play a major role in the fusion of the theoretical and empirical armamentaria of the various genetic sciences in the study of the dynamism of the interactions and coactions of the genes and environment in lifespan development (see also Baltes, this volume; Maier & Vaupel, this volume; Roberts & Caspi, this volume.) Our understanding of the architecture of development will be markedly enriched by these perspectives.

References

Arking, R. (1991). *Biology of aging: Observations and principles*. Englewood Cliffs, NJ: Prentice-Hall.
Berg, K. (1987). Genetics of coronary heart disease and its risk factors. In G. Bock & G. M. Collins (Eds.), *Symposium on molecular approaches to human polygenic disease*. Chichester, UK: Wiley.

Blizard, D. A., & Randt, C. T. (1974). Genotype interaction with undernutrition and external environment in early life. *Nature, 251,* 705–707.

Bonner, J. J., & Slavkin, H. C. (1975). Cleft palate susceptibility linked to histocompatibility-2 (*H-2*) in the mouse. *Immunogenetics, 2,* 213–218.

Bouchard, C., Tremblay, A., Despres, J.-P., Nadeau, A., Lupien, P. J., Theriault, G., et al. (1990). The response to long-term overfeeding in identical twins. *New England Journal of Medicine, 322,* 1477–1482.

Cheverud, J. M., Routman, E. J., Duarte, F. A. M., van Swinderen, B., Cothran, K., & Perel, C. (1996). Quantitative trait loci for murine growth. *Genetics, 142,* 1305–1319.

Coleman, D. L., & Hummel, K. P. (1975). Influence of genetic background on the expression of mutations at the diabetes locus in the mouse. II. Studies on background modifiers. *Israeli Journal of Medical Science, 11,* 708–713.

Cooper, R. M., & Zubek, J. P. (1958). Effects of enriched and restricted early environments on the learning ability of bright and dull rats. *Canadian Journal of Psychology, 12,* 159–164.

de Haan, G., Gelman, R., Watson, A., Yunis, E., & Van Zant, G. (1998). A putative gene causes variability in lifespan among genotypically identical mice. *Nature Genetics, 19,* 114–116.

Deitrich, R. A. (2000). Personal communication.

Dequeker, J., Nijs, J., Verstraeten, A., Guesens, P., & Gevers, G. (1987). Genetic determinants of bone mineral content at the spine and the radius: A twin study. *Bone, 8,* 207–209.

Falconer, D. S., & Mackay, T. F. C. (1996). *Introduction to quantitative genetics* (4th ed.). Essex, UK: Longman.

Ferrari, S. L., Rizzoli, R., Slosman, D. O., & Bonjour, J. P. (1998). Do dietary calcium and age explain the controversy surrounding the relationship between bone mineral density and vitamin D receptor gene polymorphisms? *Journal of Bone and Mineral Research, 13,* 363–370.

Finch, C. E., & Kirkwood, T. B. L. (2000). *Chance, development and aging.* Oxford: Oxford University Press.

Finch, C. E., & Tanzi, R. E. (1997). Genetics of aging. *Science, 278,* 407–411.

Fisher, R. A. (1918). The correlation between relatives on the supposition of Mendelian inheritance. *Transactions of the Royal Society of Edinburgh, 52,* 399–433.

Fölling, A. (1934). Phenylpyruvic acid as a metabolic anomaly in connection with imbecility. *Nordisk Medicinsk Tidsknft, 8,* 1054–1059.

Fosmire, G. J., Focht, S. J., & McClearn, G. E. (1993). Genetic influences on tissue deposition of aluminum in mice. *Biological Trace Element Research, 37,* 115–121.

Fowler, R. E., & Edwards, R. G. (1961). "Midget," a new dwarfing gene in the house mouse dependent on a genetic background of small body size for its expression. *Genetic Research, 2,* 272–282.

Fraser, F. C., & Fainstat, T. D. (1951). Production of congenital defects in the offspring of pregnant mice treated with cortisone. *Pediatrics, 8,* 527–533.

Grüneberg, H. (1952). *The genetics of the mouse* (2nd ed.). The Hague: Martinus Nijhoff.

Harrison, D. E., & Roderick, T. H. (1997). Selection for maximum longevity in mice. *Experimental Gerontology, 32,* 65–78.

Helfand, S. L., Blake, K. J., Rogina, B., Stracks, M. D., Centurion, A., & Naprta, B. (1995). Temporal patterns of gene expression in the antenna of the adult *Drosophila melanogaster. Genetics, 140,* 549–555.

Heller, D. A., de Faire, U., Pedersen, N. L., Dahlén, G., & McClearn, G. E. (1993). Reduced importance of genetic influences for serum lipids in the elderly: A study of twins reared apart. *New England Journal of Medicine, 328,* 1150–1156.

Heller, D. A., & McClearn, G. E. (1992). A longitudinal genetic study of tail tendon fibre break time. *Age and Ageing, 21,* 129–134.

Hong, Y., de Faire, U., Heller, D. A., McClearn, G. E., & Pedersen, N. (1994). Genetic and environmental influences on blood pressure in elderly twins. *Hypertension, 24,* 663–670.

Jazwinski, S. M. (1996). Longevity, genes, and aging. *Science, 273,* 54–59.

Johnson, T. E. (1997). Genetic influences on aging. *Experimental Gerontology, 32*, 11–22.

Kacser, H., & Burns, J. A. (1979). Molecular democracy: Who shares the controls? *Biochemical Society Transactions, 7*, 1149–1160.

Kamboh, M. I., Sanghera, D. K., Ferrell, R. E., & DeKosky, S. T. (1995). *APOE*4*-associated Alzheimer's disease risk is modified by alpha 1-antichymotrypsin polymorphism. *Nature Genetics, 10*, 486–488.

Keller, E. F. (1994). Rethinking the meaning of genetic determinism. In G. B. Peterson (Ed.), *The tanner lectures on human values*. Salt Lake City: University of Utah Press.

King, V., & Tower, J. (1999). Aging-specific expression of *Drosophila hsp22*. *Developmental Biology, 207*, 107–118.

Konopka, R. J., & Benzer, S. (1971). Clock mutants of *Drosophila melanogaster*. *Proceedings of the National Academy of Science, 68*, 2112–2116.

Kurapati, R., Passananti, H. B., Rose, M. R., & Tower, J. (2000). Increased *hsp22* RNA levels in *Drosophila* lines genetically selected for increased longevity. *Journal of Gerontology: Biological Sciences and Medical Sciences, 55A*, B552–B559.

Lyman, F. L. (Ed.). (1963). *Phenylketonuria*. Springfield: Thomas.

Mackie, J. L. (1974). *The cement of the universe*. Oxford: Clarendon Press.

Maddox, J. (1998). *What remains to be discovered*. New York: Free Press.

Martin, G. M. (1996). Genetic modulation of the senescent phenotype of *Homo sapiens*. *Experimental Gerontology, 31*, 49–59.

McClearn, G. E., & Hofer, S. M. (1999). Genes as gerontological variables: Uses of genetically heterogeneous stocks. *Neurobiology of Aging, 20*, 147–156.

McClearn, G. E., & Kakihana, R. (1981). Selective breeding for ethanol sensitivity: SS and LS mice. In G. E. McClearn, R. A. Deitrich, & V. G. Erwin (Eds.), *Development of animal models as pharmacogenetic tools* (DHEW Publication No. [ADM] 81-1133) (pp. 147–159). Washington, DC: U.S. Government Printing Office.

McClearn, G. E., Plomin, R., Gora-Maslak, G., & Crabbe, J. C. (1991). The gene chase in behavioral science. *Psychological Science, 2*, 222–229.

McClearn, G. E., Svartengren, M., Pedersen, N. L., Heller, D. A., & Plomin, R. (1994). Genetic and environmental influences on pulmonary function in aging Swedish twins. *Journal of Gerontology: Medical Sciences, 49*, M264–M268.

McClearn, G. E., & Vogler, G. P. (2001). The genetics of behavioral aging. In J. E. Birren & K. W. Schaie (Eds.), *Handbook of the psychology of aging* (5th ed., pp. 109–131). San Diego: Academic Press.

McClearn, G. E., Vogler, G. P., & Hofer, S. M. (2001). Environment-gene and gene-gene interactions. In E. J. Masoro & S. N. Austad (Eds.), *Handbook of the biology of aging* (5th ed., pp. 413–434). San Diego: Academic Press.

McMahon, A., Kvetnansky, R., Fukuhara, K., Weise, V. K., Kopin, I. J., & Sabban, E. L. (1992). Regulation of tyrosine hydroxylase and dopamine B-hydroxylase mRNA levels in rat adrenals by a single and repeated immobilization stress. *Journal of Neurochemistry, 58*, 2124–2130.

Miller, R. A. (1999). Kleemeier Award Lecture: Are there genes for aging? *Journal of Gerontology: Biological Sciences, 7*, B297–B307.

Miller, R. A., Austad, S., Burke, D., Chrisp, C., Dysko, R., Galecki, A, et al. (1999). Exotic mice as models for aging research: Polemic and prospectus. *Neurobiology of Aging, 20*, 217–231.

Molenaar, P. C. M., Boomsma, D. I., & Dolan, C. V. (1993). A third source of developmental differences. *Behavior Genetics, 23*, 519–524.

Mrosovsky, N. (1990). *Rheostasis: The physiology of change*. Oxford: Oxford University Press.

Murphy, E. A., & Trojak, J. E. (1983). The dynamics of quantifiable homeostasis. I. The individual. *American Journal of Human Genetics, 15*, 275–290.

Murphy, E. A., & Trojak, J. L. (1986). The genetics of quantifiable homeostasis: I. The general issues. *American Journal of Medical Genetics, 24*, 159–169.

Nesselroade, J. R. (1991). The warp and woof of development's fabric. In R. Downs, L. Liben, &

D. S. Palermo (Eds.), *Visions of development, the environment and aesthetics: The legacy of Joachim Wohlwill*. Hillsdale, NJ: Erlbaum.

Rogina, B., & Helfand, S. L. (1995). Regulation of gene expression is linked to life span in adult *Drosophila*. *Genetics, 141*, 1043–1048.

Rose, M. R. (1991). *Evolutionary biology of aging*. Oxford: Oxford University Press.

Ross, H. L. (1985). *Evidence for genetic factors in catch-up growth*. Master's thesis, Pennsylvania State University, University Park, PA.

Sattler, R. (1986). *Biophilosophy: Analytic and holistic perspectives*. Berlin: Springer.

Shmookler Reis, R. J., & Ebert, R. H., II. (1996). Genetics of aging: Current animal models. *Experimental Gerontology, 31*, 69–81.

Smith, D. M., Nance, W. E., Kang, K. W., Christian, J. C., & Johnston, C. C., Jr. (1973). Genetic factors in determining bone mass. *Journal of Clinical Investigation, 52*, 2800–2808.

Snieder, H., van Doornen, L. J. P., & Boomsma, D.I. (1997). The age dependency of gene expression for plasma lipids, lipoproteins, and apolipoproteins. *American Journal of Human Genetics, 60*, 638–650.

Vieira, C., Pasyukova, E. G., Zeng, Z. -B., Hackett, J. B., Lyman, R. F., & Mackay, T. F. C. (2000). Genotype-environment interaction for quantitative trait loci affecting life span in *Drosophila melanogaster*. *Genetics, 154*, 213–227.

Waddington, C. H. (1957). *The strategy of the genes*. New York: Macmillan.

Yates, F. E., Marsh, D. J., & Iberall, A. S. (1972). Integration of the whole organism: A foundation for a theoretical biology. In J. A. Behnke (Ed.), *Challenging biological problems: Directions toward their solution*. Fairlawn, NY: Oxford University Press.

Acknowledgment

The cited examples from the author's own work were supported variously by the MacArthur Foundation Research Network on Successful Aging; NIA grants AG04948, AG09333; AG08861, AG04563, AG10175, and AG14731; NIAAA grant AA08125; and by funds from the Center for Developmental and Health Genetics of the Pennsylvania State University.

VI
The Future of Lifespan Psychology: Comments from Related Fields and Neighboring Disciplines

17 The Future of Lifespan Developmental Psychology: Perspectives from Control Theory

Jutta Heckhausen

University of California, Irvine, CA, U.S.A.

Abstract

In this chapter, future perspectives for lifespan developmental psychology are developed on the basis of propositions of the lifespan theory of control (Heckhausen, 1999a; Heckhausen & Schulz, 1995; Schulz & Heckhausen, 1996). Four propositions about key issues in lifespan research are addressed. First, the issue of criteria for adaptive development is discussed in light of the debate about primary control striving as an anthropological constant versus as an age- and culture-dependent characteristic of human functioning. Second, processes of control and regulation in development are directed not only at the external world but also at internal representations and most important the motivational resources of the individual. These latter processes of secondary control are indispensable components of developmental regulation. Third, human ontogeny requires regulation to realize developmental potential. The three major forces—biology, culture and society, and the individual—share this regulatory requirement in different constellations of relative power across different times during the human lifespan, as well as across historical time and sociocultural setting. However, it is proposed that there is a limited set of adaptive constellations of biological, cultural and societal, and individual regulations, which are characterized by positive tradeoffs between the three forces and simultaneously minimal overdetermination. Such constellations yield systems of developmental regulation, which are both stable and productive. Fourth, an agenda for process-oriented developmental research is outlined. Key processes in developmental regulation (such as goal engagement, goal disengagement, selection and compensation) are not only recognized as potentially adaptive but are identified as tailored to specific developmental ecologies and orchestrated for specific developmental goals.

This chapter offers a perspective on the future of lifespan developmental psychology that is based on the lifespan theory of control (Heckhausen & Schulz, 1995; Schulz & Heckhausen, 1996). The lifespan theory of control was developed at a time when lifespan developmental psychology had been institutionalized as a subdiscipline in the scientific community of psychologists and neighboring disciplines (such as life-course sociology and health psychology) had begun to establish long-term cooperations with lifespan researchers.

Lifespan developmental psychology as reflected in the chapter by Baltes in this volume (see also Baltes, 1987; Baltes, Reese, & Lipsitt, 1980; Reese & Overton, 1970) has not only been highly successful in the institutionalization of the lifespan approach in research and education (for example, the West Virginia University conferences, its series of edited volumes on lifespan development, and its graduate programs in lifespan developmental psychology in several departments) but has also contributed major conceptual advances (see review in Baltes, Lindenberger, & Staudinger, 1998). The concept of development was extended far beyond childhood, thus encompassing the entire lifespan. It was also differentiated as a combined and multidimensional process of gains and losses at all ages. Moreover, the pioneers of lifespan psychology addressed the issue of intraindividual plasticity, thus opening the field of training, intervention, and lifelong learning (see review in Glück & Heckhausen, 2001). A complementary agenda for research was presented with the study of interindividual differences in developmental change, an area that drew particularly strong interest and research efforts in the field of life-course sociology (Elder, 1985). Intra- and interindividual change are best accounted for by the joint influences of three types of contextual factors: age-graded (influences associated with chronological age and experienced by all members of an age group), history-graded (influences associated with historical period and experienced by all living individuals at a given time in history), and nonnormative (influences unrelated to age or historical time and experienced by some individuals). Finally, lifespan developmental psychology focused attention on three general processes of development—the selection of areas of functioning to invest resources in, the compensation of weaknesses or losses, and the optimization of functioning in selected areas. With these conceptual and countless empirical contributions, lifespan developmental psychology laid the foundation and set the research agenda for the past three decades.

A striking characteristic of these early and fundamental propositions was their abstractness and openness for various perspectives, thus forming a metatheoretical platform with much integrative potential. As founders of a field, the early lifespan developmental researchers were ingenious in proposing proto- or metatheoretical propositions that excluded few and allowed many to project their own theoretical concepts and empirical phenomena into a common framework of lifespan developmental psychology. Hence, lifespan developmental psychology provided a broad intellectual home for many models of development in certain domains of functioning and also enticed interest in developmental questions among nondevelopmentalists in the fields of cognition, personality, and social behavior. In this way, lifespan developmental psychology became a thriving, multifaceted area of research with several subdisciplines and paradigms.

However, as the field developed, became more differentiated and elaborate, and established links to other areas of psychology, it discovered a need for up-to-date process-oriented models of development. In recent years, a set of such models was developed, each with its specific historical foundation, function, and preferred domain of application.

Some researchers opted for a research agenda, which applies the original lifespan developmental concepts of selection, optimization, and compensation (SOC) to various areas of functioning, while preserving their scope as general concepts of development and human behavior (e.g., Freund & Baltes, 1998, 2000; see also review in Baltes et al., 1998). The SOC approach is discussed in detail in the chapter by Margret Baltes and Laura Carstensen in this volume.

Another major contribution is the dual-process coping model by Brandtstädter and his colleagues (Brandtstädter, 1998; Brandtstädter & Rothermund, this volume; Brandtstädter & Renner, 1990; Brandtstädter & Greve, 1994; Brandtstädter & Rothermund, 1994; Brandtstädter, Wentura, & Greve, 1993), which is founded in action theory and distinguishes two major ways of coping with obstacles to goal attainment— assimilation and accommodation. *Assimilation* refers to active and intentional attempts to change the environment of the self, whereas *accommodation* addresses nonintentional changes in valuations of goals (such as "sour grapes") or cognitions about goal striving (such as redefining personal attributes) that reflect adjustments to objective goal blocking. The dual-process model of coping is discussed in detail in the chapter by Brandtstädter and Rothermund in this volume.

The present chapter focuses on a third approach—the lifespan theory of control (Heckhausen & Schulz, 1993, 1995; Schulz & Heckhausen, 1996)—and raises some issues that are relevant for the field and are more or less well addressed by the different approaches. Specifically, three issues are discussed—the criteria of adaptiveness in developmental regulation and its implications for a hierarchical versus parallel structure of the model; the regulation of internal processes such as motivation and emotion; and the interplay of biological, societal, and individual influences in shaping human life courses and development.

Key Propositions of the Lifespan Theory of Control

The lifespan theory of control started with theoretical propositions of control theory, a process-oriented approach to universals in human behavior. Universal mechanisms and processes involved in pursuing goals of gaining, maintaining, or extending control were proposed to operate when individuals attempt to regulate their development. In this application of control theory, the long-standing and widely used concepts of selection and of compensation as basic processes in human development (e.g., Bäckman, & Dixon, 1992; Baltes & Baltes, 1990; Baltes et al., 1998; Carstensen, 1993, Gottlieb,

1991; Salthouse, 1991; Vaughan, 1926; Waddington, 1957) are integrated with the model of primary and secondary control.

Heckhausen and Schulz (1995; Schulz & Heckhausen, 1996) have developed the lifespan theory of control, which proposes that the desire to exert control over one's environment and thus realize primary control rules the system of control behavior in humans and at least in mammals in general (for the phylogenetic roots of control behavior, see Heckhausen, 2000b). The lifespan theory of control elaborates the distinction between primary and secondary control, originally proposed by Rothbaum, Weisz, and Snyder (1982), and applies it to the human lifespan. *Primary control* is directed at the external world and comprises attempts to produce effects in the environment (for example, to solve a puzzle, write a paper, or persuade a skeptic listener). *Secondary control*, by contrast, is directed at the inner world of the individual and serves to optimize motivational and emotional resources needed for primary control striving (for example, to boost one's control beliefs when pursuing a goal, blame failure on others, or compare oneself with inferior others after having suffered a blow to self-esteem). Primary control striving is expected to remain the dominant motivator of behavior across the lifespan, while the potential to realize primary control undergoes radical changes across age (see also Heckhausen, 1999a). During childhood, adolescence, and young adulthood, primary-control potential increases substantially, reaches a maximum plateau during midlife, and declines with the loss of social roles and physical fitness associated with old age. The increasing discrepancy between primary-control striving and primary-control potential at older ages provides a challenge and potential threat for the individual, which can be managed only by disengagement from age-inappropriate goals and engagement with new more age-adapted goals. For example, older adults may have to disengage from a busy schedule of activities, which require much mobility, and focus instead on activities that can be performed closer to their homes.

Primary and secondary control strategies are orchestrated (individually and/or jointly activated and deactivated) according to action phases in cycles of action directed at attaining goals (Heckhausen, 1999a). The typical action cycle starts with the selection of a goal to pursue—for instance, the goal to achieve a promotion in one's career. In the case of developmental regulation, optimized goal choice (*optimization*) needs to take into account the opportunities and constraints for goal attainment present in the given developmental ecology. Moreover, goal choice should be optimized with regard to the implications of goal investment for other domains (such as side effects of career investments for family building) and with regard to long-term consequences. Finally, optimized goal choice will maintain moderate diversity in domains of functioning that the individual is investing in, so that vulnerability of excessive domain selection is avoided.

Once a developmental goal is chosen as one of the active goals, a specific set of control strategies that comprises goal engagement is activated (Heckhausen, 1999a; Wrosch & Heckhausen, 1999). Typically, goal engagement involves selective primary control and selective secondary control. *Selective primary control* refers to the investment of behavioral means (time, effort, and skills) into pursuing a goal. *Selective secondary control* serves to enhance and maintain motivational commitment to a chosen action goal, particularly when it is challenged by unexpected obstacles or attractive alternatives. Selective secondary-control strategies include enhanced valuation of the chosen goal, devaluation of nonchosen alternatives, as well as positive illusions about one's control potential for the chosen goal (about contrasting functions of perceived control during goal engagement and goal disengagement, see Lang & Heckhausen, 2001). In addition, *compensatory primary control* may be required when internally available behavioral resources of the individual are insufficient to attain the goal and external resources have to be recruited. Specifically, compensatory primary control addresses the recruitment of help or advice from others, the use of technical aids (such as a wheelchair), or the employment of unusual behavioral means typically not involved in the activity (lip reading to compensate for a hearing disability). Thus, when thinking in terms of the example of striving for a career promotion, the person who has set this goal for herself will invest more time and effort into work (selective primary control), imagine the positive consequences and pride that would come with achieving the promotion (selective secondary control), and seek advice from more advanced colleagues on effective strategies to foster career success.

When the individual experiences a loss of control and when the goal becomes unattainable or excessively costly, the individual needs to disengage from the goal. In contrast to the motivational mind set of goal engagement, goal disengagement requires *compensatory secondary control*. Compensatory secondary control can be attained by deactivating the obsolete goal, possibly in favor of engaging with an alternative or substitute goal. In addition, compensatory secondary control involves specific self-protective strategies, such as self-protective causal attribution (avoid self-blame) and downward social comparisons, which deflect the potential negative effects of failure experiences on important motivational resources of affective balance and self-esteem. In the context of our example about career striving, the person might find out that she was passed up for a promotion, the slots for superior level positions are used up, and the promotion is therefore unattainable. This should prompt the person to disengage from the career goal by thinking about the negative sides (such as a greater workload) of a promotion. In addition, potential threats implied in this loss of control for self-esteem need to be buffered—for instance, by looking for indications that the supervisor who made the decision strongly favors the colleague who did get promoted.

Universal Versus Relativistic Criteria for Adaptiveness

The lifespan theory of control asserts that the ultimate criterion of adaptiveness in developmental regulation and behavior in general is whether the overall control potential of the organism is optimized (Heckhausen, 1999a; Heckhausen & Schulz, 1995, 1999; Schulz & Heckhausen, 1996; 1997). The motivational system of humans is not structured in such a way as to maximize positive affect, self-esteem, or subjective well-being in general. Instead, affective responses to experiences of control gains or control losses promote persistent effort to overcome loss, while adapting swiftly to control extensions (Schulz & Heckhausen, 1997; see also Frijda, 1988). Negative changes are typically responded to by prolonged and pronounced negative affect; positive changes elicit only brief positive affect and habituate swiftly (see review in Frijda, 1988). Therefore, while an individual is proximately motivated to feel good or competent, the evolution of human emotion has formed a system of proximate motivators that as its ultimate cause promotes prolonged striving for regaining primary control after a loss and for extending primary control soon after a gain in control. Irreversible losses of control are eventually adapted to, but only to recapture control at the next level of functioning. For example, a person confronted with a severe loss in vision may give up striving for regaining the sensory function but invest in preventing the sensory loss from unduly infringing on primary control involved in activities of daily living (for example, by learning Braille or reorganizing the apartment). The tradeoff between primary control and subjective well-being is drastically illustrated by research on the relationship between pain, illness, activity restriction, and depression medication. Williamson and Schulz (1992, 1995) showed that pain and illness lead to depression only to the extent that they bring about activity restriction, especially in younger adults for whom activity restrictions imply a greater loss of primary control in their lifespan.

The SOC model (Baltes & Carstensen, this volume) and Brandtstädter's dual-process of coping model (Brandtstädter & Rothermund, this volume) formulate positions that give no priority to either objective or subjective criteria of adaptiveness. Brandtstädter's dual-process model makes no specific proposition about criteria for successful development, although the model's assumption about assimilation preceding accommodation hints to a position that gives primacy to objective over subjective criteria.

The proponents of the SOC model discuss the issue of criteria for adaptiveness at length (Baltes & Baltes, 1990; Baltes & Carstensen, this volume; Marsiske, Lang, Baltes, & Baltes, 1995). In their seminal chapter about successful development, Paul and Margret Baltes (Baltes & Baltes, 1990) assert that researchers should not attempt to establish a universal set of criteria for adaptive functioning or successful aging. Instead, they propose, "successful aging requires a value-based, systemic, and ecological perspective. Both subjective and objective indicators need to be considered within a given cultural context with its particular contents and ecological demands" (Baltes & Baltes, 1990, p. 7). In the further discussion of this issue in the context of the model of selective optimization with compensation, successful development has been defined as "realization of desired outcomes and the avoidance of undesired outcomes" (Marsiske et al., 1995) or as the "relative maximization of gains and the minimization of losses" (see Baltes, 1997, p. 367, also this volume).

Positions such as these—which define control in terms of subjective experiences of gains, and losses, which are a function of the temporal, social, and domain-specific frame of reference—are ultimately relativistic, a fact that Paul Baltes notes with assertion: "I consider it the special strength of the theory [i.e., the SOC model] that it is at the same time relativistic and universalistic" (see Baltes, 1997, p. 372, also this volume). The key feature of these criteria is that success is defined in relation to personal goals and aspirations which are thought to vary over time and sociocultural contexts. Thus, individuals who by some objective standards accomplish relatively little within a given domain or who narrowly select highly idiosyncratic goals at the expense of other major domains of functioning can experience high levels of satisfaction and success and would therefore be labeled successful developers.

Adopting these highly individualized and subjective criteria as gauges for successful development is problematic for various reasons (see also Schulz & Heckhausen, 1999). First, they open the door for any indicator to meet the criteria of success because the criteria are individually determined. Second, the absence of validity anchors for evaluating patterns of regulation leads to the conception that specific strategies of regulation such as selection or compensation are viewed as adaptive in and of themselves. However, specific strategies are adaptive only insofar as they reflect and make use of the developmental opportunities in a given developmental ecology and maximize outcomes with regard to a criterion of adaptiveness. Examples of nonadaptive selection are selections of wrong options or excessive selection, which render the individual vulnerable for defeats in the selected domain. Similarly, compensation may be unwarranted and thus undermine functioning more than promote it. Instead, a nonrelativistic stance makes clear that specific strategies need to be evaluated in light of their power to maximize desired developmental outcomes, such as high levels of functioning. Third, subjective criteria are subject to the rationalization biases characteristic of individuals when they retrospectively evaluate their own experiences and accomplishments. And fourth, a relativistic perspective fails to take advantage of the fact that all cultures are characterized by considerable consensus regarding what constitutes success.

In contrast to such a relativistic position, other approaches to successful aging and development emphasize physical functioning and absence of disability (Rowe & Kahn, 1998; Berkman et al., 1993), cognitive and intellectual performance (Lehman, 1953; Salthouse, 1991; Simonton, 1988, 1990, 1994), achievements in physical (Schulz & Curnow, 1988; Schulz, Musa, Staszewski, & Siegler, 1994; Ericsson, 1990; Ericsson & Charness, 1994), or artistic domains (Ericsson, Krampe, & Tesch-Römer, 1993; Lehman, 1953; Simonton, 1988, 1994). These paradigms focus on criteria of success that are externally measurable and include domains of functioning that have been and continue to be valued by cultures throughout time. These include physical functioning, cognitive, intellectual, affective, and creative functioning, and social relations.

Of course, tradeoffs have to be made in attempting to maximize functioning in individual or multiple domains, with the latter requiring the consideration of long-term and cross-domain consequences of engaging with or disengaging from a goal. In this context, subjective evaluations such as satisfaction with aging also play their role as one of many components of affective and intellectual functioning but are not treated as the major criteria of successful development (see Smith, this volume).

Control theory uses the potential for primary control as a summary concept of more objectified aspects of functioning. Along with physical and cognitive functioning, these include an individual's motivational and emotional resources for control. In such an approach, satisfaction, feelings of self-worth, and hopefulness not per se are viewed as adaptive but only as resources for active agency in shaping one's environment. This enables the researcher to generate specific predictions about adaptive versus maladaptive behavior and cognitions in individuals facing a developmental challenge—for example, when negotiating a life-course transition. In process-modeling terms, the regulation of development is governed by engagement with and disengagement from developmental goals that respond to the individual's developmental ecology with its opportunities and constraints (Heckhausen, 1999a). This optimized goal choice (combined goal engagement with appropriate and disengagement from inappropriate goals) guides the activation of control strategies that either serve active goal pursuit or disengagement from a goal and self-protection). Thus, optimized goal choice represents a higher-order regulatory process that activates and deactivates control strategies. The adaptiveness is produced by this process of optimized goal choice and not by the usage of control strategies themselves.

The future research agenda on developmental regulation should include a focus on the question of how cycles of goal engagement and disengagement are connected. In other words, how does the individual proceed from one cycle to choosing a new goal and domain of functioning to invest in? This question is relevant for cases of developmental loss—when the individual has to disengage from unobtainable goals and decide to invest his or her resources into adjusted or downgraded goals within the domain or into related or even remote domains of functioning. Reselection of goals also occurs when success has been accomplished. The individual can either capitalize on this success by moving along to more ambitious goals within the domain, or she can use the success to switch resources over to a domain previously neglected. Interesting models about diminishing payoffs within broader domains of psychological functioning are suggested by researchers in the tradition of rational choice (*social production function theory*) (Lindenberg, 1996; Ormel, Lindenberg, Steverink, & VonKorff, 1997; Steverink, Lindenberg, & Ormel, 1998) and from *self-determination theory* (DeCharms, 1968; see particularly *basic needs theory*, in Deci & Ryan, 1985; Ryan & Deci, 2000; Ryan, Kuhl, & Deci, 1997). Integrating such conceptions would allow control theory to move beyond studying the action cycle within the pursuit of a given goal and include the sequence and transition from one action cycle to the next. Of course, such a model would need to include interindividual differences in motive profiles and propensity for certain patterns of control processes.

Regulation of Motivational Orientation for Goal Engagement and Goal Disengagement

Goal engagement and goal disengagement require different motivational orientations. The SOC model has so far not specifically addressed the motivational processes involved in goal pursuit and goal deactivation, although recent publications have listed engagement processes such as goal commitment under the component of selection (Freund & Baltes, 1998, 2000). Brandtstädter's dual-process model and the lifespan theory of control have specifically targeted motivational processes involved in goal engagement and goal disengagement. Recent developments in this field of inquiry are discussed next.

The lifespan theory of control has been applied to developmental regulation by specifying an action-phase model of developmental goal pursuit (Heckhausen, 1999a). This conception builds on action-phase models of motivational psychology, which conceptualized motivation not as a continuous process of gradual goal engagement and disengagement but as distinct phases that are separated by critical transitions such as the "decisional Rubicon" (Gollwitzer, 1990; H. Heckhausen, 1991; H. Heckhausen & Gollwitzer, 1987). Our model conceptualizes developmental regulation as organized in action cycles of sequentially organized goal selection, goal engagement, and goal disengagement.

An important interphase transition in developmental regulation is given by age-graded developmental deadlines, which represent shifts in the opportunities to attain developmental goals. The "biological clock" is a prototypical example for such developmental deadlines (Heckhausen, Wrosch, & Fleeson, 2000). Surveys on age-normative conceptions about the timing of family events reveal that age 40 is commonly perceived as a developmental deadline for child-bearing (e.g., Settersten & Hagestad, 1996; see also Mayer, this volume). Thus, we expected that women with child-bearing goals experience urgency when approaching this age deadline and face the necessity of disengaging from their wish for a child when having passed the critical age. This implies that goal engagement will become intensified during the urgency phase, thus drawing on extra motivational investment. When passing the deadline, the individual needs to manage a radical shift from urgent goal engagement to goal disengagement in order to avoid futile striving, ruminations, and depression (see also Kuhl & Fuhrmann, 1998).

The transitions from a phase of deciding about which goal to pursue to an activated goal engagement and from urgent goal striving to postdeadline goal disengagement are conceptualized as discontinuous. Specific processes have to be involved to produce such discrete transitions from one action phase to the other. In the context of control theory, specific secondary control processes, which are processes directed at influencing motivational orientations, are associated with goal engagement and goal disengagement. As described in the section about key propositions of control theory, goal engagement is promoted by selective secondary control (such as enhanced valuation of chosen goal and devaluation of alternatives), while goal disengagement is produced by compensatory secondary control (such as devaluation of goal, goal substitution, self-protection). During phases of urgent goal engagement, the individual is expected to give highest priority to the goal at stake, devalue competing goals, and hold a positively exaggerated belief about controlling goal attainment. In contrast, during the postdeadline phase, secondary control processes such as attending to negative aspects of the futile goal and to positive aspects of competing goals should be activated.

With regard to such processes of reevaluation of goals, changes in goal hierarchies and in interpretive accounts of failures and losses, Brandtstädter has pointed out that intentional strategies may have only limited value, too limited to account for the impressive transformations in motivational orientation (Brandtstädter, 2000; Brandtstädter & Greve, 1999). Individuals can actively influence their motivation or emotional states by purposefully seeking out, creating, or avoiding relevant situational or mental conditions. For instance, they may expose and compare themselves with inferior others to enhance positive affect and self-worth. However, shifts in a goal's value, for instance, cannot be accounted for by such effortful intentional processes. As Brandtstädter asserts: "The idea that we can originate our beliefs, volitions, or emotions in the same intentional way as we can originate our actions . . . apparently has dubious consequences" (Brandtstädter, 2000, p. 6). Among the dubious consequences Brandtstädter discusses is the issue of an infinite regress of metaintentions and the transparency of self-manipulative or self-deceptive cognitions.

Brandtstädter and his colleagues have therefore studied the beneficial role of subintentional processes involved in coping with losses that serve self-protective and self-immunization functions (Brandtstädter & Greve, 1994; Brandtstädter & Rothermund, 1994; Brandtstädter, Rothermund, & Schmitz 1998; Brandtstädter, Wentura, & Greve, 1993; see also Brandtstädter & Rothermund, this volume).

In our own research program on developmental deadlines, we have taken up the challenge to study both intentional and self-reportable strategies and subintentional orientations toward biased information processing. In a study on the developmental regulation around the developmental deadline associated with the biological clock, we compared predeadline women at the age of 30 to 35 years and two postdeadline samples, ages 40 to 45 years and ages 50 to 55 years (Heckhausen, Wrosch, & Fleeson, 2001). The pattern of self-reported goals and of control strategies reflected contrasting pre- versus postdeadline motivational orientations. Predeadline women were committed to goals associated with child bearing and upbringing and family, whereas postdeadline women were more interested in career and self-development when compared to the younger women. The self-reported control strategies reflected intentional orientations that corresponded with the respective age groups—commitment to child bearing in the younger group and goal deactivation and self-protection in the two postdeadline groups. Predeadline women reported more selective primary and selective secondary-control striving, as well as higher compensatory primary-control attempts. In contrast, postdeadline women reported both more goal disengagement and more self-protective strategies of compensatory secondary control.

The congruency between reported control strategies and pre- versus postdeadline status was also investigated in terms of its relation to the women's mental health. In the urgency group, women profited from using selective primary control strategies by reducing their risk for depressive symptoms. Conversely, women in the passed-deadline groups, who reported more selective primary-control striving, suffered more depressive symptoms. This pattern of findings supports our model of adaptive control strategies in different action phases before and after passing a developmental deadline.

In order to identify subintentional differences in information processing that reflect aspects of motivational orientations probably less accessible to self-report, we included an incidental memory paradigm in our study. Subjects rated words that either were relevant or irrelevant for child bearing. After an intermediate activity, subjects were requested to recall as many words as they could remember. Women in the urgency group showed superior recall of various types of sentences about children, irrespective of positive (good things about having children) or negative (bad things about having children) valuations implied. Childless women in the passed-deadline group had particularly good recall of sentences about causal attributions, which avoid self-blame ("Having children is largely a matter of luck."). Most notably, these subintentional mind sets of biased information processing were associated with psychological well-being. Information processing mind sets that were congruent with the pre- versus postdeadline status were beneficial, and incongruent relations harmful to affective well-being. Childless women passed the child-bearing deadline, which also showed selective recall for child-related sentences, typical goals pursued by parents, and blaming the self for missing the deadline also expressed higher negative affect. In contrast, those passed-deadline women who selectively recalled substitute goals for child bearing (such as being a good aunt) and recalled fewer sentences about the benefits of having children expressed higher positive affect.

In another study on pre- versus postdeadline motivation, Wrosch (1999; Wrosch & Heckhausen, 1999) investigated control striving and subintentional biases in information processing in the partnership domain. Although for the partnership domain there is not a discrete and commonly known deadline age, the availability of potential partners drops radically from early adulthood to late midlife and old age. Subjects were young (high availability of potential partners) and late-midlife adults (low availability of potential partners) who had either recently separated from a partner or were just committed to a new partner. Developmental goals and control strategies reflected the pre- and postdeadline status of these adults. Younger adults were focused on finding a new or improving an existing partnership, whereas older adults did not report nearly as many gain-oriented goals for a partnership but focused on loss avoidance.

With regard to the control strategies, the findings of the partnership study reflect predeadline goal engagement in terms of enhanced selective primary and selective secondary control in the young adults irrespective of their partnership status. For the older midlifers, goal-engagement control strategies were high only in the group that was recently committed. Those middle-aged adults who had recently separated expressed higher compensatory secondary control and lower selective primary and selective secondary control. Moreover, in a 15-month follow-up, high ratings in compensatory secondary control (that is, disengagement from partnership goals and self-protection about a failing partnership) proved to be a differential predictor for young and older separated adults' change in affect during the 15 months period. For older midlifers, compensatory secondary-control striving was beneficial in that it predicted enhanced positive affect in the longitudinal follow-up. In contrast, young adults who had expressed disengagement with partnership goals deteriorated in positive affect over the 15 months' period.

With regard to subintentional mind sets of information processing, an incidental recall task was given using adjectives describing partnerships in positive (such as happy, important) or negative (deceptive, constraining) ways. It was found that younger separated persons recalled relatively more positive compared to negative words about partnerships, whereas older adults recalled relatively more negative words.

In summary of this section, secondary-control processes during goal engagement and goal disengagement not only comprise intentional strategies of volitional commitment and disengagement from a goal but also involve subintentional processes of shifting priorities, on-goal versus off-goal focusing of information processing, and increased availability of cognitions that deflect self-blame. The interplay of intentional and subintentional processes of secondary control and the conditions under which either of those gains priority is a fascinating topic for future research.

Moreover, the discrete nature of goal engagement and goal disengagement with their contrasting intentional and subintentional processes calls for a comparative and evolutionary analysis (Heckhausen, 2000b). Motivational modules to organize behavioral, emotional, and cognitive processes in the service of either goal engagement (the go mode) or by contrast, goal disengagement (the stop-and-retreat mode) may have evolved in early mammals and handed down as mental toolkits to primate evolution (see also Heckhausen, 2000b).

The Interplay of Biological, Societal, and Individual Influences in Shaping Human Life Courses and Development

Human development throughout the life course is jointly produced by biological maturation and aging, sociostructural channeling, and the individual striving for the attainment of goals (Heckhausen, 1999a). Addressing the conjoint regulation of these three systems of influence and therefore promoting interdisciplinary research is one of the hallmarks of the lifespan developmental perspective (see also Baltes, 1987; Baltes et al., 1980; Reese & Overton, 1970). Recent work on the SOC model has revitalized this claim and argued that all three component processes operate on multiple levels—in the individual, in social institutions and societies, and through phylogenetic evolution (Baltes, 1997).

Convergent conceptions have been developed in the framework of the lifespan theory of control (Heckhausen, 1999a; Heckhausen, 2000a; Heckhausen & Schulz, 1999). Specifically, we have focused on two fundamental requirements of human behavioral (and developmental) regulation—the *management of selectivity* and the *compensation for failure and loss* (Heckhausen & Schulz, 1998). These two requirements are jointly fulfilled by the sociocultural community and the individual along with the biological predispositions. For instance, selectivity of development is constituted by the confluence of evolution-based epigenetic pathways in biological development (Waddington, 1957), societal channeling into biographical tracks, and individual striving for developmental goals. Far from an individualistic or subjectivist perspective, control theory views sociostructural and biological constraints as adaptive constraints to the individuals' attempts to regulate her own development (Heckhausen, 1999a; see also discussion of this topic in Mayer, this volume). These constraints constitute age-graded challenges to the primary-control striving of individuals, who are prompted to organize their goal engagement and disengagement cycles in accordance with the age-timing of biological and societal transitions.

To illustrate the possible interplay of these three very different systems, it is useful to think of the analogy to the regulation of social conduct (aggression, table manners, intimacy) in social communities as analyzed by Norbert Elias (see detailed discussion in Heckhausen, 1990). Elias (1969) showed that societal enforcement of behavior regulation retreated step by step as the individual members of society internalized behavioral norms. Elias's historical analysis identified various periods of complementary waxing and waning of societal and individual regulation of behavior, always in opposing directions. The more the society regulated, the less the individual subscribed to the norm, and the more the individual constrained her behavior in accordance with social norms, the less blatant social forces were used to ensure rule obedience. The regulation of the life course can be modeled in a similar way. Where societal constraints on age-patterning of life-course transitions (such as marriage) become weaker or less specific (broader age ranges), the individual has to take up the challenge of choosing when to aim for them. This is far from the idea of a deinstitutionalized life course or the notion that life courses are entirely individualized (Beck, 1996). Instead, we propose that the specifically realized interactions of the three influencing systems—biology, society, and individual—tend to form optimally efficient regulatory higher-order systems (see also Lerner, Dowling, & Roth, this volume). In such optimized higher-order systems, regulatory mechanisms of the three systems play together in positive tradeoffs so that (relatively) stable systems contain minimized conflicts between biology, society, and individual and also entail minimized overdetermination by the three systems. Optimized systems of developmental regulation can vary with regard to the respective profile of relative influence of biology, society, and individual. However, we propose that this variability of higher-order regulatory systems is constrained to a limited repertoire of optimizable systems as a function of human phylogeny and history, in an analogous manner to individual life courses being constrained by "constrained developmental pathways" (Heckhausen & Schulz, 1993; see also "chreods" in Waddington, 1957).

The ongoing research program on developmental regulation around developmental deadlines is an example of how biological (such as the menopause-related biological clock) and sociostructural constraints (availability of partners at different ages) provide an age-sequential scaffold of developmental challenges to individuals and how individuals with their specific personal resources take up these challenges and strive for adaptive developmental progression (see also Köller, Baumert, & Schnabel, this volume). This research program is currently complemented by longitudinal studies in such deadline-related transitions and the ways in which individuals engage and disengage with developmental goals as they negotiate such transitions. Longitudinal studies of developmental regulation around deadlines and other important transitions (such as into a disability) currently underway include research about the transition from school to work (Heckhausen, 2000a; Heckhausen & Tomasik, 2002), about coping with acute and chronic illnesses (Wrosch, Schulz, & Heckhausen, 2000), about controlling the consequences of severe visual impairment (Horowitz, 2000), and about pre- versus postexam behavior in Chinese students aspiring for college qualification (Wong, 2000).

A new and promising area of research is the study of migration of individuals between societies with differing degrees of institutional regulation of behavior and the life course. From all we know, the attraction gradient is in favor of societies that provide greater opportunities for primary control to the individual (Heckhausen & Schulz, 1999). This is certainly the case for the availability of education, accessibility of careers, and thus economic upward mobility. In addition, societies differ with regard to the permeability of vocational tracks during adulthood (Hamilton, 1994). Apart from the question of which societal setting is preferred by whom, the fascinating issue is how individuals who grow up in a certain society manage to adapt their developmental regulation to a new society that is either more or less constraint and thus provides less or more room for individual control striving. Such research would provide quasi-experimental insights into the mutual fit of individual and society with regard to developmental regulation.

Conclusions for Future Research

This chapter discussed three major models of behavioral and developmental regulation—the model of selective optimization with compensation, the dual-process model, and the lifespan theory of control. The respective strengths and weaknesses of the models were examined, and future research perspectives developed (see the end of each section) with regard to three issues. First, future research should utilize explicit and nonrelativistic criteria for successful development. Nonrelativistic and objectifiable criteria of adaptiveness have important advantages, both in terms of operationalizability and in terms of explicit hierarchical conceptions about processes and their interrelation. Second, motivational and emotional processes involved in goal engagement and goal disengagement need to be investigated not only at the explicit intentional level but also in terms of subintentional processes of value shifts and selective or biased information processing. Third, the interplay of biology, society, and individual can be addressed on the basis of specific models of mutual substitutability and fit. Quasi-experimental approaches studying individuals' developmental regulation during cross-national migration may be particularly fruitful.

References

Bäckman, L., & Dixon, R. A. (1992). Psychological compensation: A theoretical framework. *Psychological Bulletin, 112*, 259–283.

Baltes, P. B. (1987). Theoretical propositions of life-span developmental psychology: On the dynamics between growth and decline. *Developmental Psychology, 23*, 611–626.

Baltes, P. B. (1997). On the incomplete architecture of human ontogeny: Selection, optimization, and compensation as foundation of developmental theory. *American Psychologist, 52*, 366–380.

Baltes, P. B., & Baltes, M. M. (Eds.). (1990). *Successful aging: Perspectives from the behavioral sciences.* Cambridge: Cambridge University Press.

Baltes, P. B., Lindenberger, U., & Staudinger, U. M. (1998). Life-span theory in developmental psychology. In R. M. Lerner (Ed.), *Handbook of child psychology*, Vol. 1, *Theoretical models of human development* (5th ed., pp. 1029–1143). New York: Wiley.

Baltes, P. B., Reese, H. W., & Lipsitt, L. P. (1980). Life-span developmental psychology. *Annual Review of Psychology, 31*, 65–100.

Beck, U. (1996). Taking your "own life" into your own hands. *Pädagogik, 48*, 40–47.

Berkman, L. F., et al. (1993). High, usual and impaired functioning in community-dwelling older men and women: Findings from the MacArthur Foundation Research Network on Successful Aging. *Journal of Clinical Epidemiology, 46*, 1129–1140.

Brandtstädter, J. (1998). Action perspectives on human development. In R. M. Lerner (Ed.), *Handbook of child psychology*, Vol. 1, *Theoretical models of human development* (5th ed., pp. 807–863). New York: Wiley.

Brandtstädter, J. (2000). Emotion, cognition, and control: Limits of intentionality. In W. J. Perrig & A. Grob (Eds.). *Control of human behavior, mental processes, and consciousness: Essays in honor of the sixtieth birthday of August Flammer* (pp. 3–16). Mahwah, NJ: Erlbaum.

Brandtstädter, J., & Greve, W. (1994). The aging self: Stabilizing and protective processes. *Developmental Review, 14*, 52–80.

Brandtstädter, J., & Greve, W. (1999). Intentionale und nicht-intentionale Aspekte des Handelns [Intention and non-intentional aspects of action]. In J. Straub & H. Werbik (Eds.), Handlungs theorie: Begriff und Erkluarning der Handelns in interdisziplinäre diskury [Theory of action: Conceptualization and explanation of action in interdisciplinary perspective] (pp. 185–212) Frankfurt am main: Campus.

Brandtstädter, J., & Renner, G. (1990). Tenacious goal pursuit and flexible goal adjustment: Explication and age-related analysis of assimilative and accommodative strategies of coping. *Psychology and Aging, 5*, 58–67.

Brandtstädter, J., & Rothermund, K. (1994). Self-percepts of control in middle and later adulthood: Buffering losses by rescaling goals. *Psychology and Aging, 9*, 265–273.

Brandtstädter, J., Rothermund, K., & Schmitz, U. (1998). maintaining self-integrity and efficacy through adulthood and Cases life: The adaptive functions of assimilative persistence and accommodative flexibility. In: J. Heckhausen & C. S. Divede (Eds.), Motivation and self-regulation across the life span (pp. 365–388). New York, NY: Cambridge University Press.

Brandtstädter, J., Wentura, D., & Greve, W. (1993). Adaptive resources of the aging self: Outlines of an emergent perspective, *International Journal of Behavioral Development, 16*, 323–349.

Carstensen, L. L. (1993). Motivation for social contact across the life span: A theory of socioemotional selectivity. In J. Jacobs (Ed.), *Nebraska symposium on motivation* (Vol. 40, pp. 205–254). Lincoln: University of Nebraska Press.

DeCharms, R. (1968). *Personal causation.* New York: Academic Press.

Deci, E. L., & Ryan, R. M. (1985). *Intrinsic motivation and self-determination in human behavior.* New York: Plenum Press.

Elder Jr., G. H. (1985). *Life course dynamics.* Ithaca, NY: Cornell.

Elias, N. (1969). *Über den Prozess der Zivilisation: Soziogenetische und psychogenetische Untersuchungen* [On the process of civilization: Sociogenetic and Psychogenetic investigations.]. Bern: Francke Verlag.

Ericsson, K. A. (1990). Peak performance and age: An examination of peak performance in sports. In P. B. Baltes & M. M. Baltes (Eds.), *Successful aging: Perspectives from the behavioral sciences* (pp. 164–196). New York: Cambridge University Press.

Ericsson, K. A., & Charness, N. (1994). Expert performance: Its structure and acquisition. *American Psychologist, 49*, 725–747.

Ericsson, K. A., Krampe, R. T., & Tesch-Römer, C. (1993). The role of deliberate practice in the acquisition of expert performance. *Psychological Review, 100*, 363–406.

Freund, A. M., & Baltes, P. B. (1998). Selection, optimization, and compensation as strategies of life-management: Correlations with subjective indicators of successful aging. *Psychology and Aging, 13*, 531–543.

Freund, A. M., & Baltes, P. B. (2000). The orchestration of selection, optimization, and compensation: An action-theoretical conceptualization of a theory of developmental regulation. In W. J. Perrig & A. Grob (Eds.), *Control of human behavior, mental processes and consciousness* (pp. 35–58). Mahwah, NJ: Erlbaum.

Frijda, N. H. (1988). The laws of emotion. *American Psychologist, 43*, 349–358.

Glück, J., & Heckhausen, J. (2001). Kognitive Trainingsstudien im Lebenslauf: Potential und Grenzen der Plastizität [Cognitive training studies over the lifespan: Potential and limits of plasticity]. In K. J. Klauer (Ed.), *Handbuch Kognitives Training* [Handbook Cognitive Training] (pp. 431–466) Göttingen: Hogrefe.

Gollwitzer, P. M. (1990). Action phases and mind-sets. In E. T. Higgins & R. M. Sorrentino (Eds.), *Handbook of motivation and cognition: Foundations of social behavior* (Vol. 2, pp. 53–92). New York: Guilford Press.

Gottlieb, G. (1991). Experiential canalization of behavioral development: Theory. *Developmental Psychology, 27*, 4–13.

Hamilton, S. F. (1994). Employment prospects as motivation for school achievement: Links and gaps between school and work in seven countries. In R. K. Silbereisen & E. Todt (Eds.), *Adolescence in context: The interplay of family, school, peers, and work in adjustment* (pp. 267–303). New York: Springer.

Heckhausen, J. (1990). Erwerb und Funktion normativer Vorstellungen über den Lebenslauf: Ein entwicklungspsychologischer Beitrag zur sozio-psychischen Konstruktion von Biographien [Acquisition and function of normative conceptions about the life course: A developmental psychology approach to the socio-psychological construction of biographies]. *Kölner Zeitschrift für Soziologie und Sozialpsychologie, Sonderheft 31*, 351–373.

Heckhausen, H. (1991). *Motivation and action.* New York: Springer.

Heckhausen, J. (1999a). *Developmental regulation in adulthood: Age-normative and sociostructural constraints as adaptive challenges.* New York: Cambridge University Press.

Heckhausen, J. (2000a, May/June). *Adolescents in the transition from school to work: Adaptive and maladaptive sequential patterns of goal orientation and control.* Paper presented at the Seventh Biennial Conference of the European Association for Research on Adolescence, Jena, Germany.

Heckhausen, J. (2000b). Evolutionary perspectives on human motivation. *American Behavioral Scientist, 43*, 1015–1029.

Heckhausen, J. (2000c). "Go" und "Stop" an den Entwicklungsfristen des Lebens ["Go" and "stop" at the developmental deadlines of life]. In Max-Planck-Gesellschaft (Ed.), *Max-Planck-Forschung* [Max Planck Research] (pp. 74–79). Munich: Max-Planck-Gesellschaft.

Heckhausen, H., & Gollwitzer, P. M. (1987). Thought contents and cognitive functioning in motivational and volitional states of mind. *Motivation and Emotion, 11*, 101–120.

Heckhausen, J., & Schulz, R. (1993). Optimisation by selection and compensation: Balancing primary and secondary control in life-span development. *International Journal of Behavioral Development, 16*, 287–303.

Heckhausen, J., & Schulz, R. (1995). A life-span theory of control. *Psychological Review, 102*, 284–304.

Heckhausen, J., & Schulz, R. (1998). Developmental regulation in adulthood: Selection and compensation via primary and secondary control. In J. Heckhausen & R. Schulz (Eds.), *Motivation and self-regulation across the life span* (pp. 50–77). New York: Cambridge University Press.

Heckhausen, J., & Schulz, R. (1999). The primacy of primary control is a human universal: A reply to Gould's critique of the life-span theory of control. *Psychological Review, 106*, 605–609.

Heckhausen, J. & Tomasik, M. (2002). Get an apprenticeship before school is out: How German adolescents adjust vocational aspirations when getting to a developmental deadline. *Journal of Vocational Behavior, 60*, 199–219.

Heckhausen, J., Wrosch, C., & Fleeson, W. (2001). Developmental regulation before and after a developmental deadline: The sample case of "biological clock" for child-bearing. *Psychology and Aging, 16*, 400–413.

Horowitz, A. (2000). *Control strategies and well-being in vision-impaired elders. Grant proposal.* New York: Lighthouse Institute.

Kuhl, J., & Fuhrmann, A. (1998). Decomposing self-regulation and self-control: The volitional components inventory. In J. Heckhausen & C. S. Dweck (Eds.), *Motivation and self-regulation across the life span* (pp. 15–49). New York: Cambridge University Press.

Labouvie-Vief, G. (1982). Dynamic development and mature autonomy: A theoretical prologue. *Human Development, 25*, 161–191.

Lang, F. R., & Heckhausen, J. (2001). Perceived control over development and subjective well-being: Differential effects across adulthood. *Journal of Personality and Social Psychology, 81*, 509–523.

Lehman, H. C. (1953). *Age and achievement.* Princeton, NJ: Princeton University Press.

Lindenberg, S. M. (1996). Continuities in the theory of social production functions. In S. M. Lindenberg & H. B. G. Ganzeboom (Eds.), *Verklarende sociologie: Opstellen voor Reinhard Wippler [Explanatory sociology: Essays for Reinhard Wippler]* (pp. 169–184). Amsterdam: Thesis.

Marsiske, M., Lang, F. R., Baltes, P. B., & Baltes, M. M. (1995). Selective optimization with compensation: Life-span perspectives on successful human development. In R. A. Dixon & L. Bäckman (Eds.), *Compensating for psychological deficits and declines. Managing losses and promoting gains* (pp. 35–79). Mahwah, NJ: Erlbaum.

Ormel, J., Lindenberg, S. M., Steverink, N., & VonKorff, M. (1997). Quality of life and social production functions: A framework for understanding health effects. *Social Science and Medicine, 45*, 1051–1063.

Reese, H. W., & Overton, W. F. (1970). Models of development and theories of development. In L. R. Goulet & P. B. Baltes (Eds.), *Life-span developmental psychology: Research and theory* (pp. 115–145). New York: Academic Press.

Rothbaum, F., Weisz, J. R., & Snyder, S. S. (1982). Changing the world and changing the self: A two-process model of perceived control. *Journal of Personality and Social Psychology, 42*, 5–37.

Rowe, J. W., & Kahn, R. L. (1998). *Successful aging.* New York: Pantheon Books.

Ryan, R. M., & Deci, E. L. (2000). Self-determination theory and the facilitation of intrinsic motivation, social development, and well-being. *American Psychologist, 55*, 68–78.

Ryan, R. M., Kuhl, J., & Deci, E. L. (1997). Nature and autonomy: An organizational view of social and neuro-biological aspects of self-regulation in behavior and development. *Development and Psychopathology, 9*, 701–728.

Salthouse, T. A. (1991). Expertise as the circumvention of human processing limitations. In K. A. Ericsson & J. Smith (Eds.), *Toward a general theory of expertise* (pp. 286–300). Cambridge: Cambridge University Press.

Schulz, R., & Curnow, C. (1988). Peak performance and age among superathletes: Track and field, swimming, baseball, tennis, and golf. *Journal of Gerontology: Psychological Sciences, 43*, 113–120.

Schulz, R., & Heckhausen, J. (1996). A life-span model of successful aging. *American Psychologist, 51*, 702–714.

Schulz, R., & Heckhausen, J. (1997). Emotion and control: A life-span perspective. In K. W. Schaie & M. P. Lawton (Eds.), *Annual review of gerontology and geriatrics* (Vol. 17, pp. 185–205). New York: Springer.

Schulz, R., & Heckhausen, J. (1999). Aging, culture and control: Setting a new research agenda. *Journal of Gerontology: Psychological Sciences, 54B*, P139–P145.

Schulz, R., Musa, D., Staszewski, J., & Siegler, R. S. (1994). The relationship between age and major league baseball performance: Implications for development. *Psychology and Aging, 9*, 274–286.

Settersten, R. A., & Hagestad, G. O. (1996). What's the latest? Cultural age deadlines for family transitions. *The Orontologist, 36*, 178–188.

Simonton, D. K. (1988). Age and outstanding achievement: What do we know after a century of research? *Psychological Bulletin, 104*, 251–267.

Simonton, D. K. (1990). Creativity and wisdom in aging. In J. E. Birren & K. W. Schaie (Eds.), *Handbook of the psychology of aging* (pp. 320–329). New York: Academic Press.

Simonton, D. K. (1994). *Greatness*. New York: Guilford Press.

Steverink, N., Lindenberg, S., & Ormel, J. (1998). Towards understanding successful ageing: Patterned change in resources and goals. *Ageing and Society, 18*, 441–467.

Vaughan, W. (1926) The psychology of compensation. *Psychological Review, 33*, 467–479.

Waddington, C. H. (1957). *The strategy of the genes*. London: Allen & Unwin.

Williamson, G., & Schulz, R. (1992). Physical illness and symptoms of depression among elderly outpatients. *Psychology and Aging, 7*, 343–351.

Williamson, G. M., & Schulz, R. (1995). Activity restriction mediates the association between pain and depressed affect: A study of younger and older adult cancer patients. *Psychology and Aging, 10*, 369–378.

Wong, W. (2000). *Control processes among Chinese students in academic pursuit: A comparative study in the predeadline and postdeadline situation*. Chinese University, Hong Kong, China.

Wrosch, C. (1999). *Entwicklungsfristen im Partnerschaftsbereich: Bezugsrahmen für Prozesse der Aktivierung und Deaktivierung von Entwicklungszielen* [Developmental deadlines in the partnership domain: Reference frame for activation and deactivation of developmental goals]. Münster: Waxmann.

Wrosch, C., & Heckhausen, J. (1999). Control processes before and after passing a developmental deadline: Activation and deactivation of intimate relationship goals. *Journal of Personality and Social Psychology, 77*, 415–427.

Wrosch, C., & Heckhausen, J. (in press). Being on-time or off-time: Developmental deadlines for regulating one's own development. In A. N. Perret-Clermont, J. M. Barrelet, A. Flammer, D. Miéville, J. F. Perret, & W. Perrig (Eds.), *Mind and time*. Göttingen: Hogrefe & Huber.

Wrosch, C., Schulz, R. & Heckhausen, J. (2002). Health stresses and depressive symptomatology in the elderly: The importance of health engagement control strategies. *Health Psychology, 21*, 1–9.

18 Without Gender, Without Self

Gisela Labouvie-Vief

Wayne State University, Detroit, MI, U.S.A.

Abstract
In this chapter, I address the model from the perspective of gender. Gender is not a part of Baltes's theory, and yet it nevertheless enters it because scientific narratives, in narrating the human condition, involve implicit assumptions about the role of gender in such cognitive and emotional aspects of development. Drawing on my previous theoretical work, I distinguish between two gendered narratives. One presents an essentially "masculine" view of the life course with an emphasis on the rise, growth, and decline of logos, activity, and internal, conscious control. The second presents an essentially "feminine" view with an emphasis on the suppression and eventual liberation of mythos—the intuitive, emotional, relational, and experiential. As do many cognitively based theories, Baltes's version of lifespan theory exemplifies a "masculine" prototype with its emphasis on autonomy and internal control, its technical rather than social-interactional view of culture, and its failure to integrate a consistent theory of emotion into his view of development across the lifespan.

Gender is a dimension about which many theories of development are strikingly silent. To point to this silence or even to break it is not always a comfortable thing to do. When attempting to articulate that silence, I sometimes find that a general theoretical message gets diluted as a result of its gender implications. Yet this polarization between sound theory and arguments about gender is the very center of part of the message I want to convey—namely, that bracketing gender out of a developmental theory can be symptomatic of a host of theoretical deletions that are far-reaching indeed.

I suggest that gender is such a natural and necessary of development that its absence itself suggests that something is amiss and been actively deleted. After all, human life is gendered, evolution has favored sexual dimorphism, and whether at the biological or psychological level, theories of evolution and development must deal with this sexual dimorphism. Selves thus are inherently gendered, and as many theories of development have realized at least implicitly, gender relationships form a metaphor *par excellence* for the basic fact that our lives are built on the generative, procreative power of gendered *relations* in development. What, then, are the theoretical consequences of deleting it from developmental theory?

Symbolic Language of Gender

My examination in this commentary begins with the proposal that the conceptual structure of human systems of thought often has at its core symbolic images that indicate an implied order of things (Labouvie-Vief, 1994; Whitmont, 1969). Although it is more usual to think of theories as abstract logical relations among constructs, the way we define and order those constructs nevertheless has rich symbolic aspects (Whitmont, 1969). By *symbol*, I here imply the meaning suggested by psychodynamic traditions and also the cognitive-developmental tradition of Jean Piaget (Piaget, 1955). In those traditions, the term *symbol* is opposed to that of *signs* and implies that the core categories by which we structure reality are based on feelings, images, stories, and other imaginative products. Piaget referred to this as the *figurative* aspect of thought— figurative in much the same sense that we sometimes speak of figurative art as something that is based in a realistic image. To speak of figurative thought similarly implies that our thought often reflects aspects of our own embodied, feeling experience. Indeed, I want to claim that this figurative element is ever present, even in our most exalted abstract ways of talking about human life. In other words, our theoretical visions of development are permeated with figurative elements, as well.

Perhaps the most basic and universal figures by which we describe aspects of life and its development are those related to gender and its procreative consequence, that of generational flow. Thus on the figurative plane, theories of development often imply a basic division of life into the categories of *masculine* and *feminine* (Labouvie-Vief, 1994; Lakoff, 1980) and *young* and *old*. On this gendered, generational conceptual structure, we base theoretical systems that are infused with core concepts and images that derive from our embodied existence. We talk of seminal ideas, of masculine (hard) and feminine (soft) forms of thinking, of incubating concepts and giving birth to them, of their marriage, longevity, aging, and ultimate death. All of those are reproductive and longevity metaphors that speak of the domain of self and mind in terms of personified images and narratives. Such metaphors can be viewed as forming themselves complex symbolic systems that complement the theories we build. In fact, it is perhaps more correct to put it more strongly, saying that reproductive and longevity metaphors form part of the basis of our theories of development. These theories thus reveal themselves as complex narratives and metanarratives commingling the language of science with that of our innermost hopes and fears.

It is, I suggest, from that language of hope and fears that ultimately arise the core developmental goals and processes around which a theory of development is structured. What is the nature of the self addressed by a theory? What is its relation to biology and culture? How does it link to the flow of generation? What are its main dreams, hopes, and fears for the lives it describes? How does is face the universal experiences of growth and aging? It is in the realm of the symbolic and metaphorical, I suggest, that ultimately such questions of the meaning of a theory are posed and eventually answered.

I suggest, then, that there exist exact parallels between theories as symbolic systems and theories as logical structures. As outlined in *Psyche and Eros: Mind and Gender in the Life Course* (Labouvie-Vief, 1994), I will refer to these dual aspects of theories by the traditional terms of *mythos* and *logos*. I suggest that while a theory of development ideally would integrate these two aspects of thinking about development, in reality, most theories are based on a dualism by which one way of describing development is preferred. The result are narratives of development that are partial, since they delete or devalue specific aspects of human experience. These part narratives express a view of relations—gender or otherwise—that is dualistic and competitive. I suggest that the most prevalent narrative—that rooted in rationalism—ultimately identifies the early lifespan with growth but prevents a meaningful definition of aging as growth and development. I suggest instead that a second narrative can construe relationships in terms of dialectical tension that can be the source of further development and of mutually enhancing relationships, and I examine how such a narrative of dynamic balance redefines growth and aging.

Modes of Knowing

Throughout history there has been a tension between two general views of mind and self (Collingwood, 1945; Simon, 1978). On one hand, there are those theoreticians for whom the self is primarily defined as a set of embodied processes. These processes are located in actual persons or selves, and such selves are subject to and even enriched by emotions; living, as they do, in a flow of time, they also are open to change. Such selves are reflected by Heraclitus's metaphor of the constantly changing river into which we step but once, or the Taoist view of the self as supported by an ever-changing ground of being (Mitchell, 1988; Russell, 1945).

The self of this embodied-mind view, then, is inherently related to its contextual and temporal surrounds. It is a union of opposites, an a-dual whole, and it often is best expressed in the language of symbols or what I term the *mode of mythos*. Mythologically and symbolically, it is often indicated not by a single image but by one that indicates a union of opposites, such as the *sacred marriage* of mythology or the yin and yang symbol of Eastern cultures (Whitmont, 1969).

In contrast to this a-dual self, we can envision a self that can step back from these constantly changing contingencies and strive for a more general, presumably even universal vision that is less dependent on the flow of the context. In so doing, we adopt the mode of logos—of detached, abstract cognitive analysis. The self, in a sense, becomes purely abstract and universal, a disembodied mind (Cassirer, 1946; Simon, 1978).

This logos self often has been identified with self and mind at their best, with the epitomy of our humanity. But whether this is a tenable position has become a matter of debate (Baynes, Bohman, & McCarthy, 1987). In that debate, an emerging solution is that both of these aspects of the mind—mythos and logos—form somewhat independent but interacting aspects of mind and self. Ideally, these two aspects work together, but in actuality, our intellectual history often has represented them in a dualistic and reductionist fashion. Depending on our inclinations, that dualism can get resolved in romantic views that favor mythos. But more generally, and especially for scientific languages, the solution is one that reduces the self to the mind—rationalism.

The Mind as Logos

The dualistic theory of rationality and the mind became institutionalized when Greek philosophers began to speculate about human nature. These efforts culminated in the work of Plato, who proposed a two-layer view of human nature and reality to supplant more ancient views (Labouvie-Vief, 1994; Simon, 1978). For more ancient views of the self as a collection of motor actions, bodily processes, or mythic-divine injunctions, Plato substituted a language of a self that is no longer primarily identified with its bodily processes and concrete actions but that is a mental agent different from its bodily manifestations. The new language was that of a self who was the author of those actions, of a psychological causal agent who was at their center and who was responsible for them (see also Mittelstrass, this volume).

Plato's dualistic, two-layered conception of the individual contrasted a layer of mind, abstract thought, soul, spirit, or ideals to a layer of body, matter, and enslavement to concrete sensory and organismic happenings. The result was a thorough reorganization of the nature of what was considered reality. No longer animated by the felt textures of the mythic and the organic, that reorganization worked by subtraction and deduction. The process of becoming rational, Durkheim claimed, was in essence a process of *demythification*—of removing from the structure of concepts the sensory, the emotional, the interpersonal, and ultimately, the mysterious and even divine. The self thus was transformed into a mere mind sans self. Thus the original a-dual unity of self was not reintegrated, but the two dimensions were put in dualistic juxtaposition. Nature versus culture, individual versus collective, body versus mind: all of these dualities have come to structure Western intellectual discourse until very recently.

Gender and Mind

Following the Greek model, many theories concerned with mind and self adopted a language of the mind that expunged mythos from discourse. All the same, the resulting language of mind was pervaded through and through with mythic imagery and metaphor. Indeed, the transformation of the new language of the mind was described not just in the development of scientific language but also in those of myth, art, religion, and poetry. In those realms, it occurred as the theme of the overthrow of original female divine figures by male godheads or heroes. These male figures were said to be the original creators, creating the world not organically, as women do, but through concepts and words (Lerner, 1986).

A well known retelling of this process of the replacement of the feminine principle is offered by the great Greek tragedies of Aeschylus (1953) and Euripides (1972) centering on the myths of Agamemnon and Orestes. These myths address the question of which of two murders was a more heinous act: was it Klytemnestra's killing of her husband Agamemnon to revenge his sacrificing their daughter Iphigenia to the gods so as to secure a good wind for his war ships, or was it their son Orestes' killing of his mother to avenge the murder of his father? The answer was that Orestes could be forgiven because he represented a new masculine order that superseded an earlier feminine order—a new paradigm in which fatherhood was said to have replaced motherhood as a principle of creation (Labouvie-Vief, 1994).

Similar myths of the displacement of archaic female powers are abundant worldwide—so much, in fact, that they have given rise to the speculation that there must have been an early historical time in which matriarchy prevailed. However, it is probably more correct to interpret such myths symbolically and socially, as part of a social order that denigrates the creative power of women (Bettelheim, 1962; Duby & Perrot, 1992–1993). Such myths usually talk about the dire consequences of letting women handle power, thereby creating cultural codes that grant men power in social life. Even though they talk about a time before the current social order, they fix that order as inalienable and invariant.

Far from being a part of the devalued mythical realm, this dismissive language of gender was widely adopted by philosophers, as well. Thus, in the *Symposium*, Plato argued that the spiritual love between men who create ideas is more valuable than the physical and material love with women, since women's creativity is merely one of bodily procreation rather than the creation of universal ideas in which men participate (Labouvie-Vief, 1994). In fact, in Plato's republic, the latter form of creativity was to be fostered by removing children from their mothers and making them wards of the state.

This association of the masculine with mind and spirit and of the feminine with body and matter widely came to characterize scientific thinking about and representations of the mind and gender. It is also pervasive in mythology and religion, literature and art (Labouvie-Vief, 1994; Ortner & Whitehead, 1981; Rosaldo & Lamphere, 1974). In all of those, one polarity of human functioning tends to be idealized and even inflated as masculine: it is based on an imagery of rise, light, and sun, and it symbolizes such psychological qualities as leadership, rational self-control, self-assertiveness, individuality, and willfulness. The other polarity, in turn, is degraded and devalued: its imagery is based on falling, being conquered and surrendering, and engulfment in dark spaces, and it symbolizes suffering, powerlessness, and entrapment in unconscious processes.

Gendered Narratives of the Life Span

This gendered dualistic notion of mind has been influential in shaping theoretical notions of development (Gilligan, 1982; Labouvie-Vief, 1994). Traditionally, development has been construed as an onward rush, a heroic and energetic striving for mental ideals and control, a triumph of conscious, abstract forms of thinking, a victory of rationality over emotions and the body. Since these features of the mind also are identified with masculinity, femininity was represented as an inferior and less developed state of being—a form, as it were, of mental and physical castration. Freud (1925/1963) was most explicit in equating development of mind and identity with a progression from the domain of the castrated mother to the potent and genital father, but most major theories of development of the past followed this same pattern of the devaluation of the emotive, imaginative, and sensory aspects of the self (Labouvie-Vief, 1994).

Such a narrative has at its core a competitive metaphor. Relationships are construed in a dualistic, either/or fashion. Images of control, castration, and even murderous overthrow describe the life course. This is evident, first, in the implied relationships of the genders. Development is not a process that encompasses both genders—each with its unique qualitative variations. Rather, growth in one gender is achieved at the expense of growth in the other. On a more symbolic level, this metaphor of overthrow is generalized to other relationships, as well. First, development is primarily identified with growth of cognitive resources, analytical skills, and intelligence. Rise of these faculties implies, at the same time, that other important resources—those linked with the vitality of the id—be displaced through control and repression.

Just as the relationship between cognitive and emotional resources is defined as a competitive one, so is that between biology and culture. True personhood is said to begin with the age of reason and ego formation, when the boy enters the realm of the phallic father, who represent culture and its demands. It is here that core processes of identification take place, as boys and girls locate themselves in this patriarchal realm— boys with a sense of phallic pride, girls with a sense of shame and deficit. In contrast, the earlier periods of development are defined as reflecting merely the realm of the maternal—the realm of our dependency and our biological heritage, all identified with the devalued mother.

Finally, generational relationships in this model also are construed as competitive. This is evident, for example, in the core myth Freud associated with development— that of Oedipus. In the myth, Oedipus's developmental path is set as his father, Laius, fearing competition with and overthrow by his son, abandons the infant to die in the wilderness. That core dynamic of competition unto death structures the young boy's identity formation with a compliant subjugation to and identification with the overidealized father. Yet this identification with the aggressor structures generational linkages between sons and fathers, and ultimately, such linkages are described by the very overturn and killing of the father. Just as Oedipus kills his father, Laius, so in *Totem and Tabu* (Freud, 1918/1952) the sons murder the generation of the fathers (e.g., Chodorow, 1978; Kaschak, 1992; Kohut, 1977).

Later theorists point out the defensive posture behind this competitive imagery. Behind the heroic bravado lies, at the core self, a profound fear of dependency and vulnerability. That fear ultimately is of the awesome power of others who hold in their hands the power of life and death over us. And that fear, in turn, is related to a compensatory devaluation of those others. Generally, this devaluation is evident in an overall neglect or denial of relationship dimensions, along with the powerful emotions these dimensions add to development. This devaluation goes along with a pervasive individualism. Ultimately, adaptation in development is measured by individual goals, such as individual well-being and survival.

One of the most profound consequences of such a theory with its devaluation of the mythic feminine is that in the end, it cannot give a truly positive account of development throughout the lifespan. There is no room for continued development in this scenario of individual pursuit in which the self is cut off from the kinds of adaptations that bind us to the social group. Rather than asserting that such adaptations are part and parcel of our developmental potential and that they form a source of genuine progression, the self envisioned in such gendered theories is rigidly defended against integrating these sources of vitality and growth. Visions of integration cannot be distinguished from issues of regression. Ultimately, the self is based on having rigidly and terminally internalized a competitive, patriarchally based vision. Transcendence beyond that vision is ruled out.

This psychology of the isolated, competitive individual is also at the core of many cognitive theories of development. Although less direct in their symbolism than psychodynamic theories, cognitive theories *traditionally* adopted a similar devaluative attitude toward relationships. Elsewhere, I discuss how this devaluative attitude appears in Piaget's theory of development (Labouvie-Vief, 1994). Ultimately, that theory is based on the individual in isolation—an individual that devalues the primacy of relationships, for whom developmental advancement is signaled by the replacement of the power or relations and emotions through an abstract formalism. As a consequence, it also is not able to deal with continued development.

The SOC Model as Part Narrative of Development

Baltes's formulation of the selection, optimization, and compensation (SOC) model and his vision of the architecture of development are profoundly rooted in this gendered view of development. The model deals primarily with the cognitive self, while the emotions and meaning are given a minor place. The resulting vision of lifespan development incorporates several structural features that make it problematic as a general theory of development: it presents the dualistic, individualistic, and competitive conception of development that characterizes other theories of the disembodied, ungendered, and unselved mind.

As is true of other traditional theories, Baltes's deletion of the emotional self— the self of mythos—has several ramifications for his account of lifespan development. That account is structured around a series of dualisms. One of those is his definition of *culture* and *biology* as opisitional categories. This opposition similarly implies a dualistic division of the mind and its faculties. Related to this view of culture is a failure to emphasize early developmental dynamics of later life development, resulting in a view of the life span as severed from its full biography. In general, what is missing from this account are mechanisms of integration—of biology and experience, of reason and emotion, of loss and gain.

Let us turn to a discussion of the role of culture first. Baltes contrasts the role of culture to the incomplete architecture of our biology. Culture thus is seen as compensating for our biological incompleteness. Moreover, Baltes suggests that as our biological resources decline: "there is an age-related increase in the need for culture," understood as "the entirety of psychological, social, material, and symbolic (knowledge-based) resources that humans have generated."

Baltes's definition of culture thus squarely places that concept into the later periods of development, those traditionally identified with the ascendancy of "reason"—or, in the case of aging, its loss. In the Platonic sense I outlined earlier, culture thus is primarily identified with human consciousness and belongs to the realm of human control and inventiveness (see also Heckhausen, this volume). It is outside of biology but represents our ability to change and operate on biology; it is primarily a technological construct, a form more or less consciously created.

If one examines the role of culture in early life, such a view of culture as system of compensatory relations—and a system doomed to fail, in the end, at that—is by no means self-evident. Contrast it, for example, with the proposition (e.g., Bowlby, 1980; Gould, 1977) that culture is a system that complements the profound immaturity of the neonate—that, in fact, forms an extension of the womb. This extension is itself supported through the biological preparedness of adults for caregiving and nurturing. Without it, we now understand, normal formation of emotional and cognitive structures could not take place: indeed, the very viability of life would be threatened. Cultural support and biological immaturity and vulnerability thus are correlative aspects of development. Together, they form a synergism that has allowed the human species to reach particularly complex levels of organization by providing an extrauterine scaffolding of development.

The interpretation I am suggesting is part of an emerging developing-systems view of development (see also Lerner, Dowling, & Roth, this volume). In that view, biology and culture or structure and context always are correlative and mutually codefining; however, in the course of development, the range of this discourse becomes progressively widened (Gottlieb, 1991). In the part narrative of development, however, the mutually enhancing and growth-producing roles of biological vulnerability and cultural support are not an integral part of the vision of lifespan development. Culture is no longer based on this synergistic, cross-fertilizing process but is the result of a perceived deficit, a mere defensive and compensatory set of relations.

This emphasis on the roots of culture in human deficiency is related to a general neglect of *early* life. The individual of the SOC model, too, is a self set against the important processes of earliest acculturation—those rooted in our dependency and vulnerability on others who secure our survival (Bowlby, 1980; Schore, 1994).

Recent knowledge about the role of early nurturance in the development of emotional competence and of the ability to form balanced and reciprocal relations of the social world (e.g., Cassidy & Shaver, 1999) is not given consideration; instead, adults are uprooted from their biographical context. This bias against emotions and the social relations in which they are embedded further creates an account of development that lacks theoretical integration with other accounts of the life span, particularly those that have elaborated its early formative dynamics.

The SOC model, as a consequence, primarily defines development in terms of cognitive competencies, just as it tends to reduce motives for development to compensatory deficiency motives. To be sure, defensive and compensatory motives are important in development, as Freud so aptly proposed. But are they able to present a view of optimal development and flexible adaptation? I suggest that such a positive view of development requires a set of *positive* motives, ones that are rooted in growth and expansion. Such nondefensive motives—examples are interest and curiosity, interdependence, joy, compassion, and love—can form a framework of progression and growth that itself provides an explanation of more defensive forms of development.

As an example, take the SOC model's interpretation of the gain and loss dynamic. When I proposed the principle of a tradeoff between growth and decline in lifespan development (Labouvie-Vief, 1980, 1981, 1982), I suggested that progressive and defensive-regressive interpretations of this principle need to be clearly differentiated. For example, how is one to differentiate between the specialization and selection that are part of growth and the successive restriction that forms mere compensation? Following Piaget and developing-systems models, I suggested that in the case of growth, specialized structures reach out to communicate with other structures, becoming part of and integrated into new systems within which they are regulated. Thus criteria for continued development are both formal and dynamic.

On the formal side, it is thus necessary to relate growth to the formal properties of the new system into which a structure has become integrated. Is the structure integrated at all? Does integration result in a system of lower or higher complexity? On the dynamic side, one needs to consider if any changes have resulted in an overall increase or decrease in homeostatic ability. In addition, one can also deal with the motives for change. Are they rooted in the striving to reach out and beyond the self with interest, with curiosity, and with the desire to view broader horizons? Or are they primarily interested in preserving the status quo?

These questions are critical in determining when specialization and selection are part of growth and when they are part of a compensatory reaction to a restriction in resources. Baltes's proposal of the selection, optimization, and compensation dynamic does not offer such a general set of criteria. Instead, his criteria are primarily concerned with whether change is voluntary or reactive in nature. But to locate criteria for growth or decline into the arena of conscious decision making affords conscious decision making a role that is altogether too exalted. It does not consider the vast knowledge about the interaction of conscious decision making and less conscious processes or the role of consciousness in distorting information. Thus, this version of the gain-loss dynamic is not a general principle of progressive development; rather, it confounds regressive and defensive processes that are called on as the organism's capacity begins to decline in later life.

One consequence of the cognitivism inherent in defining growth and decline is the Berlin model of wisdom as a form of specialized knowledge or expertise. A related consequence is the criterion of adaptive capacity that the Berlin theory of wisdom aims to address. The main criterion is that of longevity and individual survival and happiness. How relevant is that criterion? Can we gauge adaptive success by individual survival over that of species survival and the welfare of generations to follow?

Baltes and Staudinger (2000) recently noted this paradox, stating that it is necessary to balance the goals of individual and collective or species survival in a theory of wisdom and to integrate within it a theory of virtue. Yet nothing in their operationalization of wisdom indicates that the emotions that push individuals toward identification with their collective or with virtue have a part of it. Nor do the data offered by the Berlin wisdom project give evidence that "wise" individuals excel in virtue or generativity. In fact, there is much evidence to suggest that the kinds of cognitive-affective complexity that are basic to a cognitivist definition of wisdom may define individuals who cope with a basic sense of lack of purpose and identity with a hyperintellectualizing approach to reality (Labouvie-Vief & Medler, 2000). As long as wisdom is defined as cognitive expertise, the very self-processes that may foster or hinder integration of cognitive analysis and self-interest cannot be analyzed. Thus the Berlin model of wisdom ultimately remains relativistic and uncommitted to value (see Heckhausen, this volume).

Conclusions: Toward Integration in Development

One of the most remarkable and exciting phenomena of this century is the breakdown of dualistic narratives of development and their integration into a new theoretical prototype. Freud (1925/1963) envisioned such a prototype in pointing out that our very notions of cognitive and rational processes are built on the primacy of emotions. Yet while he still remained rooted in the traditional rationalism and imagined a conflicted and dualistic coexistence of logos and mythos, his followers continued his work by restoring to emotions a truly foundational significance for development.

In line with my argument that modes of knowing often are symbolically associated with gender, this restoration came in form of acknowledging the role of the maternal and its profound significance in pre-Oedipal development in the work of such theoreticians as Melanie Klein (Klein & Riviere, 1964) and Erik Erikson (1984). This restoration of the realm of the mother was evident in several features. These authors—and many to follow—called attention to the prephallic emotions of development—emotions rooted in our dependence and vulnerability as infants. The recognition of this profound dependency was followed by a focus (e.g., Bowlby, 1980; Erikson, 1984) on the complementary preparedness of adults who respond to this dependency through such emotions as love, compassion, and care. This capacity set the stage for a truly developmental approach to the life span, since it placed the study of adulthood in the more general evolutionary problem of securing continuity among generations. Accordingly, mature capacities were indicated not just by cognitive skill and expertise but by the degree to which these skills could be integrated into the virtues of generative care.

The result of this rediscovery of the "realm of the mother" was a theoretical rebalancing of the relations between masculine and the feminine. A related consequence is a rebalancing of generational relations from ones that emphasize individual survival and competitive strife to ones of nurture and care. Just as mature adult capacity flows from the capacity for care, so this capacity provides the base for the enfolding of the development of future generations (see also Cloninger, this volume). Of course, such an expanded criterion does not *guarantee* that individuals will achieve the capacity for generative care. However, it does provide a more generalized theory of development that specifies the conditions under which this capacity is fostered or stunted. Hence, the traditional part narrative becomes only one possible vision of development—and one that involves a restriction to an individualistic concern with individual survival. In contrast, more integrated visions of development imply that ultimately, growth in later life needs to be gauged by those capacities that allow the individual to integrate the awareness and acceptance of decline and death with self-transcendent motives that place the role of individual survival in the context of the well-being of future generations.

References

Aeschylus (1953). *Oresteia* (Trans. R. Lattimore). Chicago: University of Chicago Press.

Baltes, P. B., & Staudinger, U. M. (2000). Wisdom: A metaheuristic (pragmatic) to orchestrate mind and virtue toward excellence. *American Psychologist, 55*, 122–136.

Baynes, K., Bohman, J., & McCarthy, T. T. (Eds.). (1987). *Philosophy: End or transformation.* Cambridge, MA: MIT Press.

Bettelheim, B. (1962). *Symbolic wounds: Puberty rites and the envious male* (rev. ed.). New York: Collier Books.

Bowlby, J. (1980). *Attachment and loss: Depression* (Vol. 3). London: Hogarth Press.

Cassidy, J., & Shaver P. R. (Eds.). (1999). *Handbook of attachment: Theory, research, and clinical implications.* New York: Guilford Press.

Cassirer, E. (1946). *Language and myth.* New York: Harper. (Reprinted from New York: Dover, 1953.)

Chodorow, N. (1978). *The reproduction of mothering: Psychoanalysis and the sociology of gender.* Berkeley: University of California Press.

Collingwood, R. G. (1945). *The idea of nature.* Oxford: Clarendon Press.

Duby, G., & Perrot, M. (Eds.). (1992–1993). *A history of women in the West* (Vols. 1–4). Cambridge, MA: Harvard University Press.

Erikson, E. (1984). *The life cycle completed.* New York: Norton.

Euripides. (1972). *Iphigenia in Aulis* (Trans. F. M. Stawell). New York: Oxford University Press.

Freud, S. (1918/1952). *Totem and tabu* (Trans. J. Strachey). New York: Norton.

Freud, S. (1925/1963). Some psychological consequences of the anatomical differences between the sexes. In P. Rieff (Ed.), *Sexuality and the psychology of love* (pp. 183–193). New York: Macmillan.

Gilligan, C. (1982). *In a different voice.* Cambridge, MA: Harvard University Press.

Gottlieb, G. (1991). Experiential canalization of behavioral development: Theory. *Developmental Psychology, 27*, 4–13.

Gould, S. J. (1977). *Ontogeny and phylogeny.* Cambridge, MA: Belknap Press of Harvard University Press.

Kaschak, E. (1992). *Engendered lives.* New York: Basic Books.

Klein, M., & Riviere, J. (1964). *Love, hate, and reparation.* New York: Norton.

Kohut, H. (1977). *The restoration of the self.* New York: International Universities Press.

Labouvie-Vief, G. (1980). Beyond formal operations: Uses and limits of pure logic in life span development. *Human Development, 23*, 141–161.

Labouvie-Vief, G. (1981). Re-active and pro-active aspects of constructivism: Growth and aging in life-span perspective. In R. M. Lerner & N. A. Busch-Rossnagel (Eds.), *Individuals as producers of their development: A life-span perspective* (pp. 197–320). New York: Academic Press.

Labouvie-Vief, G. (1982). Dynamic development and mature autonomy. *Human Development, 25*, 161–191.

Labouvie-Vief, G. (1994). *Psyche and Eros: Mind and gender in the life course.* New York: Cambridge University Press.

Labouvie-Vief, G., & Medler, M. (2000). *Affect dampening and affect complexity as adaptive strategies.* Manuscript, Wayne State University.

Lakoff, G. (1980). *Metaphors we live by.* Chicago: Chicago University Press.

Lerner, G. (1986). *The creation of patriarchy.* New York: Oxford University Press.

Mitchell, S. A. (1988). *Relational concepts in psychoanalysis: An integration.* Cambridge, MA: Harvard University Press.

Ortner, S. B., & Whitehead, H. (Eds.). (1981). *Sexual meanings: The cultural construction of gender and sexuality.* New York: Cambridge University Press.

Piaget, J. (1955). *The language and thought of the child* (Trans. M. Gabain). New York: New American Library.

Rosaldo, M. Z., & Lamphere, L. (Eds.). (1974). *Woman, culture, and society.* Stanford, CA: Stanford University Press.

Russell, B. (1945). *A history of Western philosophy.* New York: Simon & Schuster.

Schore, A. N. (1994). *Affect regulation and the origin of the self: The neurobiology of emotional development.* Hillsdale, NJ: Erlbaum.

Simon, B. (1978). *Mind and madness in ancient Greece.* Ithaca, NY: Cornell University Press.

Whitmont, E. C. (1969). *The symbolic quest: Basic concepts of analytical psychology.* Princeton, NJ: Princeton University Press.

19 Contributions of Lifespan Psychology to the Future Elaboration of Developmental Systems Theory

Richard M. Lerner, Elizabeth Dowling, and Susanna Lara Roth

Tufts University, Medford, MA, U.S.A.

Abstract

Developmental systems theories stress that, across the human life span, development involves the integration, or "fusion," of changing relations among the multiple levels of organization that comprise the ecology of human life. These levels range from biology through culture and history. Indeed, the embeddedness of all levels within history provides a temporal component to human development; makes the potential for change a defining feature of human development; and as such assures that relative plasticity (i.e., the potential for systematic change across ontogeny) characterizes development across the human life span. Moreover, within this developmental system changes are interdependent. For instance, changes within one level of organization, e.g., developmental changes in personality or cognition within the individual, are reciprocally related to developmental changes within other levels, e.g., involving changes in caregiving patterns or spousal relationships within the familial level of organization. In turn, the reciprocal changes among levels of organization are both products and producers of the reciprocal changes within levels. These interrelations illustrate the need for integrated, multidisciplinary study across the life span of changes within and among the multiple levels of organization comprising the ecology of human life. The essence of such scholarship involves the conceptualization and investigation of the mutual regulation of change between person and context or, in other words, of the regulation of relations, of how structures function and how functions are structured over time. The lifespan model of this regulatory relational architecture–the model of selection, optimization, and compensation (SOC)–is thus an exemplary theoretical frame within which to study the human developmental system.

Across the human life span, development involves the integration, or "fusion," of changing relations among the multiple levels of organization that comprise the ecology of human life (Lerner, 1998b, 2002). These levels range from biology through culture and history (Elder, 1998). Indeed, the embeddedness of all levels within history provides a temporal component to human development, makes the potential for change a defining feature of human development, and as such ensures that relative plasticity (the potential for systematic change across ontogeny) characterizes development across the human life span (Lerner, 1984). How may such embedded, multilevel, and plastic change be conceptualized and studied?

Developmental systems theory stresses that reciprocal changes among levels of organization are both products and producers of the reciprocal changes within levels (Ford & Lerner, 1992; Sameroff, 1983; Thelen & Smith, 1998). These models suggest that a focus on process and, particularly, on the process involved in the changing relations between individuals and their contexts, is at the cutting edge of contemporary developmental theory (e.g., Baltes, Lindenberger, & Staudinger, 1998; Baltes, Staudinger, & Lindenberger, 1999; Brandtstädter, 1998; Gottlieb, 1992, 1997; Magnusson & Stattin, 1998; Sameroff, 1983; Thelen & Smith, 1998). Consistent with this suggestion, recent reviews indicate that developmental systems models have become the predominant conceptual frame for research in the study of human development (see Lerner, 1998a).

For instance, developmental systems perspectives are found in the work of Bronfenbrenner (1979; Bronfenbrenner & Morris, 1998) in regard to person-process-context-time relationships within the human ecological system; of Brandtstädter (1998, 1999) in regard to intentionality and goal pursuit in the adult and aged years; of Elder (1998) in regard to the role played by historical variation in the course of human life; of Feldman (2000) in regard to stages of cognitive development; of Fischer and Bidell (1998) in regard to cognitive and behavioral skills in childhood; of Ford and Lerner (1992) in regard to individual-family and individual-peer relations; of Gottlieb (1997) in regard to biological (such as gene-environment coactional) development; of Magnusson (1999a, 1999b), in regard to holistic person-context interactions; of Thelen and Smith (1998) in regard to infant motor development; and of Wapner (1987; Wapner & Demick, 1998) in regard to perception and motivation across life (see also Heckhausen, this volume; Labouvie-Vief, this volume).

Common across all these instances of developmental systems theory is the idea that changes within the developmental system are interdependent. For instance, changes within one level of organization (such as developmental changes in personality or cognition within the individual) are reciprocally related to developmental changes within other levels (such as involving changes in caregiving patterns or spousal relationships within the familial level of organization) (Ford & Lerner, 1992). In turn, the reciprocal changes among levels of organization are both products and producers of the reciprocal changes within levels (Brandtstädter, 1998, 1999; Brandtstädter & Lerner, 1999; Ford & Lerner, 1992; Lerner, 1982; Lerner & Busch-Rossnagel, 1981; Lerner & Walls, 1999; Sameroff, 1983; Thelen & Smith, 1998). For example, over time, parents' styles of behavior and of rearing influence children's personality and cognitive functioning and development; in turn, the interactions between personality and cognition constitute an emergent characteristic of human individuality that affects parental behaviors and styles and the quality of family life (Lerner, Castellino, Terry, Villarruel, & McKinney, 1995).

These intra- and interlevel coactions illustrate the need for integrated, multidisciplinary study across the life span of changes within and among the multiple levels of organization comprising the ecology of human life (Baltes et al., 1998, 1999; Bronfenbrenner & Morris, 1998). Given that human development is the outcome of changes in this developmental system, then, for individual ontogeny, the core process of development involves changing *relations* between the developing person and his or her changing context (Lerner, 1991).

Accordingly, a focus on the process involved in the changing relations between individuals and their contexts is of primary concern in scholarship associated with developmental systems theory (Lerner, 1998a, 1998b). Clearly, the essence of such scholarship involves the conceptualization and investigation of the mutual regulation of change between person and context or, in other words, of the regulation of relations, of how structures function and how functions are structured over time (Brandtstädter, 1998, 1999; Heckhausen, 1999).

The Nature of Developmental Regulation

The study of human development is concerned with the behavior of individuals in their environments (Lerner, 1998a, 1998b, 2002; White, 1968, 1970) and thus with the concept of developmental regulation. Developmental regulation is the process through which the components of morphological structure and behavioral function emerge and interrelate, rates of change in structure and function occur, and the direction of successive changes in the system of person-context relations (such as toward enhanced competency, health, or positive functioning) become established. By definition, developmental systems theory stresses that regulation is *systemic* (multilevel, integrated, and changing) and is predicated on the understanding that, in the phylogeny and ontogeny of human behavior and development (Gottlieb, 1992, 1997; Gottlieb, Wahlsten, & Lickliter, 1998), the relationship between biology and ecology (person and context) is a dynamic one.

The import of this dynamic for the structure and function of human development is that across their life spans, humans actualize a rich potential for psychological (such as cognitive) and behavioral plasticity (Lerner, 1984). However, the evolutionary gains in complexity (anagenesis) that underlie human plasticity have come at a price, that being neotonous development (Gould, 1977). There is an ontogenetically protracted development of humans' eventually high-level cognitive and behavioral capacities. Other organisms, whose nervous systems have lower ratios of association-to-sensory fibers (A/S ratios) (Hebb, 1949), are more stereotyped in their eventual, final level of ontogenetic functioning (Schneirla, 1957). These organisms are typically adapted to ecological niches where their behavior is strictly regulated by their context and therefore stimulus input is highly correlated with their behavioral output. Their relatively low level of ontogenetic plasticity (and their low A/S ratio) solves the problem of the regulation of organism-context relations and thus of adaptation (Hebb, 1949; Schneirla, 1957).

As Heckhausen (1999, p. 8) explains, the evolutionary gains in plasticity made by humans require greater regulation on the part of both the individual and society:

> the relative dearth of biologically based predetermination of behavior gives rise to a high regulatory requirement on the part of the human individual and the social system. The social and cultural system and the individual have to regulate behavior so that resources are invested in an organized and focused way and that failure experiences lead to an improvement rather than to a deterioration of behavioral means.

The complexity of the human nervous system and the multiple levels of potential contexts mean that there is not one, necessarily adaptive relation between context and behavior. While plasticity affords vast variation in behavior, the selection of adaptive options within the array of behaviors available constitutes the key challenge in human development. For instance, Heckhausen (1999) notes that nonhuman primates have more programmed behavioral repertoires than humans who, in turn, have evolved the ability to adapt flexibly to variation in the ecology of human development.

Successful development across life requires the regulation by individuals of relations with their complex and changing contexts. Understanding the system that links together individuals and contexts is arguably the essential intellectual problem in developmental science. As the biological underpinnings of human behavior recede in ontogenetic significance, particularly in the postreproductive years, humans make self-regulatory actions drawing on either individual (such as psychological) or collective (such as cultural) resources (means) to promote successful development (M. Baltes & Carstensen, 1998; P. Baltes & M. Baltes, 1990; see M. Baltes & Carstensen, this volume).

The focus on self-regulative actions—on the ways that the "individual is both the active producer and the product of his or her ontogeny ... [and thus on] self-regulative loops that link developmental changes to the ways in which individuals, in action and mentation, construe their personal development" (Brandtstädter, 1988, p. 807)—is the essence of action perspectives about human development and the necessary target of lifespan developmental analysis. A lifespan, action-theoretical model of this regulatory relational architecture—the model of selection, optimization, and compensation (SOC) (e.g., P. Baltes, 1997; P. Baltes & M. Baltes, 1990; M. Baltes & Carstensen, 1996, 1998; M. Baltes & Lang, 1997; Freund & P. Baltes, 1998)—is an exemplary theoretical frame within which to study the human developmental system (Lerner, Freund, De Stefanis, & Habermas, 2001).

The Baltes and Baltes SOC Model

The conception of development found in the selection, optimization, and compensation (SOC) model of P. Baltes, M. Baltes, and their colleagues (e.g., P. Baltes, 1997; P. Baltes & M. Baltes, 1990; M. Baltes & Carstensen, 1996, 1998; Freund & P. Baltes, 1998, 2000; Marsiske, Lang, P. Baltes, & M. Baltes, 1995) provides a general theoretical framework for the understanding of processes of developmental regulation across different levels of analysis (ranging from the micro to macro levels), across different domains of functioning (such as cognitive functioning or social relations), and across the entire life span. Although selection, optimization, and compensation need be considered conjointly to adequately describe and understand development, for the sake of clarifying the relation of the SOC model to developmental regulation and to developmental systems theory we introduce each process individually.

The concept of *selection* is derived from the assumption that internal and external resources such as stamina, money, and social support are constrained and limited throughout the entire life span (e.g., Baltes, 1997). By focusing and guiding resources and preventing the diffusion of resources, selection gives direction to development. The SOC model posits that a range of alternative developmental options needs to be delineated. This is termed *elective selection*. For example, to gain popularity in school, an adolescent may elect to pursue athletic goals instead of academic ones.

In order to achieve higher levels in the selected domains of functioning *optimization* needs to take place. Optimization addresses the growth aspect of development as it denotes the process of acquiring, refining, coordinating, and applying goal-relevant means or resources to the selected domains. In situations in which people seek to identify and pursue goals, typical instances of optimization are the acquisition of training of specific goal-related skills (such as weight training to enhance athletic skills) and persistence in goal pursuit.

Development is multidirectional in that it encompasses both growth and decline (P. Baltes, 1997; P. Baltes et al., 1998; Brandtstädter & Wentura, 1995; Labouvie-Vief, 1981). The SOC model addresses the aspect of decline and management of loss by stressing the importance of *compensation*. When loss or decline in goal-relevant means threatens one's level of functioning, it is necessary to invest additional resources or substitute or apply additional means geared toward the maintenance of functioning (Carstensen, Hanson, & Freund, 1995; Staudinger, Marsiske, & Baltes, 1995; Marsiske et al., 1995; see also Bäckman & Dixon, 1992).

Prototypical instances of compensation are the substitution of means or the use of external aids (such as the help of a physical trainer to excel in sports). When compensatory efforts fail or their costs outweigh their gains, the more adaptive response to loss or decline in goal-related means might be to restructure one's goal-hierarchy (such as to place academics ahead of athletics), lower one's standards (such as to settle for being a second-string athlete), or look for new goals, what is termed *loss-based selection* (such as make academics a superordinate goal instead of a means to attain, for instance, popularity among peers). This component of selection is functionally different from elective selection because it occurs as a response to a loss and typically leads to different motivational and affective consequences (Freund & Baltes, 1998, 2000).

Although it is possible to differentiate the components of SOC, successful development encompasses their coordinated integration (Freund & Baltes, 2000; Marsiske et al., 1995; see also Behrman, this volume). For instance, selection per se does not ensure high achievement if no goal-relevant means are applied to the goals that are chosen. Optimization efforts typically lead to higher levels of functioning only when they are focused on a delineated number of domains of functioning instead of being diffused among many domains. The adaptiveness of compensation is considered within the context of the entire goal system and according to the availability of resources. It is rarely adaptive to dedicate much of one's resources to relatively unimportant domains of functioning at the cost of having to neglect more important goals (Freund, Li, & Baltes, 1999).

As we have noted, the SOC model provides a conceptually nuanced and empirically productive frame for understanding across the life span the process of developmental regulation or the reciprocal influence of individuals on contexts and contexts on individuals. As such, the model extends the usefulness of developmental systems theory.

Studying Regulation Within Developmental Systems Theory: Contributions of the SOC Model

Most contemporary research about human development is associated with theoretical ideas stressing that the dynamics of individual-context relations provide the bases of behavior and developmental change (Lerner, 1991, 1996; 1998a). As such, to understand the bases of adaptive development, a key issue becomes one of specifying the nature and outcomes of individuals' actions in respect to (1) identifying, organizing, and deciding to pursue goals (which are "selection" actions), (2) developing knowledge and skills to pursue goals and to recruit social and physical resources to facilitate reaching one's goals (which are "optimization" actions), and (3) developing the ability to deal with the diversity of outcomes that actions will produce and (of special importance for the continuity of adaptive functioning across the life span) with failure. Individuals must develop the ability to accept and learn from failures and from loss and to reorganize their selection and optimization actions to enable some sort of adaptive paths to continue to be pursued (these are "compensation" actions).

Accordingly, given the significant potential use of the SOC model for understanding developmental regulation across life, it may constitute a significant tool for advancing understanding the dynamic interplay of the person with his or her contexts within the developmental system. Given this potential use, the future elaboration of developmental systems theory may involve the empirical application of the SOC model across the life span (e.g., Lerner, et al., 2001).

However, this empirical use will require methodologically triangulated research, such as that conducted in regard to the use of the model within the adult and aged portions of the life span (e.g., Baltes, 1997; Baltes et al., 1998, 1999). Moreover, such research will need to be multilevel and therefore multivariate, in order to engage variables on both "sides" of the person-context relationship involved in regulation within the developmental system. In addition, change-sensitive measures and change-sensitive (longitudinal) designs will be needed to appraise the developing goal structure and optimization and compensation strategies of youth and the import of SOC actions for adult development (see Nesselroade & Ghisletta this volume). Finally, such research will need to employ measurement and analytic techniques sensitive to diversity, both in regard to (1) intraindividual changes in goal structures and in the means used to pursue goals over the course of development and (2) interindividual differences in such intraindividual change (see Molenaar, Huizenga, & Nesselroade, this volume).

In our view, such research will underscore that the SOC model provides an integrative and potentially productive empirical frame for understanding how the basic process of human development across the life span is one of changing relations between the active, intentional individual and his or her complex social, cultural, and historical context. Thus, the SOC model of lifespan development will engage the contributions of individuals themselves to further knowledge about the issues, assets, and risks affecting their lives.

Conclusions

The SOC model extends the usefulness of developmental systems theory by providing scholars with a conceptually nuanced and empirically productive frame for understanding the influence of individuals on contexts and, reciprocally, the influence of contexts on individuals. Although it has been primarily used to elucidate developmental regulation in the adult and aged years, there is reason to believe it will become a productive frame for developmental systems research about adolescent development (Lerner et al., 2001). It may be useful, then, in elucidating the action-theoretical idea that adolescents are active producers of their own development (Lerner, 1982; Lerner & Walls, 1999; see also Köller, Baumert, & Schabel, this volume). Informed by the SOC model of lifespan development, development systems theory may evolve therefore to be a framework within which *knowledge* of the bases of research participants' successful development is coupled with programmatic *actions* by these individuals—that is, selections aimed at actively promoting their own successful development.

In this manner, the SOC model holds the promise of being a powerful conceptual tool in both understanding and, through interventions promoting the active contributions of individuals to their contexts, enhancing the developmental system. Through the SOC model, then, developmental systems theory may become a more productive frame for the *application* of developmental science across the life span. This integrated contribution to science and application would be a fitting result of the use of the SOC model, given that the formulators of this model—Paul B. Baltes and Margret M. Baltes (e.g., 1980, 1990)—have made distinguished, career-long contributions using singularly excellent developmental scholarship to enhance individuals' lives across the span of human ontogeny.

References

Bäckman, L., & Dixon, R. A. (1992). Psychological compensation: A theoretical framework. *Psychological Bulletin, 112*, 1–25.

Baltes, M. M., & Carstensen, L. L. (1996). The process of successful ageing. *Ageing and Society, 16*, 397–422.

Baltes, M. M., & Carstensen, L. L. (1998). Social-psychological theories and their applications to aging: From individual to collective. In V. L. Bengtson & K. W. Schaie (Eds.), *Handbook of theories of aging* (pp. 209–226). New York: Springer.

Baltes, M. M., & Lang, F. R. (1997). Everyday functioning and successful aging: The impact of resources. *Psychology and Aging, 12*, 433–443.

Baltes, P. B. (1997). On the incomplete architecture of human ontogeny: Selection, optimization, and compensation as foundations of developmental theory. *American Psychologist, 52*, 366–380.

Baltes, P. B., & Baltes, M. M. (1980). Plasticity and variability in psychological aging: Methodological and theoretical issues. In G. E. Gurski (Ed.), *Determining the effects of aging on the central nervous system* (pp. 41–66). Berlin: Schering.

Baltes, P. B., & Baltes, M. M. (1990). Psychological perspectives on successful aging: The model of selective optimization with compensation. In P. B. Baltes & M. M. Baltes (Eds.), *Successful aging: Perspectives from the behavioral sciences* (pp. 1–34). New York: Cambridge University Press.

Baltes, P. B., Lindenberger, U., & Staudinger, U. M. (1998). Life-span theory in developmental psychology. In R. M. Lerner (Ed.), *Handbook of child psychology*, Vol. 1, *Theoretical models of human development* (5th ed., pp. 1029–1143). New York: Wiley.

Baltes, P. B., Staudinger, U. M., & Lindenberger, U. (1999). Lifespan psychology: Theory and application to intellectual functioning. In J. T. Spence, J. M. Darley, & D. J. Foss (Eds.), *Annual review of psychology* (Vol. 50, pp. 471–507). Palo Alto, CA: Annual Reviews.

Brandtstädter, J. (1998). Action perspectives on human development. In R. M. Lerner (Ed.), *Handbook of child psychology*, Vol. 1, *Theoretical models of human development* (5th ed., pp. 807–863). New York: Wiley.

Brandtstädter, J. (1999). The self in action and development: Cultural, biosocial, and ontogenetic bases of intentional self-development. In J. Brandtstädter & R. M. Lerner (Eds.), *Action and self-development: Theory and research through the life span* (pp. 37–65). Thousand Oaks, CA: Sage.

Brandtstädter, J., & Lerner, R. M. (Eds.). (1999). *Action and self-development: Theory and research through the life span*. Thousand Oaks, CA: Sage.

Brandtstädter, J., & Wentura, D. (1995). Adjustment to shifting possibility frontiers in later life: Compensatory adaptive modes. In R. A. Dixon & L. Bäckman (Eds.), *Psychological compensation: Managing losses and promoting gains* (pp. 83–106). Hillsdale, NJ: Erlbaum.

Bronfenbrenner, U. (1979) *The ecology of human development: Experiments by nature and design*. Cambridge: Harvard University Press.

Bronfenbrenner, U., & Morris, P. A. (1998). The ecology of developmental processes. In R. M. Lerner (Ed.), *Handbook of child psychology*, Vol. 1, *Theoretical models of human development* (5th ed., pp. 993–1028). New York: Wiley.

Carstensen, L. L., Hanson, K. A., & Freund, A. (1995). Selection and compensation in adulthood. In R. A. Dixon & L. Bäckman (Eds.), *Compensating for psychological deficits and declines: Managing losses and promoting gains* (pp. 107–126). Hillsdale, NJ: Erlbaum.

Elder, G. H., Jr. (1998). The life course and human development. In R. M. Lerner (Ed.), *Handbook of child psychology*, Vol. 1, *Theoretical models of human development* (5th ed., pp. 939–991). New York: Wiley.

Feldman, D. H. (2000). *Piaget's stages: The unfinished symphony.* Manuscript, Eliot-Pearson Department of Child Development, Tufts University.

Fisher, K. W., & Bidell, T. R. (1998). Dynamic development of psychological structures in action and thought. In R. M. Lerner (Ed.), *Handbook of child psychology*, Vol. 1, *Theoretical models of human development*. (5th ed., pp. 467–561). New York: Wiley.

Ford, D. L., & Lerner, R. M. (1992). *Developmental systems theory: An integrative approach.* Newbury Park, CA: Sage.

Freund, A. M., & Baltes, P. B. (1998). Selection, optimization, and compensation as strategies of life-management: Correlations with subjective indicators of successful aging. *Psychology and Aging, 13*, 531–543.

Freund, A. M., & Baltes, P. B. (2000). The orchestration of selection, optimization, and compensation: An action-theoretical conceptualization of a theory of developmental regulation. In W. J. Perrig & A. Grob (Eds.), *Control of human behavior, mental processes and consciousness: Essays in honor of the sixtieth birthday of August Flammer* (pp. 35–58). Mahwah, NJ: Erlbaum.

Freund, A., Li, K. Z. H., & Baltes, P. B. (1999). The role of selection, optimization, and compensation in successful aging. In J. Brandtstädter & R. M. Lerner (Eds.), *Action and self-development: Theory and research through the life-span* (pp. 401–434). Thousand Oaks, CA: Sage.

Gottlieb, G. (1992). *Individual development and evolution: The genesis of novel behavior.* New York: Oxford University Press.

Gottlieb, G. (1997). *Synthesizing nature-nurture: Prenatal roots of instinctive behavior.* Mahwah, NJ: Erlbaum.

Gottlieb, G., Wahlsten, D., & Lickliter, R. (1998). The significance of biology for human development: A developmental psychobiological systems view. In R. M. Lerner (Ed.), *Handbook of child psychology*, Vol. 1, *Theoretical models of human development* (5th ed., pp. 233–273). New York: Wiley.

Gould, S. J. (1977). *Ontogeny and phylogeny.* Cambridge, MA: Belknap Press of Harvard.

Hebb, D. O. (1949). *The organization of behavior.* New York: Wiley.

Heckhausen, J. (1999). *Developmental regulation in adulthood: Age-normative and sociocultural constraints as adaptive challenges.* New York: Cambridge University Press.

Labouvie-Vief, G. (1981). Proactive and reactive aspects of constructivism: Growth and aging in life-span perspective. In R. M. Lerner & N. A. Busch-Rossnagel (Eds.), *Individuals as producers of their own development* (pp. 197–230). New York: Academic Press.

Lerner, R. M. (1982). Children and adolescents as producers of their own development. *Developmental Review, 2*, 342–370.

Lerner, R. M. (1984). *On the nature of human plasticity.* New York: Cambridge University Press.

Lerner, R. M. (1991). Changing organism-context relations as the basic process of development: A developmental contextual perspective. *Developmental Psychology, 27*, 27–32.

Lerner, R. M. (1996). Relative plasticity, integration, temporality, and diversity in human development: A developmental, contextual perspective about theory, process, and method. *Developmental Psychology, 32*, 781–786.

Lerner, R. M. (Ed.). (1998a). *Handbook of child psychology*, Vol. 1, *Theoretical models of human development* (5th ed.). New York: Wiley.

Lerner, R. M. (1998b). Theories of human development: Contemporary perspectives. In R. M. Lerner (Ed.), *Handbook of child psychology*, Vol. 1, *Theoretical models of human development* (5th ed., pp. 1–24). New York: Wiley.

Lerner, R. M. (2002). *Concepts and theories of human development* (3rd ed.). Mahwah, NJ: Erlbaum.

Lerner, R. M., & Busch-Rossnagel, N. A. (Eds.). (1981). *Individuals as producers of their development: A life-span perspective.* New York: Academic Press.

Lerner, R. M., Castellino, D. R., Terry, P. A., Villarruel, F. A., & McKinney, M. H. (1995). A developmental contextual perspective on parenting. In M. H. Bornstein (Ed.), *Handbook of parenting: Biology and ecology of parenting* (Vol. 2, pp. 285–309). Hillsdale, NJ: Erlbaum.

Lerner, R. M., Freund, A. M., De Stefanis, I., & Habermas, T. (2001). Understanding developmental regulation in adolescence: The use of the selection, optimization, and compensation model. *Human Development, 44*, 29–50.

Lerner, R. M., & Walls, T. (1999). Revisiting individuals as producers of their development: From dynamic interactionism to developmental systems. In J. Brandtstädter & R. M. Lerner (Eds.), *Action and development: Origins and functions of intentional self-development* (pp. 3–36). Thousand Oaks, CA: Sage.

Magnusson, D. (1999a). On the individual: A person-oriented approach to developmental research. *European Psychologist, 4*, 205–218.

Magnusson, D. (1999b). Holistic interactionism: A perspective for research on personality development. In L. A. Pervin & O. P. John (Eds.), *Handbook of personality: Theory and research* (2nd ed., pp. 219–247). New York: Guilford Press.

Magnusson, D., & Stattin, H. (1998). Person-context interaction theories. In R. M. Lerner (Ed.), *Handbook of child psychology*, Vol. 1, *Theoretical models of human development* (5th ed., pp. 685–759). New York: Wiley.

Marsiske, M., Lang, F. R., Baltes, P. B., & Baltes, M. M. (1995). Selective optimization with compensation: Life-span perspectives on successful human development. In R. A. Dixon & L. Bäckman (Eds.), *Compensating for psychological deficits and declines: Managing losses and promoting gains* (pp. 35–79). Mahwah, NJ: Erlbaum.

Sameroff, A. J. (1983). Developmental systems: Contexts and evolution. In W. Kessen (Ed.), *Handbook of child psychology*, Vol. 1, *History, theory, and methods* (pp. 237–294). New York: Wiley.

Schneirla, T. C. (1957). The concept of development in comparative psychology. In D. B. Harris (Ed.), *The concept of development* (pp. 78–108). Minneapolis: University of Minnesota.

Staudinger, U. M., Marsiske, M., & Baltes, P. B. (1995). Resilience and reserve capacity in later adulthood: Potentials and limits of development across the life-span. In D. Cicchetti & D. Cohen (Eds.), *Developmental psychopathology*, Vol. 2, *Risk, disorder, and adaptation* (pp. 801–847). New York: Wiley.

Thelen, E., & Smith, L. B. (1998). Dynamic systems theories. In R. M. Lerner (Ed.), *Handbook of child psychology*, Vol. 1, *Theoretical models of human development* (5th ed., pp. 563–633). New York: Wiley.

Wapner, S. (1987). A holistic, developmental, systems-oriented environmental psychology: Some beginnings. In D. Stokols & I. Altman (Eds.), *Handbook of environmental psychology* (pp. 1433–1465). New York: Wiley.

Wapner, S., & Demick, J. (1998). Developmental analysis: A holistic, developmental, systems-oriented perspective. In R. M. Lerner (Ed.), *Handbook of child psychology*, Vol. 1. *Theoretical models of human development* (5th ed., pp. 761–805). New York: Wiley.

White, S. H. (1968). The learning-maturation controversy: Hall to Hull. *Merrill-Palmer Quarterly, 14*, 187–196.

White, S. H. (1970). The learning theory tradition and child psychology. In P. H. Mussen (Ed.), *Carmichael's manual of child psychology* (3rd ed., Vol. 1, pp. 657–702). New York: Wiley.

20 The Adaptive Toolbox and Lifespan Development: Common Questions?

Gerd Gigerenzer

Max Planck Institute for Human Development, Berlin, Germany

Abstract

In this chapter, I explore the relationship between the vision of bounded rationality as an adaptive toolbox (e.g., Gigerenzer, Todd, & the ABC Research Group, 1999) and the vision of development as selection-optimization-compensation (Baltes, 1997, this volume). Both approaches are metatheories that advise us as to what questions to ask and what kinds of models to build. Both have an affinity for the use of evolutionary thinking as a guideline for what problems to address. Beyond this, however, are there similar ideas? Contradictions? And most important, is there a fruitful transfer of ideas and questions?

Visions of Rationality

Developmental, economic, and philosophical theories postulate, explicitly or implicitly, models of rational behavior and cognition. The Enlightenment view of rationality—that the laws of thought and the laws of probability are two sides of the same coin—has left its fingerprints on contemporary theories of human thinking that assume that mature thinking is content-independent, just as are the laws of logic and probability. For instance, Piaget and Inhelder (e.g., 1975) modeled the development of thinking in children as a cumulative process that ends at age 12 to 15 at the level of formal operations—at least in Geneva. Whereas Piaget, Inhelder, and many contemporary researchers in their wake have conducted experiments with textbook-type problems assuming that only logical operations, but not the content of the problem, should matter, others studied rationality in the real world where content-related knowledge does matter (cf. Wellman, this volume).

The move away from simple deductive or inductive reasoning problems has often resulted in visions of rationality in which organisms are assumed to be capable of computing probabilities and their joint distributions and also of having substantial knowledge about their environment, sometimes to the point of clairvoyance. Optimal foraging theory, for instance, models ants and bees *as if* they knew the distribution of all resources, conspecifics, and predators and could compute differential equations to choose the optimal patch and the moment to switch to the next patch (see Goodie, Ortmann, Davis, Bullock, & Werner, 1999). Real animals, of course, have to rely on rules of thumb (e.g., Seeley, 2001). Not only is the rationality of animals modeled by omniscience and massive mental computations; that of humans is portrayed in this way, too. Theories of human categorization, for instance, assume that a person stores all instances of, for example, cars she has ever seen—all Chevrolets, Hondas, Fords, Mazdas, and so on—in a multidimensional space of huge proportions. To categorize a new object—say, the car that just passed by—humans represent the new object as a new point in the same space. They then, ostensibly, compute the Euclidean distances between the new object and all stored ones and finally classify the new object as an instance of that class of stored objects that minimizes the average Euclidean distance (see Berretty, Todd, & Martignon, 1999). In many a vision, the rationality of cognition is equated with the three Os—omniscience, omnipotence, and optimization.

In Figure 20.1, I distinguish between two visions of rationality—*demons* and *bounded rationality*. Demons involve the three Os and enjoy great popularity in the social and behavioral sciences. There are two species of demons—those that exhibit *unbounded rationality* and those that *optimize under constraints*. Unbounded rationality describes decision strategies that ignore the fact that humans (and other animals) have

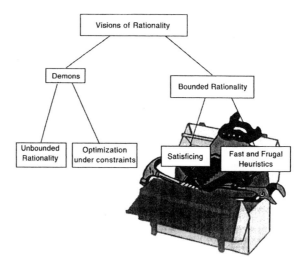

Figure 20.1   Visions of Rationality Underlying Cognitive Theories (from Gigerenzer, 2001; reprinted with permission of University of Nebraska Press).

limited time, knowledge, and computational capacities. In this framework, the question is, If humans were omniscient and had all eternity at their disposal, how would they behave? Maximizing expected utility, Bayesian models, Piaget's formal operations, and *Homo economicus* are examples of unbounded rationality frameworks. Unbounded rationality recreates humans in the image of God or in a secularized version thereof—Laplace's superintelligence. The weakness of unbounded rationality is that it does not describe the way real people think—not even philosophers, as the following anecdote illustrates. A philosopher from Columbia University was struggling with whether to accept an offer from a rival university or to stay where he was. His colleague took him aside and said: "Just maximize your expected utility: you always write about doing this." Exasperated, the philosopher responded: "Come on, this is serious."

In 1961, the economist George Stigler made the image of *Homo economicus* more realistic. He introduced the fact that humans need to search for information—rather than being omniscient—which costs time and money (cf. Behrman, this volume). However, Stigler chose to retain the ideal of optimization and assumed that search is stopped when the costs of further search exceed its benefits: in other words, an optimal stopping point is calculated. This vision of rationality is known as *optimization under constraints* (such as time) and is prominent in models of domains ranging from animal foraging to human memory (Anderson & Milson, 1989). Even devoted proponents of optimization under constraints, however, have pointed out that the resulting models generally become more demanding than models of unbounded rationality, both mathematically and psychologically: The more constraints one introduces, the more complex the optimization calculations become. In optimization under constraints, humans are recreated in the image of econometricians, one step above the gods.

Most theories of cognition are based, at least implicitly, on the assumption of unbounded rationality: they do not model the search for information or stopping rules but rather assume that the organism already has all the relevant information (omniscience). The trick in the experiments is to use reasoning problems that exclude information search because (1) they have no content, as with logical problems, or (2) they have content, but it consists of artificial stimuli that vary only on two or a few dimensions, thereby excluding search for relevant knowledge. Textbooks on thinking and reasoning overflow with this type of problem. In the rare cases where search for information is actually modeled, optimization under constraints seems to be the favorite model.

An alternative vision is that of bounded rationality (see Figure 20.1). Herbert Simon (e.g., 1956, 1992), the father of "bounded rationality," argued that a theory of rationality has to be faithful to the actual cognitive capacities of humans—to their limitations in knowledge, attention, memory, and other resources. To Simon's dismay, his term *limitations* has mostly been taken to mean "constraints," and the term "bounded rationality" became confused with "optimization under constraints." In personal conversation, he once remarked, with a mixture of humor and anger, that he had considered suing authors who misused his concept of bounded rationality to construct even more complicated and unrealistic models of the human mind.

The Adaptive Toolbox

I propose the concept of the *adaptive toolbox*, which can help to avoid the misapprehension that making rationality more realistic just means making optimization more difficult. The adaptive toolbox of a species contains heuristics, not a general optimization calculus. These heuristics do not compute utilities, nor do they involve optimization. When used in the proper environment, these heuristics can be fast and effective. The heuristics consist of building blocks—such as rules for search, stopping search, and decision—and these building blocks can be recombined to generate new heuristics (see Gigerenzer & Selten, 2001; Gigerenzer & Todd, 1999). Some are inherited; others are learned or designed.

In Figure 20.1, I list two classes of tools in the adaptive toolbox. One class, Simon's *satisficing*, involves search and an aspiration level that stops search. For instance, when searching for a house, satisficers search until they find the first house that meets their aspiration level, stop search, and go for it. No attempt is made to compute an optimal stopping point (where the costs of further search exceed its benefits). A second class are fast and frugal heuristics (see Gigerenzer et al., 1999). The difference is this: satisficing involves search across alternatives, such as houses and potential spouses, assuming that the criteria are given (the aspiration level). Fast and frugal heuristics, by contrast, search for criteria or cues in situations in which the alternatives are given. For instance, classifying heart attack patients into high- and low-risk categories is such a situation: the alternatives are given (high or low risk), and one has to search for cues that indicate the alternative category a patient belongs to (Gigerenzer & Todd, 1999). A heuristic is said to be *fast* when it does not involve much computation and *frugal* when it searches for only some of the information.

The adaptive toolbox contains heuristics that help humans to deal with their social and physical environments. Heuristics are simple strategies—shortcuts or rules of thumb that can solve a class of problems, even when there is only limited time, knowledge, and other resources.

An example of a fast and frugal heuristic is the recognition heuristic. This heuristic is in the adaptive toolbox of both animals and humans. For instance, when a wild Norway rat has to choose between two foods—one that it recognizes because it had tasted it before and another that it does not recognize—the rat prefers the recognized food. Similarly, when humans choose between two similar goods—one whose brand name they recognize and one that they do not recognize—they tend to prefer the first. More generally, consider the class of tasks required to infer which of two alternatives has a higher value on a criterion and those situations in which recognition is positively correlated with the criterion (for example, having heard of a city indicates that it has a larger population). If a person recognizes one alternative but not the other, the recognition heuristic advises inferring that the recognized alternative has the higher value on the criterion. The heuristic is, of course, not foolproof; the proportion of correct inferences can be theoretically predicted on the basis of an individual's knowledge and empirically tested (Goldstein & Gigerenzer, 2002).

The adaptive toolbox is, in two respects, a Darwinian model of human functioning:

- *Domain-specificity* Heuristics are domain-specific, not domain-general. Evolution does not follow a grand plan but results in a patchwork of solutions for specific problems. The same holds for the adaptive toolbox. Like hammers and wrenches, its tools—the heuristics—are specifically designed to solve a class of problems but not all problems.
- *Ecological rationality* Heuristics are not good or bad or rational or irrational per se. Their performance is relative to an environment, just as adaptations are not good or bad per se but are relative to an environment. The rationality of the adaptive toolbox is not logical but *ecological*.

For instance, the recognition heuristic is domain-specific in the sense that it can help to quickly solve problems that involve choosing between known and unknown objects. If one has to choose between two colleges—one that has a good reputation and the other that does not have a recognizable name—mere name recognition is a valid (although never perfect) cue for the quality of education. More generally, competitive situations—such as in stock markets, education, and sports—belong to the domain of the recognition heuristic. This heuristic can be used only by people who are sufficiently ignorant about the task at hand. An expert who knows all colleges, all brand names, or all sports teams cannot use the recognition heuristic: she has to rely on knowledge beyond recognition. And in a class of situations that have been defined, not being able to use the recognition heuristic can cause the counterintuitive less-is-more effect: more knowledge leads to less accurate inferences (Goldstein & Gigerenzer, 2002).

Ecological Rationality

The human color-constancy mechanism—which allows us to see an object as having the same color in the bluish sunlight at noon as well as the reddish light of the setting sun—is an adaptation. An adaptation is always with respect to an environment: it is not a good or bad mechanism per se. For instance, in situations with certain artificial lights, such as sodium vapor lamps in parking lots, our color-constancy mechanism breaks down. Those who have seen their green car turn blue know of this shocking experience. More generally, a Darwinian notion of rationality is always relative to an environment—that is, rationality is not logical but ecological. Face recognition, voice recognition, and name recognition are adaptations that help us to identify conspecifics that engage with us in social exchange and cooperation and to ostracize cheaters, among other functions. The recognition heuristic feeds on these psychological adaptations; it is not derived from logic, nor does it use an optimization calculus. The use of this heuristic is ecologically rational in environments where recognition is correlated with the criterion one wants to know—that is, where the recognition validity is better than chance (see Goldstein & Gigerenzer, 2002).

Domain-specificity and ecological rationality go hand in hand. In fact, the concept of ecological rationality provides a quantitative framework for understanding which structures of environments a heuristic can exploit. It also helps us to better understand the notion of domain-specificity and, moreover, define it mathematically (Martignon & Hoffrage, 1999). So far, however, domain-specificity has meant many things to many people (e.g., Hirschfeld & Gelman, 1994).

Simon expressed the ecological nature of bounded rationality by using a pair of scissors as a metaphor. The cognitive capabilities are one blade; the other is the structure of environments. One blade alone does not cut. Studying solely the cognitive capabilities—as most research in cognitive, developmental, and social psychology still does—will not help us understand how the mind works. Without ecological rationality, the study of bounded rationality is reduced to that of irrationality.

The Adaptive Toolbox in Lifespan Development

Thus far, I have briefly introduced the vision of bounded rationality as an adaptive toolbox—a collection of fast and frugal heuristics that uses simple rules for search, stopping, and decision as building blocks. I have also discussed the concept of ecological rationality rather than logical rationality and a toolbox with domain-specific, middle-range heuristics rather than one general-purpose tool. In what follows, I suggest several questions, not answers, that emerge from the intersection of the study of bounded rationality and the selection, optimization, and compensation framework.

What Is in the Adaptive Toolbox at Birth?

What heuristics are present at birth, and which emerge in the course of early development? Which social and physical environments are helpful in eliciting prepared heuristics? One challenge is to describe the content of the adaptive toolbox in early infancy in a precise and testable way (cf. Singer, this volume; Wellman, this volume). A description of a heuristic involves (1) its initial purpose (which may generalize later), (2) the environmental stimuli (including social stimuli and, if necessary, the inner physiological states of the infant) that elicit the heuristic, and (3) the search, stopping, and decision rules of which the heuristic consists. A baby's social smile, for instance, can be seen as a heuristic that emerges after a few months for the purpose of eliciting a parent's commitment, bonding, and the emotion of parental love. Once elicited, parental love prevents a parent from acting like *Homo economicus* making a cost-benefit analysis every morning of whether to invest time and resources in an infant or in some more promising venture or offspring.

The heuristics in the adaptive toolbox are concrete instructions to both infants and parents telling them what to do, not general capabilities or attitudes. The notion of a theory of mind, for instance, is not a heuristic; it is a description of a capability, just like episodic memory or fluid intelligence.

Are Heuristics Acquired and Lost During Development?

I distinguish four ways to acquire new heuristics. Heuristics can be genetically coded or prepared, they can be acquired during the life course by learning, they can be designed, and they can be created from the building blocks of other heuristics. Let me give one example of each of these.

Female guppies choose between two potential mates using a simple heuristic that decides using only one reason, such as whether they have seen the one candidate mating with another female but not the other (Dugatkin & Godin, 1998). These females prefer the male that other females also preferred. This mate copying is genetically coded, although not observable at birth. Note that mate copying exemplifies the *interaction* between culturally based preferences and genetic preferences. Social copying heuristics can also be observed in humans, from the pop idols whom teenagers favor to the hiring of star professors.

When you learn to fly an airplane, you are taught a heuristic for avoiding collisions: when another plane approaches, look at a scratch in your windshield and see whether the other plane moves relative to that scratch. If it does not, dive away quickly. This heuristic is faster and more frugal than the "rational" procedure of computing the trajectories of both planes in four-dimensional space (including time) and determining whether they intersect. Learning, including observational learning, imitation, and instruction, is a second way to acquire new heuristics.

Besides observation and imitation, there is a third possibility for designing heuristics from scratch. For instance, emergency room physicians must decide whether a patient with suspected acute ischemic heart disease should be admitted to the coronary care unit. The Heart Disease Predictive Instrument (HDPI) has a documented validity for this decision and consists of a logistic formula for calculating the probability that the patient has the disease from a table with almost 50 probabilities. Because of this complexity, however, physicians tend neither to use nor to understand this tool and often rely on pseudodiagnostic cues that lead to inferior predictions. Yet there is a third method aside from confusion through complexity and mere intuition. Green and Mehr (1997) designed a fast and frugal heuristic, based on the Take The Best heuristic (Gigerenzer & Goldstein, 1996), which turned out to be more accurate in classifying patients than the HDPI and, moreover, could easily be understood and used by physicians.

Finally, new heuristics can be constructed from the building blocks—rules for search, stopping, and decision—of old heuristics. This recombination of the building blocks is described in Gigerenzer et al. (1999).

One might assume that, during development, the adaptive toolbox becomes more and more filled with new tools and that nothing gets lost. Can heuristics or their building blocks ever be lost? When and to what degree this happens is still an open question. Tasks in which children outperform adults suggest that there might indeed be heuristics that are lost between childhood and adult life.

Do Heuristics Change in Old Age?

Old age is characterized by losses in several functions, and the concept of compensation in the SOC framework refers to these losses. One form of compensation can be the shifting of tools in the adaptive toolbox so that certain classes of tools are on the top—that is, more often used. For instance, when the daily activities and the organization of a social life become difficult to manage because of losses in sensory and motor functions, heuristics that involve less planning and less attention to the outside world may be preferred. Heuristics involving routines and imitation rather than judgments and informed choice may become more frequent (cf. Kliegl, Krampe, & Mayr, this volume). If this change of heuristics does not occur automatically, one might systematically teach older people to reorganize their adaptive toolbox and switch to more robust heuristics that can reduce complexity into manageable parts. The divide-and-conquer heuristic is one example. When complex tasks (such as maintaining a conversation while maneuvering around an obstacle) tend to become difficult with age, the divide-and-conquer heuristic advises splitting such tasks into manageable parts or sequences (for example, first maneuver around the obstacle while stopping the conversation, and then take up the conversation again). This heuristic can prevent a type of accident in older people that results from their trying to solve everyday problems in the same way as they did when they were young.

A second heuristic whose scope might increase in old age is the recognition heuristic. Aging affects recall more than recognition memory. For instance, at a party, a friend of mine once wanted to introduce his wife to a colleague and said, "This is my wife—um, ah, um . . . " at which point his wife helped him out and said, "Susan." Note that recall, not recognition, of her name was the problem. In general, the more recall fades, the more an aging person has to rely on mere name recognition in everyday life. For instance, when information about the quality of products becomes hard to recall, aging consumers nevertheless do not have to rely on guessing; they can choose among the products in supermarkets and department stores using the recognition heuristic: buy the product you recognize. Therefore, older people, just like younger and yet fairly ignorant people, may have a great use for the recognition heuristic to guide their decision making.

How Should Environments Be Designed During the Life Span?

Theories of thinking and problem solving assume that solving a problem occurs inside a person's head. The concept of ecological rationality, in contrast, emphasizes that the structure of the environment can do part of the work when a person solves a problem. For instance, consider a person who takes a hemoccult test, a screening test for colorectal cancer, that comes out positive. He wants to know his chances for actually having colorectal cancer. When we gave experienced physicians the relevant information in conditional probabilities, which is common in medical training, their answers varied from 1% to 99%. When we gave the physicians the same information in natural frequencies, all of them gave the same answer of about 5%, which is consistent with Bayes's rule (Gigerenzer, 2002; Hoffrage & Gigerenzer, 1998). Insight comes, in part, from outside—in this case, how one presents information in the physicians' environments.

If it is true that heuristics and their building blocks change in a predictable way during lifespan development, one can imagine designing environments so that these heuristics can work better at each stage of development. For instance, if in old age routines dominate everyday affairs, then it may be important to not change a person's home environment with new technology, even if this would improve a younger adult's life.

What Is the Role of Emotions as Heuristic Strategies over the Course of Life?

Heuristics can include cognitive and emotional building blocks. Emotions can fulfill the same functions in the adaptive toolbox as do cognitive building blocks. They can provide tools for search (what information to look for), stopping search, and decision making, in order to prevent the organism from getting stuck in an endless search for information or a cost-benefit analysis. But why would one need emotion in addition to cognition? There is a class of adaptive problems in which emotions can guide decisions more effectively than cognitive building blocks. Consider three women searching for a partner to start a family and rear children.

Ms. Economicus proceeds by rational-choice theory. She first tries to determine all possible partners and list for each all possible consequences—whether he likes children, will help parenting, be tender, be humorous, become an alcoholic, beat her up, get depressed, divorce her, and so on. Then she must do extensive research with each candidate to reliably determine the probability of each of the consequences actually occurring. Next, she needs to estimate quantitative utility for each of these consequences—say, helping parenting is plus 4 and becoming an alcoholic is minus 3. Finally, she multiplies the probabilities by the utilities of each consequence, sums these up to the expected utility for each candidate, and chooses the man with the highest expected utility. When she is finished with her research, she may be years older, and the chosen man happily married to someone else who was less rational.

Ms. Satisficing, in contrast, gets things done because she does not attempt to optimize. She simply has an aspiration level, which experience may modify, and she picks the first man that meets her aspiration level. So far, so good. However, when another man comes around the corner and looks even better, nothing keeps Ms. Satisficing from dropping her current husband and embracing the next one. Satisficing does not result in commitment.

Ms. Love, our third woman, is similar to Ms. Satisficing in that she does not try to maximize expected utility but rather uses a sequential search process. However, she has a different stopping rule: she stops her search by falling in love. Unlike the cognitive process of comparing a man to an aspiration level, love stops search more efficiently and for a longer time and, most important, can generate a high degree of commitment to the loved one.

This example illustrates that emotions can be highly effective tools for decision making. Emotions are involved in important adaptive problems, such as finding a mate, caring for children, or choosing food. Since the relevance of some of these adaptive problems rises and declines over the life course, the kinds of emotions that are in a person's repertoire may change in accordance to intensity and frequency of use over the life course (cf. Roberts & Caspi, this volume).

Concepts

Recently, Baltes and Freund (in press) suggested interpreting SOC in terms of heuristics. One way to do this is to specify strategies of, say, selection of means and ends and then to specify their building blocks, such as search, stopping, and decision rules. Here, I use the three key concepts of SOC and investigate what these terms mean in the bounded rationality framework. The meanings can differ substantially, and to recognize this is a first step to exploring the relationship between the two frameworks.

Selection

In the adaptive toolbox, selection occurs at three levels—the selection of cues for making a decision, the selection of an alternative or action (the decision itself), and the selection of a heuristic (which defines both of these selections) from those available in the adaptive toolbox. The selection of cues is defined by two rules: a *search rule* that determines where to look for cues and what cues to look at first, and a *stopping rule* that determines when to end search. The selection of an object or an action is determined by one rule, the decision rule. For instance, the Take the Best heuristic searches cues in the order of their subjective validity and stops search the moment a cue is found that provides evidence for one alternative but not for the other. The decision rule uses just this reason (one-reason decision making) and does not integrate several reasons (it is noncompensatory). The selection of a particular heuristic over another depends on extent of knowledge about cues (some heuristics assume less, others more knowledge), on the task (heuristics are domain-specific and can be applied to a bounded class of tasks), and on earlier experience with various heuristics. The general concept of "selection" in the SOC framework can easily be connected with the more specific models of search, stopping, and decision rules in the adaptive toolbox.

Optimization

The concept of optimization, however, means different things in the two frameworks. In mathematics, statistics, and the theory of fast and frugal heuristics, optimization means computing a maximum or minimum of a function, such as to maximize the expected utility of alternative actions. Fast and frugal heuristics differ from models of unbounded rationality and optimization under constraints in that they do *not* involve optimization computations (see Figure 20.1). Heuristics and optimization are opposites of each other.

Optimization as a computational process needs to be distinguished from an *optimal* outcome. Heuristics try to achieve good-enough outcomes without optimization. They do so by exploiting the structure of environments. Note that heuristics do not try to get a complete representation of the environment in the first place; they just "bet" that it has the right structure—and learn from failure. Note also that optimization (as a process) does not guarantee an optimal outcome. The reason is that most real-world environments are highly uncertain, unpredictable, and incompletely known; therefore, one has to make simplifying assumptions in order to be able to apply the differential calculus. As a consequence, optimization has to "bet" on the assumptions, and that bet may prove wrong, just as with a heuristic. In SOC theory, optimization seems to refer to choosing the right tool for the right goal. Thus, it may refer to the outcome of behavior and not to an underlying optimization computation. If so, the term is used in opposite ways, but the underlying ideas need not be contradictory.

Compensation

The notion of compensation in the SOC framework refers to situations in which losses of goal-relevant means occur and in which a person acquires and invests in alternative means. Compensation here means *substitution* in the sense of vicarious functioning: one strategy is substituted for another. Compensation of means (as opposed to goals) would correspond to the substitution of one heuristic, or class of heuristics, for another one. For instance, cognitive heuristics that require amounts of memory that are no longer available due to age-dependent losses might be substituted with emotion-driven heuristics that exhibit anger or induce feelings of guilt to achieve the same goal.

In the theory of fast and frugal heuristics, compensation has a second, different meaning. A heuristic can process reasons (or cues, predictors) in a compensatory or noncompensatory way. Most cognitive models assume compensatory processing—that is, a negative or positive value on one reason can always be compensated by the values on other reasons. Multiple regression, neural networks, analysis of variance, factor analysis, Euclidean distances, and the expected utility calculus are all examples of models that specify how several reasons or cues are combined—that is, they assume compensatory cognitive processes. But not all cognitive, emotional, and moral processes are compensatory in nature; not everything can be reduced to one common currency. Love, honor, military medals, and Ph.D.s are said to be without price: You cannot buy them with money. Many of the heuristics we study are noncompensatory: only one reason decides, and no attempt is made to weight and sum all possible reasons. Is this distinction between compensatory and noncompensatory strategies a relevant issue for lifespan development? It may well be. Noncompensatory forms of decision making pose fewer demands on memory because they typically involve only a limited search for information. Thus, noncompensatory heuristics may be particularly fit to guide decisions at that point of the life span where recall memory gets more and more difficult to access.

Bringing Ideas Together

It is evident that there are both parallels and differences between SOC and the adaptive toolbox. These can be observed at various levels—as a metatheory, as concrete models of heuristics, and in the terminology. My attempt to explore some of the parallels in this chapter is very preliminary. But it may provide a starting point for a deeper exploration of the potential of a connection between the two frameworks. And both research programs can benefit. First, the study of bounded rationality could eventually be extended into a lifespan perspective. That is, one can study the ontogenetic change of the adaptive toolbox of *Homo heuristicus*. Such a developmental perspective is still missing today, just as the program of unbounded rationality has never been concerned about what happens when their demons are aging. And demons, after all, do not seem to age. Second, the study of bounded rationality with its emphasis on decision making with limited time and resources can provide a heuristics perspective to lifespan development. Because the individual heuristics are not just verbally but also formally defined, the study of the adaptive toolbox can also provide a new analytic framework for modeling the cognitive and emotional processes in development.

References

Anderson, J. R., & Milson, R. (1989). Human memory: An adaptive perspective. *Psychological Review, 96,* 703–719.

Baltes, P. B. (1997). On the incomplete architecture of human ontogeny: Selection, optimization, and compensation as foundation of developmental theory. *American Psychologist, 52,* 366–380.

Baltes, P. B., & Freund, A. M. (in press). Human strength as the orchestration of wisdom and SOC. In L. G. Aspinwall & U. M. Staudinger (Eds.), *A psychology of human strengths: Perspectives on an emerging field.*

Berretty, P. M., Todd, P. M., & Martignon, L. (1999). Categorization by elimination: Using few cues to choose. In G. Gigerenzer, P. M. Todd, & the ABC Research Group, *Simple heuristics that make us smart* (pp. 235–254). New York: Oxford University Press.

Dugatkin, L. A., & Godin, J. J. (1998). How females choose their mates. *Scientific American, 278,* 46–51.

Gigerenzer, G. (2001). The adaptive toolbox: Toward a Darwinian rationality. In J. A. French, A. C. Kamil, & D. W. Leger (Eds.). *Nebraska Symposium on Motivation: Evolutionary psychology and motivation. Vol. 47:* (pp. 113–143). Lincoln: University of Nebraska Press.

Gigerenzer, G. (2002). *Calculated risks: How to know when numbers deceive you.* New York: Simon & Schuster.

Gigerenzer, G., & Goldstein, D. G. (1996). Reasoning the fast and frugal way: Models of bounded rationality. *Psychological Review, 103,* 650–669.

Gigerenzer, G., & Selten, R. (Eds.). (2001). *Bounded rationality: The adaptive toolbox.* Cambridge, MA: MIT Press.

Gigerenzer, G., & Todd, P. M. (1999). Fast and frugal heuristics: The adaptive toolbox. In G. Gigerenzer, P. M. Todd, & ABC Research Group, *Simple heuristics that make us smart* (pp. 3–34). New York: Oxford University Press.

Gigerenzer, G., Todd, P. M., & ABC Research Group (1999). *Simple heuristics that make us smart.* New York: Oxford University Press.

Goldstein, D. G., & Gigerenzer, G. (2002). Models of ecological rationality: The recognition heuristic. *Psychological Review, 109,* 75–90.

Goodie, A. S., Ortmann, A., Davis, J. N., Bullock, S., & Werner, G. M. (1999). Demons versus heuristics in artificial intelligence, behavioral ecology, and economics. In G. Gigerenzer, P. M. Todd, & ABC Research Group, *Simple heuristics that make us smart* (pp. 327–355). New York: Oxford University Press.

Green, L., & Mehr, D. R. (1997). What alters physicians' decisions to admit to the coronary care unit? *Journal of Family Practice, 45,* 219–226.

Hirschfeld, L. A., & Gelmano, S. A. (Eds.). (1994). *Mapping the mind: Domain specificity in cognition and culture.* Cambridge: Cambridge University Press.

Hoffrage, U., & Gigerenzer, G. (1998). Using natural frequencies to improve diagnostic inferences. *Academic Medicine, 73,* 538–540.

Laplace, P.-S. (1951). *A philosophical essay on probabilities* (F. W. Truscott & F. L. Emory, Trans.). New York: Dover. (Original work published 1814).

Leibniz, G. W. (1951). *Towards a universal characteristic* (Ed. P. P. Wiener). New York: Scribner's Sons. (Original work published 1677).

Martignon, L., & Hoffrage, U. (1999). Why does one-reason decision making work? A case study in ecological rationality. In G. Gigerenzer, P. M. Todd, & ABC Research Group, *Simple heuristics that make us smart* (pp. 119–140). New York: Oxford University Press.

Piaget, J., & Inhelder, B. (1975). *The origin of the idea of chance in children* New York: Norton. (Original work published 1951).

Seeley, T. (2001). Decision making in superorganisms: How collective wisdom arises from the poorly informed masses. In G. Gigerenzer & R. Selten (Eds.), *Bounded rationality: The adaptive toolbox* (pp. 249–261). Cambridge, MA: MIT Press.

Simon, H. A. (1956). Rational choice and the structure of environments. *Psychological Review, 63,* 129–138.

Simon, H. A. (1992). *Economics, bounded rationality, and the cognitive revolution.* Aldershot UK: Elgar.

Stigler, G. J. (1961). The economics of information. *Journal of Political Economy, 69,* 213–225.

21 The Nature-Nurture Problem Revisited

Wolf Singer

Max Planck Institute for Brain Research, Frankfurt am Main, Germany

Abstract

The plan is to describe the changes in neuronal mechanisms that are associated with two important transitions in brain development—the transition from prenatal to postnatal life and the transition from puberty to adulthood. Until birth, developmental processes are controlled mainly by biochemical signaling systems that read structural information from genes and regulate gene expression as a function of developmental progress. This process continues until puberty but gets progressively more under the control of electrical activity generated by the maturing nerve nets. Since sense organs become functional after birth, this electrical activity is modulated to a large extent by sensory signals, and hence experience assumes the role of an important shaping factor for the development of neuronal architectures. During this phase of development, experience leads to irreversible modifications of the genetically determined blueprint of neuronal connections. In this process, cognitive and motor functions are adapted to the actual requirements of the encountered environment, and neuronal resources become assigned to particular functions as a result of exercise. Around the time of puberty, the developmental processes proper such as the formation and breaking of synaptic connections come to an end, but experience continues to modulate the functions of the now crystallized anatomical substrate by modifying the strength of established synaptic connections. This process is the basis for adult learning. Particular emphasis is laid on the evidence that these adaptive processses are all supervised by central gating systems that permit changes only in response to activity patterns that are identified as concordant with genetically prespecified expectancies of the developing brain and that are identified as behaviorally relevant. Together with the well-defined rules that govern experience-dependent modifications of the neuronal architecture and of synaptic weights, this constrains the range of modifications that can be induced by early imprinting and subsequent learning. Also explored is the extent to which the knowledge about these constraining factors is relevant for educational programs intended to unfold latent capacities, to encourage the development of special skills, and to rescue functions that have either failed to develop or were lost as a consequence of disease.

A Swinging Field

Few scientific questions have stirred up as many unsettled controversies and attracted as much popular interest as the nature-nurture problem (cf. McClearn, this volume; Molenaar, Huizenga, & Nesselroade, this volume). And few matters have had opinions shift back and forth between extreme positions for so long and have been exploited so shamelessly to ground ideological positions in scientific arguments. Now that the Human Genome Project has come to a preliminary end, naturalist positions have experienced a renaissance. Although the mere deciphering of the nucleotide sequences of the coding part of our genome is providing in itself no new arguments in favor of or against the prevalence of genetic determinants, genes have attained an unprecedented popularity, and as a consequence genetic determinism is in vogue. In a recent seminar that we organized for high school teachers, we heard the argument more than once: "Why bother with educational efforts beyond the unavoidable disciplinary measures if characters and personalities are determined genetically anyway and will express themselves with or without our contribution?" Thirty years ago, one would have heard quite different opinions. The nurture view dominated. The brain was considered as a freely instructable tabula rasa. All that mattered was appropriate instruction. Essential traits of personalities—such as aggressiveness, tolerance, emotional competence, and even intelligence as defined by the scores achieved in the respective tests—were considered as variables that depend crucially on instructions provided by social environment and education. Accordingly, deviations from normal and unwanted traits were considered to be the result of inappropriate environmental influences and hence of specific cultural traditions. Aggressiveness figured as the consequence of early experience with vetos, authorities, and frustrations. Mental disorders such as are associated with schizophrenia were attributed to subconscious double-binding strategies applied by the nurturing environment. The mothers were to blame when children developed schizophrenia or autism. These views were not perturbed by the fact, already known at that time, that the incidence of schizophrenia is about the same across all cultures despite of the diversity of nurturing conditions and educational systems.

These few examples illustrate the far-reaching consequences of positions in the nature-nurture debate with respect to judgments about the role of education and the responsibility of caretakers. It is imperative, therefore, to constantly reevaluate these positions on the basis of established scientific facts and to clearly define the borders between the known and the hypothetical.

Some Facts

It is probably undisputed by now that all behavior of organisms, including the highest cognitive and mental functions in human subjects, is the result of the functional architecture of the nervous system. A full description of the functional architecture of a brain would have to comprise a detailed blueprint of all connections between the neurons, the efficiency and polarity of the respective connections, and the integrative properties of the various neuron types. Proof that this functional architecture specifies all behavioral and psychological traits of an individual comes from the fact that reversible blockade of the electrical activity circulating in the brain—which can be achieved by cooling or deep anaesthesia—neither interferes with memories nor alters personality features. The nature-nurture problem can thus be reduced to the question of to what extent the functional architecture of the brain is determined by genetic instructions, on the one hand, and environmental influences, on the other.

Unfortunately, this distinction is notoriously difficult because of the lack of appropriate controls. The functional architecture of an individual brain is the result of a self-organizing developmental process, the trajectory of which is the consequence of a large number of nonlinear interactions (cf. McClearn, this volume). Developmental processes are based on myriads of intertwined decisions on which bifurcation is to be followed next. As every next decision is constrained by the preceding ones, small fluctuations in initial conditions can lead to widely differing trajectories. Nature (evolution) has implemented a wealth of control mechanisms that detect gross deviations and permit subsequent redirection of developmental trajectories to compensate for errors. However, this does not invalidate the view that developmental trajectories do follow idiosyncratic courses even if initial genetic dispositions are identical and environmental influences perfectly controlled (cf. Molenaar, Huizenga, & Nesselroade, this volume). The deep reason for this is that genes do not function as instructors that specify phenotypes in a one-to-one relation. Rather, the genes are only elements of a highly interactive and extremely complex network that as a whole contains in its relations the information required for the initiation of the developmental self-organizing process that eventually leads to a new organism. An impressive demonstration for this is provided by experiments in which a particular gene has been knocked out from the genome. There are now numerous examples that the knockout of a gene coding for a protein thought to be essential for the functioning of cells is fully compatible with the development of a phenotypically normal animal. Apparently, the network interactions allow for sufficient flexibility to fully compensate for the loss of an essential molecule.

Because of these uncontrollable fluctuations in developmental trajectories, it is thus not possible to conclude that all differences between genetically identical organisms are necessarily due to specific environmental influences. All that can be said with confidence is that differences must be attributed to epigenetic influences. These, however, include not only the usually cited environmental influences impinging on the developmental organism from outside (such as maternal stress hormones, malnutrition, or postnatal deprivation) but also the environment that the organism provides for its own genes. There is no read-out of genes without epigenetic influences. When and in which sequence genes are read out is determined from the very beginning by factors in the cellular environment of genes and hence by epigenetic cues. The first source of epigenetic variability is thus the composition of molecules in the maternal egg. The issue is further complicated by the fact that the numerous mitochondria in the cytoplasm of the egg contain genetic information that is exclusively of maternal origin.

Finally, there is the problem of appropriate controls. It is a frequently employed strategy in the investigation of epigenetic influences to manipulate, in most cases, impoverished environmental conditions. If this leads to modifications in the development of the brain and the behavior of the organism, it is assumed that the development of the modified traits is under epigenetic rather than genetic control. However, this conclusion can be challenged because it is not possible to infer from deprivation experiments whether experience has an instructive or simply permissive role. In the former case, specific experience would actually be required to instruct the development of functional architectures and hence the emergence of functions that have not been anticipated by genetic determinants. In the latter case, experience would simply serve as the incentive to develop and maintain functions that are entirely prespecified by genetic instructions. It will be impossible in most instances to find out whether a deprivation-induced impairment of function is due to the arrest of a genetically preprogrammed developmental process or to an actual lack of information.

This distinction is even difficult in animal experiments where changes can be studied at the level of neuronal circuits. Here, there is ample evidence that manipulation or abolition of signals provided by the sense organs leads to sometimes dramatic modifications of a developmental process. Connections can get misrouted or fail to attain selectivity, and these abnormalities are paralleled by specific functional losses. For some of these conditions, it could be shown that neuronal activity was necessary only to permit the nerve cells to read the molecular signals that they had to recognize for path-finding and to take up the nutrients that they required for their survival. Neuronal activity is not only used as a carrier of information in computational processes but also serves as the vehicle for the exchange of trophic substances and the uptake of nutrients. And this explains why it is so difficult to draw clear lines between genetic and epigenetic determinants of developmental processes.

In contrast to strategies based on deprivation, a promising alternative strategy to disentangle experiential from genetic determinants on human development is improving environmental conditions. A good example for such a strategy is the so-called testing-the-limits procedure frequently used in the field of lifespan plasticity research. Individuals of different ages are exposed to extensive performance-enhancing training programs until they reach the limits of their potential. Two main findings arise from such studies. On the one hand, both young and older adults benefit from experiential and practice factors; on the other hand, asymptotic performance levels of older adults are clearly lower than of younger participants. Such findings of age-related differences in maximum levels of performance are then usually attributed to genetically determined factors rather than to differences in experiential exposure (Baltes & Kliegl, 1992; Baltes, 1987, 1998, this volume).

Strictly speaking, however, distinctions between genetic and epigenetic determinants of performance are possible only in thought experiments but are of little heuristic value when it comes to concrete experiments because genes do not exist in isolation. They are always embedded in environment, and epigenetic control of gene expression is an integral part of development and learning. The performance of an organism is the result of the dialogue between two partners that have equal rights and equal importance— the genome and its environment. If either of the two is missing, there is neither development nor learning, and if either of the two changes, behavioral trajectories change.

Some Pragmatic Considerations

Although the developmental process depends at all times on environmentally controlled gene expression, the relevant environmental cues change in the course of development. The nature-nurture question can thus be rephrased in a more pragmatic way by asking which kind of nurture needs to be provided at which stage of development. It is now well established—and from what has been said above, it comes as no surprise—that all phases of pre- and postnatal development are highly susceptible to epigenetic modifications. There is ample clinical evidence of functional deficits that can be traced back to epigenetic modifications of developmental trajectories, and for some of them the underlying mechanisms have been elucidated in animal experiments. I shall leave aside the many accidents that can occur throughout embryonic development—the ensuing malformations, compensatory processes, and functional abnormalities. Rather, I concentrate on epigenetic influences that lead to more subtle changes in the functional architecture of the developing brain and still can lead to quite dramatic alterations of functions.

Here are some examples that illustrate the consequences of epigenetic modifications during prenatal development. Malnutrition of the mother is one frequent factor. It interferes with the development of the embryo's brain and leads to irreversible impairment of cognitive functions. Another factor is stress. Mothers experiencing stress have elevated stress hormones circulating in their blood. These traverse the placental barrier, influence the development of the embryo's brain, and permanently alter the stress response of the offspring. Likewise, there appear to be critical phases in embryonic development where exposure to sexual hormones determines not only the later phenotype but also patterns of sexual behavior.

Because of the more obvious and often also more dramatic consequences of sensory deprivation, much effort has been put into the investigation of epigenetic influences on postnatal development. Most of the alarming observations on the crucial role of sensory experience in the development of normal cognitive functions came from ophthalmology. Clinicians knew for a long time that children fail to acquire or lose irreversibly the ability to fuse the images in the two eyes into a common percept if they suffer from early onset strabismus (von Noorden, 1990). Even if the visual axes of the eyes are corrected by optical means, children remain unable to fuse the images and to extract depth information from comparing the signals arriving from the two retinas. Clinicians also knew that squinting children frequently avoid the problem of double vision by attending only to the signals provided by one of the two eyes and that this leads to an irreversible degeneration of the functions of the neglected eye. These children develop amblyopia, and again, this deficit cannot be rescued if therapy begins only at school age.

The most dramatic impairments do, however, result from complete visual deprivation. If contour vision is prevented from birth because of corneal opacities or other disturbances of the eyes' optical media and if these deficits persist over the first years of life, then vision is irreversibly lost, even if the optical media of the eyes are corrected by later surgical intervention. These clinical observations served as proof that sensory experience plays a pivotal role in the development of cognitive functions and introduced the notion of critical periods. Abnormal experience influences developmental processes only during well-defined windows. When inflicted beyond puberty, deprivation causes no lasting impairment of sensory functions.

Complementary evidence for the influence of early experience on later behavior came from studies on filial imprinting pioneered by Konrad Lorenz. It is well established by now that in many species the choice of later mating partners depends on early exposure to the appropriate templates. Likewise, the acquisition of species-specific vocalization patterns or songs is due to experience-dependent shaping of the song-producing neuronal networks (Tchernichovski, Mitra, Lints, & Nottebohm, 2001).

These observations triggered a large number of developmental studies in which the influence of experience on the expression of the structural and functional properties of neurons was investigated. And these led to detailed insights into the mechanisms through which sensory experience influences developmental processes and gene expression.

Evidence from Animal Studies

Sensory stimulation entrains a specific patterning of neuronal activity in afferent pathways, and these patterns assume a number of different functions in development. To appreciate these different effects, it is important to recall that mammals (including humans) are born with surprisingly immature brains. Although the full set of neurons is already available at birth, connections are still rudimentary and only coarsely specified, and especially in the cerebral cortex the majority of connections are still lacking (Assal & Innocenti, 1993; Galuske & Singer, 1996). Hence, postnatal development is characterized by the morphological differentiation of neurons, the extension of dendritic and axonal processes, and the formation of ever more complex connectivity patterns. In mammals, these proliferative processes decline only toward the end of puberty. Thus, in humans they extend at least over the first 15 years of life (Burghalter, Beranrdo, & Charles, 1993).

It is well established by now that these developmental processes are influenced by electrical activity and hence by all factors that contribute to the patterning of activity. These factors comprise sensory experience but also self-generated actions that are associated with distinct neuronal activation patterns, such as self-initiated motor acts, attentional shifts, and memory retrieval. The prevailing role of activity patterns consists in biasing the outcome of competitive processes. During circuit formation, there is competition for synaptic target space. Molecular and hence genetically determined markers specify which neurons ought to become interconnected, but the fine details of the wiring are left to activity-dependent competition (Changeux & Danchin, 1976; Stent, 1973). In most instances, more connections are initially formed than will eventually consolidate, and which of these connections survive is determined by the activity patterns that they convey. Selection occurs on the basis of a correlation analysis. Circuits tend to stabilize if they connect neurons that have a high probability of being active in temporal synchrony, while connections tend to destabilize between neurons that rarely exhibit correlated discharge patterns (Rauschecker & Singer, 1979, 1981; Singer, 1995). This selection algorithm has a number of implications. First, afferents conveying correlated activity have a competitive advantage over inputs that are active in a less coherent manner. Second, frequently coactivated neurons become permanently associated with one another through selectively stabilized connections. Third, among the many connections converging onto a particular neuron, those will be stabilized preferentially that respond with about the same latency to a particular event.

Evidence indicates that this correlation-based selection is used for the fine tuning of functional architectures in developmental processes that require functional validation (Antonini & Stryker, 1993; Frost & Innocenti, 1986; Goodman & Shatz, 1993; Löwel & Singer, 1992). This is the case, for example, when precise correspondence needs to be established between representations whose final expression does in turn depend on epigenetic influences and hence cannot be fully specified a priori by genetically determined molecular markers. A much investigated developmental problem is the establishment of precise correspondence between the representations of the two retinas in the visual cortex. For simple trigonometric reasons, correspondence depends on the interocular distance and the exact position of the eyes in the orbit. These variables change throughout development and are subject to unpredictable variations. The only way to identify afferents originating at precisely corresponding retinal loci is to rely on functional criteria. By definition, corresponding retinal loci are stimulated by the same contours when the two eyes fixate on the same object, and hence signals originating from corresponding retinal loci will show a high degree of temporal correlation. Exact correspondence between representations can thus be ensured by consolidating selectively connections that convey optimally correlated activity (Singer, 1990). Similar selection processes serve the establishment of correspondence between somatosensory, auditory, and visual maps and between sensory and motor representations in polymodal brain regions (King, Hutchings, Moore, & Blakemore, 1988; King & Moore, 1991). Functional matching criteria are used to establish selective associations between points in the various maps that correspond to the same loci in personal or extrapersonal space.

Here, then, is an interesting tradeoff between the option to realize ever more sophisticated polymodal associations—one of the prerequisites for higher cognitive functions—and the vulnerability of the developmental process. Because these adaptive processes require that connections be susceptible to use-dependent modifications, disturbances in the uptake of sensory signals have deleterious effects on the maturation of the corresponding neural networks. If circuits do not get confirmed because of deprivation, they are identified as inappropriate and get removed altogether, although in their imprecise expression they could have supported at least some rudimentary functions.

Because of the competitive nature of the use-dependent selection processes, early practice can also lead to an extension of the neuronal substrate devoted to a particular function. Practice enhances the amount and the coherence of activity in the corresponding neuronal networks, and this leads to preferential consolidation of the involved circuits and within limits also to an expansion of the territories in the neocortex that become recruited for the realisation of the practiced function (Elbert, Pantev, Wienbruch, Rockstroh, & Taub, 1995; Galuske, Schlote, Bratzke, & Singer, 2000; Jenkins, Merzenich, Ochs, Allard, & Guic-Robles, 1990). Conversely, deprivation within one modality can lead to the recruitment of the respective cortical areas by other modalities (Rauschecker, 1995, 1999; Rauschecker & Korte, 1993). Examples for this are the expansion of the representation of the left hand in the somatosensory cortex of violinists if they start to practice well before the end of puberty and the recruitment of visual cortical areas for somatosensory functions in blind subjects who are trained in Braille reading (Pascual-Leone & Torres, 1993; Sadato et al., 1996).

Gating by Value-Assigning Systems

An important aspect of all of these experience-dependent developmental processes is that they are supervised by attentional mechanisms and are not simply taking place as a consequence of passive exposure. Availability of sensory signals is alone not sufficient to support these use-dependent developmental processes. The brain actually needs to attend to the respective signals and has to use them for the control of behavior (Held & Hein, 1963). Otherwise, the sensory activity does not support appropriate circuit selection. This is, of course, necessary to avoid modifications in response to accidental, behaviorally irrelevant signals. The supervisory systems that gate developmental plasticity as a function of attention and behavioral relevance are well studied, and it appears that they are identical with those that also supervise the learning processes that continue to alter the functional architecture of the brain once development has come to an end (for a review, see Singer, 1990, 1995). Among these gating systems are the cholinergic, noradrenergic, dopaminergic, and serotoninergic projections that liberate their transmitters as a function of arousal, attention, and behavioral relevance of stimuli.

Thus, there is an interesting parallel between experience-dependent development and adult learning. In both cases, the brain actively selects the activity patterns that are enabled to induce modifications of functional architectures. Similarities extend even further since the processses that are thought to underlie adult learning appear to follow the same correlation rules as those supporting developmental circuit selection.

Adult learning is supposed to depend on differential strengthening and weakening of synaptic connections, and there is uncontroversial evidence that these synaptic gain changes depend on a correlation analysis (Gustafsson & Wigstroem, 1988; Singer & Artola, 1995). Evidence is also available that adult learning leads to rather durable if not permanent structural modifications in synaptic connections and hence to permanent modifications of functional architectures (Engert & Bonhoeffer, 1999).

These similarities raise the question of whether it is really possible to determine when development comes to an end. So far, we use the operational definition that development ends when the proliferation of new connections stops. However, recent data indicate that new synapses can still form in the adult and that in some brain regions even new neurons can be generated and integrated in the circuitry (Kono & Raff, 2000; Shors et al., 2001). There are, thus, lifelong changes not only in the functions of neurons, their integrative properties, and their synaptic efficacy but also in the fine-grained architecture of connections. Differences between early and late phases of development and adulthood might, thus, be considered to be more quantitative in nature rather than qualitative. As development proceeds, modifications of circuitry get restricted more and more to short-range projections, and structural as well as functional modifications get reduced to changes at the molecular scale. But the basic principles—according to which genetic and epigenetic influences interact with one another in order to guarantee homeostasis of the system and its adaptation to the ever-changing demands of the environment—remain essentially the same. At least up to the point in time when degenerative processes accelerate, when the loss of connections and neurons increases, when the molecular mechanisms subserving learning and plasticity slow down, and when repair processes become inefficient, one might consider being as becoming.

In conclusion, the evidence from studies of neuronal development and plasticity is in general agreement with propositions derived from lifespan investigations (Baltes, 1987, 1997). Ontogenetic development is best conceptualized as the result of a complex interaction between both biological-genetic and cultural-environmental factors. Thus, lifespan changes in neuronal and behavioral functions can be considered as the result of a continuous interplay between proliferative and degenerative processes, the latter prevailing more and more as the organism ages. However, there appear to be at least three distinct phases that are related to the reproductive potential of the organism. Until puberty, proliferative, truly developmental processes dominate; throughout the reproductive life span, proliferative and degenerative processes are balanced, and thereafter, degenerative processes prevail. The obvious explanation for the postreproductive decline is that evolutionary selection pressure is no longer affecting organisms once they stop to contribute to reproduction and raising of offspring. Given that life expectancy is rapidly increasing in industrialized countries, the challenge of future plasticity research will be the investigation of nurture conditions that optimize the balance between degenerative and proliferative processes in favor of the latter during the third phase of life.

References

Antonini, A., & Stryker, M. P. (1993). Rapid remodeling of axonal arbors in the visual cortex. *Science, 260,* 1819–1821.

Assal, F., & Innocenti, G. M. (1993). Transient intra-areal axons in developing cat visual cortex. *Cerebral Cortex, 3,* 290–303.

Baltes, P. B. (1987). Theoretical propositions of life-span developmental psychology: On the dynamics between growth and decline. *Developmental Psychology, 23,* 611–626.

Baltes, P. B. (1997). On the incomplete architecture of human ontogeny: Selection, optimization, and compensation as foundation of developmental theory. *American Psychologist, 52,* 366–380.

Baltes, P. B. (1998). Testing the limits of the ontogenetic sources of talent and excellence. *Behavioral and Brain Sciences, 21,* 407–408.

Baltes, P. B., & Kliegl, R. (1992). Further testing of limits of cognitive plasticity: Negative age differences in a mnemonic skill are robust. *Developmental Psychology, 28,* 121–125.

Burghalter, A., Beranrdo, K. L., & Charles, V. (1993). Development of local circuits in human visual cortex. *Journal of Neuroscience, 13,* 1916–1931.

Changeux, J.-P., & Danchin, A. (1976). Selective stabilisation of developing synapses as a mechanism for the specification of neuronal networks. *Nature, 264,* 705–712.

Elbert, T., Pantev, C., Wienbruch, C. Rockstroh, B., & Taub, E. (1995). Increased cortical representation of the fingers of the left hand in string players. *Science, 270,* 305–307.

Engert, F., & Bonhoeffer, T. (1999). Dendritic spine changes associated with hippocampal long-term synaptic plasticity. *Nature, 399,* 66–70.

Frost, D. O., & Innocenti, G. M. (1986). Effects of sensory experience on the development of visual callosal connections. In F. Lepore, F. M. Ptiti, & H. H. Jasper (Eds.), *Two hemispheres, one brain.* New York: Liss.

Galuske, R. A. W., Schlote, W., Bratzke, H., & Singer, W. (2000). Interhemispheric asymmetries of the modular structure in human temporal cortex. *Science, 289,* 1946–1949.

Galuske, R. A. W., & Singer, W. (1996). The origin and topography of long-range intrinsic projections in cat visual cortex: A developmental study. *Cerebral Cortex, 6,* 417–430.

Goodman, C. S., & Shatz, C. J. (1993). Developmental mechanisms that generate precise patterns of neuronal connectivity. *Cell, 72 (Suppl.)* 77–98.

Gustafsson, B., & Wigstroem, H. (1988). Physiological mechanisms underlying long-term potentiation. *TINS, 11,* 156–162.

Held, R., & Hein, A. (1963). Movement-produced stimulation in the development of visually guided behavior. *Journal of Comparative and Physiological Psychology, 56,* 872–876.

Jenkins, W. M., Merzenich, M. M., Ochs, M. T., Allard, T., & Guic-Robles, E. (1990). Functional reorganization of primary somatosensory cortex in adult owl monkeys after behaviorally controlled tactile stimulation. *Journal of Neurophysiology, 63,* 82–104.

King, A. J., Hutchings, M. E., Moore, D. R., & Blakemore, C. (1988). Developmental plasticity in the visual and auditory representations in the mammalian superior colliculus. *Nature, 332,* 73–76.

King, A. J., & Moore, D. R. (1991). Plasticity of auditory maps in the brain. *TINS, 14,* 31–37.

Kono, T., & Raff, M. (2000). Oligodendrocyte precursor cells reprogrammed to become multipotential CNS stem cells. *Science, 289,* 1754–1757.

Löwel, S., & Singer, W. (1992). Selection of intrinsic horizontal connections in the visual cortex by correlated neuronal activity. *Science, 255,* 209–212.

Pascual-Leone, A., & Torres, F. (1993). Plasticity of the sensorimotor cortex representation of the reading finger in Braille readers. *Brain, 116,* 39–52.

Rauschecker, J. P. (1995). Compensatory plasticity and sensory substitution in the cerebral cortex. *Trends in Neuroscience, 18,* 36–43.

Rauschecker, J. P. (1999). Auditory cortical plasticity: A comparison with other sensory systems. *Trends in Neuroscience, 22*, 74–80.

Rauschecker, J. P., & Korte, M. (1993). Auditory compensation for early blindness in cat cerebral cortex. *Journal of Neuroscience, 13*, 4538–4548.

Rauschecker, J. P., & Singer, W. (1979). Changes in the circuitry of the kitten visual cortex are gated by postsynaptic activity. *Nature, 280*, 58–60.

Rauschecker, J. P., & Singer, W. (1981). The effects of early visual experience on the cat's visual cortex and their possible explanation by Hebb synapses. *Journal of Physiology (London), 310*, 215–239.

Sadato, N., Pascual-Leone, A., Grafman, J., Ibanez, V., Deiber, M.-P., Dold, G., & Hallett, M. (1996). Activation of the primary visual cortex by Braille reading in blind subjects. *Nature, 380*, 526–528.

Shors, T. J., Miesegaes, G., Beylin, A., Zhao, M., Rydel, T., & Gould, E. (2001). Neurogenesis in the adult is involved in the formation of trace memories. *Nature, 410*, 372–376.

Singer, W. (1990). The formation of cooperative cell assemblies in the visual cortex. *Journal of Experimental Biology, 153*, 177–197.

Singer, W. (1995). Development and plasticity of cortical processing architectures. *Science, 270*, 758–764.

Singer, W., & Artola, A. (1995). The role of NMDA receptors in use-dependent synaptic plasticity of the visual cortex. In H. Wheal & A. Thomson (Eds.), *Excitatory amino acids and synaptic transmission* (2nd ed.). London: Academic Press.

Stent, G. S. (1973). A physiological mechanism for Hebb's postulate of learning. *Proceedings of the National Academy of Science USA, 70*, 997–1001.

Tchernichovski, O., Mitra, P. P., Lints, T., & Nottebohm, F. (2001). Dynamics of the vocal imitation process: How a zebra finch learns its song. *Science, 291*, 2564–2569.

von Noorden, G. K. (1990). *Binocular vision and ocular motility: Theory and management of strabismus.* St. Louis, MO: Mosby.

22 Secondary School as a Constraint for Adolescent Development

Olaf Köller

Fredrich-Alexander-Universitat, Nürnberg, Germany

Jürgen Baumert

Max Planck Institute for Human Development, Berlin, Germany

Kai U. Schnabel

University of Michigan, Ann Arbor, MI, U.S.A.

Abstract

In this chapter, we describe and discuss the extent to which schools as external socializers influence development in early adolescence. Although we are aware of theories and research on how children and adolescents actively shape their environments, including their parents and schools, we concentrate here on schools as important socializers of adolescents. After describing major findings of research on school effectiveness in general, we focus on the concrete role of schools in shaping individual development. In this part of the chapter, we briefly refer to the concept of *executive functioning*, introduced in cognitive psychology to describe and understand how individuals plan, organize, evaluate, monitor, coordinate, and execute cognitive tasks. Schools are conceptualized as executive functionaries helping learners to manage the flow of information coming into the cognitive system and thus fostering the acquisition of new knowledge (cf. Zelazo & Frye, 1998). Whenever a mismatch occurs between the individual's executive system and socially organized executive functioning, negative effects on individual development are to be expected. The developmental "stage and environment-fit" model proposed by Eccles and colleagues (e.g., Eccles & Midgley, 1989) and research in situated cognition (e.g., Resnick, 1994) are presented as two prominent theoretical approaches conceptualizing consequences of a mismatch between individual needs and their school environments. Finally, we present some ideas on how the selection, optimization, and compensation model, a framework for the understanding of human development (e.g., Baltes, 1997), can be applied to students' development under the institutional constraints of school.

The successful development of human beings across the entire life span is dependent both on their individual (internal) characteristics and on external socializers such as significant others and social institutions. The relative importance of internal and external promoters varies across the life span and between the areas of individual functioning. Parents, for example, play a dominant role in their children's development during infancy, childhood, and early adolescence. Family management theorists (e.g., Furstenberg, Cook, Eccles, Elder, & Sameroff, 1999) argue that parents play a critical role in orchestrating their children's daily lives, providing them with opportunities and resources and protecting them from risks and dangers. These experiences have a major impact on both the domain-specific knowledge and skills and the self-regulatory skills that children acquire as they mature. The influence of parents, however, decreases during adolescence and often ceases entirely in adulthood.

Particularly in the domain of academic learning and, more generally, cognitive development, the social institution of school plays an important role during childhood and adolescence. There is no doubt that the opportunities to learn provided by the school environment are highly important sources for knowledge acquisition in the first 20 years of life (e.g., Opdenakker & Van Damme, 2000; Rutter, Maughan, Mortimore, & Ouston, 1979; Scheerens & Bosker, 1997). Furthermore, it is often suggested (e.g., Brookover & Lezotte, 1979; Eccles et al., 1993) that schools not only influence the development of academic skills during adolescence but that they impact on the formation or development of motivation, emotions, attitudes, and other characteristics. This reflects the assumption prevailing in almost all modern industrialized societies that noncognitive variables are explicit goals of education (e.g., Brookover, Beady, Flood, Schweizer, & Wisenbaker, 1979; Opdenakker & Van Damme, 2000; Rutter et al., 1979).[1]

In this chapter we describe and discuss the extent to which schools as external socializers influence development in early adolescence. Although we are aware of theories and research on how children and adolescents actively shape their environments, including their parents and schools (e.g. Lerner, 1987), we concentrate here on schools as important socializers of adolescents. From the perspective of institutionalized education, in particular, our approach seems to be justified, in that schools provide many developmental opportunities but at the same time impose many constraints on students (take, for example, the lesson timetables regulating the school subjects taught and the number of lessons per week).

After describing major findings of research on school effectiveness in general, we focus on the concrete role of schools in shaping individual development. In this part of the chapter, we briefly refer to the concept of *executive functioning*, introduced in cognitive psychology to describe and understand how individuals plan, organize, evaluate, monitor, coordinate, and execute cognitive tasks. Schools are conceptualized as executive functionaries helping learners to manage the flow of information coming into the cognitive system and thus fostering the acquisition of new knowledge (cf. Davis-Kean & Eccles, 1998; Zelazo & Frye, 1998). Schools thus represent learning environments in which students can acquire skills such as reading, mathematics, and science literacy that are of great importance for a successful academic or occupational career. Whenever a mismatch occurs between the individual's executive system and socially organized executive functioning, negative effects on individual development are to be expected (see also Lerner, Dowling, & Roth, this volume). A prominent and elaborated approach conceptualizing the negative motivational consequences of the mismatch between individual and school is the developmental "stage and environment fit" model proposed by Eccles and colleagues (e.g., Eccles & Midgley, 1989; Eccles et al., 1993), which posits that negative effects on students' affect and motivation are to be expected when the environment does not fit their needs. Another prominent approach focusing on the cognitive consequences of a mismatch between the individual and social executive system is research into situated cognition (e.g., Resnick, 1987, 1994), which argues that the artificial learning situations in schools do not help students to master everyday problems. Both approaches are described in this chapter, since they currently exert the most far-reaching influence in both theoretical and practical discussions on how to optimize students' cognitive and noncognitive development in school environments. Greater emphasis is placed, however, on the "stage and environment-fit" model.

Finally, we present some ideas on how the selection, optimization, and compensation model, a framework for the understanding of human development (e.g., Baltes, 1997; Baltes & Baltes, 1990), can be applied to students' development under the institutional constraints of school.

Effects of School Environments on Individual Development: Major Findings of School-Effectiveness Research

In traditional school-effectiveness research, schools are assumed to be important socializers of children and adolescents. Many studies have attempted to quantify the influential power of schools on students by estimating the amount of variance in interindiviual differences in cognitive and social development that can be explained by school and class characteristics. The underlying assumption of all these studies is that organizational, structural, and instructional characteristics differ among schools and that these school or class variables influence students' development in cognitive, motivational, emotional, and social variables (see Sheerens & Bosker, 1997, for an overview). As an illustrative example, Figure 22.1 displays Cremer's (1994) basic model of educational effectiveness. This particular model concentrates mainly on the quality of instruction.

Although many more models of educational effectiveness have been proposed, a couple of influential studies conducted in the 1960s and 1970s cast doubt on the assumption that school environments really do influence students' development. The

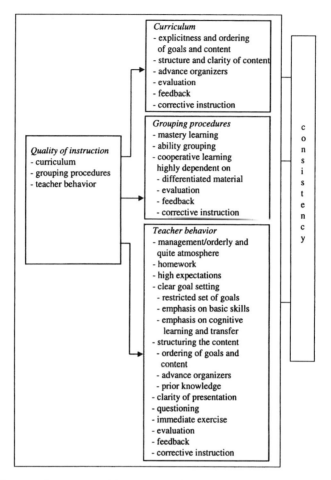

Figure 22.1   Cremers's (1994) Model of the Quality of Instruction

most frequently cited study in this respect was conducted by Coleman et al. (1966). The authors provided estimates for the relative importance of the school factor in accounting for differences in students' academic achievement. After correcting for intake differences between the schools and differences in students' socioeconomic status, the estimated school effects on math achievement, measured in explained variance, were about 5% for white students and about 9% for black students. As such, the Coleman report led to a rather pessimistic view of what could be achieved by schools and institutionalized education. This pessimistic view was reinforced by other studies published at the beginning of the 1970s. Jencks and others (1972), for example, found an effect size of $d < .20$ for academic achievement after controlling for prior knowledge and hence concluded that schools do not have much impact on student achievement. Numerous studies have since readdressed the issue of school effectiveness, coming to different conclusions from Jencks and colleagues. Scheerens and Bosker (1997), for example, reported a metaanalysis based on 89 studies with a mean effect size of $d = .31$. The amount of achievement variance explained by differences between schools was approximately 12%. Scherens and Bosker, however, argued that this effect size underestimates the true effect of schools for at least two reasons—the unreliability of the achievement tests administered in school-effectiveness studies and their unsatisfactory curricular validity.

In terms of Cohen's effect sizes, the mean effect size of $d = .31$ reported by Sheerens and Bosker (1997) indicates a small effect. From the perspective of experimental psychology, one might argue that this effect is almost trivial. On the other hand, longitudinal studies in German secondary schools (e.g., Köller, 1998) have shown that about one school year of instruction is required for an average achievement gain of $d = .30$. Furthemore, it is often overlooked that although schools differ to some extent in their educational effectiveness, all of them provide young people with the knowledge needed to meet most requirements of the highly complex modern societies. In modern industrialized countries, at least, there is no doubt that schools in general afford students the opportunity to acquire the relevant knowledge in terms of reading, mathematics, and science literacy, enabling them to cope with everyday problems and to succeed in their occupational careers (see Baumert, Bos, & Lehmann, 2000, for more details). Schools more or less have a monopoly on the systematic teaching of these central skills.

Although traditional research on school effectiveness has focused primarily on cognitive outcomes—especially language, mathematics, and science achievement—a body of research has investigated noncognitive outcomes (e.g., Brookover et al., 1979; Opdenakker & Van Damme, 2000; Rutter et al., 1979). These outcomes (such as self-esteem, academic self-concepts, and interests) are often seen as educational aims in themselves, and modern schools always strive to enhance students' development in these areas. Furthermore, social learning has become an important issue in education. The effects of the school setting on noncognitive outcomes, however, seem to be substantially smaller than the effects on achievement. In a recent study, Opdenakker and Van Damme (2000) investigated the effects of schools on students' achievement and well-being at the end of the first grade in secondary education in Belgium. Multilevel analyses revealed that 56% of the total variance in mother tongue and 43% of the total variance in mathematics achievement was due to differences between schools and classes, while only 5 to 11% of the total variance in students' well-being was explained by differences between schools and classes. Similar findings have been reported for the United States (e.g., Teddlie & Springfield, 1993) and for Germany (e.g., Köller, Baumert, & Schnabel, 1999). Schools and classes are thus most influential in academic domains (mathematics, languages, science), in which they provide opportunities in the form of systematic instruction, while their impact is much less pronounced in social domains, in which alternative socializers (parents and peers) seem to be more important for development in adolescence.

Schools as Executive Functionaries for Adolescents

Why are some schools more effective than others in enhancing cognitive and noncognitive outcomes? One answer to this question refers to different levels of schools' *executive functioning*. In their recent work, Davis-Kean and Eccles (2002) have provided a theoretical framework describing how social actors shape young people's development. In this approach, young people are assumed to learn by interacting with their physical and social environments. They take in and process information, leading to cognitive and social learning (e.g., Flavell, 1999). Early in life, this information is usually managed by parents, both in their daily practices and in the decisions they make on the types of information and resources to which the child is given access (e.g., Eccles, 1992). As the child matures, school comes to exert a particular influence on the flow of information and the resources available to the child. This flow of information is not necessarily restricted to curriculum-based knowledge but can also relate to motivation, opinions, attitudes, moral judgment, and so on. Thus, over childhood and adolescence, school becomes more and more important in the management of the information and resources available to both inform children about their world and shape their growing knowledge and skill repertoire.[2] In this respect, schools are *executive functionaries* for adolescents.

In cognitive psychology, *executive functioning* is defined as the planning, organizing, evaluating (task analysis), monitoring, coordinating, and executing of cognitive tasks (e.g., Borkowski & Burke, 1996; Fletcher, 1996; Zelazo, Carter, Resnick, & Frye, 1997). Executive functioning is the management of information and resources coming into and being distributed within the cognitive system; the performance of various subsystems is constantly evaluated and monitored, and necessary adjustments are made for required tasks to be performed. Effective executive functioning is critical for the management of both the flow of information coming into the cognitive system from the physical and mental world and the flow of information coming out of the brain to the relevant subsystems of the body.

Metacognition research suggests that children become better executive functioners on their own behalf as they mature, leading to improved independent problem-solving and self-regulated learning and behavior (Zelaszo & Frye, 1998). Note, however, that the system starts out at a fairly immature level. Initially, efficient executive control of children's interactions with their external world needs to be scaffolded by more matured individuals or social institutions for two reasons: (1) to protect the child and make sure the child has the resources necessary for survival and growth and (2) to help the child learn both the content-specific skills and knowledge and the executive-functioning skills necessary to manage their own survival.

The idea of socially organized executive functioning is a continuation and incorporation of these traditions with an explicit focus on the management (or mismanagement) of children's lives and development. The analogy to the cognitive executive functions is that parents, significant individuals, and institutions act as external executive functionaries responsible for the organization, evaluation, and distribution of information and resources for children as they develop. In this respect, the school setting is conceived as a specific structure of opportunities and constraints for individual learning and development. Teachers support students in their management of information and resources coming into and being distributed within the cognitive system. Furthermore, teachers provide social support, discipline, attention, motivation, teaching, as well as psychological and physical resources. To be effective executive functionaries for the child, schools must coordinate their functioning with the executive functioning of the students and the family-level caregivers. When the schools manage resources and information well for the child, the child should become a self-regulating, socially integrated adult. When there is a "failure" in the socially organized executive-functioning system, it is increasingly likely that the child will have problems in acquiring the information or resources needed to develop into a self-regulating adult. The two theoretical frameworks presented in the following emphasize the negative consequences that schools' "failure" to adequately perform the task of executive functionaries for their students may have on the students' development.

Reducing the Mismatch Between Artificial Learning Situations in School and the Cognitive Requirements of Everyday Problems: The Situated-Cognition Approach

Several authors (e.g., Lave, 1988) have severely criticized traditional classroom instruction. In their view, one of the major shortcomings of instruction is that learning arrangements are very artificial in that they do not provide the cognitive skills needed to solve real-world problems. As a consequence, cognitive development in terms of knowledge acquisition and problem-solving skills often remains below its optimum, and students fail to master applied problems beyond the school context. Research on situated learning (e.g., Clancey, 1993; Greeno, Smith, & Moore, 1992; Resnick, 1987, 1994) thus emphasizes the idea that much of what is learned is specific to the context in which it is learned. The following ideas are central to situated learning:

- Learning is grounded in the concrete situation in which it occurs—that is, knowledge or skill acquisition is specific to the context in which a learning task is performed.
- Knowledge does not transfer between tasks—that is, once it has been learned in a specific context or domain, knowledge cannot and will not be transferred to another domain, especially not to real-life situations.
- Training by abstraction is of little use—for instance, abstract calculating rules taught in mathematics cannot help students to solve numerical problems in everyday life.
- Instruction needs to be done in complex, social environments, since people spend most of their time in social environments and must solve complex problems.

With respect to social executive functioning, the situated-cognition approach claims that successful cognitive development in adolescence is possible only if students' information processing, and thus their skill acquisition, is managed by open and real-life-oriented instruction in school. However, research conducted within the aptitude, treatment, interaction paradigm (e.g., Harrison, Strauss, & Glauman, 1981) suggests that this type of instruction is cognitively demanding. As a result, positive effects of situated learning may be more likely for older and for brighter students.

Explaining the Decline in Motivation over Adolescence by Reference to School Characteristics: The Developmental "Stage and Environment-Fit" Model

A body of research suggests that, for many students, the early adolescent years mark the beginning of negative developmental trends in both cognitive and motivational characteristics. For example, Simmons and Blyth (1987; see also Eccles et al., 1993) found a remarkable decline in early adolescents' school grades as they moved from primary to secondary school. Similar declines were observable for such motivational constructs as academic interest (Baumert & Köller, 1998), intrinsic motivation (Harter, 1981), task orientation (Köller, 2000), and self-concepts of ability (Eccles, Midgley, & Adler, 1984). At the same time, increases in undesirable motivational characteristics such as test anxiety (Hill, 1980) and ego orientation (Köller, 2000) have been reported. Authors agree that it is both the age of the students and the transition from elementary to secondary school that is primarily associated with the decline in motivation, self-esteem, and self-concept. During early adolescence, children experience the biological and social changes associated with puberty at more or less the same time as they move from primary to secondary school. In other words, biological and social changes coincide with changes in the school environment (cf. Simmons & Blyth, 1987; Simmons, Blyth, van Cleaves, & Bush, 1979). In particular, adolescents' needs for autonomy increase during this time, and peers become more important, while adults such as parents and teachers lose a certain amount of their influence. The developmental "stage and environment-fit" model proposed by Eccles and colleagues (e.g., Eccles et al., 1993; Eccles & Midgley, 1989) posits that negative effects on students' motivation, self-esteem, and subjective well-being are to be expected when the environment does not fit their needs. Exposure to developmentally appropriate environments would facilitate both motivation and cognitive growth. With respect to the instructional setting, Hunt (1975) "suggested that teachers need to provide the optimal level of structure for children's current level of maturity while at the same time providing a sufficiently challenging environment to pull the children along a developmental path toward higher levels of cognitive and social maturity" (Wigfield, Eccles, & Pintrich, 1996, p. 161). In particular, the highly competitive classroom climate of secondary schools seems to undermine students' needs for competence and intrinsic learning motivation and to reduce their self-concepts of ability. Marsh and Peart (1988) have demonstrated that an environment fostering competition and social comparison leads to lower self-concepts than settings that encourage cooperation and a focus on individual improvement. Ames (1992) also noted that social comparisons encourage unfavorable evaluations of ability, self-concept, and effective learning strategies. In a strong critique of competitive environments, Covington (1992) argued that competition reduces levels of academic achievement and undermines self-worth. Furthermore, Eccles and colleagues have argued that in early years of secondary school, students' rates of participation decrease, and most exercises are less demanding than in primary school, resulting in a misfit between the students' needs for autonomy and competence and their learning environments. This misfit combined with a stronger focus on out-of-school-activities in puberty often results in negative effects on academic outcomes such as achievement and learning. Coming back to the question of why some schools are more effective than others in enhancing cognitive and noncognitive outcomes, we can answer that the better the stage and environment match between the school context and individuals' needs and desires, the more positive the cognitive and noncognitive development of the students particularly in early adolescents will be.

There is relative little research on long-term effects of secondary schooling on students' development in later adolescence (see Wigfield et al., 1996, for an overview), but authors agree that the negative effects on motivation, self-esteem, and affective variables observed in early adolescence tend to disappear in later years. Research on the development of self-esteem in particular (e.g., McCarthy & Hoge, 1982) shows that students' self-esteem increases in late adolescence and early adulthood. Although this positive trend has been replicated in many studies (e.g., Wigfield et al., 1996), it remains unclear whether it is caused primarily by students' compensational strategies or by changes in the school environment.

Selection, Optimization, and Compensation in School

As we have outlined above, understanding the process of developmental regulation in childhood and adolescence requires models and theories that focus on individual resources and developmental opportunities and also on constraints provided by families, peers, and particularly schools. In the following, we present some ideas how the process of selection, optimization, and compensation (SOC) (e.g., Baltes, 1997; Baltes & Baltes, 1990; see also Baltes, this volume) can be moderated by the school context.

The starting point of the concept of selection, optimization, and compensation is the assumption that individual internal and external resources are limited. These individual or environmental limitations force selection processes—for example, in terms of goal settings—that provide a basis for goal attainment by means of optimization and compensation (cf. Wiese & Freund, 2000; see also Marsiske, Lang, Baltes, & Baltes, 1995, for a more detailed overview of the SOC approach). Today, there is overwhelming evidence (e.g., Freund & Baltes, 1998) that "(1) selecting from a pool of alternative developmental projects (selection), (2) allocating resources as means of achieving one's goals (optimization), and (3) applying means in order to counteract actual or impending losses (compensation) are key factors for the successful mastery of lifespan demands in different domains of functioning, including the family and professional domains" (Wiese & Freund, 2000, p. 182). Schools, however, usually provide an environment in which students are not free to define and optimize their goals. The institutional setting offers a variety of developmental opportunities but at the same time excludes others. It defines the framework for individual gains, losses, and the possibilities of compensation. Educational goals both in several academic domains and in terms of social learning are, at least in primary and middle school, prescribed entirely by curricula, meaning that students do not really have any degree of freedom in the selection process. The same is true with respect to optimization. When students try to optimize only the academic domains that are of special interest to them, compensating for this extra effort by concentrating less on some other domains, perhaps even ignoring them, their behavior is punished by poor grades in the subjects they did not focus on. One might argue that the mismatch between individuals goals and the normative goals of schools causes the negative effects in development described by the stage and environment-fit model above. On the other hand, schools provide opportunities to learn many skills that prepare young people for successful life careers. Here, the question arises of how the educational system can achieve a balance between individuals' needs and the normative learning goals defined by the institution. The German school system offers an interesting way to combine individual SOC behavior and the constraints of the normative educational system. When students at academically selected high schools (in German, *Gymnasien*) change from lower secondary level (usually grades 5 to 10) to upper secondary level (typically grades 11 to 13), the system enables them to systematically choose between advanced and basic courses for the first time. At the lower secondary level, students are not allowed to drop any classes in accordance with their own abilities or interests. As a consequence, they cannot avoid classes with a heavy workload. The picture changes at the beginning of upper secondary level, however, when students have the opportunity to choose advanced courses in two or three domains and basic courses in the remaining domains. Advanced courses usually comprise five to six lessons per week, whereas basic courses involve two to three lessons per week. Students are then able to optimize outcomes in the domains of special interest in which they feel particularly competent, while reducing their investment in domains of lesser interest. From the perspective of school policy and educational planning, it is assumed that students aged 16 or older are more or less able to autonomously and responsibly define the areas of special interest in which they would like to optimize (maximize) their knowledge. With respect to the SOC model, this suggests that, at least in adolescence, selection and optimization in academic contexts are always strongly driven by both individual needs *and* the constraints of the school environment (see also Mayer, this volume). And since primary and early secondary schools define academic goals and the means of optimizing these goals, one can expect students' subjective well-being to be negatively affected by these constraints, particularly in early secondary school years (see, however, the argument advanced by Wellman, this volume). This assumption is empirically supported by the findings of Eccles and colleagues, who have repeatedly reported a decline in motivational variables and indicators of subjective well-being during the early years of middle school (e.g., Eccles & Midgley, 1989; see also the section on the stage-environment mismatch above).

These findings highlight the necessity for research of SOC behavior—in adolescence, at least—to take into account the context in which young persons define and optimize their goals (for example, within the environmental constraints of schools).

Notes

1. Beyond enhancing students' knowledge and their cognitive and social development, schools in modern industrialized countries have the function of selection, in that final examinations and certificates at the end of secondary school regulate students' access to universities and to the labor market.
2. Note that students spend about 15,000 hours of their young life at school (estimation by Rutter et al., 1979).

References

Ames, C. (1992). Classroom goals, structures, and student motivation. *Journal of Educational Psychology, 84*, 261–271.

Baltes, P. B. (1997). On the incomplete architecture of human ontogeny: Selection, optimization, and compensation as foundations of developmental theory. *American Psychologist, 52*, 366–380.

Baltes, P. B., & Baltes, M. M. (1990). Psychological perspectives on successful aging: The model of selective optimization with compensation. In P. B. Baltes & M. M. Baltes (Eds.), *Successful aging: Perspectives from the behavioral sciences* (pp. 1–34). New York: Cambridge.

Baumert, J., Bos, W., & Lehmann, R. (2000). *TIMSS/III. Dritte Internationale Mathematik-und Naturwissenschaftsstudie. Mathematische und naturwissenschaftliche Bildung am Ende der Schullaufbahn.* [TIMSS/III. Third International Mathematics and Science Study. Mathematics and science achievement at the end of upper secondary school]. Opladen, FRG: Leske+Budrich.

Baumert, J., & Köller, O. (1998). Interest research in secondary level I: An overview. In L. Hoffmann, A. Krapp, K. A. Renninger, & J. Baumert (Eds.), *Interest and learning* (pp. 241–256). Kiel, FRG: IPN.

Borkowski, J. G., & Burke, J. E. (1996). Theories, models, and measurements of executive functioning: An information processing perspective. In G. R. Lyon & Krasnegor, N. A. (Eds.), *Attention, memory, and executive function* (pp. 235–261). Baltimore: Brooks.

Brookover, W., Beady, C., Flood, P., Schweizer, J., & Wisenbaker, J. (1979). *Schools, social systems, and student achievement: Schools can make a difference.* New York: Praeger.

Brookover, W. B., & Lezotte, L. W. (1979). *Changes in schools' characteristics coincident with changes in student achievement.* East Lansing: Michigan State University. (ERIC Document Reproduction Service No. ED 181 005).

Clancey, W. J. (1993). Situated action: A neuropsychological interpretation response to Vera and Simon. *Cognitive Science, 17*, 87–116.

Coleman, J. S., Campbell, E. Q., Hobson, C. F., McPartland, J., Mood, A. M., Weifeld, F. D., & York, R. L. (1966). *Equality of educational opportunity.* Washington, DC: U.S. Government Printing Office.

Covington, M. V. (1992). *Making the grade: A self-worth perspective on motivation and school reform.* Cambridge: University Press.

Cremers, B. P. M. (1994). *The effective classroom.* London: Cassel.

Davis-Kean, P., & Eccles, J. S. (2002/under review). *It takes a village to raise a child: An executive function and community management perspective.*

Eccles, J. S. (1992). School and family effects on the ontogeny of children's interests, self-perceptions, and activity choice. In J. Jacobs (Ed.), *Nebraska symposium on motivation, 1992: Developmental perspectives on motivation* (pp. 145–208). Lincoln: University of Nebraska Press.

Eccles, J. S., & Midgley, C. (1989). Stage/environment fit: Developmentally appropriate classrooms for early adolescents. In R. E. Ames & C. Ames (Eds.), *Research on motivation in education* (Vol. 3, pp. 139–186). New York: Academic Press.

Eccles, J. S., Midgley, C., & Adler, T. (1984). Grade-related changes in the school environment: Effects on achievement motivation. In J. G. Nicholls (Ed.), *The development of achievement motivation* (pp. 283–331). Greewich, CT: JAI Press.

Eccles, J. S., Midgley, C., Wigfield, A., Buchanan, C. M., Reuman, D., Flanagan, C., & Mac Iver, D. (1993). Development during adolescence: The impact of stage environment fit on young adolescents' experiences in schools and in families. *American Psychologist, 48,* 90–101.

Flavell, J. H. (1999). Cognitive development: Children's knowledge about the mind. *Annual Review of Psychology, 50,* 21–45.

Fletcher, J. M. (1996). Executive functions in children: Introduction to the special series. *Developmental Neuropsychology, 12,* 1–3.

Freund, A. M., & Baltes, P. B. (1998). Selection, optimization, and compensation as strategies of life management: Correlations with subjective indicators of successful aging. *Psychology and Aging, 13,* 531–543.

Furstenberg, F. F., Jr., Cook, T. D., Eccles, J., Elder, G. H., Jr., & Samcroff, A. (1999). *Managing to make it: Urban families and adolescent success.* Chicago: University of Chicago Press.

Greeno, J. G., Smith, D. R., & Moore, J. L. (1992). Transfer of situated learning. In D. Detterman & R. J. Sternberg (Eds.), *Transfer on trial: Intelligence, cognition, and instruction* (pp. 99–176). Norwood, NJ: Ablex.

Harrison, J.-A., Strauss, H., & Glaubman, R. (1981). Who benefits from the open classroom? The interaction of social background with class setting. *Journal of Educational Research, 75,* 87–94.

Harter, S. (1981). A new self-report scale of intrinsic versus extrinsic orientation in the classroom: Motivational and informational components. *Developmental Psychology, 17,* 300–312.

Hill, K. T. (1980). Motivation, evaluation, and educational test policy. In L. J. Fyans (Ed.), *Achievement motivation: Recent trends in theory and research* (pp. 34–95). New York: Plenum Press.

Hunt, D. E. (1975). Person-environment interaction: A challenge found wanting before it was tried. *Review of Educational Research, 45,* 209–230.

Jencks, C., Smith, M. S., Ackland, H., Bane, M. J., Cohen, D., Grintlis, H., Heynes, B., & Michelson, S. (1972). *Inequality: A reassessment of the effect of family and schooling in America.* New York: Basic Books.

Köller, O. (1998). *Zielorientierungen und schulisches Lernen.* [Goal orientations and academic learning]. Münster, Germany: Waxmann.

Köller, O. (2000). Goal orientations: Their impact on academic learning and their development during early adolescence. In J. Heckhausen (Ed.), *Motivational psychology of human development: Developing motivation and motivating development* (pp. 129–142). Oxford: Elsevier.

Köller, O., Baumert, J., & Schnabel, K. (1999). Wege zur Hochschulreife: Offenheit des Systems und Sicherung vergleichbarer Standards Analysen am Beispiel der Mathematikleistungen von Oberstufen-schülern an Integrierten Gesamtschulen und Gymnasien in Nordrhein-Westfalen [Paths into higher education: Openness of the system and ensuring comparable standards. Illustrative analyses on the mathematics achievement of upper secondary school students attending comprehensive and Gymna-sium schools in North Rhein-Westphalia]. *Zeitschrift für Erziehungswissenschaft, 2,* 385–422.

Lave, J. (1988). *Cognition in practice: Mind, mathematics, and culture in everyday life.* New York: Cambridge University Press.

Lerner, R. M. (1987). A life-span perspective for early adolescence. In R. M. Lerner & T. T. Foch (Eds.), *Biological-psychosocial interactions in early adolescence: A life-span perspective.* Hillsdale, NJ: Erlbaum.

Marsh, H. W., & Peart, N. (1988). Competitive and cooperative physical fitness training programs for girls: Effects on physical fitness and on multidimensional self-concepts. *Journal of Sport and Exercise Psychology, 10,* 390–407.

Marsiske, M., Lang, F. R., Baltes, P. B., & Baltes, M. M. (1995). Selective optimization with compensation: Life-span perspectives on successful human development. In R. A. Dixon & L. Bäckman (Eds.), *Compensating for psychological deficits and declines. Managing losses and promoting gains* (pp. 35–79). Hillsdale, NJ: Erlbaum.

McCarthy, J. D., & Hoge, D. R. (1982). Analysis of age effects in longitudinal studies of adolescent self-esteem. *Developmental Psychology, 18,* 372–379.

Opdenakker, M.-C., & Van Damme, J. (2000). Effects of schools, teaching staff and classes on achievement and well-being in secondary educations: Similarities and differences between school outcomes. *School Effectiveness and School Improvement, 11,* 165–196.

Resnick, L. B. (1987). Learning in school and out. *Educational Researcher, 16,* 13–20.

Resnick, L. B. (1994). Situated rationalism: Biological and social preparation for learning. In L. Hirschfeld & S. Gelman (Eds.), *Mapping the mind: Domain specificity in cognition and culture* (pp. 474–493). New York: Cambridge University Press.

Rutter, M., Maughan, B., Mortimore, P., & Ouston, J. (1979). *Fifteen thousand hours: Secondary schools and their effects on children.* London: Open Books.

Scheerens, J., & Bosker, R. (1977). *The foundations of educational effectiveness.* Oxford: Elsevier.

Simmons, R. G., & Blyth, D. A. (1987). *Moving into adolescence: The impact of pubertal change and school context.* Hawthorne, NY: Aldine de Gruyter.

Simmons, R. G., Blyth, D. A., van Cleaves, E. F., & Bush, D. (1979). Entry into early adolescence: The impact of school structure, puberty, and early dating on self-esteem. *American Sociological Review, 38,* 553–568.

Teddlie, C., & Springfield, S. C. (1993). *Schools make a difference: Lessons learned from a 10-year study of school effects.* New York: Teachers College Press.

Wiese, B. S., & Freund, A. M. (2000). The interplay of work and family in young and middle adulthood. In J. Heckhausen (Ed.), *Motivational psychology of human development: Developing motivation and motivating development* (pp. 176–192). Oxford: Elsevier.

Wigfield, A., Eccles, J. S., & Pintrich, P. R. (1996). Development between the ages of 11 and 25. In D. C. Berliner & R. C. Calfee (Eds.), *Handbook of educational psychology* (pp. 148–185). New York: MacMillan Library Reference USA.

Zelazo, P. D., Carter, A., Resnick, J. S., Frye, D. (1997). Early development of executive function: A problem-solving framework. *Review of General Psychology, 1,* 198–226.

Zelazo, P. D., & Frye, D. (1998). Cognitive complexity and control: II. The development of executive function in childhood. *Current Directions in Psychological Science. 7,* 121–126.

23 The Sociology of the Life Course and Lifespan Psychology: Diverging or Converging Pathways?

Karl Ulrich Mayer

Max Planck Institute for Human Development, Berlin, Germany

Abstract

Lifespan psychology and life-course sociology concern themselves to a considerable extent with separate areas of interest and separate lines of research. Life-course sociology aims to understand the evolution of life courses primarily as the outcome of institutional regulation and social structural forces. Lifespan psychology views development across the life span primarily as changes of genetically and organically based functional capacities and as behavioral adaptation. In life-course sociology and lifespan psychology, however, there is also a considerable overlapping of interests and a need for synthesis and integration.

Introduction

In the last twenty to thirty years, both lifespan psychology and the sociology of the life course have experienced a great and long takeoff with regard to theory building and conceptualization, methodological advances, and empirical studies. Within sociology but also partly in demography, economics, and social policy studies, a cohort and life-course perspective, event history analysis, and microanalytic longitudinal data have become almost predominant (Mayer, 1990, 2000; Riley, Kahn, & Foner, 1994). Baltes, Staudinger, & Lindenberger (1999, p. 473) note, for instance, that lifespan psychology became more prominent due to, among other reasons, "a concern with lifespan development in neighboring social science disciplines, especially sociology. Life course sociology took hold as a powerful intellectual force."

At the beginning of this development, there were great expectations that the disciplines involved in this "life-course turn"—especially life-course sociology and lifespan psychology—would grow together in a parallel trajectory and that there would be co-evolution in the direction of a truly interdisciplinary or even transdisciplinary paradigm on human development. Volumes such as the one edited by Kohli (1978), Sørensen,

Weinert, and Sherrod (1986), or the series on *Lifespan Development and Behavior* edited by Baltes, Featherman, and Lerner (1978–1990) bear ample witness to this view. This expectation was also not in any way ill-founded.

On the one hand, there were earlier developmentalist traditions where psychological and sociological orientations were closely tied (Bühler, 1931, 1959). On the other hand, there was a reemergence of a kind of social-psychological study of the life cycle (Clausen, 1986) in which the variation of external conditions and psychological characteristics were connected to their later consequences. Glen Elder's now classic study on the *Children of the Great Depression* (1974) and the consequent research of his group count among the best examples. Many of the actors personally knew each other, frequently interacted, and sometimes cooperated. There were also several attemps to provide something like a common theoretical frame (Featherman, 1983; Elder & Caspi, 1990; Baltes, 1997, in this volume; Baltes et al., 1999; Heckhausen, 1999; Diewald, 1999). Even some identity blurring appears to have taken place, since some labeled as psychologists by sociologists were labeled as sociologists by psychologists.

In retrospect, despite all the strong mutual recognition and reinforcement, surprisingly little convergence and intergration has actually occurred. Lifespan psychology and life-course sociology now seem to stand further apart than in the seventies. The main purpose of this comment is to reconstruct and understand this impasse as seen from the point of view of a sociologist. The major questions to be raised are whether and to what extent these divergences are necessary and legitimate and whether they should be seen as mutual and detrimental shortcomings that should be and can be overcome. I approach these questions not so much as matters of principle and of general theory but more from the point of view of practical empirical research. I proceed in the following steps. First, I describe what life-course sociologists actually do and what goals they pursue. Second, I portray how lifespan psychology appears to a sociologist. Third, on this basis, I discuss how the two disciplinary perspectives tend to be restrictive and shortsighted in some of the areas where they intersect. Fourth, I outline more systematically how psychological developemnt should come into the sociological study of the life course and how life-course sociology could enrich and broaden the psychological study of the life span. I use examples from existing and potential research to illustrate these points.

The Life Course from the Perspective of Sociology

For sociologists, the term *life course* denotes the sequence of activities or states and events in various life domains that span from birth to death. The life course is thus seen as the embedding of individual lives into social structures primarily in the form of their partaking in social positions and roles—that is, with regard to their membership in institutional orders. The sociological study of the life course, therefore, aims at mapping, describing, and explaining the synchronic and diachronic distribution of individual persons into social positions across the lifetime. One major aspect of life courses is their internal temporal ordering—that is, the relative duration times in given states as well as the age distributions at various events or transitions.

How do order and regularities in life courses come about? Sociologists look primarily for three mechanisms to account for the form and outcomes of life courses. The first mechanism is the degree and manner to which societies are internally differentiated into subsystems or institutional fields (Mayer & Müller, 1986). This is often taken to be the most obvious and important one. The second mechanism is seen in the internal dynamic of individual lives (in group contexts). Here, one searches for conditions of behavioral outcomes in the prior life history or in norm-guided or rationally purposive action. The third mechanism derives from the basic fact that it is not simply society on the one hand and the individual on the other that are related to each other but that aggregates of individuals appear in the form of populations such as birth cohorts or marriage cohorts (Mayer & Huinink, 1990).

Let me illustrate each of these three life-course mechanisms in turn. How do institutions shape life courses? The educational system defines and regulates educational careers by its age-graded and time-scheduled sequences of classes, its school types and streams, and its institutions of vocational and professional training and higher learning with their hierarchical and time-related sequence of courses and certificates. Labor law defines who is gainfully employed and who is unemployed or out of the labor force and thus employment trajectories. The occupational structure defines careers by conventional or institutionalized occupational activities, employment statuses, and qualification groups. The supply of labor determines the opportunity structure and thus the likelihood of gaining entry into an occupational group or of change between occupations and industrial sectors. Firms provide by their internal functional and hierarchical division of labor career ladders and the boundaries for job shifts between firms and enterprises. In a similar manner, the institutions of social insurance and public welfare define the status of being ill, the duration of maternity leave, the age or employment duration until retirement, and so on. Family norms and law constitute the boundaries between being single or in nonmarital unions, married, and divorced. Finally, the spatial structure of societies as well as forms of property define the interaction with family roles and forms of household trajectories of residential mobility, household changes, and migration.

The second mechanism for shaping life courses focuses on life trajectories and their precedents. Research tends, when being descriptive, to concentrate on transition or hazard rates—that is, the instantaneous rates at which a well-defined population at risk makes certain transitions (such as into first employment, first motherhood, or retirement) within a given time interval (such as a month or a year but across larger spans of a lifetime). The explanatory question for life-course research, then, is whether situational, personal, or contextual conditions shape a certain outcome, and also whether outcomes are shaped by experiences and resources that are acquired at earlier stages of the biography, such as incomplete families in childhood (Grundmann, 1992), prior job shifts (Mayer, Diewald, & Solga, 1999), prior episodes of unemployment (Bender,

Konietzka, & Sopp, 2000), educational careers (Henz, 1996), or vocational training and early career patterns (Konietzka, 1999; Hillmert, 2001). There is one important additional point to be made in this context. Looking for "causal" mechanisms on the microlevel of the individual biography does not resolve the issue as to whether the individual is more an active agent or more a passive object in the processes that shape the life course or—to put it in different terms—whether selection or adaptation by choice is of primary importance (Diewald, 1999, ch. 2). Sociologists tend to be split on this issue. Some would emphasize cultural scripts, some would stress social norms, and others would bet on rational choice. But on the whole, sociologists tend to believe more in selection than in choice. First of all, the institutional contexts as described above already narrow down to a large extent which life avenues are open and which are closed. Second, within given institutional contexts, individuals are probably more frequently being selected than doing the selecting themselves. This is related to another sociological axiom: If material resources, power, authority, information, and symbolic goods are distributed very unequally within given societies, then it follows that more people have to accommodate than have the opportunity to exert control.

The third mechanism that one can look for when unraveling patterns in life courses has to do with the fact that it is not single individuals but populations that are allocated to and are streamlined through the institutional fabric of society across the lifetime. One example of this is cohort size (one's own as well as the preceding and succeeding cohorts), which influences individual opportunities way beyond individual or situational conditions (Ryder, 1965, 1980; Macunevic, 1999). Another example is the dynamics of union formation and marriage where one's own chances of finding a partner change over time depending on the behavior of others searching at the same time (Hernes, 1972, 1976).

From the perspective of sociology, then, life courses are considered not as life histories of persons as individuals but as patterned dynamic expressions of social structure. These apply to populations or subsets of populations, are governed intentionally or unintentionally by institutions, and are the intentional or nonintentional outcomes of the behavior of actors. Patterns of life courses are, however, not only products of societies and a part and parcel of social structure; they are at the same time also important mechanisms for generating social structures as the aggregate outcome of individual steps throughout the life course. One example of this that is intuitively easy to grasp is that the age and cohort structures of a population are the highly consequential result of a multitude of fertility behaviors and decisions. Likewise, the employment structure is the outcome of a multitude of individual employment trajectories.

Finally, the relationship to historical time is crucial for the sociological study of life courses. They are embedded in definite strands of historical periods but also in the collective life histories of families and birth cohorts. They are subject to historical circumstances at any time but are also subject to the cumulative or delayed effects of earlier historical times on the individual life history or the collective life history of birth cohorts (or marriage cohorts or employment entry cohorts).

Our heuristics for the study of life courses are thus guided by four sign posts (Mayer & Huinink, 1990; Huinik, 1995, pp. 154–155). First, individual life courses are to be viewed as part and product of a societal and historical multilevel process. They are closely tied to the life courses of other persons (parents, partners, children, work colleagues) and the dynamics of the social groups of which they are a member. They are highly structured by social institutions and organizations and their temporal dynamics. Second, the life course is multidimensional. It develops in different mutually related and mutually influencing life domains such as work and the family. It also unfolds in the context of biological and psychological maturation and decline. Third, the life course is a self-referential process. The person acts or behaves on the basis of, among others, prior experiences and resources. We must, therefore, expect endogenous causation already on the individual level. This then becomes via aggregation also true for the collective life course of birth cohorts or generations. Their past facilitates and constrains their future. This is the meaning of the phrase *die Gleichzeitigkeit des Ungleichzeitigen,* which characterizes the interdependency of generations. The various age groups live together in a common present, but each brings its own particular past to it. Fourth, through the manner in which persons live and construct their own individual lives, they reproduce and change social structures. This can either happen via "simple" aggregation processes or via immediate or intermediate institution formation. An example of the latter would be that a growing proportion of fully employed mothers exerts electoral pressure to change schools into institutions that take care of children for most of the day.

One might also ask in which sources sociologists of the life course expect the greatest share of variance in life-course outcomes to be explained. The largest part of variation will usually be expected to reside in those external structures within society that are closely tied to the division of labor—that is, the occupational structure, the structure of employment in various industrial sectors, and the educational systems. The reason for this is that both the distribution of initial resources (of resulting income rewards) and the distribution of positions that form the basic opportunity structure (and into which people are sorted) are intimately tied to these institutional fields. Thus, life-course patterns are expected to vary greatly across social classes or status groups (Carroll & Mayer, 1986). The second-largest source of variation sociologists would tend to locate would be in the division of labor within households—the way women and men in families and other unions allocate their lifetime for economic and family roles (Sørensen, 1990; Ben-Porath, 1980). The third important source of variation that life-course sociologists would look for relates to the differential intervention of the state in the form of the modern welfare state (Mayer & Müller, 1986; Huinink et al., 1995; Mayer, 2001b). It is, therefore, the so-called welfare mix—the relative importance and manner of the interconnection of economic markets, the family, and the state across historical time and across contemporary societies—that sociologists would see as the major determinant of life-course patterns (Esping-Andersen, 1999).

Now we have come to the stage where we can formulate the major research questions for sociological life-course research. What are the patterns of life courses, and how do they differ between women and men, social classes and groups, nation states, birth cohorts, and historical periods? What are the determinants of and influences on life courses resulting either from the past individual or collective life history or from socioeconomic contexts and conditions and institutional constraints? What are the consequences of changing life-course patterns for social structure and institutions?

Thus one direction of research is descriptive and exploratory. A second direction runs from the macro level down to the micro level and asks how macro conditions of an institutional or structural kind affect individual lives. A third direction moves horizontally on the individual level and asks how earlier conditions have an impact on later outcomes, and a fourth direction focuses on the way micro outcomes affect macro configurations from the bottom upward.

Lifespan Psychology as Seen from Sociology

At first glance, the psychology of the life span and the sociology of the life course share the same object of scientific inquiry—the lives of women and men from birth to death. If they happen to tell different stories, it may seem as if they are just behaving like the blind men describing an elephant. One touches the snout, one touches the foot, and a third touches an ivory tusk. In contrast to this analogy, I would like to argue in this section how divergent their respective fields of study really are. Lifespan psychology "deals with the study of individual development (ontogenesis) . . . as lifelong adaptive processes of acquisition, maintenance, transformation, and attrition in psychological structures and functions" (Baltes et al., 1999, p. 472). At the center of interest stand changes in highly biologically based functional capacities and personality, such as cognitive abilities, memory, emotion, perception, information processing, attachment, or resilience. Many of these functional capacities and their overall changes across the lifetime can be fruitfully thought of as being the fairly universal results of evolutionary selection. Therefore, lifespan psychology can—at least on a general theoretical level— make a close and productive connection between phylogenesis as the evolution of the species and ontogenesis as individual development (cf. Kirkwood, this volume; Maier & Vaupel, this volume). Accordingly, often a relatively large share of the interindividual variability in functional trajectories and behavioral outcomes is generally attributed to genetically founded constraints. These biological and genetic constraints vary across the lifetime (Kirkwood, this volume; cf. Baltes, 1997, this volume). They are likely to be highest, on the one hand, in infancy and early childhood and, on the other hand, in late age, and (as the testing-the-limits research on cognitive functioning impressively demonstrates) age differences between young adults and old persons can rarely be offset even by intensive learning and intervention (cf. Singer, this volume).

Lifespan psychology views development as based both on biology and culture and therefore as a "nature" as well as as a "nurture" discipline, while from its perspective the sociology of the life course appears as a somewhat narrow "nurture" discipline that would need to expand its horizon to acknowledge genetic factors to overcome a simple environment-based conception of social forces. Conversely, the sociology of the life course sees itself as an endeavor combining both "nurture" and "institutions" and views lifespan psychology as needing to include the complexities of institutions for more precise accounts of contexts.

Thus, lifespan psychology and life-course sociology do not only diverge with regard to the level of the unit of analysis, the major life dimensions, and dependent variables at stake; they also diverge with regard to the broad causal forces that can be seen at work. Clearly, life-course sociology is much more agnostic in regard to main areas of interest of psychology, since it almost dogmatically abhors thinking beyond the last one or two centuries back to evolution and (equally dogmatically) tends to exclude evolutionary, biological, and genetic factors from its explanatory toolbox (see, in contrast, Runciman, 1998). The same applies to a large extent to concurrent psychological traits and functional capacities. Durkheim's formula—according to which sociology is to explain the social by the social—still reigns in the realm (Lukes, 1972, 2001).

In contrast, lifespan psychology commands within its conceptual apparatus a good number of open doors to the variability brought about by history, society, and culture such as plasticity, malleability, interindividual variation, environment, coevolution, and culture. However, as seen from sociology, if we go beyond the social-psychological level of interpersonal relationships, these categories tend to be something of undifferentiated residuals that display little explanatory power. The same charge very much applies to the distinction within lifespan psychology between age-graded, history graded, and nonnormative changes across life (Baltes, 1987). Whereas *historical* denotes nonsystematic ideographic circumstances and *nonnormative* tends to be residually defined as nonregularities, *age-graded* changes are primarily seen by developmental psychologists as the outcome of either biological changes or the outcome of age norms as rules of convention like the proper age for marriage, motherhood, and fatherhood. The latter view is forcefully argued by Heckhausen (1999, p. 35): "life-course patterns would be expected to have become increasingly regulated by internalized norms about age-appropriate behavior . . . as societal regulation became more lenient. Thus, age-normative conceptions about the life course internalized by individuals may gradually have replaced external regulations based on objectified institutions. . . . Age-normative conceptions may have committing power as internalized, naturalized, and thus unquestionable ways of thinking about human lives." In contrast, sociologists will always search for external, institutional constraints first and will tend to view age norms as epiphenomenal cognitions deriving from them. Thus, instead of, for instance, asking survey respondents about the proper ages for starting gainful work, they would set out to determine how educational, vocational, and professional tracks of various duration allow persons to enter labor markets at varying ages and how these medians add up in a given population. This debate does not play out on an ontological level. The issue, therefore, is not whether age norms exist or do not exist and whether institutional regulation exists or does not exist. The issue is, rather, what ought the importance of institutional and other kinds of socioeconomic regulation assumed to be relative to the rise, persistence, and change of normative orientations. Marriage behavior may again serve as our example. If we are to believe the lifespan psychologist, changes in the median age at marriage should be primarily the consequence of changes in age norms. In contrast, the sociologist of the life course would look first at changes in the duration of education and training, the relative affluence in given historical periods, the incentives provided by family assistance policies, and so on.

If we review the evidence of the recent German changes in the median age at marriage, there is some consolation for both sides. On the one hand, the lowest median cohort ages at marriage in the last century occurred for the 1945 birth cohort of men and the 1947 cohort of women (Mayer, 2001a). There is little doubt that this outcome was the result of two forces. One force was the relatively high economic affluence and high economic growth rates of the late 1960s and thus the income development and the opportunities on the labor market. The other force was indeed a norm but not an age norm—the still binding norm at that time that sexual unions should take place. within marriage. The later rapid increase in the ages at marriages from the early 1970s onward was again not an outcome of changes in age norms but was the outcome of increasing ages of leaving education and employment as well as of the effectiveness and accessibility of birth control and the tolerance of nonmarital unions. Similarly, the dramatic changes of the very low ages at marriage in East Germany after German unification were an effect not of normative changes but of changes in economic circumstances, in housing scarcity, and in family assistance pay (Huinink, 1995). Although there is little doubt that the differential opportunities for early marriage and early fertility in East Germany did in fact give rise to corresponding age norms, the persistence of these norms under the new conditions after unification is doubtful. If age norms are primary and constitutive rather than derivative and epiphenomenal, then one should expect that East German couples will return to and persist in lower ages at marriage and first birth in comparison to couples in West Germany. So far the demographic data do not support this hypothesis (Sackmann, 1999). This is not to deny the importance of social norms in guiding behavior relative to rational action based on the calculation of personal interest. For instance, in a recent study on the differences in the rates of nonmarital fertility in East and West Germany, Huinink (1998) concludes that differential incentives cannot fully account for the fact that East German couples have many more children out of wedlock and therefore that different norms must be assumed. The consequence of norms on nonmarital fertility is not least their impact on age at marriage and age at first birth. The important point in the context of our present discussion, however, is that these are not age norms but rather observed age profiles that are the outcome of both other kinds of behavioral norms and institutional incentives.

Jutta Heckhausen, in her recent book on *Developmental Regulation in Adulthood* (1999; cf. Heckhausen, this volume), has probably gone furthest as a lifespan psychologist to meet life-course sociologists halfway. It is, therefore, useful to take up where she sees the closest connections. What she terms *sociostructural constraints* falls into three areas—lifetime-related, chronological age-based, and age-sequential. At this point, sociologists would already ask for conceptual clarification, since what is called *sociostructural* here throws together structural and institutional constraints. For a sociologist, structural constraints arise from the distribution of resources, positions, and opportunities, whereas institutional constraints arise from explicit and relatively permanent social rules that are often tied to specific organizational settings.

Lifetime constraints relate to the overall life span and thus the impressive fact that both institutions and individual persons have to achieve their goals and tasks within a finite time. This is reflected in what Kohli (1985) and others have called the *tripartite structure of the life course*—(1) socialization, education, and training, (2) gainful employment and reproductive roles, and (3) retirement and old age. The length of the lifetime puts limits on the amount of time available for achieving life goals. The lengthening of the life span or at least of the years without severe functional impairment therefore makes it plausible, for instance, to see why the duration spent in initial schooling and training is lengthening and why many—especially gerontopsychologists—call for an extended and more flexible age of transition to retirement. It is also plausible that longer lives would lead to a sequence of occupations or a sequence of marital or nonmarital unions. The sociologically more interesting fact is, however, that the institutional partitioning of the life course often runs counter to the lengthening of the lifetime. The concentration of education and training in the years until early adulthood is persisting despite many campaigns of lifelong learning (Mayer, 1996). Likewise, modern society still concentrates the formative years of occupational careers and the crucial years of family formation within a very short (and ever shorter) time span in young adulthood. And in most advanced societies, the median age at retirement drops rather than increases (Kohli, Rein, Guillemard, & van Gunsteren, 1991; but see also Burkhauser & Quinn, 1997). This may reflect what Matilda Riley (Riley et al., 1994) has called a *structural lag* between demographic and institutional development that will be adjusted in the foreseeable future. It is as likely, however, that institutional mechanisms shape the age at retirement quite independently from overall trends in length of the life span and in the opposite direction. While the need to finance pensions individually or collectively will provide a push for later retirement ages, the inclination of employers and employees to look for exits well before the legal retirement age is powerfully influenced by the high rate of occupational and sectoral restructuring. In addition to the lifetime as such, Heckhausen explicitly acknowledges that deadlines are also frequently imposed by institutions formally and informally, such as restrictions in the length of university studies, the length of time it takes to reach the grade of major in the military, or age deadlines until one has to have made it to full professor in the German university system.

The second kind of sociostructural constraint Heckhausen (1999, p. 30) introduces is *chronological-age-based*: "In most human societies, the life course is composed of an age-graded structure, which stratifies the society into age strata and involves age norms for important life events and role transitions." There is little dissension about the fact that both formally and informally age and age groups form an important basis of differentiation within societies and that age is often used in legal or quasi-legal norms to regulate entry into and exit from social positions. As already argued above, however, lifespan psychology tends to overemphasize, from a sociological point of view, social distinctions based on age—at least if they are taken to be directly explanatory as a consequence of age norms rather than descriptive regularities. Behind many apparent age regularities, they would argue, are regularities brought about by institutional time scheduling. Thus, age at entry into employment varies widely depending on the length of prior schooling. In many countries, age at retirement is contingent on years of service rather than age per se. It is exactly the highly institutionalized and regulated intersection of education, vocational training, and employment in Germany (rather than age per se) that imposes such a demanding developmental task. I would seriously question whether the category of chronological age-based constraints is an effective way of introducing a social-structural dimension into lifespan psychology, since it presumes an unrealistic degree of unmediated institutionalization of age differentiation.

The third type of sociostructural constraints is called *age-sequential*. By this term, Heckhausen (1999, pp. 31–32) refers to the fact that states and events across the lifetime are not randomly distributed but that the choice or experience of a prior transition or state narrows down options and probabilities for consequent steps. It remains unclear, however, how this kind of endogenous causation occurs. Heckhausen speaks of "segregated life-course paths demarcated by social structure" and "commonly shared notions of normal or desirable biographies." In this respect, sociology (and economics) could offer more precise and elaborated concepts. Let us take as the most important example the area of employment and occupational careers. Continuities in occupational trajectories can come about via the individual investment in human capital and the accumulation of human capital in education, training, or work. Initial mismatches between acquired human capital and the job available on the labor market tend to lead to a series of job shifts until the level of skill matches what is taken to be an adequate reward in terms of status or income (Sørensen & Tuma, 1981; Carroll & Mayer, 1986). Career contingency can also occur, however, as a result of restrictions on the demand side. When labor markets are true markets, all market participants have in principle access to vacant positions. Everybody competes with everybody. But very often labor markets are segmented into submarkets defined by skills, sectors, or organizations. Occupationally segmented labor markets require credentials for entry and often additionally impose career ladders like apprentice, journeyman, and master. Firm-segmented labor markets tend to restrict access to positions to workers already in the firm and thus create well-defined internal career ladders. Gender-segregated labor markets restrict women from access to male-dominated jobs and occupations.

The challenge sociology would pose to lifespan psychology would then focus on how adaptive tasks vary between different institutional frameworks and settings and how these select and modify psychological characteristics across the lifetime.

Lifespan Psychology as a Challenge for the Sociology of the Life Course

Lifespan psychology poses a threefold challenge to the sociology of the life course. First, it questions the usefulness of an exclusively or excessively sociostructural and institutional perspective on conceptualizing and explaining life courses. Second, it allows the hidden cognitive, volitional, and emotional mechanisms to be revealed. By so doing, actors can be seen as translating structural and institutional constraints and incentives into their own behavior and can thus offer a more than rhetorical idea of how persons shape their own lives. Third, lifespan psychology can offer concepts, theories, methods, and measurement that can supplement and modify sociological explanatory models. Let me elaborate on these three issues in sequence.

Why would it be shortsighted and indeed misleading to restrict oneself to a view of life courses where these would be seen exclusively as the outcome of social role playing, structural constraints, institutional regulation, and the socioeconomic circumstances of given historical periods? An initial answer is that as much as life courses are the products of culture, society, and history, they are also the product of persons as natural organisms, individual decision makers, and personalities (Diewald, 1999, pp. 18–43). One might well argue, therefore, that the genetic, physical, and personality constraints and the interindividual variations resulting from them—on how people live out their lives—are not only nonnegligible but probably overwhelming in comparison to those determinants resulting from sociocultural differences (Rutter, 1997). In this respect, however, one might at least tender the hypothesis that across evolution, social and cultural construction and elaboration would tend to increase in their relative weight and that other factors would recede in importance. Thus, it is a long way from small segmented societies (where the structure of life courses and the functional division of labor is intimately and immediately tied to aging as a trajectory of physical ability and of a sequence of reproductive roles) (Linton, 1939) to current societies (where nurseries, schools, labor organizations, social security systems, and welfare provisions intervene in this process).

In stark contrast, however, Heckhausen (1999, pp. 33–37) develops a powerful argument as to why psychological modes of regulation of the life course should become more important than structural or institutional constraints. She makes a distinction here between external and internal regulation. External regulation is equated with social conditions that might be legal sanctions, group pressure, or organizational rules. Internal regulation is equated with relatively stable psychological dispositions with regard to modes of adaptation and coping or with regard to substantive preferences. Analogous to the theory of the civilizing process of Norbert Elias (1969), she claims that "external enforcement via societal power has gradually, over centuries, been transformed into internalized rules and norms of conduct and behavior. This process of internalization renders the need for external societal enforcement obsolete. . . . Modern anthropologists argue that social conventions become transformed into institutionalized ways of thinking. Social constructions of reality provide societal stability and predictability as well as subjective certainty about a mutually habitualized, and thereby institutionalized, foundation of individual action" (Heckhausen, 1999, pp. 34–35). Heckhausen's position appears to be strongly supported by sociologists' claim that life courses become deinstitutionalized, that cognitive biographical scripts about the normal life course become more important (Kohli, 1985), that institutions and traditional collectivities lose their binding power, that therefore individualization increases (Beck, 1986), and that more subtle forms of psychological influence have replaced the crude mechanisms of physical force and material incentives in controlling behavior (Foucault, 1977; Pizzorno, 1991).

Although one can hardly deny the historical thrust of the argument à la Elias and Foucault, I have many doubts as to its applicability to modern life courses as far as the role of normative orientations is concerned. As John Meyer has argued, internalized and strongly religiously based norms in guiding life courses may have been appropriate and widespread in the seventeenth to nineteenth centuries, but they would be highly dysfunctional in present-day societies where very flexible situational adaptation is required (Mayer, 1988; Meyer, 1986). The relative importance that persons and cultures accord to their lives as an overall developmental project is itself highly variable (Brandtstädter, 1990). The debate on this issue is still very much open. On the one hand, we find good arguments in favor of increasing decollectivization and individualization. In particular, increasing material resources should support the rise of individual life projects. On the other hand, however, we also see a decline in cultural expectations according to which persons are expected to be the definer and defendant of meaningful and coherent life designs (Jaspers, 1979; Mayer & Müller, 1986; Riesman, Glazer, & Denney, 1950).

This brings us to the second challenge that lifespan psychology poses for the sociology of the life course—how to fill the black box of the actor. If they do so at all, sociologists tend to rely on action models based on variants of rational-choice theory (Coleman, 1990; Braun, 1998; Voss & Abraham, 2000). The disadvantage of these models is that, on the one hand, they assume "modal" actors (they are more interested in average group behavior than individual behavior) and, on the other hand, they assume that (apart from investment and consumption theories) (Becker, 1976) the life course is nothing but a series of unrelated decision situations. Lifespan developmental psychology offers remedies to both of these deficits. It investigates a set of psychological processes that is of particular interest in the first of these two contexts—control and goal striving (Heckhausen & Schulz, 1995; Brandtstädter, 1990; Brandtstädter & Rothermund, this volume), control beliefs (Bandura, 1977, 1992), and selective optimization with compensation (Baltes & Baltes, 1990; M. Baltes & Carstensen, this volume; cf. Behrman, this volume).[1]

Control theories start with the basic assumption that persons want to be the masters of their own destinies—that they want to pursue their own goals and that they do so by exerting control over their environment. Primary control strategies relate to the active shaping of one's own development and to efforts to bring one's environment into line with one's own needs and goals. Secondary control strategies help the person accept that certain circumstances are not easily changeable and that it is, therefore, wiser to adapt desires and goals to those that can be realistically obtained (Elster, 1983).[2] Schulz and Heckhausen (1996) assume that with increasing age external restrictions increase and that persons, therefore, employ more secondary control strategies at higher ages in order to protect their sense of self-worth, their belief in their self-efficacy, and thus their motivation for primary control.

The second group of psychological processes relate to the person's beliefs in the efficacy of his own actions and the related degree to which persons invest in goal attainment and persist in their efforts. Numerous studies have shown that high self-efficacy beliefs lead to more intense and persistent efforts in goal pursuit. The relation of such control beliefs to aging is less obvious. On the one hand, beliefs in self-efficacy and tenaciousness are the consequence of prior experiences and should, therefore, accumulate either positively or negatively across the life course. On the other hand, negative experiences will tend to become more frequent in advanced age and will eventually also affect self-efficacy negatively (Brandtstädter, 1990). Finally, the behavioral strategy of selective optimization with compensation presumes a double mechanism of successful adaptation. On the one hand, goals are selected in view of their relatively good returns or remain theoretically undetermined. On the other hand, goals that cannot be obtained are substituted by others more attainable, and resulting losses are covered by partially offsetting compensation. The latter model has been explicitly developed as a powerful explanatory and interpretative tool for adaptive behavior in aging. This model rests on three assumptions about universally shared basic developmental goals—growth, maintenance and resilience, and regulation of losses. Growth relates to behavior that is directed toward achieving higher levels of functioning or adaptive potential. Maintenance and resilience relate to behavior that is directed toward keeping or regaining prior levels of functioning in the context of new adaptive challenges and losses. The regulation of losses relates to behavior that has the aim of safeguarding functional capacity on a lower level, if maintenance is no longer possible. Physical and cognitive aging constitute per se major developmental tasks for persons across the life course. Growth creates potential that can be differentially realized or missed as opportunities in given social contexts. Maintenance can be differentially successful. Decline may be compensated with specialization and increased effort or by changing goals (Baltes & Baltes, 1990; Baltes, this volume; cf. M. Baltes & Carstensen, this volume; Brandtstädter & Rothermund, this volume; Salthouse, this volume).

Bringing this ensemble of psychological processes into the framework of the sociology of the life course would have a number of advantages. First of all, it quite clearly demonstrates that a pure "sociologistic" construction of the life course is untenable, since it would postulate that actors are largely influenced by external factors (or chance) and that they would also generally believe in the low efficacy of their own actions in comparison to external conditions. This would result in pervasive low self-esteem and low life satisfaction and is therefore inconsistent with the empirically well-founded assumption of psyches as positively equilibrating systems. It becomes rather both an explanandum and an explanatory variable that groups of persons tend to follow using primary or secondary control strategies; where various groups perceive the locus of control, how they differ in beliefs of self-efficacy and tenaciousness, and how good people are at shifting from primary to secondary control strategies and from unrealistic to realistic action goals.

I have defined above the third challenge of lifespan psychology to the sociology of the life course to actually include psychological variables in its models and to test their gross and net influences. I see in this two major goals. One goal is to increase the proportion of variance to be explained in life-course outcomes by the preceding life history by adding psychological variables measured at an earlier point in time. The second goal is to show how psychological characteristics themselves have to be seen as malleable outcomes rather than stable conditions in life-course processes. There are relatively few good examples of either of these research strategies. One example is the studies by Diewald, Huinink and Heckhausen (1996) and Diewald (1999). In the context of a study of life courses during the transformation of East Germany after the fall of the Berlin wall (Mayer et al., 1999), Diewald et al. (1996) examined first how control beliefs, control strategies, and feelings of self-respect varied between groups of different age and different occupational experiences before 1989 and between 1989 and 1993. Second, Diewald (2000) tested whether control beliefs had a net impact on unemployment, downward mobility, upward mobility, and occupational shifts between 1989 and 1993. As in earlier research (Heckhausen, 1999; Mayer, Kraus, & Schmidt, 1992), a number of significant covariations were found between age, other sociostructural variables, and beliefs of control and self-respect. Most important and unexpected was the result that positive attitudes did not simply covary with age in a monotonic fashion but that the oldest cohort groups, which was about 60 in 1989, did best, while those of approximately 50 years of age in 1989 did worst. There are probably two complementary explanations. The first relates to the fact that the oldest group did—for historical reasons—experience superior career opportunities in the GDR before 1989 (Mayer & Solga, 1994). The second explanation is based on the circumstance that practically all of the oldest group lost their employment due to labor-market policies of early retirement, whereas the approximately 50-year-olds experienced the turbulent labor market after unification. The oldest group could externalize the locus of control and keep their sense of prior achievements and self-respect intact, while the group that found itself as the relatively oldest one remaining in the labor market faced the relatively worst employment conditions and reacted accordingly. It is noteworthy, however, that scrutinizing labor-market experiences before 1989, gender and age control cognitions (as measured in 1993 and presumed to be prior and stable) played an important role in preventing unemployment but that they had no significant effects on upward and downward mobility. For the two variables already measured in 1991—internal control and fatalism—only fatalism showed any effect at all and it showed effect on only one of the four dependent variables (unemployment). In general, then, the evidence from these studies points on balance more to psychological dispositions as outcomes of (in our case dramatic) life-course events rather than a strong selectivity of life-course adaptation due to prior psychological dispositions.

Life-Course Sociology and Lifespan Psychology: An Agenda for Research

Lifespan psychology and life-course sociology concern themselves to a considerable extent with separate areas of interest and separate lines of research. Life-course sociology aims to understand the evolution of life courses primarily as the outcome of institutional regulation and social structural forces. Lifespan psychology views development across the life span primarily as changes of genetically and organically based functional capacities and as behavioral adaptation. In life-course sociology and lifespan psychology, however, there is also a considerable overlapping of interests and a need for synthesis and integration. If my above assessment is correct, then this common ground is mutually both poorly understood and underresearched. I, therefore, want to outline an agenda for joint research.

For lifespan psychology, it would be crucial from my point of view to exploit sociology in order to gain a more refined and a more differentiated repertoire of institutionally regulated developmental tasks and their consequences beyond generalized notions of age norms, developmental goals, and cognitions. In general, this will require cross-national comparative and longitudinal research in order to systematically vary the institutional contexts. One good example is the transition between general education and employment. In Germany and other countries with an important segment of a dual system of vocational training, this transition involves a highly stratified linkage between school achievement and accessible training positions—a two- or sometimes three-step transition between school, training, and early career positions and a highly differentiated system of certification. In Britain, most young people transit from school to work directly within a very narrow age range and receive most of their training on the job. These two transition regimes require and reward different psychological resources and should have different consequences for psychological disposition and personality (Hillmert, 2001; for a similar German-U.S. comparison, see Alfeld-Liro, Schnabel, Baumert, Eccles, & Barber, in press).

For life-course sociology, in contrast, the open agenda should aim to bring back the person. The questions to be addressed are given biographical resources and structural opportunities, how are persons of varying psychological makeup being selected, how do they cope differentially with given developmental tasks, and what are the consequences of specific life-course experiences for psychological dispositions such as developmental goals and control beliefs. This would involve measuring both objective life courses—as routinely is done in sociological life history studies (Brückner & Mayer, 1998)—as well as strategic psychological variables in prospective longitudinal studies.

Notes

1. Brandtstädter (1990, p. 339) makes the distinction between development-related perceptions and beliefs, development-related goals and values, and development-related control beliefs.
2. An important aspect of control theories is attributions about the locus of control—oneself, external factors, or chance.

References

Alfeld-Liro, C., Schnabel, K. U., Baumert, J., Eccles, J. S., & Barber, B. L. (in press). Educational structure and development during the transition to adulthood in the U.S.A. and Germany. *Journal of Vocational Behavior*.

Baltes, P. B. (Ed.). (1978). Life-span development and behavior (Vol. 1). New York: Academic Press.

Baltes, P. B., & Brim, O. G., Jr. (Eds.). (1979, 1980, 1982, 1983, 1984). Life-span development and behavior (Vol. 2–6). New York: Academic Press.

Baltes, P. B., Featherman, D. L., & Lerner, R. M. (Eds.). (1986, 1988, 1990). Life-span development and behavior (Vol. 7–10). Hillsdale, NJ: Erlbaum.

Baltes, P. B. (1987). Theoretical propositions of life-span developmental psychology: On the dynamics between growth and decline. *Developmental Psychology, 23*, 611–626.

Baltes, P. B. (1997). On the incomplete architecture of human ontogeny: Selection, optimization, and compensation as foundation of developmental theory. *American Psychologist, 52*, 366–380.

Baltes, P. B., & Baltes, M. M. (1990). Psychological perspectives on successful aging: The model of selective optimization with compensation. In P. B. Baltes & M. M. Baltes (Eds.), *Successful aging: Perspectives from the behavioral sciences* (pp. 1–34). New York: Cambridge University Press.

Baltes, P. B., Staudinger, U. M., & Lindenberger, L. (1999). Lifespan psychology: Theory and application to intellectual functioning. *Annual Review of Psychology, 50*, 471–507.

Bandura, A. (1977). Self-efficacy: Toward a unifying theory of behavioral change. *Psychological Review, 84*, 191–215.

Bandura, A. (1992). Exercise of personal agency through the self-efficacy mechanism. In R. Schwarzer (Ed.), *Self-efficacy: Though control of action* (pp. 3–38). Washington, DC: Hemisphere.

Beck, U. (1986). Risk society. On the road to another modern society. Frankfurt: Suhrkamp.

Becker, G. (1964). *Human capital.* New York: National Bureau of Economic Research, Columbia University Press.

Becker, G. (1976). *The economic approach to human behavior.* Chicago: University of Chicago Press.

Bender, S., Konietzka, D., & Sopp, P. (2000). Transition to flexibility or marginalization? The course of employment 'beyond the normal working relationships' in the job market of the 1990s, *Kölner Zeitschrift für Soziologie und Sozialpsychologie, 3*, 475–499.

Ben-Porath, Y. (1980). Families, friends and firms and the organisation of exchange. *Population and Development Review, 6*, 1–30.

Brandtstädter, J. (1990). Development across the life-span. Life-span developmental psychology and the personal self-regulation of development. *Kölner Zeitschrift für Soziologie und Sozialpsychologie, 31*, 322–350. In K. U. Mayer (Ed.), Life Courses and Social Change (pp. 322–350) Opladen: Westdeutscher Verlag.

Braun, N. (1998). The rational choice attempt in sociology. In I. Pies & M. Leschke (Eds.), Gary Becker's economic imperialism (pp. 147–173). Tübingen: Mohr & Siebeck.

Brückner, E., & Mayer, K. U. (1998). Collecting life history data: Experiences from the German life history study. In J. Z. Giele & G. Elder Jr. (Eds.), *Methods of life course research: Qualitative and quantitative approaches* (pp. 152–181). Thousand Oaks, CA: Sage.

Bühler, C. (1931). Childhood and youth. Genesis of consciousness. Leipzig: Hirzel.

Bühler, C., with Mitarbeit von H. Harvey & E. Kube. (1959). The human life course as a psychological problem. Göttingen: Verlag für Psychologie Dr. C. J. Hogrefe.

Burkhauser, R. V., & Quinn, J. F. (1997). Pro-work policy proposals for older Americans in the twenty-first century. *Policy Brief, 9*. Syracuse, NY: Center for Policy Research, Maxwell School, Syracuse University.

Carroll, G. R., & Mayer, K. U. (1986). Job-shift patterns in the Federal Republic of Germany: The effects of social class, industrial sector, and organisational size. *American Sociological Review, 51*, 323–341.

Clausen, J. A. (1986). *The life course: A sociological perspective*. Englewood Cliffs, NJ: Prentice-Hall.

Coleman, J. S. (1990). *Foundations of social theory*. Cambridge, MA: Belknap Press of Harvard University Press.

Diewald, M. (1999). *Devaluation, Revaluation, Enhancement. The course of East German employment between continuity and change*. Habilitation Thesis for Sociology, Faculty of Political and Social Sciences, Free University, Berlin.

Diewald, M. (2000). Continuities and breaks in occupational careers and subjective control: The case of the East German transformation. In J. Bynner & R. K. Silbereisen (Eds.), *Adversity and challenge in life in the New Germany and in England* (pp. 239–267). London: MacMillan Press.

Diewald, M., Huinink, J., & Heckhausen, J. (1996). Radical social change of life courses and personality development: Fates of cohorts and control beliefs in East Germany after 1989. *Kölner Zeitschrift für Soziologie und Sozialpsychologie, 48*, 219–248.

Elder, G. (1974). *Children of the great depression*. Chicago: University of Chicago Press.

Elder, G., & Caspi, A. (1990). Human development and social change: An emerging perspective on the life course. *Kölner Zeitschrift für Soziologie und Sozialpsychologie, 31*, 22–57. (Life courses and social change [K. U. Mayer, Ed.]).

Elder, G., & O'Rand, A. M. (1995). Adult lives in a changing society. In K. S. Cook, G. A. Fine, & J. S. House (Eds.), *Sociological perspectives on social psychology* (pp. 452–475). Needham Heights, MA: Allyn & Bacon.

Elias, N. (1969): *Ueber den Prozess der Zivilisation: Soziogenetische und psychogenetische Untersuchungen* [On the process of civilization: Sociogenetic and psychogenetic investigations]. Bern: Francke.

Elster, J. (1983). *Sour grapes: Studies in the subversion of rationality*. Cambridge: Cambridge University Press.

Esping-Andersen, G. (1999). *Social foundations of postindustrial economies*. Oxford: Oxford University Press.

Featherman, D. L. (1983). Life-span perspectives in social science research. In P. B. Baltes & O. G. Brim (Eds.), *Life-span development and behavior* (Vol. 5, pp. 1–57). New York: Academic Press.

Foucault, M. (1977): *Discipline and punish: The birth of the prison*. New York: Pantheon Books.

Grundmann, M. (1992). Family structure and life course. Historical and social conditions of individual development. Frankfurt am Main/New York: Campus Verlag.

Heckhausen, J. (1999). *Developmental regulation in adulthood: Age-normative and sociostructural constraints as adaptive challenges*. New York: Cambridge University Press.

Heckhausen, J., & Schulz, R. (1995). A life-span theory of control. *Psychological Review, 102*, 284–304.

Henz, U. (1996). Intergenerational mobility. Methodological and empirical analyses (Studies and Reports, No. 63). Berlin: Max-Planck-Institut für Bildungsforschung.

Hernes, G. (1972). The process of entry into first marriage. *American Sociological Review, 37*, 513–547.

Hernes, G. (1976). Structural change in social processes. *American Journal of Sociology, 82*, 513–547.

Hernes, H. M. (1984). Women and the welfare state: The transition from private to public dependence. In H. Holter (Ed.), *Patriarchy in a welfare society* (pp. 26–45). Oslo: Universitetsforlaget.

Hillmert, S. (2001). Education, training systems and the job market. A cohort comparison of life courses in Great Britain and Germany. Wiesbaden: Westdeutscher Verlag.

Huinink, J. (1995). Education, work, and family patterns of men: The case of West Germany. In H.-P.

Blossfeld (Ed.), *The new role of women: Family formation in modern societies* (pp. 247–262). Boulder: Westview Press.

Huinink, J. (1998). Single parenthood of young women and men in the East and West. *Leipzig Sociological Studies*, No. 1, 301–320.

Huinink, J., et al. (1995). Life courses in the GDR and after the fall of the Wall. Berlin: Akademie Verlag.

Jaspers, K. (1979). The intellectual challenge of the present. Berlin: de Gruyer.

Kohli, M. (Ed.). (1978). Sociology of the life course. Neuwied: Luchterhand.

Kohli, M. (1985). The institutionalization of the life course. Historical facts and theoretical arguments. *Kölner Zeitschrift für Soziologie und Sozialpsychologie, 37*, 1–29.

Kohli, M., Rein, M., Guillemard, A.-M., & van Gunsteren, H. (Eds.). (1991). *Time for retirement: Comparative studies of early exit from the labour force.* Cambridge: Cambridge University Press.

Konietzka, D. (1999). Education and occupation. The birth years 1919–1961 from school to work, Opladen: Westdeutscher Verlag.

Linton, R. (1939). A neglected aspect of social organization. *American Journal of Sociology, 45*, 870–886.

Lukes, S. (1972). *Emile Durkheim: His life and work.* New York: Harper and Row.

Lukes, S. (2001). Emile Durkheim (1858–1917). In N. J. Smelser & P. B. Baltes (Eds.), *International encyclopedia of the social and behavioral sciences* (Vol. 6, pp. 3897–3903). Oxford: Elsevier Science.

Macunevic, D. J. (1999). The fortunes of one's birth: Relative cohort size and youth labor market in the United States. *Journal of Economics, 12*, 215–272.

Mayer, K. U. (1988). Structure of Society and the Life Course. In K. U. Mayer, U. Schimank, & W. Schumm (Eds.), Biography or life course? On the suitability of two concepts (course unit 1) (pp. 21–40). Hagen: Fernuniversität Hagen.

Mayer, K. U. (Ed.). (1990). Life courses and social change (Special edition of the Kölner Zeitschrift für Soziologie und Sozialpsychologie, volume 31).

Mayer, K. U. (1996). Education and work in an aging population. In A. Burgen (Ed.), *Goals and purposes of higher education in the twenty-first century* (pp. 69–95). London: Kingley.

Mayer, K. U. (2000). Promises fulfilled? A review of twenty years of life course research. *Archives Européennes de Sociologie, 51*, 259–282.

Mayer, K. U. (2001a). Life Course. In B. Schäfers & W. Zapf (Eds.), Concise dictionary on German society, 2nd edition. (pp. 446–460). Opladen: Leske & Budrich.

Mayer, K. U. (2001b). The paradox of global social change and national path dependencies: Life course patterns in advanced societies. In A. E. Woodward & M. Kohli (Eds.), *Inclusions and exclusions in European societies* (pp. 89–110). London: Routledge.

Mayer, K. U., Diewald, M., & Solga, H. (1999). Transitions to post-communism in East Germany: Worklife mobility of women and men between 1989 and 1993. *Acta Sociologica, 42*, 35–53.

Mayer, K. U., & Huinink, J. (1990). Age, period, and cohort in the study of the life course: A comparison of classical A-P-C-analysis with event history analysis or farewell to LEXIS? In D. Magnusson & L. R. Bergman (Eds.), *Data quality in longitudinal research* (pp. 211–232). Cambridge: Cambridge University Press.

Mayer, K. U., Kraus, V., & Schmidt, P. (1992). Opportunity and inequality: Exploratory analyses of the structure of attitudes towards stratification in West Germany. In F. C. Turner (Ed.), *Social mobility and political attitudes* (pp. 51–78). New Brunswick, NJ: Transaction.

Mayer, K. U., & Müller, W. (1986). The state and the structure of the life course. In A. B. Sørensen, F. E. Weinert, & L. R. Sherrod (Eds.), *Human development and the life course: Multidisciplinary perspectives* (pp. 217–245). Hillsdale, NJ: Erlbaum.

Mayer, K. U., & Solga, H. (1994). Mobility and Legitimacy. A comparison of the opportunity structures in the old GDR and the old FRG or: Have mobility chances contributed to the stability and breakdown of the GDR? *Kölner Zeitschrift für Soziologie und Sozialpsychologie, 46*, 193–208.

Meyer, J. (1986). The self and the life course: Institutionalization and its effects. In A. B. Sørensen, F. E. Weinert, & L. R. Sherrod (Eds.), *Human development and the life course: Multidisciplinary perspectives* (pp. 199–217). Hillsdale, NJ: Erlbaum.

Pizzorno, A. (1991). Social control and the organization of the self (a summary of the original paper). In P. Bourdieu & J. S. Coleman (Eds.), *Social theory for a changing society* (pp. 232–234). New York: Sage.

Riesman, D., Glazer, N., & Denney, R. (1950). *The lonely crowd*. New Haven, CT: Yale University Press.

Riley, M. W., Kahn, R. L., & Foner, A. (Eds.). (1994). *Age and structural lag. Society's failure to provide meaningful opportunities in work, family, and leisure*. New York: Wiley.

Runciman, W. G. (1998). The selectionist paradigm and its implications for sociology. *Sociology, 32*, 163–188.

Rutter, M. (1997). Nature-nurture integration: The example of antisocial behavior. *American Psychologist, 52*, 390–398.

Ryder, N. (1965). The cohort in the study of social change. *American Sociological Review, 30*, 843–861.

Ryder, N. (1980). *The cohort approach: Essays in the measurement of temporal variations in demographic behavior*. New York: Arno Press.

Sackmann, R. (1999). Is an end of the fertility crisis in East Germany foreseeable? *Zeitschrift für Bevölkerungswissenschaft, 24*, 187–211.

Schulz, R., & Heckhausen, J. (1996). A life-span model of successful aging. *American Psychologist, 51*, 702–714.

Sørensen, A. (1990). Gender and the life course. Life courses and social change (special edition of the Kölner Zeitschrift für Soziologie und Sozialpsychologie, volume 31), 304–321. (Sonderheft: Lebensverläufe und sozialer Wandel [K. U. Mayer, Ed.]).

Sørensen, A. B., & Tuma, N. B. (1981). Labor market structures and job mobility. In R. Robinson (Ed.), *Research in social stratification and mobility* (Vol. 1, pp. 67–94). Greenwich, CT: JAI Press.

Sørensen, A. B., F. E. Weinert, & L. R. Sherrod (Eds.). (1986). *Human development and the life course: Multidisciplinary perspectives*. Hillsdale, NJ: Erlbaum.

Voss, T., & Abraham, M. (2000). Rational-choice theory in sociology: A survey. In S. Quah & A. Sales (Eds.), *The international handbook of sociology* (pp. 50–83). London: Sage.

24 Philosophy or the Search for Anthropological Constants

Jürgen Mittelstrass

Constance University, Constance, Germany

Abstract

Philosophy deals with the lifespan architecture of human development in the areas of both theoretical and practical philosophy. In the area of theoretical philosophy, it is mainly the development of human understanding (in the disciplinary framework of logic and epistemology) that plays the central role in philosophical analysis; in the area of practical philosophy, it is mainly the development of moral behavior (in the disciplinary framework of ethics) that is at issue here. The traditional focus of philosophy on human development has been the development of reason (from theoretical and practical perspectives). In terms of a lifespan architecture, this model is complemented by the development of a form of life (*Lebensform*) that also includes aspects of different periods of life such as aging and old age. Here, it is of particular philosophical interest to ask whether the self or self-consciousness ages like the body or whether it remains unchanged. This again is one of the reasons that philosophy often deals with the lifespan architecture of human development primarily in essentially anthropological, not in behavioral terms. This and related issues are discussed in this chapter.

Philosophy deals with the lifespan architecture of human development both theoretically and practically. The development of human understanding (in the disciplinary framework of logic and epistemology) plays the central role in theoretical philosophy (see Salthouse, this volume; Wellman, this volume). The development of moral behavior (in the disciplinary framework of ethics) is at issue in practical philosophy (see Cloninger, this volume; Labouvie-Vief, this volume). Traditionally, philosophy has focused on the development of reason (from theoretical and practical perspectives). In terms of a lifespan architecture, this model is complemented by the development of a form of life (*Lebensform*) that includes aspects of all periods of life, including aging and old age. Here, it is of particular philosophical interest to ask whether the self or the self-consciousness ages like the body or whether it remains unchanged (see Roberts & Caspi, this volume). This again is one of the reasons that philosophy often deals with the lifespan architecture of human development primarily in essentially *anthropological*—that is, nonempirical, sometimes even normative—terms and not in behavioral or historical terms. It deals with universal human properties—nature, not social, cultural, or historical circumstances.

In philosophy, as a rule, there is no state of the art in the sense of determining the discipline's common position on evaluating what has already been achieved and what next steps must still be taken. This also holds for questions of anthropology. There are anthropological conceptions in philosophy, both old and new, but no anthropological research agenda provides the framework for identifying successes and failures and growing textbook knowledge. This makes it difficult to say something about lifelong development that is representative of this discipline. Therefore, in the following I do not provide a textbook presentation but make only some brief remarks on the keywords *anthropological basic situation, temporal forms of life, age and aging, consciousness,* and *finitude.* The choice of these keywords is based on the assumption that a philosophical anthropology is fundamentally concerned with the analysis of the particular situation of humankind, as an expression of its nature, and that this situation is essentially characterized by temporal categories (among them, those that refer to aging processes) and by categories of consciousness and finitude (as a particular expression of human incompleteness).

The Anthropological Basic Situation

The goal of a philosophical anthropology—its main rationale—is to search for and to determine those *anthropological constants* that, independent of concrete social, cultural, and historical circumstances and developments, constitute the components or properties of being human. Human nature (or essence) allows various conceptions—namely, "(1) nature in the sense of biologically (or more generally scientifically) describable dispositions and the behavior patterns they explain; (2) in the sense of ancient or even prehistoric rules for human action (and possibly also the normative notions that legitimate these rules), and (3) in the sense of man's 'life world'—that is, the experiences available to everyone" (Schwemmer, 1980, p. 126). What is common to these different approaches to human nature is that common or similarly applicable determinations are made that—as *universal* determinations—can be understood as conditions of every social, cultural, historical, and intellectual development in the form of anthropological constants.

In answer to the objections of *historical* anthropology (which is usually oriented toward philosophy of history and seeks to represent such constants as properties brought forth by historical developments), let me point out that we are considering properties here that even a historical explanation must presuppose as biologically or phenomenologically given, and even the appeal to lifeworld, cultural or historical realities, has no relativizing consequences. On the contrary, the lifeworld-constituted character of the human condition reveals to us the unavoidable presuppositions of historical approach. In this sense, which was elaborated on by Martin Heidegger (1977), albeit from an ontological perspective, a philosophical anthropology embraces social, cultural, historical, and other empirical aspects—among them the results of physical, historical, and cultural anthropology (Lévi-Strauss, 1958)—but it attempts to present their achievements in understanding and explanation as open varieties of a deeper-lying structure of humanity or to derive them from the analysis of universal presuppositions (anthropological constants). These, in turn, are looked for in lifeworld dispositions (*Befindlichkeiten*) (Heidegger, 1977) or, with the same results, elaborated on in the form of ethics (Kamlah, 1973).

Modern philosophical anthropology takes its point of departure from two opposing theorists—Max Scheler (1927) and Helmut Plessner (1928). According to Scheler, philosophical anthropology is nothing but the quintessence of philosophy itself; according to Plessner, it follows the structure of the empirical sciences in the form of an "integrative" discipline. Scheler harkens back to traditional determinations of humans as *animal rationale*; Plessner is oriented toward the state of biological, medical, psychological, and, in the extended sense, social-scientific research and does this with the conceptual goal of a *structural theory* of humans. Common to both is the concept of *world openness*, which includes openness of development.

According to Scheler, humans are the "X that can behave in a world-open manner to an unlimited extent" (1927, p. 49); according to Plessner, humans are characterized by an "eccentric positionality" (1928, pp. 288), whereby an eccentric existence that possesses no fixed center is described as the unity of mediated immediacy and natural artificiality. Accordingly, Plessner formulates three *fundamental laws of anthropology*: (1) the law of natural artificiality, (2) the law of mediated immediacy, and (3) the law of the utopian standpoint (Plessner, 1928, pp. 309–346; see Lorenz, 1990, pp. 102 f.). Similarly, Arnold Gehlen states the thesis that humans by nature are cultural beings (1961, p. 78), whereby cultural achievements are seen as compensation for organs and humans are defined as creatures of defect (*Mängelwesen*) (1972, p. 37).

Stipulations of a similar kind can also be found in the history of philosophical anthropology. Thus humans are called creatures without an archetype by the Italian Renaissance philosopher Giovanni Pico della Mirandola: humans according to the will of their creator, are to determine the "form"—that is, the cultural form in which they wish to live (1942, p. 106). According to Immanuel Kant, the question "What is man?" can be answered only if we already have answers to the questions, "What can I know?" "What ought I to do?" and "What may I hope?" (*Logik* A 25; 1958, vol. 3, p. 448). The attempt to determine "(1) the source of human knowledge, (2) the extent of the possible and profitable use of knowledge, and finally (3) the limits of reason" is itself an anthropological research goal, and against the background of the critical philosophy of Kant, the goal is open-ended, shaped by what can be achieved in theory and practice. For Friedrich Nietzsche, finally, man is the not yet determined animal (1968, p. 79), whereby science too is seen as the expression of human endeavor "to determine himself" (1973, p. 533). Furthermore, human beings can reflect about themselves. As Heidegger says, a human is a creature "that in its being relates understandingly to its being" (1977, pp. 52 f.) or is "concerned in its being with this being itself" (1977, p. 12). This opens up a broad horizon of possible self-interpretations and a wide array of answers to the question, "What is man?" This essential openness of man can be called the *anthropological basic situation.*

This openness, which is primarily practical but is reflected on in theoretical terms, affects all phases of human development, both ontogenetic and phylogenetic. There is no "natural" fate in the individual or the species that might be definitely determined by biological laws, even though the schema (that is, biological regularities) of this development is given. There is no adulthood before childhood, no reverse aging, no Achilles who is young until he dies. But there is a realization that these phases are possibilities—a horizon, not a predetermined system of paths and stopping points (see Kirkwood, this volume; Singer, this volume). In psychological terminology, the architecture of human ontogeny is incomplete and throughout a lifetime. I use here Paul Baltes's terminology (Baltes, 1977, this volume), although in speaking about the incomplete architecture of human ontogeny, Baltes primarily refers to the fact that old age and aging still need to become optimized and "completed" because, as a mass phenomenon, they are quite new in human history. In my view, as well as in Plessner's view, "incompleteness" is a result of the "constructive" nature of man and is therefore an anthropological constant.

The opposing but at the same time complementary concepts of *nature* (or causal relation) and *culture* (or institutional relation) make clear two recipocal approaches to analysis: "Causal and intentional regularities constitute strictly distinct ranges of objects that must be studied by the disciplines of natural science and cultural science with different scientific methods. Causal regularities are constrained by initial conditions; intentional regularities are determined by goal representations that due to their social mediation normally do not become conscious. The disputed question—whether and to what extent sociocultural behavior is naturally biologically determined or vice versa—is actually a dispute about whether some empirically observed behavior is to be taken as 'natural' (belonging to nature) or as 'cultural' (belonging to culture)" (Lorenz, 1990, p. 23).

Certain tensions are involved in all forms of philosophical anthropology. They all conceive of themselves rightly (inside and outside philosophy) as fundamental but also integrative (similar to Plessner's approach)—namely, they take knowledge acquired by other (empirical) disciplines into account. For example, certain temporal categories (as was pointed out at the beginning) determine what is here called the anthropological basic situation.

Temporal Forms of Life

The accustomed distinctions between childhood, youth, adulthood, and old age are expressions of a measure constituted by biological, medical, psychological, and other elements just as much as by cultural, economic, and legal elements. If we view humans from the point of view of their development merely as biological creatures, we have misunderstood the cultural self-understanding that lies in these distinctions. The same holds for all the other elements. Times of life are forms of life and at the same time, in Plessner's words, are "forms of fate" because "they are essential to the development process. Forms of fate are not forms *of* a being but rather *for* a being. Being undergoes them and submits to them" (Plessner, 1928, p. 154; on the following, see Mittelstrass, 1992). Youth and old age but also farewell and fortune are not properties of (an individual) life but *forms, gestalts, times* that a life undergoes (the term *gestalt* is used here for the shape things take; it has no holistic connotations often associated with the term in psychology). The time of a life is determined from its "nature"; life is not simply a temporal process. In other words, *the time of life is its times.*

One of the philosophical insights of Greek thought was that life has temporal gestalts—for instance, childhood, youth, adulthood, and old age—and not simply a temporal structure. According to this insight, life does not consist of time but of times— that is, of temporal gestalts. The fact that Achilles remains young until he dies means that his life has only one gestalt—youth. The alternative to such a view would be a continuum model of time or the picture of time's arrow. But these conceptions belong to a different world, the world of physics. It is not time that flows but things that flow and that change themselves in time—albeit gestalt-like. The Aristotelian theory of time, the most exacting theory in Greek thought, does not allow such notions as are expressed in phrases like "time passes." In Aristotle's physics, time is a form of motion. But in motion, time does not move; only *duration* grows proportionally to the space traversed in a motion (see Janich, 1980, p. 255).

Thus the Greek constructions of time—the time lived and the time represented in myth and everyday language—correspond to their age. What might seem archaic here is rather the expression of an experience in dealing with human time that has not yet taken the path either to an abstract physical theory or to the soul. The fact that we seem to have different experiences today is due to the fact that other constructions of time, such as everyday physical conceptions, influence us. The need to coordinate concrete times—including times of action, times of nature, times of life—to be able at any time to move from one temporal gestalt to another leads to an "abstract time" that is everywhere the *same* and everywhere *one* time. Theories of time, which as a rule are theories of an abstract time in this also everyday physical sense, have this practical background.

Gestalt-like conceptions of time were preserved up into modern times. This holds particularly within the framework of a philosophy of times of life. Here, ancient notions, in which human life displays an orderly sequence of temporal gestalts, determine decisively the development of a philosophical and literary anthropology (Boll, 1913; Rosenmayr, 1978). An archaic division of life into two gestalts, youth and old age, oriented toward the cycles of the sun (daily and yearly rhythms) is followed by a division into three gestalts of life (see Martianus Capella, 1983, p. 23). From the two-part division, there developed (probably in the Pythagorean tradition, see Klibansky et al., 1964, pp. 3–15, pp 55–66) a division into four gestalts that correspond to the four seasons, which now reflect the gestalts of life. Ptolemy takes up the Aristotelian notions, compares times of life with seasons and sense qualities, and, for reasons of (recent) astronomy and (older) calendar-making, increases the four life stages to seven. The seven days of the week and the seven planets known to antiquity constitute the fundament on which Ptolemy now seeks directly to represent relationships between the properties of the planets and the properties of times of life (Ptolemaios, 1980, pp. 436 ff.; see Macrobius, 1963, p. 50).

Medieval and early modern conceptions take these notions of gestalt-like times of life as their point of departure (see Burrow, 1986; Sears, 1986). Some well-known examples are the use of the seven planet analogy in Sir Walter Raleigh's *History of the World* of 1614 (see Burrow, 1986, pp. 51 f.) and in Jaques' speech in Shakespeare's *As You Like It* (Shakespeare, 1975, 55–57, lines 139–166), as well as the reintroduction of the conception of four times of life in Dante's *Convivio* (Dante, 1980, pp. 316–343). A notion of life times based on decades is joined to old wheel-of-life representations that are often also used in connection with the four-time conceptions and since the sixteenth century also with the picture of a stairway of life in which a child on one side sets his foot and ascends and on the other side a very old man or woman descends and leaves the stairs. What is decisive for an anthropological perspective, such as has been explicated here on the example of the temporal forms of life, is the fact that in all cases the times in which life appears possess a gestalt-like character. Cultural forms and self-understandings overlay the biological forms.

Aging and Old Age

What has been said here about the temporal forms of human life in a general anthropological or philosophical perspective applies as well to every temporal form—in particular, for instance, to old age and the process of aging. In a recent introduction to a collection of three essays on the philosophy of aging, the editor rightly notes that philosophy has been remarkably silent on the theme of aging and the corresponding developments in modern gerontology and that in its academic form philosophy has made no contribution in the field (Baars, 1997, p. 259). The reason for this he sees in the fixation of philosophy on the concept of subjectivity (Baars, 1997, p. 260). In fact, as I emphasized at the start, philosophy's conceptions of universality, which also constitute the core of a philosophical anthropology, are intended to be "timeless." Their subject is (as in Scheler) the rational human being, not the growing and aging human being; their goal is (as in Plessner) a structural theory of humanity. The *conditio humana* described by philosophical anthropology gives the impression of being cleansed of everything empirical, although it means precisely those empirical boundary conditions in which—in the classical tradition—the rational individual or rationality as the distinctive nature of man is formed.

It is no wonder then that the philosophical tradition has marginalized the perception of aging people, especially the later phases of life, by shunting it into a *Lebensphiloso-phie* that purchases its closeness to everyday and average forms of life by the loss of (in principle) generality and of philosophical systematicity (for instance, in the area of epistemology and ethics). Wherever human kind in general is not the object of philosophy and human contingent dispositions step to the fore, the empirical gains the upper hand over thought and the speculative. This was the opinion of Hegel: "The empirical phenomenon becomes too much for thought, which now only stamps on its sign of possession but cannot any longer actually penetrate it" (Hegel, 1971, pp. 197 f.). And on the other hand, the speculative is conceived as the triumph of thought and theory over the empirical.

Applied to aging and old age, this means that these two are rather understood as belonging to the contingent conditions to which human beings are exposed and not as something that belongs to the definition of being human. And this applies even to death, to the property of being mortal, if this is not incorporated into the human essence as the definitive element of finitude. This changes essentially only with Heidegger's determination of existence as a being-toward-death (Heidegger, 1977, pp. 235 ff.). Death here becomes part of (human) life; it is no longer its absolute limit. Nonetheless, in this conception, too, aging and old age do not occur. The general aspect of temporality, which according to Heidegger determines all structures of human existence, makes evolutionary processes like aging appear to be something derivative and therefore not relevant for philosophical analysis. Furthermore, in Heidegger's anthropology, which is not supposed to be an anthropology but an ontology, death is always alien death— that is, the death of others and the other of one's own life: " 'Death is encountered as a well-known event occurring within-the-world. ... 'one dies', " and "this one is *the nobody*" (Heidegger, 1977, p. 253). Even Plato was able to conceive of death only as the transition from (lived) life to the pure (philosophical) life of reason (*Phaed.* 64cff.). As simple death, with which everything is over, death is nobody's death.

Conceptions of this kind basically preserve ancient Greek notions of the temporal forms of life. In these temporal forms (therefore, also in the late phases of life), we find reflected a *bios*—in the sense of a unified form of life but above and beyond this also in the sense of "general" forms of life that a particular life takes on. In this sense, the Greeks distinguished, for instance, between a *bios praktikos*, an active, practical-political life (*vita activa*) and a *bios theoretikos,* a contemplative, "theoretical" life (*vita contempla-tiva*). An individual *bios* gives such general forms of life an individual expression—in every phase of life. This is also the way that developmental psychology sees it, even if it emphasizes the independence of the individual *bios*: "A critical developmental- and social-psychological consideration of aging stresses ... the inner uniformity of an individual Bios, even in old age, in contrast to the often expected and too easily discovered superindividual uniformity of a life phase" (Thomae, 1968, p. 16). Here the individual *bios* steps in front of the general *bios* without losing its general gestalt-form.

Old age brings us closer to the "end of all things"; death becomes an individual judgment day. Or so did Kant describe the real end of all things "in time" while at the same time giving it an old moral meaning: as far as a man knows himself, "reason leaves him no other perspective on eternity than what his own conscience opens up for him at the end of his life based on the life he has lead" (Kant, 1958, vol. 6, p. 178; see Borngräber, 1990, pp. 238 ff.). Kant calls this a mere "judgment of reason" because humans are in fact not in a position to survey their entire lives and to do this in an objective and judgmental fashion. Thus, old age and death are condensation forms of life and at the same time a submission to the inevitable. But this in turn is only one side of dealing with growing old; *shaping* the developmental potentials that still lie in old age is the other side. Just as no youth is the same, so, too, no old age is the same; not even dying is the same. But death is the great equalizer—albeit only when it actually occurs. Its anticipation by life (Heidegger's being-toward-death) leads to just the opposite—to great diversity of opportunity.

Aging and old age along with sickness are expressions of the *finitude* of humans, old age and death its most extreme forms of reality (see Rentsch, 1992). Therefore, in antiquity it was not the form of existence of a god that was the ideal of human aspiration but rather Achilles, who was a youth until his death. It was not the finitude but the process of aging and growing old that was negated.

Consciousness and Finitude

Old age is the result of a history—a biological and an "individual cultural" history. In this sense, aging means the progression of a history that began with birth. This is not meant deterministically, although such a history, especially in its biological and medical parts, does include deterministic elements. Rather, it is meant in the sense of a life history, the biography of an individual expressed in the individual sphere (as personal course of life) and in the general sphere (as generalizable process of growing older or old). What we are is always also what we have been as members of the human race and as individual forms of life.

This history in turn is played out in the framework of a philosophical anthropology in differing scenarios. One of these scenarios is, for instance, the distinction between *Körper* and *Leib*, between the body as a physical object and the body as experienced phenomenologically. According to Plessner (1970, p. 238), man *is* a phenomenological body (*Leib*) and *has* it as a physical body (*Körper*); he is a *Leib im Körper* as opposed to an animal that is its (physical) body and has this as its phenomenological body. As difficult as this distinction is, it stands against an all too restricted notion of body that reduces it (in the Cartesian tradition) to a mere mechanism. An example of this is the connection to the (medical) concept of disease in the following characterization: "(1) The organism is not guided by special vital forces, there is *no vital force*. (2) The processes of life are in principle *physical and chemical* processes. ... (3) The interconnection of these functional parts is strictly *determined* and governed by natural law. ... Natural laws are causal laws. ... (7) The knowledge of the conditions under which parts of a living creature operate allows us ... to find ways arbitrarily to *influence* and guide the life processes. ... (10) Sickness is a disturbance of life processes that as a rule is secondarily expressed in the morphological structure. ... (11) Process disturbances rest on relations governed by natural law that can with adequate means be objectively demonstrated. ... (13) One should not be satisfied with the analysis of law-like relations in the healthy or sick body until one has acquired a *knowledge complete enough for the repair of the causal relations*" (Rothschuh, 1978, pp. 417–419).

This concept of body is today biologically and medically dated, but it nonetheless still determines our usual notions of body, sickness, and—extended to the process of growing old and older—old age. Our physical abilities grow weaker; the living body becomes increasingly a function of the physical body alone. Humans adapt themselves to their decreasing biological capacities, to the circumstance "that the benefits resulting from evolutionary selection evince a negative age correlation" (Baltes, 1997, p. 367, this volume), through the fact that (individual) selection, optimization, and compensation become determining factors of this life phase much more concretely than in previous stages of life. *Selection* is understood here not only as an element of natural evolution and thus generally of all natural developmental processes but also as a cultural element that makes individuality possible in the first place; the same holds for *optimization*, without which all abilities both in the individual and in general would remain average. *Compensation* finally is the answer to, for instance, the age-linked decline of the powers of selection and optimization (see also Baltes & Carstensen, this volume).

Philosophically speaking, these are not separate processes but rather different aspects of man's dealings with the world and with himself (see also Behrman, this volume). Thus, optimization is also always an element of compensation (compensation optimizes under given defective situations), and compensation is always also an element of optimization (optimization increases given abilities and compensates given defects). Both of these in turn are aspects of selection, which is also an effect of optimization and compensation.

Behind the concepts of selection, optimization, and compensation lurks Gehlen's concept of the creature of defect. Biologically defective creature and culturally superendowed creature, these are the two poles between which the *conditio humana* is spread. At the same time, these two poles determine themselves in a dialectical fashion in man's process of self-becoming: "In the process of a dialogically progressing self-understanding and world understanding, man's being self-produced becomes 'objectivizable' so as to determine a being able to produce himself—that is, a higher order of self-generated being. We can, in general, speak of 'natural abilities' 'of humans'— of precisely those abilities for instrumental and communicative action that serve the elimination of natural defects. Correspondingly, in the same dialogical process, man's self generated being, as a suffered self-generation or a 'being stamped' (that is, a higher order of being self-produced), is 'appropriated'—which allows us once again to speak

in general of 'cultural defects' that put limits on the expansion of cultural abilities"
(Lorenz, 1990, p. 68).

With this, it once again becomes clear that philosophical anthropology—even
where it refers with the concepts of selection, optimization, and compensation to empirical relations and thus to aspects of finitude—remains true to its original program
of determining anthropological constants. The philosophical interest is directed in the
sense of Plessner to a structural theory of humanity, but in such a way that the results of empirical disciplines can also be taken into consideration. This holds even
where philosophy is, so to speak, at home—namely, in the analysis of the *ego* and of
self-consciousness. Here, the results of psychology and neuroscience are increasingly
included in philosophical reflection (see Singer, this volume), but still the (anthropological) thesis remains unaffected that the ego does not age. One could also say:
consciousness does not age, at least not in the form of self-consciousness. Since the
ego is a philosophical construction, albeit a construction without which the concepts of
consciousness and self-consciousness lose their meanings, there is no empiricist way
around the ego.

Returning once more to the question of aging and old age, we can say that the ego
perceives processes of aging but does not participate in them. That one can be young
in old age is thus not surprising because "young" here means to be different from
the aging body in one's consciousness and the forms of life guided by consciousness.
No new dualism, such as still determines the mind-body problem and the research
program of philosophy of mind, is intended by this, rather only the circumstance that
consciousness, the ego, participates in the development of humans in a different manner
than does the body.

Karl Popper and John Eccles, albeit in the framework of a strictly dualistic conceptual scheme, also expressed this idea, arguing that on the one hand the self or
self-consciousness is a product of evolution but that on the other hand the brain belongs to the self, not the self to the brain. The self is the programmer of the computer
"brain"—the pilot, not the piloted (Popper & Eccles, 1977, p. 120; see Carrier &
Mittelstrass, 1991, pp. 115–125). Eccles translates this idea of the self into neurobiological language. According to him, the self controls and interprets the neuronal processes; it actively seeks brain events that lie in its domain of interest and integrates them
into a unified and conscious experience. It constantly scans the collective interactions
of large numbers of neurons ("cortical modules"), which are open to an interaction
with mental states and events, the so-called World 2 ("liaison brain"). The unity of
conscious experience "is provided by the self-conscious mind and not by the neural
machinery of the liaison areas of the cerebral hemisphere" (Popper & Eccles, 1977, p.
362). That is to say, the mind uses a liaison brain to bridge the psychophysical gap to
influence the brain mechanism that resides in the world of physical bodies (the so-called
World 1).

This is, admittedly, an extreme position, which—unsurprisingly—is opposed by
other, monistic conceptions. But it shows—precisely by its extremism—that philosophy

even in connection with modern scientific approaches (here, neuroscience) still makes its own way, even when dealing with questions of human development and its architecture. This "way" need by no means always lead to a dualism (which is also for philosophical reasons objectionable). It is sufficient here to point out that a determination of the *conditio humana* can also be carried out with philosophical means, in this case with those of a philosophical anthropology. In our context, along with the point of view of the development of reason (from a theoretical but also from a practical perspective), we find the point of view of the development of the self or the self-consciousness (see Labouvie-Vief, this volume). It is here, in connection with an analysis of the anthropological basic situation of humankind and the determination of anthropological constants, that the anthropological question of the finitude and with it the question of the incomplete nature of man is decided.

References

Baars, J. (1997). The reinterpretation of finitude: An introduction to three articles on the philosophy of aging. *Journal of Aging Studies, 11*, 259–261.

Baltes, P. B. (1997). On the incomplete architecture of human ontogeny: Selection, optimization, and compensation as foundation of developmental theory. *American Psychologist, 52*, 366–380.

Boll, F. (1913). Die Lebensalter. Ein Beitrag zur antiken Ethologie und zur Geschichte der Zahlen. *Neue Jahrbücher für das Klassische Altertum, 31*, 99–154.

Borngräber, U.-W. (1990). *Alter in Gerontologie und Philosophie*. Dissertation, Freie Universität Berlin, Berlin.

Burrow, J. A. (1986). *The ages of man: A study in medieval writing and thought*. Oxford: Oxford University Press.

Carrier, M., & Mittelstrass, J. (1991). *Mind, brain, behavior: The mind-body problem and the philosophy of psychology*. New York: de Gruyter.

Dante Alighieri. (1980). *Convivio* (ed. P. Cudini). Mailand: Garzanti.

Gehlen, A. (1961). *Anthropologische Forschung: Zur Selbstbegegnung und Selbstentdeckung des Menschen*. Reinbek: Rowohlt.

Gehlen, A. (1972). *Der Mensch: Seine Natur und seine Stellung in der Welt* (1940) (9th ed.). Wiesbaden: Athenaion.

Hegel, G. W. F. (1971). *Werke in zwanzig Bänden* (ed. E. Moldenhauer & K. M. Michel, Vol. 19, *Vorlesungen über die Geschichte der Philosophie* II). Frankfurt am Main: Suhrkamp.

Heidegger, M. (1977). *Sein und Zeit* (1927) (14th ed.). Tübingen: Niemeyer.

Janich, P. (1980). *Die Protophysik der Zeit: Konstruktive Begründung und Geschichte der Zeitmessung*. Frankfurt am Main: Suhrkamp.

Kamlah, W. (1973). *Philosophische Anthropologie: Sprachliche Grundlegung und Ethik*. Mannheim: Bibliographisches Institut.

Kant, I. (1958). *Werke in sechs Bänden* (ed. W. Weischedel). Darmstadt: Wissenschaftliche Buchgesellschaft.

Klibansky, R., et al. (1964). *Saturn and melancholy: Studies in the history of natural philosophy, religion and art*. London: Nelson.

Lévi-Strauss, C. (1958). *Anthropologie structurale*. Paris: Plon.

Lorenz, K. (1990). *Einführung in die philosophische Anthropologie*. Darmstadt: Wissenschaftliche Buchgesellschaft.

Macrobius (1963). *Commentarii in somnium scipionis* (ed. J. Willis). Leipzig: Teubner.

Martianus Capella (1983). *De nuptiis philologiae et mercurii* (ed. J. Willis). Leipzig: Teubner.

Mittelstrass, J. (1992). Zeitformen des Lebens: Philosophische Unterscheidungen. In P. B. Baltes & J. Mittelstrass (Eds.), *Zukunft des Alterns und gesellschaftliche Entwicklung* (Akademie der Wissenschaften zu Berlin. Forschungsbericht 5, pp. 386–407). New York: de Gruyter.

Nietzsche, F. (1968). *Jenseits von Gut und Böse.* In F. Nietzsche, *Werke. Kritische Gesamtausgabe* (ed. G. Colli & M. Montinari, Vol. 6/2). Berlin: de Gruyter.

Nietzsche, F. (1973). *Nachgelassene Fragmente Frühjahr 1881 bis Sommer 1882. Werke. Kritische Gesamtausgabe* (ed. G. Colli & M. Montinari, Vol. 5/2). Berlin: de Gruyter.

Pico della Mirandola, G. (1942). *De hominis dignitate. Heptaplus. De ente et uno, e scritt vari* (ed. E. Garin). Florence: Vallecchi.

Plessner, H. (1928). *Die Stufen des Organischen und der Mensch: Einleitung in die philosophische Anthropologie.* Berlin: de Gruyter.

Plessner, H. (1970). Immer noch Philosophische Anthropologie? (1963). In H. Plessner, *Gesammelte Schriften* (Vol. 8, *Conditio humana*). Frankfurt am Main: Suhrkamp.

Popper, K. R., & Eccles, J. C. (1977). *The self and its brain.* New York: Springer.

Ptolemaios, K. (1980). *Tetrabiblos* (ed. F. E. Robbins). Cambridge, MA: Harvard University Press.

Rentsch, T. (1992). Philosophische Anthropologie und Ethik der späten Lebenszeit. In P. B. Baltes & J. Mittelstrass (Eds.), *Zukunft des Alterns und gesellschaftliche Entwicklung* (Akademie der Wissenschaften zu Berlin. *Forschungsbericht* 5, pp. 283–304). Berlin: de Gruyter.

Rosenmayr, L. (1978). Die menschlichen Lebensalter in Deutungsversuchen der europäischen Kulturgeschichte. In L. Rosenmayr (Ed.), *Die menschlichen Lebensalter: Kontinuität und Krisen* (pp. 23–79). Munich: Piper.

Rothschuh, K. E. (1978). *Konzepte der Medizin in Vergangenheit und Gegenwart.* Stuttgart: Hippokrates-Verlag.

Scheler, M. (1927). *Die Stellung des Menschen im Kosmos.* Darmstadt: Otto Reichl.

Schwemmer, O. (1980). Anthropologie. In J. Mittelstrass (Ed.), *Enzyklopädie Philosophie und Wissenschaftstheorie* (Vol. 1). Mannheim: Bibliographisches Institut.

Sears, E. (1986). *The ages of man: Medieval interpretations of the life cycle.* Princeton, NJ: Princeton University Press.

Shakespeare, W. (1975). *As you like it* (ed. A. Latham). London: Methuen.

Thomae, H. (1968). Zur Entwicklungs- und Sozialpsychologie des alternden Menschen. In H. Thomae & U. Lehr (Eds.), *Altern: Probleme und Tatsachen* (pp. 3–17). Frankfurt am Main: Akademische Verlagsgesellschaft.

AUTHOR INDEX

"p" after a page number indicates that the author is also found on the following page; "pp" after a page number indicates that the author is also found on the next following pages. Numbers set in italics indicate the reference page.

SUBJECT INDEX

"p" after a page number indicates that the keyword is also found on the following page; "pp" after a page number indicates that the keyword is also found on the next following pages.

Cognition, cognitive (*Continued*)
  Gf/Gc theory (fluid, crystallized), 4, 160, 177,
    307, 332
  mechanics vs. pragmatics, 4, 30p, 93, 160,
    266, 307
  migration hypothesis, 267, 270p, 282pp
  performance, 4, 10, 22, 73p, 87, 234, 267pp,
    279pp, 291pp
  sensory deprivation hypothesis,
    441p
  sets, 109
  situated, 455p
  training, 22
Coherence (*see* Personality)
  therapy, 172p
Cohort, 69, 105, 112, 120, 371p, 465pp
Collaboration
  across disciplines, 2, 36, 38, 394
  social, 93
Compensation (as a psychological process; *see also*
SOC), 18, 25, 27pp, 87pp, 93pp, 110pp, 120,
  146pp, 190p, 226, 270, 296, 307, 309p, 395, 409,
  417pp, 430, 433p, 457p, 491p
Computation, mental, 281, 294, 424pp, 440
Conditio humana, 488, 491pp
Conscientiousness (*see* Personality)
Consciousness, 161p, 174pp, 190pp, 408pp
Constraints, 8, 26p, 32, 107p, 136, 147, 251, 259,
  290, 297p, 386
  enabling, 8
  institutional, 450pp, 469, 473
  structural (of the life course), 395p, 471pp
Context, developmental, 4pp, 60, 95, 108pp, 185,
  193, 203, 216pp, 226, 229, 384, 408p, 414pp
Contingency, 195
Continuity, continuous (*see also* Discontinuity), 9,
  10, 107, 117pp, 161, 176, 185pp, 198pp, 221,
  276pp, 407, 472
Control
  beliefs (*see also* Self efficacy), 9, 90, 108pp,
    115p, 223, 227pp, 386pp, 474pp
  primary, 11, 28, 386pp, 390, 395p
  proxy, 93
  secondary, 11, 28, 91, 386pp, 391pp
  lifespan theory of, 383pp
Coping, coping style, 86, 91p, 108pp, 114, 385
  flexible goal adjustment (FGA), 108, 112,
    114p
  tenacious goal pursuit (TGP), 108
Cost-benefit-ratio, 111, 143, 428p

Costs, 128, 130
  marginal, 130pp, 142pp
Creativity, 171pp, 405
Critical life events, critical events, 53, 89, 108, 117
Culture, cultural, 1pp, 8p, 21p, 30, 38, 60p, 72, 83,
  120p, 146p, 151, 408, 416, 486
  differences, 29, 86, 221

D

Deadline, developmental (*see* Development)
Death, 107, 111, 136, 177, 406, 489p
  rates, age-specific, 60pp, 69pp, 65
  gender-specific, 65
Decline, developmental (*see* Development)
Defense, defensive,
  mechanisms (*see also* Coping), 169, 191,
    408pp
Demography, demographic, 35, 470p
Deoxyribonucleic acid (DNA), 48, 365p
Dependency in old age, 25, 93, 95, 226
Design
  research, 6p, 192, 324pp, 341, 349, 353
  cross-sectional, 221, 230, 322, 325, 343
  longitudinal (*see also* Factor analysis,
    longitudinal), 110pp, 169, 184p, 187p,
    193p, 200, 203, 221, 227, 321, 325p, 341,
    396
Desirability, desirable, of developmental outcomes,
  7, 23p, 107, 113, 121, 218pp, 224p 228pp, 388p
Development, developmental,
  architecture of, 8, 17, 19pp, 38, 127, 136,
    147pp, 160pp, 226, 368, 483
  deadline, 391pp, 471
  decline, 1, 8, 81pp, 215pp, 220pp, 250,
    267pp, 296p, 300, 306p, 409pp, 417, 456
  domain-specificity vs. domain generality,
    217, 225p, 247, 251pp, 282, 292p, 427pp
  dynamic systems models, 232
  early, 4, 246pp
  economic model, 127pp, 146pp
  efficiency of interventions, 8, 22, 74p, 147
  environmental influences, 9, 135, 247p, 385p,
    439pp, 450pp
  gains, 3, 18, 23pp, 38, 64, 74, 82pp, 110pp,
    126, 130pp, 147, 159, 217pp, 246pp
  gain-loss dynamic, 3, 18, 23pp, 38, 87pp,
    110pp, 215pp, 278, 388, 409
  genetic influences, 46pp, 129pp, 148, 361pp,
    438pp